# ASP.NET 2.0

## Kathleen Kalata

THOMSON

COURSE TECHNOLOGY

Australia • Canada • Mexico • Singapore • Spain • United Kingdom • United States

**THOMSON**

**COURSE TECHNOLOGY**

## ASP.NET 2.0

is published by Course Technology

**Vice President, Technology and Trades ABU:**
Dave Garza

**Director of Learning Solutions:**
Sandy Clark

**Acquisitions Editor:**
Amy Jollymore

**Content Project Manager:**
Summer Hughes

**Development Editor:**
Jill Batistick

**Marketing Specialist:**
Victoria Ortiz

**Manufacturing Coordinator:**
Justin Palmeiro

**Composition House:**
GEX Publishing Services

**Cover Designer:**
Mike Tanamachi

# TABLE OF
# Contents

PREFACE                                                                    XIII

## CHAPTER ONE
## Introduction to Web Programming                                          1

Introducing Visual Web Developer Tools                                      2
    Exploring Visual Web Editors                        2
    Exploring the Individual Windows                     2
    Create a New Web Application                         6
Introduction to HTML                                                        8
    The Fundamentals of Tags and Attributes             9
    HTML Structure                                      10
    Tags that Contain or Format Text                    13
    Tags for Elements Other than Pure Text              15
    Create a New Web Page with a Web Editor             20
Introduction to XML                                                        26
    XML Standards                                       26
    XML Rules                                           27
    Markup Validation of XML Documents                  30
    Creating and Validating XML Documents in the XML Designer   33
    Displaying Images with an XML File                  35
    Web Site Accessibility                              35
Introduction to ASP.NET Server Programming                                 36
    Before There Were Client-Server Applications        36
    Processing ASP.NET Applications                     37
    Server Controls                                     38
    HTML Tags and HTML Controls                         41
    Web Controls                                        42
    Creating a Web Page Using a Web Editor              43
Help Resources                                                             46
Chapter Summary                                                            47
Review Questions                                                           48
Hands-on Projects                                                          51
Case Projects                                                              57

## CHAPTER TWO
## Introduction to Programming                                             61

Integrating Programming and Web Forms                                      62
    Configuring the Page Directive                      62
    Where to Place Your Programming Statements          62
Using Variables and Constants in a Web Form                                64
    Declaring a Variable                                64
    Declaring Constants                                 66

Working with Different Data Types                                                           66
  Working with Text Data                                                                    66
  Working with Numeric Data                                                                 67
  Working with the Date and Time                                                            69
  Converting Data Types                                                                     71
  Working with Collections                                                                  71
Working with Web Objects to Store Data                                                      77
  Using the Request Object to Retrieve Data from the Header                                 77
  Retrieving Data from a Form with the Request Object                                       77
  Accessing Form Field Data                                                                 78
  Working with the Response Object                                                          79
  Session Objects                                                                           79
  Saving Data Using a Session Object                                                        80
Designing .NET Web Applications                                                             82
  Web Application Architecture                                                              82
  Organization of Classes in the .NET Framework                                            83
Programming with Visual Basic .NET                                                          83
  Creating a Class in ASP.NET                                                               83
  Using a Procedure                                                                         85
  Creating a Property Method                                                                88
  How Web Applications Interact with the Systems.Drawing.Graphics Class                     89
  Using the Systems.Drawing.Graphics Class                                                  90
  Dynamically Creating Server Controls                                                      92
  Dynamically Creating a Hyperlink Control                                                  92
Programming Control Structures                                                              93
  If Then Statement                                                                         95
  Select Case Statement                                                                     95
  While Loop                                                                                96
  Do Loop                                                                                   96
  For Next Loop                                                                             97
  For Each Loop                                                                             97
  Nested Statements                                                                         97
Introduction to Web Configuration and Debugging                                             98
  Exception Handling                                                                        98
  Using Exception Classes to Identify Exception Errors                                      99
  Common Error Status Messages                                                             100
  Creating a Custom Error Message                                                          100
  Using the Web Site Administration Tool                                                   101
  Configuring the Web Application to Use the Debugger Tool                                 103
  Programming Best Practices                                                               104
Chapter Summary                                                                            105
Review Questions                                                                           106
Hands-On Projects                                                                          109
Case Projects                                                                              115

CHAPTER THREE
Designing Web Applications                                                                 119
  Creating Cascading Style Sheets                                                          120
    Overview of CSS Style Rules                                                            120
    Comments Within CSSs                                                                   124
    Cascading Priority with Rules                                                          124
    Creating Classes                                                                       125

Using the Style Builder 126
Using the Color Picker Feature 127
XSLT Stylesheets 129
Understanding the Structure of an XSLT Stylesheet 129
Customizing XSLT Stylesheets 135
Inserting and Configuring the XML Control in a Web Form 144
Master and Content Pages 147
Creating the Master Page 147
Creating the Content Page 148
Using Master and Content Pages 150
Creating a Navigational System 151
The Site Map 151
Building Breadcrumb Trails with the SiteMapPath Control 155
TreeView Control 158
The Menu Control 161
Using the MultiView Control 165
Chapter Summary 168
Review Questions 169
Hands-On Projects 173
Case Projects 176

**CHAPTER FOUR**
**Custom Designing Web Applications**                                   **181**
Customizing the Presentation Layer 182
Using Style Sheets to Configure a Web Page Dynamically 182
Using Skins to Format a Web Form 184
Using Themes to Create a Uniform Web Page 187
User Controls 197
Understanding User Controls 198
Creating and Registering a User Control 200
Web Parts and Portals 202
Web Parts 202
Web Portals 211
The Use of Third-Party Controls 213
Dot Net Nuke 213
FreeTextBox 213
Telerik 214
Other Third-Party TextBox Controls 214
Retrieving Information from a TextBox Control 215
The Value of Retrievable Data 216
Chapter Summary 217
Review Questions 217
Hands-On Projects 220
Case Projects 223

**CHAPTER FIVE**
**Advanced Web Controls**                                               **225**
The AdRotator Control 226
The Role of the Advertisement File 226
Modifying the Advertisement File 228
Understanding the Properties of the AdRotator Control 230

Inserting the AdRotator Control into a Web Page                                231
Creating the Web Page to Display the AdRotator                                232
The Calendar Control                                                           233
Supported Properties, Methods, and Events                                     234
Creating a Program to Interact with the Calendar Control                      235
Working with Multiple Dates                                                    237
Using the FileUpload Control                                                   238
Uploading a File with the FileUpload Control                                  239
Creating the File Upload Page                                                 240
Changing Security Permissions to the Upload Folder                           242
Sending E-Mail from the Web Page                                              244
Security and Privacy Issues Related to E-Mail                                245
The Role of the E-Mail Server                                                 245
Configuring the E-Mail Server                                                 246
CDONTS and E-Mail Objects                                                     250
Sending an E-Mail Message from an ASP.NET Web Page                           254
Troubleshooting the Sending of E-Mail Messages                               256
Storing and Retrieving Data in the Web Server's File System                  257
Working with Directories and the DirectoryInfo Class                         257
Creating and Deleting Directories with the DirectoryInfo Class               260
Creating and Reading Files from an ASP.NET Page                              263
Security Issues Related to Building Web Applications                          268
Chapter Summary                                                               270
Review Questions                                                              271
Hands-On Projects                                                             276
Case Projects                                                                 282

CHAPTER SIX
Securing the ASP.NET Application                                              285
Building Information Management Security Policies                             286
Security Policies                                                             287
Privacy Policies                                                             289
Passing Valid Data from a Web Form                                           289
Understanding Validation Controls                                            290
Building Regular Expressions                                                 294
Validating Form Data with Validation Controls                               299
Maintaining State                                                            303
Maintaining State with Client-Side Cookies                                  304
Maintaining State with HTTP Cookies                                         307
Maintaining State without HTTP Cookies                                      311
Storing Session Data                                                         313
Storing and Retrieving Session Data                                         314
Storing Session Data                                                         316
Application Configuration                                                    323
Viewing and Understanding the Web Server Property Sheets                    323
Understanding Application Configuration Files                               327
Membership Services                                                         337
Implementing Authorization                                                  337
Authenticating Users with Forms Authentication                             338
Implementing Authentication                                                 345
Using Web Controls to Maintain Security                                     348
Chapter Summary                                                             350

Review Questions                                                            351
Hands-On Projects                                                           356
Case Projects                                                              358

## CHAPTER SEVEN
## Managing Data Sources                                                   361
Working with Database Applications                                          362
    Characteristics of a Relational Database           362
    Relationships Between Tables                        363
    Applications That Store Relational Data             367
Visual Studio .NET Built-in Database Tools                                 368
    Creating a SQL Server Database in Visual Studio .NET   368
    Using the Table Designer                           369
    Creating a Relationship with the Database Diagram  376
Views and Queries                                                          378
    Using Views and Queries                            378
    Building a View with the Query and View Designer    379
    Using the Query and View Designer                   380
SQL Statements                                                             382
    Creating Search Conditions                         382
    Building SQL Queries to Insert, Update, and Delete Data   384
SQL Stored Procedures and SQL Server Scripts                               387
    Input and Output Parameters                        387
    The Return Code                                     388
    Creating Stored Procedures with the SQL Editor      388
    Creating a Stored Procedure with an Input Parameter   390
    Inserting a New Record with a Stored Procedure      392
    Using Wildcard Characters to Search for a Matching Value in a Column   393
    Modifying a Stored Procedure with the SQL Editor    394
    Using Built-in Views and Stored Procedures         394
    Using and Building SQL Server Scripts               395
Database Connections                                                       396
    Understanding the Connection String                 396
    Storing Connection Strings in the Web Configuration File   397
    Creating a Connection to a Database from a Web Page   399
    Creating a Connection to a Microsoft Access Database   403
    Creating a Connection to XML Data                   405
    Moving Data to SQL Server                           406
Chapter Summary                                                            409
Review Questions                                                           410
Hands-On Projects                                                          412
Case Projects                                                             416

## CHAPTER EIGHT
## Binding Data to Web Controls                                            419
Designing a Web Data Application in the .NET Framework                      420
    Data Access Components                              422
    Creating DataSets and DataAdapters                  423
    Data Binding Techniques                             428
    Binding Data to Web Controls                        429
    Repeated-Expression Binding                         432

Binding Data to Web Controls and Data Controls                                 432
    Binding Data in a Collection to a Web Control                          433
    Binding Data to a Data Control                                         434
Automatic Binding Techniques                                                    437
    Binding Data to a DataList Control                                     438
    Binding Relational Data to a GridView Control                          440
Overview of the ADO.NET Data Model                                             443
    ODBC and OLE DB                                                        444
    .NET Providers                                                         445
Retrieving Data in the .NET Framework                                          447
    Using the DataReader to Retrieve Data from a Database                  448
    Using the DataSet to Retrieve Data from a Database                     453
    Using the DataSet Object to Retrieve Data from an XML File             454
    The DataView Object                                                    455
Chapter Summary                                                                459
Review Questions                                                               460
Hands-On Projects                                                              462
Case Projects                                                                  465

**CHAPTER NINE**
**Customizing Data with Web Controls**                                         **467**
Templates and Styles Available to the Data Controls                            468
    Templates Available to Data Controls                                  468
    Styles Available to Data Controls                                      473
    Modifying the DataList Control Using Styles                            474
Modifying Data Controls Using Templates                                        476
    Using Templates to Modify the Repeater Control                         477
    Using Templates to Modify the DataList Control                         479
Using the GridView Control to Display Data                                     480
    GridView Columns                                                       480
    Column Properties                                                      482
    Column Data                                                            483
    Modifying the GridView Control Columns and Templates                   484
Building a Master-Detail Page with GridView and DetailsView Controls           487
Creating Custom Templates                                                      489
Chapter Summary                                                                492
Review Questions                                                               492
Hands-On Projects                                                              496
Case Projects                                                                  500

**CHAPTER TEN**
**Managing Data with ASP.NET**                                                 **503**
Inserting, Modifying, and Deleting Records                                     504
    Using the GridView Control to Maintain a Database                      504
    Filtering Data with the GridView Control                               505
    Sorting Data with the GridView Control                                 509
    Editing a New Record with the GridView Control                         510
    Deleting a New Record with the GridView Control                        515
    Inserting a New Record with the DetailsView Control                    515
    Using a FormView Control                                               516
    Using Templates and Styles with the FormView Control                   518

Data Management                                                      520
    Using Stored Procedures with a GridView Control                 520
    Using Stored Procedures with a FormView Control                 523
Securing Databases                                                  528
    Securing Databases                                              528
    Detecting Database Errors                                       529
Chapter Summary                                                     530
Review Questions                                                    531
Hands-On Projects                                                   535
Case Projects                                                       539

**CHAPTER ELEVEN**
**Advanced Web Programming                                          541**
Building Reusable Code                                              542
    Creating Reusable Code with Classes                            542
    Calling the Class from the Web Page                            543
    Creating and Using Classes                                     544
    Using Code Snippets                                            548
    Compiling the Application                                      551
    Third-Party Components                                         553
Building a Complete Application                                     555
    Starter Kits                                                    556
    Planning Your Web Application                                   557
    Analyzing Project Requirements                                 558
    Designing the User Interface and Programming Requirements      560
    Developing the Web Application                                  562
    Testing the Web Application                                     563
    Maintaining the Web Application                                 563
New Tools and Technologies                                         564
    AJAX                                                            564
    Atlas                                                           565
    Integrating ASP.NET into Current Business Applications         566
Deploying an ASP.NET Web Application                                566
Chapter Summary                                                     568
Review Questions                                                    568
Hands-On Projects                                                   572
Case Projects                                                       574

**CHAPTER TWELVE**
**Extending Web Applications                                        577**
Overview of Web Services                                            578
    Communicating Between Applications with Web Services            578
    Applying Web Services to Business Applications                  580
    Using Web Editors to Create and Consume Web Services           583
Web Services Standards and Protocols                                593
    Programming Web Services with .NET Development Editors          593
    The SOAP Contract                                               593
Creating a Web Service                                              595
    Creating a Web Service to Display Data from a Database          597
    Previewing the Web Service Home Page                            599

Using a Web Service                                                       602
    Locating a Web Service                                                602
    Consuming a Web Service from a Web Page                               604
    Locating Third-Party Web Services                                     605
Securing Web Services                                                     607
Working with Alternative Platforms: PDAs and Mobile Devices               609
    Creating a WML Document                                               609
    Building PDA and Mobile Applications in .NET Development Tools        610
    Using Mobile Controls in an ASP.NET Application                       612
Chapter Summary                                                           616
Review Questions                                                          617
Hands-On Projects                                                         621
Case Projects                                                             625

**APPENDIX A**
**.NET Development Editor Requirements, Setup, and Configuration    627**
Software Requirements – In Brief                                          628
Software Requirements – In Detail                                         628
    Operating System                                                      628
    Web Server                                                            629
    .NET Development Editors                                              629
    MSDN Library                                                          630
    Database Server                                                       630
    Database Application                                                  630
Hardware Requirements                                                     631
    Visual Studio .NET Professional Installation on Windows XP Professional  632
    Installing Visual Studio .NET on Windows Vista                        633
Compatibility Issues with Visual Studio .NET                              634

**APPENDIX B**
**Troubleshooting Data Connectivity Issues                          635**
Installing and Configuring the Database Server                            636
Database Connectivity for Web Applications                                637

**APPENDIX C**
**Working with Project and Solution Files                           639**
Managing Projects and Solutions                                           640
Using the Data Files and Solution Files                                   640
Setting up Alternative Configurations for Classroom Instruction           640
    Web Server Connection Methods Used to Publish Web Projects            642

**APPENDIX D**
**ASP.NET Controls                                                  643**
Control Hierarchy                                                         644
    HTML Server Controls                                                  644
    Web Controls                                                          645
Building Web Controls                                                     649

**APPENDIX  E**
**Using  C#**                                                          **651**
    Editors to Support Building Applications                              652

**INDEX**                                                                 **655**

# Preface

This book will familiarize you with ways to create dynamic Web applications using server-side programming technologies. A well-rounded Internet programmer needs to be able to integrate server technologies to produce Web applications that not only interact with visitors, but also integrate other computer applications.

Web sites today need to validate form data, as well as provide ways of interacting with visitors. In the past, you might have used JavaScript to create client-side scripts. You may have worried about which browser application and browser version would support your web site. Today, with the wide range of Internet-enabled devices, Internet applications must support devices such as mobile phones and hand-held devices that do not support JavaScript. Your challenge is to create applications that can be used in a variety of settings and on a variety of devices. Two .NET development editors that are commonly used to create ASP.NET applications are Visual Studio .NET and Visual Web Developer Express. You can create ASP.NET Web applications with both .NET development editors that are portable. These applications can be displayed on a simple hand-held device, or in the latest browser.

In the early days of the World Wide Web, a company might have created a web presence consisting of a few web pages that contained general information about the company. Today, companies are building Web applications to manage and deliver information to their customers and business partners. They are using databases to store, retrieve, and display data on the web. Although the need for business-to-business applications was recognized early, Internet programmers did not have the tools or skills to develop these types of web sites. Large companies could afford to build custom applications, while small to medium size businesses lacked the resources to develop Internet business applications. Microsoft's solution to building e-business applications with a new type of Internet application is known as a Web service. Web services are built on Internet standards and allow companies to share data and build applications that communicate over the Internet. Microsoft provides tools within the .NET development editors and ASP.NET to build Web services.

In this book, you will learn how to use ASP.NET to process form data from the client, and to send out e-mail from a web page. You will also learn how ASP.NET can be used to interact with other computer applications on the server. You will learn how to use ASP.NET to read and write information to a file on the server, and how ASP.NET can also be used to build Web applications that interact with a database. Finally, you will learn how to develop Web services and mobile Web applications.

## The Intended Audience

This book is intended for the individual who wants to create dynamic Web applications. You should be familiar with the Windows operating system and know how to use Internet Explorer to view web pages. A basic understanding of the Internet and HTML is recommended. No prior knowledge of programming is required. This book has been successfully used in a variety of settings including online. Students will get the most out of this book when it is used in conjunction with an instructor-led course. Clearly, the level of student's application of this topic will vary greatly with their programming ability.

This book provides background chapters on beginning programming concepts, including object-oriented programming and Visual Basic .NET, as well as the .NET Framework and the ASP.NET model. No prior knowledge of server programming is required. In later chapters, the book describes how to create web pages that interact with a Microsoft Access database and a SQL Server database. When you install either of the .NET development editors, a version of SQL Server Express is installed for free. These chapters explain relational database concepts, and use the Access database environment to upsize your database to SQL Server. No prior knowledge of database programming is required.

It is recommended that instructors structure the class presentations, course objectives, and class assignments to the level of experience of the students. Students who have a stronger background in web programming concepts, client-side programming, Visual Basic .NET, networking, and database programming will be able to develop more complex ASP.NET Web applications than a beginner. For these students, some of the content provided will be useful as a review of the programming concepts that they have already mastered. However, students who do not have prior knowledge of these topics will be able to accomplish all of the chapter objectives and successfully perform all of the in-chapter and hands-on project exercises.

## What's New

This book can be used with either Visual Studio .NET Professional 2005 or Visual Web Developer Express 2005, running on Windows XP Professional or Windows Vista. To aid instructors, difficult topics such as software installation and database connectivity have been included in Appendix A and Appendix B. Instructors will want to refer to Appendix C to get ideas on how to organize student projects and solutions on their web server.

There have been many new editions to this version and some of the content has been reorganized to provide basic programming concepts in Chapter 2, and more hands-on activities in Chapter 1. To clarify some of the more complex topics, such as ADO.NET, security, and web server configuration, the text has been expanded with additional samples, graphics, and screenshots. There are new ways to structure web sites. New master pages allow you to provide reusable content across your web site. New themes, skins, and style sheets allow you to dynamically change the look and feel of your web site. New navigation controls allow you to create breadcrumb trails, menus and site maps from XML data. There are several new editions to the data controls. A new GridView replaces the DataGrid, and DetailsView now makes it easy to create master-detail pages. The data controls support a simpler binding method, requiring no manual programming in most instances. Template editing is even easier in this edition. You can use the graphical template editors or edit the code manually in HTML view. User controls also remain part of ASP. However, a new set of controls allows you to create WebParts. This allows you to create sections of the page that can be combined, moved, deleted, and added by the user. Security is a major topic with .NET today. Within ASP.NET, security can easily be controlled using a Membership Service and Personalization Service. New Login controls allow you to easily design a membership system that secures the web site in combination with the Web.config files. Site counter controls allow you to manage and monitor usage of the site. New wizards allow you to set up roles, users, and rules manually or programmatically using global.asax and the code in the page. Authentication can still be based on either forms authentication or Windows. In the second edition, both scenarios were provided with examples of configuring web sites using each technique. With ASP.NET 2.0, forms authentication becomes easy to set up and configure.

The Teaching Tools have been updated to reflect the new edition. All of the databases that the students create are included within the solution files. One of the benefits of the new version of ASP.NET is the ability to create web sites without project and solution files. This makes setting up your data files easier than in previous editions. Furthermore, both the SQL Server and Access databases required for each chapter are already set up in the App_Data folder for each chapter. Instructions on how to use these files are included within the Instructor's Manual. A project assignment sheet in an HTML page is provided in the Teaching Tools. It includes hyperlinks to all of the solutions to the exercises in the book. Instructors can have students use this page to keep track of their activities or can customize this page for their own course requirements.

Students will not need to import data files. They should be able to copy the data files to their own student directory. We have included a swooping arrow as the line continuation character to indicate to students when to continue typing on the subsequent line. We have decreased the amount of typing required in many of the exercises. We have also included a text file with each chapter in the Teaching Tools. This file contains the text that is displayed in the figures. This will enable faculty to quickly copy and paste code into their applications during an in-class demonstration.

## The Approach

To facilitate the learning process, this book presents content and theory integrated with sample exercises. Each chapter includes a summary and review questions that highlight and reinforce major concepts that were presented. The hands-on projects are guided activities that let you practice and reinforce the techniques presented in the chapter. They also enhance your learning experience by providing additional ways to apply your knowledge in new situations. At the end of each chapter, there are several case projects that allow you to use the skills that you have learned in the chapter to solve real-world problems. These cases can be used by beginner developers who need to learn to apply concepts learned in the chapter. The instructor can add additional requirements to these case studies. Therefore, they can also be used in an advanced course to allow students to build and develop more robust programming applications.

The examples provided in each chapter were developed to provide you with the opportunity to practice the skills discussed within the chapter. They are not dependent upon successful completion of the previous chapter. Therefore, you can always move ahead to another chapter, while still reviewing content presented in a previous chapter.

The approach and sequence of topics was chosen based upon experience teaching ASP.NET in the classroom. Beginning ASP.NET developers need to have a strong grasp of the basic concepts. They need to see a variety of techniques that are used in real-world applications. In this book, a layering approach is integrated within the chapters. Instead of jumping into web databases, this book begins with form processing and validation. Then, it moves to binding data using controls and data structures such as ArrayLists and HashTables. In later chapters students take another step to bind to data objects such as the DataReader and DataSet. Then, they extract this knowledge to build a data component in Visual Basic .NET. Finally, they expose their web database application as a Web service. By using this layered approach, students build upon the knowledge that they learned in previous chapters. This helps them review the information as well as focus on learning new concepts and skills.

There are several ways to accomplish the same task within the .NET development editors. This book uses several different methods to import data files, create connection strings, insert Web controls, configure Web applications, and preview web pages. Students are presented with different techniques so that they can select the ones that they prefer and that will match the business case.

Too much variety in a complex course tends to be difficult for students because they cannot focus on the learning objectives, and instead spend more time on assessment of the case study. Therefore, the majority of this book uses a sample fictional store called Tara Store as the focus of the hands-on activities. This is not a running case study. It provides a conceptual framework for students so that they can focus on learning the material, but are not reading about a new company in each chapter. Additional projects are included to provide some variety for students.

## Overview of this Book

The examples, hands-on exercises, projects, and cases in this book will help you achieve the following objectives:

- Describe the architecture of the .NET Framework and the ASP.NET object model
- Create basic web pages using ASP.NET and .NET development editors
- Use Server controls to create dynamic Web applications
- Validate form data using server-side Validation controls
- Use server-side programming to process forms, send e-mail from a web page, and read and write to files on the server
- Locate Internet resources that include information ASP.NET and .NET development editors
- Create XML documents and transform them into XHTML using XSLT style sheets
- Become familiar with object-oriented programming and Visual Basic .NET programming techniques
- Become familiar with relational database concepts and learn how to create queries using SQL
- Create and manage databases using Microsoft Access and SQL Server
- Create dynamic Web applications that interact with a database using server-side programming
- Create reusable server components to retrieve data from SQL Server using stored procedures and Visual Basic .NET
- Configure your Web applications to optimize web performance and minimize security risks
- Become familiar with methods to debug and troubleshoot your Web application.
- Create Web services that allow your Web application to interact with other server-based applications
- Create Web applications that can be displayed on mobile devices

In **Chapter 1**, you will learn about the ASP.NET object model. You will also learn about the new HTML and ASP.NET Server controls, and about how Visual Basic .NET programs are integrated with ASP.NET pages. You will use the .NET development editor tools to create a Web application. You will locate Internet resources that provide additional information on ASP.NET, and you will learn about the architecture of the .NET Framework. You will have hands on exercises to create a Web application and content items. You will learn about HTML as well as XHTML and XML. In

**Chapter 2**, you will learn how to program using Visual Basic .NET. You will learn basic object-oriented programming concepts such as how to create classes, functions, and procedures. You will learn how to create code to handle server events and store data. You will use decision control structures to alter the execution order of a program and looping control structures to repeat blocks of code. You will learn to create User controls to store reusable content and code. You will create ASP.NET pages using HTML Server controls. You will build cascading style sheets using the Style Builder tool. You will learn how to customize the toolbox. In **Chapter 3**, you will create ASP.NET pages with web server controls. You will create, validate, and process forms. You will use master and content pages to manage your web site content. You will use navigation controls such as TreeView, breadcrumb trails, and Menu controls. In **Chapter 4**, you will learn how to enhance your Web application using themes, skins, and style sheets. You will learn how to manage content with WebParts and User controls. In **Chapter 5** you will create an XML file to store your web site banner ads, and use an AdRotator control to manage your banner ads. You will learn how to insert and style the Calendar control, and integrate data with the calendar. You will learn how to send outbound e-mail from your web page. You will use the FileUpload control to upload files to the web server without requiring a file transfer program. You will also learn how to create programs that interact with the file and directory systems. You will create XML data files, XSLT style sheets, and transform them into an XHTML page using the XML control. You will also use a MultiView control to display dynamic content.

There are three chapters that focus specifically on web databases. **Chapter 6** provides information on form validation, maintaining state, web site configuration, personalization and membership services, and role management. You will learn how to store your user login information in various data structures. In **Chapter 7**, you will learn about relational databases. You will learn how to create database connections, create Access and SQL Server databases, and build SQL scripts and stored procedures. You will also learn to use the database tools to create your table structures and build SQL queries. You will create data-driven web pages. You will learn how to create stored procedures and build connection strings. **Chapter 8** describes how to build more complex web database applications. You will learn how to use different Data objects to bind and display various types of data. This chapter explains how to bind a Data object to various Data controls that are located within the web page. You will also learn to work with a variety of new Data controls such as a DataGrid and Repeater. You will learn more about the ADO.NET Framework.

In **Chapter 9**, you will learn how display your data using a variety of templates, styles, and style sheets. You will build a master-detail page using a variety of data controls. In **Chapter 10**, you will learn how to manage data. You will insert, modify, and delete data using a variety of tools and controls, including stored procedures and parameter queries. You will learn how to secure your SQL Server databases. In **Chapter 11**, you will learn to build reusable components. You will locate and consume third party web components from a web page. You will also learn about how to build and deploy a complete Web application. In **Chapter 12**, you will learn to create Web services. You will describe the standards and protocols used to create Web services. You will locate and consume third party Web services from a web page. You will learn how to manage files and directories on the server and to store and retrieve data from a file on the server. You will learn how to send e-mail from a web page. Finally, you will create web pages that can be viewed on mobile devices using Mobile Server controls.

**Appendix A** details the software and hardware requirements, provides guidelines for installing Windows XP Professional and the Web server, and provides step-by-step instructions for installing Visual Studio .NET 2005 Professional. While Chapter 7 covers database concepts and how to use the database tools within the editors, **Appendix B** covers troubleshooting installation, configuration, and data connectivity issues with SQL Server. **Appendix C** provides detailed information working with projects and solution files, using the data and solution files, and alternative ways to configure the classroom servers. You will find that with the new edition and new software, managing projects is easier in classrooms and labs. **Appendix D** discusses control hierarchy, Server controls, third-party controls, and custom controls. **Appendix E** provides information on differences with C# and Visual Basic .NET with respect to Web application development.

## Features

- **Chapter Objectives:** Each chapter in this book begins with a list of the important concepts to be mastered within the chapter. This list provides you with a quick reference to the contents of the chapter as well as a useful study aid.

- **Step-By-Step Methodology:** As new concepts are presented in each chapter, tutorials are used to provide step-by-step instructions that allow you to actively apply the concepts you are learning. Many of the hands-on projects at the end of the chapter also provide step-by-step instruction. Students often need additional cases to apply the concepts learned in the chapter. These hands-on activities provide a great way to reinforce the material.

- **Modular Approach:** Each chapter contains exercises, hands-on projects, and case projects that are self-contained. Many of the chapters can be taught in a different scope and sequence. For example, a course in web databases may only need to cover Chapters 1, 2, 7, 8, 9, and 10. A course in Visual Basic .NET may want to use this book to teach about web programming and include only a subset of chapters, such as Chapters 1, 2, 3, 4, 5, and 11. This book can be used to teach two separate courses in ASP.NET using Chapters 1–6 without web databases in the first course and 7–12 in the second course.

- **Figures and Tables:** Figures help you visualize web-architecture components and relationships, and other basic concepts. Tables list examples of code components and their variations in a visual and readable format.

- **Tips:** Chapters contain tips designed to provide you with practical advice and proven strategies related to the concept that is being discussed. Tips also provide suggestions for resolving problems you might encounter while proceeding through the chapters.

- **Chapter Summaries:** Each chapter's text is followed by a summary of chapter concepts. These summaries provide a helpful way to recap and revisit the ideas covered in each chapter.

- **Review Questions:** End-of-chapter assessment begins with a set of approximately 20 review questions that reinforce the main ideas introduced in each chapter. These questions ensure that you have mastered the concepts and understand the information you have learned. The end of the chapter includes multiple-choice questions to provide a method to assess a student's knowledge of the basic concepts and short answer questions that provide a method to assess a student's ability to apply the concepts learned in the chapter.

- **Hands-On Projects:** Along with conceptual explanations and step-by-step tutorials, each chapter provides hands-on projects related to each major topic aimed at providing you with practical experience. Some of the hands-on projects provide detailed instructions, while others provide less detailed instructions that require you to apply the materials presented in the current chapter with less guidance. As a result, the hands-on projects provide you with practice implementing web programming in real-world situations.

- **Case Projects:** Approximately four cases are presented at the end of each chapter. These cases are designed to help you apply what you have learned in each chapter to real-world situations. They give you the opportunity to independently synthesize and evaluate information, examine potential solutions, and make recommendations, much as you would in an actual business situation.

## TEACHING TOOLS

The following supplemental materials are available when this book is used in a classroom setting. All of the Teaching Tools available with this book are provided to the instructor on a single CD-ROM.

**Electronic Instructor's Manual.** The Instructor's Manual that accompanies this textbook includes additional instructional material to assist in class preparation, including items such as sample syllabi, chapter outlines, technical notes, lecture notes, quick quizzes, teaching tips, discussion topics, and key terms. Each chapter includes references to additional Internet resources in the Instructor Manual. It is very useful to layer a project on top of this course.

Students can build their web project as they learn new features and skills during the course. Many of the case studies provide opportunities to assign students learning activities that could be integrated into a course project. Sample guidelines for assigning and grading a course web project are found in the Instructor Manual.

**ExamView**®. This textbook is accompanied by ExamView, a powerful testing software package that allows instructors to create and administer printed, computer (LAN-based), and Internet exams. ExamView includes hundreds of questions that correspond to the topics covered in this text, enabling students to generate detailed study guides that include page references for further review. The computer-based and Internet testing components allow students to take exams at their computers, and also save the instructor time by grading each exam automatically.

**PowerPoint presentations**. This book comes with Microsoft PowerPoint slides for each chapter. These are included as a teaching aid for classroom presentation, to make available to students on the network for chapter review, or to be printed for classroom distribution. Instructors can add their own slides for additional topics they introduce to the class.

**Solution Files**. Solutions to steps within a chapter and end-of chapter exercises are provided on the Teaching Tools CD-ROM and may also be found on the Course Technology web site at *www.course.com*. The solutions are password protected.

**Distance Learning**. Course Technology is proud to present online test banks in WebCT and Blackboard to provide the most complete and dynamic learning experience possible. Instructors are encouraged to make the most of the course, both online and offline. For more information on how to access the online test bank, contact your local Course Technology sales representative.

# ACKNOWLEDGMENTS

No book is written on an island. So, I would like to thank Jill Batistick, Developmental Editor, Tricia Coia, and the entire Course Technology team for making this book happen. Thank you to the reviewers who provided invaluable comments and suggestions during the development of this book. These include: Mike Michaelson, Palomar College; Pat Paulson, Winona State University; Bonnie Ryan, New Brunswick Community College; Paul Sbraccia, Macomb Community College.

The Tara Store case study is modeled after Joy of Ireland (*www.JoyOfIreland.com*), which was a real brick and mortar store well known for its customer service, quality products, and vast product line. I'd like to thank the owner Mike Joy for allowing me to use the photographs of his store and products in the fictitious Tara Store. Slainte!

Thank you to my husband John. I'd like to dedicate this book to Vincent Kalata and Christy Kalata, whose sacrifices, love and support have always been greatly appreciated. May all your dreams come true. Go raibh maith agat. (Thank you.)

# Read This Before You Begin

## To the User

You can use your own computer to complete the exercises, hands-on projects, and case projects in this book. To use your own computer, you will need the following:

- **Microsoft Windows XP Professional or Windows Vista.** Your computer must be configured so that you can connect to the Internet. Your login user account will need to be able to modify NTFS security permissions to folders and files and have access to administrative tools that are installed with Windows XP. The book was tested on Windows XP Professional; however, you may use Windows Vista to run the editors and ASP.NET 2.0.

- **A .NET Development Editor.** You may use either Visual Studio .NET professional 2005, or Visual Web Developer Express 2005 (VWD). The VWD editor has the same look and feel as Visual Studio .NET, with additional new features and is downloadable for free from *www.asp.com*. The visual database and mobile control tools are now available within VWD. You can select the default installation. It is recommended that you install all of the documentation locally so that you do not need the CD each time you view a Help file. You should read the ReadMe file that comes with the installation disks. Appendix A provides a step-by-step guide for installing the software.

- **Web Server.** If you use either .NET development editor, you do not need to install a separate web server. The web server is packaged with the editors. If you do not have one of these editors, you will require a web server that is compatible with ASP.NET such as Internet Information Server. In this case, you may also have to enter all of the code manually for some activities in the application, and manage the databases using native database tools.

- **Microsoft Access XP or Microsoft Access 2007.** You will use Access XP to create the database tables and queries and upsize your database to SQL Server. However, you can work through all of the exercises without Access. You can learn more about the features in Access at *www.microsoft.com/office/access*.

- **SQL Server.** SQL Server Express 2005 comes with both .NET development editors for free. SQL Server Express is needed to create the database tables, queries, and stored procedure. Appendix B contains useful information on troubleshooting database connectivity problems with the SQL Server. Alternately, you can use the full version of SQL Server. If you use Visual Web Developer Express, you will not be able to work with remote SQL Server databases.

■ **Student Data Files.** To complete the steps and projects in the chapters, you will need data files that have been created specifically for this book. You may obtain these files from your instructor. You may also download them from the Course Technology web site by going to *www.course.com*, and then searching by title or ISBN. You will need a place to store your data files. The data files are named after the chapter, for example Chapter01Data, Chapter02Data, etc. Projects and solutions no longer maintain pointers to all of the files in the project. What that means is that projects are folder-based. Students can keep their projects on a disk or web site, and not in the IIS folder structure. They can test them locally, and optionally transfer them to a web server at a later date. It is useful to keep each project and case data and solution files in their own folders within the chapter folder.

■ **Web Folder on a Web Server.** Because a web server is installed with the editor, you do not need to use a live web server for testing. However, once you log off the computer and leave the editor, the web server is no longer running. You may be required to post your solutions to a live web server. In each chapter, you will create a single project named after the chapter, for example, Chapter1, Chapter2, and Chapter3. You will be creating many files as you proceed through the tutorials, hands-on projects, and case projects within this single project. This way you will be able to manage all of your files for the chapter within a single location. Appendix C contains additional setup information for organizing Web applications on the web server. The book uses the local web server to publish the chapter web projects. If you use a remote web server, you will need to either FTP your projects or use FrontPage extensions to upload your projects to the remote web server. You should work with your network system administrator to setup permissions to your Web server and to configure your editor.

■ **Visual Basic .NET.** Visual Basic .NET was selected as the primary language for this book because of its ease of use for beginners, and its integration with other courses that are often taught at the beginning programming level. Appendix E provides additional information on some of the differences in syntax between Visual Basic .NET and C#. All of the exercises in this book use classes that are available within the .NET Framework to both programming languages. Therefore, all of the examples in this book can be recreated using C#. Additional information on this is provided in the Instructor Manual. In an advanced class, this is often an exercise that can be assigned for practice learning in both .NET languages.

## A NOTE ON SYNTAX

The exercises in this book often contain code statements that the user must type in the web page. These statements are sometimes too long to fit on one line in a book, and must be split over two lines. A swooping arrow character is used to identify when the code statement is split across two or more lines. It is important that you type the code statement on a single line. An example of using the swooping arrow is as follows:

```
<%@ Page Language="vb" AutoEventWireup="false" ⤵
Codebehind="WebForm1.aspx.vb"
Inherits="TaraStore.WebForm1"%>
```

## TO THE INSTRUCTOR

To complete all the exercises and chapters in this book, your users must work with a set of files, called a Data Disk, and download software from web sites. The data files are included on the Instructor's Resource CD. They may also be obtained electronically through the Course Technology web site at *www.course.com*. Follow the instructions in the Help file to copy the user files to your server or standalone computer. You can view the Help file using a text editor, such as WordPad or Notepad.

After the files are copied, you can make Data Disks for the users, yourself, or tell your students where to find the files so they can make their own Data Disks. Make sure the files are set up correctly by having students follow the instructions in the "To the User" section of Read This Before You Begin.

These are some of the software issues that you will need to consider when setting up your course. You should thoroughly read Appendices A, B, and C before you plan your course. These appendices will provide additional information required to create remote web projects and configure Visual Studio .NET.

## COURSE TECHNOLOGY DATA FILES

You may only use the data and solution files and content from the Teaching Tools if the course has included the textbook as a required text for the course. You are granted a license to copy the data files to any student personal computer or school local computer network used by individuals who have purchased this book so that they can complete the exercises. Please do not place these files in an unprotected site on the Internet. If they are distributed to students electronically, they should be password protected.

## VISIT OUR WORLD WIDE WEB SITE

Additional materials for your course may be available at the Course Technology Web site. Go to *www.course.com* and search for this book by title, author, or ISBN for more information and materials to accompany this text.

# 1

# INTRODUCTION TO WEB PROGRAMMING

### In this chapter you will:

♦ Learn about Web developer tools

♦ Work with the basics of HTML

♦ Work with the basics of XML

♦ Understand the role of ASP.NET server programming

♦ Locate Help resources

In the past, Web development courses focused on teaching specific technical skills such as how to create a Web page. While this knowledge remains important in the Web development profession, Web development is no longer just focused on developing Web pages for a browser. It now requires the integration of Web development concepts with networking, programming, design, content management, project management, business, entrepreneurship, and other disciplines.

In the past, browser applications did not support the same versions of HTML and companies had to develop different Web sites for each software platform. The latest version of HTML, called XHTML, aims to help provide unified standards to present content. In this chapter, you will learn how to create and build basic Web pages using HTML, XHTML, and a Web server-based technology called ASP.NET. ASP.NET is a language-independent technology that is used to develop Web applications. This technology will allow you to create Web applications that are run on the server, but can send out standard HTML or XHTML to the client software. As a result, companies can develop a single Web application that will be supported by a variety of software applications.

## INTRODUCING VISUAL WEB DEVELOPER TOOLS

Where applications were once hand-coded by developers, rapid application development tools now allow developers to build higher-quality applications more quickly. These tools allow developers to create prototypes, develop reusable software components, and facilitate communication and file management.

There are many text and Web page editors that can be used to create Web applications. You can create your Web application using a basic text editor, and then copy or upload the application to a Web server using a basic file transfer program (FTP). However, you will be more productive if you use an ASP.NET-compatible Web editor such as **Visual Studio .NET** or **Visual Web Developer Express (VWD)**. While all the code in this book was created with VWD, it is compatible with the code created by Visual Studio .NET. VWD was chosen as a platform for this book because it contains the same basic ASP.NET features as Visual Studio .NET, and is freely available by download from Microsoft. For more information on how to set up your computer with these Web developer tools, check out Appendix A.

In the following sections, you will explore some of the features available in the visual Web editors and their associated windows.

## Exploring Visual Web Editors

Using Visual Studio .NET and VWD provides Web developers and windows programmers a consistent programming model. All of Microsoft's major programming languages share this single developing environment.

As you can see in Figure 1-1 there are many windows, controls, and toolbars within the user interface. When you start your program, a **Start Page** provides access to your recently created applications and links to the MSDN support site, additional tools, and tutorials available for download. After you have created a Web application, you can click the application name on the Start page to reopen the application quickly. If you have closed the Start Page and want to reopen it, click View on the menu bar, select Other Windows, and then click Start Page.

## Exploring the Individual Windows

The **Properties window** is used to set properties for objects, controls, and classes. When you click a control, such as an image in a Web page, the properties for that image is displayed in the Properties window. Many properties can be set through the Properties window during the design of the Web pages, as shown in Figure 1-2. However, some properties of Web pages and controls can only be set programmatically. In later chapters, you will learn to set properties of the controls and the Web page using the Properties window and programmatically in the code.

The **Main window**, as was shown in Figure 1-1, is used to view your project files. When you open multiple documents in the main window at the same time, a document tab appears

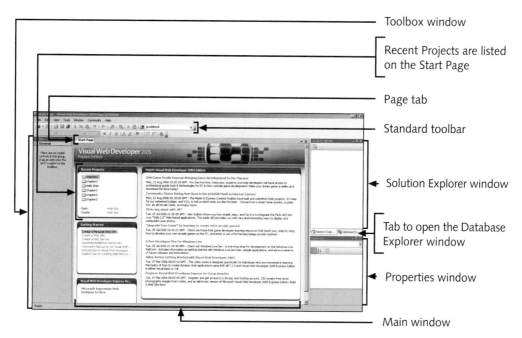

**Figure 1-1**   The Visual Web Developer user interface

in the main window to allow you to switch between documents easily. If you open a large number of documents, you can use the next and previous buttons to navigate through the other tabs. (Note: These buttons appear to the right of the document tabs.)

The **Solution Explorer window** is used to manage all of the files and resources within your Web application. The **Database Explorer window** is used to create and manage connections to databases and to manage data objects such as tables and stored procedures.

The **Toolbox window** (commonly called the **Toolbox**) contains frequently used controls. These controls are organized using tabs. If you create code that you plan to reuse, you can customize the Toolbox and add the code to the General tab.

Note the following about the General and other tabs of the Toolbox:

- **Standard tab:** Contains many of the ASP.NET controls that are used within ASP.NET pages.

- **Data tab:** Provides access to data controls used to display data, and data source controls.

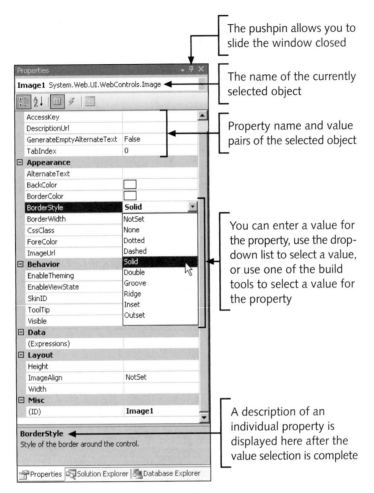

The pushpin allows you to slide the window closed

The name of the currently selected object

Property name and value pairs of the selected object

You can enter a value for the property, use the drop-down list to select a value, or use one of the build tools to select a value for the property

A description of an individual property is displayed here after the value selection is complete

**Figure 1-2**   The Properties window

- **Validation tab:** Provides access to controls used to validate Web page forms. Validation controls are a form of ASP.NET controls that allow you to assign validation rules to other controls. You can build custom validation rules to validate your form fields, or use one of the prepackaged form field Validation controls.

- **Navigation tab:** Provides access to controls used to create site maps, menus, and tree views.

- **Login tab:** Provides access to controls that are used to create a login, password recovery and change password forms, controls to view the visitors' login status, and wizards to create users.

- **WebParts tab:** Provides access to create and manage a new way of organizing Web pages using Web Parts and Web Zones.

- **HTML tab:** Provides access to the traditional HTML tags. This tab does not include basic HTML tags such as the anchor tag or formatting tags such as the heading tag. These items are located within an HTML toolbar.

- **General tab:** Does not contain any controls by default. This tab is used to store user created controls and snippets of code that you might want to reuse.

Some windows, such as the **Task List window**, are not visible by default. This window allows you to manage a list of user tasks and comments within your application. You can mark code so that you can locate it quickly. To open the Task List window, click the View menu and select Task List. If any of these windows are not open, you can reopen them by clicking the View menu and then selecting the name of the window.

The Standard tab and the Task List window are shown in Figure 1-3.

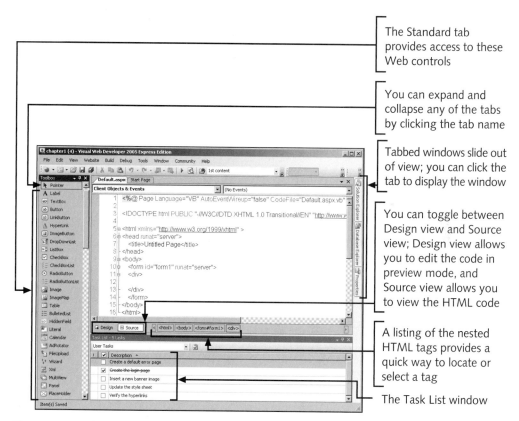

**Figure 1-3**   The Standard tab and the Task List window

## Auto Hide Property

The **Auto Hide property** is a new feature that allows you to store the window on the desktop as a tab. The tab is labeled with the name of the window. When you click the tab or drag the pointer over the tab, its associated window slides open. For example, the Properties window can be hidden as a tab. The Properties window slides out when you drag the pointer over the Properties window tab. When you drag your pointer outside of the Properties window tab, the Properties window will collapse. To turn this feature off and make the window stick to the desktop, click the pushpin icon on the window's menu bar; the pushpin changes so that it is facing down. To turn this feature back on, click the pushpin icon again. You can also set this feature by right-clicking the Properties window title bar and selecting Auto Hide.

## Dockable Property

Windows have additional properties that allow you to customize the layout of your user environment. The **Dockable property** allows windows to be moved to other locations on the desktop and to be placed on top of one another. When one window is docked on top of another window, the user interface creates several tabs that you can use to move back and forth between each window.

## Floating Property

The **Floating property** allows you to select the window and drag and drop it to any location on the desktop; the window does not have to be placed on top of another window. It is useful to practice moving the windows. If you want to return to the default window layout, click the Window menu, and then click Reset Window Layout. An alert box will ask you to confirm your selection; you should click Yes.

# Create a New Web Application

In this exercise you will create a basic Web application. Doing so will give you a feel for the user interface for your visual Web developer program. Remember that in this book, all the exercises will refer to [*your student folder*], as discussed in Appendix A. Your instructor will provide you with the location where you are to create and save your projects.

To create a new Web application:

1. Start your Web editor application.

2. To create a new project, click the **File** on the menu bar and click **New Web Site**. The New Web Site window opens. ASP.NET Web Site is selected by default and is used to create a blank ASP.NET Web site. By default, File System is selected in the Location drop-down list and Visual Basic is selected in the Language drop-down list, as shown in Figure 1-4.

3. To locate [*your student folder*], click the **Browse** button, which opens the Choose Location window, as shown in Figure 1-5.

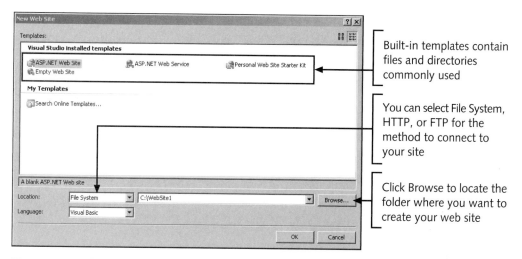

Built-in templates contain files and directories commonly used

You can select File System, HTTP, or FTP for the method to connect to your site

Click Browse to locate the folder where you want to create your web site

**Figure 1-4**   The New Web Site window

You can create the site on the local file system, or use FTP or HTTP to create the site on a remote system

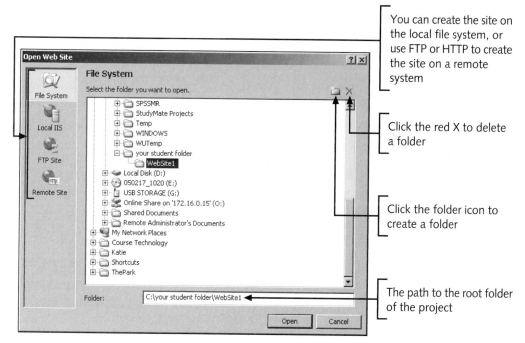

Click the red X to delete a folder

Click the folder icon to create a folder

The path to the root folder of the project

**Figure 1-5**   The Choose Location window

4. Navigate through your file system to locate and click **[*your student folder*]**.

5. You now need to create a new folder within [*your student folder*] to store your first Web application. To do so, click the **Create New Folder** icon, type

**WebSite1**, and then press **Enter**. The complete file path to your new Web application will be displayed in the Folder text box.

6. Click **Open**, which closes the Choose Location window.

7. Click **OK** to create your Web application and close the New Web Site window.

8. To close the Web application, click **File** on the menu bar and then click **Close Project**.

9. To exit, click **File** on the menu bar and click **Exit**.

In the next section, you will learn how to use HTML to create a Web page.

## Introduction to HTML

**Hypertext Markup Language (HTML)** is a markup language that provides an easy means to locate and access cross-platform documents called Web pages. Today the most common Web browsers are Internet Explorer, FireFox, America Online, and Netscape Browser. The browser, which allows you to view Web pages on the Internet, is an example of a client application. A **client application** runs on your local computer, and the Web browser allows your computer to view many types of files including Web pages.

HTML is based on **Standard Generalized Markup Language (SGML)**, which defines the data in a document independent of how the data will be presented. HTML uses tags to instruct browsers how to format (or render) the Web page. Browsers use HTML to create Web pages. These Web pages are viewable no matter which computer platform you use.

You may feel that a review of HTML is not necessary for your career as a Web programmer; however, you will find this knowledge useful in situations such as customizing your Web database applications and using skins and style sheets to modify your Web site design.

**NOTE**

HTML tags are used to display and format static content in the Web page. Browser software interprets HTML tags and formats the output. A static Web page displays the same content for all users because the Web server sends the same code to all the browsers. However, different browsers may render (or manipulate the visual appearance) of the content differently. Basic Web pages end in a file extension .htm or .html. As shown in Figure 1-6, when the browser requests the Web page (1), the request is directed to the Web server (2). The Web server receives the request, locates the file, and sends the HTML to the browser (3), which then renders the HTML (4).

The following sections demonstrate how to use basic HTML tags to create a Web page. Web pages can be created in a simple text editor program, such as Notepad, or a Web editor such as FrontPage, Visual Web Developer Express, Visual Studio .NET, or Dreamweaver MX. Web

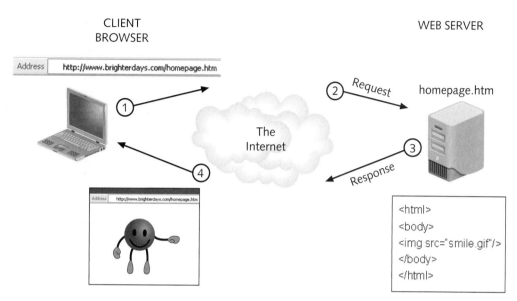

**Figure 1-6**   Processing a request for a static Web page

editors provide a graphical user interface that allows you to easily manipulate the HTML, layout, design, and features within a Web page.

## The Fundamentals of Tags and Attributes

There are two basic parts to an HTML tag: the opening tag and the closing tag. They are always enclosed within angle brackets (<>).The closing tag is differentiated from the opening tag with the forward slash (/) character within the tag name.

Content to be manipulated by tags must be between the two tags. An example of HTML is `<b>Course Technology</b>`. The `<b>` tag tells the browser to bold the subsequent text until the browser finds a closing tag `</b>`. Note that tags can be classified as inline or block. Inline tags apply only to a single tag within the page; block tags apply to multiple text items, such as multiple paragraphs or list items.

Within many HTML tags, you can specify additional attributes within the opening tag. These attributes provide a means of altering the tag in some way. In order to be compliant with the latest version of HTML, which is called XHTML, note that you must place the attribute values in quotation marks, even if the value is numeric. Some common attributes include the following:

   ■ The **id attribute** is used to provide a unique identifier for the tag within that document. The id attribute is an identifier of type ID and replaces the name attribute used in previous versions of HTML. In XHTML 1.1—and the next version of XHTML, which is 2.0—the use of the name attribute is not allowed.

- The **class attribute** is a space-separated list of cascading style sheet classes.
- The text in the **title attribute** is often used as an advisory title to the end user.

# HTML Structure

Static Web pages generally begin with the `<html>`tag and end with the `</html>` tag. There are two parts to a Web page, as follows:

- The **body section**, which is nested within the html tags. The body section is identified by a pair of body tags (`<body></body>`). Tags in the body section are used to provide the content that is displayed in the Web page.
- The **heading section**, which is identified by a pair of head tags (`<head></head>`). Tags used in the heading section provide additional functionality.

HTML code now needs to be compliant with XML standards, which allow Web content to be ported to an increasing variety of browsers and devices, such as cellular phones. The **xmlns attribute** in the opening head tag is used to identify the version of the standards that was used to create the Web page. The standards are maintained by the **World Wide Web Consortium (W3C)**. For more information on XHTML, visit the World Wide Web Consortium at *www.w3.org*.

Although HTML tags are not case sensitive, XML is case sensitive and XML requires that the case for the opening and closing tags match. In other words, XML considers `<HEAD>` and `<head>` to be different elements. It is important to note that with XHTML, you must use lowercase for all HTML tags and attributes. In this book, all HTML tags and properties are written in lowercase.

When you create Web pages only with HTML, you can preview the file locally with a Web browser without having to transfer the file to a Web server or place it on the Internet. Figure 1-7 is an example of a basic Web page with static content.

In the following sections, you learn more about what type of tags and content are used in the heading section and body section of a page.

## The Heading Section

In the heading section, the **title tags** (`<title></title>`) identify the page name in the title bar, in the history list, and in the favorites list within the browser application. The title tags are required in all XHTML-compliant Web pages. In the heading section, client-side programs within the **script tag** (`<script>`), written using JavaScript, are used to provide interactivity and validate forms. **Style sheets** within the `<style>` tags (or identified in an external file using the **link tag** (`<link>`)) are used to format the contents of the page. For example, the code `<link type="text/css" href="ch_sample1.css" />` will link the style sheet to the current page. Using the link tag allows you to use external style sheets, which can be applied across multiple pages within your Web site.

The Design and Source buttons allow you to toggle between editing the page and previewing the page

The xmlns attribute identifies that the page follows the XHTML standards

The tag hierarchy shows the nesting order of the tags

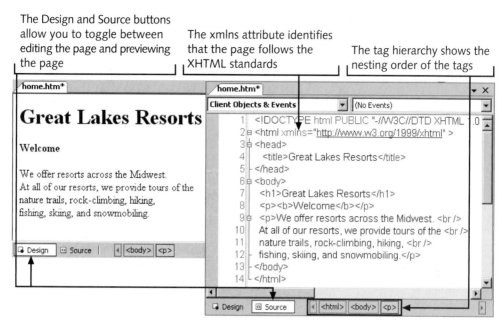

**Figure 1-7**   Static Web page created with HTML

The **meta tag** (<meta />) can be used to force the browser to identify keywords and other global values, reload the page, and identify the character encoding scheme. If the content attribute is set to zero, the Web page identified in the URL attribute will reload in the browser.

Note that the process of loading a new page into the browser is known as client-side redirection. When a Web page uses client-side redirection, as shown in the following code, you can see the original page before the browser loads the new page:

```
<meta http-equiv="refresh"
content="0;url=http://www.course.com" />
<meta name="keywords" content="Course Technology, ASP.NET" />
<meta name="description" content="Introduction to ASP.NET" />
```

You can split the HTML code into separate lines, but never split the attribute values within quotation marks.

**CAUTION**

You can use meta tags to dictate the character encoding set that will be used on a page. The **ISO 8859** family of character codes is used to encode many different types of languages, as follows:

- ISO 8859-1 is often defaulted because it is used for English and most Western European languages.

- ISO 8859-16 adds many Eastern European languages including Albanian, Croatian, Hungarian, Polish, Romanian, and Slovenian, as well as Irish Gaelic and Finnish.

- ISO 8859-6 is used for Arabic languages.
- ISO 8859-8 is used for Hebrew and Yiddish.

## The Body Section

In the body section, the **body tag** (<body></body>) can alter the format of the entire document. The current version of the body tag allows you to change the color of the background, or use an image as the background. Both are discussed in the following subsections.

**Colors for the Background**    To have any significance to the browser, the opening body tag must contain an attribute. The **bgcolor attribute** is used to change the color of the background. The value of the bgcolor attribute is assigned using the = sign. You should always place quotation marks around the value of the attribute because some browsers will not recognize the attribute values without the quotation marks. The HTML to create a Web page with a black background is as follows:

```
<body bgcolor="black">
```

HTML tags are sometimes referred to as HTML elements, and the attributes are referred to as properties. The current version of HTML, which is XHTML, requires all elements and attributes to be in lowercase.

**TIP**

In HTML, a color value can also be identified by the hexadecimal number associated with the color. A pound sign always precedes the hexadecimal value. Some browsers do not support color names as values of an attribute. Therefore, it is better to use the hexadecimal number associated with a color than it is to use the color name itself. The hexadecimal number associated with the color black is 000000.

**Images for the Background**    The background attribute of the body tag can be used to identify a background image for the Web page. If you insert a background image, the image will tile across and down the page by default. The **bgproperties attribute** allows you to set the background image to a fixed position. So, if the user scrolls down the page, the background image will not scroll. It will remain in place while the content of the page changes.

Images that are commonly supported by browsers have a .gif or .jpg extension. The background attribute identifies the location of the image. If the image is on the same Web server, you can use a relative address. A **relative address** identifies the path to the image in relation to the Web page. The location of the image can also be identified with a complete Web address known as the **Uniform Resource Locator (URL)**.

The following is an example of the common attributes used with the body tag:

```
<body bgcolor="#000000" background="images/disk.gif" ⤶
link="#FFFFFF" text="#33CC00" vlink="#FFFF66" ⤶
alink="#FF0066">
```

Now that you have learned how to change the background the next sections will show you how to format the content on your page.

**TIP**

## Tags that Contain or Format Text

In the body section, some HTML tags were created to act as containers for text and other content. This section will review some of the tags that have been commonly used in traditional HTML.

### Tags for Headings

**Heading tags** are used in the body to format a line of text with one of six predefined formats. The heading tag is <hn></hn>, where *n* represents a number from one through six. Heading 1 (<h1></h1>) will display the title in the largest font size, and Heading 6 (<h6></h6>) is displayed in the smallest font size.

### Tags for Paragraphs

A paragraph is defined by a set of **paragraph tags** (<p></p>). The closing paragraph tag indicates where a hard return will occur in the Web page. When you use this tag set, there will be a slight vertical space visible between the paragraphs. If you want to insert a blank line between two lines of text that do not include this vertical space, you can use the **line break tag** (<br />) instead.

The **blockquote tags** (<blockquote></blockquote>) indent text. Such indenting is often used to provide a visual emphasis for the text by separating the text from the main content. However, note that most developers use the tag only for indicating quotations.

The **span tags** (<span></span>) and the **div tags** (<div></div>) are container tags used to separate content into logical blocks. They are container tags, because they are primarily used to contain content and other tags. The difference between div and span is that the div tag will place a carriage return at the end of the content, causing the content following the div tag to start on a new line. The span tag formats the content within the current line.

A common use of the div tags is to position controls absolutely in the page. For instance, you can surround your controls with a pair of div tags. Then, in the opening div tag, set the style attribute to a string that will contain other attributes. Inside this string you would set the position attribute to absolute and set the z-index attribute to 0. (The z-index is used to determine which control to display on top when controls overlap.) You can then assign values for the width and height attributes of the div section in pixels. The top and left attributes will identify the number of pixels from the top of the page and from the left of the page.

The code following this paragraph shows how to place controls using the div tags. The paragraph tag uses absolute positioning without a div tag. The paragraph contains an image instead of text. The style attribute could have also been applied directly to the image tag. The first div tag provides a way to group the text box control Text1. The absolute positioning is within the style attribute of the text box control. The second div tag uses the style attribute to position the control absolutely. While the content of this div control is simply the text "Name," it could have been any control.

```
<p style="z-index: 101; position: absolute; ⤴
left: 8px; top: 4px"><img src="images/header.jpg"
width="809" height="83" alt="header" /></p>
<div><input id="Text1" style="z-index: 105; ⤴
left: 342px; position: absolute; top: 92px"
type="text" name="Text1" /></div>
<div style="display: inline; z-index: 107; ⤴
left: 165px; width: 70px; postition: absolute; ⤴
top: 96px; height: 15px">Name</div>
```

## Tags to Format Characters

The **bold tag** (<b>), the **italic tag** (<i>), and the **underline tag** (<u>) are used to modify the presentation of individual or groups of characters. Note, however, that in the current version of XHTML, the underline tag is no longer supported and content can be formatted as underline using style sheets.

Additional presentational tags include the **big tag** (<big>) to increase the font size, the **small tag** (<small>) to decrease the font size, the **sub tag** (<sub>) and the **sup tag** (<sup>) to include subscript and superscript, respectively, and the **tt tag** (<tt>) to include text in a typewriter font such as courier.

**TIP**

When you use a Web editor to create your Web page, the format toolbar contains buttons used to format the text as bold, italic, and underline. If you select your text and press the bold button, your HTML page might use the bold tag or the strong tag, depending on the version of the HTML standard that your Web editor supports. The bold tag is considered a presentational tag that presents a specific way to format the content. Structural tags, such as strong, are now preferred today over presentational tags. Structural tags allow more flexibility when creating content that might be displayed on various types of devices. For more information on strong tags, check the documentation that came with your Web editor.

## Tags for Creating a Horizontal Line

If you want to insert a horizontal line, you can use the **hr tag** (<hr />). The horizontal line was also referred to as a horizontal rule, which is where the hr tag originally obtained its name. The height of the horizontal line is set with the size attribute and the color of the line with the color attribute.

In previous versions of HTML, some attributes did not require a value to be set. These attributes included compact, nowrap, ismap, declare, noshade, checked, disabled, readonly, multiple, selected, noresize, and defer. As an example of their use, consider a situation in which you wanted a horizontal line to appear solid. In such a situation, you would use the noshade attribute with no value assigned. Thus, the code `<hr size="10" noshade />` would have displayed a solid line. These attributes were known as Boolean attributes. In the current version of XHTML, all Boolean attributes must be written using a name and a value. Thus, the code to insert the horizontal line would be rewritten as `<hr size="10" noshade="noshade" />`.

## Tags for Elements Other than Pure Text

Tags can also be used to format the presentation of the text and to insert non-textual content. In the following sections, you will learn how such tags can be used to format tables, insert hyperlinks, and perform other presentation tasks.

### Creating Tables

Creating a table with HTML tags is more complicated than inserting text. Tables require **table tags** (`<table></table>`) to identify the beginning and ending of the table. The table tag uses attributes to set the table width, height, border, and background color and background image.

Nested within the table tag are one or more **table row tags** (`<tr></tr>`) used to define the beginning and ending of a row. Nested within each table row tag is one or more **table cell tags** (`<td></td>`). Additional tags such as **table heading cell tags** (`<th></th>`) can be used to identify the table heading cells and will by default display their contents as bolded text.

The **table heading**, **table body**, and **table footer tags** (`<thead></thead>`, `<tbody></tbody>`, and `<tfoot></tfoot>`, respectively) are used to identify the table header, body, and footer sections. You can include a caption for the table using the **caption tags** (`<caption></caption>`). The **colgroup tags** (`<colgroup></colgroup>`) are used as the parent tags for one or more **column tags** (`<col></col>`). These column tags are empty elements that are primarily used to contain attributes such as the column width.

### Generating Forms

**Forms** are commonly used to allow users to register on a Web site, to log in to a Web site, to order a product, and to send feedback. Forms are defined by a set of **form tags** (`<form></form>`).

Forms contain many types of form elements, such as text boxes, radio buttons, check boxes, and drop-down lists. Each form element (or form field) has traditionally been assigned a name with the name attribute. Users enter values into the text boxes, or make selections from the radio buttons, check boxes, and drop-down lists. When the user clicks the submit button, the values he or she enters or selects are passed with the name of the form element to the Web server. In previous versions of HTML there could be more than one form in the page as long as they were identified using different names. However, in the current version of XHTML 1.1, the name attribute is not permitted. With the next version of XHTML, 2.0, the entire group of form elements is subject to a radical change to a new method known as **XForms**. However, this standard is not yet approved by the W3C or widely accepted.

## Creating Numbered and Bulleted Lists

Lists can be formatted using **unordered list tags** (`<ul></ul>`) and **ordered list tags** (`<ol></ol>`). Unordered lists do not convey significance in the order in which the elements appear; ordered lists are often used when you want to indicate a series or sequence of steps. Nested within the unordered and ordered list tags are **list item tags** (`<li></li>`) for each element in the list. You can modify the type of bullet or character used or the starting number with attributes.

## Images and Image Maps

The **image tag** (`<img/>`) is used to add a graphic image to the Web page. The image tag contains several attributes, such as width and height, that identify the dimensions of the image. The tag can also contain the following attributes:

- The **align attribute** is used to identify where the image is placed in relation to the current line. Frequently the image is aligned to the right or left of the text. To force the text to continue below the image, you can use the **line break tag** with the **clear attribute** (`<br clear="all" />`).

- The **src attribute** is the location to the image on the Internet using an absolute or relative Web address.

- The **hspace** and **vspace attributes** allow you to create horizontal and vertical padding (or whitespace) around the image when it is surrounded by text.

- The **border attribute** is used to specify a border around the image.

- The **alt attribute** is used to specify alternative text that is displayed when the browser does not support images, or when the user places the mouse over the image. This attribute is important to use for sites that must comply with accessibility policies within the American for Disabilities Act (ADA) and therefore is a required attribute for XHTML 1.1.

- The **usemap attribute** is useful for images that are called image maps. **Image maps** allow you to click one part of an image, and then send you to a different Web page, depending on which area of the image you clicked. The name of the image map is preceded with the pound sign.

1

The following code shows some of these attributes in action:

```
<img src="images/disk.gif"
alt="Blue Floppy Disk"
width="50" height= "50" border= "1"
hspace="5" vspace= "5"
align="right" />
```

**CAUTION** In XHTML 1.1 many of these attributes, such as border and align, are no longer supported within the image tag. You can use style sheets to provide formatting for these tags. The align attribute can be mimicked using the float property within a cascading style sheet. In XHTML 2 the W3C has modified the concept of an image. For example, in the table tag, you can include the src attribute to define an image. The code would appear as `<table src="corporate.jpg">`. If the device supports images, it will display the image; otherwise, it will display a table.

## Hypertext Links and Bookmarks

The **anchor tags** (`<a></a>`) are most often used to create a hyperlink to another document. When the user clicks the content defined between the anchor tags, the browser opens the location or Web page identified by the href attribute. The href attribute indicates the absolute or relative Web address to the new location or Web page.

You can force the browser to open the Web page in a new browser window by specifying the target window in the target attribute of the anchor tag. The target window can be identified as _blank, _self, _parent, or _top. (Note: The current version of XHTML 1.1 does not support the target attribute.) The syntax for creating a basic hyperlink is as follows:

```
<a href="url/pagename.htm" target="_blank"> ⤶
Displayed content goes here.</a>
```

You can also use the anchor tag to create a bookmark within a Web page. Bookmarks are used to specify a location within a Web page. In traditional HTML, there were two steps to create a bookmark (also known as an internal anchor). First, you had to create the bookmark in the page using the anchor tag and the name attribute. The name attribute was used to identify the name of the bookmark. For example, the bookmark `<a name = "top">` might be used to create a bookmark at the top of the page. Then, at the bottom of the page, you had to create a hyperlink using another anchor tag and set the URL to the bookmark. The value of the href attribute is a pound sign (#) appended with the name of the bookmark. In this case the HTML code might be `<a href="#top">Click here to return to the top of the page</a>`.

**CAUTION** In XHTML 1.1, bookmarks are not created using the name attribute. Instead, the id attribute is used to identify the bookmark. Thus, `<a name = "top">` would be changed to `<a id = "top">`. However, some browsers do not support the new method of creating a bookmark. Therefore, the Web programmer should learn both methods.

## Special Characters

A special character is one that cannot be entered using the basic keyboard settings. These characters cannot be automatically displayed in the browser. You must tell the browser to display the special character. Special **characters entities** such as the ones listed in Table 1-1 are entered using their named markup code or decimal code. The **named markup** is most often used to represent a character entity within the Web page. If the character does not have a named markup code, you must use the decimal code. Some Web editors will allow you to enter the special character in Design view; the Web editor will insert the markup code into the HTML code.

**Table 1-1**   Common HTML elements

| Description | Character | Decimal Code | Named Markup |
|---|---|---|---|
| Quotation Mark | " | &#34; | &quot; |
| Currency | $ | &#36; | N/A |
| Percent | % | &#37; | N/A |
| Ampersand | & | &#38; | &amp; |
| Apostrophe Mark | ' | &#39; | &apos; |
| Less-than sign | < | &#60; | &lt; |
| Greater-than sign | > | &#62; | &gt; |
| At Symbol | @ | &#64; | N/A |
| Carriage Return | N/A | &#10; and &#13 | N/A |
| Blank Space | N/A |   |   |
| Cent sign | ¢ | &#162 | &cent; |
| Pound | £ | &#163; | &pound; |
| Currency | ¤ | &#164; | &curren; |
| Yen sign | ¥ | &#165; | &yen; |
| Copyright | © | &#169; | &copy; |
| Not sign or Discretionary Hyphen | ¬ | &#172; | &not; |
| Registered Trademark sign | ® | &#174; | &reg; |
| Tilde | ~ | &#126; | &tilde; |
| Euro | € | &#8364; | &euro; |

## Ruby Markup

The latest browser versions and XHTML provide Ruby (or agate) markup support, which is a requirement for East-Asian languages such as Chinese, Japanese, and Korean. These small notations are often placed above or beside the letter and used to assist the reader in pronunciation. The W3C provided the first recommendations for Ruby Annotation in 2001 and provides documentation on ruby at *www.w3.org/TR/ruby*.

**1**

Essentially, the **ruby tag** (`<ruby>`) contains the common core attributes of class, id, and title, and several international attributes including charset, dir, hreflang, and xml:lang. The charset attribute is the name of the character set, and hreflang identifies the language used to display the content.

**CAUTION**  You can find the language and character set codes listed in several places on the Internet including *www.loc.gov/standards/iso639-2/langcodes.html*. These attributes are used to help the browser or application identify the language used. They do not perform any language translation!

The ruby tag nests the **ruby base text tag** (`<rb>`) and the **annotated ruby text tag** (`<rt>`). You can also use the **rtc tag** (`<rtc>`) to span the annotation across several elements. The **ruby parenthesis tag** (`<rp>`) can be used to include parentheses. Older browsers will then render the annotations after the base text within parentheses and newer browsers will display the annotations above the base text without the parenthesis.

The top of the code in Figure 1-8 is an example of ruby markup displaying the time and temperature. The bottom of the code in Figure 1-8 shows how to use the ruby markup to display content using a different language. The code in Figure 1-8 would be rendered by the browser in the Chinese version of the text "World Wide Web" in Pinyin over the Chinese version of the text "World Wide Web" in Chinese Simplified. The browser settings must be set up for the Chinese Simplified language. In Internet Explorer, you can change your language settings to Chinese Simplified by clicking View on the menu bar, then Encoding, More, and Chinese Simplified (HZ). As you can see in Figure 1-8, the characters are displayed in both languages.

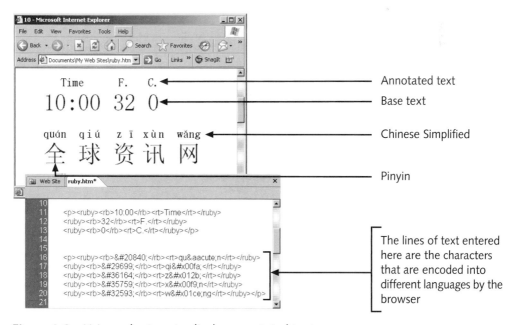

**Figure 1-8**  Using ruby tags to display annotated text

## The Role of IntelliSense

Although you can use the Property window to assign values to the attributes, you can also type the attributes and values directly into the opening HTML tags. Your Web editor supports a new feature called IntelliSense, which improves the speed that you are able to enter attributes and values, and decreases the chance of inserting a syntax error. **IntelliSense** detects what you have typed and tries to predict what you will type next. IntelliSense detects built-in keywords and properties, as well as third-party controls installed with your application. Drag-and-drop controls and IntelliSense are available for all languages within .NET. Because you can select the keyword from a predefined list, IntelliSense helps prevent syntax errors in your HTML code.

If you are editing inside of the HTML tag, as shown in Figure 1-9, pressing the space bar will cause the list of attributes to be displayed. You can use the arrow keys on the keyboard to select an attribute. You can also jump to the listings that begin with "b" by typing "b." If you press the equal sign, the equal sign, a pair of quotation marks, and the list of possible values are displayed. You can use your arrow keys again to select the value or type the value. If you hit the space bar again, another set of attributes appears. Once you have completed editing the tag, the Web editor will automatically insert the closing tag when you close the opening tag.

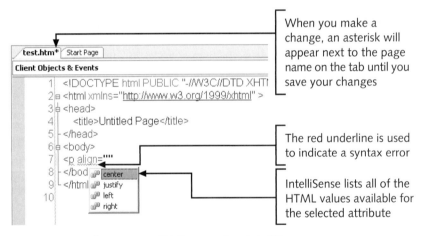

**Figure 1-9**    Selecting an HTML tag using IntelliSense

# Create a New Web Page with a Web Editor

In this exercise you will open an existing Web application and create a basic Web page. In this book, the exercises will refer to [*your student folder*].

To create a simple HTML document:

1. Start your Web editor.

2. To open an existing project, click **File** on the menu bar and click **Open Web Site**.

3. Navigate through your file system to locate [*your student folder*].

4. Click **chapter1** located in [*your student folder*] and click **Open**.

5. To create a new Web page, click **File** on the menu bar and click **New File**. The Add New Item window opens, displaying templates of typical Web project files that were installed with your editor.

6. Click **HTML Page**.

7. In the Name text box, highlight the existing content. Type **ch1_sample.htm**, as shown in Figure 1-10, and then click **Add**. (Note: The default file extension for Web pages is htm.) The Web page is added to the project and opens in the main window.

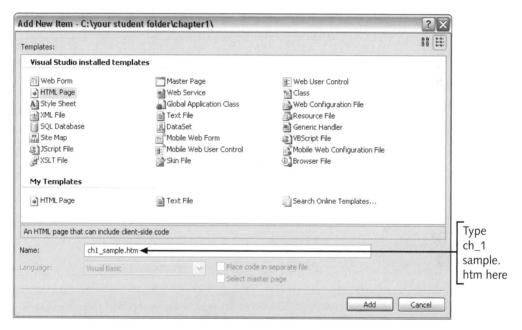

**Figure 1-10**   The Add New Item window

8. Enter the html tags and attributes between the two body tags, as shown in Figure 1-11.

9. Click **File** on the menu bar, and then click **Save All**. (Note: You can save files individually, or save all the files at one time.)

10. Click the **Design** tab to view the page in the graphical editor. In the Properties window, change the selection in the drop-down list from LI to **Document**.

11. In the Properties window, change the value of the Title property of the document from Untitled Page to **Dictionary**.

```
<img class="left" height="105"
   src="images/clover.gif" width="90" />
<h1>Online Dictionary</h1>
<p>Click on a term. <br />
A window will open with the definition.</p>
<ul>
<li><a href="ch1_dom.htm" >Document Object Model</a></li>
<li><a href="ch1_objects.htm" >Objects</a></li>
<li><a href="ch1_encapsulation.htm" >Encapsulation</a></li>
<li><a href="ch1_eventhandler.htm" >Event Handler</a></li>
<li><a href="ch1_methods.htm" >Methods</a></li>
</ul>
```

Type this
code

**Figure 1-11**   HTML sample code

12. Click the clover image. In the Properties window, change the value of the Alt property from clover to **crystal**.

13. Click **File** on the menu bar, and then click **Save All**.

14. Click **File** on the menu bar, and then click **View in Browser**. Your screen should resemble Figure 1-12.

15. Click **File** on the menu bar and click **Close** to close any open pages.

## Customizing Source Code View

The Web editor provides options for how the developer wants to format Source Code view including the color, font, case and structure of HTML tags and attributes. Some Web editors will reformat the code according to predefined preferences. In your Web editor you can preserve your code as it was entered or allow your Web editor to reformat the HTML according to your predefined preferences. To access the options, click Tools on the menu bar, and then click Options.

In the Environment properties, the General options allow you to change the window layout from tabbed documents to multiple documents. Multiple documents allow you to view documents side by side in the main window. The Fonts and Colors options shown in Figure 1-13 allow you to change the appearance of many objects including the line numbers, collapsed text, comments, and so on. As an example why you may want to change your preferences, suppose you preview the page in the browser and then want to view the source code from the client's browser. The Web Browser options allow you to view the client's source code in the built-in editor, the HTML editor, or an external editor such as Notepad or Microsoft FrontPage. Web editors such as Microsoft FrontPage color-code the HTML tags, making it easier to locate potential HTML errors. To show all of the options available, you will need to click the Show all settings check box in the Options window, as shown in Figure 1-13.

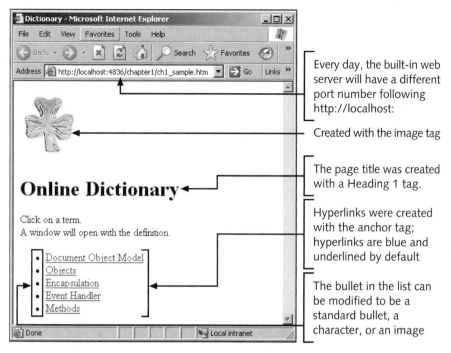

Every day, the built-in web server will have a different port number following http://localhost:

Created with the image tag

The page title was created with a Heading 1 tag.

Hyperlinks were created with the anchor tag; hyperlinks are blue and underlined by default

The bullet in the list can be modified to be a standard bullet, a character, or an image

**Figure 1-12**   Previewing the HTML page in the browser

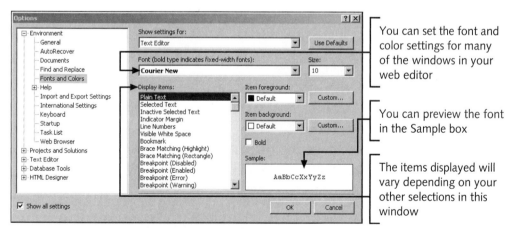

You can set the font and color settings for many of the windows in your web editor

You can preview the font in the Sample box

The items displayed will vary depending on your other selections in this window

**Figure 1-13**   Fonts and Colors options

This window has many features, many of which are discussed in the following subsections.

## Projects and Solutions Options

Below the General options are the Projects and Solutions options. These options allow you to change the default folder for the projects and templates. This is the path that appears in the dialog box when you first created your project. If you are running your Web editor in a network environment, this setting may have been changed to your individual user folder.

## Text Editor Options

Below the Projects and Solutions options are the Text Editor options. The Text Editor options allow you to set the preferences for all of the text editors globally with the General settings. You can also set the preferences for a specific language such as Visual Basic, C#, CSS, HTML, SQL Script, T-SQL, and XML. You can set the ability to auto-list the members as you type, enable word wrapping, and display the line numbers. You can specify how to format the layout of the code, including the indent size, line length, and whether to use block indenting. You can modify the formatting options for specific client and server tags in the Tag Specific Options window.

## Validation Options

As shown in Figure 1-14, the Validation options are important because you can set the format for the page code to be validated with a specific target. The default setting is to target the Internet Explorer browser version 6. Note that you can also change the settings to require that your page only support the XHTML 1.1 standards.

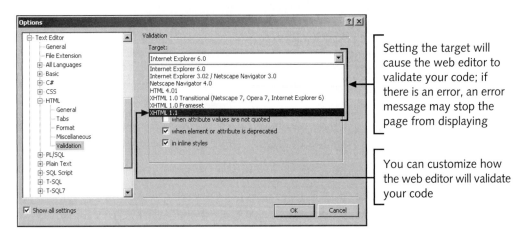

**Figure 1-14**   Validation options

No matter what version you are using, it is useful to ensure that tags are lowercase, well-formed, with quoted values. You should avoid any inline styles and use of deprecated elements. Deprecated elements are elements that are no longer supported in the standards. However, some browsers may continue to support the tags. HTML designer options allow you set the default view, and other properties related to the HTML editor.

## Previewing Your Web Page

Basic HTML pages do not require that you preview the page using a Web server. However, ASP.NET pages will require that you preview the page with a Microsoft-compatible Web server. Microsoft Windows Professional XP comes with a free Web server called **Internet Information Services (IIS)**. For your Web server to recognize the ASP.NET pages, you must have installed the Web server before you installed ASP.NET.

When you installed ASP.NET and your Web editor, a Web server was also installed. This internal Web server was written using managed C# code. It can handle multiple requests and makes it easier to preview your pages. It is also free, but it will only accept local requests by default. By accepting requests only from the local server, you are not at risk of Web service attacks.

The internal Web server can be referred to as the **localhost**. It can also be referenced by the local IP address of your computer's network interface card or by the default IP loopback address of 127.0.0.1. However, this Web server does not work on port 80 where most Web servers are located. (Note that each day, the local Web server uses a different port number.) There are several ways to preview the current page in the browser.

- You can right-click a single page and select View in Browser. This will open up the page in the browser from within the Web editor program. The complete URL including the localhost and port number is displayed in the URL text box at the top of the page.

- You can go to the File menu and select View in Browser. This will also open the current page in the browser.

- You can press the Control, Shift, and W keys simultaneously to open the current page in the browser.

## Changing Your Browser

You can set your Web pages to open in any browser by clicking File on the menu bar and then clicking Browse With. In Figure 1-15, you can see that the two choices are Internal Web Browser and Microsoft Internet Explorer (Default). As seen in Figure 1-15, the browser window size can be preset. You can also add other browsers to this list by clicking the Add button and entering the path to the other browser.

## Preparing to Preview a Web Application

The Web application includes all of the files and resources within the root folder. During the development phase, when you have an application such as a shopping cart, you may want to preview the pages in a specific order. After you select a specific page you can press the Control key and the F5 key simultaneously to open the page in the browser. This action will run the Web site without debug mode. You can assign the page that opens in the browser when the application is first opened by right-clicking the file name in the Solution Explorer window and selecting Set As Start Page.

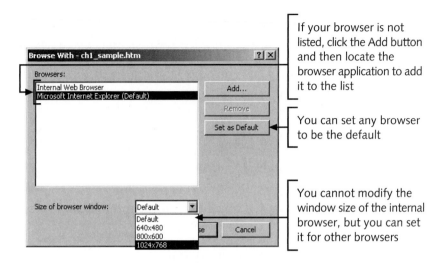

If your browser is not listed, click the Add button and then locate the browser application to add it to the list

You can set any browser to be the default

You cannot modify the window size of the internal browser, but you can set it for other browsers

**Figure 1-15**   Changing the default Web browser

If you are already familiar with programming, you may have previewed programs in debug mode. **Debug mode** will compile the program, identify errors, and open the program. To run the program in debug mode, you first have to change the Web configuration file (named Web.config) to enable debug mode. The chapter1 Web application has debug mode turned off. Debugging is not enabled by default and should be turned off before your site is published because it can significantly slow down your application. Pressing the F5 key will cause the browser to open the current page in debug mode.

## INTRODUCTION TO XML

There are many technologies that work with XML documents in addition to XHTML. For example, XML documents can store data that can be accessed from your Web page. Because XML has become such an integral part of building Web applications, an introduction to XML is provided for you in the following subsections.

## XML Standards

**Extensible Markup Language (XML)**, like HTML, is a markup language that provides access to structured content and provides a universal format for structured documents and data. But, unlike HTML, XML is not limited to a set of tags or to being displayed in a browser. XML allows you to define your own tags (or elements). XML documents can also be shared across applications, file systems, and operating systems. Because XML enables cross-platform interoperability, XML is a powerful tool for developing Internet applications.

The XML standards are maintained by the World Wide Web Consortium (*www.w3.org*).

The XML standards allow you to add content, referred to as data, to an XML document. However, an XML document can also include information that describes the data, which is known as the data structure or schema. The XML standards contain the **XML Document Object Model (DOM)**, which is a standard language-neutral interface for manipulating XML documents from a script or program. This is important because although you can view an XML document using a simple text editor, such as Notepad, any program or script can access and update the content, structure, and style of an XML document. For example, the Microsoft Internet Explorer browser contains a built-in XML parser (known as Microsoft XML Core Services) that allows you to read and display XML documents.

The Microsoft XML Developer Center at *http://msdn.microsoft.com/xml* contains information on XML technologies and software.

# XML Rules

As you learned before, XHTML must conform to the XML rules. If the document follows the XML rules, it is referred to as a well-formed document. A well-formed document follows XML standards and can therefore be read by any XML parser. Let's look at some of the parts and rules of an XML well-formed document.

## Prologue

When you create a well-formed XML document, you must first select which version of XML standards you will be working with. The first section document, known as the **prologue**, may contain the version, formatting information, and schema definitions.

## XML Declaration

The first line in an XML document is called the **XML declaration**. It specifies the version of XML, using the version property, as shown in the code following this paragraph. The question mark indicates that this tag, xml, is a processing instruction and therefore does not contain data. (Note: There is no space between the question mark and the xml tag.) The version property identifies the XML standards version to be used to read the document. The character encoding property describes any coding algorithms that are used within the page and is utf-8 by default. If this XML declaration is not included, the document can only implement the default character encodings UTF-8 or UTF-16.

```
<?xml version="1.0" encoding="utf-8" ?>
```

It is important to note that with XHTML, you must use lowercase for all HTML tags and attributes. XML is case sensitive and `<LI>` and `<li>` are considered different elements.

## External Style References

Immediately below the prologue, you can insert a reference to an **external cascading style sheet (CSS)** or an **Extensible Stylesheet Language (XSL)** file. XHTML files can be formatted using cascading style sheets only. XML documents can use either. Both CSS and XML files contain instructions for how to format or display the XML document. For example, `<?xml-stylesheet type="text/css" href="ch1_sample.css"?>` adds a relative reference to a CSS style sheet in an XML document using the href attribute.

In the IT industry, all cascading style sheets are referred to as style sheets. All XSLT stylesheets are referred to as stylesheets.

## XML Characters

In XML, certain characters are not supported within the tags because they are used to create and separate XML elements. In other words, these characters have non-textual uses with XML. Thus, if you want to use these characters for textual uses, you must replace them with their equivalent element markup codes. Table 1-2 lists common XML characters and their markup codes.

**Table 1-2**    Common XML characters and their markup codes

| XML Character | XML Character Markup Code |
|---|---|
| ' | &apos; |
| " | &quot; |
| & | &amp; |
| < | &lt; |
| > | &gt; |

## Nesting Elements

Like HTML, XML documents must have a logical structure. The XML body of the XML file contains the elements (tags), attributes, and data in the XML document. In XML the tags are referred to as **elements**. In an XML document, you must define a root container element to carry all the elements and data in the file. The root tag in an XML document is also known as the **root node** or **root element**. All tags must be nested within the root node. In other words, if the root node is html, then all tags are nested within the opening and closing html tags. A node that contains other elements is also referred to as a branch node, while a node that does not contain other elements is referred to as a leaf node.

A container element is an element in which other elements can nest. The root node is a container element because all elements must be nested within the root. In a Web page, the html tag is the root element and is a container element because it contains nested child elements such as the head and body tags. In this case, the html element is also called the parent element for the head and body tags and the head and body tags are referred to as the child elements.

**CAUTION**    You cannot mix or overlap the nesting element order. For example, in older versions of HTML, you could write Welcome to <i>Tara Store</i>. In XHTML, this statement is illegal. You must rewrite the statement as Welcome to <i>Tara Store</i>.

Figure 1-16 shows a simple XML document named ch1_sample.xml.

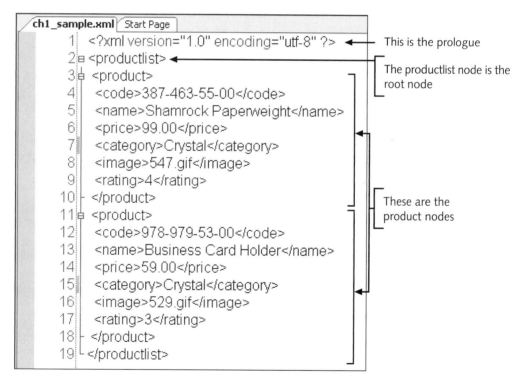

**Figure 1-16**    Sample XML file

## Well-Formed XHTML

There are several ways to verify that your XML code is well formed. Web editors such as Visual Studio .NET, Visual Web Developer Express, and FrontPage 2003 can verify that your document is well-formed during development. These programs indicate if you have a formatting or syntax error in your file as you enter the elements and data.

If you are using a basic text editor to create your Web pages, you can save the Web page as an XML file with the .xml file extension. When you open the file in Microsoft Internet Explorer, the browser will parse the file and inform you if there are formatting errors. If there are no formatting errors found, the browser will display the code. Note that this only indicates that the file is well-formed; it does not validate the data.

Figure 1-17 shows the previous sample XML document viewed from the browser. Notice how both views allow you to expand and collapse the container element nodes, which include product and productlist.

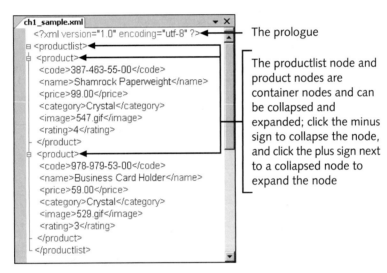

**Figure 1-17**   Sample XML file viewed in a browser

Today, XHTML is considered a content language and not just a markup language, because the target may not be a Web browser but a diverse collection of computing platforms such as cellular phones and portable digital devices. XHTML 1.0 and 1.1 organize the elements into several collections of abstract modules grouped by functionality. Each module will list the set of element types included, attribute-list declarations, and content model declarations. Individual devices can specify which collection of modules they support. Then, programmers can work without being concerned about which individual elements are supported by a particular device.

## Markup Validation of XML Documents

One of the benefits of XML is that it allows you to define your own markup language. You can create a document that contains a set of rules and share them with other programmers. Of course, you have to be careful when XML documents to follow the same set of rules. For example, one XML document may use <p> to mean a paragraph, and another XML document may use <p> to represent a person.

To eliminate confusion when working with multiple XML documents, XML documents can identify a set of rules, or namespace, associated with the document. This namespace is called a **schema**. Schemas are used to define the structure, content, and semantics of XML documents. The schema can be written in a **document type definition (DTD) document** or in a **schema document**. When you create your XML document, you can point to the rules that the document will follow. The reference to the rules is placed in the prologue of the XML document. Then, the XML parser uses the rules to validate the structure of the XML document and the data.

## Document Type Definitions

Document type definition (DTD) is an older method used to identify the rules used to structure a document. Now, Web pages require a **Doctype declaration**, which is the document type definition identified on the first line in the Web page before the beginning html tag. The W3C maintains a list of recommended Doctypes at *www.w3.org/QA/2002/04/valid-dtd-list.html*. You can download these files by typing the Web addresses shown into the browser and saving the files to your desktop.

Which version of the DTD should you choose? Well, the three options that are supported in HTML 4.0 are as follows:

- HTML 4.01 Strict is more often applied to newer browsers. It emphasizes structure over presentation, and therefore does not support many of the deprecated presentational elements or attributes, frames, and link targets.

- HTML 4.01 Transitional is more robust because it adds the presentational attributes, deprecated elements, and link targets that were missing in HTML 4.01 Strict.

- HTML 4.01 Frameset is a version of HTML 4 Transitional that is used for Web pages that contain frames.

The Doctype for Web pages that comply with the HTML 4.01 Strict standards is shown in the following code:

```
<!DOCTYPE html PUBLIC
"-//W3C//DTD HTML 4.01//EN"
 "http://www.w3.org/TR/html4/strict.dtd">
```

XHTML 1.0 also has several versions of the Doctype: XHTML 1.0 Strict, Transitional, and Frameset. These are all versions of HTML Strict, Transitional, and Frameset that are XML-compliant. The Doctypes for Web pages that comply with the XHTML 1.0 standards are shown in the code following this paragraph. The string is case sensitive, so make sure that you enter the code in exactly as shown:

```
<!DOCTYPE html PUBLIC
"-//W3C//DTD XHTML 1.0 Strict//EN"
"http://www.w3.org/TR/xhtml1/DTD/xhtml1-strict.dtd">
```

```
<!DOCTYPE html PUBLIC ⤶
"-//W3C//DTD XHTML 1.0 Transitional//EN" ⤶
"http://www.w3.org/TR/xhtml1/DTD/xhtml1-transitional.dtd">
<!DOCTYPE html PUBLIC ⤶
"-//W3C//DTD XHTML 1.0 Frameset//EN" ⤶
"http://www.w3.org/TR/xhtml1/DTD/xhtml1-frameset.dtd">
```

Below is the DTD for the current version of XHTML, version 1.1, published in 2001:

```
<!DOCTYPE html PUBLIC "-//W3C//DTD XHTML 1.1//EN" ⤶
"http://www.w3.org/TR/xhtml11/DTD/xhtml11.dtd">
```

## XML Schemas

The XHTML standards are upgrading document type definition files to a newer format called XML schemas. An **XML schema** is like a DTD document in that they both are ways to structure elements. Data that has its structure defined is often referred to as a **typed dataset**. The W3C defines XML schemas as a shared vocabulary (*www.w3.org/XML/Schema.html*). The **xmlns attribute** of the root node is used to identify the XML schema document associated with the document. The following sample code shows the namespace from the W3C that is associated with XHTML:

```
<html xmlns="http://www.w3.org/1999/xhtml">
```

Microsoft also has a schema. The Microsoft XML schema is extensible because you can add elements to a document without invalidating the document, which is not possible within the W3C schemas. The Microsoft XML schema document file extension is .xsd. You can create your own schemas for your XML documents and set the xmlns attribute to the path to the XML schema.

Built into the .NET Framework are many tools and utility programs. The XML Schema Definition (Xsd.exe) tool automatically generates your XML schema or classes from several sources, including your XML and XSD files. The xmlns attribute of the root node is used to identify the XML schema document associated with the document.

## Validation Services

There are several programs that can be used to validate your markup against a set of rules. The W3C provides a free **Markup Validation Service**, which validates Web documents in formats like HTML and XHTML. The service is available at *http://validator.w3.org/*. You can submit a URL, upload a file, or copy and paste the code into a form and submit the form. If your page passes the W3C validation, you are able to place the W3C valid icon on your Web page, as shown in Figure 1-18.

There have been many changes in XHTML 1.1 from the original version of HTML. In XHTML 1.1, all deprecated elements such as presentational tags and framesets have been removed. Presentation of Web pages is now only controlled by cascading style sheets. Previous HTML versions allowed elements like <br /> to be placed anywhere within the body. With XHTML 1.1, some elements are defined as child elements and must be nested

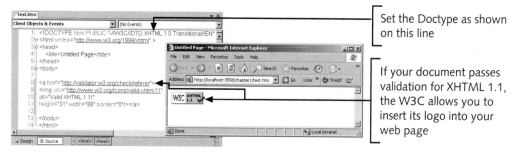

**Figure 1-18**  Sample XML file viewed in a browser

within a parent element. Thus, `<br />` cannot be a parent element by definition and must be nested within a parent element, such as an anchor, button, or table heading cell.

**CAUTION**

**XHTML 2.0** is currently in development. It is important for you to be aware of its changes, as they will impact your ability to develop sites that are compliant with the new standards.

## Creating and Validating XML Documents in the XML Designer

In this exercise you will modify a basic XML file and validate the data using an XML schema. In this chapter, the exercises will refer to [*your student folder*]\chapter1 folder.

To create a simple XML document:

1. In the Solution Explorer window, double-click the **ch1_inventory.xml** file. The XML file opens in the main window. In this view, the file has many products already entered for you.

2. Enter the XML tags and attributes for the first product, as shown in Figure 1-19.

3. Click **File** on the menu bar, and then click **Save All**.

4. In the Solution Explorer window, double-click the **ch1_inventory.xsd** file. The XML schema opens in the main window. You are currently in Design view.

5. Right-click in the main window and select **View Code**. Notice that the date type for the instock property is xs:positiveInteger, as shown in Figure 1-20. Although you can define your own data types, positiveInteger is one of the many default XML data types defined within this schema.

6. Click the **ch1_inventory.xml** tab to return to the XML file. For the first product, change the value of the instock tag from 5 to **0**.

7. Click **File** on the menu bar, and then click **Save All**. Notice that a blue line appears under the closing instock tag. If you mouse over the tag, an error message appears indicating that the value was invalid.

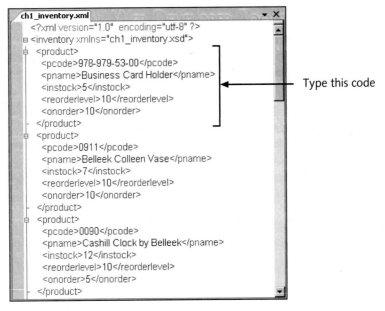

Figure 1-19    Modifying XML data

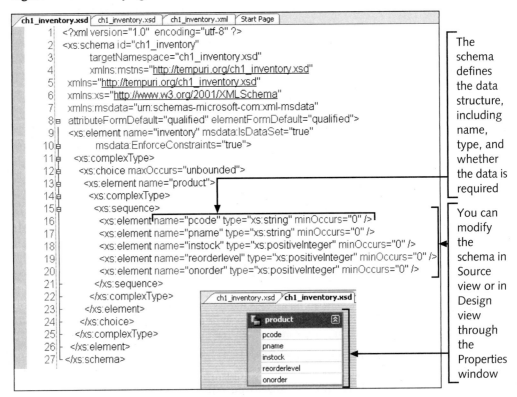

Figure 1-20    Sample XML schema

8. Change the value of the instock tag back to **5**. Click **File** on the menu bar, and then click **Save All**.

9. Click the **Close** buttons to close ch1_inventory.xml and ch1_inventory.xsd.

You can validate the document by placing the xmlns attribute in the root tag of the xml file and setting the value to the location of your schema. Then, when you view the document in a browser or validation program, the parser will use the rules in the schema file to validate your file. As you can see, XML documents, including XHTML, can be validated against rules and standards.

## Displaying Images with an XML File

There are many ways that XML documents can be used with Web applications. In the following exercise, you will see how a simple XML file can be used to display images.

To view an XML document that is used to display banner ads:

1. In the Solution Explorer window, right-click **ch1_addisplay.aspx** and select **View in Browser**. The image in the ch1_addisplay.aspx page was created from an advertisement file.

2. Click the image and a new page named ch1_adshow.aspx will appear displaying the image.

3. In the Solution Explorer window, double-click the **ch1_addisplay.xml** file that contains the banner ads.

4. Close all of the open files.

The banner ad XML file is required to follow rules. The nodes and elements are case sensitive and must be named with specific names. Schemas and DTDs help you develop Web applications that are compliant with standards and have fewer syntax errors.

## Web Site Accessibility

The Internet provides access to vital information and resources. Web sites must comply with state, federal, and industry regulations such as accessibility, privacy, and security. Government regulations include the Americans with Disabilities Act (ADA), the California Online Privacy Protection Act (COPPA), the Data Protection Act, and the Disability Discrimination Act. Today, several governments have instituted regulations that require equal access to all visitors. The U.S. government's Section 508 and the UK's Disability Discrimination Act are commonly used to build Web site accessibility standards within public and private organizations.

The **Web Accessibility Initiative (WAI)** of the W3C provides **Web Content Accessibility Guidelines (WCAG)** that address broad accessibility issues. The WCAG 2.0 is currently in a working drafts version and addresses the needs of individuals who have a variety of disabilities including blindness, low vision, color deficit or distortions, deafness and hearing loss, learning disabilities, paralysis, and photo sensitive epilepsy. This version will also include requirements that may be applied across technologies such as XML and cascading style sheets (CSS). There are three levels of W3C WCAG compliance based on three priority levels in Web content accessibility.

Web designers and developers are responsible for meeting accessibility standards. Creating a page that simply prints text does not provide a similar experience for a person with a disability. A person with access needs requires assistive technologies to interpret the Web page code. Some individuals who are blind use JAWS for Windows (*www.freedomscientific. com/fs_products/software_jaws.asp*) or the IBM Home Page Reader (*www-3.ibm.com/able/hpr. html*) to read the Web site out loud. Some individuals who have trouble using their hands can control their interactions on the Web site using only their voice with the help of the Dragon Naturally Speaking software (*www.nuance.com/naturallyspeaking/*).

Many e-commerce, government, and educational sites choose to use third-party software to validate their site for accessibility requirements. The W3C provides a list of several accessibility validation tools at *www.w3.org/WAI/ER/tools/*. Watchfire provides WebXACT, a free online service that lets you test single pages of Web content for quality, accessibility, and privacy issues at *http://Webxact.watchfire.com/*. Bobby provided free online accessibility validation. Bobby was first available from the Center for Applied Special Technology (CAST) at *www.cast.org/bobby/* and was acquired by Watchfire in 2002. Watchfire provides an updated version of Bobby as a Web accessibility desktop testing tool. Bobby will spider through a Web site and check over 90 accessibility problems, including readability by screen readers and alternative text for all multimedia.

## INTRODUCTION TO ASP.NET SERVER PROGRAMMING

Programming that makes it possible for client applications to communicate with server applications in a network is referred to as **client-server programming**. Today, the Internet is a network of networks and supports many types of client-server applications. In this section you will use a technology created by Microsoft called Active Server Pages .NET—or simply ASP.NET—to create client-server applications. Because these client-server applications communicate primarily through the Internet, they are simply referred to as Web applications.

### Before There Were Client-Server Applications

As the Internet expanded from governments and universities to businesses and individuals, Web applications needed to become more dynamic. A dynamic Web application enables the user to interact with the application in ways that change the appearance or the content of the Web page. Examples of dynamic Web applications include shopping carts, membership databases, online catalogs, and personalized Web sites.

Unfortunately, you cannot create dynamic Web applications using HTML alone. However, you can use many other different technologies along with HTML, including client- and server-side scripting and server-side programming, to create dynamic Web applications. Of course, a major limitation of client-side scripting is browser dependency, because client-side scripts are executed via the browsers' scripting engines and not all browsers support all scripting languages.

Another major limitation of client-side scripting is security. The user of the client can easily view the scripts within the Web page. In a recent situation involving this issue, a large not-for-profit organization created a Web application to deliver an online course. The programmer processed the login using client-side JavaScript. During a security analysis, a Web consultant was able to obtain the registration, login, and credit card information for each participant. Reason? The programmer used client-side redirection, which was easily bypassed by using a slower Internet connection and stopping the redirection by pressing the escape key. In other words, the programmer processed the registration form using JavaScript and FrontPage, but did not protect the data on the server.

In contrast to HTML, server-side programs allow you to create dynamic Web applications that can process a form or manage a database. With server-based applications, you can create a secure Web site because the programs are run on the Web server. The Web server sends static HTML to the client's browser. Because the processing of the program occurs on the server, you can hide code from the client.

## Processing ASP.NET Applications

A basic Web page created with ASP.NET is referred to as a **Web Form**. Web Forms allow you to quickly develop and process forms on Web pages and develop cross-browser Web applications. Web Forms are Web pages identified with the file extension .aspx. Any page ending in .aspx is directed to the ASP.NET engine, which is located on the server in a file named aspnet_isapi.dll. Your Web application may include special application directories to store resources such as programming code and data. An example of an ASP.NET application is a shopping cart. Web Forms can be used to target any browser or device without requiring you to write a separate application for each.

Note that when you build the application, any server programming code is compiled on the server. Figure 1-21 shows how ASP.NET Web pages are processed on the Web server. The developer creates the Web page (1), which is stored on the Web server. Programming code can be precompiled into the assembly (2) or compiled at the first runtime. The assembly contains a language- and computer-independent representation of your code called the **Microsoft Intermediate Language (MSIL)**. When the visitor first requests a page (3), the ASP.NET engine dynamically compiles the assembly (4) and on subsequent requests the page is translated into computer-specific instructions (5) with the output sent back to the browser.

Each application directory in your Web application is compiled into a single file called an assembly. The main directory and subdirectories are compiled into a single assembly named [*your_application_name*].dll by default. You can also precompile code using the ASP.NET

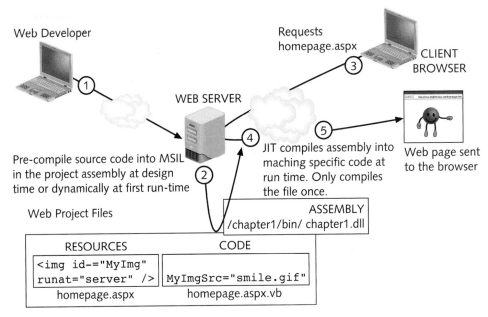

**Figure 1-21** Processing an ASP.NET application

compiler tool (ASPNET_Compiler.exe), and place it in the bin directory of your application, which frees you from having to store the source code files on the Web server. Then when you are ready to publish your site, you only have to deploy your ASP.NET and additional resource files, configuration files, and the dll files.

## Server Controls

As you learned previously, the Toolbox is used to group controls logically into tabs according to their common functions. The HTML tab provides many of the basic HTML tags that can be used in static HTML pages or ASP.NET pages. These HTML tags are simply passed from the Web server to the Web browser unchanged. HTML tags can be used in static HTML pages.

ASP.NET provides a way to use server controls. These server controls are objects on the Web server built from classes that were installed when you installed the .NET Framework. These server controls, such as HTML controls and ASP.NET controls, can be used only within ASP.NET pages—that is, within pages that end in .aspx.

Note that an object is a set of related methods and properties that are compartmentalized. Properties are used to set the value of a variable defined within an object. You change the values of the properties of the server objects by using the Properties window in the Web editor. Object-oriented programming allows you to use these objects, which can be accessed by other programs, including Web pages. With HTML alone, it is difficult for the server to retain the values and properties of the HTML tags across page requests. With server controls, the state of the server controls can be maintained using ASP.NET. You can access the properties of these server controls by using programs that run on the Web server.

It is important to understand that the server controls will generate the output that is compatible with the browser. Server controls can be configured to target a specific browser, or version of HTML. In Figure 1-22, you can see how the server controls will generate the output as HTML.

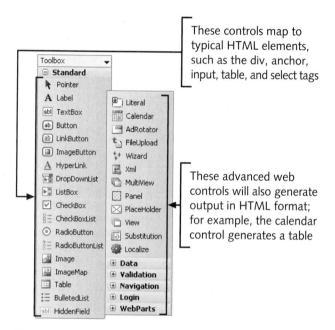

These controls map to typical HTML elements, such as the div, anchor, input, table, and select tags

These advanced web controls will also generate output in HTML format; for example, the calendar control generates a table

**Figure 1-22**   Server controls on the Standard tab in the Toolbox

These server controls generate the necessary HTML tags, JavaScript, and Dynamic HTML (DHTML), which are supported by the client. DHTML allows you to interact with the user when they complete a form or click a hyperlink. There are various levels of browser support for JavaScript. With these server controls, you do not have to write the client-side script. Rather, you write the code to configure the properties and events of the server controls.

By using a server control, you generate output that is supported by the client. If the client's browser supports JavaScript and DHTML, the output is generated using JavaScript and DHTML. Events such as form validation could be performed on the client. If the browser does not support JavaScript and DHTML, then the output is HTML, and events such as form field validation are performed on the server. When the HTML tag in the browser detects an event, such as a mouse click, the browser can respond to the event by using an event handler, which executes code statements when the event occurs. The server controls generate the HTML tag, as well as JavaScript to capture events on the client (these events include the onchange and onclick events). If you have a basic label, text box, and button control on a page, the ASP.NET controls generate a hidden input field named

__EVENTVALIDATION. However, if you insert other Web controls such as a link button, the control generates a hyperlink, and the hyperlink click can be intercepted by the browser. Therefore, there needs to be client-side code in the browser to intercept the request.

In the sample code in Figure 1-23, the Web page contains hidden fields that are used to determine which tag called the function and what parameters were passed with the tag back to the server.

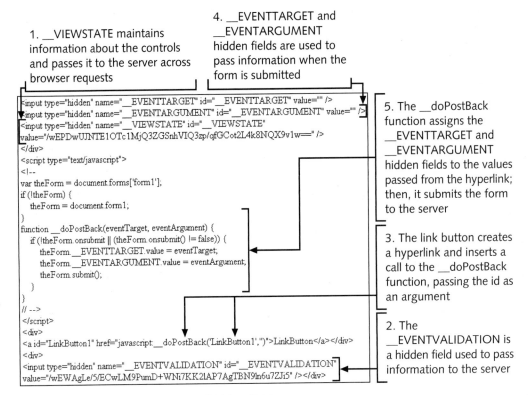

**Figure 1-23**  Web page contains hidden fields

__VIEWSTATE (1) and __EVENTVALIDATION (2) contain information about the controls in the page. In the page, the hyperlink control intercepts the event when the user clicks on the hyperlink, calls the JavaScript function __doPostBack (3), and passes the id and any arguments from the hyperlink control. A function is a named grouping of one or more programming statements. This JavaScript function only occurs once in the page, no matter how many server controls are used. This function is used to assign values passed from the hyperlink control to the __EVENTTARGET and __EVENTARGUMENT hidden fields (4) and submit the form that will pass information in all of the hidden fields to the Web server (5).

# HTML Tags and HTML Controls

HTML controls are similar to HTML tags, except that they are programmable by the server. In a traditional HTML page the developer creates a text box by writing <input id="Text1" type="text">. HTML tags are sent unaltered to the browser. You only need to add runat ="server" to the tag to transform the HTML tag into an HTML control. In this case, you would write <input id="Text1" type="text" runat="server"/>. When the value of the runat property is set to server, the control is processed by the server. For HTML controls, the attributes are referred to as properties. The properties can be assigned values in the Properties window, within the opening tag, or in the server programming code. The HTML controls generate the HTML tags that are sent to and then rendered in the browser.

By transforming HTML tags to HTML controls, you can create server-side programs that interact with the control before it is rendered as a plain HTML tag and sent to the browser. When you refer to the HTML control in your code behind the page, you need to set the runat property. If you have not set the runat property, the compiler displays an error message that the control is not declared. You cannot set the runat property using the Properties window. You must either manually enter in Source Code view; in Design view you can right-click the tag and then click Run As Server Control. (Note: A small green arrow appears in Design view on any HTML or other server controls.)

In the .NET Framework, classes are organized into logical hierarchical treelike structure groupings used to categorize the base class types called namespaces, which are split across several physical files. **Namespaces** are a hierarchical way to organize objects. All HTML controls inherit from the same class in the .NET Framework named System.Web.UI. HTMLControl (called the HTMLControl class), which is located in the System.Web namespace in system.Web.dll. Thus, all HTML controls inherit the same properties and methods from the System.Web.UI.HTMLControl class. HTML controls can be further subdivided within this class. Although each HTML control inherits these common properties, each subgroup of HTML controls has additional properties specific to that group of controls.

The properties and methods common to all HTML server controls can be found in the documentation for the System.Web.UI.HTMLControl class. For example, all HTML server controls inherit a property called Visible. The Visible property can be assigned a Boolean value that indicates whether the HTML control is rendered as an HTML tag on the page. All HTML controls are visible by default because the Visible property is True by default. Another commonly used property is the Style property. The Style property retrieves a collection of all cascading style sheet (CSS) rules applied to a specified HTML control. The Style property can be configured by using a cascading style sheet or by using the Style Builder.

# Web Controls

There are a variety of server controls that can be used within ASP.NET pages. Web controls allow you to render HTML output and provide more flexibility than HTML controls when you are creating your programs. Web controls will create the HTML tags that are sent to the browser.

Web controls are usually identified with the prefix `asp:` followed by the name of the control. For example, the code to create a Button control is `<asp:Button ID="Button1" runat="server" Text="Show the message" />`. In previous versions of ASP.NET, these server controls were called Web Server Controls, Server Controls, ASP.NET Web Controls, or simply Web Controls. In this book, we will use the term Web controls to represent the aggregate group of built-in controls in ASP.NET, and classify the controls according to their location within the Toolbox tabs.

Web controls have different properties than their HTML control counterparts. Web controls can interact with client-side events such as the user clicking a button. When the event occurs, the Web control can trigger a script to run on the server.

HTML controls and Web controls use different properties to generate output. In the sample code following this paragraph, the HTML Label control named Message1 contains an InnerHTML property that is used to assign the value to an HTML tag. However, the Web Label control named Message2 uses the Text property to assign the value to the HTML tag. (Note: A Label control that is a Web control is simply referred to as a Label control. Unless stated, you can assume that the controls used in this book are Web controls.)

```
Message1.InnerHTML="Product 1"
Message2.Text="Product 2"
```

**CAUTION** It is very important that you look at the browser source code of each ASP.NET page that you create in order to understand what the Web server is sending to the browser. ASP.NET code is never sent to the browser, only HTML tags, along with client-side scripts. Many errors are related to the syntax of the HTML tags—such as a missing closing tag or a missing quotation mark—sent to the browser. By viewing the source code in the browser, you can more quickly locate the HTML syntax errors. Sometimes it is also useful to paste the code into an editor such as FrontPage, which can help you locate and identify HTML errors quickly.

Web Forms inherit from the Web Control class, which is found in the System.Web.UI. WebControls namespace. Web controls are similar to HTML controls, but they support additional properties, methods, and events. Some properties are assigned values that are not of type string. For example, color is a class that inherits its properties from System.Drawing. Color properties must be assigned using a different syntax. So, to retrieve a color, you have to directly or indirectly inherit from System.Drawing.Color. You can assign the value by the known color name, a 32-bit value, a hexadecimal value, or a property of an object. In the sample code following this paragraph, the BorderColor property is assigned Green. Green is one of the known colors that you can refer to by name.

```
MyControl.BorderColor = System.Drawing.Color.Green
```

You can select the property using the known color name, such as Green, or from a value from another object. The following sample code shows how to assign the color value from the text box:

```
MyControl.BackColor = Color.FromName(txtBackColor.Value)
```

Some of the properties of Web controls require a numeric value and not a string. You cannot simply assign the numeric value dynamically; ASP.NET requires that you use a new object, known as a **Unit object**. The unit class represents numeric values for the properties of other objects. You need to use the keyword New to create the Unit object, and then pass the numeric value to the class. The following sample code assigns the BorderWidth property using the Unit object:

```
MyBtn.BorderWidth=New Unit(4)
```

## Creating a Web Page Using a Web Editor

When you create a Web Form in your Web editor, there are several options that can be configured. First, the programming code that relates to the page can be placed in a separate file called the "code behind the page" or in the same Web page. When you create the code within the page, you will see the default server script tags (<script runat="server"></script>) inserted for you in the heading section. Second, you can select a master page that will act as a main template for the new page. In this exercise you will create a Web Form, insert Web controls, preview the page in a browser, and validate the HTML output.

To create a simple Web Form:

1. Click **File** on the menu bar and click **New File**. The Add New Item window opens. The Add New Item window displays templates.

2. Click **Web Form** in the Add New Item window.

3. In the Name text box, highlight the existing content, type **ch1_sample.aspx**, and then click **Add**. The Web Form is added to the project and opens in the main window in Source Code view. Notice that by default the DTD applied is the transitional for version XHTML 1.0.

4. Type the code shown in Figure 1-24.

5. Click **File** on the menu bar, and then click **Save All**.

6. Click **File** on the menu bar, and then click **View in Browser**.

7. Right-click the page in the browser and click **View Source**. This is the code that is pushed out to the browser or client application. Your page will appear in your default browser source code editor.

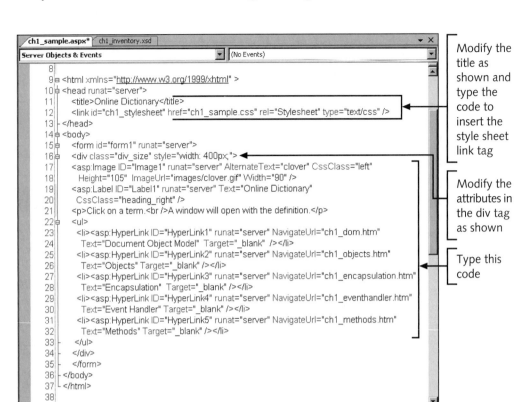

**Figure 1-24**   Creating a Web Form

8. Select all of the text in Source Code view. In Notepad you can click **Edit** on the menu bar and click **Select All**. Then, click **Edit** on the menu bar and click **Copy**.

9. Open a browser window, type **http://validator.w3.org/** in the address text box, and then press **Enter**. The Markup Validation Service Web page opens.

10. Scroll down to the Validate by Direct Input text box, right-click inside the text box, and click **Paste**. Then, click the **Check** button. The page is validated; a message will be displayed that says "This Page Is Valid XHTML 1.0 Transitional!" If the page had failed the validation, the number of errors is displayed along with information about each error.

11. Close the browser and all of the open files in your Web editor.

## Using the Postback Process

When a user fills out a form and clicks the Submit button, the data is sent to the Web server for processing. If the user enters an invalid value, the form is redisplayed to the client. Such maintenance of information across browser requests is known as **maintaining state**. To maintain state, the server code must retrieve the values from the initial page and merge them with the code for the subsequent page.

Server controls allow you to send data to the browser without writing the data-gathering and data-rendering code. By default, the server control automatically supports the posting of data back into the form, a process known as postback. When the user enters the data into a text box on a form, the server collects the value and re-renders the text box with the data.

A hidden form field named __VIEWSTATE is a very long encoded string that contains information required to maintain the form data across multiple page requests. Therefore, the value of __VIEWSTATE changes each time the form is reposted back to the server and each time the Web server decodes the value of the field. Then, the values are stored with the page, even if it is redirected to a different Web server.

In an enterprise network, it is common to have a group of Web servers called a **Web farm**. In a Web farm, when one server stops, the clients are redirected to another server. By storing the information on the client and not on the server, you enable the information to travel with the client across page requests and across servers. This string is not encrypted (which means the data is scrambled using a mathematical algorithm so that others cannot retrieve the data), which means you should not expect information stored here to be private. If you need to send information securely across the Internet, you can do this with ASP.NET if you enable the Secure Sockets Layer (SSL) protocol when you request your page using https:// instead of http://. Your network administrator will need to set up the SSL protocol for your Web application.

You can turn the postback feature on or off by setting the EnableViewState property to true or false within the @Page directive. The **@Page directive** is located on the first line of every Web Form and is used to modify the settings for the entire page. You can also turn the EnableViewState property on or off by setting the property for any individual server control. In addition, you can turn the EnableViewState property on or off for the entire application by setting the property in the application configuration files. In the following sample code, the property is turned off for the entire page for all server controls:

```
<%@ Page EnableViewState="false" %>
```

## Creating Item Templates

Templates are used by your Web editor to create projects and items based on your project type, programming language, and business decisions. All of the templates are available in the Add New Item window. Your Web editor-installed templates are stored by default at `C:\Program Files\Microsoft Visual Studio 8\Common7\IDE\VWDExpress\ItemTemplates\Web\VisualBasic\1033`.

There are many other templates for purchase and freely available on the Internet from the developer community. These templates—and the ones that you create on your own—will appear in the My Templates section in the Add New Item window. To create an item template, create the template file for the item and an XML-compliant metadata file (named *.vstemplate) that can be used to define how to display the project item in the Web editor. These two files are compressed into a .zip file and placed in the template directory.

## HELP RESOURCES

There are numerous Web sites that provide help, documentation, support, sample code, and sample applications. One of the early sample ASP.NET applications was an online catalog and shopping cart application for a company that provided an online catalogue and shopping cart for spyware products. The site was created to help developers learn about using Web Forms, accessing a database from the Web, and creating a simple Web Service. Today, Microsoft provides several starter-kits, which are applications for developers to learn new techniques and to use as building blocks within their own applications. These are available from the *www.asp.net* Web site.

Some of the applications created by Microsoft and third-party developers are located in the QuickStart Web site. Once installed, you can install this site locally at *http://localhost/ quickstart*, or view the site on the Web at remote sites such as *www.asp.net/Tutorials/quickstart. aspx*. You may want to visit the older versions at *http://samples.gotdotnet.com/quickstart/* because they provide a richer description and samples of the Web controls and basic ASP.NET programming techniques.

There are many help resources within the Web editor in addition to the Start Page mentioned earlier. **Dynamic Help**, as shown in Figure 1-25, provides help for the currently selected item. **Search Help** provides a text box to enter a search phrase. **Index Help** provides a dictionary index that lets you search for a term alphabetically. **Contents Help** allows you to navigate the help documentation using a table of contents. All help methods provide results in a ranked list. You can double-click the items in the list to view the documentation from within the user interface. You do not have to leave the Web editor application to locate help or documentation. You can view the actual URL of the help files in the URL drop-down list box on the Web toolbar.

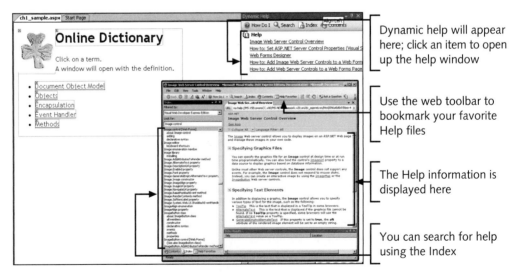

**Figure 1-25**  Dynamic Help search results

# CHAPTER SUMMARY

❏ You can use a variety of editors to create ASP.NET pages. However, you do need a Web server that supports the .NET Framework to run your pages. Visual Web Developer Express is a scaled down version of Visual Studio .NET 2005 and is used to create ASP.NET applications.

❏ The Solution Explorer window allows you to manage all of your project files from one location. You can also set properties of object in the code manually or use the Properties window.

❏ The Toolbox contains several sets of commonly used controls, which are organized into tabs. You can customize the Toolbox to include your own custom controls.

❏ HTML is a markup language that uses tags to identify how to format and present the content. Web pages created with HTML can end in .htm or .html. You can only use HTML tags when creating a static Web page. The two parts to a Web page created with HTML are the head and body. Web pages use HTML tags to create forms that can be used to collect information from the visitor. These form elements include text boxes, check boxes, and drop-down lists. You can use HTML tags to create tables that can be used to create a more definitive page layout. You can write the HTML code directly in HTML view, or use Design view and drag-and-drop HTML tags from the HTML tab in the Toolbox.

❏ Web Forms are Web pages created with ASP.NET. Web Forms allow you to build dynamic Web pages by using new server-side controls. Visual Studio .NET allows you to create Web Forms using HTML tags, HTML controls, and Web controls. Web Forms end in .aspx. ASP.NET controls enhance the user interface and increase interactivity within Web pages. HTML controls are HTML tags where the runat attribute has been set to server. Server controls provide you with more flexibility on creating output for the Web page because the server control will generate the HTML output to the browser.

❏ XHTML is a version of HTML that is XML-compliant. XML files can be formatted with cascading style sheets or XSLT stylesheets. XML files are required to follow a specific set of rules. XML files must be well formed. There is only one root element in any XML document. XHTML requires that tags such as <br> be closed in the first tag <br /> or include a closing tag <br></br>. XML elements are case-sensitive and all elements have an opening and closing tag. An XML schema is a set of rules used to define document format and structure of the data. Industries can create their own schemas and define their own sets of tags. Validation tools are used to verify that the XML code is compliant with the schema.

❏ Web Content Accessibility Guidelines (WCAG) address broad accessibility issues related to Web access and standards.

❏ The .NET framework is the architectural framework in which ASP.NET applications are created. NET applications are compiled into a Microsoft Intermediate Language (MSIL) and stored in assemblies. Namespaces are a hierarchical way to organize classes within the assemblies. The assembly is the file that is used to store the programming code.

❏ Additional features such as Dynamic Help and IntelliSense help programmers prevent syntax errors.

## REVIEW QUESTIONS

1. Which tab in the Toolbox is most commonly used to insert custom code fragments?

   a. HTML

   b. General

   c. Web Form

   d. Standard

2. What feature supplies context-sensitive help?

   a. Index

   b. Start Page

   c. Dynamic Help

   d. Contents

3. Which of the following is the file extension for a Web Form page?

   a. .api

   b. .html

   c. .aspx

   d. .xhtm

4. What is the name for the hierarchical treelike structure used to categorize the base class types within the .NET Framework?

   a. namespace

   b. postback

   c. toolbox

   d. quickstart

5. What property transforms an HTML control to an HTML server control?

   a. runat

   b. id

   c. target

   d. xmlns

6. You have just created a page named StoreFront.htm. If your project folder name is Baker, and you created your project using the Web editor default settings where the port number is 6394, where can you view your page in a browser?

   a. *www.baker.com:6394/StoreFront*

   b. *http://localhost:6394/baker/StoreFront.htm*

   c. *http://localhost:6394/StoreFront.htm*

   d. *http://127.0.0.1/6394/ghost.htm*

7. What tag is used to attach an external style sheet to a Web page?
   a. `<link>`
   b. `<inherits>`
   c. `<href>`
   d. `<style>`

8. Which tag is used to create a hyperlink?
   a. `<link>`
   b. `<target>`
   c. `<a>`
   d. `<name>`

9. Who is responsible for the maintenance of the XML standards?
   a. Microsoft
   b. IBM
   c. W3C
   d. Sun Microsystems

10. Which property is used to uniquely identify the server controls?
    a. id
    b. control
    c. name
    d. meta

11. DTD stands for _____ .
    a. design time data
    b. data transformation definition
    c. digital transform document
    d. document type definition

12. Which DTD allows use of presentational attributes, deprecated elements, and link targets that were missing in HTML 4.01 Strict?
    a. XHTML 1.0
    b. HTML 4.01 Transitional
    c. XHTML 1.1
    d. HTML 4.01 Frameset

13. Which is the preferred method to close the line break element in an XHTML 1.1 document?

    a. `<br><\br>`

    b. `</br>`

    c. `<\br>`

    d. `<br />`

14. What is the name of the input tag that is used to store encoded information about controls across browser requests?

    a. `__VIEWSTATE`

    b. `__doPostBack`

    c. `__EVENTTARGET`

    d. `__EVENTARGUMENT`

15. Which XHTML 1.1-compliant tag will form the text as bold in most browsers?

    a. `<bold>`

    b. `<strong>`

    c. `<style="bold">`

    d. `<font-bold>`

16. What version of character encoding is used for most Western European languages?

    a. ISO 8859-1

    b. ISO 8859-6

    c. ISO 8859-8

    d. ISO 8859-16

17. Which of the following tags is not supported in XHTML 1.1?

    a. `<u></u>`

    b. `<sub></sub>`

    c. `<rt></rt>`

    d. `<hr />`

18. The named markup for & is _____ .

    a. `&#38;`

    b. ` `

    c. `&amp;`

    d. `&target;`

1

19. Which standards address broad accessibility issues?

   a. SVG

   b. Web.UI

   c. WCAG

   d. XSD

20. Programming that makes it possible for client applications to communicate with server applications in a network is referred to as _____ .

   a. peer-to-peer networking

   b. bipolar networking

   c. client-server programming

   d. Web farms

21. Explain how a client request for a Web Form is processed on the server and delivered to the client.

22. Compare how HTML tags and server controls are used in Web pages.

23. Compare client-scripting using JavaScript and client-server programming.

24. Explain how you would ensure that your Web site would be accessible to the widest possible audience.

25. Explain why Web page standards have moved from a markup language model to a content language model.

26. Ruby tags will translate Chinese words into a Western European language. True or False?

27. All browsers will render the static content from HTML tags the same way. True or False?

## HANDS-ON PROJECTS

HANDS-ON
PROJECTS

### Project 1-1

One of the basic functions of a Web page is to provide methods for the visitor to interact with the Web site, and to communicate with the company. In this project, you will create a feedback form on a Web page with your Web editor using HTML. The page will comply with the XHTML 1.0 transitional standards.

   1. Start your Web editor and open your chapter1 Web site if necessary.

   2. Create a new HTML page named **ch1_proj1.htm** in the ch1_proj1 folder. Verify that the Doctype is set to the XHTML 1.0 transitional standards.

   3. Add a title to the page using the title tag that says **Feedback Form**.

4. Add to the Web page the **header.jpg**, **menu.gif**, and **customersupport.jpg** images located in the images folder.

5. Add a heading that says **Feedback Form** using the Label tag on the HTML tab of the Toolbox. Format the text as **Heading2**. Drag the handles of the control to show the text on one line.

6. Add HTML Text controls to collect the user's name and e-mail address. Add labels for each of the Text controls that say **Name** and **E-mail Address**.

7. Add a Label control that says **How did you hear about our Web site?**

8. Add a drop-down list box containing five choices such as **Magazine**, **Radio**, **E-mail**, **Friend**, and **Television**. Right-click the drop-down list box and then click Properties to display the Select Property Pages dialog box. Enter the value for the options. The options should be the same value as the text. You must click the **Insert** button after each text and value pair you enter. Leave the Allow multiple selections check box unchecked. Change the Size property to **1**. Click **OK**.

9. Add a Label control that says **What products are you interested in?**

10. Add three check boxes and corresponding Label controls that say **Jewelry**, **Clothing**, and **China**. (Note: You may add additional check boxes and option buttons to enhance the form.)

11. Add a Submit button that says **Send Your Comments**.

12. You can make it look presentable and professional by adding color and by changing the text fonts, graphics, and style sheets. For each of the items on the page, you can use the div tags and style attributes to position the items absolutely. Your page should look similar the one in Figure 1-26.

13. Go to the **File** menu and select **Save All**.

14. View your page in a browser. View the source code to examine how the elements are rendered. From the browser, print the page and Source Code view.

15. Close any open pages.

**Figure 1-26**   Creating a feedback form with XHTML

## Project 1-2

Companies store data in a variety of sources, including databases and recently in XML files. In this project, you will create an XML data file to store product data. The images are stored in your chapter1 folder.

1. Create a new XML document in your text editor named **ch1_proj2.xml** in the ch1_proj2 folder.

2. On the second line, create a root node named **ProductCategories**.

3. Create a child node named **Category** for each of the eight product categories.

4. Create elements named **ImageURL**, **CategoryID**, and **CategoryName** for each product category.

5. Add the data to each of the category nodes using the information in Table 1-3. (Hint: You will have to replace each of the ampersands (&) with the character code &amp;.)

**Table 1-3**   Data for the category nodes

| ImageURL | CategoryID | CategoryName |
|----------|------------|--------------|
| 21.jpg | 1 | Irish & Celtic Gifts |
| 22.jpg | 2 | Jewelry |
| 23.jpg | 3 | Crystal & China |
| 24.jpg | 4 | Pottery & Handblown Glass |
| 25.jpg | 5 | Foods from Ireland & England |
| 26.jpg | 6 | Irish Clothing |

**Table 1-3**   Data for the category nodes (continued)

| ImageURL | CategoryID | CategoryName |
|----------|------------|--------------|
| 27.jpg | 7 | Books, Music & Video |
| 28.jpg | 8 | Bridal Department |

6. Save the file. Open the page in your browser. Print the page from the browser.

7. In your chapter1 folder is the ch1_proj2.xsd file that contains the schema for this data file. Open this file and print the schema.

8. Insert the **xmlns** attribute in the XML file to point to this XML schema file. Validate your XML data file structure by viewing the page in a browser. (Note: If you have an error, go back and review the XML file for typos and syntax errors. Make sure you have included the XML prologue and only one root node, which includes an opening and closing tag. All elements must be well formed.)

9. Close the files and your Web browser window.

**HANDS-ON PROJECTS**

## Project 1-3

A large portion of revenue on the Internet comes from advertisements. In this project, you will create an XML file to store banner advertisement data. In a later chapter you will learn how to use this file within a Web page.

1. Create a new XML document in your text editor named **ch1_proj3.xml** in the ch1_proj3 folder.

2. Next, add the root node called **Advertisements**.

3. Create five nodes called **Ad**. Create elements within each Ad node named **ImageUrl**, **NavigateUrl**, **Height**, **Width**, **AlternateText**, **Keyword**, and **Impressions** for each advertisement.

4. Locate information to create five banner advertisements. This data can be used to create an image hyperlink. You will need to collect the following data listed in the bulleted list following this paragraph. (Note: Although the URLs can be relative in a banner advertisement, use absolute URLs for this assignment.) You can enter the collected information in Table 1-4. You can use your favorite graphics program to create the banners, locate a free banner on the Internet, or use a banner that your instructor has provided. The banners can be of any size. (Note: Your instructor may also provide you with the advertisement information to include in your file.)

   - **ImageUrl:** The absolute URL of the image that you want to display, which is used to create the SRC property in the image tag.

   - **NavigateUrl:** The absolute URL of the page to go to when the AdRotator control is clicked. This value identifies the URL to which the browser will be directed when the user clicks on the image. NavigateUrl is used to create the href property in the hyperlink created in the anchor (<a>) tag. The NavigateUrl page is also known as the ad response page, the target page, or the destination page. NavigateURL corresponds to the href property in the hyperlink created by the anchor (<a>) control.

1

- **Height:** The height of the image in pixels.
- **Width:** The width of the image in pixels.
- **Alternate Text:** Used to create the ALT property of the image tag. If the user's browser does not support images, the text is displayed instead of the image.
- **Keyword:** Used to indicate one or more words that categorize the banner ad. The category for the ad is used to filter the file to display specific groups of ads.
- **Impressions:** Indicates the frequency with which the banner ad is displayed. A numeric value (a weighting number) that indicates the likelihood of how often the ad is displayed. For this project, the total of all of the values of the impressions in the file should be 100.

**Table 1-4**   Elements of the Advertisement file

| ImageUrl | NavigateUrl | AlternateText | Impressions | Keyword | Height | Width |
|---|---|---|---|---|---|---|
|  |  |  |  |  |  |  |
|  |  |  |  |  |  |  |
|  |  |  |  |  |  |  |
|  |  |  |  |  |  |  |
|  |  |  |  |  |  |  |

5. Place the data from each of the banner ads in your table into the case-sensitive XML file using the structure shown in the sample snippet code below. (Note: Do not enter the code following this paragraph. Use this as a sample of what your code will look like.)

```
<Ad>
<ImageUrl>http://www.course.com/books.gif</ImageUrl>
<NavigateUrl>http://www.course.com/</NavigateUrl>
<AlternateText>Course Technology</AlternateText>
<Impressions>50</Impressions>
<Keyword>Books</Keyword>
<Height>150</Height>
<Width>150</Width>
</Ad>
```

6. Save the document. View the file in the browser to ensure that there are no formatting errors. Close the file and your Web browser window.

HANDS-ON
PROJECTS

## Project 1-4

Companies today are expanding to alternative platforms to display their content. Companies must change their current content to conform to standards that can be used across diverse platforms. In this project, you will validate a Web page and fix the errors so that the page conforms to the XHTML 1.1 standards.

1. Right-click the **ch1_proj4.aspx** page and select **View in Browser**.

2. View the source code for **ch1_proj4.aspx** in the ch1_proj4 folder. Change the Doctype to point to the XHTML 1.1 DTD. (Note: Use the Doctype for XHTML 1.1 shown earlier in this chapter.)

3. Preview the page in the browser and view the source code from the browser. Depending on your browser, the page will display a feedback form.

4. Select all of the code from the browser, copy it, and validate it using the W3C Markup Validation Service or other validation application or service.

5. If the page has errors, return to your editor and correct the errors, and then revalidate your page. The page should contain the same layout and functionality as the original page. Here are a few items that you should correct: all tags should have a beginning or closing tag or be minimized, all form controls and main tags such as the form, body, and the head tag should have the runat attribute set to server, all name attributes should be changed to ID, and attributes such as text, bgColor, and align need to be converted using a style attribute (style="color: #993333; background-color: #FFFF99;" or style="text-align: center;").

6. Repeat Steps 3 and 4 until your page is validated. For now, you may still have one error. ASP.NET puts a name attribute inside of the form tag.

7. Close all of the open files and the browser.

**HANDS-ON PROJECTS**

## Project 1-5

Currently, many companies are converting their sites to support the accessibility standards required by law in many institutions, states, and countries. It is common for Web developers to have to convert sites from one platform to another. You will want to validate and update pages in your site. In this project, you will validate a Web page and fix the errors so that the page conforms to the accessibility standards. Use Priority level 1 or A-level compliance for WCAG as the minimum standard for your Web page.

1. Read HTML Techniques for Web Content Accessibility Guidelines 1.0 at *www.w3. org/TR/WCAG10-HTML-TECHS/*. Visit the Web Accessibility Initiative (WAI) site at *www.w3.org/WAI/* to confirm the current version for the guidelines.

2. Open the **ch1_proj5.htm** page in the ch1_proj5 folder in the browser. (Note: Your instructor may provide you an alternative file, or direct you to a URL for a page located on the Web.)

3. Validate your page for WCAG. (Note: You may use WebXACT, a free online service that lets you test single pages of Web content for quality, accessibility, and privacy issues at *http://Webxact.watchfire.com/*. However, you will have to copy this file onto any live Web site first.)

4. If the page has errors, return to your Web editor and correct the errors, and then revalidate your page. You should target minimally compliance with the Priority 1 - A level for quality and accessibility. The page should contain similar layout and functionality as the original page. (Note: You may want to remove tables or use captions and other tools to support the table. You can read about how tables are supported at *www.w3.org/TR/WCAG10-HTML-TECHS/#identifying-table-rows-columns.*)

5. Close your browser window and the ch1_proj5.htm file.

## CASE PROJECTS

CASE PROJECTS

### Project 1-1

You are hired as the Web developer for a new Web site called MyStore. You are responsible for creating the home page for the Web site. Use your Web editor to create a home page in the ch1_case1 folder. Add at least three graphics, three hyperlinks, a bulleted list, and a table. Use the Properties window to modify the appearance of the controls and the Web page. Format the page using additional graphics, content, fonts, and color to enhance the appearance of the page. You may change the name of the store. Save the home page as ch1_case1.aspx in the ch1_case1 folder. Validate your pages conforms to XHTML 1.1 standards. View your Web page in your browser. Print your Web page and the source code from the browser.

CASE PROJECTS

### Project 1-2

As project manager, you are required to implement the goals and policies of the organization. In many institutions such as schools, and government Web sites, accessibility is not a luxury, it is the law. Administrators often do not understand the implications of how HTML 1.1 and accessibility standards can impact operations and the costs that can be incurred for upgrading and maintaining Web sites to these standards. Visit the W3C site and other sites to learn more about accessibility standards and XHTML 1.1. Write a paper in a Web page that presents the situation to non-programmers, and how you would recommend meeting these requirements. Place this in your in the ch1_case2 folder.

Create a Web page, named ch1_case2.aspx. Provide a summary of the information you learned about the topics you researched. In your Web page, provide step-by-step instructions how to customize the development environment to support accessibility and standards. Modify the presentation of the pages using the toolbars, Toolbox, and Properties window. View each Web page in your browser. Validate that your page conforms to XHTML 1.1 standards. Print each Web page and the source code from the browser.

## Project 1-3

You are responsible for developing a survey for your Web site. Develop a survey Web page that uses multiple choice, true and false, short answer, and open-ended questions. Use your Web editor to create the form in an ASP.NET page named ch1_ase3.aspx in the ch1_case3 folder. The form should consist of questions that use a variety of form controls such as text boxes, option buttons, check boxes, drop-down lists, and command buttons. Add hyperlinks and images to the Web page. Modify the presentation of the page using the toolbars, Toolbox, and Properties window. View the Web page in your browser. Validate your page conforms to XHTML 1.1 standards. Print the Web page and the source code from the browser.

## Project 1-4

In today's market your company will have to work with customers and businesses outside of their own culture or nation. The World Culture Foundation has hired your company to create a Web site to promote cultural awareness and diversity. The project manager has asked you to create a sample Web site using your Web editor. Select a culture that you are interested in and visit Web sites that discuss your topic. Create a Web site containing information you researched in the ch1_case4 folder. Provide at least one phrase in the language of the culture that can be displayed in the Web page. (You may not use a graphic image to display the phrase or select English!) Use only XHTML 1.1-compliant tags to create the Web pages. (Hint: Go back and read the sections on character sets and language attributes.) Save the Web pages as ch1_case4.aspx. Validate your page conforms to XHTML 1.1 standards. Print out your Web pages and the source code for the ASP.NET page and the code behind the page.

## Project 1-5

In the beginning, Web pages were created using basic HTML tags and targeted mainly two browsers. Today, Web sites have to be flexible to deliver content to a variety of platforms. What new skills are required of Web developers today? View Web sites such as the World Organization of Webmasters (WOW) at *www.joinwow.org*. Is Web development a profession with a discrete set of skills? How do WOW and the W3C impact the Web profession? Write a paper in a Web page that presents your findings and what you think. Save the paper as ch1_case5.aspx in the ch1_case5 folder.

## Project 1-6

Your store provides Belleek products to a distributor. The distributor would like you to provide an XML file of your Belleek product inventory. In your Web editor, you will use the information in Table 1-5 to create an XML file named ch1_case6.xml in the ch1_case6 folder. The root node should be ProductNode. The elements should be named ProductID, SubCatID, ModelName, ProductImage, UnitCost, and Thumbnail. The data in the table has been provided for you in a tab delimited form in the ch1_case6.txt file. Create a schema for your XML file. Validate your XML file using the schema. When you are finished, go to your browser and view the XML file and print out the view from the browser. View the schema in the browser and print the schema from the browser.

**Table 1-5**   Product information

| Product ID | SubCat ID | Model Name | Product Image | Unit Cost | Thumbnail |
|---|---|---|---|---|---|
| 550 | 16 | Marriage Blessing Plate | 550.jpg | 75.00 | 550.gif |
| 551 | 16 | Claddagh Plate | 551.jpg | 45.00 | 551.gif |
| 552 | 16 | Irish Blessing Plate | 552.jpg | 75.00 | 552.gif |
| 554 | 15 | Shamrock Picture Frame | 554.jpg | 70.00 | 554.gif |
| 555 | 15 | Cashill Clock | 555.jpg | 110.00 | 555.gif |
| 557 | 15 | Killarney Clock | 557.jpg | 70.00 | 557.gif |
| 559 | 15 | Child's Picture Frame - Boy | 559.jpg | 50.00 | 559.gif |
| 561 | 17 | Glendalough Vase | 561.jpg | 45.00 | 561.gif |
| 564 | 17 | Tall Daisy Vase | 564.jpg | 65.00 | 564.gif |
| 568 | 19 | Shamrock Creamer | 568.jpg | 50.00 | 568.gif |
| 570 | 19 | Cup | 570.jpg | 48.00 | 570.gif |
| 571 | 19 | Saucer | 571.jpg | 35.00 | 571.gif |
| 573 | 18 | Claddagh Bud Vase | 573.jpg | 30.00 | 573.gif |
| 556 | 15 | Oval Shamrock Picture Frame | 556.jpg | 50.00 | 556.gif |
| 560 | 15 | Child's Picture Frame - Girl | 560.jpg | 50.00 | 560.gif |
| 563 | 17 | Claddagh Bud Vase | 563.jpg | 30.00 | 563.gif |
| 565 | 17 | Galway Vase | 565.jpg | 25.00 | 565.gif |
| 566 | 17 | Colleen Vase | 566.jpg | 34.00 | 566.gif |
| 567 | 19 | Shamrock Sugar | 567.jpg | 50.00 | 567.gif |
| 572 | 19 | Dinner Plate | 572.jpg | 80.00 | 572.gif |
| 574 | 18 | Claddagh Plate | 574.jpg | 45.00 | 574.gif |
| 575 | 18 | Claddagh Makeup Bell | 575.jpg | 25.00 | 575.gif |

**Table 1-5**    Product information (continued)

| Product ID | SubCat ID | Model Name | Product Image | Unit Cost | Thumbnail |
|---|---|---|---|---|---|
| 576 | 18 | Heart-Shaped Trinket Box | 576.jpg | 30.00 | 576.gif |
| 578 | 18 | Heart-Shaped Claddagh Dish | 578.jpg | 40.00 | 578.gif |
| 579 | 20 | Kylemore Trinket Box | 579.jpg | 35.00 | 579.gif |
| 580 | 20 | Shamrock Ring Holder | 580.jpg | 35.00 | 580.gif |
| 581 | 20 | Kylemore Bowl | 581.jpg | 100.00 | 581.gif |
| 582 | 20 | Claddagh Makeup Bell | 582.jpg | 25.00 | 582.gif |
| 583 | 20 | Daisy Candle Holder | 583.jpg | 45.00 | 583.gif |
| 584 | 20 | Child's Cup for a Girl | 584.jpg | 25.00 | 584.gif |
| 585 | 20 | Child's Cup for Boy | 585.jpg | 25.00 | 585.gif |
| 553 | 16 | Mother's Blessing Plate | 553.gif | 65.00 | 553.gif |
| 569 | 19 | Shamrock Teapot | 569.jpg | 250.00 | 569.gif |

# 2

# INTRODUCTION TO PROGRAMMING

---

### In this chapter, you will:

- ◆ Integrate programming and Web Forms
- ◆ Store data in variables and constants
- ◆ Compare data types in Visual Studio .NET
- ◆ Work with Web objects to store data
- ◆ Design .NET Web applications
- ◆ Create programming structures using Visual Basic .NET
- ◆ Use programming control structures
- ◆ Locate runtime errors using debugging tools and programming code

---

Today, many companies expect their programmers to create their Web applications. As you learned in the previous chapter, building a Web application can be more complicated than building a traditional desktop application. Companies want Web programs that can be easily maintained and integrated with other applications. Companies need to build reusable programs with different data sources. To accomplish this, programmers use object-oriented programming techniques to encapsulate the business logic. Then they create applications that can access the business logic, regardless of how the program was written.

ASP.NET code can be written using a variety of programming languages. In this chapter, you will learn how to use object-oriented programming techniques and Visual Basic .NET within an ASP.NET application. In this chapter, you will learn about the .NET Framework, the Visual Basic .NET programming language, and how to create classes, store data using several data structures, access the data using functions and methods using Visual Basic .NET, and debug your application.

## INTEGRATING PROGRAMMING AND WEB FORMS

The Web Form is a Web page that can contain the HTML controls, client-side scripts, and ASP.NET controls. Web Forms contain compiled server programs which can be written inline with the Web Form, or written in a separate file known as the code behind the page. These server programs can be simple programming statements or complex programs.

The `<% %>` tags or the `<script runat="server"></script>` block tags are used to indicate **inline server code** within a Web Form. If you contain all of your code inline within the Web Form, the server will compile your pages for you and place the compiled files into a temporary directory at runtime.

The **code behind the page** contains programming routines that are directly related to the various server controls on a Web Form. Only server controls can interact with the code behind the page. The filename for the code behind the page has the extension .aspx.vb, if the code is written in Visual Basic .NET. Separating the server programming and Web Form allows you to alter your presentation tier without interfering with how the page is processed by the business programming code. Because of this separation of presentation and business logic, the graphic designer could work on the Web page layout at the same time the Web programmer is modifying the server code.

### Configuring the Page Directive

Both the inline and code behind programming models contain a Page directive. The **Page directive** allows you to set the default properties such as the default language for the entire page. If the programming code is written using the code behind programming model, the location of the code behind the page is identified by a property that is set on the first line in the page, using the Page directive. The default **Language property** is set to VB to indicate that the code behind the page is written in Visual Basic .NET. The file location is identified by the **CodeFile property**. The **Inherits property** indicates that the code behind the page inherits the partial class. In ASP.NET, the code to create objects such as a Web Form is stored in a partial class. **Partial classes** allow you to divide the definition of the class across several declarations or Web Forms. When the page is compiled, the code from the partial classes is joined into a single class. All the partial classes from these Web Forms must be located within the same assembly and the same namespace as the Web Forms.

### Where to Place Your Programming Statements

In the following exercise you will place your programming statements inline and in the code behind the page.

1. Start your Web development editor.
2. Click **File** on the menu bar, and then click **Open Web Site**. This opens the Open Web Site window. Locate the **chapter2** folder from your student folder and click **Open**.

2

3. In the Solution Explorer window, right-click the **ch2_inline.aspx** page and click **View Code**. After the page opens, on the first line, enter the code below to insert the Page directive and assign Visual Basic .NET as the default language:

```
<%@ Page Language="VB" %>
```

4. On the line after the comment 'Insert the code here,' enter the code below to display a message in the Label control when the user clicks the button. Click the **Save All** icon on the toolbar.

```
<script runat="server">
Protected Sub Button1_Click(ByVal sender As Object, _
ByVal e As System.EventArgs)
Label1.Text = "Welcome " & TextBox1.Text & _
". <br />Your password is: " & TextBox2.Text & "."
End Sub
</script>
```

**NOTE**

When the code is very long, use an underscore to continue the code to the next line. It is important not to break the contents of a string across multiple lines, unless each string is contained within its own pair of quotation marks and the string is concatenated.

5. Right-click the **ch2_ inline.aspx** page and click **View in Browser**.

6. Type **admin** in the Member ID text box and **password** in the Password text box and then click the **Sign In** button. The login information is displayed in the Web page.

7. In the Solution Explorer window, right-click the **ch2_codebehind.aspx** page and click **Open**. After the page opens, on the first line, enter the code below to insert the Page directive and the page properties. Click the **Save All** button.

```
<%@ Page Language="VB" AutoEventWireup="false"
CodeFile="ch2_codebehind.aspx.vb"
Inherits="ch2_codebehind" %>
```

8. Click the **Design** tab to change the view. Double-click the **Sign In** button.

9. The code behind page named ch2_codebehind.aspx.vb opens and displays the button click event handler. Locate the comment that says 'Insert the code here.' On the next line, type the code shown after this paragraph of instruction. Then click the **Save All** button.

```
Label1.Text = "Welcome " & TextBox1.Text & _
". <br />Your password is: " & TextBox2.Text & "."
```

10. In the Solution Explorer window, right-click **ch2_codebehind.aspx** page and click **View in Browser**. Type **admin** in the Member ID text box and **password** in the Password text box and then click the **Sign In** button. The login information is displayed in the Web page.

11. Close all of the windows.

## Using Variables and Constants in a Web Form

**Variables** store data that can be retrieved at a later time. For example, a variable might store a value that is to be used during a calculation. If you need to calculate several values, compare values, or perform multiple operations on a value, then it is worthwhile to use variables to store them, in lieu of using the values themselves. The program can then refer to the variable instead of the value.

A **variable declaration** consists of three parts: the declaration keywords, a variable name, and a data type. Declaration keywords define what parts of the Web application will have access to the variable. The **variable name** refers to the name of the variable as well as a section of memory in the computer. It is not necessary to know the exact location of the variable in the computer's memory because you can refer to the location by using the name of the variable. The **data type** identifies what kind of data the variable can store. For example, a variable might be an **integer** used in a calculation, or it might be a **string** of characters that is used to store the name of the company.

## Declaring a Variable

When you declare a variable, the computer reserves the memory required to store the variable. **Declaring** a variable is the process of reserving the memory space for the variable before it is used in the program.

Where your Web application defines the variable determines where the variable can be used within the application. For instance, **local variables** are defined within a procedure and can be used only by the procedure in which they were declared. Local variables persist in memory only while the procedure in which they were declared is being executed. Local variables are more readable, easier to maintain, and require less server memory resources than module-level variables. Therefore, you should choose local variables unless multiple procedures require the same variable.

**Module-level variables** are defined in the class but outside of the procedures, and can be used by any of the procedures within the page. Module-level variables are not available to other Web Forms or other classes within the application. When the page loads, the memory is allocated to the variable and the contents are assigned to the memory location. Any procedure within the Web Form can read or change the value of the variable. After the page has been unloaded and discarded, the memory can be reallocated to other resources.

If Dim is used, and the context is not specified, then the variable is public by default. You use the keywords in the following list to specify the scope of the variable. The **scope** identifies what context of the application can access the variable.

- **Dim:** With no other keyword, its use will mean the variable is public.
- **Public:** This is used to declare a variable global or public, and therefore available to other locations within the same Web page or from outside the Web Form.

- **Friend:** This defines variables that are used only within the current Web application or project.

- **Protected:** This defines variables that can be used only by the procedure in which they were declared.

If you have multiple variables to declare, you can declare each one on a separate line, or use a single line. To declare several variables on a single line, use the Dim keyword once, followed by the list of variables separated by a comma. The following examples illustrate how to declare multiple variables in Visual Basic .NET:

```
Dim intQuantity, intPrice As Integer
Dim strName, strEmail As String
```

By default you must declare all variables before the variables can be used. The **Explicit property** of the Page directive is used to configure the page to require you to declare all variables before they are used. Declaring variables before they are used makes it easier to debug your code. For example, it helps you catch spelling and syntax errors. If you type in the wrong name for a variable, the program will not run until you declare the variable with the correct name.

## Naming Variables

When naming variables, there are certain naming rules to which you must adhere. Violations of the following conventions result in errors in your programs:

- You cannot use any of the Visual Basic .NET commands or keywords as your variable name.

- Variable names must begin with a letter.

- You cannot use a period or space within a variable name.

- Avoid using any special characters in a variable name except for the underscore.

Variables are more useful if you name them with a standardized naming convention. This makes them easier to identify, and also makes spelling and syntax errors less likely. Visual Basic .NET commands and variables are not case sensitive. Variable names often consist of two or more combined words with the first letter of each word capitalized, for example, the variable named LastName.

It is useful to provide your variables with a descriptive name, one that has some meaning or association with the contents or purpose of the variable. Your company may also have a standard for naming objects and variables. For example, the variable that holds the price of a product can be named IntPrice to indicate that the variable contains an integer that describes the price.

## Assigning Values to Variables

You can store values in variables using the **assignment operator**, which is the equal sign (=). To assign a value to a variable, enter the name of the variable on the left side of the assignment operator, and enter the new value on the right side of the assignment operator. You can assign the value to the variable when you declare the variable, or after the variable has been created. The following sample code shows you how to declare multiple variables at the same time, and how to assign a value to a variable when the variable is declared:

```
Dim CompanyName As String = "Barkley Builders"
Dim CompanyName As String
CompanyName.Text = "Barkley Builders"
```

## Declaring Constants

You can use a **constant** instead of a variable when you want to assign a value that does not change. For example, you can use constants for tax rates, shipping fees, and values used in mathematical equations. The **Const keyword** is used to declare a constant. The naming rules for variables also apply to constants. However, the names of constants are usually all uppercase, as shown in the code that follows this paragraph. In addition, when you declare a constant, you need to assign the value to the constant.

```
Const TAXRATE As Integer = 8
```

# WORKING WITH DIFFERENT DATA TYPES

In your Web programs you will need to know how to store and manipulate different types of data. Each data type has special characteristics and capabilities. In the following subsections, you will learn about the most common types of data and how they are stored and used within your Web page.

## Working with Text Data

Character text is stored in data types called strings and chars. The **Char data type** allows you to store a single text value as a number between 0 and 65,535. The Char data type can be used to create new character sets for other types of languages that use Unicode standards.

The **String data type** is used to store one or more text characters, which can consist of numbers and characters. Number values not used in mathematical expressions are more efficiently stored as strings. Social Security numbers, zip codes, and phone numbers are typically stored as strings. However, strings are stored as basic text, and must be explicitly converted to a numerical data type before a string value can be used in an arithmetic expression. When you assign a string a value, the value must be within quotation marks. All strings are stored as Unicode and are variable in length. Therefore, you don't have to specify the number of characters in the string when you create the string object. In the following subsections you will learn how to modify strings.

## Methods Used to Modify Strings

In Visual Basic .NET, strings can be manipulated using different methods that are built into the String object, as follows:

- The **Ltrim**, **Rtrim**, and **Trim methods** remove the blank spaces from the preceding, ending, and both ends of the string, respectively.

- The **Asc method** provides the string's ANSI (American National Standards Institute) character equivalent.

- The **Chr method** provides the ASCII (American Standard Code for Information Interchange) character equivalent. Chr is a useful method when you want to create control characters such as carriage returns.

- The **Replace method** replaces one string with another.

- The **Split method** returns a string that has been split, using a delimiter to identify where to split the string.

- The **Concat method** allows you to join strings together without using the concatenation operator.

- The **Compare method** allows you to compare two strings. If they are equal, the method returns 0. If the value on the left side is less than the value on the right side, then a negative integer is returned; otherwise a positive integer is returned.

- The **LCase** and **UCase methods** convert the case to lowercase and uppercase, respectively.

## Concatenating Strings

**Concatenation** is the process of joining together one or more strings. The string can be a literal string, the result returned from an expression, or a variable that contains a String data type. You can also use built-in methods to determine the length of the string, locate characters within the string, and truncate the spaces at the beginning or end of the string. In the sample code that follows this paragraph, the variable is used to store the result of an expression. The expression is built using the values from the properties, concatenated with a line break tag. The ampersand is used to concatenate the expression to one single string.

```
Dim ContactEmail As String = CompanyEmail.ToString() & "<br />"
```

**NOTE**    You can also use the plus sign (+) for concatenation of strings. However, because the plus sign also represents the addition operator for mathematical equations and because it can be used with non-strings, it's recommended to use the ampersand as the concatenation operator.

# Working with Numeric Data

The numeric data type you use depends on the values anticipated and the amount of memory available. Whole numbers are stored in numeric data types such as Byte, Short,

Integer, and Long. Real number data types are represented by the types Single, Double, and Decimal. Consider the following:

- The **Byte data type** stores an integer between 0 and 255. A byte data type is stored in a single byte.

- The **Short data type** is a 16-bit number. Therefore, a short data type can only store values from −32,768 to 32,767. It uses two bytes of memory to store the value.

- The **Integer data type** is a 32-bit whole number and is the preferred data type for representing a 32-bit number on a 32-bit operating system. It uses four bytes of memory to store the value.

- The **Long data type** is a 64-bit number and is the preferred data type for representing a 64-bit number on a 64-bit operating system. It uses eight bytes of memory to store the value.

- The **Single data type** represents a single-precision floating point number, which means that it can include decimal points. It uses four bytes of memory to store the value.

- The **Double data type** supports larger numbers than the Single data type. It also includes decimal points but requires eight bytes of memory to store the value.

- The **Decimal data type** can store numbers up to 28 decimal places and is often used to store currency data. Variables that store monetary values have a subtype called Decimal. (*Note:* In previous versions of Visual Basic .NET this data type was known as **currency**. You can use formatting methods to change the appearance of the Decimal data type to currency.)

There are many built-in mathematical methods that can be used with your numeric data. Some of these mathematical methods include absolute value (Abs), divide and provide the remainder (DivRem), exponents, logarithmic, and power methods (Exp, Log, Log 10, and POW), floor, ceiling, minimum, and maximum values (Floor, Ceiling, Min, and Max), and square root, round, and truncate (Sqrt, Round, and Truncate). Other methods directly available with the various numeric classes include Add, Equals, Divide, Multiply, and Subtract, and you can also use the arithmetic operators (such as + = / * - ).

As you may recall, the **Format method** of the String class allows you to format the numeric value. In general, there are two ways to use the Format method. You can use the Format method with predefined format styles listed below, or you can create your own user-defined format style.

- Number (N) is used to format the number using commas.

- Currency (C or c) will insert the dollar symbol and two decimals.

- Percent (P) will format the number as a percent.

- Fixed number (F or f ) represents a fixed number with two decimals.

You can use the full name of the format, such as Percent, or the abbreviation, such as P. The sample code that follows this paragraph illustrates how to use a predefined format such as currency and percentage:

```
System.String.Format("{0:C}", 1234.45)
String.Format("{0:P}", 1234.45)
Format("Percent", 1234.45)
```

You can use a mask to create your own numeric format using 0 to represent a digit, pound (#) to represent a digit or space, or insert characters such as a comma (,), percent sign (%), or dollar sign ($). In the sample below, the numbers would be displayed as 1,231 and $24.99 and 5.54%.

```
Format(1231.08, "#,###")
Format(24.99, "$#,###.##")
Format(0.0554, "0.00%")
```

## Working with the Date and Time

The **DateTime data type** is a .NET data type located in System.DateTime and used to store dates and times. The date value is enclosed within a pair of pound signs. Visual Basic .NET can store any date between 01/01/0001 and 12/31/9999. The Web server will display the local time by default. You can configure the date to display based on the Coordinated Universal Time (UTC). UTC was previously known as Greenwich Mean Time (GMT). You can format the DateTime object using one of the built-in properties such as Date, Day, DayOfWeek, DayOfYear, Month, Year, Hour, and Minute. You can display the date in a DateTime object based on local time, or use the UtcNow property to display the Coordinated Universal Time. The date and time values are stored in the formats mm/dd/yyyy and hh:mm:ss. You can retrieve or assign a value to the date using the pound sign before and after the date, as shown in the following sample code:

```
Dim MyBirthday As DateTime
MyBirthday = #3/22/2008#
```

### Formatting the Date and Time

You can use the Format method of the String class to format the date and time. You can use a predefined format by passing a standard mask to the Format method with the DateTime object. For example, the d and D masks represent the short and long date formats. You can use t or T masks to represent the short and long time formats. The r or R masks will display the date as Coordinated Universal Time (UTC). As shown in the following code, the first would display the date as 3/12/2008 by using the Short format.

```
Dim ShippingDate As DateTime = #3/12/2008#
Format(ShippingDate, "d")
```

To build a custom format for the date and time, you can use masks to represent the values for the day, year, month, minutes, and the time of day, like so:

- *d*: Represents the weekday by a number. Using *dd* will display a leading 0 if needed. Sunday is 1.

- *ddd*: Represents the first three letter abbreviations of the day of the week, while *dddd* represents the full day name such as Wednesday.

- *m* and *mm*: Represents the month numerically. Using *mm* will display a leading 0 if needed.

- *MMM* and *MMMM*: Represents the month abbreviation and full name.

- *y*, *yy*, or *yyyy*: Represents the year.

- *h*, *m*, and *s*: Represents hours, minutes, and seconds.

- *H*: Is used for the 24-hour clock often used with military, financial, and healthcare applications.

- *t* or *tt*: Represents the time of day using A.M. or P.M. abbreviations.

To build a custom format for the date and time you can use masks such as a colon (:) for separating time elements, and a forward slash (/) for separating date elements. You can force insertion of leading zeroes for single digits using *dd*, *yy*, *hh*, *mm*, and *ss*. Table 2-1 shows some of the common formats applied to the date and time.

**Table 2-1**   Formatting date and time

| Format | Appearance |
| --- | --- |
| Format(*MyDT*, *"h:m:s"*) | 5:2:34 |
| Format(*MyDT*, *"hh:mm:ss tt"*) | 05:02:34 PM |
| Format(*MyDT*, *"d-MMM"*) | 7-Dec |
| Format(*MyDT*, *"d-MMMM-yy"*) | 7-December-07 |
| Format(*MyDT*, *"dddd, MMM d yyyy"*) | Sunday, Sep 9 2007 |
| Format(*MyDT*, *"HH:mm:ss"*) | 17:02:34 |
| Format(*MyDT*, *"d MMMM"*) | 9 September |
| Format(*MyDT*, *"h:mm:ss t"*) | 5:02:34 P |
| Format(*MyDT*, *"H:mm"*) | 21:45 |
| Format(*MyDT*, *"m/d/yyyy H:mm"*) | 9/9/2007 17:34 |

## Using the Boolean Data Type

A **Boolean data type** has only two possible values: True or False. Typically, in binary math, 1 represents True and 0 represents False. However, when a Boolean value is used within a mathematical expression, the value of the Boolean variable is converted to a number. When these values are converted to an integer, the True value is converted to -1, and the False value is converted to 0. In the next section you will learn how to convert different types of data.

# Converting Data Types

As you learned, the number 1 and the character 1 are different data types. When you collect data from a form field such as a text box, the value is a string. In order to use the numeric character in an equation, you need to convert the value from the String data type to a numeric data type.

Some data types can be converted using intrinsic methods. So, you can use `MyTotal.ToString()` to provide the value of some objects as a string. Strings are not implicitly converted to numbers. You could convert the string to an integer using the System.Convert class or you could use the CInt function to convert the string as in CInt(strVariable).

Problems can occur when you convert data types. If you attempt to convert one type to another, which isn't allowed, no conversion will occur, and an InvalidCastException exception will be thrown.

When you convert a decimal to an integer, you may lose some data. If you convert 23.50 to 23, you lose the .50. In this case, an overflow exception is thrown, signaling that there is data that is at risk of being lost if the conversion were to occur. These are called **narrowing conversions** and are not allowed by default because data could be lost. On the other hand, when you convert 23.00 to 23, no data is lost because the .00 digits are considered not significant. No exception is thrown. This example of **narrowing conversions** is allowed, because there is no data loss. If you convert an integer such as 25 to a single such as 25.00, no data is lost. This is an example of a **widening conversion**. Widening conversions are always allowed because no data loss occurs.

You can set the **Strict property** of the Page directive to True so that any narrowing conversion that would result in data loss is halted. You would then need to convert data types explicitly when narrowing conversions would occur.

# Working with Collections

A **collection** is an object that can store different types of data. Each item in the collection is also referred to as an **element**. A collection is like a movie theatre. The collection and the movie theatre are both containers. You can refer to the movie theatre as a whole or to an individual seat in the movie theatre. Each seat in the movie theatre has its own number so that the patrons can locate their seat. In the same way, you can refer to the collection as a whole, or to each item—such as a piece of data—within the collection.

The items in the collection can be any valid data type such as a string or an integer, an object, or even another collection. For example, a list of employee names, a list of states, or a list of tax rates could all be stored within a collection. Although this data could be stored in other types of structures, such as a database, this would often require significant processing every time the Web application had to retrieve the list, because it would need to return to the database to get the values.

The Systems.Collections namespace defines several types of collections including the ArrayList, HashTable, SortedList, Queue, and Stack. You will learn more about collections in the subsections that follow.

## The ArrayList

The **ArrayList** is a collection object that stores each item in sequential order, and each item is indexed with a number. The ArrayList is declared using the keyword Dim, the name of the array, and the keyword New. You must specify that the collection is an ArrayList. These items are grouped together using a group variable name.

When you declare the ArrayList, you do not need to specify the size. The **Capacity property** of the ArrayList is the number of items the list can hold. As items are added to an ArrayList, the capacity is automatically increased as required. Therefore, you do not have to worry about defining the size of the ArrayList when you create the array, add items, or remove items. The ArrayList is **zero-based**, which means that the counting of items in the ArrayList starts at 0 and not 1. The first item in the ArrayList is at position 0. So, if an ArrayList size is 3 the ArrayList has four items. If the Capacity property is explicitly set to zero, the CLR sets the Capacity property to a default capacity of 16.

The **Count property** determines the actual number of items in the ArrayList. Each item in the ArrayList is identified using an index number that indicates its position within the ArrayList. The ArrayList stores the items in an Items Collection. The items within the ArrayList are not required to be of the same data type.

Assigning values to elements in an ArrayList is called **populating** the ArrayList. To populate the ArrayList, specify the index number, and then pass the value for each element. You can add items to the ArrayList by using the Add method of the Items collection. The **Clear method** can be used to clear the values of all of the elements in the array. The sample code that follows this paragraph illustrates how to create an ArrayList named StateAbbrev. The ArrayList is populated with three elements.

```
Dim StateAbbrev As New ArrayList
StateAbbrev.Add("IL")
StateAbbrev.Add("MI")
StateAbbrev.Add("IN")
```

After the ArrayList is populated, the program can retrieve the value of any element in the array. To retrieve the value of an ArrayList element in the ArrayList, you use the ArrayList name and the index number of the element. You can then use this value in an expression, display it in a Web page, or assign it to a variable. You can create an ArrayList and rotate through the list using the For-Next loop.

The following is a list of methods that apply to the ArrayList collection:

- The **Add** and **Remove methods** add or delete a single element.
- The **Insert** and **RemoveAt methods** add and remove elements at a specific location preceding the ArrayList. You can insert or remove an element at a specific index position within the ArrayList by specifying the element's index position number.

- The **AddRange** and **RemoveRange methods** allow you to add or remove a group of elements. When you remove a range, you must specify the index number of the first element you want to delete, and then the number of elements you want to delete.

- The **IndexOf property** returns an integer which represents the index position of the element in the list. A value of –1 means that the element was not found in the list.

- The **Count property** identifies the number of items in the array, which will be the largest index number plus 1.

- The **IsArray function** returns True if the variable is an ArrayList; otherwise, it returns False.

- The **Erase method** is used to clear the values of all of the elements.

- The **Clear method** allows you to remove all of the elements within the ArrayList. It's useful to clear the items from the list anytime you are beginning a list.

In the following sample code, an ArrayList is inserted into the first position and then removed:

```
StateAbbrev.Insert(0, "OK")
StateAbbrev.Remove("OK")
```

ArrayList elements can be directly manipulated, or the values of the ArrayList elements can be assigned to variables and the variables can be manipulated. In the sample code that follows this paragraph, the index position of the OK element is retrieved and all of the values are written to a single textbox control:

```
Dim iPos as Integer
iPos = StateAbbrev.IndexOf("OK")
Dim MyCount As Integer
MyCount = StateAbbrev.Count
For I = 0 to MyCount -1
  MyStates.Text = StateAbbrev(I) & "<br />"
Next
```

## The HashTable

The HashTable is a collection object where the order in which the items are stored is based upon a built-in set of rules known as the **hashing algorithm**. The HashTable creates the index of items using an alphanumeric key. In other words, each item is referenced by an alphanumeric key, like an encyclopedia. The keys are a collection of alphanumeric values, and the values are a collection of items.

You can create a HashTable by declaring the object using the keyword Dim, the name of the HashTable, and the keyword New. You do not need to identify the number of items in the HashTable. You can add and remove items using the Add and Remove methods. The items are added using a key and value pair. The code to add a value to the HashTable is

HashTableName.Add(*key, value*) You can use variables instead of the actual values. The **key** is the first parameter and is passed using quotation marks indicating that the key is a string. The second parameter is the **value** parameter. The value parameter is separated from the key parameter with a comma. You can use the key in your programming to retrieve the value for a particular item.

The sample code following this paragraph would create a hashtable that stores information about a piece of property. You can retrieve the key value using "{0}:" or the Key property of the item, and you can retrieve the value using "{1}:" or the Value property of the item. The code loops through each item in the array collection using the For-Each statement, retrieves the value, and concatenates the value to the CustomerLabel string. The code between the For-Each and Next statements will be executed for every item in the array collection.

```
Dim HT1 As New HashTable()
HT1.Add("1", "Mrs. Marijean Richards")
HT1.Add("2", "1160 Romona Rd")
HT1.Add("3", "Wilmette")
HT1.Add("4", "Illinois")
HT1.Add("5", "60093")
Dim CustomerLabel as String
For each Customer in HT1
CustomerLabel &= Customer.Value & "<br />"
Next Customer
```

The Clear method allows you to delete all of the items in the HashTable. The **ContainsKey** and **ContainsValue methods** can help you determine if a key or value exists. These methods are often used before adding or removing an item. For example, you might only want unique values in the HashTable. You could use the ContainsKey method to verify that the element does not already exist before calling the Add method. If the key or value exists, the method returns True.

When you want to retrieve the hash key and value when you bind the data to a control, you will need to specify what you want to do with the key and value. In data controls, **DataValueField** is used to create the value for the control and is usually assigned to the value in the HashTable, but it's not required. In some cases you may want the key of the HashTable to be sent as the value of the control. Data controls also have a **DataTextField**, which is used to create the text displayed for the control; in most instances it's the text that is displayed on the page. This is usually assigned to the key in the HashTable, but it's not required. In some cases you may want the value to be displayed in the control. In the next section you will learn about other types of collections available within the .NET Framework.

## Other Collections

There are other types of collections available in the .NET Framework, as follows:

- The **SortedList** is a collection object that is indexed by both the key and the item. Because the sorting of the list is based on the key, the index position of the element changes frequently. Therefore, you cannot insert the element based on its index position.

- The **Queue** is a collection object that can only be used to provide sequential access to the elements. This is similar to a waiting list at a restaurant. Typically, the people at the top of the list are seated first. This sequential ordering system is known as first in, first out (FIFO).

- The **Stack** is a collection object that provides sequential access but stores the elements in last in, first out (LIFO) order. The stack is similar to the seating policies in an airplane. The first one to board the airplane is the last one to exit the airplane.

## Binding Collections to Web Controls

You can easily bind controls to a collection with your code behind the page. If you want to assign the values in the collection to a TextBox control, you can retrieve the values using a For Next loop, and assign the values to a variable. Then you would assign the variable to the Text property of the TextBox control.

Check boxes, radio buttons, and drop-down lists allow you to select from lists of options. The **Checked property** can be used to determine which radio button was checked. The difference between check boxes and radio buttons is that you can select only one option from a group of radio buttons. You can select none, one, many, or all options from a group of check boxes. Therefore, the radio button group must all be identified with a single name.

The drop-down list can be created using the DropDownList control, which will create the HTML code, including the select (`<select></select>`) tags and the option (`<option> </option>`) tags for each item displayed in the control. The drop-down list displays a list one item at a time, and a list box displays multiple items at a time. Option tags are used to create each individual item in the list. A value can be associated with each item in the list. The value of the item does not have to match the displayed text of the item.

The position of each item in a drop-down list is represented by the index number. The index number of the first element in the list is 0. You can access the item that was selected by the user by retrieving the **SelectedIndex property**. If nothing has been selected, the SelectedIndex property returns the value -1. In the next section you will modify a Web Form to implement an ArrayList and HashTable.

## Using Collections in a Web Form

In the following exercise you will add items to a Web control in a Web Form using the Add method. You will also add items using an ArrayList and HashTable collection, which will then be used to insert the items into a control in the Web Form.

1. In the Solution Explorer window, right-click the **ch2_dropdown.aspx** page and click **View Code**. Notice that the code adds the items in the HTML Dropdown control named CatList using the Add method of the Items collection. To insert the code to add a new item, Gifts for Women, type **CatList.Items.Add("Gifts for Women")** on the next line after the line 'Insert the code here. Click the **Save All** button.

2. In the Solution Explorer window, right-click the **ch2_ dropdown.aspx** page and click **View in Browser**. Select **Gifts for Women** from the drop-down list and then click the **Submit** button. The CatList is replaced with the ProductList control, the ProductList control displays gift ideas for women, and the lblTitle message is changed.

3. In the Solution Explorer window, right-click the **ch2_select.aspx** page and click **View Code**. To insert the code to add a new item named Bridal, type the code **dlCategory.Items.Add("Bridal")** on the next line after the comment 'Insert the code here. Click the **Save All** button.

4. In the Solution Explorer window, right-click the **ch2_ select.aspx** page and click **View in Browser**. Select **Bridal** from the drop-down list and then click the **Select a Category** button. The label and image will be replaced with the Bridal department content.

5. In the Solution Explorer window, right-click the **ch2_rbl.aspx** page and click **View Code**. Notice that the item is inserted using an ArrayList. To insert the code to add a new item named Sports in Ireland, type the code **AR1.Add("Sports in Ireland")** on the next line after the comment 'Insert the code here. The DataBind method of the RadioButtonList control will bind the ArrayList data to the RBL control. Click the **Save All** button.

6. In the Solution Explorer window, right-click the **ch2_rbl.aspx** page and click **View in Browser**. Notice that the new item was inserted. Click the **Sports in Ireland** radio button and then click the **Submit** button. The sports in Ireland will appear in the right panel.

7. In the Solution Explorer window, right-click the **ch2_ cbl.aspx** page and click **View Code**. Notice that the items are inserted using a HashTable. The DataTextField property of the CheckBoxList control is set to the value of the hash table, and the DataValueField property is set to the key of the hash table. To insert the code to add a new item named Sports in Ireland, type the code **HS1.Add(5, "Sports in Ireland")** on the line after the comment 'Insert the code here. The DataBind method of the CheckBoxList control will bind the hash table data to the CBL control. Click the **Save All** button.

8. In the Solution Explorer window, right-click the **ch2_cbl.aspx** page and click **View in Browser**. Notice that the item is inserted using the hash table. Check the check boxes labeled **Hiking in Ireland**, **Fishing in Ireland**, and **Sports in Ireland**, and then click the **Submit** button. The items will appear in the right panel.

9. Close each of the open pages.

## WORKING WITH WEB OBJECTS TO STORE DATA

HTTP is one of the protocols used to send and receive data over the Internet. With each request from the browser, and response from the Web server, certain data is transmitted in the header. The **header** is the portion of a data packet that describes how and where to send the file. The header includes the date and time, the type of request (Get or Post), the page requested, and the HTTP version. Additional data includes the default language, the referring page, the IP address of the client, the cookies associated with that domain, and the user agent. The **user agent** can be used to identify the client software. Additional data can be sent with the header, such as the values entered into a form. You can programmatically access the information that is transferred with the request and response using various programming objects. In this next section you will learn how data can be sent in the header using server variables.

## Using the Request Object to Retrieve Data from the Header

HTTP collects information and stores the values as a collection of **server variables**. The **Request object** of the Page class allows you to retrieve any data sent by the browser, including the names and values of form fields and the server variables. Server variables can be retrieved by using an HTTPRequest object with Request.ServerVariables("*VARIABLE_NAME*"). The server variable name is always in uppercase.

The System.Web.HttpRequest class is mapped directly to the Request property of the Page object. So, instead of using the server variables to retrieve the header data, you can use Page.Request.*PropertyName* or Request.*PropertyName*. To retrieve the URL requested, the IP address of the client, the physical path to the file, and the domain name of the previous page that contained the link to the current page, use Request.Url, Request.UserHostAddress, Request.PhysicalPath, and Request.UrlReferrer.Host.

For example, the user agent provides a string that can be used to detect the browser version. However, the string must be parsed to locate the browser application name and version. The System.Web.HttpBrowserCapabilities class provides the ability to detect more specific browser features. With the **Browser property** of the Page class, you can directly access the browser application's name and version without the user agent. The following sample code uses the Browser property to retrieve and display the client browser's version, the short name of the browser application, the version number, and the operating system version.

```
Dim MyBrowser as String = Request.Browser.Browser & "<br />" & _
Request.Browser.Type & "<br />" & _
Request.Browser.Version & "<br />" & _
Request.Browser.Platform
```

## Retrieving Data from a Form with the Request Object

Although the form field names and values can be accessed from the header, the Request object of the Page class allows you to access the values. The Request object contains a **Form collection** and **QueryString collection** that allow you to retrieve form data from the header. If you use HTML elements to create your form, you must request the Form or QueryString collections to retrieve the form field values.

If the value of the form method identified in the HTML Form element is Post, then the form is sent as part of the HTTP request body. To retrieve the value of a field named CompanyName, you would enter `Request.Form("CompanyName")`.

If the value of the form method identified in the HTML Form element is Get, then the form results are HTML encoded and appended with a question mark to the URL requested as a single string called the **QueryString**. In the code below, the CompanyName form field name and value are passed in the QueryString:

```
www.course.com/index.aspx?
CompanyName=Green%20River&Industry=Electronics
```

The value of the CompanyName form field is retrieved and assigned to a Label control using code shown below:

```
Label1.Text = Request.QueryString("CompanyName")
```

The QueryString can contain only valid URL characters, has a fixed limit length, and is not appropriate to be used to send sensitive or personal information. Although the user may have entered "Course Technology" in the form field, the QueryString would send the value as "Course%20 Technology" because the URL will not support spaces and special characters. You can manually encode a string using `Server.UrlEncode("The String")` and decode the QueryString using `Server.UrlDecode("The%20String")`. If you would like to see a listing of server variables and properties available with the request property, view the System.Web.HttpRequest class list using the Quickstart Class Browser at *www.asp.net/QuickStart/util/classbrowser.aspx*.

## Accessing Form Field Data

If you are processing server controls on the Web page, you can access the value properties of the form field directly from your Web page code. The property name that you use to access the value is different for each type of server control. Note, however, that accessing the property value works only with server controls. To retrieve the value of the form field, you simply use the name of the object and the property that stores its value, such as `CompanyName.Value`. Likewise, you can assign a value to the form field such as `CompanyName.Value = "Green River Electronics"`.

**Cross-page posting** allows you to send data from one form to another. Essentially, you set the PostBackUrl property of an ImageButton, LinkButton, or Button control to the new page. You can detect if the user came from another page by determining if the Page.Previous property is null.

## Working with the Response Object

The Page class also contains a Response object, which is used to send information to the browser. Remember that the Response object is mapped to the System.Web.HttpResponse class. All data sent to the browser is sent via the HttpResponse class or via the Response object. For example, the IP address of the server and the name and version number of the Web server software are sent to the client. The Cookies collection is used to send cookies to the browser, which are then written by the browser in a cookie file within the client's cookie directory. A status code is sent to indicate whether the browser request was successful or encountered an error. You can access status codes with a custom error message page.

The Response object has several methods to send content to the browser. The **WriteFile method** allows you to send the entire contents of a text file to the Web page. The **Write method** allows you to send a string to the browser. You can send text, HTML tags, and client script to the browser using the Write method. For example, the code to write a string to the Web page is Response.Write("Green River Electronics<br/>"). You can use a variable or expression to store the string. In the following code example, the Write method is used to write out a string using a variable:

```
Dim strMessage as String = "Green River Electronics<br/>"
Response.Write(strMessage)
```

The Response object allows you to redirect the browser to another page. You can use the Response object to create server-side redirection. Because this redirection occurs on the server, the visitor never knows that he or she has been redirected to a new page. Although technically the browser is redirected using the HTTP headers, it is not classified as client-side redirection, so the user cannot stop the page redirection. The sample code that follows shows how to redirect the visitor to another page:

```
Response.Redirect("http://www.course.com/")
```

Another method that you can use to change to a new page is Server.Transfer. To keep the ViewState information, insert "true" as the second parameter:

```
Server.Transfer("Page2.aspx", true)
```

In the next section you will learn how to store data in the Session object.

## Session Objects

One of the biggest challenges in creating interactive Web pages is maintaining the state of the user. User information can be tracked across user sessions and across the entire application. Some of this information is retrieved from the properties of the Session object, such as the **SessionID**, which is a unique identifier that identifies each session. Although the SessionID is determined by several factors, including the current date and the IP addresses of the client and server, it is technically possible—though improbable—for the SessionID to repeat. You cannot change the value of the SessionID property. A special session cookie is used to maintain the session information. When the session ends, the cookie is discarded. If the user opens a new session, a new SessionID is issued. Therefore, a SessionID can be used to track a user across a single session, but not across multiple sessions.

To track a user across multiple sessions, the SessionID can be stored in a client-side cookie or in a database that contains the identity of an individual. Some of the information that Web sites track is retrieved from forms submitted by users. Once the user logs on with a user ID, the information collected can be correlated with past visits. As an example of using the Session object, the following code will retrieve the SessionID and the number of session variables, and extend the timeout to 30 minutes:

```
Session("Session ID") = Session.SessionID
Session("Number") = Session.Count.ToString
Session.Timeout = "30"
```

The Session object is used to maintain session state across a single user's session. The session variables are also stored in the server's memory. However, session variables can be accessed only within the session that declared and assigned the session variables. When the session ends, the session variables are released from memory. The application variables are released from memory only when the Web application is stopped, when the Web server is stopped, or when the server is stopped. The following code will store form field data, server variables, and session data, and will request properties in session variables:

```
Session("Member ID") = TextBox1.Text
Session("Date of visit") = DateTime.Now.ToShortDateString
Session("URL requested") = Request.Url.ToString
Session("Server") = _
Request.ServerVariables("SERVER_NAME").ToString
```

You can save your state information in session variables or directly within the __VIEWSTATE form field. The __VIEWSTATE form field contains the ViewState, which is information that is persisted across browser requests because it is stored with HTML code that is delivered to the client. The __VIEWSTATE form field stores information only about the server controls. The ViewState is serialized into a base64-encoded data string and is not encrypted, so, it is possible to view the contents. For instance, you can save a value in a variable named Publisher in ViewState with:

```
ViewState("Publisher") = "Course Technology"
```

To retrieve the value, you would place ViewState("Course Technology") within an expression or programming statement such as:

```
Dim MyPublisher As String = CStr(ViewState("Publisher"))
```

## Saving Data Using a Session Object

In the following exercise you will use the Request object to retrieve information about the client and server, and the session object to store data and to modify the timeout property and the ViewState contents. The Clear the controls button will remove the session objects and changes in the ViewState.

1. In the Solution Explorer window, right-click the **ch2_state.aspx** page and click **View Code**. A comment ('Insert the code here.) is used to indicate the point after which your code should be placed. Type the code shown in Figure 2-1 to retrieve the values from the text boxes, the date, and client and server data.

Retrieves the value from the
text box and stores it in a
session variable

Retrieves the data from the header using the
Request object and stores it in a session variable

**2**

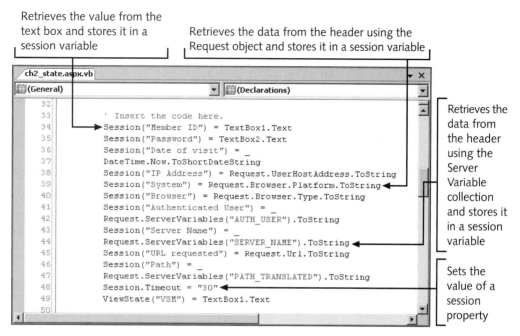

```
ch2_state.aspx.vb                                                              ▾ ×
(General)                                    ▾  (Declarations)                   ▾
   32
   33            ' Insert the code here.
   34         ▸ Session("Member ID") = TextBox1.Text
   35            Session("Password") = TextBox2.Text
   36            Session("Date of visit") = _
   37            DateTime.Now.ToShortDateString
   38            Session("IP Address") = Request.UserHostAddress.ToString
   39            Session("System") = Request.Browser.Platform.ToString ◂
   40            Session("Browser") = Request.Browser.Type.ToString
   41            Session("Authenticated User") = _
   42            Request.ServerVariables("AUTH_USER").ToString
   43            Session("Server Name") = _
   44            Request.ServerVariables("SERVER_NAME").ToString ◂
   45            Session("URL requested") = Request.Url.ToString
   46            Session("Path") = _
   47            Request.ServerVariables("PATH_TRANSLATED").ToString
   48            Session.Timeout = "30" ◂
   49            ViewState("VSM") = TextBox1.Text
   50
```

Retrieves the
data from
the header
using the
Server
Variable
collection
and stores it
in a session
variable

Sets the
value of a
session
property

**Figure 2-1**   Saving state using the session object

2. Click the **Save All** button.

3. In the Solution Explorer window, right-click the **ch2_state.aspx** page and click **View in Browser**. In the Member ID and Password text boxes, type **admin** and **password**, respectively. The password is a password text box and does not display the contents locally, but it is still passed as clear text to the server.

4. Click the **Session variables** button. Notice how the information from the text boxes is displayed in the browser. Click the **Clear the controls** button.

5. In the Member ID and Password text boxes, type **admin** and **password**, respectively, and then click the **Event handler** button. Notice how the session values are still available using an event handler. Click the **Clear the controls** button.

6. In the Member ID and Password text boxes, type **admin** and **password**, respectively, and then click the **__ViewState** button. Notice how the value that was entered into the text box is now stored in the ViewState. Click the **Clear the controls** button.

7. Close each of the open pages.

## DESIGNING .NET WEB APPLICATIONS

Web applications are different than Windows application because in a Web application you are designing the application to be used in a browser or an Internet-enabled device. Visual Basic .NET is used as the programming language for both types of applications. ASP.NET is the technology used to develop dynamic Web applications within the .NET Framework. The .NET Framework consists of a common language runtime (CLR) and a hierarchical set of base class libraries. A class is a named logical grouping of code. The class definition contains the functions, methods, and properties that belong to that class. In the next section you will learn how Web applications are designed and you will learn how to design a tiered application.

## Web Application Architecture

In the past, programmers were trained to take advantage of a **tiered hierarchical framework** when designing the architecture for Web applications in order to take advantage of the hardware efficiencies. One example of a tiered application would be to store the data on a data server on a separate physical computer. Today even if the entire application is stored on one computer box, the application can still be designed with a tiered framework where the presentation, business, and data layers are separated. Figure 2-2 shows how both the logical and physical tiers are related in an enterprise environment.

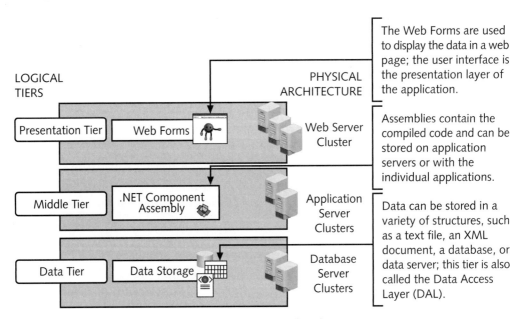

**Figure 2-2**   Comparing the logical tier and physical architecture in enterprise environments

As you can see in the figure, the **presentation tier** contains the user interface. The business programming logic, such as the formulas to calculate interest rate, are implemented in components at a **middle tier**. It is useful to create the business components to isolate the programming logic so that changes within the visual layer would not impact the programming code. The **data tier** often consists of one or more data servers such as SQL Server. Making the application support a larger number of visitors is called **scaling**. Scaling may require adding more Web servers to handle the requests, to deliver applications, and to store and cache data. Scaling the application should not result in recoding a well-designed application. Rather, the server and configuration files may simply need to be modified to locate the appropriate Web application resources. In the next section you will learn how your program code is managed within your Web pages.

## Organization of Classes in the .NET Framework

Your Web application will reference classes that you create, or that are built into the .NET Framework. The **base class libraries** are groups of commonly used built-in classes stored in executable files. These classes can be accessed from any .NET application. They contain fundamental code structures and methods that allow you to communicate with the operating system software and other applications. Your Web programs are written in Visual Basic .NET and access these built-in classes.

The base class libraries are organized into hierarchical logical groupings of code called **namespaces**. The System namespace is at the top of the namespace hierarchy, and all built-in classes inherit from it. For example, the Web controls are objects created by classes that are located within the System.Web.UI.Control.WebControl namespace.

## PROGRAMMING WITH VISUAL BASIC .NET

In the very early days of BASIC (the precursor to Visual Basic), each line of code was given a number, and these **programming statements** were executed sequentially in a single file. Later, decision control structures, functions, and procedures were used to control the execution order of the program. **Decision control structures** used conditional expressions to determine which block of code to execute. The block of code is a group of one or more programming statements. If a condition is met, then a block of code is executed; otherwise, an alternate block of code is executed. This type of programming was often referred to as procedural programming. Today, these programming methods are stored in classes that can be reused throughout your Web application. In this part of the chapter, you will learn to create a class and call it from the Web page code.

## Creating a Class in ASP.NET

Today an ASP.NET application stores programming statements in **classes**. Within a Web application, the code behind the page is contained within the page class. In **object-oriented programming**, you create custom objects based on the object definition, and then you can access the procedures and properties of the object across multiple Web pages. An **object** is a set of related, compartmentalized code that is based on a class. In addition to the page class, you can create a user-defined class with no visual component but with global variables, properties, and procedures. Your classes are often used to store access to the data and business logic for your Web application.

The creation of an object consists of two separate tasks. The first task is to create the object definition, also called the base class or **class definition**. The class is not accessed directly; it is the code that will be used to create the procedures and properties of the object. Once you define the class, you can create many objects based on the class definition. In other words, the class is the template for the new object. When you create an object, you are really creating an instance of the class. **Instantiation** is the process of declaring and initializing an object from a class.

The source file for the class ends in .vb, and by default it is placed in a directory named **App_Code**. You can create more than one class in the source file. You can restrict which applications can have access to the class using these additional keywords:

- Public: Can interact with other objects outside of the base class
- Private: Can only be called within the base class
- Protected: Can be called from within the base class and within subclasses; subclasses are used to create a class that inherits from a base class
- Friend: Can be called anywhere from within the same application

You can create classes using an external file or component, or create the class inline within the Web Form or in the code behind the page. A **component** is a class with a visual or graphical user interface. The code that follows is a sample of how to create a class definition named MyClass in a Web application named GreenRiverWeb:

```
Public Class MyClass
  Private CompanyName As String = "Green River Electronics"
End Class
```

If you want to use a class that is located in a different file, you need to import the class into the Web page, and then create a new object using the class. In the class in the sample code below, the MyClass class is imported into the code behind the page:

```
Imports MyClass()
```

You must use the keyword **Dim** to declare a variable in which to store the object, and the keyword **New** to identify that this is an object based on a class definition. In the class in the sample code below, the MyNewClass object is based on the MyClass class:

```
Dim MyNewClass As New GreenRiverWeb.MyClass()
```

After the object is created, it can access all of the variables, properties, functions, and procedures defined within MyClass. In the class in the sample code below, the company name is displayed in a Label control based on the CompanyName variable in the MyNew-Class object:

```
Label1.Text = MyNewClass.CompanyName
```

# Using a Procedure

Some programming statements are action statements; for example, they change the value of a text box. Some programming statements are decision control structures, which allow you to organize the order in which the code is executed. **Procedures** are used to contain one or more programming statements. Procedures are executed only when they are called by another procedure or when an event occurs. It is important to note that the order in which procedures are declared does not affect the order of their execution. Procedures always execute in the order in which they are called, not the order in which they are created. There are two types of procedures: subprocedures and functions. Both are considered a named grouping of one or more action and control statements.

You can pass zero or more arguments, called **parameters**, to a procedure or other type of programming structure. Parameters can be passed in a comma-delimited list within a pair of parentheses. You must also pass the type of data stored in the parameter. If no arguments are passed, you use an empty pair of parentheses. You can call the procedure several times, passing different arguments each time. In the following four subsections you will learn the different types of procedures used in Web applications.

## Creating Subprocedures

A **subprocedure** is a procedure that can be called from other locations. By using multiple subprocedures instead of combining them into one, each subprocedure can be reused without having to rewrite entire sections of code. Subprocedures do not return values and cannot be used in an expression value. Variables declared within the subprocedure are local and are available only to the subprocedure.

When you create the subprocedure, you declare it public or private. The keyword **Public** is used to explicitly declare the subprocedure available to all other procedures in the application, while private subprocedures are only available to other subprocedures in the context in which they are declared, such as the class. Subprocedures are declared using the keyword **Sub**. You can use the Exit Sub statement to stop the subprocedure. The syntax for a subprocedure is shown in the code that follows this paragraph:

```
Sub SubprocedureName(CompanyName As String, _
 TotalEmployees As Integer)
 Programming statements go here
End Sub
```

The subprocedures are executed in the order they are called by specifying the name of the subprocedure or using the keyword **Call** and passing any parameters required. You can pass the values as variables containing values, or use the value. The code following this paragraph is the syntax for calling a method:

```
[Call] SubprocedureName("Green River Electronics", 3400)
```

## Creating Event Procedures

An **event procedure** is a type of subprocedure that is attached to an object with events. An event procedure is not executed until triggered by an event. The event procedure is the code that will execute when the event handler intercepts an event, such as a button click. Note that the event procedure is not called, but rather is triggered, when the event occurs for that specific object. The object calls the event procedure when it detects that the event has occurred.

Different objects have different events. Event procedure names are based on the name of the object and the event name. An underscore (_) is used to separate the object name and the event name. For example, if you create a button named btnExit that calls an event procedure when it is clicked, you name the event procedure btnExit_Click.

When an event such as a button click occurs in the browser, the client-side script passes the name of the event procedure and the parameters to the server. The Sender As Object parameter identifies the object in the page that initiated the event. The EventArgs, represented as an e, is the set of parameters that was sent with the object. Many objects can send several different types of parameters, depending on the type of event that was triggered. Your event procedure needs to identify the parameters that correspond to the event that was triggered. An event procedure does not return a value. The following is the syntax for creating a basic event procedure:

```
Sub objectName_event(Sender As Object, e As EventArgs)
  Programming statements go here
End Sub
```

## Page Events

A static HTML page interprets the code line by line. However, a Web Form contains programming code and server controls in addition to HTML. A Web Form will process the code in a different order. The **page lifecycle** is the order that the Web Form is processed on the server and rendered in the browser. Page-related events will occur as part of page lifecycle. For example, the Page_Load event is triggered when the page is loaded into memory on the server. You can intercept the event handlers for the page events within code behind the page by writing an event procedure.

A page event is, quite simply, an event that occurs within the page lifecycle. The first time a page is requested by a client, a series of page events occurs, as follows:

- The **Page_Init event** initializes the page framework hierarchy, creates all of the controls, deserializes the ViewState, and applies the previous settings to the controls.

- The **Page_Load event** loads any server controls into memory and occurs every time the page is requested. You can determine if the page has previously been loaded by using the Page.IsPostback property.

- The **Page_PreRender event** occurs immediately before the control hierarchy is rendered and sent to the browser. The browser sees only the rendered client controls, such as HTML and client-side script.
- When the **Page_Unload event** occurs, the page is removed from the server's memory. You can use the Page_Unload event handler to close database connections, close files, and release any programming variables or objects.

Not all controls need to be rendered to the client. For example, to decrease the amount of code downloaded by the browser, you may not want to render a control to the browser until the user completes the login form correctly. You can use the Panel control to group controls, and set the Visible property to False to prevent the controls from being rendered to the browser.

You can view the order in which the server controls are rendered to the Web page by turning on the Trace feature. The **Trace feature** allows you to view the page controls, the order in which they are loaded, and the time it takes to load each control. To turn on the Trace feature, set the **Trace property** in the Page directive to true.

## Creating Functions

A **function** is a block of code that is grouped into a named unit. There are hundreds of built-in functions available within the .NET Framework including mathematical, date and time, string, and formatting functions, among others. You can also create your own function. The function declaration is identified by a unique name and declared as public, private, protected, or friend before the Function keyword. The End Function statement is used to identify the end of the function. You can leave the function at any time by inserting the Exit Function statement. Functions return a value—one value only—to the program that called the function by using the Return statement. You can return the value specifically or send the value that was stored in a variable or expression. The data type returned is identified in the function declaration. In the sample code below, if the customer lived in Michigan, the customer is given a $10 discount in his or her membership dues:

```
Public Function GetDiscount(CustomerState As String) As Integer
     Dim MyDiscount as Integer
     If CustomerState = "MI" then
          MyDiscount = 10
     Else
          MyDiscount = 5
     End If
     Return MyDiscount
End Function
```

If a parameter is required by the function, then it must be passed with its data type when you call the function, as shown in the following code:

```
Dim MembershipFee As Integer
MembershipFee = 100 - GetDiscount("MI")
```

## Creating a Property Method

A **Property method** sets the value of a variable defined within an object and is often used to expose private variables that are defined within the class. Some properties are assigned to the object by default within the object definition. Then all new objects inherit the same properties as the original object definition. However, if an object does not assign a value to a property, and a new object is created without assigning a value to the property, the property is assigned the default value "undefined." You can also assign values to properties that are declared in the class when you create the object from the class and after the object is created.

To use an instance variable from a different class, you need to use the Property method. These values may be stored within a variable within the class. You can use the Property method to make the instance variable available to code outside of the class. The following sample code shows how a property is defined within a class:

```
Public ReadOnly Property StoreName() As String
 Get
 Return StoreName
 End Get
End Property
```

Property methods are identified by the name of the object, followed by a period, followed by the name of the property, as shown to the left of the equal sign in the following code:

```
lblContact.Text = ch2_classname.StoreName.ToString()
```

### Using a Property to Retrieve and Set the Value of a Variable

In the code that follows this paragraph, the Property method retrieves the value of the internal instance variable named StoreName. By having the Property method store the value of the variable, the internal variable is not exposed outside of the class. Property methods keep private the variables that are internal to your code. You can simply return the value as a String data type using the Return statement. You must identify the data type of the variable that is returned to your main code. You can use the Property method to retrieve and set the value of the variables. In the sample code that follows, the value of the variable is set using the Property method:

```
Public Class MyClass
 Private StoreName As String = "Green River Electronics"
 Public Property NewStoreName() As String
 Get
 Return StoreName
 End Get
 Set(ByVal NewValue As String)
 NewStoreName = NewValue
 End Set
 End Property
End Class
```

**NOTE**

You should not declare the variable public or friend, because that directly exposes the variable outside of the class. Rather, you can use the property to retrieve the variable within the class. Then only the property is exposed outside of the class. You can set the property to read-only by using the keyword ReadOnly. This prevents you from writing to the property.

### Using the Object Browser to View Classes, Properties, and Methods

The **Object Browser** can be used to display the classes, properties, and methods built into the namespaces within the .NET Framework. In addition to the System classes, the Object Browser will also show the classes for other namespaces, including the Microsoft.VisualBasic namespace. (*Note:* To open the Object Browser window, open your solution, go to the View menu, and select Object Browser. To view classes within a namespace, you can expand the list by clicking the plus sign next to the namespace.) For example, DateAndTime is a specific class within Visual Basic .NET and is not the same DateTime object within the .NET System namespace.

## How Web Applications Interact with the Systems.Drawing.Graphics Class

Because your output is XHTML, your image files are sent using a Web-acceptable format. Windows programmers are used to working with the Systems.Drawing.Graphics class, which is referred to as the GDI+ or simply the Graphics class. With the **Graphics class**, you can create visual objects such as lines, and shapes such as rectangles and ellipses, paint the background, include and scale existing images, build custom objects, and even insert charts into your Web applications.

The application drawing objects are first created as an in-memory bitmap using the **Bitmap class**. Then you need to define a graphic object using the FromFile method of the System.Drawing.Image class, which acts as your drawing board. There are many additional classes that can be used to display content in the graphic, as follows:

- The **DrawString class** is used to draw text to the bitmap. You can pass the value as a literal or variable.

- The **FillRectangle method** is used to create rectangles and squares.

- The **FillPolygon method** is used to create polygon shapes such as triangles, trapezoids, and octagons.

- The **Point class** is used to create and connect individual points within the polygon.

- The **FillEllipse method** can be used to create circles and ovals.

- The **Font class** can be used to set the font type and size for a text message. The client is not required to have the font installed on their system because the font will be converted to a graphic.

- The **Brushes enumerator** is used to change the color of the brushes.

- The **Pen class** is used to draw; you can choose different styles of pens using the LineCap and DashStyle properties.

- The **LineCap property** indicates how to start and end the line. Examples of LineCap properties include Flat, Square, Round, Triangle, SquareAnchor, Round-Anchor, DiamondAnchor, and ArrowAnchor.

- The **DashStyle property** is used to alter the line style and can be Solid, Dash, Dot, DashDot, DashDotDot, or Custom.

- The **SmoothingMode property** can be set to AntiAlias, which will smooth any curves.

- The **DrawString class** actually draws the graphic into the bitmap.

- The **Dispose method** closes the image and releases the memory so that the image source file can be used with other applications.

Image formats most widely supported on the Web include JPEG, GIF, and PNG. The Graphics class now has the ability to save the image to the HTML output stream as other formats such as JPEG using the Save method, as shown below:

```
MyImage.Save(Response.OutputStream, System.Drawing.Imaging.
ImageFormat.Jpeg)
```

## Using the Systems.Drawing.Graphics Class

In the following activity, you will use the Graphics class to create a graphic dynamically for a Web Form. The menu was created dynamically from a collection, and the clock image is an example of an icon from the Microsoft image library.

1. In the Solution Explorer window, right-click the **ch2_gdi.aspx** page and click **View Code**.

2. Insert the code shown in Figure 2-3 in the Page_Load event handler in the line under the comment 'Insert the code here. This code will create a hash table, and will draw the menu using the values in the hash table. (*Note:* This page could easily be modified to grab the values from another type of data collection, file, or database.)

3. Click the **Save All** button.

4. In the Solution Explorer window, right-click the **ch2_ gdi.aspx** page and click **View in Browser**. Your page should appear as shown Figure 2-4. (Note: You may need to maximize your browser window to view the entire graphic.)

5. Close each of the open pages.

Although the menu was created with a HashTable, it could easily have been created using other types of data structures such as a collection or database.

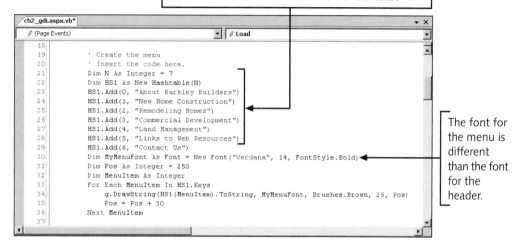

The font for the menu is different than the font for the header.

**Figure 2-3**   Creating a menu in a graphic with a collection

You can use an existing image as the drawing board, or create a blank drawing board; you can change the resolution of the image by modifying the properties of the drawing board.

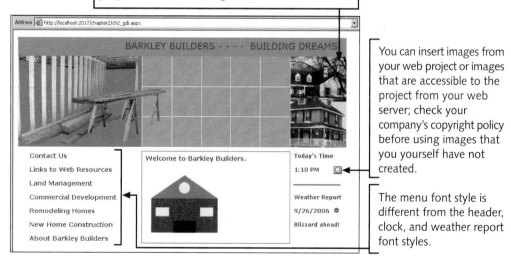

You can insert images from your web project or images that are accessible to the project from your web server; check your company's copyright policy before using images that you yourself have not created.

The menu font style is different from the header, clock, and weather report font styles.

**Figure 2-4**   Viewing a Web page created with the Graphics class

## Dynamically Creating Server Controls

The **Placeholder control** is used as a container to store dynamically added server controls. The Placeholder control inherits from the Control class. The Placeholder control does not produce any visible output without the use of other controls. The Placeholder control is created with the code `<asp:PlaceHolder ID="PlaceholderID" runat="server"></asp:PlaceHolder>`.

To add, insert, or remove a control from the Placeholder control, you can use the Control class of the control namespace. To do this, you must know how to use the constructor to create a control dynamically. For example, say you create and initialize a new instance of the Button class. This won't display anything. You have to add it to the Controls Property collection of the Placeholder class. Then, the page will display the control in its place and format the Button properties.

The **Panel control** can contain other controls and creates a DIV tag to enclose the contents. You can set properties such as wrapping, absolute positioning, font type, and scroll bars. For example, if you want to add some text to a panel, simply add a Label control within the panel tags or enter the text directly into the panel. The Label control creates contents within a Panel control using the SPAN tag. You use the Text property to display text in a Label control.

You can also use a **Literal control** to write content directly to the page. Literal controls are often used to add client-side HTML and text to the page. Any non-server code, such as HTML tags or tags without an ID property assigned, is placed within Literal controls when the page is rendered.

The **HyperLink control** is used to create an anchor tag that can link to another page or a target by using the **ImageURL property**. The displayed text is configured using the **Text property**. The Text property also becomes the ToolTip by default. The **ToolTip** is a new property that is used to display a message when the user places the pointer over the object. Notice that the image hyperlink does not have to be any specific size, color, or font. You can change the **Target property** of the hyperlink. The **target** is the window or frame used to load the Web page linked to when the HyperLink control is clicked. The default value for the target is String.Empty. You can change the target to any named window, or one of the reserved window names. The named window must begin with a letter in the range of a through z and is case sensitive. The reserved windows are as follows:

- **_blank:** Renders the content in a new window without frames
- **_parent:** Renders the content in the immediate frameset parent
- **_self:** Renders the content in the frame with focus
- **_top:** Renders the content in the full window without frames

## Dynamically Creating a Hyperlink Control

In the following activity, you will dynamically create a HyperLink control and add it to the Placeholder control. The Literal control is used to send HTML line break tags to the browser. The Placeholder control is created within a Panel control, which is used to position the controls on the Web Form.

1. In the Solution Explorer window, right-click the **ch2_placeholder.aspx** page and click **View Code**.

2. On the first line after the comment 'Insert the code here,' type the code in Figure 2-5, which will dynamically create and configure a hyperlink and add it to the Placeholder controls collection.

The new control is added to the Placeholder control using the Add method of the Controls collection; you can then modify the properties of the new control.

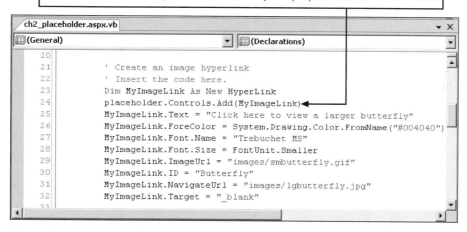

```
ch2_placeholder.aspx.vb
(General)                                    (Declarations)
20
21        ' Create an image hyperlink
22        ' Insert the code here.
23        Dim MyImageLink As New HyperLink
24        placeholder.Controls.Add(MyImageLink)
25        MyImageLink.Text = "Click here to view a larger butterfly"
26        MyImageLink.ForeColor = System.Drawing.Color.FromName("#004040")
27        MyImageLink.Font.Name = "Trebuchet MS"
28        MyImageLink.Font.Size = FontUnit.Smaller
29        MyImageLink.ImageUrl = "images/smbutterfly.gif"
30        MyImageLink.ID = "Butterfly"
31        MyImageLink.NavigateUrl = "images/lgbutterfly.jpg"
32        MyImageLink.Target = "_blank"
33
```

**Figure 2-5**   Dynamically creating a HyperLink control within a Placeholder control

3. Click the **Save All** button.

4. In the Solution Explorer window, right-click the **ch2_placeholder.aspx** page and click **View in Browser**. Your page should appear as shown in Figure 2-6.

5. Click the image to view the larger graphic in a new window.

6. Close each of the open pages.

## PROGRAMMING CONTROL STRUCTURES

Most of you will have taken another programming language before learning ASP.NET. You may use this section as a review of programming control structures and to view the syntax for how Visual Basic .NET codes these programming statements. **Control statements** allow you to conditionally determine whether and how an action statement is executed, and the order in which action statements are executed.

In addition to the two types of statements, there are two types of control structures. Decision control structures allow you to alter the execution order of action statements on the basis of

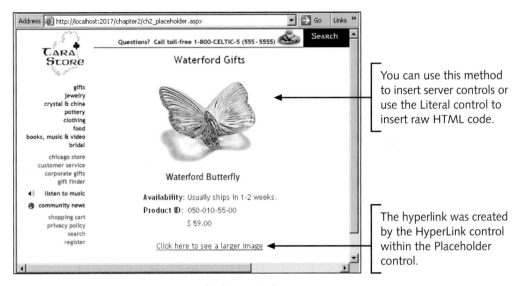

**Figure 2-6**   Creating server controls dynamically

conditional expressions. A **conditional expression** is an expression that is evaluated by the program as true or false. The If Then and Select Case statements are examples of decision control structures.

Loop structures allow you to repeat action statements on the basis of conditional expressions. The While, Do While, For Next, and For Each are examples of loop structures. You can also nest any of these programming control structures.

Using a loop structure, you can repeat action statements or control statements any number of times. For example, to list 100 elements in an array would take 100 statements without a loop structure but only a few statements with a loop structure. The statements contained in the loop are called the body of the loop, and may consist of a single statement or several statements.

The Loop structure repeats a block of statements while a Boolean condition is true or until the condition becomes true. Each repetition of a loop is called iteration. The number of iterations is referred to as a loop index variable. An update statement is used to determine how to change the loop index variable. If you never update the loop index variable, the loop will continue to run without a natural ending; this is called an infinite loop. The loop uses a conditional expression to determine when to stop. The loop stops when the conditional expression is true. It is important to understand that the loop could repeat thousands of times, depending on the business logic that has been built into the code. The following subsections will discuss commonly used programming control structures and how to nest programming control structures.

# If Then Statement

The **If Then statement** is the most frequently used decision control structure. It allows only two options for altering the order in which statements are executed. The If Then statement allows a script to alter the execution order on the basis of a conditional expression. The conditional expression tests whether a certain condition is true or false, and therefore is often known as a Boolean expression, because Boolean variables can only be resolved to true or false. If the condition in the conditional expression is met, then the expression is evaluated as true, and the script immediately following the conditional expression is executed. The following code is an example of how the If Then statement can be used in a program:

```
If (MyBrowser.ToString = "IE") Then
  Response.Write("You are running Internet Explorer.")

Else
  Response.Write("You are running a different browser.")

End If
```

Conditional expressions often consist of two expressions and a comparison operator such as equal to (=), not equal to (<>), less than (<), greater than (>), less than or equal to (<=), and greater than or equal to (>=). Below are some commonly used conditional expressions used in an If Then statement:

```
If (MemberDuesPaid.Checked = True) Then
If (Page.IsPostback = True) Then
If (DuesPaid.Value < DuesOwed.Value) Then
If (RadioButtonList1.SelectedIndex > -1) Then
```

A **logical operator** is used to compare two or more conditional expressions at the same time. Logical operators are And, Or, and Not. The And operator is used to determine if each expression is true. If all expressions are true, the result is true. If just one expression is false, the result is false. The Or operator is used to determine if one or more of the expressions are true. If at least one expression is true, the result is true. If all expressions are false, the result is false. The Not operator is used to negate a single expression. If the expression is true, the result is false. If the expression is false, the result is true.

The following statements demonstrate how to include logical operators in the conditional expressions:

```
If ((a = 1) And (b = 2)) Then
If ((a = 1) Or (b = 2)) Then
If Not Page.IsPostBack Then
```

# Select Case Statement

The **Select Case statement**, an extension of the If Then statement, is used to include more than two conditions in the conditional expression. The statement could be broken into many nested If Then statements, but if you use a Select Case statement, your code will be shorter and easier to maintain. Below is an example of using the Select Case statement:

```
Select Case TxtRole.Value
 Case "Manager"
 Response.Redirect("Manager.aspx")
 Case "Admin"
 Response.Redirect("Admin.aspx")
 Case Else
 Response.Redirect("Member.aspx")
End Select
```

## While Loop

The **While loop** will repeat a block of code for as long as a conditional expression is evaluated as true. If the condition statement is Nothing, it is treated as false. **Exit While** can be used to escape the loop and is often used to stop an infinite loop. What follows is an example of the While loop:

```
Dim I As Integer = 0
While i < 10
 i += 1
 Response.Write(i)
End While
```

## Do Loop

**Do loops** are used when you want to repeat statements an indefinite number of times, until a conditional expression is true. **Do While** will repeat the loop until the condition is false. **Do Until** will repeat the loop until the condition is true.

The Do loop structure is similar to the While loop structure. The only difference is that the conditional evaluation is done at the end of the loop, which means there will be at least one iteration loop. (To repeat statements a specific number of times, For Next loops are a better option; see the next subsection.) The variable i is initialized to zero, and this will be incremented each time the loop is executed. The variable i will represent the loop index variable. **Exit Do** can be used to escape the loop and is often used to stop an infinite loop. Note that in some languages, a unary operator such as ++ is used to increment (or decrement by using --) a value by one. In Visual Basic .NET you can achieve this same functionality with 1 += i. Below in an example of a Do While loop:

```
Dim i As Integer = 0
Do While i < 10
 i += 1
 Response.Write(i)
Loop
```

## For Next Loop

The For Next loop, like the Do While loop, repeats action statements for a fixed number of times. However, the syntax is very different. The **For Next loop** identifies not only the conditional expression but also the loop index number and the update statement as parameters in the "For" statement. Your code must define the loop index using the start number, end number, and step number. **Exit For** can be used to exit the loop. Below is an example of a For Next loop:

```
Dim StartNum, EndNum, StepNum, i As Integer
StartNum = 0
EndNum = 5
StepNum = 2
For i = StartNum To EndNum Step StepNum
 Response.Write(i)
Next
Loop
```

## For Each Loop

The **For Each loop** is often used to access elements of a collection, array, or object properties where you may not know the number of elements in the collection. Exit For can be used to exit the loop. In the sample code that follows the CBL is a CheckBoxList control. If the SelectedIndex is greater than –1 then the user selected at least one option. Although Items.Count is the number of items in the list, you need to subtract one because the count always starts at 0. For each item, if it was selected, add the value to the Result variable. When the code has looped through each item, display the Results variable in a Label control. Below is an example of a For Each loop:

```
Dim Result As String
If CBL.SelectedIndex > -1 Then
 Result = "You selected "
 Dim i As Integer
 For i = 0 To CBL.Items.Count - 1
 If CBL.Items(i).Selected Then
 Result += CBL.Items(i).Text + "<br />"
 End If
 Next
Else
 Result = "You did not select a category."
End If
lblTopics.Text = Result
```

## Nested Statements

You can nest statements within other programming control structures. For example, you can nest one If Then statement within another If Then statement. The process of nesting can be done indefinitely. The code that follows shows a nested If Then statement. The welcome message is displayed the first time the visitor opens the page. If the visitor clicks the Submit button, the form is posted back to the server. The code checks to see if the member login status is current, and displays a custom message. However, if the status is not current, then the login message is displayed.

```
If (Page.IsPostback = True) Then
 If (MemberLoginStatus.ToString = "Current") Then
 Label1.Text = "Welcome member!"
 Else
 Label1.Text = "Please log in!"
 End If
Else
 Label1.Text = "Welcome."
End If
```

## INTRODUCTION TO WEB CONFIGURATION AND DEBUGGING

You may have had experience creating Windows applications with Visual Basic .NET. When the application has been completed, the application is tested for errors. Today, customers demand that Web sites run without errors all of the time. Therefore, it is important to build Web applications that are error-free. When an error does occur, the Web developer tools should quickly allow you to detect, locate, and fix the error. **Debugging** is the process of detecting programming errors within the application.

**Error handling** is a collection of techniques that allow you to identify programming errors in your code, which are often called **bugs**. Many programming errors are caused by incorrect syntax or spelling errors and can be detected during development using tools such as IntelliSense. However, some errors, such as programming logic errors, are more difficult to detect because they are not detected until **runtime**, when the application is running. To handle errors that arise during program execution, you can write code that interprets error messages and executes when an error is detected, even generating custom error messages and global error handlers.

### Exception Handling

As mentioned, some errors may not occur until the application is running. ASP.NET uses language-independent, structured exception handling to handle runtime errors that may occur. An **exception** is an object that is thrown when a predefined runtime error occurs. The Try-Catch-Finally statement is the structure that is used to handle these exceptions.

The .NET System contains an Exception class that acts as the base class for all exceptions. The exception object forces you to deal with certain types of errors called exceptions when they occur. For example, if the page cannot connect to the database, then an exception pointing to a problem with the database connection is thrown. If an exception is raised and you don't explicitly handle the exception, a general ASP.NET exception will occur, forcing the application to terminate without allowing the code to continue executing, resulting in an error page. Catching exceptions can help you quickly identify errors in your Web application.

To use the exception object, you can use a programming structure called Try-Catch-Finally. The Try-Catch-Finally statement allows you to attempt to run a block of code that detects when an error has occurred. The goal of the Try-Catch-Finally statement is to gracefully recover when an exception occurs. Rather than have an error message occur, you can customize the code that is executed. You can even log the error information captured from the error. The Try statement attempts to run a block of code. If there is an error, an exception object is created. The Catch statement catches the error as an exception object. You can use the Catch statement multiple times to catch multiple types of errors. The Finally statement allows you to execute a block of code no matter what happens in the Try-Catch block. In the next section you will learn about the different types of exceptions that occur.

## Using Exception Classes to Identify Exception Errors

These predefined exception errors are categorized in the SystemException class and ApplicationException class. The **SystemException class** is the base class for all predefined exceptions. The **ExternalException class** allows other classes to indirectly inherit from the SystemException class. The **ApplicationException class** provides a base class to create user-defined exception objects. There are several predefined exceptions that are derived from the SystemException class. You can also use a general exception handler to catch general exceptions.

Common exceptions that are handled with the Try-Catch-Finally statement are included in the following list:

- SqlException is thrown when an error occurs from the SQL Server DataAdapter. This exception is often thrown when the database server does not exist.

- OleDbException is thrown when an error occurs from the OleDbDataAdapter.

- NullReferenceException is thrown when an error occurs when a null object is referenced.

- IndexOutOfRangeException is thrown when an Array object is improperly indexed.

When the exception object is created from the SystemException class, several properties and methods derived from the SystemException class will give you information that can help identify the source of the error, as follows:

- The Message property returns the error message.

- The TargetSite property returns the name of the method that threw the exception.

- The HelpLink property returns the help file associated with the exception object.

- The StackTrace property returns the location where the exception occurred.

■ The InnerException property returns the first exception within the error stack.

■ The ToString method returns the fully qualified name of the object, as well as the other properties.

■ The HRESULT property returns a coded numerical value that represents a specific exception.

■ The Source property returns the name of the application or object that raised the exception.

## Common Error Status Messages

Every time a browser requests a Web resource, such as a Web page, from a Web server, a status message is returned. This status message indicates a successful or unsuccessful response from the Web server. If the resource is received and returned, then a Status Code 200 is returned to the browser in the header.

Table 2-2 contains a listing of the common status codes exposed by the **HttpStatusCode property** of System.Net. These are the same status codes that are used by the Web server that is running the HTTP protocol. The property values are enumerations and correlate to the HTTP Status Message Codes. For example, when the browser requests a page that does not exist on the Web server, an HTTP Status Message Code is sent with the HTTP response back to the client. You can retrieve this information using the HttpStatusCode property.

**Table 2-2**   Common status codes

| Status Code | Code Name | Description |
| --- | --- | --- |
| 200 | OK | The request was received and returned by the Web server successfully. |
| 301 | Moved | The URL requested was moved to a new URL. |
| 400 | BadRequest | The server did not understand the request. |
| 401 | Unauthorized | The request required authentication. |
| 403 | Forbidden | Access to the resource was forbidden. This is usually because the Access Control List (ACL) refused access to the resource. The ACL is the list of valid users who have access to a resource, as defined by the Windows file system. |
| 404 | NotFound | The server cannot locate the resource. |
| 405 | MethodNotAllowed | The method Post or Get is not allowed. |
| 500 | InternalServerError | A generic error occurred on the server. |
| 503 | ServiceUnavailable | The server is unavailable. |

## Creating a Custom Error Message

The **ErrorPage property** of the Page directive can be used to identify an error page that is displayed when an error occurs on that page. When an error occurs, the client is redirected

2

to this error page. You can customize the error messages for the entire Web site by using the customErrors node in the Web.config file. You can edit this file manually or use the **Web Site Administration Tool (WSAT)**.

Within the Web.config file, the **customErrors node** (<customErrors>) configures a generic error-handling page with the **defaultRedirect attribute**. When the **Mode attribute** of the customErrors node is set to RemoteOnly, then only remote clients are redirected to the new page. If you are viewing the Web site locally using the local Web server (localhost), the browser will still display the default error message. This is important because you want to be able to see the specific details about the error on the default error page.

The customErrors node can contain zero or more Error elements (<error>). The statusCode identifies the status code of the error, and the redirect attribute identifies the URL to redirect the browser. These status codes used in the Web.config file correspond to the status codes shown in Table 2-2.

When the application encounters an error, a status code is generated, and the application can be redirected to a new page. The resulting URL will be the URL of the error page, appended with a question mark and a QueryString. The QueryString consists of the name aspxerrorpath and the virtual path to the page that was requested. For example, if you were looking for a page named garden.aspx, and the name of the custom error page was error.aspx, the resulting URL would be *http://localhost:1234/Chapter2/error.aspx?aspxerrorpath=/chapter2/garden.aspx.*

## Using the Web Site Administration Tool

In the following exercise, you will modify the Web configuration file to use a custom error message using the WSAT. You will change the Web configuration file to redirect the browser to a custom error page when the page requested cannot be found. The location of these error files are configured with a tilde and forward slash (~/), which indicates that the file is located off of the root directory of the Web application.

1. Click **Website** on the menu bar in the Web application editor and then click **ASP.NET Configuration**. The Web Site Administration Tool opens. Click the **Application** tab. Under the Debugging and Tracing heading, click the link labeled **Define default error page** as shown in Figure 2-7. The port number for the WSAT is identified in the URL and will vary every day you open the program.

2. Click the **Specify a URL to use as the default error page** radio button. Scroll down to find the **ch2_genericerror.aspx** page as shown in Figure 2-8 and click the **Save** button. When your settings are saved a message will appear that says: The default error page setting has been saved. Click the **OK** button and close the Web Site Administration Tool. This will only change the defaultRedirect property.

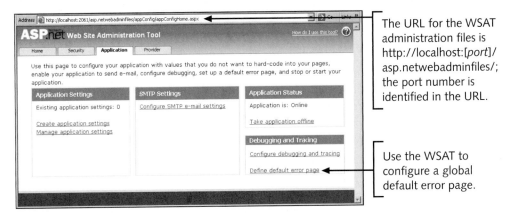

The URL for the WSAT administration files is http://localhost:[*port*]/asp.netwebadminfiles/; the port number is identified in the URL.

Use the WSAT to configure a global default error page.

**Figure 2-7**    Creating custom error messages in the Web configuration file

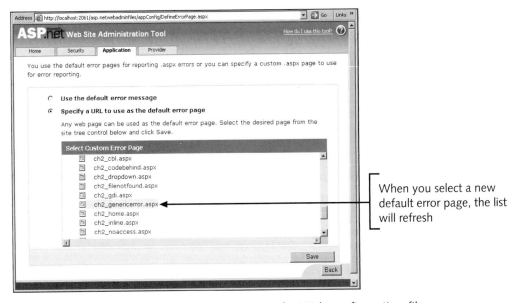

When you select a new default error page, the list will refresh

**Figure 2-8**    Creating custom error messages in the Web configuration file

3. In the Solution Explorer window, right-click the **Web.config** file and click **Open**. Note that the code below was placed within your Web configuration file:

```
<customErrors
defaultRedirect="~/ch2_genericerror.aspx" />
```

4. To customize the error pages for different status codes, delete the code shown in Step 3 and replace it with the code shown below. The code redirects the visitor to a custom error page when a file has not been found.

```
<customErrors defaultRedirect="~/ch2_genericerror.aspx"
mode="On">
 <error statusCode="403"
redirect="~/ch2_noaccess.aspx" />
 <error statusCode="404"
redirect="~/ch2_filenotfound.aspx" />
</customErrors>
```

5. Click the **Save All** button.

6. In the browser, go to **http://localhost:[port]/chapter2/ch2_test.aspx/** where the port is the port number for the WSAT. The page should be redirected to the ch2_filenotfound.aspx custom error page. If you wait 30 seconds, the page will be redirected to the ch2_home.aspx page.

7. Click the **File** menu and select **Save Web.config As**. In the Save File As dialog box, change Web to **ch2_Web2** and click the **Save** button.

8. Open the **Web.config** file and delete the entire customErrors node. Click the **Save All** button. This will return the Web configuration file to the default configuration.

9. Close any open pages.

## Configuring the Web Application to Use the Debugger Tool

One of the most difficult problems programmers traditionally faced was debugging their Web applications. Now debugger tools can help. A **debugger** tool allows you to step through the application at **breakpoints**, which are defined points in the program where processing stops so that you can view the variables, properties, and other application settings. This data can be helpful when trying to locate programming logic errors.

To debug your application, you must first enable the page to support debugging. The Page directive includes an attribute named Debug, which allows you to turn on support for debugging. The following sample code shows how to turn on debugging for a single page:

```
<%@ Page Debug="True" %>
```

You can also turn on debugging for the entire application by configuring debugging in the Web configuration file. The following sample code shows how to turn on debugging for the entire Web application using the Web configuration file:

```
<?xml version="1.0" encoding="UTF-8" ?>
<configuration>
 <system.Web>
 <compilation
 debug="true" defaultLanguage="vb"
 explicit="true" strict="true" >
 </compilation>
 </system.Web>
</configuration>
```

Once the application is in debug mode, you can use the following Debug menu commands to configure how you want to step through the code:

- Step Over (F10) allows you to execute the current line of code. Use this command to step through the code line by line.

- Step Into (F11) allows you to step into a method that is being called on the current line.

- Step Out (Shift+F11) allows you to leave the method and return to the function call.

- Run to Cursor (Ctrl+F10) allows you to execute all the code between the current line and the current cursor position.

Once you have stepped into the application, you can view the variables, properties, and application data using one of the debugger windows. The following are some of the windows used within the debugger:

- The Locals window and the Auto window display the variables. Local variables are defined within the scope of the current method.

- The Me window displays the properties of the current object.

- The Watch window displays variables that you have specifically requested.

- The Call Stack window displays a hierarchical list of methods that have been called. The Call Stack window allows you to identify which statement called the method.

## Programming Best Practices

**Best practices** are commonly accepted activities within a given discipline. Within Web programming, many of the best practices are similar to those used in Windows programming. For example, within Web programming, you should do the following:

- Add comments to document the structure and purpose of your programs to decrease the time required to maintain your program.

- Use appropriate data types and programming structures to increase the efficiency of your program.

- Avoid narrowing conversions to avoid data conversion errors.

- Use explicit conversion techniques to avoid data conversion errors.

- Use error-handling and exception-handling techniques when there are likely to be runtime errors such as with database connections.

In addition to traditional best practices, you will learn in this book that there are additional activities that Web programmers take to ensure that their program functions correctly. Remember that Web programmers must integrate knowledge from a variety of disciplines such as networking, programming, internetworking, graphic design, database management, computer security, and Web development. You will want to learn about the best practices in each of these areas before creating your commercial Web applications. Remember that desktop applications are maintained on either a single computer or a group of computers that are networked. Web programmers work with Web servers, which communicate with other devices as well as computers. They must learn how these output devices work, and how they are expecting to receive the data. So, although there are many Windows Form controls that work with a Windows application, they may not work with Web applications.

## CHAPTER SUMMARY

- Variables are used to store data. You must assign a data type to a variable when the variable is created. You can also assign a value to the variable when the variable is created. You cannot start a variable with a number. You can start the name of a variable with an underscore or letter.

- Constants are used to store values in variables that do not change within the application. The keyword Const is used to declare the constant. The value must be specified when the constant is declared.

- The concatenation operator in Visual Basic .NET is the ampersand. In C# the concatenation operator is the plus sign. In Visual Basic .NET there is no line termination character. If you write code that expands over multiple lines you must use the line continuation character, which is the underscore.

- Properties are used to set the value of a variable defined within an object. Public means that the properties, variables, and methods can interact with other objects outside of the base class. Private variables can only be called within the base class. Protected variables can be called from within the base class and within subclasses. Friend variables can be called from anywhere within the same application or project.

- A property is a method that is used to get and set values. You can directly manipulate variables within a class, or you can use a property to indirectly read and change the variable.

- ArrayLists, HashTables, SortedLists, Queues, and Stacks are examples of collections. When you create a collection, you must declare the name of the collection first. Each item in the Array or HashTable collections is referred to by its index position, which is in parentheses.

- Server controls can be modified programmatically. Some controls can be created or populated programmatically.

- Procedures are used to organize the order in which the code is executed. The event handlers are used to execute code when an event occurs. The Functions are used to return values. Subprocedures do not return a value to the code that called it. Functions use the keyword Return to return the value to the code that called the function.

- The values that are passed to the subprocedure or function are called parameters. Multiple parameters are separated by commas when they are passed to the procedure.

- Error handling is a collection of techniques that allow you to identify programming errors, called bugs, in your code.

- Status message codes are exposed by the HTTPStatusCode property.

- The SystemException class is the base class for all predefined exceptions. The ApplicationException class provides a base class to create user-defined exception objects.

- You can configure custom error pages within the Web page using the Page directive. You can configure custom errors for the application within the Web configuration file. The most common error message is the File Not Found (status code 404) error message.

## REVIEW QUESTIONS

1. Which of the following is the only variable name that is allowed in Visual Basic .NET?

    a. My_ImageName

    b. Public

    c. Image Name

    d. $NewImage

2. What is the concatenation operator in Visual Basic .NET?

    a. $ (dollar sign)

    b. ' (single quotation mark)

    c. '' (quotation marks)

    d. & (ampersand)

3. Which collection is used to store the sort index and the key?

    a. HashTable

    b. Variables

    c. Properties

    d. Parameters

4. Which access modifier makes an element available anywhere to any class?

    a. Public

    b. Private

    c. Friend

    d. Protected

5. Which term, when used in code, requires you to declare all variables before they are used?

    a. instantiation

    b. instance

    c. option explicit

    d. option strict

6. Which of the following returns a value?

    a. subprocedure

    b. procedure

    c. event procedure

    d. function

7. What is used to separate multiple arguments passed to a function?

    a. ; (semicolon)

    b. : (colon)

    c. / (forward slash)

    d. , (comma)

8. Which are possible values for a Boolean variable?

    a. 0 or 1

    b. T or F

    c. True or False

    d. On or Off

9. Which numeric data type is a 32-bit number?

    a. Byte

    b. Short

    c. Long

    d. Integer

10. Which data type stores values between –32,768 and 32,767?

    a. Byte

    b. Short

    c. Long

    d. Integer

11. Which keyword is used to declare a constant variable?

    a. Var

    b. Dim

    c. Con

    d. Const

12. A _____ is a program used to locate errors.

    a. virus detection program

    b. debugger

    c. dewormer

    d. bug checker

13. You can step through the application at defined points called
    _____ .

    a. breakpoints

    b. stops

    c. hops

    d. endpoints

14. To turn debugging on for the entire application, you must configure the
    _____ attribute in the compilation node of the Web.config file.

    a. debug

    b. Error

    c. customError

    d. system.Web

15. What method is used to remove all the items in a Dropdown List control?

    a. Remove

    b. Delete

    c. Clear

    d. none of the above

16. The Label control is assigned to HTML controls that do not have the runat=server
    property configured. True or False?

17. The Panel control is used as a container to store dynamically added server controls to
    the Web page. True or False?

18. Assign the target property to _blank to open a new window for a hyperlink. True
    or False?

19. The _____ window is used to display variables that are within the scope
    of the current method.

    a. Locals

    b. Watch

    c. Call Stack

    d. a or b

20. Programming logic errors are not detected by the Web development editor. True
    or False?

21. The 650 status error code is used to indicate that the server is unavailable. True or False?

22. Explain five ways to prevent or detect errors in your programming code.

23. List five pieces of data you might collect in a shopping cart and then identify the data type you would select to store the information.

24. Compare the differences between storing data in a HashTable and an ArrayList.

25. Compare the differences between storing state information in the session variable or the ViewState.

# HANDS-ON PROJECTS

**HANDS-ON PROJECTS**

## Project 2-1

In this project, you will create a class and use the variable defined within the class in a Web Form.

1. Start **your Web development editor** and open your **chapter2** Web site, if it is not already open.

2. Create a new class item in your project and name it **ch2_proj1_class.vb**. After it is created, your Web development editor will store the class in the App_Code directory.

3. Open the class **ch2_proj1_class.vb** file. Create a public instance variable named **StoreAddress** that is a String data type. Assign the value **555 Michigan Avenue, Chicago, IL 60016** to the variable.

4. Click the **Save All** button to save the class file.

5. In the Solution Explorer window, right-click the **ch2_ proj1.aspx** page in the ch2_proj2 folder and click **View Code**.

6. In the Page_Load procedure add the code that follows to create a new object named **ch2_proj1_newclass**, based on the ch2_proj1_class. Because the variable contains an object, the keyword New must be used to instantiate the object from a class. As you type each period, notice that the IntelliSense list box appears.

```
Dim ch2_proj1_newclass As New ch2_proj1_class
```

7. Type the code that follows to retrieve the values from the new class and assign the variable from the class to the text property of the lblContact label control in the Web page. (*Note:* You need to use the ToString method to retrieve the value from the string stored in the variable.)

```
lblContact.Text = ch2_proj1_newclass.StoreAddress.ToString
```

8. Click the **Save All** button. In the Solution Explorer window, right-click the **ch2_proj1.aspx** page and click **View in Browser**. Right-click the page and click **View Source** to view the client-side code sent from the Web server to the browser.

9. Print the Web page and the client-side code, the ch2_proj1.aspx code behind the page, and the ch2_proj_1class.

10. Close any open pages.

**HANDS-ON PROJECTS**

## Project 2-2

In this project, you will create a custom error message and enable your Web application configuration file to detect HTTP status errors.

1. Start **your Web development editor** and open your **chapter2** Web site, if it is not already open.

2. Open the code behind the page for the Web.config file. Locate the customErrors node and modify the code (as shown in the code that follows) to redirect the visitor who has been denied access to a Web resource. (*Note*: Do not create a new custom-Errors node.)

```
<customErrors defaultRedirect="~/ch2_home.aspx" mode="On">
 <error statusCode="404"
redirect="~/ch2_proj2/ch2_proj2_404.aspx" />
</customErrors>
```

3. Create a new Web page named **ch2_proj2_404.aspx** in the ch2_proj2 folder. Add graphics and content to indicate to the visitor that the resource has not been found. Provide the visitor with a link back to the ch2_home.aspx page. (*Hint*: You can use the NavigateUrl property of the HyperLink control to configure the URL.)

4. Click the **Save All** button.

5. View the Web page in an external browser. In the URL, change the ch2_proj2.aspx to **ch2_proj2_test.aspx** and press the **Enter** key (or click the Go button in some browsers). Since this page does not exist, you should be redirected to the ch2_proj2_404.aspx page.

6. Print your source code for the ch2_proj2_404.aspx page and the source code for the Web.config file.

7. Save your Web.config file as **ch2_proj2_Web.config** in the ch2_proj2 folder. Then open the Web.config file and delete the entire customErrors node. Click the **Save All** button. This will return the Web configuration file to the default configuration.

8. Close any open pages.

**HANDS-ON PROJECTS**

## Project 2-3

The IT Department at Michigan Lakeside University has a login page that they would like you to rewrite for their ASP.NET application. In this project you create a Web page that retrieves user login information, authenticates the user, and then redirects the user to the appropriate student or administration home page. In ch2_proj3.aspx in the ch2_proj3 folder, you will replicate the same features as the login.htm page without using client-side JavaScript.

1. Start your Web development editor and open your **chapter2** Web site, if it is not already open.

2. In the Solution Explorer window, right-click the **ch2_proj3_login.htm** page in the ch2_proj3 folder and click **View in Browser**. The page retrieves the user login information, then uses that information to redirect the user to his or her home page. If the username and password is admin and password, then it is redirected to the ch2_proj3_admin.aspx home page. If the username and password is student and password, then it is redirected to the ch2_proj3_student.aspx home page. Otherwise, the browser is redirected back to the ch2_proj3_login.aspx home page.

3. In the Solution Explorer window, right-click the **ch2_ proj3_login.aspx** page and click **View Code**.

4. Insert the code in the Submit1_ServerClick event handler as shown in Figure 2-9. This code will retrieve the values of the form fields when the user clicks on the button, determines if the username is the admin or student, and determines if the password field matches "password". If the password does not match, redirect the user to the login page. You will need to repeat the Case-Select and If-Then-Else control structures for each user that you allow in the site.

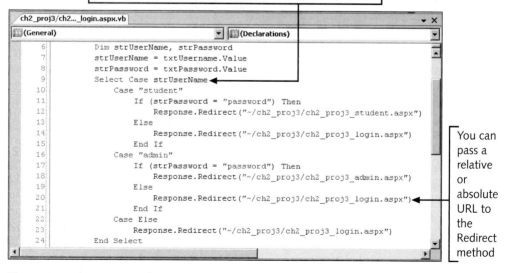

Figure 2-9  Using nested programming control statements

5. Click the **Save All** button. Open the page in the browser. Print the Web page, the ASP.NET source code, and code behind the page within VWD.

6. Close any open pages.

# Project 2-4

Your company owns stores in New York and Chicago. You want the user to be able to customize his or her page using the user's home store location. In the following exercise, you will create two classes and use them within your application. The classes will set the values for the Label and Image controls using properties and variables. Then, in the code behind the Web page, you will create two objects based on these classes, and retrieve the properties based on the user's selection from a radio button list.

1. Start your Web development editor and open your **chapter2** Web site, if it is not already open.

2. Open the **ch2_proj4_class.vb** file in the App_Code folder. Below the End Class statement, create two classes named chicago and newyork and set the values for the variables and properties as in Figure 2-10.

3. In the Solution Explorer window, right-click the **ch2_proj4.aspx** page in the ch2_proj4 folder and click **View Code**. Insert the code as shown in Figure 2-11 to create two objects based on the two classes. Select the class to create based on what the user selected in the RadioButtonList control. Then, use the values from the object properties to retrieve values that are assigned to the image and label controls.

4. Click the **Save All** button. Preview the page in the browser.

5. Click the **Tara Store in New York** and **Tara Store in Chicago** radio buttons to verify that the label control and image values changed.

6. Print the code behind the page and the ch2_proj4_class.vb file. Close any open pages.

# Project 2-5

Your project manager has asked you to create the main category list for the Tara Store Online Catalog. The current page simply changes the image. Create a Web page that displays the category list as a RadioButtonList control, as shown next. In the markup view of the ch2_proj5.aspx page, the values for the RadioButtonList control were generated by modifying the ListItem tag. When the visitor clicks a Submit button, its associated category page should open. The catch is that the project manager has been known to add or change the items on the menu list. Therefore, you elect to store the information in a central class file, and retrieve the values using functions.

1. Start your Web development editor and open your **chapter2** Web site, if it is not already open.

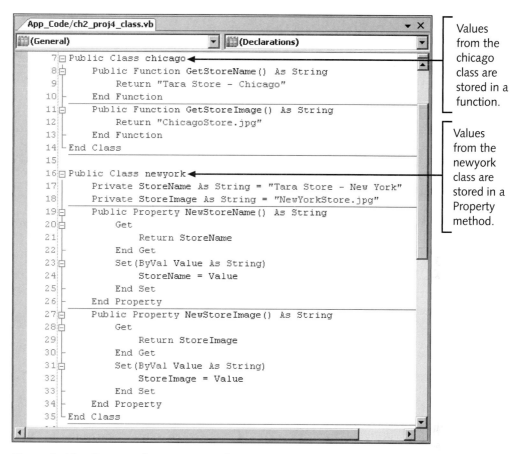

```
App_Code/ch2_proj4_class.vb                                    ▼ ✕
(General)                          ▼   (Declarations)               ▼
     7 ⊟ Public Class chicago ◄
     8 ⊟     Public Function GetStoreName() As String
     9           Return "Tara Store - Chicago"
    10 └     End Function
    11 ⊟     Public Function GetStoreImage() As String
    12           Return "ChicagoStore.jpg"
    13 └     End Function
    14 └ End Class
    15
    16 ⊟ Public Class newyork ◄
    17       Private StoreName As String = "Tara Store - New York"
    18       Private StoreImage As String = "NewYorkStore.jpg"
    19 ⊟     Public Property NewStoreName() As String
    20 ⊟         Get
    21               Return StoreName
    22 └         End Get
    23 ⊟         Set(ByVal Value As String)
    24               StoreName = Value
    25 └         End Set
    26 └     End Property
    27 ⊟     Public Property NewStoreImage() As String
    28 ⊟         Get
    29               Return StoreImage
    30 └         End Get
    31 ⊟         Set(ByVal Value As String)
    32               StoreImage = Value
    33 └         End Set
    34 └     End Property
    35 └ End Class
```

Values from the chicago class are stored in a function.

Values from the newyork class are stored in a Property method.

**Figure 2-10**   Creating functions in a class

2. In the Solution Explorer window, right-click the **ch2_ proj5.aspx** page and click **View in Browser.** Notice that the image source is changed when the user clicks on a radio button. Instead of changing the image, your boss wants you to redirect the user to another page.

3. In the Solution Explorer window, create a new class named **ch2_ proj5_class.vb** page, which will be stored in the **App_Code** directory. Insert the code as shown in Figure 2-12 into the page to create a function named GetCatList, which creates the basic HashTable object. In the same class file, insert a function named GetPageName that can be used to retrieve the name of the Web page to be redirected to. The function will use the value from the selected item in the RadioButtonList to determine which page name to send.

4. Click the **Save All** button.

You must declare a new object based on the chicago class and use that new object to retrieve the default values from the chicago class.

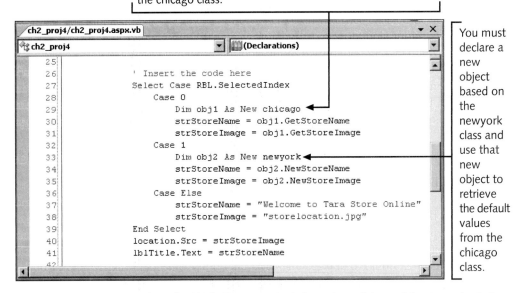

```
ch2_proj4/ch2_proj4.aspx.vb                                           ▼ ×

ch2_proj4                              ▼    (Declarations)                ▼

25
26            ' Insert the code here
27            Select Case RBL.SelectedIndex
28                Case 0
29                    Dim obj1 As New chicago
30                    strStoreName = obj1.GetStoreName
31                    strStoreImage = obj1.GetStoreImage
32                Case 1
33                    Dim obj2 As New newyork
34                    strStoreName = obj2.NewStoreName
35                    strStoreImage = obj2.NewStoreImage
36                Case Else
37                    strStoreName = "Welcome to Tara Store Online"
38                    strStoreImage = "storelocation.jpg"
39            End Select
40            location.Src = strStoreImage
41            lblTitle.Text = strStoreName
42
```

You must declare a new object based on the newyork class and use that new object to retrieve the default values from the chicago class.

**Figure 2-11**    Setting values for Web Form controls based on data and business logic in a class

5. View the **ch2_proj5_redirect.aspx** page in the browser and make sure that each of the radio buttons redirects the visitor to the new page. Print out the ch2_proj5_class.vb page.

```
Public Function GetCatList() As Hashtable
    Dim HS1 As New Hashtable(9)
    HS1.Add(21, "Gifts")
    HS1.Add(22, "Jewelry")
    HS1.Add(23, "Crystal")
    HS1.Add(24, "Pottery")
    HS1.Add(25, "Food")
    HS1.Add(26, "Clothing")
    HS1.Add(27, "Books")
    HS1.Add(28, "Bridal")
    Return HS1
End Function
Public Function GetPageName(ByVal rbl As String) As String
    Dim PageName As String
    Select Case rbl
        Case "21"
            PageName = "ch2_proj5_gifts.aspx"
        Case "22"
            PageName = "ch2_proj5_jewelry.aspx"
        Case "23"
            PageName = "ch2_proj5_crystal.aspx"
        Case "24"
            PageName = "ch2_proj5_pottery.aspx"
        Case "25"
            PageName = "ch2_proj5_food.aspx"
        Case "26"
            PageName = "ch2_proj5_clothing.aspx"
        Case "27"
            PageName = "ch2_proj5_books.aspx"
        Case "28"
            PageName = "ch2_proj5_bridal.aspx"
        Case Else
            PageName = "ch2_proj5_redirect.aspx"
    End Select
    Return PageName
End Function
```

**Figure 2-12**    Storing the menu data in a class

# CASE PROJECTS

## Project 2-1

The World Culture Foundation has hired your company to create a Web site to promote cultural awareness and diversity. The project manager has asked you to create a sample Web site stored in a folder named ch2_case1. Select a culture that you are interested in (or that you have been assigned by your instructor). Visit Web sites that discuss your topic. Create a Web site containing at least five Web pages that present the information you researched. One of the Web pages should contain an annotated list of your references cited using APA or MLA format. Use only server controls to create the Web pages. At least one of the pages must contain a form that contains at least three types of form fields, and is processed using the code behind the page programming model. After the user completes the form and clicks the Submit button, the values are displayed in the Web page (but not within the form!). The users may click a button to submit the data, or click a button that will return to the form and allow the user to make changes. Add graphics and content to enhance the appearance of the Web site. Your instructor may provide you with additional directions for submitting and printing out your assignment.

**CASE
PROJECTS**

## Project 2-2

Now that you have learned how to create and process forms using ASP.NET, your manager would like you to create a basic Web site. In the ch2_case2 folder, create at least 10 pages in your Web site. The content of your Web site should be related to a business or commercial topic, such as an online store, a department Web site, a corporate Web site, or a not-for-profit Web site. You instructor may provide you with additional criteria related to the content for this exercise. Your Web site should contain a menu that links to all of the pages in the site and at least two forms. You should use Visual Basic .NET programming techniques to store reusable data and procedures. You should implement at least 10 programming techniques that you learned in this chapter, such as server-side redirection, error handling, and classes. Add graphics, color, content, and text to enhance the appearance of your Web site. Add one page named that contains the description of the programming tools and techniques you used to create your site. Your instructor may provide you with additional directions for submitting and printing out your assignment.

**CASE
PROJECTS**

## Project 2-3

Your project manager has requested that you create a method to manage errors on your company Web site. Create a basic Web site stored in the ch2_case3 folder. Create a home page and a site map of all the pages you created. Your Web site potentially has many different problems, from too many users connecting at once to the server, to invalid hyperlinks. You have been asked to create a system to manage the errors on your Web site. You must not only handle the errors, but you must also display custom error messages to the user. Refer to Table 2-2 to view a list of status codes. The custom error messages should indicate what the problem was, if known, and the contact information for additional help. The error messages should also provide links for the user to return to what they were doing, or to return to the home page. If the error is a file not found error, you must also provide a link or redirection to the site map. Add graphics and content to enhance the appearance of the Web site. Modify the configuration file to support the new error pages that are displayed when the client visits the Web site. Print source code for each of the Web pages and the Web configuration file. Your instructor may provide you with additional directions for submitting and printing out your assignment.

**CASE
PROJECTS**

## Project 2-4

Your coworker suggests that you learn Visual Basic .NET because the company plans to use the Microsoft .NET platform to create its Web applications. Your coworker doesn't know if other companies are planning to use Visual Basic .NET and is concerned that it won't help his career. Visit at least three of the Web sites in the following list to locate information on Web programming careers:

- Chicago ComputerJobs.Com: *www.chicago.computerjobs.com*

- CNET Online Career Center: *www.cnet.com/techjobs/0-7067.html?tag=boxhl1*

- Dice.com: *www.dice.com*

- IT Headhunter.com: *www.itheadhunter.com*

- Techies.com: *www.techies.com*

- Monster: *www.monster.com*

After reading the information, create a Web page named ch2_case4.aspx in your ch2_case4 folder that discusses your findings. Provide information about three specific jobs. Discuss each position available, including the salary and job descriptions. Discuss what programming skills and languages, certifications, degrees, and educational requirements are required. Explain how you will acquire the education and skills necessary for this type of position. Add graphics, color, content, and text to enhance the appearance of your Web page. Print out the Web page and the source code of the Web page.

**CASE
PROJECTS**

## Project 2-5

Your project manager has asked you to create the product list page for an online catalog. In your ch2_case5 folder, create a form that displays the product list. The data for the product list should be retrieved from a collection that is stored in a class. Display a default graphic when the page loads. When the visitor clicks the Submit button, the related product image should be displayed in place of the default graphic. (*Hint:* You should review the Placeholder control before attempting this assignment.) Because the user can select more than one item, you must retrieve the value for each check box checked and create an image for each check box checked. For each item checked in the check box list, you will create an Image control and a Literal control. The Image control will be assigned to the value of the check box control. One way to do this is to assign the ImageUrl property to the images directory and concatenate the value from the items collection in the CheckBoxList control. If no item in the list is selected, then show the default image. Add graphics, color, content, and text to enhance the appearance of your Web page. You may use the images in the chapter2\images folder. Print out your Web page and the source code for the ASP.NET page and the code behind the page.

## Project 2-6

Your project manager has asked you to create a sample Web site that displays products. In your ch2_case6 folder, create a form that displays at least five product images, along with their product name, price, and product number. Add a Submit button that is labeled "Add to My Cart" below each of the products. Display the quantity ordered as a single text box. You can add additional form fields and ASP.NET controls as needed. When the visitor clicks the Submit button, calculate the price by using the quantity times the cost of the item. Allow the user to store his or her order using one of the methods discussed in this chapter (such as session variables or the ViewState). Include a field for the user to enter their state. In a separate class file, store the tax rates in a collection. Display the product cost, total tax, and total cost to the user. Add graphics, color, content, and text to enhance the appearance of your Web page. You may use the images in the chapter2\images folder. Print out your Web page and the source code for the code behind the page.

# 3

# DESIGNING WEB APPLICATIONS

**In this chapter, you will:**

♦ Create cascading style sheets (CSSs)

♦ Explain the benefits for using external style sheets to manage your Web site design

♦ Create an XSLT stylesheet that is used to format XML data

♦ Create master and content pages that control the appearance of the Web site

♦ Compare and contrast the different navigation controls available to ASP.NET applications

Many businesses currently use ASP.NET to build real-world business applications. As the number of Web pages, content, and visitors grow, it is important to provide efficient ways to manage the layout, navigation, and content of a Web site. In this chapter, you will learn about some of the problems and issues that companies have encountered when designing the navigation, layout, usability, and structure of their Intranet and Internet-based Web sites and some of the alternatives that ASP.NET provides. That is, you will learn how to use the ASP.NET tools to enhance the organizational and navigational structures within your Web applications. You will use cascading style sheets to format the site appearance, master pages to enforce standard layout and designs, and menu controls to manage the site navigation.

## CREATING CASCADING STYLE SHEETS

Most Web applications use **cascading style sheets (CSSs)** to store information about how to present a Web site. These CSSs can be used with Web pages created using HTML, XML, and ASP.NET. Web sites that use CSSs are easier to maintain. For example, when you need to make a change to the font color of the H1 tag, you simply can change the color property within the CSSs. The change is reflected immediately across the entire Web site. Because CSSs can be used to help manage the presentation of the Web site, it is important to plan and create your CSSs before you start developing your application.

**NOTE**

The World Wide Web Consortium (*www.w3.org*) is responsible for developing and maintaining the CSS standards.

Both Visual Studio .NET and Visual Web Developer Express help you create and maintain CSSs. You can create your CSS manually or use a Style Builder graphical user interface to create it. The Style Builder allows you to build and preview complicated style sheets quickly. In the following sections, you will learn how to create and store style sheets, insert comments within CSSs, and describe how the style rules are applied when there are multiple style sheets referenced by the Web page.

**TIP**

Some terms in Web development sound the same, but have slight differences in their meaning. For example, if a Web page created with HTML contains a style rule, the style rule is referred to as a style sheet. As you go through this chapter, however, you will learn that ASP.NET supports XSLT stylesheets. XSLT stylesheets contain XSLT commands and other content used to format and transform the contents of one XML file into another file. Furthermore, mobile controls, which are used to display Web content on a mobile device, use StyleSheet controls to store style information. As you can see, there are many variations of the term "style sheet," and the spelling of terms used in Web development is defined by where the terms are used. (You also see this issue arise with the naming of controls, such as the text box control in a Web page, Input control in HTML code, and TextBox control in a Web Form. They all are used to represent a box used to insert content in a Web page.) Many students find it useful to create a personal glossary of terms and definitions while taking this course, including where and how each term is used.

## Overview of CSS Style Rules

A **style rule** is the information that is applied to a single HTML tag. The syntax for the style rules varies depending on where the style rule is located. In the following sections, you will learn how style rules can be inline rules, embedded rules, and external rules, all of which can be implemented within CSSs. When they are so implemented, they are referenced as inline CSSs, embedded CSSs, and external CSSs.

## Inline Styles or CSSs

**Inline styles** format a single HTML tag. When referring to an HTML tag within a style sheet, the tag is referred to as an **element**. The style information is stored with the HTML tag using the keyword style. In the style rule, you separate the name of the property and the value that is assigned to that property with a colon. You can format multiple style rules by separating each name and value pair with a semicolon. The following is the syntax for using an inline style rule (note that not all tags contain content):

```
<tagname style="property1:value;property2:value2;">
    Content goes here
</tagname>
```

In the following sample code, the HTML uses the color property of the <font> tag to format the color of the text:

```
<font color="green">
    <h1>Welcome to Tara Store!</h1>
</font>
```

Using CSSs, you can format a heading using an inline style rule. For instance, you could format the color property using the color style rule, as shown in the code that follows this paragraph. In this case, there is no need to include the <font> tag.

```
<h1 style="color:green;">Welcome to Tara Store!
</h1>
```

## Embedded Styles or CSSs

**Embedded styles** are style rules that are placed in the heading section of the HTML page. Because embedded styles are placed in the heading section, they can be applied to more than one tag within the HTML page.

Following this paragraph is the syntax for inserting embedded styles. All style rules are contained within a pair of style tags. In the code, the *ElementName* represents any valid XML or HTML control. Examples of HTML controls are <h1>, <p>, and <div>. The entire listing of property names and values are enclosed within a single pair of curly braces. The *PropertyName* represents any property that is valid for that control. For example, you can format the font color with the color property. The value represents any value that is valid for that property.

```
ElementName {
    PropertyName: value;
    PropertyName: value;
}
```

**NOTE** Although some programmers prefer to write all the rules on a single line, it is a good idea to enter only one style rule per line. Then, you can easily detect if there is a colon or semicolon missing from the style rule. You can also easily detect if there is a missing curly brace.

Embedded styles are useful when you need to create custom style rules that apply to all elements within the same page. The code in Figure 3-1 shows an embedded style. With this embedded style, all of the <h1> tags that will appear on the Web page will appear as 12 point, green.

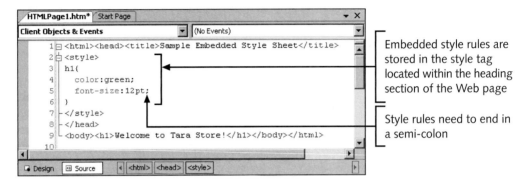

**Figure 3-1**    Embedding style rules within a Web page

## External Styles or CSSs

**External styles** apply across multiple Web pages. Each Web page must include a reference to the external style using a <link> tag. The benefit of using an external style is that if you need to make a change to a style rule, you have to make the change in only one location. All of the Web pages that use that style would instantly display the new style. Because this is an efficient way to manage style rules, external styles are commonly used in business Web sites because they provide the greatest flexibility.

Figure 3-2 shows code for an external style. The format for external styles is the same as the format for embedded styles. In this case, however, you do not need to include the style (<style>, </style>) tags. The name of the file holding the external styles ends with the extension .css.

The <link> tag is an HTML tag that is used to identify the location of the external CSS. When using external styles, the style tags are omitted because the **rel property** indicates that the linked file is a style sheet. The **type property** is used to indicate the MIME type of the linked file. The MIME type is used to indicate which types of programs can open the files. The MIME type, text/css, indicates that the file is a text file and contains cascading style information. The **href property** is used to indicate the location of the external styles. The URL can be the absolute URL, such as *http://www.domain.com/path/StyleSheetName.css*, or a relative URL, such as */includes/StyleSheetName.css*. The URL should be placed within quotation marks.

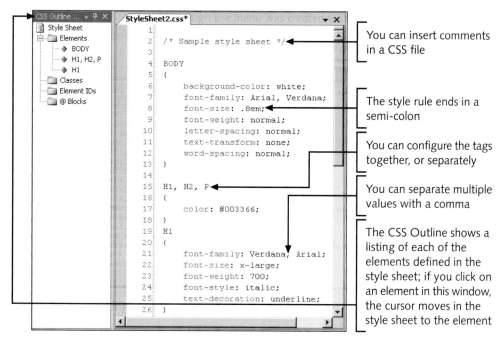

**Figure 3-2**   An external style sheet

The following code shows the syntax for adding the external style to the Web page using the `<link>` tag:

```
<link rel=stylesheet type="text/css" href="StyleSheet.css" />
```

Another method is to include the @import statement within the style sheet. You can specify the URL of the CSS to import. You can read more about @import at *www.w3.org/TR/REC-CSS2/cascade.html#at-import*. The following code is an example of applying the @import statement:

```
<style type="text/css">
<!--
@import url("StyleSheet.css");
-->
</style>
```

The code in Figure 3-3 uses the `<link>` tag to insert the external style into the Web page.

The code for the `<link>` tag is entered on one line within the heading section and because it has no content, the opening tag is closed using a forward slash at the end of the line (`/>`)

The href is the absolute or relative location of the style sheet; if you click and drag the stylesheet onto the Design view, the editor creates the link tag and configures the href attribute

HTMLPage2.htm* | Start Page | ▾ ✕

Client Objects & Events | (No Events) | ▾

```
1 <html><head><title>Sample External Style Sheet</title>
2 <link rel="stylesheet" type="text/css" href="MyStyle.css" />
3 </head>
4 <body><h1>Welcome to Tara Store!</h1></body></html>
5
```

Design   Source

**Figure 3-3**   Inserting an external cascading style sheet into a Web page

## Comments Within CSSs

You can add comments to external CSSs or embedded CSSs. You can add a single-line comment or multiline comment by adding the symbol /* before the comment and adding */ after the comment. The code in Figure 3-4 uses comments to document an external CSS.

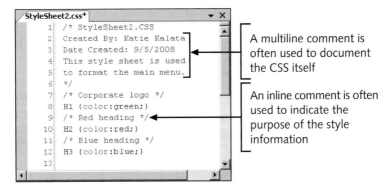

StyleSheet2.css* | ▾ ✕

```
 1  /* StyleSheet2.CSS
 2  Created By: Katie Kalata
 3  Date Created: 9/5/2008
 4  This style sheet is used
 5  to format the main menu.
 6  */
 7  /* Corporate logo */
 8  H1 {color:green;}
 9  /* Red heading */
10  H2 {color:red;}
11  /* Blue heading */
12  H3 {color:blue;}
13
```

A multiline comment is often used to document the CSS itself

An inline comment is often used to indicate the purpose of the style information

**Figure 3-4**   Inserting comments in a CSS

## Cascading Priority with Rules

Each of the three types of CSSs can contain style rules that conflict with the style rules of another CSS. These conflicts are resolved through the use of **cascading priority**. In most cases, inline style rules take precedence over embedded style rules, and embedded style rules take precedence over external style rules.

In the following exercise, you will view a Web page that demonstrates cascading priority. In this example, the external style sheet indicates that the heading tag is to be formatted in blue, the embedded style sheet indicates that the heading tag is to be formatted in green, and the inline style sheet indicates that the heading tag is to be formatted in red. The heading tag displayed in the browser is formatted in red.

1. Open your Web editor application, and then open the **chapter3** Web site located in your student folder.

2. Right-click the **ch3_cascading.htm** file in the Solution Explorer window and then select **Open**. The related cascading priority is shown in Figure 3-5.

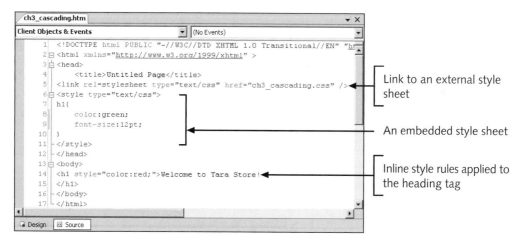

**Figure 3-5**   Cascading priority of rules

3. Right-click the **ch3_cascading.htm** file in the Solution Explorer window and then select **View in Browser**. The Welcome to Tara Store heading will appear in red.

# Creating Classes

What if your company requires all headings to be size 12 point, but allows the departments to select the color? Classes can be used to manage multiple styles applied to a group of different tags or a subgroup of a specific tag. You will find them useful in situations such as when different styles must be applied to multiple groups of elements across a Web site, in which the use of inline styles would be too cumbersome to maintain.

In the embedded or external style sheet, the class is defined with a period followed by the name of the class. The style rule is provided using the same notation as other HTML elements. If you want to restrict the use of the class to a specific HTML tag, you will insert the name of the tag before the period. To use the class in the Web page, you would insert the class attribute into the HTML tag and then set the value of the class attribute to the name of the class.

In the following exercise, you will use classes to customize the color of the headings in a Web page. The heading 1 tag is set to green by default in the style sheet. The showblue class changes the color of all heading 2 tags in the document to blue where the class is showblue. The showred class changes the color of all heading 3 tags in the document to red where the class is showred. The showyellow class changes the color of all heading 3 tags in the document to yellow where the class is showyellow. However, neither the showred or showyellow classes can be used on any other HTML element other than the heading 3 tag.

1. Return to the chapter3 Web site in your Web editor.

2. Right-click the **ch3_class.htm** file in the Solution Explorer window and then select **Open**.

3. Type the code as shown in Figure 3-6. The first group of code will create the style rules and classes. The second group of code will create the Web page content and assign classes to the heading tags.

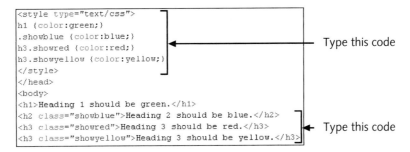

```
<style type="text/css">
h1 {color:green;}
.showblue {color:blue;}                          Type this code
h3.showred {color:red;}
h3.showyellow {color:yellow;}
</style>
</head>
<body>
<h1>Heading 1 should be green.</h1>
<h2 class="showblue">Heading 2 should be blue.</h2>
<h3 class="showred">Heading 3 should be red.</h3>     Type this code
<h3 class="showyellow">Heading 3 should be yellow.</h3>
```

**Figure 3-6**   Using classes to manage style rules

4. Click the **Save All** button.

5. Right-click the **ch3_class.htm** file in the Solution Explorer window and select **View in Browser**. The headings display as green, blue, red, and yellow, respectively.

6. Close any open files.

## Using the Style Builder

A CSS editor uses a graphical user interface to represent Web page elements and properties. A CSS editor called the **Style Builder** is built into your Web development editor. You can create the style sheets, view the CSS code, and preview the output within the Style Builder, as shown in Figure 3-7.

The Background property is often used to add a color or image to the background of an object; in browsers, the background applies to the entire line, not just the text; by specifying margins, you can specify where the background color is implemented

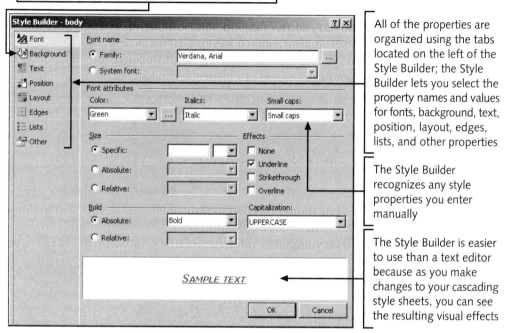

All of the properties are organized using the tabs located on the left of the Style Builder; the Style Builder lets you select the property names and values for fonts, background, text, position, layout, edges, lists, and other properties

The Style Builder recognizes any style properties you enter manually

The Style Builder is easier to use than a text editor because as you make changes to your cascading style sheets, you can see the resulting visual effects

**Figure 3-7**   Using Style Builder to build style rules

## Using the Color Picker Feature

The Style Builder includes a **Color Picker** feature, which can be used to help you select a color. The Color Picker is useful because you can select your colors from a predefined palette based on your design and business objectives. It is useful to test your Web application to ensure that the colors applied in your Web site are acceptable on different browsers and platforms.

As shown in Figure 3-8, there are four tabs in the Color Picker. The tabs that follow identify how the colors are commonly used:

- **Web Palette tab:** Provides the 216 basic Web colors.
- **Named Colors tab:** Provides the 16 Windows colors and the 122 other named colors.

- **System Colors tab:** Allows you to select a color that matches the colors used to create system graphical user interfaces such as windows, menus, scroll bars, and buttons. For brevity, the details of this tab are not shown in Figure 3-8. Your instructor can provide additional information about system colors.

- **Custom Color tab:** Allows you to use three slider controls to select the red, green, and blue (RGB) values for the color.

Some Web sites prefer to use only the Web colors; the Web colors are 216 colors that are supported by the majority of computers and browsers; therefore, if you select a color from the Web Colors palette, you can be confident that the end users see the same color on their monitors

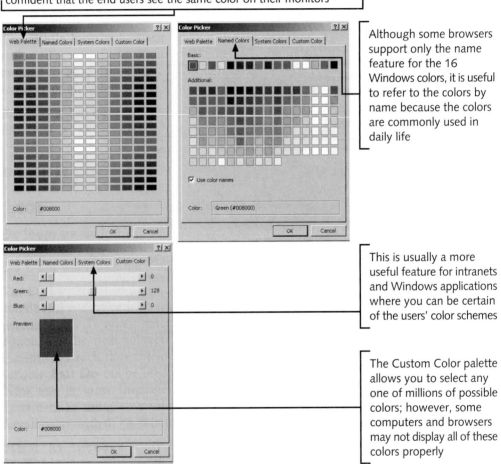

Although some browsers support only the name feature for the 16 Windows colors, it is useful to refer to the colors by name because the colors are commonly used in daily life

This is usually a more useful feature for intranets and Windows applications where you can be certain of the users' color schemes

The Custom Color palette allows you to select any one of millions of possible colors; however, some computers and browsers may not display all of these colors properly

**Figure 3-8** Using the Color Picker

# XSLT STYLESHEETS

In Chapter 1, you learned how to create XML documents and XHTML documents. Both XML and XHTML documents can be formatted using CSS. XML documents, however, can be formatted using a style sheet known as an **XSL Transformations (XSLT) stylesheet**. (XSLT is a language for transforming XML documents; XSL stands for Extensible Stylesheet Language.) Transformation is the process where XSLT stylesheets retrieve and format individual elements, or groups of elements within the XML document. Although the browser is requesting an XML file, the XML file refers to the XSLT stylesheet that will process the XML file.

You can insert an XSLT stylesheet directly into an XML document and view the formatted output using an XML parser such as a browser. If you do this, however, the stylesheet is hard-coded into the XML document. If you want to switch to a new XSLT stylesheet, you would have to change the code manually in the XML document. Alternatively, you create a Web Form that formats the XML document using an external XSLT stylesheet. This method allows you to change the XML document source, or the XSLT stylesheet programmatically, without directly altering the XML document.

In the following subsections, you will learn what type of formatting information is stored within an XSLT stylesheet, how to use the XML control to manipulate which XSLT stylesheet is applied, and how to modify an XSLT stylesheet.

## Understanding the Structure of an XSLT Stylesheet

The XSLT stylesheet can contain HTML, style rules, and XSLT commands. Because the XSLT stylesheet is an XML document, it must be formatted according to the XML standards. The first line identifies the version of XML. A root node is used to indicate that the document is an XSLT stylesheet.

The code in the following exercise shows the basic code required to create an XSLT stylesheet. The usual file extension for a cascading stylesheet is .css. The file extension for the XSLT stylesheet is usually .xsl, however.

1. Right-click the **ch3_sample.xsl** file in the Solution Explorer window and select **Open**. The XSLT Stylesheet appears as shown in Figure 3-9.

2. Close the page.

In the following subsections, you will learn how to format the main template and its associated elements.

### Using XSLT Stylesheets to Format the Main Template

With your stylesheet, you can format all the elements in the XML document at the same time by using the generic template, or you can specify how you want to format each element within the document with the custom template. XSLT provides **processing instructions**, which are used to retrieve data from the XML file. For example, the **xsl:for-each** statement

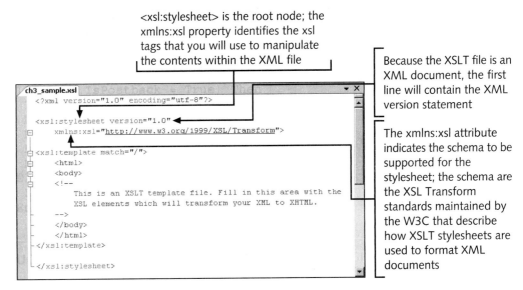

**Figure 3-9**   An XSLT stylesheet

is a processing instruction that retrieves data from each of the nodes in the XML file. In this example, for each product node, the product name element, a colon, and the product category element would be written, followed by a line break tag.

The following exercise formats several of the elements within the XML document. In this example, the productlist element in the XML file is the root node.

1. Right-click the **ch3_products_generic.xml** file in the Solution Explorer window and select **Open**. Figure 3-10 shows the XML data file that will be formatted by the XSLT stylesheet.

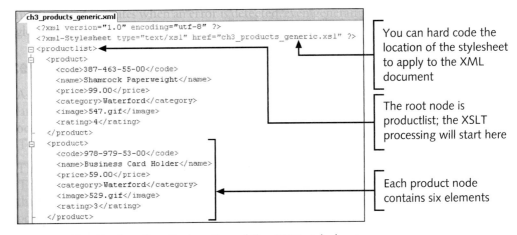

**Figure 3-10**   Hard-coding the location of the XSLT stylesheet

3

2. Right-click the **ch3_products_generic.xsl** file in the Solution Explorer window and select **Open**. The first template, which is shown in Figure 3-11, will start applying the template, using the root node in the XML document. (*Note*: You do not have to use the entire XML document when formatting the page.)

This is the main template, as indicated by the match attribute with a forward slash, and is used to format the XML document; you must match the root node of the existing XML document; this is used by the XSLT processor to read the document and to know where to start formatting the document

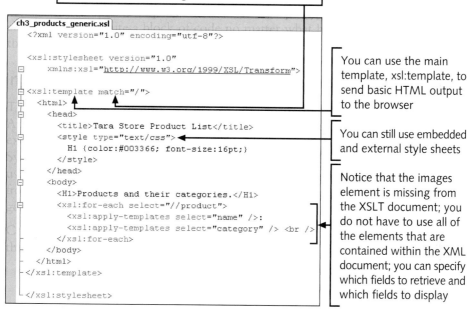

You can use the main template, xsl:template, to send basic HTML output to the browser

You can still use embedded and external style sheets

Notice that the images element is missing from the XSLT document; you do not have to use all of the elements that are contained within the XML document; you can specify which fields to retrieve and which fields to display

```
ch3_products_generic.xsl
    <?xml version="1.0" encoding="utf-8"?>

<xsl:stylesheet version="1.0"
    xmlns:xsl="http://www.w3.org/1999/XSL/Transform">

<xsl:template match="/">
    <html>
        <head>
            <title>Tara Store Product List</title>
            <style type="text/css">
                H1 {color:#003366; font-size:16pt;}
            </style>
        </head>
        <body>
            <H1>Products and their categories.</H1>
            <xsl:for-each select="//product">
                <xsl:apply-templates select="name" />:
                <xsl:apply-templates select="category" /> <br />
            </xsl:for-each>
        </body>
    </html>
</xsl:template>

</xsl:stylesheet>
```

**Figure 3-11**   A generic template in an XSLT stylesheet

3. In the Solution Explorer window, right-click the **ch3_products_ generic.xml** file and select **View in Browser**. The XML document is formatted and displayed in the browser as shown in Figure 3-12.

4. Close the page.

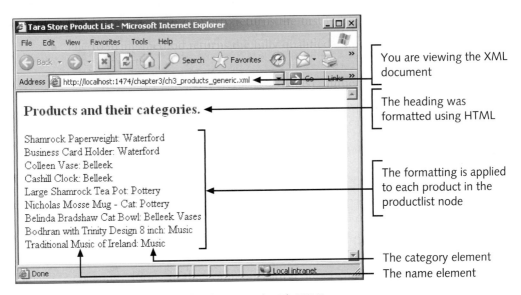

**Figure 3-12**   Viewing an XML file formatted with XSLT

## Using a Main Template with Element Templates

Your main template will be used to format the entire XML file. After using the main template, you can define individual templates for individual elements within the product nodes. These individual templates are called **element templates**. In the sample code after this paragraph, a template is defined for each element. The match attribute indicates the name of the element to apply the template. When the name element template is called, a string is displayed, along with the value of the contents within the name element. The xsl:value-of attribute is used to retrieve the value of the element from the XML document. If you want a template to apply to all the other elements in the node, you can use an asterisk as the value for the Match property, as follows:

```
<xsl:template match="*">
  <div class="product"><xsl:value-of select="."/></div>
</xsl:template>
```

To display the contents of any node, just use a period, which means that everything within the node is selected:

```
<xsl:template match="value">
  <b><xsl:value-of select="." /> </b>
</xsl:template>
```

In the following exercise, you view the main template in an XSLT stylesheet, which corresponds to the root node of the ch3_products_main XML document. Then, you will view the individual styles for each child element within the product node. For each product node in the XML file, different formatting can be applied to each child element within the product node.

1. Right-click the **ch3_products_main.xsl** file in the Solution Explorer window and select **Open**. Figure 3-13 shows the XSLT code.

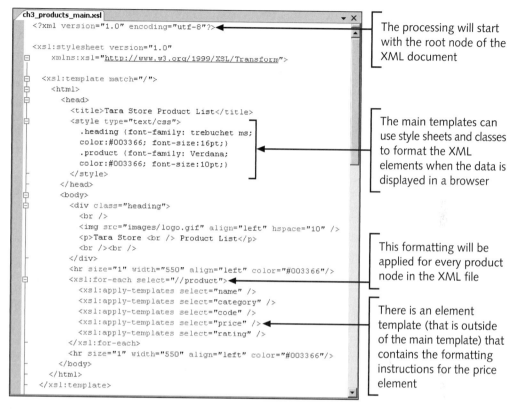

```
ch3_products_main.xsl                                    ▾ ✕
  <?xml version="1.0" encoding="utf-8"?>

<xsl:stylesheet version="1.0"
    xmlns:xsl="http://www.w3.org/1999/XSL/Transform">

  <xsl:template match="/">
    <html>
      <head>
        <title>Tara Store Product List</title>
        <style type="text/css">
          .heading {font-family: trebuchet ms;
          color:#003366; font-size:16pt;}
          .product {font-family: Verdana;
          color:#003366; font-size:10pt;}
        </style>
      </head>
      <body>
        <div class="heading">
          <br />
          <img src="images/logo.gif" align="left" hspace="10" />
          <p>Tara Store <br /> Product List</p>
          <br /><br />
        </div>
        <hr size="1" width="550" align="left" color="#003366"/>
        <xsl:for-each select="//product">
          <xsl:apply-templates select="name" />
          <xsl:apply-templates select="category" />
          <xsl:apply-templates select="code" />
          <xsl:apply-templates select="price" />
          <xsl:apply-templates select="rating" />
        </xsl:for-each>
        <hr size="1" width="550" align="left" color="#003366"/>
      </body>
    </html>
  </xsl:template>
```

The processing will start with the root node of the XML document

The main templates can use style sheets and classes to format the XML elements when the data is displayed in a browser

This formatting will be applied for every product node in the XML file

There is an element template (that is outside of the main template) that contains the formatting instructions for the price element

**Figure 3-13**   The XSLT code

2. Scroll down the **ch3_products_main.xsl** file to view the individual templates, as shown in Figure 3-14. Element templates are applied to the name, category, product code, price, and rating elements. Each of the elements defined in the for-each code in the main template references the style template.

3. In the Solution Explorer window, right click the **ch3_products_main.xml** file and select **View in Browser**. The XML document is formatted and displayed in the browser as shown in Figure 3-15.

4. Close the page.

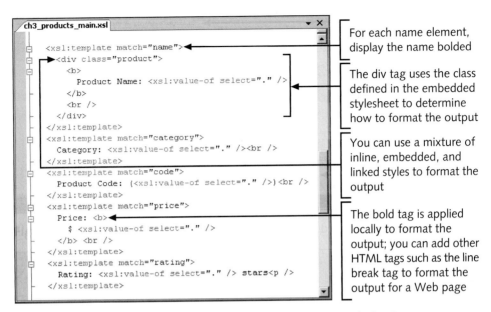

For each name element, display the name bolded

The div tag uses the class defined in the embedded stylesheet to determine how to format the output

You can use a mixture of inline, embedded, and linked styles to format the output

The bold tag is applied locally to format the output; you can add other HTML tags such as the line break tag to format the output for a Web page

**Figure 3-14**    The individual element templates in an XSLT stylesheet

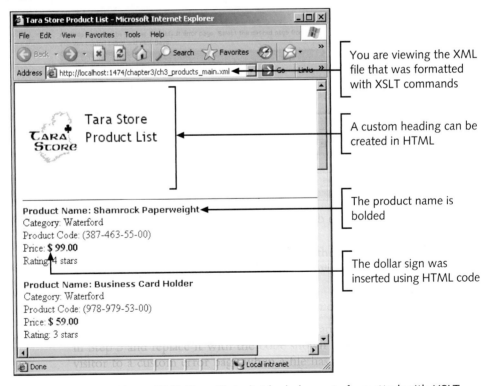

You are viewing the XML file that was formatted with XSLT commands

A custom heading can be created in HTML

The product name is bolded

The dollar sign was inserted using HTML code

**Figure 3-15**    Viewing an XML file with individual elements formatted with XSLT

# Customizing XSLT Stylesheets

To customize an XSLT stylesheet, you can insert HTML, CSS, and XSLT processing instructions. You can insert images, tables, and hyperlinks within an XSLT stylesheet. When you want to mix the XML data within an HTML tag, however, you need to use the **xsl:attribute** processing instruction. In the following exercise, you create an ASP.NET page that displays the XML data with an XSLT stylesheet. All of the project files for this exercise will be placed in the appropriate directory.

1. Double-click **ch3_products_customize.xml** in the Solution Explorer window to open the XML file. The root node is productlist. For each of the 33 products, there is a products node. In each products node, the elements are code, name, price, image, and rating.

2. Right-click **ch3_products_customize.xsl** in the Solution Explorer window and select **Open**.

3. After the comment <!--Insert code here-->, type the code shown in Figure 3-16. This code will display the product elements inside the table.

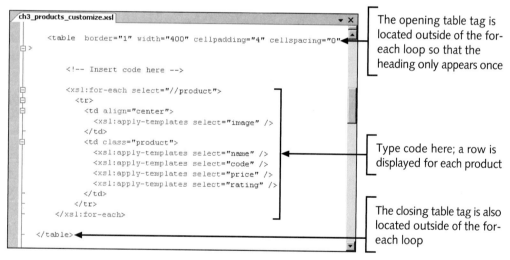

**Figure 3-16**   Customizing XML data with a table

4. Scroll down the page to the next <!--Insert code here--> comment and type the code shown in Figure 3-17.

5. Click the **Save All** button. Right-click the **ch3_products_customize.xml** file in the Solution Explorer window and select **View in Browser**. The page should appear as shown in Figure 3-18. Click a hyperlink to see the main image change to a new category image.

6. Close all of the pages.

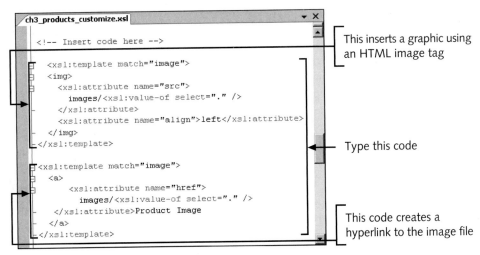

**Figure 3-17** Customizing an HTML attribute with XML data in an XSLT file

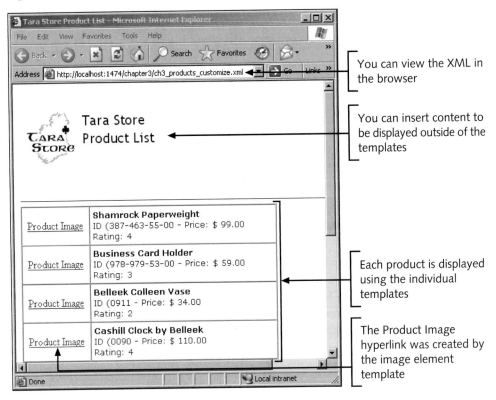

**Figure 3-18** Viewing the output

## Nesting XSLT Stylesheets

In this exercise, you will nest one template inside of another. In this example, the values being used are the same. You can use the XPath notation from Chapter 1 for navigating through elements and nodes within an XML file. In this example, you will create a thumbnail image, which is displayed as a hyperlink.

1. Double-click **ch3_ categories_nesting.xml** in the Solution Explorer window to open the XML file. The root node is ProductCategories. For each of the six ProductCategories, there is a Category node. In each Category node, the elements are ImageUrl, CategoryID, and CategoryName.

2. Right-click **ch3_categories_ nesting.xsl** in the Solution Explorer window and select **Open**.

3. Scroll down the page and after the comment <!--Insert code here-->, type the code shown in Figure 3-19 that will display the elements as images and hyperlinks.

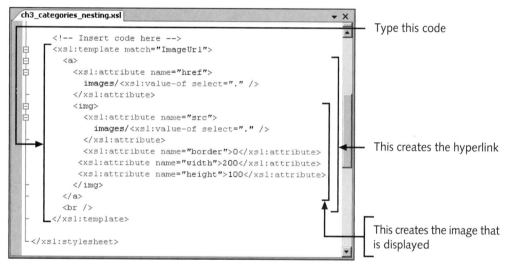

**Figure 3-19**   Customizing XML data with a table

4. Click the **Save All** button. Right-click the **ch3_ categories_nesting.xml** file in the Solution Explorer window and select **View in Browser**. The page should appear as shown in Figure 3-20. Click a thumbnail image to see the larger image.

5. Close all of the pages.

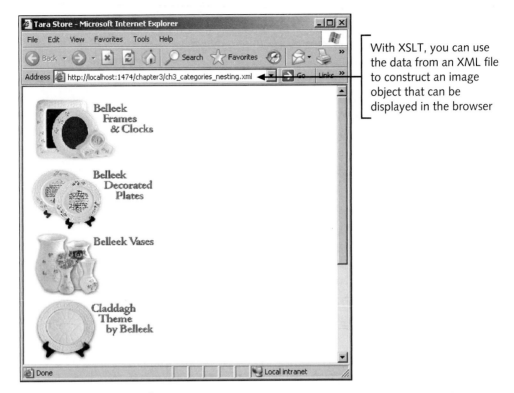

With XSLT, you can use the data from an XML file to construct an image object that can be displayed in the browser

**Figure 3-20**   Viewing the page

## Writing Literal Output to the Web Page

The **xsl:text** instruction is used to write out the value of the text to the Web page. In the following exercise, you will create the hyperlink and query string in the XSLT file. The processing page retrieves and displays the image name.

1. Double-click **ch3_products_literal.xml** in the Solution Explorer window to open the XML file.

2. Double-click **ch3_products_literal.xsl** in the Solution Explorer window, and then type the code shown in Figure 3-21.

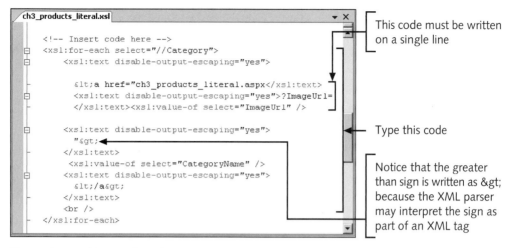

**Figure 3-21** Writing literal text

**TIP**  The disable-output-escaping attribute is used to generate characters without escaping. Therefore, you can use this instruction to write out literal text, as well as special control characters such as the at (@) symbol and create a hyperlink with a query string using the XML data. You need to be careful not to split the xsl:text instruction across multiple lines because the XML parser will process the carriage return and blank spaces. In this step sequence, the text is wrapped to illustrate how the code is spliced across XSLT instructions.

3. Click the **Save All** button. Right-click the **ch3_products_literal.xml** file in the Solution Explorer window and select **View in Browser**. The page should appear as shown in Figure 3-22. Click a hyperlink to see the main image change to a new category image. The processing page named ch3_products_literal.aspx simply retrieves the data from the query string and displays the image.

4. Close all the files.

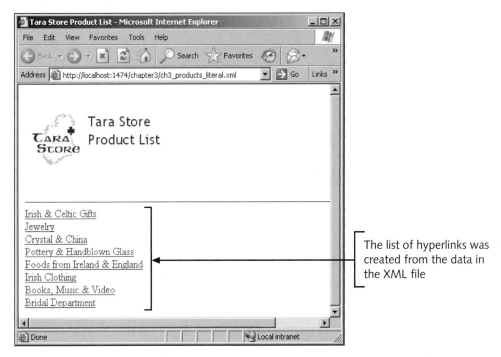

The list of hyperlinks was created from the data in the XML file

**Figure 3-22**   Using XML data in a query string

## Processing XML Data with an XSLT Stylesheet

In addition to retrieving the data and formatting the output, the XSLT stylesheet can analyze the contents of an element and perform actions on that element. For example, if the product rating is equal to or greater than 4, then the page displays a clover image and the message "Excellent!" The text is formatted using a class called over, which is defined in the embedded style sheet. If the product rating is 3, then only the message "This is within current projections" is displayed. No special formatting is applied to the message. If the product rating is equal to or less than 2, then a message is displayed that says "WARNING: Below target!" This message is formatted using the over class, which is defined in the embedded style sheet.

In the following exercise, you will create the stylesheet to process the rating and to display different images and text based on the value of the rating. You will use the **xsl:choose** processing instruction to analyze the value of the rating. You will include the **xsl:when** processing instruction and a test attribute to determine if that product should be chosen. If the test attribute is met, the code in the xsl:when is processed. If the first condition is met, then the formatting within the statement occurs. Otherwise, the parser moves to the next condition. The **xsl:otherwise** statement is used to format any data that may not apply to the other choices listed.

1. Double-click **ch3_products_process.xml** in the Solution Explorer window to open the XML file. This is the same data as that in the ch3_products_customize.xml file.

2. Double-click **ch3_products_process.xsl** in the Solution Explorer window to open the XSLT stylesheet. Type the code shown in Figure 3-23.

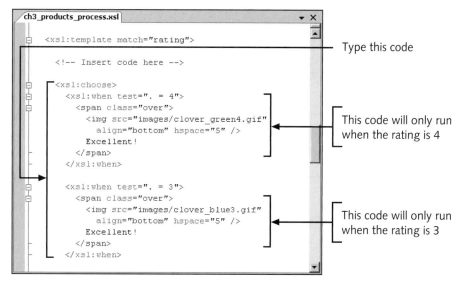

```
ch3_products_process.xsl                            ▾ ✕

    <xsl:template match="rating">                         ──── Type this code

        <!-- Insert code here -->

    <xsl:choose>
        <xsl:when test=". = 4">
            <span class="over">
                <img src="images/clover_green4.gif"       ──── This code will only run
                    align="bottom" hspace="5" />                when the rating is 4
                Excellent!
            </span>
        </xsl:when>

        <xsl:when test=". = 3">
            <span class="over">
                <img src="images/clover_blue3.gif"         ──── This code will only run
                    align="bottom" hspace="5" />                when the rating is 3
                Excellent!
            </span>
        </xsl:when>
```

**Figure 3-23**   Using XSLT processing instructions

3. Click the **Save All** button. Right-click the **ch3_products_process.xml** file in the Solution Explorer window and select **View in Browser**. The page should appear as shown in Figure 3-24.

4. Close all the files.

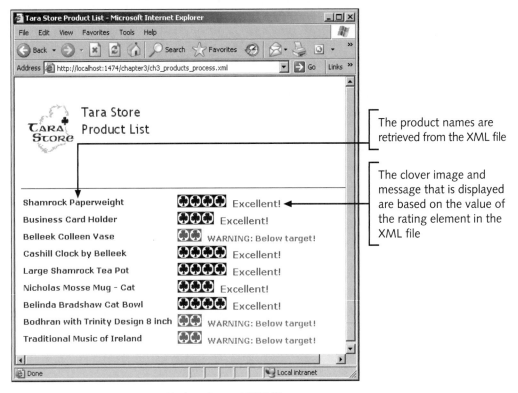

**Figure 3-24**   Processing XML data in an XSLT file

## Using Processing Instructions

With XSLT stylesheets, many other processing instructions are available for use. For instance, you can create and use variables and parameters with XSLT instructions, as described in the following list and demonstrated in the subsequent code:

- You can sort the data by using the **xsl:sort** command.

- You can use the test instruction to determine if a condition has been met—for example, to determine the length of the element. The sample code following this bulleted list tests to see if the length of the element named ProductImage is greater than zero.

- You can use the period (.) to represent the element data or the element name.

- You can also use &gt; to represent the greater than (>) symbol.

- You can use the **xsl:if** statement, which is similar to the xsl:if-else-end if control statement, but does not run unless the conditional statement resolves to true, as shown in the code sample following this bulleted list.

```
<xsl:template match="ProductImage">
<xsl:if test="string-length(ProductImage)>0">
```

```
<img><xsl:attribute name="src">
     <xsl:value-of select="." />
   </xsl:attribute></img>
</xsl:if>
</xsl:template>
```

In the previous exercise, you used an arbitrary value to determine the content to change on the page. However, all of the products were displayed. In the following exercise, you will use the xsl:when statement to process the data from the SubCatID field and only display a subset of data from the XML file.

1. Double-click **ch3_products_subset.xml** in the Solution Explorer window to review the structure of the XML file.

2. Double-click **ch3_products_subset.xsl** in the Solution Explorer window to open the XML file. Type the code shown in Figure 3-25.

The processing instruction looks for a specific value from the SubCatID element to determine whether to display the product     Type this code

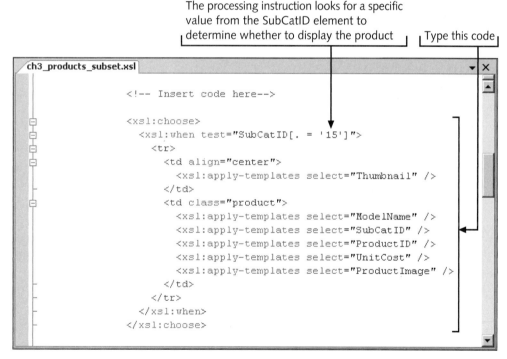

**Figure 3-25**   Using XSLT processing instructions

3. Click the **Save All** button. Right-click the **ch3_products_subset.xml** file in the Solution Explorer window and select **View in Browser**. The page should appear as shown in Figure 3-26.

4. Close all the files.

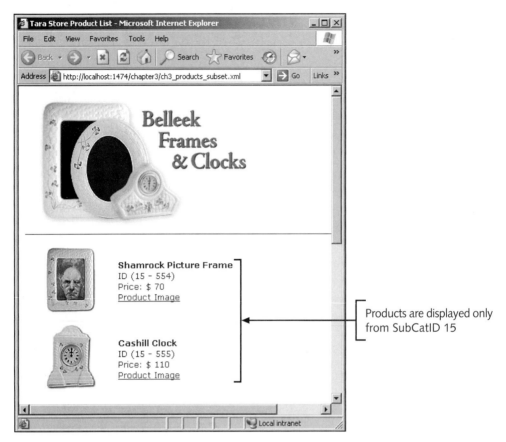

**Figure 3-26**  Processing XML data in an XSLT file

# Inserting and Configuring the XML Control in a Web Form

In this section of the chapter, you will learn how to use the XML control properties to set the XML document and XSLT stylesheet programmatically. The **XML control** allows you to read, process, and display XML data using an XSLT stylesheet. Knowing how to do this is helpful in situations when your data may not be stored in a static XML file; rather, it may be created as a stream of data in the computer memory, or it may be a file that is created dynamically.

In the following exercise, you will learn how to insert the XML control. The Web Form displays an XML document named ch3_xml_control.xml using an XSLT stylesheet named ch3_xml_control.xsl.

1. Right-click **ch3_xml_control.aspx** in the Solution Explorer window and select **View Markup**.

2. Locate the <!--Insert code here--> comment, and type the code shown in Figure 3-27.

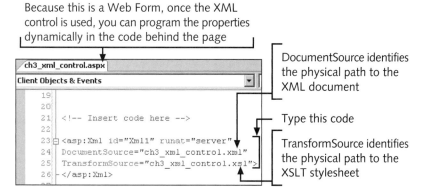

Because this is a Web Form, once the XML control is used, you can program the properties dynamically in the code behind the page

DocumentSource identifies the physical path to the XML document

Type this code

TransformSource identifies the physical path to the XSLT stylesheet

**Figure 3-27** Setting the properties of the XML control

**TIP** You also can use the graphical tool in the Toolbox to insert the XML control and set the DocumentSource and TransformSource properties in the Properties window. You can type in the names of these files, or you can use the Build button to open the dialog box and browse to locate the file.

3. Click the **Save All** button. Right-click the **ch3_xml_control.aspx** file in the Solution Explorer window and select **View in Brower**. Your Web Form will look like the one in Figure 3-28.

4. Close all of the pages you have created.

Note that the three attributes that can be configured in the XML control to locate the XML data are as follows:

- **DocumentSource:** Allows you to identify a physical or virtual path to the XML document.

- **Document:** Indicates that the XML data is located in an object called **XMLDocument**.

- **DocumentContent:** Indicates that the XML data is a string containing the entire text of the XML document.

You can also set the DocumentSource property in code to System.XML.XMLDocument, which is an XML string object. Then, you would have an XML input stream as the DocumentSource property instead of a physical file. The XML input stream could be a string that contains the entire XML file, which is read into the DocumentSource property.

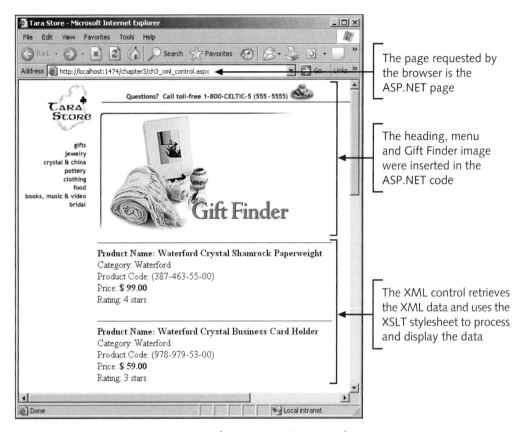

Figure 3-28 showing the Tara Store page in Internet Explorer with the following annotations:
- The page requested by the browser is the ASP.NET page
- The heading, menu and Gift Finder image were inserted in the ASP.NET code
- The XML control retrieves the XML data and uses the XSLT stylesheet to process and display the data

**Figure 3-28**   Viewing a page created using an XML control

The three attributes that can be configured in the XML control to locate the XSLT stylesheet are as follows:

- **TransformSource:** Identifies the physical or virtual path to the XSL or XSLT stylesheet.

- **Transform:** Allows you to use an object called **XSLTransform**, which contains the XSL or XSLT stylesheet. This stylesheet then is used to transform the document before displaying it.

- **TransformArgumentList:** Contains a reference to an object called **XsltArgumentList** that contains the arguments to be passed to the stylesheet.

You can also set the TransformSource property programmatically to an object from System. XML.XSLTransformObject. This would allow you to use a stream that contained the XSL style information without having a physical file. The XSLT input stream could be a string that contains the entire XSLT file, which is read into the TransformSource property.

## MASTER AND CONTENT PAGES

In the past, content in a Web page was displayed using a flow-based layout in which the HTML tags were processed and displayed in the order in which they appeared within the source code. Typically, tables were used to control the page layout. With ASP.NET 2.0, Microsoft introduced a new method to manage the Web site layout and design using master and content pages. This method decreased the cost of Web site maintenance and easily bound different pages dynamically at runtime. The **master page** is used to provide hierarchical control of content, layout, and design. The master page will contain one or more ContentPlaceHolder controls. **ContentPlaceHolder** controls are used to identify locations where content may be inserted in a content page. **Content pages** contain content controls that map to the ContentPlaceHolder controls. Content pages can insert content only within areas defined by the ContentPlaceHolder controls of the master page.

This technology is useful in corporate sites when multiple departments can choose their own layout and design, based on the master template. With such a setup, individual departments would be in compliance with corporate directives and marketing plans across an organization while still being able to add custom content and design. In today's marketplace, the end user may be using multiple devices to access the Web site. Companies can use master and content pages to create a device-specific master page. For example, the Web site could have different master pages for browsers and Internet phones. In the next sections, you will learn how to build a master page and a content page.

### Creating the Master Page

In the following exercise, you will insert a ContentPlaceHolder control in a master page.

1. Right-click **ch3_sample.master** in the Solution Explorer window and select **View Markup**. Type the code after the <!--Insert code here--> comment, as shown in Figure 3-29.

**Figure 3-29**   Editing the master page

2. Click the **Save All** button. Click the **Design** tab. Your Web Form in Design view will look like the one in Figure 3-30.

3. Close any open files.

The ContentPlaceHolder control will be used by the content page to identify where to insert the content from the content page; content pages reference the master page as the basic framework for the content page; content pages insert content only within areas defined by the ContentPlaceHolder controls of the master page; this configuration creates a parent-child relationship between the content and master pages

You can have multiple ContentPlaceHolder controls on a single page but each has to have a unique ID that will match up with the respective Content control in the content page

Any relative path mentioned within the master page will look for images and other resources in the MasterPages folder or relative to the master page

Default content in the ContentPlaceholder can be overridden by the content page by simply including content in the control

If you use a relative address with the tilde (~), the image will not be displayed when you are editing the page, but the path will remain valid if the Web site is moved

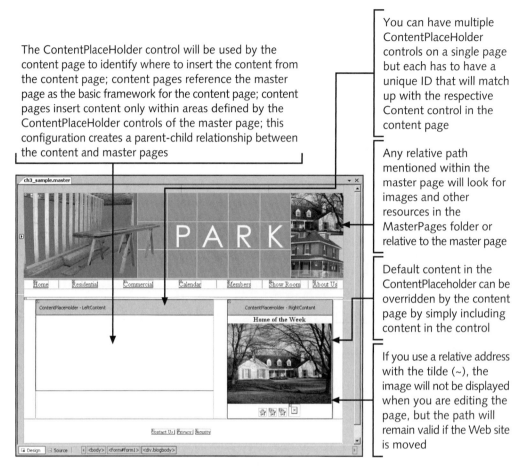

**Figure 3-30**  Viewing the master page in Design view

## Creating the Content Page

The content page is the Web page where you will insert your page-specific content. In the following exercise, you will create a content page based on the master page you just finished editing.

1. Right-click the **chapter3** icon in the Solution Explorer window and then click **Add New Item**. Select **Web Form** in the Visual Studio installed templates dialog box and in the Name text box replace Default.aspx with the new name for the page, **ch3_sample.aspx**. Check the **Select master page** check box and **Place code in separate file**. Click the **Add** button.

2. In the Select a Master Page window, you need to locate the master page. In the right pane, click **ch3_sample.master** and then click the **OK** button. The page opens in Source code view. Two content controls have been inserted for you.

3. Right-click **ch3_sample.aspx** in the Solution Explorer window and select **View Markup**. Type the code as shown in Figure 3-31.

The content page uses the MasterPageFile property in the page directive to identify which master page to use

Type this code to insert the content into the left content control

Type this code insert the content into the right content control

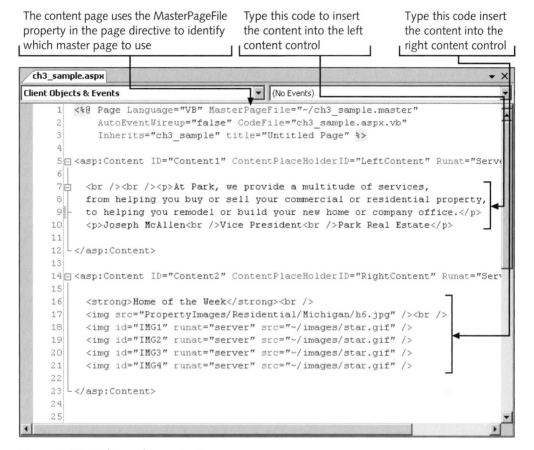

```
ch3_sample.aspx

Client Objects & Events                              (No Events)

 1    <%@ Page Language="VB" MasterPageFile="~/ch3_sample.master"
 2        AutoEventWireup="false" CodeFile="ch3_sample.aspx.vb"
 3        Inherits="ch3_sample" title="Untitled Page" %>
 4
 5    <asp:Content ID="Content1" ContentPlaceHolderID="LeftContent" Runat="Serve
 6
 7        <br /><br /><p>At Park, we provide a multitude of services,
 8        from helping you buy or sell your commercial or residential property,
 9        to helping you remodel or build your new home or company office.</p>
10        <p>Joseph McAllen<br />Vice President<br />Park Real Estate</p>
11
12    </asp:Content>
13
14    <asp:Content ID="Content2" ContentPlaceHolderID="RightContent" Runat="Ser
15
16        <strong>Home of the Week</strong><br />
17        <img src="PropertyImages/Residential/Michigan/h6.jpg" /><br />
18        <img id="IMG1" runat="server" src="~/images/star.gif" />
19        <img id="IMG2" runat="server" src="~/images/star.gif" />
20        <img id="IMG3" runat="server" src="~/images/star.gif" />
21        <img id="IMG4" runat="server" src="~/images/star.gif" />
22
23    </asp:Content>
24
25
```

**Figure 3-31**   Editing the content page

4. Click the **Save All** button. Click the **Design** tab. Your Web Form in Design view will look like the one in Figure 3-32.

5. Click the **Save All** button. Right-click **ch3_sample.aspx** in the Solution Explorer window and select **View in Browser**. Notice the changes. Close any open pages.

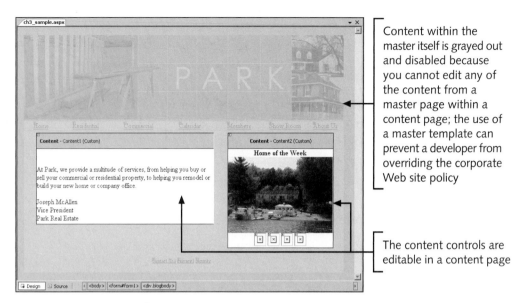

Content within the master itself is grayed out and disabled because you cannot edit any of the content from a master page within a content page; the use of a master template can prevent a developer from overriding the corporate Web site policy

The content controls are editable in a content page

**Figure 3-32**   Viewing the content page in Design view

## Using Master and Content Pages

You can also force the Web site to apply a specific master page globally. In the pages node of the Web configuration file, insert the code MasterPageFile = "[*master page path and file name*].master" that changes the MasterPageFile property for all pages. Although this page can be configured globally, it still can be overridden locally by setting the MasterPageFile property in the individual Web pages.

You can have nested master and content pages. You can use the designer to edit the content pages if the content page is not nested within multiple master pages. Content within nested master pages cannot be edited in Design view because Design view actually renders the master page within the content page at design time.

The code within the content page can interact with the master page. However, you must understand that the code within the content page will run before the code in the master page. Each of these pages has its own page event model. In other words, the Web server will process the code in the content page load event handler before it will process the code in the master page load event handler. Therefore, you can change the master page at runtime if the master page is assigned within the PreInit event handler. The **PreInit** event handler is one of the page events that occurs every time a page is requested. Notice that because the page has not been built yet, the page cannot be identified using Page in the PreInit event handler, but is identified using the keyword, Me. Then the master page is compiled as part of the final version of the content page. Being able to do this is beneficial because you can change the master page based on criteria, such as the department name or the user status. When a user logs in, you may want to provide different master templates for employees, partners, customers, and visitors.

## CREATING A NAVIGATIONAL SYSTEM

Welcome to dynamic navigation! ASP.NET now provides a new dynamic navigation method to create not only menus, but other navigational controls that can change in appearance and content. ASP.NET has the ability to expose XML data, which can be bound to new navigational controls. This hierarchical navigation data is made available to the controls through the use of a site map. The site map is an XML file that contains the navigation data. The **XMLSiteMapProvider** will parse the site map file.

Now that you have created the framework for your Web site, in the following subsections you will learn how to create the site map file, use the site map file, use the SiteMapData-Source control, build breadcrumb trails, and use the site map file in conjunction with various controls to create navigational tools for the Web site.

## The Site Map

The **site map** is an XML file that stores your Web site navigation data. It is named **Web.sitemap** by default. The site map file represents your hierarchical Web site map, as shown in Figure 3-33.

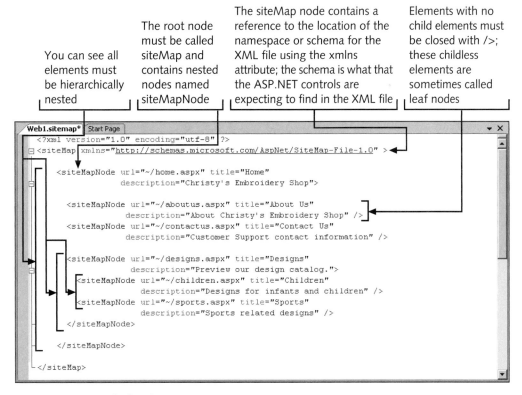

**Figure 3-33** Code for the site map

Each siteMapNode element can contain string values for the following properties:

- **Title:** Displays the title of the page on the title bar.

- **Description:** Is used by the navigation controls to display text and a ToolTip when the user hovers the mouse over the link.

- **Roles:** Provides a list of roles that can view the node and multiple roles can be used if they are separated by a comma or semicolon.

- **URL (URL):** Represents a unique key for the siteMapNode and is required. No two nodes can have the same URL. If two nodes do end up with the same URL, an error message will appear in any Web page that uses the site map.

- **SiteMapFile attribute:** Identifies an external file that contains additional siteMapNodes. The Web site map configuration is not limited to a single file. You can create a hierarchy of nested nodes from several files.

- **Provider attribute:** Identifies the name of a site map provider that can contain additional nodes. The site map data can be obtained from the site map XML file or another data structure such as a database. Thus, you can use a mixture of data sources for your siteMapNodes.

There are some limitations to the site map:

- You must use valid URLs; each URL must be unique and valid or the page will not render the navigation controls.

- You can't use the site map files across Web sites.

- You will not use multiple Web site maps in the same application unless you create your own providers.

- You can work with multiple Web.sitemap files in one application. You will need to register them in the Web configuration file, however, and then set the SiteMap-Provider property for the SiteMapPath control.

Because of these limitations you will need to save your old site map files each time you modify them for a new activity in this chapter. In this next section, you will create a site map file.

## Creating the Site Map File

In this exercise, you will modify the site map file.

1. Right-click **Web.sitemap** in the Solution Explorer window and then click **Open**.

2. Insert the code after the <!--Insert code here--> comment, as shown in Figure 3-34.

3. Click the **Save All** icon. Close any open pages.

**Figure 3-34**    Modifying the site map file

## The SiteMapDataSource Control

The siteMap class provides access to the SiteMapDataSource control and the SiteMapPath control. The **SiteMapDataSource control** is used to identify the site map file for the TreeView and Menu navigation controls, but not the SiteMapPath control. (The SiteMapPath control is discussed later in this chapter.) The navigation controls use the SiteMapDataSource control to create a hierarchical data source that mirrors the structure of the site map. You can bind the SiteMapDataSource to other controls that support data binding, such as the DropDownList and GridView.

The TreeView and Menu controls do not interact or query the Web.sitemap file directly. You can bind the TreeView and Menu navigation controls to the site map by setting the **DataSourceID property** to the SiteMapDataSource control. This layer of abstraction allows you to build Web applications that can be easily modified. The SiteMapDataSource will look for the default Web.sitemap file for the siteMapNode data.

## Using the SiteMapDataSource Control

In this exercise, you will modify the Web configuration file to include use your site map file as the default site map for your Web site and then insert the SiteMapDataSource control into a master page.

1. Right-click **web.config** file in the Solution Explorer window and then click **Open**.

2. Type the code shown in Figure 3-35.

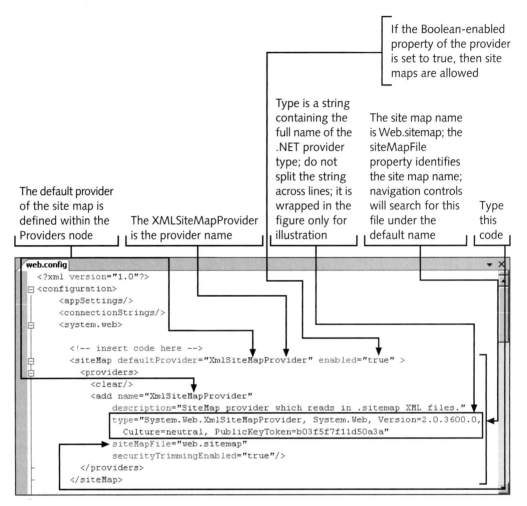

**Figure 3-35** Modifying the configuration file

3. In the Solution Explorer window, right-click the **MasterPage.master** in the MasterPages folder and then click **View Markup**.

4. Insert the code shown in Figure 3-36 to create a data source for your Web site map.

5. Click the **Save All** icon.

6. Go back to the MasterPage.master and click the **Design** tab. The menu on the right was created based on the information in the site map file.

7. Close any open files.

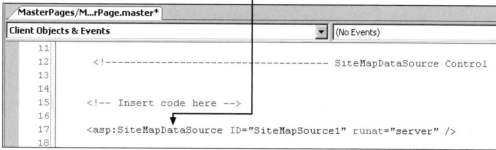

**Figure 3-36**   Inserting a SiteMapDataSource control

By default, the SiteMapDataSource control can be configured with additional properties:

- **ShowStartingNode:** To show or hide the starting node, which is usually the root node.

- **StartingNodeOffset:** To specify the URL of the node where to start in the data file.

- **StartingNodeUrl:** Where to start in the data file. The starting node is always set at 0.

- **StartFromCurrentNode:** To modify the control to start from the current node. For sites with very long directory structures, you may want to limit the depth to the parent by setting the property to -1.

# Building Breadcrumb Trails with the SiteMapPath Control

In the Joy of Ireland online store, there were eight main categories, but over a hundred nested subcategories and thousands of products. Many products appeared across multiple categories. It is essential that the visitor be able to locate the categories and products. With a breadcrumb trail, your can show your visitors the current location of the Web page and how to navigate within the Web site. The **SiteMapPath** control is used to create this breadcrumb trail and is frequently located at the top and bottom of your Web pages. In the following subsections, you will see how to insert the breadcrumb trail and how to configure the various properties of the SiteMapPath control.

## Creating a Breadcrumb Trail

In this exercise, you will create a second breadcrumb trail using the SiteMapPath control in the master page.

1. Right-click **MasterPage.master** in the **MasterPages** folder and then click **Open.**

2. In the Source view near the bottom of the page, enter the code shown in Figure 3-37 to insert the breadcrumb trail using the SiteMapPath control. Notice that no source has to be identified because it already was defined earlier in the page.

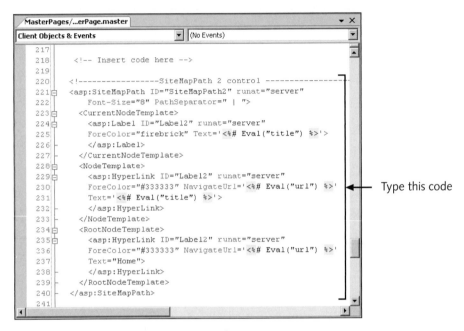

```
MasterPages/...erPage.master                                    ▼ ✕
Client Objects & Events              ▼  (No Events)                ▼
   217
   218        <!-- Insert code here -->
   219
   220     <!-----------------SiteMapPath 2 control ---------------
   221     <asp:SiteMapPath ID="SiteMapPath2" runat="server"
   222          Font-Size="8" PathSeparator=" | ">
   223       <CurrentNodeTemplate>
   224         <asp:Label ID="Label2" runat="server"
   225         ForeColor="firebrick" Text='<%# Eval("title") %>'>
   226         </asp:Label>
   227       </CurrentNodeTemplate>
   228       <NodeTemplate>
   229         <asp:HyperLink ID="Label2" runat="server"        ◄──── Type this code
   230         ForeColor="#333333" NavigateUrl='<%# Eval("url") %>'
   231         Text='<%# Eval("title") %>'>
   232         </asp:HyperLink>
   233       </NodeTemplate>
   234       <RootNodeTemplate>
   235         <asp:HyperLink ID="Label2" runat="server"
   336         ForeColor="#333333" NavigateUrl='<%# Eval("url") %>'
   237         Text="Home">
   238         </asp:HyperLink>
   239       </RootNodeTemplate>
   240     </asp:SiteMapPath>
   241
```

**Figure 3-37**   Inserting another control

3. Click the **Save All** icon.

4. In the Solution Explorer window, right-click the **Default.aspx** page in the **Home folder** and click **View in Browser**. Scroll to the bottom of the page to view the breadcrumb trail. Only the home node is displayed as plain text.

5. In the Solution Explorer window, right-click the **Default.aspx** page in the **Commercial folder** and click **View in Browser**. Scroll to the bottom of the page to view the breadcrumb trail, as shown in Figure 3-38. Close all of the open pages.

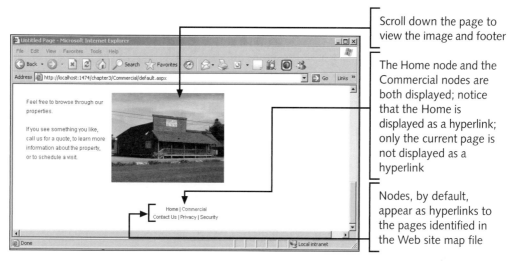

Scroll down the page to view the image and footer

The Home node and the Commercial nodes are both displayed; notice that the Home is displayed as a hyperlink; only the current page is not displayed as a hyperlink

Nodes, by default, appear as hyperlinks to the pages identified in the Web site map file

**Figure 3-38**   Viewing the results of the control

## Properties of the SiteMapPath Control

The SiteMapPath control contains many additional properties or attributes to configure the appearance of the SiteMapPath control. These include the following:

- **PathSeparatorStyle** and **PathSeparatorTemplate:** Used to set the style or template for the PathSeparator.

- **RenderCurrentNodeAsLink:** Set this to False to give visitors an indication that they are on the current page. Do not display the node as a link, because it would just link to the current page.

- **HoverNodeStyle:** Alters the style when the mouse hovers over the hyperlink.

- **ShowToolTips:** Set to False to hide ToolTips for the hyperlinks.

As you get further into working with the SiteMapPath control, you'll realize that you can customize the ordering of the node hierarchy in the breadcrumb trail. This is useful in situations such as displaying different navigation for different types of users. Here are additional attributes of the SiteMapPath control:

- **ParentLevelsDisplayed:** Allows you to specify a certain number of parent levels to display. In large Web sites with multiple levels, you may want to set this so that the breadcrumb trail does not extend over a line, because at this point navigation can become confusing to the user. The default is -1, which means that all of the levels are shown.

- **PathDirection:** Is used to return or assign the nodes displayed. By default, the root nodes are shown on the left, and the rest of the hierarchy of nodes, such as the parent and root nodes, are shown on the right. If you set the PathDirection to CurrentToRoot, the current node starts on the left, and the hierarchy of nodes are to the right of the current node.

## TreeView Control

The **TreeView control** allows you to display the site map data using a format that looks like a tree when all of the nodes are displayed. When the user clicks a hyperlink, he or she is redirected to a new page. When the user clicks the image next to the hyperlink, the node will expand and list any child nodes.

You can control the appearance of the TreeView control using styles through a TreeView styles class. Some styles are used to set the layout of the TreeView control globally and the spacing between nodes. These styles properties can be set as attributes of the TreeView control, as individual properties, or programmatically. In the next chapter, you will learn to combine your knowledge of styles with other technologies to enhance the appearance of your Web controls. The TreeView control does not support style templates per se. However, style properties can be specific to the level of the node within the XML file, and the type of node.

### Creating a TreeView Control

In this exercise, you will insert a TreeView control into the master page for the Web site. In the master page there are two ContentPlaceHolder controls, LeftContent and RightContent, and a lot of content within the master page. The content includes a common banner, a department banner, a horizontal line, a static menu, and footer content. The TreeView control will be placed in the right side of the page, above the RightContent control so that it can be used across all pages in the site.

1. Right-click **MasterPage.master** in the **MasterPages** folder and then click **Open.**

2. In Source view, after the <!--Insert code here--> comment, insert the Tree-View control, as shown in Figure 3-39. (Note: The comment is located in the middle of the page, around line 158.)

3. Click the **Save All** icon.

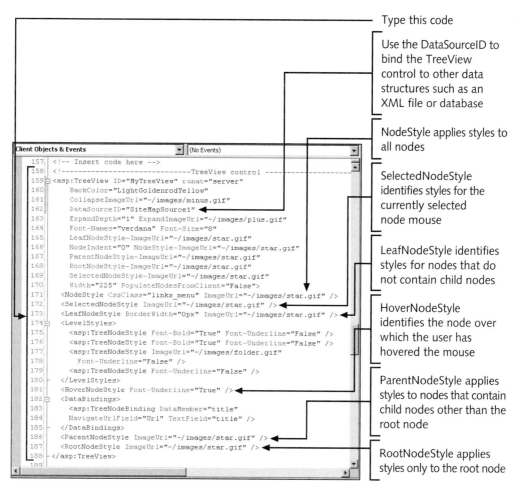

Type this code

Use the DataSourceID to
bind the TreeView
control to other data
structures such as an
XML file or database

NodeStyle applies styles to
all nodes

SelectedNodeStyle
identifies styles for the
currently selected
node mouse

LeafNodeStyle identifies
styles for nodes that do
not contain child nodes

HoverNodeStyle
identifies the node over
which the user has
hovered the mouse

ParentNodeStyle applies
styles to nodes that contain
child nodes other than the
root node

RootNodeStyle applies
styles only to the root node

**Figure 3-39**   Inserting a TreeView control

4. Right-click the **Default.aspx** page in the **Home folder** and select **View in Browser**. Click each of the nodes to expand the nodes. Your TreeView control is displayed as shown in Figure 3-40.

5. Click the **Close** button to close any open pages.

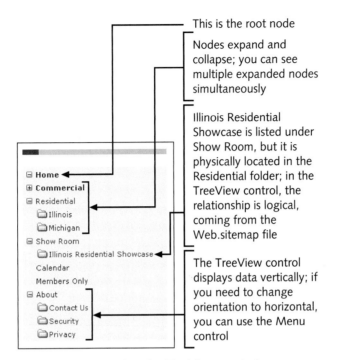

This is the root node

Nodes expand and collapse; you can see multiple expanded nodes simultaneously

Illinois Residential Showcase is listed under Show Room, but it is physically located in the Residential folder; in the TreeView control, the relationship is logical, coming from the Web.sitemap file

The TreeView control displays data vertically; if you need to change orientation to horizontal, you can use the Menu control

**Figure 3-40**   Viewing the TreeView control

## TreeView Properties

The TreeView is a very flexible control. You can set the default target window for all nodes with the **Target property**. You can configure the global properties of the TreeView and the properties of the individual nodes. The following is a list of common properties that can be set globally:

- **ImageUrl:** The image that is shown next to the node
- **NodeSpacing:** The space between the current node and the ones above and below
- **VerticalPadding:** The space above and below the node
- **HorizontalPadding:** The space to the right and left of the node
- **ChildNodesPadding:** The space between the last child node and the next parent
- **NodeIndent:** The number of pixels (from the left) to indent the nodes

Some of the attributes that you can set for individual nodes are in the following list:

- **Text:** Text value displayed in the node
- **ToolTip:** Text displayed when the user hovers over the node
- **Value:** A non-displayed value that is passed when the user clicks on the node
- **NavigateUrl:** A URL to which to forward the user when the node is clicked

- **Target:** Set NavigateUrl to include the target window
- **ImageUrl:** Image display next to the node text
- **ImageToolTip:** Text displayed when the user's mouse hovers over the image

There are events and methods associated with the TreeView control. For example, you also can add nodes to the TreeView control programmatically using the code Treeview1. Nodes(0)ChildNodes.Add(newNode). In selection mode, a click posts back to the server and raises the TreeView.SelectedNodeChanged event. In navigation mode, a click sends the request to redirect the user to the new page in the URL attribute, unless it is set to an empty string.

# The Menu Control

The **Menu control** allows you to display hierarchical data in a menu. The Menu control allows you to display only a single submenu at any one time. The Menu control can display the root node, parent nodes, and child nodes using fly out menus. The **static menu** appears showing the root level items when the menu is first generated. Then, **dynamic menus** are created that will fly out when an item in the root menu is selected. Each of these menus can be configured using styles or templates. You can modify the individual item, the mouse hover item, or the selected style.

Unlike the TreeView control, the Menu control allows you to use templates to give more control over the styles. Menu control styles can be set using the style base classes named **MenuStyle** and **MenuItemStyle**. The Menu control styles can be set using CSS. If you color the default hyperlink text in a CSS, the CSS will override the Menu style setting. While the Menu control supports templates, it does not support using check boxes to indicate which item is selected.

The Menu control can be bound to several types of sources of data, including the site map file. You can fill the Menu class declaratively or programmatically using the **DataBindings property**. The Menu control allows you to customize the data binding method such as another XML file instead of the default site map file. You can create custom methods to look up the siteMapNode based on the URL that was clicked. For example, you can retrieve and use multiple pieces of data within the Menu control; these pieces can include the title and description. Remember that you can alter the nodes that are displayed using the **ShowStartingNode property** of the SiteMapDataSource control. You also can hide the root node so that your menu starts with the second level node.

## Creating a Menu Control

In the following example, you will create a Menu control.

1. In the Solution Explorer window, right-click the **MasterWithMenu.master** file in the **MasterPages** folder and then click **View Markup**.

2. Below the Insert the Menu control here comment, insert the code as indicated in Figure 3-41.

XmlDataSource control identifies the location of
the XML file with the DataFile attribute

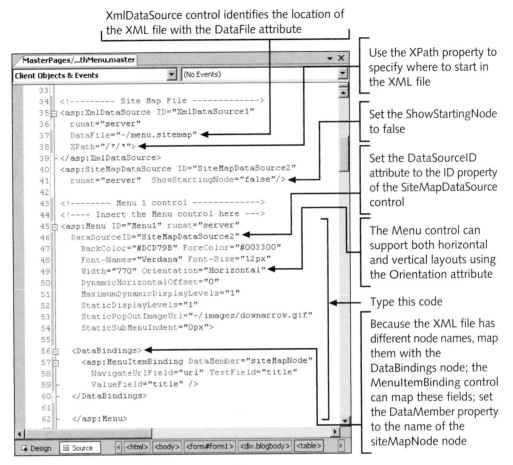

Use the XPath property to
specify where to start in
the XML file

Set the ShowStartingNode
to false

Set the DataSourceID
attribute to the ID property
of the SiteMapDataSource
control

The Menu control can
support both horizontal
and vertical layouts using
the Orientation attribute

Type this code

Because the XML file has
different node names, map
them with the
DataBindings node; the
MenuItemBinding control
can map these fields; set
the DataMember property
to the name of the
siteMapNode node

**Figure 3-41**  Creating the Menu control

3. Click the **Save All** icon.

4. Right-click the **homewithmenu.aspx** file in the **Home folder** in the Solution Explorer window and then click **View in Browser**.

5. On the first menu at the top of the page, place your mouse on the **Residential** link. The Illinois and Michigan links will appear. Place your mouse on the **Michigan** link. No change occurs.

6. On the second menu at the bottom right side of the page, place your mouse on the **Residential** link. The Illinois and Michigan links will appear. Place your mouse on the **Michigan** link. When you placed your mouse on each link, the background color changed.

7. Close any open files.

## Layouts and Properties of the Menu Control

Each item within the menu is called a **MenuItem control**. The basic properties of a MenuItem control include the **Text**, **ToolTip**, **Value**, **NavigateUrl**, **Target**, **ImageUrl**, and **ImageToolTip** properties. All are used as they are with the items in the TreeView control. You can also set the target attribute for individual menu items, or for the entire Menu control. Additional properties include the following:

- **Selectable:** Is a Boolean value that allows you to select the menu item. If false, you cannot select the menu item and it therefore becomes a basic heading.
- **PopOutImageUrl:** Used to display an image if the MenuItem contains subitems. By default this is an image of a solid arrow.
- **SeparatorUrl:** Used to display an image under each menu item.
- **StaticPopOutImageUrl:** May include a default graphic, which appears to the right of the static menu item.

There are also events associated with the Menu control. For example, when you click a particular item, the Menu control will redirect you to the new page, or initiate a **Menu.MenuItemClick** event.

## Changing the Properties of the Menu Control

In the following exercise, you will change the properties for the Menu control.

1. If necessary, open the **MasterWithMenu.master** file in Source view.
2. Locate the code you inserted in the previous exercise. After the blank line, insert the code as shown in Figure 3-42.

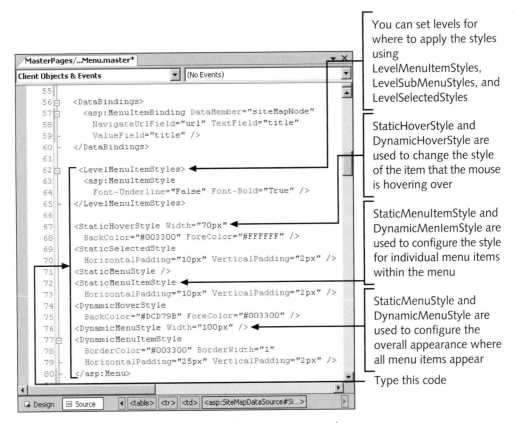

You can set levels for where to apply the styles using LevelMenuItemStyles, LevelSubMenuStyles, and LevelSelectedStyles

StaticHoverStyle and DynamicHoverStyle are used to change the style of the item that the mouse is hovering over

StaticMenuItemStyle and DynamicMenIemStyle are used to configure the style for individual menu items within the menu

StaticMenuStyle and DynamicMenuStyle are used to configure the overall appearance where all menu items appear

Type this code

**Figure 3-42** Changing the properties for a Menu control

3. On the first menu at the top of the page, place your mouse on the **Residential** link. The Illinois and Michigan links will appear as shown in Figure 3-43.

4. Place your mouse on the **Michigan** link. When you placed your mouse on each link, the background color changed. Close any open pages.

5. Close any open pages.

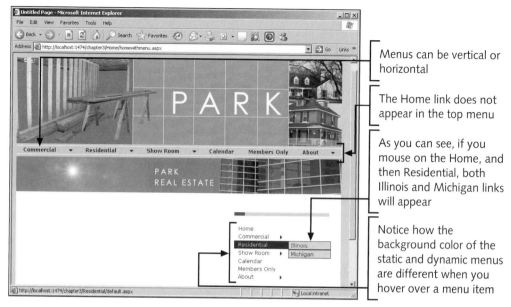

Menus can be vertical or horizontal

The Home link does not appear in the top menu

As you can see, if you mouse on the Home, and then Residential, both Illinois and Michigan links will appear

Notice how the background color of the static and dynamic menus are different when you hover over a menu item

**Figure 3-43**   Viewing the Menu control

## Using the MultiView Control

The **MultiView control** allows you to control when to display content. The MultiView control is one way to present multiple pieces of content from a single page and often is used for presentations and processing forms. This commonly is used when creating interactive presentations or content that can be provided based on the user's selections. With the MultiView control, you do not need to write the underlying navigational code. (*Note:* If you want a more complex control, the Wizard control is useful in building very complex multipage forms.)

Once you have created the MultiView control, you can nest zero or more **View** controls. The Views collection is the entire group of controls nested within the MultiView control. Each View control is like the box around your content. You can include Server controls, Data controls, HTML controls, graphics, and text. The navigation between these View controls is through controls and events. You can use buttons and links to insert a control that can trigger the switch view event. You can iterate through the multiple views similar to how you would through a PowerPoint slide presentation.

In this activity, you will configure the MultiView control to update the active view to the next view. All of the views contain a static image.

1. Right-click **Illinois_Showcase.aspx.vb** in the **Residential** folder in the Solution Explorer window, and then click **Open**.

2. Locate the <!--Insert code here--> comment, and type the code as shown in Figure 3-44. This will insert the first two View controls in the MultiView control.

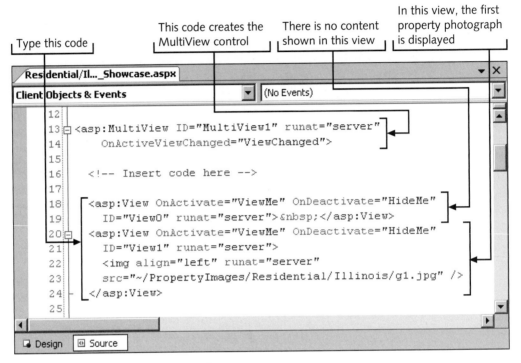

This code creates the MultiView control

There is no content shown in this view

In this view, the first property photograph is displayed

Type this code

```
12
13  <asp:MultiView ID="MultiView1" runat="server"
14      OnActiveViewChanged="ViewChanged">
15
16    <!-- Insert code here -->
17
18    <asp:View OnActivate="ViewMe" OnDeactivate="HideMe"
19      ID="View0" runat="server"> </asp:View>
20    <asp:View OnActivate="ViewMe" OnDeactivate="HideMe"
21      ID="View1" runat="server">
22      <img align="left" runat="server"
23      src="~/PropertyImages/Residential/Illinois/g1.jpg" />
24    </asp:View>
25
```

Residential/Il..._Showcase.aspx

Client Objects & Events          (No Events)

Design     Source

**Figure 3-44**   Creating View controls

3. Click the **Design** tab to view the control in Design view. The MultiView control appears as shown in Figure 3-45.

4. Click the **Save All** icon. Right-click **Illinois_Showcase.aspx.vb** in the **Residential** folder in the Solution Explorer window, and then click **View in Browser**.

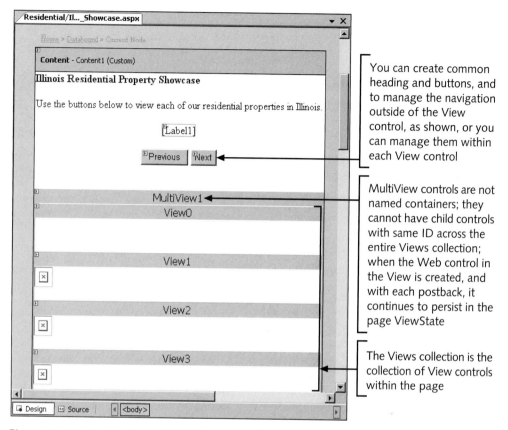

Figure 3-45   Previewing a MultiView control in Design mode

5. Click the **Previous** and **Next** buttons several times to rotate through the pictures, as shown in Figure 3-46.

6. Close any open pages.

The ActiveViewIndex is the index position of the current view being displayed. If the ActiveViewIndex is by default set to -1, no view is displayed. To set the first view to be the default, simply change this value to 0.

**TIP**

You can switch the views based on their index number or by their ID by setting the CommandName to **SwitchViewByIndex** and **SwitchViewByID**. Then you can include arguments with the CommandArgument attribute, such as the index number or ID of the view to display. In other words, you can name a view "View_Month." Then, in another view control, you can set the attributes of a button or hyperlink to change the view to the View_Month view. To do so, you would configure the button CommandName attribute to SwitchViewByID and the CommandArgument attribute to "View_Month."

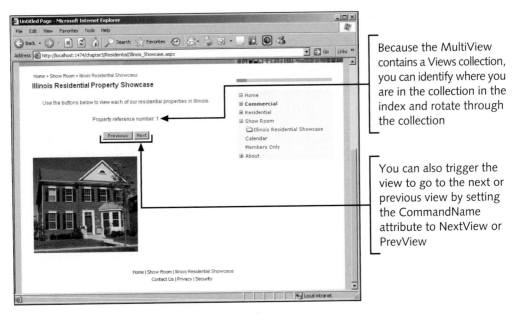

Because the MultiView contains a Views collection, you can identify where you are in the collection in the index and rotate through the collection

You can also trigger the view to go to the next or previous view by setting the CommandName attribute to NextView or PrevView

**Figure 3-46**   Viewing the MultiView control

## CHAPTER SUMMARY

- There are three types of CSSs that format the styles of elements on a Web page. The inline style sheet rules apply only to a single element. The embedded style sheet rules can be applied to multiple elements within the same page. A linked style sheet contains rules that can be applied to multiple pages. CSSs can be created manually or with the Style Builder. CSSs follow a set of rules that determines which style is expressed when styles conflict.

- XML files can be formatted with CSSs or XSLT stylesheets. XSLT stylesheets format the XML document using a main template and individual element templates. Processing instructions such as xsl:for-each allow you to retrieve information from each of the nodes in the XML file. You can use processing instructions such as xsl:choose or xsl:if to select a subset of data from the XML file. The resulting file is displayed. This process of applying the content and processing instructions to the XML file is known as transformation. The XML control allows you to configure the Web Form to load XML data and XSLT stylesheets dynamically.

- Master and content pages are used to manage a consistent layout and design of a site. The master page contains placeholders created by the ContentPlaceHolder control, which allow you to define areas that can be edited in the content page. When you edit the content page, you cannot alter content in the master page that is not within a ContentPlaceHolder control. Both types of pages can interact and have their own page event model.

- The site map is an XML file that contains nested nodes named SiteMapNodes, which store your Web site navigation data. The default site map is Web.sitemap and is found in the root level of your Web site. The site map is configured in the Web configuration file. The SiteMapDataSource is used to link the page to the site map. Navigation controls on the Web Form use the DataSourceID to identify the SiteMapDataSource control that should be used.

❑ The SiteMapPath control is used to create a breadcrumb trail and is frequently located at the top and bottom of your Web site to provide navigation information.

❑ The TreeView control allows you to use the site map data to create a navigational menu that looks like a tree, because the user can expand the nodes in the TreeView control.

❑ The Menu control allows you to display a vertical or horizontal menu based on the site map data. Multiple levels of static and dynamic menus can be configured. Templates provide you with the ability to modify the appearance of the Menu control.

❑ The MultiView control can be used to display interactive content, one view at a time. The View control contains navigational tools, or you can build your own navigation in the MultiView control.

## REVIEW QUESTIONS

1. What is the file extension for the default file that contains site navigation content?
   a. siteMap
   b. siteMapNode
   c. rootNode
   d. rootSiteMapNode

2. What is the file extension for a master page?
   a. .aspx
   b. .content
   c. .aspm
   d. .master

3. What control is used in the master page to identify where content can be placed by content pages?
   a. Content
   b. ContentPlaceHolder
   c. Panel
   d. PlaceHolder

4. What characters are used in the URL to represent the relative address for the resource in relationship to the Web application?
   a. /*
   b. #
   c. ~/
   d. <!--

5. What is the default name for the file that contains the data for the navigation controls?

    a. Web.sitemap

    b. web.config

    c. sitemap.api

    d. sitemap.xml

6. Which node in the navigation configuration file is used to identify who can view the node?

    a. description

    b. title

    c. roles

    d. URL

7. You cannot use a relative path in the navigation configuration files. True or False?

8. Which is not a method to redirect the page to a new page without the user performing any action?

    a. URLMappings node

    b. Response.Redirect

    c. Server.Transfer

    d. Hyperlink

9. Which property is used to identify the data location for the SiteMapDataSource control?

    a. ID

    b. DataBind

    c. DataSource

    d. DataSourceID

10. Which control is configured to change the ShowStartingNode to False to hide the root node?

    a. SiteMapDataSource control

    b. Menu control

    c. TreeView control

    d. Hyperlink control

11. Which attribute is used to configure how to separate nodes displayed in the SiteMapPath control?

    a. NodeStyle

    b. LinkStyle

    c. ItemSeparator

    d. PathSeparator

12. What is one of the unique benefits of the TreeView control over the other navigation controls?

 a. It is based on an XML data file.

 b. It can be configured to hide the root node.

 c. It can display all the nodes at one time.

 d. You can set the default window with the Target property.

13. What attribute is used to modify the layout for the Menu control to horizontal?

 a. Horizontalpadding

 b. HorizontalLayout

 c. Layout

 d. Orientation

14. Which attribute is used to display an image if the static menu in the Menu control contains a submenu?

 a. SeparatorUrl

 b. PopOutImageUrl

 c. Selectable

 d. DynamicHoverStyle

15. If you use an XML file instead of a site map, what node must you include in the Menu control to identify the corresponding node names?

 a. DataBindings

 b. XPath

 c. XMLDataSource

 d. StaticMenu

16. Which navigation control allows you to interact dynamically with the user?

 a. SiteMapPath

 b. MultiView

 c. TreeView

 d. All of the above

17. Explain the relationship of the XmlSiteMapProvider, siteMapProvider, site map API, the Web.sitemap file, and the navigation controls.

18. Compare the benefits and disadvantages for using the SiteMapPath, TreeView, Menu, and MultiView controls.

19. List five benefits of using styles and template navigation controls.

20. List five benefits of using a server-side navigation control over a client-side JavaScript control.

21. Compare why content and master pages are more efficient and cost effective for maintaining complex sites.

22. Explain five reasons to use a breadcrumb trail.

23. Which prefix is used to indicate that the XML document should use a cascading style sheet?

    a. xml:css

    b. xml-stylesheet

    c. asp:stylesheet

    d. type = css

24. Which XML processing instruction retrieves the contents of any element within the node?

    a. <xsl:value-of select="." />

    b. <xsl:apply-templates select="*" />

    c. <xsl:template match="/*">

    d. <xsl:apply-templates select="." />

25. Which property is used to identify the XSL stylesheet in an XML control?

    a. DocumentContent

    b. TransformSource

    c. Href

    d. XML:CSS

26. Which type of style sheet takes precedence over all other style rules?

    a. inline

    b. external

    c. linked

    d. embedded

27. What tag is used to attach an external style sheet to a Web page?

    a. Link

    b. MIME

    c. Rel

    d. Href

28. What is the character that separates the name and values within a style rule?

    a. :

    b. *

    c. { }

    d. ,

29. Which style element can be applied to more than one element?

    a. Class

    b. ID

    c. H2

    d. None of the above

30. What is the file extension of a cascading style sheet?

    a. .css

    b. .ccs

    c. .html

    d. .ascx

**3**

# HANDS-ON PROJECTS

**HANDS-ON PROJECTS**

## Project 3-1

Your boss has created static Web pages that are time consuming to maintain. In this project, you will use master and control pages to modify the layout and design of the Web pages, which will make it easier for him to maintain. All of the project files for this assignment will be placed in this folder and the chapter3/images folder.

1. Open your browser and view the current page for Tara Store at **ch3_proj1.htm** in your **ch3_proj1** folder. The ch3_proj1.htm page contains a table with all of the products available on the Web site. Click the **Vases & Bowls** hyperlink. The page refreshes to ch3_proj1_sc9.htm. All of the pages for subcategories 9, 10, 11, and 12, are set up in the same format. Click the **Belleek Tabletop Pieces** hyperlink.

2. Create a subcategory master page named **ch3_proj1.master**, a new home page named **ch3_proj1.aspx**, and a content page for each of the subcategories, named **ch3_proj1_sc_9.aspx**, **ch3_proj1_sc_10.aspx**, **ch3_proj1_sc_11.aspx**, **ch3_proj1_sc12.aspx**.

3. Insert the contents of the home page so that it looks the same as in the ch3_proj1.htm, except you will need to change the links to the subcategory pages.

4. In the subcategory master page, the heading, left menu, and color of the background should not be changed by the content pages. You will need to make sure the left menu hyperlinks link to the new content pages.

5. Save all of your pages and view them in a browser.

## Project 3-2

Your boss created a series of Web pages in HTML. He created the Web Forms and started the style sheet. He has made some changes in the style of the hyperlinks, but would like to finish creating the style sheet and change the default style of the text. The default font should be changed to Arial size medium. He anticipates that the styles will have to change again in two months. In this project, modify the external cascading style sheet to make it easier for you to maintain the styles within your Web pages. You will create and use classes to store style information. All of the project files for this assignment will be placed in this folder and the chapter3/images folder.

1. To view his existing Web pages, view **ch3_proj2.htm** in your **ch3_proj2** folder in a browser. Click the **Vases & Bowls** hyperlink. Notice the layout and format of the page. Click the **Belleek Tabletop Pieces** hyperlink.

2. Open the style sheet named **ch3_proj2.css**. Some of the HTML elements and classes already are inserted for you. After the "Insert code here" comment, add the following elements and values to the style sheet that are shown in Table 3-1.

**Table 3-1**  Configuring Styles with a Cascading Style Sheet

| HTML Tag or Class | Style Sheet Property | Value |
|---|---|---|
| body | background-color | #669999 |
| | text-align | center |
| | font-family | Arial |
| | font-size | Medium |
| | color | :#003300 |
| .BigTable | padding | 5 |
| | width | 794px |
| | background-color | #ffffff |
| | text-align | Center |
| .SmallTable | padding | 5 |
| | width | 587px |
| | text-align | center |
| | background-color | #ffffff |
| | border-width | 1px |
| | border-style | solid |
| | border-color | #669999 |
| .GreenCell | text-align | center |
| | height | 18px |
| | background-color | #669999 |
| | color | #ffffff |
| | font-weight | bold |

3. Create a subcategory page for each of the subcategories named **ch3_proj2_sc_9.aspx, ch3_proj2_sc_10.aspx, ch3_proj2_sc_11.aspx, ch3_proj2_sc12.aspx,** and a home page named **ch3_proj2.aspx.**

4. Insert the cascading style sheet into the new Web pages using the HTML link tag.

5. In each of the four subcategory pages, assign the following classes to the HTML elements.

- Assign BigTable to the first table element

- Assign SmallTable to the second table element

- Assign GreenCell to the first row element inside the second table element

- Assign MainCatLink to the first hyperlink that says Belleek Tabletop Pieces

- Assign SubCatLink to the other four hyperlinks

6. Click the **Save All** icon.

7. Preview the style sheet. Print the first subcategory page and the style sheet.

HANDS-ON
PROJECTS

## Project 3-3

In this project, you will create an XSLT stylesheet to process XML data. Then you will use the XML control in a Web Form to change dynamically the XSLT stylesheet that applies to the XML file. The manager and employee XSLT files have been created for you. All of the project files for this assignment will be placed in the ch3_proj3 directory.

1. Double-click the **ch3_proj3.xml** file in the Solution Explorer window to view the listing of product inventory.

2. Open **ch3_proj3_customer.xsl**. After the first comment, insert a **xsl:for-each** statement to retrieve data on every product. Use the **xsl:apply-templates** to insert templates for the **instock**, **pname**, and **pcode** elements, and insert a **line break**.

3. Insert an item template for the **instock** element. Use the **xsl:choose** statement to determine if the product is in stock. (*Note*: Make sure to use the **&gt;** instead of the greater than sign (>)). If the value is greater than 0, display the **clover.gif** image in the images folder; otherwise, display the **clover_red.gif** image.

4. Insert an item template for the product **name** element and bold the value. Then, insert a **colon**. Insert an item template for the **pcode** element and put the value inside a **pair of parentheses**. Click the **Save All** icon.

5. Open the **ch3_proj3.aspx** file in Source view. After the second comment, insert the code for an **XML control**. The ID should be xml1.

6. Open the code behind the page. Create an event procedure for the Page_Load event. When the drop-down list is changed, the page is reloaded. Assign the **DocumentSource** property for the XML control to the inventory XML file. If the value is a customer, assign the **TransformSource** property for the XML control to the customer XSLT file. If the value is an employee, assign the TransformSource property for the XML control to the employee XSLT file. If the value is a manager, assign the TransformSource property for the XML control to the manager XSLT file.

7.  Click the **Save All** icon. View your work, as shown in Figure 3-47. Print your source code and each of the pages from the browser. Close all of the pages.

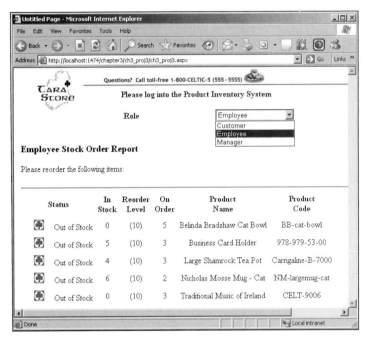

**Figure 3-47**    Dynamically changing XSLT stylesheets

# CASE PROJECTS

**CASE PROJECTS**

## Project 3-1

Your company has created thousands of Web pages in over 6 divisions and 30 departments. After polling your customers, you found that the majority of them were not able to locate the information they were looking for on your Web site. This has resulted in thousands of dollars worth of expenses related to simple customer support issues. Your customers are unhappy because they report that they have spent an average of 30 minutes on your Web site looking for information, which was confirmed by your Web site log analysis.

Your task is to design a new Web site. Create a master page for the entire company, and child masters for each of the main divisions. Create child masters for the different departments. The user should be able to identify where they are in relation to the other sections on the site through the use of navigation controls and layout and design. You can download the graphics and product information from the Web. Format the pages using graphics, content, fonts, and color to enhance the appearance of the page. You may change the name of the company. Insert at least one navigation control in the super master page that contains links to each page in the site.

All of your files will be placed the ch3_case1 folder . You may create any folder hierarchy structure within this folder. Create a home page named default.aspx and a Web page for each of the departments and divisions and store them in the ch3_case1 folder.

The six divisions and their departments are shown in Table 3-2:

Table 3-2   Company Information

| Marketing | Finance | Operations | Customer Support | Adminis-tration | Information Technology |
|---|---|---|---|---|---|
| Public Relations | Accounting | Manufac-turing | Customer Care Center | Executive Administra-tion | Help Desk |
| Investment Relations | Accounts Payable | Shipping and Receiving | Continuous Quality Improve-ment | Board of Directors | Networking and Hardware Support |
| Media and Press Support | Budget Director | Research and Devel-opment | Sales | Strategic Planning | Application Develop-ment |

## Project 3-2

You are hired as the Web developer for a company that sells products over the Web. They have experienced a decline in their sales volume, which according to the research department is directly related to the lack of the ability for the visitor to locate their products. You are to create a proposal and a sample demonstration site showing how the current site can be improved using the navigation technologies that you have learned in this chapter.

Create a project folder named ch3_case2 inside the chapter3 folder. All of your files will be placed in this directory. You may use a master page and multiple content pages, and any of the navigation controls. You can download the graphics and product information from the Web. Format each page using graphics, content, fonts, and color to enhance the appearance of the page. The user should be able to identify where they are in relation to the other sections on the site through the use of navigation controls, layout, and design. Create a name for the company and place it in the master page. Write up a three-page summary explaining your choices of navigation controls and how they will benefit the sales in your company. Save this paper as ch3_case2.doc in your ch3_case2 folder.

## Project 3-3

You are a Web developer for a software company that creates online course management systems using ASP.NET technology. You have been given the task to create a small Web site that contains links to resources from *www.microsoft.com*, *msdn.microsoft.com*, *www.asp.net*, and other Web sites. Then, create a folder named ch3_case3 in your chapter3 project folder. All of your files will be placed in this directory. Visit these Web sites and select at least 20 Web pages. You may add more pages and sections if you need to. List the name of the page, the

URL, and a short description on a single page and then save this to your folder. Because you expect that this list will expand over time, you use a master page and multiple content pages, navigation controls, and styles and templates to layout and format your Web site. When the user clicks the link, the user will be redirected to the site in a new window. Format each page using graphics, content, fonts, and color to enhance the appearance of the page. The user should be able to identify where they are in relation to the other sections on the site through the use of navigation controls, layout, and design. Create a name for the company and place it in in the master page.

## Project 3-4

Your company has just started on the Web. They are a late entry, so they have no graphics, content, structure, or resources. Your task is to create their Web site. Create a folder named ch3_case4 in your chapter3 project folder. All of your files will be placed in this directory. Use a master page and multiple content pages, navigation controls, and styles and templates to layout and format your Web site. Format each page using graphics, content, fonts, and color to enhance the appearance of the page. The user should be able to identify where they are in relation to the other sections on the site through the use of navigation controls, layout, and design. Create a name for the company and place it in the master page.

## Project 3-5

Your company has just started on the Web. The customer support has been asked to create an online presentation that covers basic computer and Web technology concepts. Create a folder named ch3_case5 in your chapter3 project folder. All of your files will be placed in this directory. Create 10 views in a Web page using the MultiView control. Review what you learned in previous courses and in the first three chapters of this book, and then create the content for each of the 10 views. Use a master page and multiple content pages, navigation controls, and styles and templates to lay out and format your Web site. Format each page using graphics, content, fonts, and color to enhance the appearance of the page. The user should be able to identify where they are in relation to the other sections on the site through the use of navigation controls, layout, and design. Create a name for the company and place it in the master page.

## Project 3-6

You are hired as the Web developer for a new Web site. Your store manager has requested that you make several product category pages. Choose at least five product categories such as shirts, accessories, china, jewelry, or books. Create a Web page for each product category. On each Web page, include a menu that lists all product categories. Each category listed contains a hyperlink to the specific category page. You may use the data from the Tara Store database, or create up your own data.

Create a style sheet that formats the category menu and the product listing. Add a link from the external style sheet to each of the Web pages using the link tag. Create a folder named ch3_case6 in your chapter3 project folder. All of your files will be placed in this directory. You may also use a master page and multiple content pages, navigation controls, and styles and templates to layout and format your Web site. Format each page using graphics, content, fonts, and color to enhance the appearance of the page. Create a name for the store and place it in the master page. View your Web pages in your browser. Print each Web page and the source code from the browser.

## Project 3-7

You are to create an XML file that will store information about your department. You have been asked to present your data in three different formats. Create a Web page to view the XML data and format using one of the XSLT stylesheets that you will create. First, create an XSLT stylesheet to read and format the data. Create a second stylesheet to use the thumbnail data to create an image that is displayed in the Web page. Create a third stylesheet to format the price of the products with a dollar sign. You should format the data using a table. Save these stylesheets as ch3_case7_style1.xsl, ch3_case7_ style2.xsl, and ch3_case7_style3.xsl.

Create a Web page named ch3_case7.aspx. Add the XML control and a DropDownList control to the Web page. Change the DocumentSource property to ch3_case7.xml. Change the TransformSource property to a style sheet based on what the user selects in the drop-down list.

All of your files will be placed in the ch3_case7 folder. You may also use a master page and multiple content pages, navigation controls, and styles and templates to layout and format your Web site. Add your company logo, graphics, color, and content to enhance the appearance of the page. Format each page using graphics, content, fonts, and color to enhance the appearance of the page. Create a name for the company and place it in the master page. Print out your Web page and the source code. Print out the XSLT stylesheets.

# 4

# CUSTOM DESIGNING WEB APPLICATIONS

## In this chapter, you will:

♦ Create a web application that uses themes and skins to modify dynamically the design of a Web site

♦ Create a User control that can be reused across a Web site

♦ Create Web Parts that can allow the user to modify the Web site appearance and layout

♦ Locate third-party controls that may be integrated within your Web application

**B**usinesses today need to provide custom solutions for their technology savvy clients. These custom solutions include not only data, but also presentation and usage of the web content. Companies realize that clients use their web sites for different purposes. In this chapter, you will learn how to use themes and skins to allow your clients to select a custom appearance for your web site. Their custom themes and skins can be stored with their user profiles, databases, or other data structures, and then retrieved and applied at subsequent visits to your web site. Later in the chapter, you will learn how to create your own User control. Then you will use Web Parts to create a Web site where the user can customize the layout and appearance of controls within the Web site. Last, you will become familiar with third-party controls so that you will understand how they can be integrated into your applications. By the end of this chapter, you'll be on your way to creating a Web site that has a custom design.

## Customizing the Presentation Layer

In this section, you will learn how to select a method to manage the presentation layer of your Web site. In the first subsection, you will learn when to use external style sheets and how to modify style sheets dynamically. In the following subsection, you will learn how to apply skins to an ASP.NET page to configure the styles for Web controls. Finally, you will learn how to group skins into themes that can be applied throughout your entire Web site.

## Using Style Sheets to Configure a Web Page Dynamically

Style sheets commonly are used to customize the presentation layer of a Web application. Style sheets allowed you to customize the styles of the HTML controls. Inline styles allowed you to configure the appearance of a single control, while internal and external style sheets allowed you to manage the appearance of one page or an entire Web site. If you are working with only HTML content, then you would use Cascading Style Sheets to customize the presentation layer of your Web site. Generally, if the site is larger than 10 pages, you should use an external style sheet. After 10 pages, it generally becomes more labor intensive to maintain the same Web design using inline styles.

Generally, if you are working with an HTML page, you cannot change the class or style of an HTML control dynamically. Because HTML controls are client-side objects, you cannot modify their properties using server side programming. You can modify properties only of server controls such as Web controls. Cascading Style Sheets do not directly support configuring the styles of Web controls. You can assign a class to a Web control, however, and when the Web control is rendered as HTML controls, the class is applied to the HTML controls. In a Web Form, you can dynamically change the style class of a Web control in the page code. For example, you may want to change the font color or the background image based on the user's role.

In the following exercise, you will view how styles can be dynamically based on the user preference and changed using an external style sheet.

1. Start your Web development editor.

2. Click **File** on the menu bar, and then click **Open Web Site**. Browse through your file system until you locate your chapter4 data folder. Select the folder and click the **Open** button.

3. Right-click the **ch4_styles.aspx** page in the Solution Explorer window and select **View in Browser**.

4. Change the drop-down list item to **Red** and click the **Change the hyperlink color** button. The label will change and indicate the style sheet class selected was named links_red, as shown in Figure 4-1, and the Course Technology link will be displayed in a red font.

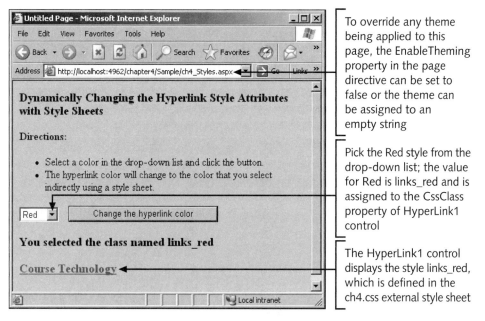

To override any theme being applied to this page, the EnableTheming property in the page directive can be set to false or the theme can be assigned to an empty string

Pick the Red style from the drop-down list; the value for Red is links_red and is assigned to the CssClass property of HyperLink1 control

The HyperLink1 control displays the style links_red, which is defined in the ch4.css external style sheet

**Figure 4-1**   Previewing the ch4_styles.aspx page in the browser

5. Right-click the **ch4_styles.aspx** page in the Solution Explorer window and select **View Code**. Notice in Figure 4-2 how the CssClass property for the HyperLink1 control was determined by the value selected in the DropDown-List1 control.

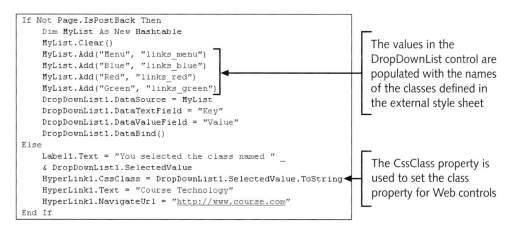

```
If Not Page.IsPostBack Then
    Dim MyList As New Hashtable
    MyList.Clear()
    MyList.Add("Menu", "links_menu")
    MyList.Add("Blue", "links_blue")
    MyList.Add("Red", "links_red")
    MyList.Add("Green", "links_green")
    DropDownList1.DataSource = MyList
    DropDownList1.DataTextField = "Key"
    DropDownList1.DataValueField = "Value"
    DropDownList1.DataBind()
Else
    Label1.Text = "You selected the class named " _
    & DropDownList1.SelectedValue
    HyperLink1.CssClass = DropDownList1.SelectedValue.ToString
    HyperLink1.Text = "Course Technology"
    HyperLink1.NavigateUrl = "http://www.course.com"
End If
```

The values in the DropDownList control are populated with the names of the classes defined in the external style sheet

The CssClass property is used to set the class property for Web controls

**Figure 4-2**   Dynamically changing styles based on user input

6. Close all the open pages.

You can see that customizing an entire page of controls would require significant time. Although customizing in this manner is possible, the time and cost to create a customizable application has prevented some Web sites from offering personalized services. Today with themes and skins, however, we can dynamically change the class or style of not only a control, but an entire Web site. The first step is to create a collection of skins for your Web site. In the next section, you will learn how to create and use skins to configure the appearance of your Web site.

## Using Skins to Format a Web Form

A **skin** is a file that contains style and other properties that are used to format Web controls. While Cascading Style Sheets are used only for HTML controls, skins can be used for any of the Web controls. You can use skins to set up default values so that you do not have to configure the style property of every Web control on every page in your Web site.

In the skin file, you will insert one or more Web controls. Each Web control within the skin file is referred to as a skin. For example, you can have three Label controls in a single skin file. You can then assign a **SkinID property** to each of the Label controls. The SkinID is used to identify each skin.

**TIP**    Skin has two meanings; it refers to the file itself, and to the controls within the file. The skin file can be added to your Web project from the Add Items templates. Skin files end with the extension .skin. Skin files are stored in a subfolder within the App_Themes folder. Each subfolder is referred to as a theme.

You can format the skin by using properties within the control or by using the Style tag. You can include most of the properties for the control and values in the skin file, but you can't include methods such as onSelectionChanged. You can insert comments within the skin file using the syntax <%-- comment goes here --%>.

In the skin file shown in Figure 4-3, three HyperLink controls are configured. The first HyperLink control is not assigned a SkinID and is therefore the default skin. If a HyperLink control in the Web page is not assigned to a skin, then this default skin will be used as the template to format the control in the Web page. In the second HyperLink control the SkinID is set to Red, and in the third HyperLink control the SkinID is set to Green.

In the Web page, you must set the EnableTheming property to true and assign a theme in the page directive. You can configure the HyperLink controls to use (or not use) one of the skins in the skin file. In the code displayed in Figure 4-4, you can see how several HyperLink controls are configured. Properties such as Text and NavigateUrl are configured in the page, because if they were configured in the skin, then each HyperLink control that used the skin would have the same values. We don't want each control to link to the same page, so the values are assigned within the Web page.

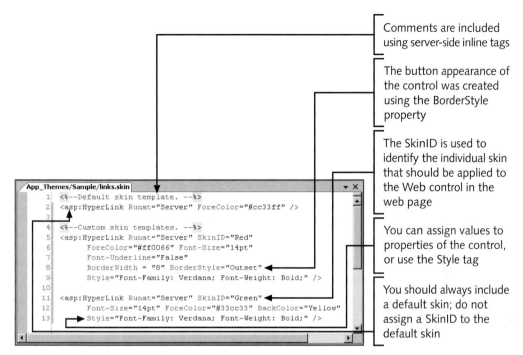

Comments are included using server-side inline tags

The button appearance of the control was created using the BorderStyle property

The SkinID is used to identify the individual skin that should be applied to the Web control in the web page

You can assign values to properties of the control, or use the Style tag

You should always include a default skin; do not assign a SkinID to the default skin

```
App_Themes/Sample/links.skin                               ▼ ×
 1  <%--Default skin template. --%>
 2  <asp:HyperLink Runat="Server" ForeColor="#cc33ff" />
 3
 4  <%--Custom skin templates. --%>
 5  <asp:HyperLink Runat="Server" SkinID="Red"
 6       ForeColor="#ff0066" Font-Size="14pt"
 7       Font-Underline="False"
 8       BorderWidth = "8" BorderStyle="Outset"
 9       Style="Font-Family: Verdana; Font-Weight: Bold;" />
10
11  <asp:HyperLink Runat="Server" SkinID="Green"
12       Font-Size="14pt" ForeColor="#33cc33" BackColor="Yellow"
13       Style="Font-Family: Verdana; Font-Weight: Bold;" />
```

**Figure 4-3**   Creating a skin file

**TIP**   If you put a value in the skin for a control, it can override the value defined in the Web page.

In Figure 4-5, you can see how the code from Figure 4-4 would appear in a browser.

## SkinIDs

You can have two Label controls defined in a single skin file and can set the SkinID to red in one control, and then set it to blue for another control. A skin file can contain the skins for many types of Web controls. So, in a single skin file, you can configure the properties of Label controls and HyperLink controls. All of the SkinIDs within a single skin file, however, must be unique within the same type of controls. For example, you can't have the SkinID set to red for two Label controls in the same skin file. This restriction exists because the SkinID is used to identify which skin to apply to the Web control. It is the link between the Web controls in the Web page and the properties defined in the skin in the skin file.

The first control, which links to the Home page, is not assigned to a skin; therefore, the default skin will be used

To add space within the buttons, you can use  

You can use   to add space between the buttons

You must assign the ID value in the Web page and not in the skin; you cannot name any control with the same ID in the same page

You can see that although the second and third HyperLink Web controls are assigned to the same SkinID, they have different values for the ID

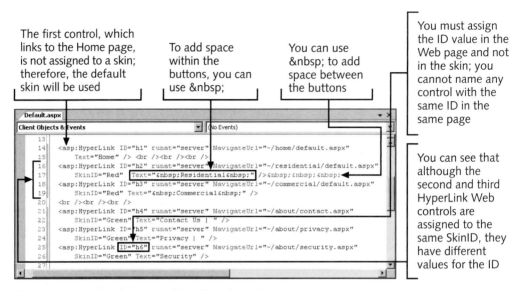

```
13
14  <asp:HyperLink ID="h1" runat="server" NavigateUrl="~/home/default.aspx"
15      Text="Home" /> <br /><br /><br />
16  <asp:HyperLink ID="h2" runat="server" NavigateUrl="~/residential/default.aspx"
17      SkinID="Red" Text=" Residential " />   
18  <asp:HyperLink ID="h3" runat="server" NavigateUrl="~/commercial/default.aspx"
19      SkinID="Red" Text=" Commercial " />
20  <br /><br /><br />
21  <asp:HyperLink ID="h4" runat="server" NavigateUrl="~/about/contact.aspx"
22      SkinID="Green" Text="Contact Us | " />
23  <asp:HyperLink ID="h5" runat="server" NavigateUrl="~/about/privacy.aspx"
24      SkinID="Green" Text="Privacy | " />
25  <asp:HyperLink ID="h6" runat="server" NavigateUrl="~/about/security.aspx"
26      SkinID="Green" Text="Security" />
27
```

**Figure 4-4**   Assigning a HyperLink control to a skin

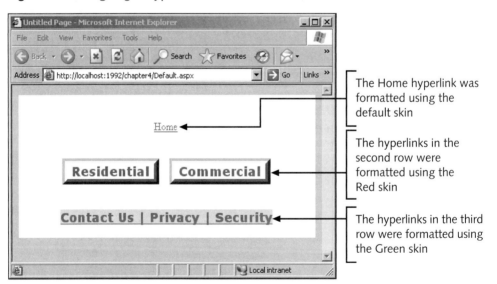

The Home hyperlink was formatted using the default skin

The hyperlinks in the second row were formatted using the Red skin

The hyperlinks in the third row were formatted using the Green skin

**Figure 4-5**   Previewing HyperLink controls that were configured with skins

**TIP**

Note that HTML server controls, such as the table cell, cannot be formatted using a skin defined within a theme. Instead, you must use Web control versions of these controls. A compatible Web control is available for each HTML server control.

4

### Grouping Controls within Skins

In most situations, you will create multiple skin files with different file names for each type of control. Often developers group controls within the skins based on the type of controls, such as buttons and labels. By separating the controls into separate skins, it is easier to maintain and modify the styles. Within the skin files, it is important to include a default skin with no SkinID specified. This will allow you to configure the control in the Web page when no SkinID is specified.

If you use a skin that requires a path to a resource such as an image, you can use a relative path. You can also use the ~/ character combination, which will identify a path relative to the root folder of the Web application. With a relative path, your Web site is easier to maintain because you can copy and paste the theme when you want to create a new theme. For example, you could use the sample code `ImageUrl="~/App_Themes/Default/images/banner.jpg"` or `ImageUrl="images/bar.gif"` to insert your images into an image Web control. Most programmers prefer to maintain their images within a separate images folder within each theme folder.

## Using Themes to Create a Uniform Web Page

Although you can use skins without themes, it is useful to group skins within a theme. A **theme** is a collection of skin files along with style sheets and image resources. The theme files are stored together within a named folder that is named after the theme. The theme folder is nested within the special themes folder named **App_Themes**. It is from this folder that you provide themes for your site. Figure 4-6 shows theme folders within the App_Themes folder.

### Style Sheets and Themes

It's useful to insert the style sheet using a theme, because you don't have to insert the link to the style sheet manually in the Web page. To insert the style sheet using a theme, however, your heading tag within the Web page must have the runat property set to server because the style sheet is configured within the heading section of a normal Web page. To allow the server to configure the heading section, you need to change it to a server control.

While you can create multiple themes within a single Web application, you can configure only one theme at a time for any given page. Therefore, you cannot implement more than one theme within a single page. However, you can apply a single theme across several pages or an entire site. You can apply multiple themes across multiple pages and folders within a Web site.

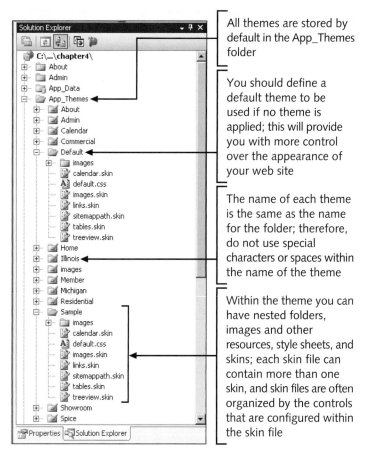

Figure 4-6    The App_Themes folder

The style sheet can be set at the page level using StyleSheetTheme property. The **StyleSheetTheme property** allows you to select the styles for some controls, such as the GridView, using an auto format template. Style sheet themes are like Cascading Style Sheets, in that the style defined within the style sheet can override the values defined locally within the Web page. Therefore, you may not want to configure some controls, such as ImageUrl or NavigateUrl, within the theme. Doing so would conflict with the styles defined within the style sheet.

## Applying the Theme to a Folder or Web Application

You can configure the theme to be applied statically in the Web configuration file, which would apply to the entire directory or Web site, or globally to all sites on the Web server. To configure the theme to be applied at the directory level, include a Web configuration file within the directory and specify the theme within the configuration file. To configure the theme to be applied to the entire Web site, specify the theme within the configuration file at the root of your Web application. Figure 4-7 shows a sample of a theme configured within the Web configuration file for a Web site.

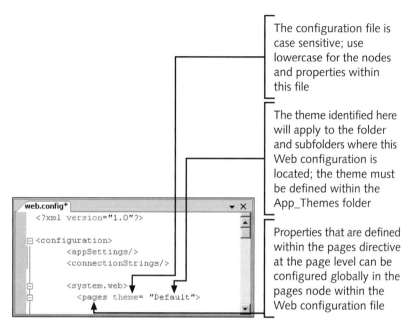

The configuration file is case sensitive; use lowercase for the nodes and properties within this file

The theme identified here will apply to the folder and subfolders where this Web configuration is located; the theme must be defined within the App_Themes folder

Properties that are defined within the pages directive at the page level can be configured globally in the pages node within the Web configuration file

**Figure 4-7**    Applying a theme using the Web configuration file

You can specify the theme within an individual page within the pages directive. Simply set the code to `Theme= "MyTheme" styleSheetTheme= "MyStyles"`. When you configure the theme at the page level, it overrides the theme configuration in the Web site or folder configuration. As you can see in Figure 4-8, if you defined your themes before you created your Web page, a list of the available themes appears when you enter `Theme=`.

## Configuring Multiple Themes in the Web Configuration File

There is an alternative to applying the theme within each Web configuration file in each folder in your site. You can include a Web configuration file in the root folder, but you must create a location element for any folder that would have a different theme. The **location element** in the Web configuration file can nest other elements, such as pages.

There can be many location elements included within your Web configuration file, as shown in Figure 4-9. Using this method allows you to centralize the configuration of your themes within a single configuration file. A central configuration file is easier to maintain.

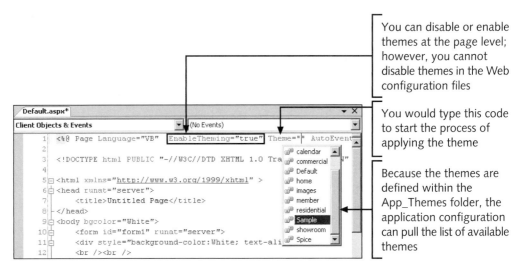

You can disable or enable themes at the page level; however, you cannot disable themes in the Web configuration files

You would type this code to start the process of applying the theme

Because the themes are defined within the App_Themes folder, the application configuration can pull the list of available themes

**Figure 4-8** Applying a theme within the Web page

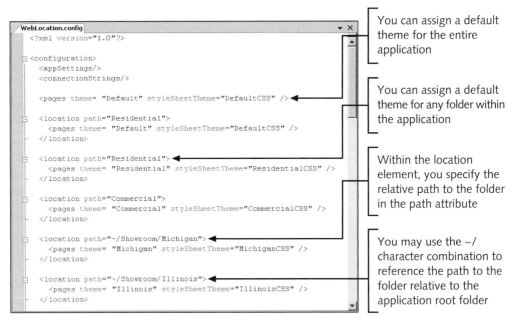

You can assign a default theme for the entire application

You can assign a default theme for any folder within the application

Within the location element, you specify the relative path to the folder in the path attribute

You may use the ~/ character combination to reference the path to the folder relative to the application root folder

**Figure 4-9** Defining a theme for several folders in the Web site configuration file

You can set the **allowOverride attribute** within the location element to false to prevent the page level configuration from overriding the Web configuration file.

**TIP**

4

## Configuring Themes in the Machine Web Configuration File

You can configure the theme to be available to all of the Web applications within a server by placing them in the [*Web server root*]\aspnet_client\system_web\[*version*]\Theme\[*theme name*] folder. By default, the Web server root is C:\Inetpub\wwwroot\ and the current version of the .NET Framework is 2_0_50727. On the default settings, the location of a theme named RealEstate would be C:\Inetpub\wwwroot\aspnet_client\system_web\[*version*]\Theme\RealEstate\. To apply the default theme to all Web applications running on a server, you would modify the machine Web configuration file, which is by default located at C:\WINDOWS\Microsoft.NET\Framework\[*version*]\CONFIG\web.config. The reason you would configure the default theme here is to provide a way to guarantee that all Web applications would use the same theme. Such a situation might occur if you were building an intranet Web site where other users would be allowed to add Web pages and folders. This would configure each Web folder to apply the default Web theme automatically, thus providing consistency across your Web application.

## Applying the Theme to a Master and Content Page

If you use master and content pages, you should be very careful when planning your Web site. The path identified in the location element in the Web configuration file is the path to the master page, not the content page. While you can enable or disable themes within a master page, you cannot directly apply the theme to the master page. You can directly configure the theme only within the content page.

Although it may seem that you cannot use themes with master content pages, there are ways to configure the master and content page to use themes without directly configuring each content page. For instance, to configure a theme to apply to a subset of pages, you would place the pages within the same folder, and include a Web configuration file with the new theme specified in the pages node. This technique will work with master and content pages if you place the Web configuration file within the folder that contains the content pages. When the page is assembled, the theme referred to the Web configuration file in the content page would be used to format the page.

**TIP**

When you are editing pages, you may see a green underline under the SkinID for any controls because the theme will be applied programmatically when the content and master page are merged.

## Disabling the Use of Themes

Your Web application and Web pages will support themes by default. Several ways exist to disable the use of themes. You can disable the application of a theme on a specific control by setting the **EnableTheming property** of the control to false. If you want to disable a group of controls, you can use a panel control to group all of the controls and set the EnableTheming property of a control to false; your action will apply to child controls within the panel control. If you want to disable themes for an entire page, you can set the EnableTheming property within the page directive to false.

**TIP**
Remember that you don't have to configure all of the properties within the skin. You can define some of the properties within the skin and some of them within the Web page.

## Creating a New Theme

One of the common techniques is to create your skins for a single theme and then copy the entire group of skins to another theme. Then you can change the value for the skins in the new theme. In the following exercise, you will copy an existing theme, modify the skins, and identify the differences between the themes.

1. In the Solution Explorer window, expand the **About** folder, right-click the **Default.aspx** file, and click **View in Browser**. The page is displayed, as shown in Figure 4-10.

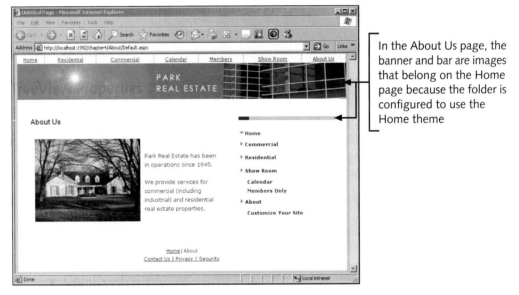

In the About Us page, the banner and bar are images that belong on the Home page because the folder is configured to use the Home theme

**Figure 4-10**   Previewing a Web page configured with a theme

2. In the Solution Explorer window, expand the **App_Themes** folder, right-click the **Home** folder, and then select **Copy**. Right-click the **App_Themes** folder and select **Paste**. Right-click the **Copy of Home** folder and select **Rename**. Type **About** and press the **Enter** key. Expand the **About** folder that contains the skin files.

3. In the Solution Explorer window, immediately under the chapter4 project, expand the **About** folder, and double-click the **web.config** file. (*Note:* Do not expand the About theme; expand the About folder located in the root of the Web project.)

4. Locate the pages element and change the theme from home to **About**.

5. In the Solution Explorer window, if necessary, expand the **App_Themes** folder and then expand the **About** folder. Double-click the **images.skin** file. The code to create the banner and bar images is shown in Figure 4-11.

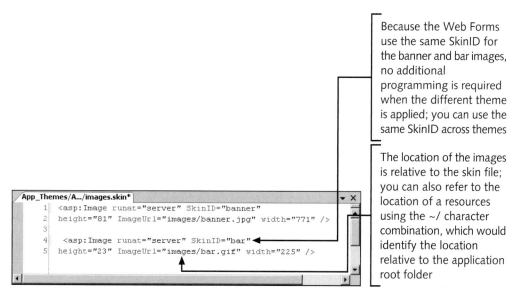

Because the Web Forms use the same SkinID for the banner and bar images, no additional programming is required when the different theme is applied; you can use the same SkinID across themes

The location of the images is relative to the skin file; you can also refer to the location of a resources using the ~/ character combination, which would identify the location relative to the application root folder

```
App_Themes/A.../images.skin*
1    <asp:Image runat="server" SkinID="banner"
2    height="81" ImageUrl="images/banner.jpg" width="771" />
3
4    <asp:Image runat="server" SkinID="bar"
5    height="23" ImageUrl="images/bar.gif" width="225" />
```

**Figure 4-11**    Creating the banner and bar image skins

6. In the Solution Explorer window, if necessary, expand the **App_Themes** folder. Expand the **images** folder and then expand the **About** folder. Click the **banner.jpg** file. Holding the **Shift** key down, click the **bar.gif** files to select both files. Right-click the **banner.jpg** file and select **Copy**. Right-click the **About** theme folder, and select **Paste**. You will need to confirm that you are overwriting existing files. The files are named the same but are different images. The files are now copied to the new About theme.

7. Click the **Save All** button.

8. Go back to your **default.aspx** page, right-click the page, and then click **Refresh**. The page now appears with the new banner and bar image, as shown in Figure 4-12.

9. Close any open pages.

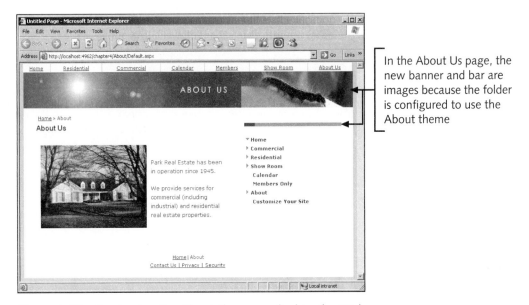

In the About Us page, the new banner and bar are images because the folder is configured to use the About theme

**Figure 4-12**   Previewing the About theme applied to the Web page

Using themes can allow you to manage the presentation layer of your Web site efficiently. In the first version of the Park Real Estate Web site, the master page required two procedures to retrieve the name of the requested file and its parent directory; the master page then used this information to retrieve the corresponding images for the banner and bar image. By using skins and themes, the master page was not required to have any code behind the page. Furthermore, the images and resources used for the themes can be stored with the theme.

## Programmatically Applying a Skin or Theme

You can assign the SkinID for a control programmatically or change the theme. For example, you could enter `HyperLink2.SkinID="MainMenuLink"` to assign the Main-MenuLink skin to be used to format the style for the HyperLink2 control. You need to assign the value prior to or within the Page PreInit event, however, which occurs before the control is created.

**TIP**   Because the controls in the content page do not exist until they are merged with the master page, you cannot modify the SkinID of a control programmatically in a content page.

You have learned how to create server controls dynamically. If you want to apply a theme to a control that is dynamically created, however, you must apply the theme before it is added to the control collection for the page. You would have to apply the skin before the page postback event. The most common way to do this is to use the page preinit event handler, which is the event that occurs before the controls are created. If you attempt to build a page that allows the user to select the theme, when you retrieve the value from the QueryString or Forms, you then will apply the value in the page preinit event handler. In the following activity you will learn how to modify the SkinID and theme programmatically.

1. In the Solution Explorer window, expand the **Sample** folder, right-click the **ch4_ChangeSkin.aspx** file, and then click **View Code**. Type the code as shown in Figure 4-13.

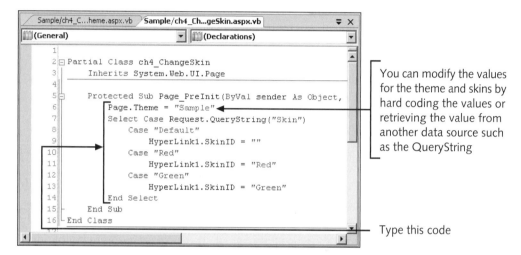

**Figure 4-13**   Changing the theme and SkinID programmatically

2. Click the **Save All** button.

3. Right-click the **ch4_ChangeSkin.aspx.** file and click **View in Browser**. The page appears with the hyperlink displayed using the default style.

4. Change the URL by appending the QueryString **?Skin=Red**. The page appears with the HyperLink1 control displayed as a button, as shown in Figure 4-14.

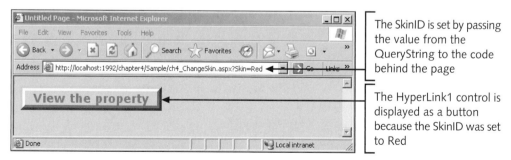

**Figure 4-14**   Passing the SkinID from the QueryString

5. In the Solution Explorer window, open the **Sample** folder, right-click the **ch4_ChangeTheme.aspx** file, and then click **View Code**. Type the code as shown in Figure 4-15.

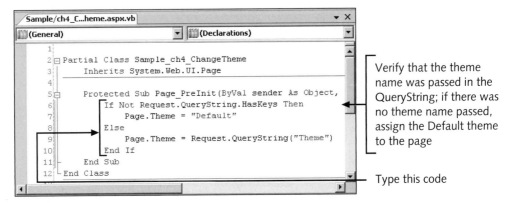

Figure 4-15 showing code editor:

```
Sample/ch4_C...heme.aspx.vb
(General)                                          (Declarations)
1
2  Partial Class Sample_ch4_ChangeTheme
3      Inherits System.Web.UI.Page
4
5      Protected Sub Page_PreInit(ByVal sender As Object,
6          If Not Request.QueryString.HasKeys Then
7              Page.Theme = "Default"
8          Else
9              Page.Theme = Request.QueryString("Theme")
10         End If
11     End Sub
12 End Class
```

Verify that the theme name was passed in the QueryString; if there was no theme name passed, assign the Default theme to the page

Type this code

**Figure 4-15** Changing the theme programmatically in a content page

6. Click the **Save All** button.

7. Right-click the **ch4_ ChangeTheme.aspx** file and click **View in Browser**. The page appears with the default theme.

8. Change the URL by appending the QueryString **?Theme=Home**. The page appears with the Home theme applied. Change the Querystring to **?Theme=Member** and refresh the page. The page appears with the Member theme applied.

9. In the Solution Explorer window, open the **Sample** folder, right-click the **ch4_RetrieveThemeList.aspx** file, and then click **View Code**. Type the code as shown in Figure 4-16.

10. Click the **Save All** button.

11. Right-click the **ch4_ RetrieveThemeList.aspx** file and click **View in Browser**. The page appears with the default theme, and the drop-down list is populated with the names of the themes available. In the drop-down list, select **Calendar** and click the **Change my theme!** button. The theme changes to the Calendar theme.

12. Close any open pages.

In Chapter 2, you learned how to create and use classes, properties, and objects. User preferences are often stored within a profile object. You can create your own profile object or use the built-in profile object. ASP.NET provider allows you to store user profiles in a variety of data sources such as the SQL Server. You can store the theme preferences in a property of the profile object. Later, when the user accesses the page, you can assign the theme for the user

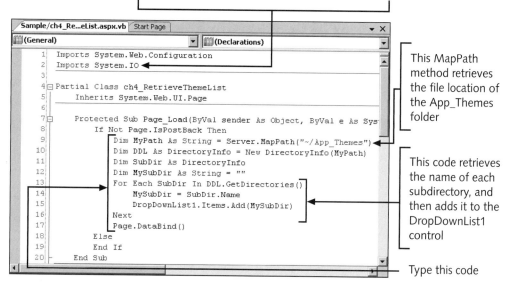

Figure 4-16    Retrieving the list of themes

to a theme defined within the profile in the page preinit event using the code `Page.Theme` = `Profile.Theme`.

# USER CONTROLS

A **User control** is a container where you can insert server controls, HTML markup, and programming code. The User control is inserted into a Web Form. User controls are used to store content that can be reused in other parts of the Web application. The User control may be as simple as a heading image or as complicated as a list of records returned from a database. The User control can be reused in other Web pages within the same application and across projects.

User controls make it easier to maintain Web pages. For example, you might use a User control to display a header image throughout the hundreds of pages on your Web site. The User control contains an image tag with the name of the file that contains the image. If the file name changes, you need only modify the name of the image in the User control and not in the hundreds of pages on the Web site.

**NOTE** It is important to plan your Web application before you start to develop the code. After planning the desired outcome of your Web site, you can try to identify areas where code can be reused. Then, you can create User controls to replace this code. The User control can be inserted into any Web Form page, including master and content pages.

## Understanding User Controls

The User control must have the .ascx file extension. The first line of the User control must identify the file as a User control with the keyword Control. All User controls are identified with this keyword. Because the User control can contain programming code, it also contains a reference to the code behind the page. You can place the server code within the code behind the page, or you can include the code within HTML view. You cannot include the `<html>`, `<head>`, `<body>`, or `<form>` elements in the User control.

The code in Figure 4-17 creates a User control that displays a list of months in a drop-down list. The code to populate the DropDownList1 control is located in the code behind the page identified with the CodeFile property.

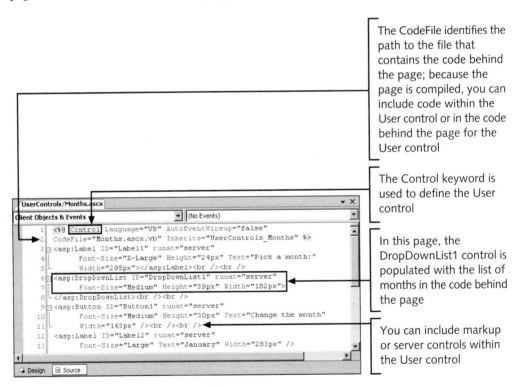

The CodeFile identifies the path to the file that contains the code behind the page; because the page is compiled, you can include code within the User control or in the code behind the page for the User control

The Control keyword is used to define the User control

In this page, the DropDownList1 control is populated with the list of months in the code behind the page

You can include markup or server controls within the User control

**Figure 4-17** Defining a User control

User controls are compiled by Visual Studio .NET and must be registered with each ASP.NET page. Within each Web Form that contains the User control, you must register the User control. To register the control, the first line of the page must contain the **@Register directive**. The @Register directive allows you to include the file as a User control. The sample code in Figure 4-18 shows how you would register the User control from the code sample in Figure 4-17.

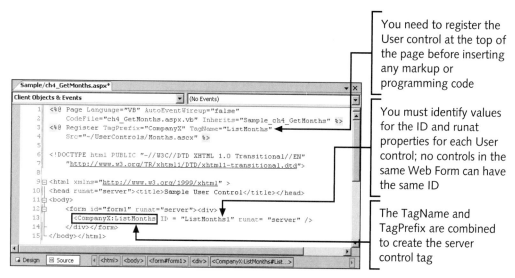

You need to register the User control at the top of the page before inserting any markup or programming code

You must identify values for the ID and runat properties for each User control; no controls in the same Web Form can have the same ID

The TagName and TagPrefix are combined to create the server control tag

**Figure 4-18**   Registering and inserting a User control within a Web Form

**TIP**  You also can add the code to register and insert the User control by dragging the User control from the Solution Explorer window to the Web page in Design view. This adds the register code and the User control tags to the new Web page. You can still edit the markup code manually.

Once the User control has been registered, you can use the new tag anywhere in the Web page. You can reuse any User control many times within the same page. You must provide a unique ID, however, for each User control instance. The tag for the new User control will be `< [TagPrefix] : [TagName] />`.

**TIP**  User controls are set up to use the flow layout mode as the default. You can change the layout to grid layout so that you can use absolute positioning of controls. To do this, you open the HTML tab on the Toolbox and add a Grid Layout Panel control. Then, you can position the elements within the panel. This places the items within a `<div>` tag in the resulting Web page.

## Creating and Registering a User Control

The following exercise illustrates how to implement User controls. The User control contains an image map and some basic code. Image maps allow you to define hot spots using coordinates. When the user clicks the hot spot, you can program your page to react to the click event and navigate to another page, or you can post back the information to the Web page. In this example, the user will be redirected to the Michigan and Illinois residential pages if he or she clicks on the Upper Michigan or Illinois areas. Otherwise, the information is posted back to the Web site, and a message is displayed in the Label controls. In this exercise, you will implement the User control in the content page.

1. In the Solution Explorer window, expand the **Residential** folder, right-click the **Default.aspx** page, and then click **Open**. The Content control on the left is named Content1 and the Content control on the right is named Content2.

2. In the Solution Explorer window, expand the **UserControls** folder, right-click the **park.ascx** page, and then click **View Markup**. Markup allows you to edit the page in Source Code view. As you can see in Figure 4-19, the User control is defined with the control declarative instead of the page declarative.

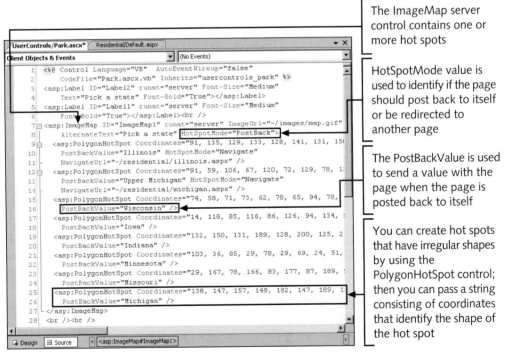

The ImageMap server control contains one or more hot spots

HotSpotMode value is used to identify if the page should post back to itself or be redirected to another page

The PostBackValue is used to send a value with the page when the page is posted back to itself

You can create hot spots that have irregular shapes by using the PolygonHotSpot control; then you can pass a string consisting of coordinates that identify the shape of the hot spot

**Figure 4-19**   Creating an image map in a User control

3. In the Solution Explorer window, left-click the **park.ascx** page. Hold the mouse button down, and drag the **park.ascx** page to the Content2 control on the Residential default page. The User control will be automatically registered in the page and the content will be displayed.

4. Click **File** on the menu bar, and then click **Save All**.

5. Right-click the **Residential Default.aspx** page and click **View in Browser**. Click **Minnesota**, which is the top-left state that is colored green. Your page should appear as shown in Figure 4-20.

**4**

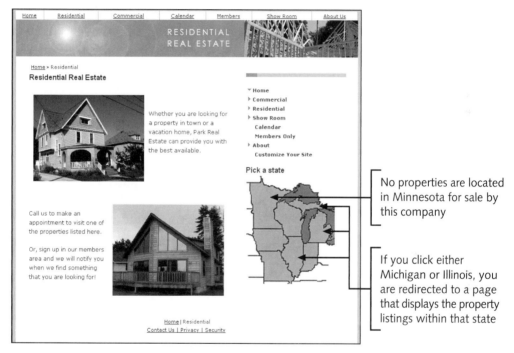

**Figure 4-20**   Viewing a Web page that implements a User control

6. Close any open pages.

**TIP**
Remember that the User control has its own page events and can contain its own code behind the page. You can implement User controls to contain code only in this code behind the page and with no visual presentation to the end user.

The use of User controls allowed companies to build reusable controls. Controls could be used throughout an application and across applications. In the next section, you will learn how Web Parts and Web portals also are used to enhance the functionality of your Web application.

# WEB PARTS AND PORTALS

In the last version of ASP.NET, Microsoft introduced its version of Web Parts and Web portal applications. **Web Parts** are a collection of controls. Web Parts can contain User controls and Web controls. Within a Web Form, you can load Web Parts dynamically. The Web Parts can be configured to allow the end user to control the display layout dynamically and edit the content loaded on the page. Web portals are often used in conjunction with Web Parts. **Web portals** provide ways that users can access other applications through a single interface. The Web portal may contain one or more Web Parts.

Many colleges and universities have implemented applications that support Web Parts and portals. The Web portal may allow students access to the registration system and library databases. The Web portal can allow faculty access to the student information system to record grades. Web parts allow the students to determine which content areas of the Home page that they want to view when they log in. Web parts allow the system administrators the ability to predefine which controls are loaded into the Web page and which controls users can optionally add into the Web page.

With this technology, administrators can lock Web Parts on the Home page so that all students have easy access to the information on the Home page. For example, administrators may want to keep a section for announcements on everyone's Home page. In addition, different groups of users may want to view different content. For instance, faculty may want to keep links to their record-keeping software on their Home page. A student in an online class needs a link to have access to his or her online course software, but a student on campus may not need this link. Instead, a student on campus may want to keep the information on the campus activities on his or her Home page.

In the next sections, you will learn how to create and use Web Parts, and how businesses can use Web portals to enhance their Web applications.

## Web Parts

In ASP.NET, each Web Part is called a **Web Part control**. ASP.NET contains several tools to allow you to create and manage your Web Parts. Within your Web page, the Web Part controls are stored in structures called WebZones, or simply **zones**. You will need to add one or more **WebZone controls** to your Web page wherever you intend to insert a zone. You can then add your own User control or Web control to the zones.

### Using the WebPartManager Control

The **WebPartManager control** is used to configure the Web Parts and WebZones. The WebPartManager control can be inserted anywhere in the Web page, and it uses **modes** to control how the content is displayed.

The default mode for a WebPartManager control is **browse mode**. In browse mode, if you were to view your page in the browser, you would be able to only minimize or close the zone. **Minimize** allows the user to collapse the control so that only the non-content area of the zone is displayed. This non-content area is called the **chrome** and consists of the border, title bar, and buttons used to open, close, and minimize the zone.

Buttons located in the upper-right corner of the zone may appear as links. When they appear as links, they are called **verbs**. Verbs allow you to close and minimize windows. If the user selects **Close**, the zone will close, and the user won't be able to reopen the zone without additional programming. If the user minimizes the zone, he or she can use the menu and select **Restore**, which redisplays the Web Part controls. You can allow users to select their mode using a menu, bullet list, or drop-down list.

In order to do more with the Web Part controls, you need to modify the WebPartManager to change the view to an alternative mode and insert additional zone controls. You can change the WebPartManager display mode in your code by changing the **DisplayMode property**. If the WebPartManager is in the Design mode, you can move a Web Part control from one zone to another by clicking and dragging the Web Part control to another zone. You can insert the code to create the WebPartManager control in Code view, or you can click and drag the WebPartManager control from the Toolbox to the Web page. The list of Web Part controls available in the Toolbox is shown in Figure 4-21.

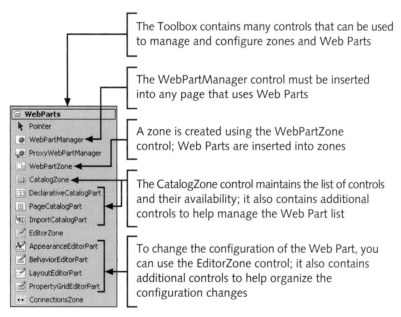

**Figure 4-21**   Web Part controls available in the Toolbox

## Display a Web Part List with the CatalogZone Control

The end user may want to do more than rearrange the Web Part controls on the page. To manage the list of available Web Part controls within the entire page, you need to add a CatalogZone by inserting a **CatalogZone control** to the page. Then in the CatalogZone, the user can add or remove a Web Part control by simply selecting it from the Web Part list. You can select the Web Parts from the catalog list and add it to one of the zones. Using the CatalogZone control will allow your user to add Web Part controls dynamically to any of the zones defined within the page.

Within the CatalogZone, you can insert additional controls to manage the Web Parts:

- **DeclarativeCatalogPart control:** This control is used to instantiate each Web Part control. The **EditTemplate** of the DeclarativeCatalogPart control is used to insert Web Part controls in Design view and will instantiate a version of the Web Part control. It is this instantiated version that will be managed by the CatalogZone.

- **PageCatalogPart control:** This control uses a catalog to maintain the references to all Web Part controls and server controls within the zones that have been closed by the user. The difference between the DeclarativeCatalogPart and PageCatalogPart controls is that the PageCatalogPart control displays only currently closed Web Part controls. DeclarativeCatalogPart controls display all of the controls within the list, even if they are already present in a zone. The PageCatalogPart control allows you to add the closed Web Part control back to the page. One of the main reasons to include the PageCatalogPart control is for users who may have accidentally closed the Web Part control. They will need to use the PageCatalogPart control to locate the closed Web Part control and to re-add it to the zone. Therefore, if you do not use the PageCatalogPart control, it is possible that the user could add multiple Web Part controls.

- **ImportCatalogPart control:** This control allows users to share the same settings for Web Part controls. The ImportCatalogPart control uses an imported description file for a Web Part control, which can be used to add the control using pre-assigned settings.

## Using the EditorZone Control

The **EditorZone control** is used to change the configuration of the Web Part controls. Using the EditorZone, you can use one of the editors to modify the appearance, layout, behavior, and property grid of the zone. After you insert an EditorZone control in the page, you can add one of the editors to the Editor Zone. When you preview your page, by default each of the Web Part controls will display "Edit" on the menu or list of links created by the WebPartManager control. When the user clicks the Edit link, the editors you selected within the zone appear. The user can modify the properties within the EditorZone such as the title and chrome type. The **chrome type** allows you to control the display of the title and border surrounding the Web Part.

The **PropertyGridEditorPart control** is used within the EditorZone to modify properties defined within the Web Part control. These properties can be modified and then later reset for the individual user. The properties can be stored locally using a personalization application or other data storage.

**TIP**

Because each user can have different views of the page, their preferences can be stored remotely in data storage such as SQL Server.

**4**

## Managing Web Parts

In the following exercise, you will learn how to create Web Parts, insert the WebPartManager control, and configure the zones. You will modify a page that will allow the user to manage Web Parts. Two zones exist for displaying Web Parts. By default, the first zone will contain a User control that contains a Calendar control and Label control. When the user clicks a date, information about events on that date will appear. The Calendar User control contains a property that is used to retrieve a date from the visitor and redisplays the calendar for that date. The second zone contains the real estate property search User control. In this exercise you will use the EditorZone to modify the appearance of the Web Part control. (*Note:* You will need your local copy of SQL Server 2005 Express to be running or you will not be able to view the page in the browser.)

1. Expand the **WebParts** folder in the Solution Explorer window, right-click the **Default.aspx** page, and then click **View Markup**.

2. Type the code as shown in Figure 4-22. This code registers each of the User controls that will be available to the user as Web Parts and inserts the WebPart-Manager control.

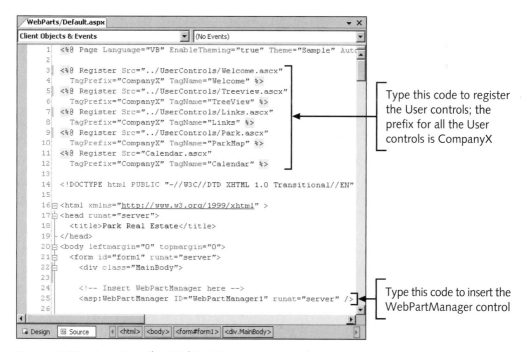

**Figure 4-22**   Inserting the WebPartManager control

3. Type the code as shown in Figure 4-23. This code inserts a new zone named WebPartZone1, inserts a default control, and configures the properties and style of the zone.

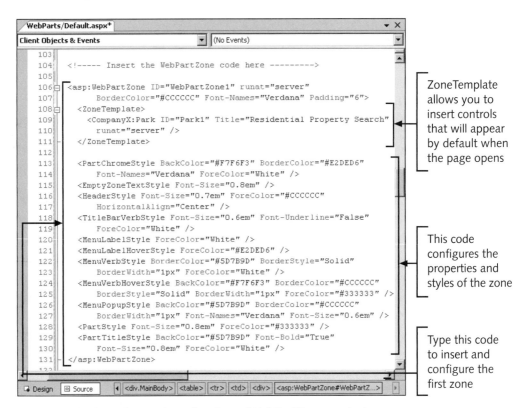

**Figure 4-23**    Inserting and configuring a WebPartZone control

4. The second zone, WebPartZone2, already has been inserted and configured for you. Type the code as shown in Figure 4-24 to insert the Welcome control into the zone template.

5. Type the code as shown in Figure 4-25. This code inserts a CatalogZone. There are three User controls and one Web control loaded into the control list by default.

6. Type the code as shown in Figure 4-26. This code inserts an EditorZone control and an AppearanceEditorPart control.

7. Click **File** on the menu bar, and then click **Save All**.

4

Notice that each zone must have a unique ID

The Welcome User control is inserted into the zone and will be displayed by default when the page opens

Type this code to insert the zone and control

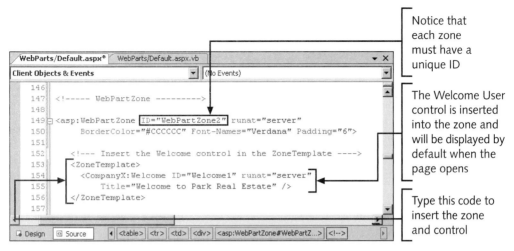

**Figure 4-24**  Inserting a control into a zone

The DeclarativeCatalogPart control displays all of the controls within the catalog list

Type this code

The Calendar1 control is a Web control and will display the default calendar

The Calendar2 control is a custom User control that uses a skin to modify the appearance of the control

The title is used to identify the control in the catalog list; if your editor displays a line under Title, it is most likely not an error; the title is used by the Web Part and isn't necessarily defined within the control

The PageCatalogPart control maintains the references to all controls within the zones that have been closed by the user

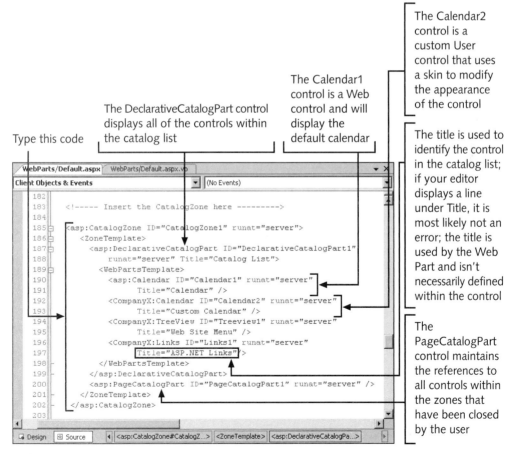

**Figure 4-25**  Inserting a CatalogZone control

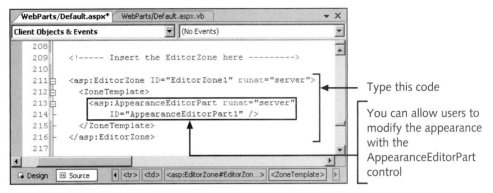

**Figure 4-26** Inserting an EditorZone control and an AppearanceEditorPart control

8. In the Solution Explorer window, right-click **Default.aspx** and click **View Code**. Type the code as shown in Figure 4-27.

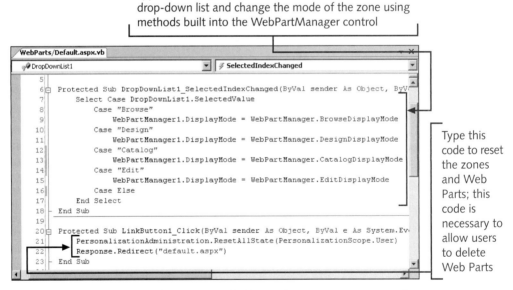

**Figure 4-27** Configuring the zones with the WebPartManager control

9. Click **File** on the menu bar, and then click **Save All**.

10. Right-click the **Default.aspx** page and click **View in Browser**. The browser displays the page as shown in Figure 4-28. The first zone contains the Park-Map control and the second zone contains the Welcome User control. You are in Browser mode by default.

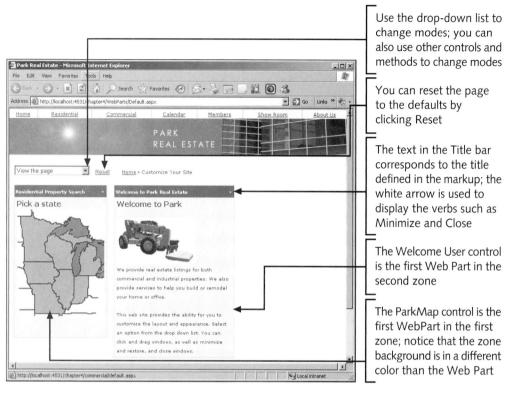

Use the drop-down list to change modes; you can also use other controls and methods to change modes

You can reset the page to the defaults by clicking Reset

The text in the Title bar corresponds to the title defined in the markup; the white arrow is used to display the verbs such as Minimize and Close

The Welcome User control is the first Web Part in the second zone

The ParkMap control is the first WebPart in the first zone; notice that the zone background is in a different color than the Web Part

**Figure 4-28**   Viewing Web Parts and zones on a Web page

11. Click the small white arrow on the ParkMap title bar, and then click **Minimize**. The entire zone minimizes. Click the white arrow again, and then click **Restore**. The zone expands to its original size.

12. In the drop-down list, select **Move windows around**. This puts the zones in Design mode. Click the blue title bar in the first Web Part and drag the control to the bottom of the second zone. When you release the mouse button, the Web Part appears in the second zone.

13. Click the **Reset** hyperlink to return the page to the default mode.

14. In the drop-down list, select **Add and remove windows**. This puts the zones in CatalogDisplay mode. All four of the controls you added earlier are listed.

15. Click the check box for **Calendar**, and then click the **Add** button. The default calendar is added to the first zone.

16. Click the check box for **Custom Calendar**, change the drop-down list to **WebPartZone2**, and then click the **Add** button. The custom calendar that was created by the Calendar User control is added to the second zone, as shown in Figure 4-29. Click the **Reset** hyperlink to return the page to the default mode.

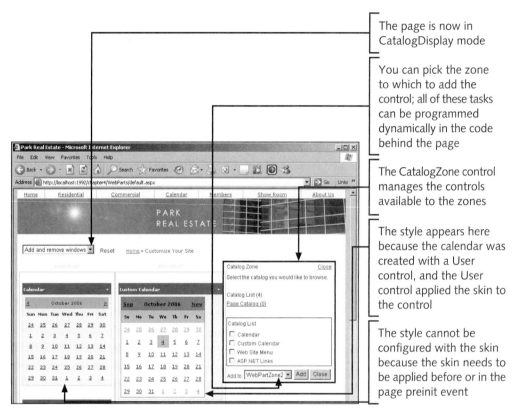

**Figure 4-29** Comparing how styles are applied to Web Parts

17. In the drop-down list select **Modify the window layout**. This puts the zones in Edit mode. Click the small white arrow on the Residential title bar, and then click **Edit**. In the text box, change Residential to **Midwest** as shown in Figure 4-30, and then click the **OK** button. The title bar changes to Midwest Property Search.

18. Close the browser window and any open pages.

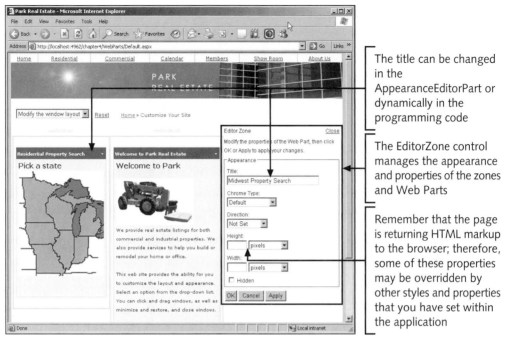

The title can be changed in the AppearanceEditorPart or dynamically in the programming code

The EditorZone control manages the appearance and properties of the zones and Web Parts

Remember that the page is returning HTML markup to the browser; therefore, some of these properties may be overridden by other styles and properties that you have set within the application

**Figure 4-30** Modifying the appearance and properties of the Web Parts and zones

## Web Portals

You have learned how useful it is to build reusable controls and Web Parts that can be inserted into your Web page. However, when you have many users and many applications it is useful to have these disparate applications integrated into a single user interface. Companies attempt to have a single sign-on for their users, so that the end user does not have to sign in to multiple information systems. Web portals provide ways that users can access other applications through a single interface. For example, students and faculty can access various library resources through a portal to an online database. These online database programs allow you to search for items such as journal articles, newspaper articles, books, and media. The school library pays a subscription fee for access to the online database. Students can log into their school Web site using a single sign-on. Then, when they click on the database link, they are directed to the portal software, which validates their credentials and allows them access to the online database.

The key to building a successful portal application is to be able to isolate your application from the other application, and to clearly provide methods that the Web programmer can use to interact with your application. In many instances, you will be building your application and connecting to a portal. A technology that provides a similar framework for multiple application communication is Web services. It is vital that you read the documentation that is provided by the portal developer. Many sample applications are available that provide programmers the framework for a portal application. The general principles of working with portals is the same across industries. Companies that build portals, however, tend to work within specific industries. For instance, Jenzabar (*www.jenzabar.com*) refers to the portal application called the Internet Campus Solution as a dashboard. Its portal application is designed to work with many information systems that are used in higher education.

Companies often rename their Web portal so that it is more in line with the corporate culture. At Park University, the portal is called PirateNet because its mascot is a pirate. At Oakton Community College, the portal is called OakStar. At some schools they prefer a more personal name to the portal, such as MyNMU at Northern Michigan University, or GoWMU at Western Michigan University. The names of the products does not impact the technology but can help assist the transition to the new technology.

The ASP.NET Portal Starter Kit provides a good starting point for looking at the potential of the user of Web parts and Web portals. This ASP.NET Portal Starter Kit provides 10 basic portal modules with the ability to expand to custom portal modules, an online administration module, and role-based security. The ASP.NET Portal Starter Kit site can be viewed live at *www.asp.net/StarterKits/StarterKitRedirect.aspx?Item=PortalLive*. You can read more about the portal at *www.asp.net/StarterKits/StarterKitRedirect.aspx?Item=PortalWhitepaper* and in the developer forum at *www.asp.net/StarterKits/StarterKitRedirect.aspx?Item=PortalForum*.

The portal shown in Figure 4–31 provides the ability for the end user to connect to different applications through one sign-in and user interface.

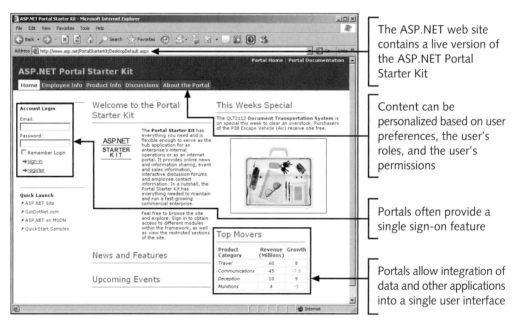

The ASP.NET web site contains a live version of the ASP.NET Portal Starter Kit

Content can be personalized based on user preferences, the user's roles, and the user's permissions

Portals often provide a single sign-on feature

Portals allow integration of data and other applications into a single user interface

**Figure 4-31**    Sample Web Portal application

There are many companies, such as SnowCovered.com, that provide add-on modules that work with the portal applications. When you want to modify your application to support Web Parts and portals, it is useful to diagram your site into logical functions and try to determine which combinations of content are likely to be included. Many Web developers will use a basic table to lay out the Web Parts in order to control the design of the Web page.

## THE USE OF THIRD-PARTY CONTROLS

Microsoft provides many Web controls and sample applications for developers as learning tools, and as a starting point for developers. These applications demonstrate their view of best practices in Web programming. In this part of the chapter, you'll learn a bit about what kinds of third-party controls and applications are available for ASP.NET applications in the market today.

## Dot Net Nuke

**Dot Net Nuke** is a community-supported sample kit and is frequently used as the foundation for commercial Web sites, corporate intranets and extranets, online publishing such as blogs, and other custom applications. Dot Net Nuke integrates Web Parts, zones, and portals, and provides modules that can be integrated with the Web application. You can find more information about DNN and links to many showcase Web sites that implement DNN at *www.dotnetnuke.com*.

**TIP**

Sample applications are referred to as **starter kits** and can be located at *www.asp.net/default.aspx?tabindex=5&tabid=41*.

## FreeTextBox

FreeTextBox is a control available for free from *www.freetextbox.com*. The text box can be displayed as a multi-line text box, along with multiple toolbars that are used for formatting the content. The toolbars can be styled to appear similar to the toolbars in Microsoft Word XP or 2003. You can customize which buttons appear on the toolbars, and the order and placement of the toolbars. The end user would type his or her content into the text box, and then format the content using the buttons on the toolbar, as the user normally would using Microsoft Word.

This type of user interface allows end users with very little training the ability to enter Web content into a content management system without knowing about HTML. This control is very robust, and it also features the ability for the end user to upload items to your site, such as graphics, and insert them into the text box. You can preview the images within the text box. For advanced users, there is a button that allows the user to switch into the HTML mode to modify the code manually. The free version does not provide support for tables and other advanced controls.

With many industries, it is imperative that the HTML code be compliant with the current XHTML standards and ADA regulations. One issue that arises with content management systems is the ability for the end user to cut and paste into the TextBox control. While many of these third-party TextBox controls support this feature, there are problems that can arise. Copying and pasting from a Microsoft Word document will bring not only the content, but also the formatting of the document. The formatting will be inserted using tags because the User controls where they place the content, however, it's possible that the end user could insert the content outside of the standard HTML control tree. In other words, the HTML control tree defines the order in which tags can be placed. You previously learned that with XHTML, the tags must be nested in a hierarchical structure. Pasting from Microsoft Word can break this hierarchical nesting pattern. One of the tools available on the toolbars in some of the third-party TextBox controls is the ability to strip out the formatting from Microsoft Word. Your end user would have to reformat the page. This will create a more stable and usable application.

## Telerik

Many other companies provide custom controls. A competitor to FreeTextBox is Telerik. Telerik provides many types of third-party controls in addition to the TextBox editor control called r.a.d. editor. It is more expensive, but offers additional features and product support that are not available with FreeTextBox. When you are comparing products, make sure to compare not only the price and features, but also the customer support.

## Other Third-Party TextBox Controls

Companies such as Blackboard and eCollege create content management systems for educational institutions that offer courses and training programs online. The faculty member can enter Web page content using the default text box. However, the faculty member would have to enter the HTML tags manually in order to perform any formatting that would be displayed in the Web page. The default text box Web control only allows the user to enter text. You can use the validation controls to verify the contents of the text box. If your user is entering data such as HTML tags, scripting commands, or server controls, however, you will want to build a control that has robust validation. You do not want a hacker to insert malicious code into your form. A popular method is to integrate a third-party TextBox control with your application. Several companies provide more robust text-editing controls.

**NOTE** As you learned in this chapter, you can create your own User controls. Many companies provide third-party controls and applications. These third-party controls may have other names for their TextBox control. You can locate these companies through the www.asp.net Web site at http://www.asp.net/default.aspx?tabindex=5&tabid=41. Click Control Gallery to view the various types of controls available.

4

# Retrieving Information from a TextBox Control

After the user has completed entering and formatting content within the TextBox control, the next step is to retrieve the information and either use it or store it. Retrieving the information from the TextBox control usually involves simply assigning the contents to a string variable. If you plan to store the information in a file or database, however, you may want to screen the content to ensure that it does not contain any inappropriate HTML tags, scripts, or server code.

If you intend to store the value from the text box in a database, you also will want to verify the length of the TextBox control. Some TextBox controls will provide the number of characters that were entered. In SQL Server, you can store the information using the text or ntext data types, or in Microsoft Access you may store the information in a memo field. These data types are used to store large amounts of textual content. You can also pick one of the other text data types and specify a limit to the number of characters in properties of the TextBox control.

**NOTE** Some TextBox controls will convert special characters such as < and > to &gt; and &lt;.

If you place a limit on the number of characters, you should also inform the users what the limit is in the page before they submit their content. At the same time, you should also be informing the user on how much time they have to complete the form. The **server timeout property** is set to 30 minutes by default. If the user is inactive after the number of minutes set in the server timeout property, the session with the browser will end, and the user will have to log in again before the form can be sent.

Of course, timeout errors can cause frustration on the part of the user. Although you can increase the timeout property, you may also want to recommend that the end user type the content in a basic text editor such as Microsoft Notepad, and then copy the information into the TextBox control. That TextBox control is where they can finish formatting the content. Notepad will not insert any HTML characters because it is a simple text editor. If you choose to store the information in a file, you will need to ensure that the Web server administrator allows the ASP.NET user account to write to the folder where the file will be stored. Later in your application, you can retrieve the value from the database or file, as you would any other data.

## The Value of Retrievable Data

Web developers in companies should educate the business departments on the capabilities for using the Web to store and create collaborative documents. For example, at Park University's School for Online Learning, the FreeTextBox control was used to create a collaborative document creation form so that faculty could create a single file via a Web interface.

Of course, one of the challenges at Park University was determining how to store the information for historical and backup purposes. The documents were stored in separate files, because only the current version was required to be displayed via the Web. In this case, the faculty member opened the page with the TextBox control, and the contents of the current file were displayed within the control automatically. The faculty member made their changes and clicked the Submit button. Once submitted, a copy of the newly edited version was saved in a backup folder and in the current document folder, which overwrote the previous edition. This small application was templated to provide the ability to expand its use to other projects and institutions. So, with the use of a third-party control and ASP.NET, they were able to create a small Web application to create and manage content collaboratively.

Although many Web developers end up working on large projects within their institution, it's important that they learn to think creatively on how they can use and implement these tools with very little impact on the organization's budget. Figure 4-32 is the sample of a collaborative document creation form, which uses the FreeTextBox control.

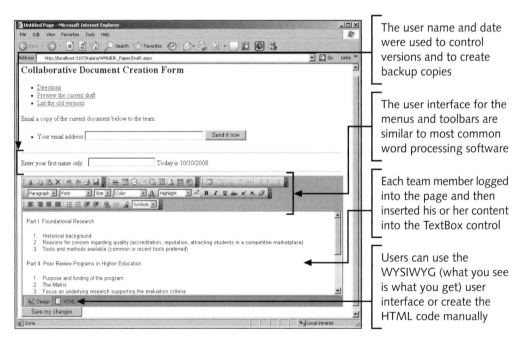

**Figure 4-32**    Implementing a FreeTextBox control to create a collaborative document creation form

4

To work with the FreeTextBox control, you would need to download several files from the Web site. You would need to place the executable within your bin directory. Then, you need to copy the aspnet_client folder that contains the necessary image files and other resources to the root of your Web application for the control to work. Depending on your system, you may have to alter the web.config file to configure the application to recognize the control.

## CHAPTER SUMMARY

- Skins and themes are used to customize the appearance of the Web page. The skin is a file that ends in .skin and contains the style information. Server controls can be configured using skins.

- Themes are collections of skins, style sheets, images, and other resources used to customize the page appearance. Themes must be stored in the App_Themes folder. Only one theme can be selected at a time. Themes can be configured at the page level, folder level, Web site level, or Web server level.

- You can create your own custom controls called User controls. User controls can contain HTML code and programming code. User controls must be registered within an ASP.NET page before they can be used. Once a tag has been registered as a User control, you can use the tag throughout the Web page. User controls are compiled and can be reused across multiple pages within the same application.

- Web Part controls are User controls or server controls that can be configured by the end user through the use of zones. Some zones allow the user simply to view the controls, while others allow you to move, modify, or edit the control. The WebPartManager maintains the mode state. You can configure the controls and modes using the graphical user interface, or programmatically.

- Web portals provide a single user interface that integrates multiple User controls, Web Parts, and other applications.

- Third-party controls are available free, and for purchase from a variety of vendors. It is important to remember that the application of the controls fit the purpose of the activity.

## REVIEW QUESTIONS

1. Which keyword is used to define a User control?
   a. control
   b. pagelets
   c. fragments
   d. register

2. Which tag type cannot be included within a User control?

   a. html

   b. head

   c. body

   d. all of the above

3. Explain how third-party TextBox controls can impact the ability for the Web content to meet XHTML standards.

4. Which Microsoft Web site provides access to a list of companies and third-party User controls?

   a. *msdn.microsoft.com*

   b. *www.microsoft.com/downloads*

   c. *www.asp.net*

   d. *www.freetextbox.com*

5. Your boss would like you to create a feedback form using a third-party TextBox control. List three steps necessary to protect your Web site from hackers inserting malicious code into your form.

6. Which Web control allows the user to manage the layout and appearance of items on your Web page?

   a. User control

   b. WebPartManager control

   c. Web Security Zone control

   d. Windows Form control

7. Which control is used to encapsulate the content from a Web control, User control, or custom control?

   a. Zone Editor control

   b. Web Part control

   c. Import Zone control

   d. CustomManager control

8. Which editor provides the ability to modify a property in a Web Part?

   a. Property editor

   b. PropertyGridEditorPart

   c. Property Smart Builder

   d. Style Editor

9. Which attribute is used to prevent the developer from overriding the theme?

    a. AllowOverride

    b. DisallowOverride

    c. ThemeOverride

    d. AllowTheme

10. What is the file extension for a skin?

    a. .skin

    b. .ascx

    c. .theme

    d. .css

11. If your theme is named Garden and the skin is named Roses, what folder path would you use to set the theme in your Web configuration file?

    a. `path = "garden/roses"`

    b. `path = "roses"`

    c. `path = "~/roses"`

    d. `path = "garden"`

12. What attribute of the pages element is used in the Web configuration file to set a style sheet for the theme?

    a. styleSheetTheme

    b. StyleSheet

    c. Theme

    d. Style

13. Which object consists of the border, title bar, and buttons used to open, close, and minimize zones?

    a. verbs

    b. chromes

    c. banner

    d. template

14. If the end user changes the value of a property in a zone, by default the property will change for all users. True or False?

15. Graphics created in Microsoft Word will convert to gif formats when the file is uploaded to the Web server. True or False?

16. What is the file extension of a User control?

    a. .usr

    b. .ascx

    c. .cstm

    d. .custom

17. Which keyword is used to declare a User control?

    a. control

    b. page

    c. custom

    d. register

18. Which tag type cannot be included within a User control?

    a. html

    b. head

    c. body

    d. all of the above

19. Briefly explain three differences between Web controls and User controls.

20. Briefly explain three differences between User controls and Web Parts.

21. Provide five reasons a business should consider implementing a Web portal.

22. Briefly explain three differences between style sheets and skins.

23. Describe three benefits of using third-party controls.

24. Describe the role of the WebPartManager control.

25. Describe three benefits of using third-party controls.

# HANDS-ON PROJECTS

**HANDS-ON PROJECTS**

## Project 4-1

In this project, you will create a theme, several skins, and configure the page to use the theme and the controls to use the skin.

1. Expand the **ch4_proj1** folder, right-click **Default.aspx**, and then select **View in Browser** to preview the page.

2. In the App_Themes folder, create a new theme named **ch4_proj1**.

3. In the theme, create a skin named **Label**. In the Label skin, create two skins called **Heading1** and **Heading2**, which is used to format the Label controls. Heading1 should set background color as **#003300**, font family name as **verdana**, font size as

**x-large**, forecolor as **white**, and width as **500px**. Heading2 should set background color as **#003300**, font family name as **verdana**, font size as **larger**, forecolor as **white**, and width as **500px**.

4. In the theme, create a skin named **Table**. In the Table skin, create a default skin with the border width set to **0**, background color as **#003300**, cellpadding as **5**, cellspacing as **0**, horizontal align as **center**, and width at **500px**.

5. In the theme, create a skin named **Image**. In the Image skin, set the SkinID to **Image1**, background color as **#003300**, and border width as **5px**.

6. In the theme, create a skin named **LinkButton**. In the LinkButton skin, create a default skin that is used to format all of the LinkButton controls. Set the width to **200px**, height to **25px**, background color to **#003300**, font family name to **Arial Black**, and the forecolor to **white**.

7. Right-click **Default.aspx** and select **View Markup**. Set the theme for that page to **ch4_proj1**. Insert the SkinID as **Image1** for the Image control, and **Heading1** and **Heading2** for the Label controls.

8. Click **File** on the menu bar, and then click **Save All**.

9. Right-click the **Default.aspx** page and select **View in Browser**.

10. Close any open pages and the browser window.

## Project 4-2

In this project, you will create a User control and insert it into a content page.

1. Expand the **ch4_proj2** folder. Right-click the **calculate.ascx** page and click **Open**. Type the code as shown in Figure 4-33.

**Figure 4-33**    Create the User control

2. Change the page to **Design** view. Double-click the **Calculate my commission** button. In the click event handler for the button control, insert the code to calculate the commission and assign the results to the Label control. The formula is **(txtH.Text * txtR.Text) / 100**. You should display a message with the results: **Your commission is $**.

3. Click **File** on the menu bar, and then click **Save All**.

4. Expand the **ch4_proj2** folder. Right-click the **Default.aspx** page and click **Open**. Click and drag the **ch4_proj2.ascx** to the left content control in the page. The User control is registered and inserted into the content page.

5. Click **File** on the menu bar, and then click **Save All**.

6. Right-click the page and select **View in Browser**. In the first text box, enter **100,000**, enter **6** in the second text box, and then click the **Calculate my commission** button. A message saying, "Your commission is $6000" should be displayed in the browser.

7. Close any open pages and the browser window.

**CASE PROJECTS**

## Project 4-3

In this project, you will create a page that implements Web Parts. The ch4_proj3 folder contains several User controls, which you will include as Web Parts in your Web page.

1. Expand the **ch4_proj3** folder. Right-click the **Default.aspx** page and click **Open**.

2. Click and drag a **WebPartManager** control to the Web page and insert it into the left control.

3. Click and drag a **WebPartZone** control to the Web page and insert it into the left control. Click the smart tag control on the CatalogZone control and select **Auto Format**. Click **Professional** and click the **OK** button.

4. Click and drag the **HouseofWeek.ascx** control to the Web page and insert it into the left control.

5. Right-click the **HouseofWeek** page and select **Open**. Locate the WebPartsTemplate for the HouseofWeek. Insert the title property and set it to **Residential Property of the Week**.

6. Click the **Design** tab to return to Design mode.

7. Click and drag a **CatalogZone** control to the Web page and insert it into the right control. Click the smart tag control on the CatalogZone control and select **Auto Format**. Click **Professional** and click the **OK** button.

8. Click and drag a **DeclarativeCatalogPart** control to the Web page and insert it into the CatalogZone control.

9. Click the smart tag for the DeclarativeCatalogPart control and select **Edit Templates**. The WebPartsTemplate appears.

10. Click and drag the **ListAgents.asxc**, the **Business.ascx**, and the **Vacation.ascx** User controls and place them inside the WebPartsTemplate. You will need to insert a new line after each control is inserted in the WebPartsTemplate.

11. Right-click the page and select **View Code**. Locate the WebPartsTemplate for the DeclarativeCatalogPart. For each User control, insert the title property. For

> ListAgents, insert **List Agents**, for Businesses, insert **List Businesses**, and for Vacation, insert **Show Vacation Homes**.
>
> 12. Click the **Design** tab to return to Design mode.
>
> 13. Click and drag a **PageCatalogPart** control to the Web page and insert it below the DeclarativeCatalogPart control.
>
> 14. Click and drag an **EditorZone** control to the Web page and insert it below the CatalogZone control.
>
> 15. Click the smart tag for the EditorZone control and select **Auto Format**. Click **Professional** and click the **OK** button.
>
> 16. Click and drag the **AppearanceEditorPart** control and place it inside the EditorZone.
>
> 17. Click **File** on the menu bar, and then click **Save All**.
>
> 18. Right-click the page and select **View in Browser**. Preview each of the Web Part modes as you did earlier in the chapter.
>
> 19. Close any open pages and the browser window.

**4**

## CASE PROJECTS

### Project 4-1

You are hired as the Web developer for a new corporate intranet Web site. You are responsible for creating the Home page for each department within the Web site. The departments include human resources, finance, marketing, manufacturing, administration, and customer services. Add at least three graphics, three hyperlinks, a bullet list, and a table in a master page. Use controls to create the individual department pages. Create a theme for each of the departments. Create Web configuration files for each folder, and configure the theme for each department. You may format each page using additional graphics, content, fonts, and color to enhance the appearance of the page. Save the files in the ch4_case1 folder. View your Web page in your browser. Print your Web page and the source code from the browser.

### Project 4-2

You are hired as the Web designer for a Web site. You are to use a site that you have previously created and modify it using themes and skins. Allow the user to select a skin or theme from a drop-down list or radio bullet list. Create at least three themes. Each theme should have at least three skin files. You also are required to use master and content pages to organize the Web site content. You will need to modify the theme dynamically in the page code. You may format each page using additional graphics, content, fonts, and color to enhance the appearance of the page. Save the files in the ch4_case2 folder. View your Web page in your browser. Print your Web page and the source code from the browser.

CASE
PROJECTS

## Project 4-3

Your store manager has requested that you make several product category pages. However, you don't have the budget to create custom pages and to maintain individual pages. Create a Web page for each product category. Create three User controls for the header, menu, and contents. In the header control, add a banner graphic. Create a menu in the Menu control. The menu should list at least five product categories. Each category listing should contain a hyperlink to the category Home page. Within each page, register the three controls, and insert them into the page. You may format each page using additional graphics, content, fonts, and color to enhance the appearance of the page. Save the files in the ch4_case3 folder. View each Web page in your browser. Print each Web page and the source code from the browser.

CASE
PROJECTS

## Project 4-4

Your store manager has requested that you allow the end user to modify the appearance and layout of your Web site. Using a Web site that you have previously created, or a new site, you must insert at least two WebPartZone controls. Then, allow the user to modify the appearance and layout of the page using the zone controls. You may format each page using additional graphics, content, fonts, and color to enhance the appearance of the page. Save the files in the ch4_case4 folder. View each Web page in your browser. Print each Web page and the source code from the browser.

HANDS-ON
PROJECTS

## Project 4-5

You are required to complete your Web site by tomorrow. One of the features that you have yet to implement is a content management system. Using a Web site that you have previously created, or a new site, create a page that allows the end user to insert content into a Web page to demonstrate that you can collect the information from the user. Allow the user to modify the heading title, meta tags for description, keyword, and author. The Web page should contain the author information as well as the date the file was created. The body of the page should be created using a third-party control such as FreeTextBox. You will need to download the control, insert the assembly into the bin directory, configure the Web configuration file, and download and install additional configuration files and resources. It is important to read the documentation that comes with the third-party control. For this activity, you need to gather the information required above and display it in a Web page. You may format each page using additional graphics, content, fonts, and color to enhance the appearance of the page. Save the files in the ch4_case5 folder. View each Web page in your browser. Print each Web page and the source code from the browser.

CHAPTER

# 5

# ADVANCED WEB CONTROLS

> **In this chapter, you will:**
>
> ♦ Create a rotating banner advertisement using the AdRotator control
> ♦ Create an interactive calendar using the Calendar control
> ♦ Create Web pages that allow you to upload a file to the Web server
> ♦ Send e-mail from the Web application
> ♦ Store and retrieve data from the Web server's file system

**T**oday businesses need to be able to enhance the appearance of their Web pages, as well as to manage the data within the Web site. In this chapter, you will learn about the Web controls that will enhance your Web pages, not only in appearance, but also by providing the user with more information and interactivity. You will use the Web controls to create XML-based rotating banner ads and display an interactive calendar. You will also learn to upload files from a Web page. In this chapter, you will learn how to use these controls, and other advanced Web controls, to enhance the interactivity within your Web site.

# THE ADROTATOR CONTROL

The **AdRotator control** allows you to display a banner ad on a Web page. When you refresh the page, the banner ad is changed to another image. The AdRotator control is created from the `System.Web.UI.WebControl.AdRotator` namespace.

The **advertisement file** is an XML document that stores the ad information. This file is also known as the rotation file because it includes the information about the rotating ads. You will see each ad for the proportion of time that you indicate in the advertisement file. The **banner ad** is a hyperlinked image. You need to obtain your graphics and import them into your Web application. You can create your own image using a graphics software package, such as PhotoShop or Paint Shop Pro, or use an existing graphic. You don't have to use the dimensions in a traditional banner ad. You can use any type of rectangular graphic.

You can find several books on Web graphics and Photoshop at *www.course.com*.

**NOTE**

## The Role of the Advertisement File

The information used to create the banner ad is stored in an external file called the advertisement file. The advertisement file is an example of an XML document. The advertisement file contains information that creates the HTML image tag, which inserts the image in the Web page. The file also contains information that creates the hyperlink using an anchor tag. When you click the banner ad, you are redirected to the URL defined within the hyperlink. The image source and the URL for the hyperlink are defined within the advertisement file. Each time the page is displayed, the AdRotator class retrieves a different image and hyperlink from the advertisement file.

The XML document can be edited with a basic text editor such as Notepad or an XML editor. Visual Studio .NET contains an editor that can create and edit XML documents such as the advertisement file. Because the advertisement file is an XML document, the file name has the file extension .xml.

The first line of the advertisement file indicates the version of the XML document. The following is the syntax for defining the XML version that is used in the XML document. It follows the same format as all XML documents.

```
<?xml version="1.0" encoding="utf-8" ?>
```

The rest of the file is contained within a root node named **Advertisements**. In an XML document, all tags must be nested within the root node. The root tag in an XML document is also known as the **root node**. Contained within the Advertisements node are one or more Ad elements. The **Ad element** contains the individual properties for the ad.

Each ad contains several properties that are used to create the image and hyperlink tags within the Web page. The **ImageUrl element** identifies the absolute or relative location of the image. Only images in the JPEG, GIF, or PNG formats currently are supported on most browsers. The ImageUrl is used to create the SRC property in the image tag. The ImageUrl is the only required property for the AdRotator control. The **NavigateUrl element** identifies the URL to which the browser will be directed when the user clicks on the image. The NavigateUrl is used to create the href property in the hyperlink. The NavigateUrl page is also known as the target page, or the destination page. The **AlternateText element** identifies the text that is displayed when the user places the mouse icon over the image. AlternateText is used to create the ALT property of the image tag. If the user's browser does not support images, the text is displayed instead of the image. The advertisement file has several new properties available. For instance, the **Height property** and **Width property** allow you to define the ad dimensions separately from the AdRotator control.

**TIP**   The advertisement file is an XML file. Therefore, the elements and properties within the file are case sensitive. You can also edit the file in Data view if you are working with Visual Studio .NET.

Remember that the NavigateUrl corresponds to the href property in the hyperlink created by the anchor (`<a>`) control. You may want to redirect the user to a Web site outside of your Web site, or to another page within your Web site. You can also pass additional information with the hyperlink in a hard-coded query string. For example, you could use the value `getproduct.aspx?id=529.jpg`. The query string is separated by the URL with a question mark. When the user clicks on the image, the hyperlink takes them to the getproduct.aspx page and passes the query string to the next page. The next page can retrieve the name and value pairs in the query string using the Page.Request.Querystring collection.

## Properties with No Corresponding HTML Function

There are two properties that do not have a corresponding HTML function. The **Impressions element** is used to indicate the frequency with which the banner ad is displayed. The advertisement file may contain data for thousands of banner ads. You can indicate how often you would like each banner ad to be displayed. Then, when the banner ad is created, the AdRotator class selects a banner ad from the XML file based upon the Impressions property. The Impressions property identifies the relative frequency with which the ad should be displayed. If there are three banner ads defined in the file, and the first banner ad Impressions property is 20, and the other banner ads' Impressions properties are 35 and 45, then the total number of impressions would be 100. The first banner ad would appear in the Web page 20 times out of 100 page views. The total number of impressions is the total number of times the banner ad is displayed. The higher the number of impressions in relation to the total number of impressions, the more often the banner ad will be displayed. (*Note*: The total of all of the ad impressions does not have to add up to 100. This is a relative weight value, not a percentage.) This property is important because you can configure the number of times that a banner ad should be displayed. You can refer to your log files to determine the exact number of times that the ad was displayed.

The **Keyword element** is used in the advertisement file to indicate one or more words that categorize the banner ad. The AdRotator class uses the keyword to group the banner ads. For example, a newspaper Web site may contain one area that is for adults and another area for children. The adult Web site can display all of the banner ads. Not all of the banner ads may be appropriate for children, however. The newspaper can configure the AdRotator control using the KeywordFilter property. In the children's area on the Web site, the banner AdRotator would screen the banner ads in the XML file for those where the Keyword property matched the KeywordFilter property defined in the AdRotator control. Children would only be able to see age-appropriate content. Thus, one advertisement file can be used to create the banner ads in multiple pages. If you want a banner ad to belong to multiple categories, you can create an additional entry with the other keywords.

Figure 5-1 displays a sample of the code used to display two banner ads. The Keyword element is used to separate the ads into books and software.

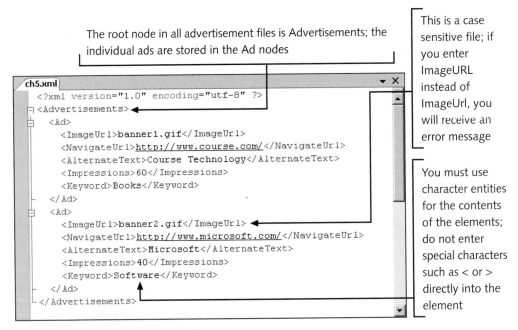

**Figure 5-1** The advertisement file

## Modifying the Advertisement File

In the following example, you will use the XML editor to add a new banner ad to the advertisement file.

1. Open the **chapter5** project in Visual Web Developer Express.

2. Double-click the **ch5_ads/ch5_ads.xml** file in the Solution Explorer window. Notice that you can edit the XML code manually. Under the opening Advertisements tag, add the code in Figure 5-2 to create a new banner ad element.

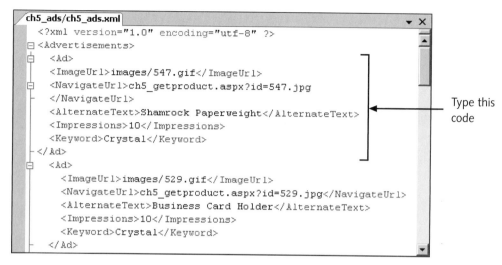

Figure 5-2 Inserting a new banner ad element

3. Click the **Save All** button. Close the ch5_ads.xml file.

## Useful New Elements

Today, many companies want to track the number of times that an ad is displayed, which is called **impressions**, and when the user clicks on the ad, which is referred to as the **clickthrough**. You can use some of the new properties built into the AdRotator control to track the visitor clicks. The **CountClicks**, **CountViews**, and **TrackNavigationUrl** **properties** are Boolean values that can be tracked with the SiteCounters table or Site-Counters API.

AdRotators traditionally have been banner ads. Recently companies use them to create **pop-up ads**, which are ads that appear in a separate window. (*Note*: some browsers and third-party software products do allow the user to block the pop-up ad.) To configure the banner to be a pop-up ad, you need to set the **AdType property** to Banner, PopUp, or PopUnder. If you set AdType to PopUp, then you can set the **PopPositionTop property** and the **PopPositionLeft property** to the number of pixels from the top and left of the window. If no value is set, the position will center in the screen. The **PopFrequency property**, which contains the value 100 by default, is the percentage of times that the PopUp would be displayed.

You can customize the advertisement file by adding custom elements defined within the Ad node. This might be used to pass information such as the product, caption for the image, product identification numbers, or price. You can pass this information from the custom elements in the query string to the next page instead of building the query string in the NavigateUrl property. Then, when the ad is created, the **AdCreated event** occurs, and these elements are passed in the **AdCreateEventArgs arguments** as the **AdProperties value**. Note the modifications to the file, as shown in Figure 5-3.

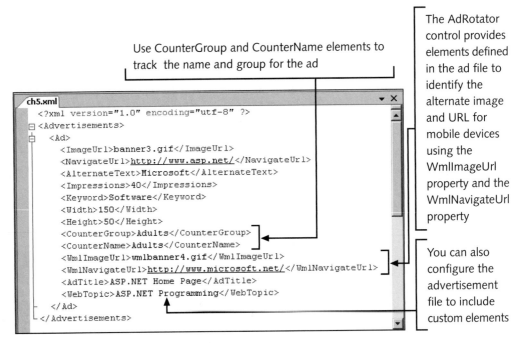

The AdRotator control provides elements defined in the ad file to identify the alternate image and URL for mobile devices using the WmlImageUrl property and the WmlNavigateUrl property

You can also configure the advertisement file to include custom elements

Use CounterGroup and CounterName elements to track the name and group for the ad

```
ch5.xml                                                              ▼ ✕
  <?xml version="1.0" encoding="utf-8" ?>
⊟ <Advertisements>
⊟    <Ad>
         <ImageUrl>banner3.gif</ImageUrl>
         <NavigateUrl>http://www.asp.net/</NavigateUrl>
         <AlternateText>Microsoft</AlternateText>
         <Impressions>40</Impressions>
         <Keyword>Software</Keyword>
         <Width>150</Width>
         <Height>50</Height>
         <CounterGroup>Adults</CounterGroup>
         <CounterName>Adults</CounterName>
         <WmlImageUrl>wmlbanner4.gif</WmlImageUrl>
         <WmlNavigateUrl>http://www.microsoft.net/</WmlNavigateUrl>
         <AdTitle>ASP.NET Home Page</AdTitle>
         <WebTopic>ASP.NET Programming</WebTopic>
      </Ad>
  </Advertisements>
```

**Figure 5-3**   Modifying the advertisement file

## Understanding the Properties of the AdRotator Control

By default the AdRotator looks for the XML file in the **AdvertisementFile property**. The **Height property** and **Width property** define the height and width of the image that will be displayed. If you want to display images that have different Height and Width properties, then you should not set the Height and Width property of the AdRotator control. If you use the AdRotator control from the Toolbox within Visual Studio .NET, however, note that the default Height and Width are 468px and 60px.

You can also use the **Style property** within Visual Studio .NET to configure the styles for the AdRotator control. Recall that the AdRotator control inherits the properties from the Web control class. Therefore, you can configure many of the basic Web control style properties that you learned in the previous chapter, such as BorderColor, BorderWidth, BorderStyle, Visible, TabIndex, and Absolute Positioning.

By default, when your end user clicks a hyperlink, the browser opens the new URL in the current window. You can force the browser to open the new URL in a different window or frame by using the **Target property**. The Target property is set to _top by default. When the target is set to _top, the URL is displayed in the current, unframed window. If the target is set to _blank, the URL is displayed in a new unframed window. If the hyperlink is within a frame, you can set the target to display the URL in the current frame, or in the parent frameset. The _self value displays the URL in the current frame, and the _parent value displays the URL in the parent frameset. The Target property also can place the URL in the Search window by changing the value to _search.

The **KeywordFilter property** retrieves only those banner ads from the XML document whose keyword matches exactly. Because the property can contain one or more words, the keyword value should be contained within quotation marks. The **ToolTip property** is used to provide more information about the banner ad. The ToolTip property stores a message as a string. The browsers display the message in the ToolTip when the user holds the mouse over the banner image.

### Integrating your AdRotator with a Database

You do not have to use an XML text file for your ad data storage. You can choose to set the DataSource, and assign an alternative data source such as a database. If you choose to use a database, you should also set the **DataMember property** and **DataSourceID property** when you work with a database. These properties are used to identify which data table to map to the AdRotator control. You simply create a database with the same names for the fields as the XML file. Then, set the DataSourceID property to the data source control that connects to the database.

## Inserting the AdRotator Control into a Web Page

To insert the banner ad in the Web page, you must insert the banner ad control, which is called **AdRotator control**. Recall that because this is a Web control, the control is identified with the prefix asp and a colon. In the AdRotator control, you must set the runat property to server to indicate that the control is a server control. Also, you must configure the AdvertisementFile property to point to the location of the advertisement file.

You can insert the AdRotator control manually by entering the code in the source view, or you can drag and drop the AdRotator control from the Toolbox on to the Web page in Design view. If you use the latter, you will need to configure the properties for the AdRotator control using the Properties window. The code following this paragraph is an example of how you manually insert an AdRotator control in a Web page.

```
<asp:AdRotator runat="server" id="AdRotator1"
AdvertisementFile="~/ch5_ads/ch5_ads.xml"
KeywordFilter="Crystal" />
```

**NOTE**   The ID property should be explicitly assigned to each Web control. If you do not assign an ID, the code behind the page still recognizes the object, and the Web server assigns an ID to the control. You cannot create programs to interact with the control, however.

## Creating the Web Page to Display the AdRotator

In Visual Studio .NET, you can insert the AdRotator control directly in the HTML code, or drag and drop the control from the Web Forms tab in the Toolbox. In the following exercise, you create a banner advertisement in a Web page using the AdRotator control from the Toolbox. This page will contain two banner ads. One of the ads will display only Waterford products, and one will display only Belleek products. You will accomplish your task by using the KeywordFilter property. Both ads will use the same advertisement file. When the user clicks the banner ad, he or she is redirected to a new page that retrieves the product ID and displays the large product image. In an actual application, this page would also display product information, such as price.

1. Double-click the **ch5_ads/ch5_adrotator.aspx** file to open the page in the main window.

2. In the Toolbox, click the **Standard** tab, if necessary, and then drag the **AdRotator** control to the page, placing it to the right of the AdRotator1 control. In the Properties window, change the KeywordFilter property to **Belleek**. Change the AdvertisementFile property to **ch5_ads.xml**. Delete the values listed for the Height and Width properties.

3. Click the **Save All** button.

4. Right-click the page, and then click **View in Browser**. Click **View** on the menu bar, and then click **Refresh** to reload the page. Note which image is displayed.

5. Repeat the previous step 10 times, noting each time which image is displayed for each AdRotator control. Figure 5-4 shows how the banner advertisement appears in the Web page.

6. Click either image created by the AdRotator2 control. The ch5_getproduct. aspx page should open, displaying a larger picture of the product.

7. Close all of the pages.

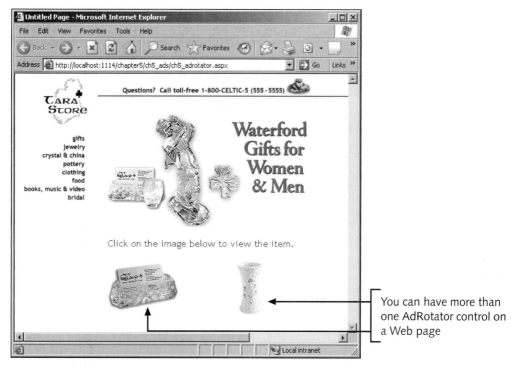

**Figure 5-4**    Inserting an AdRotator control into a Web page

## THE CALENDAR CONTROL

You can use the **Calendar control** to insert and configure an interactive calendar within the Web page. The Calendar control is useful for allowing a user to select dates for plane, hotel, and conference reservations. The Calendar control can also be used to display event data such as the location and time of the event. You may also want to use the Calendar control to help project managers to keep track of the project timelines.

The Calendar control is created by the calendar class. The calendar class is System.Web. UI.WebControls.Calendar. The calendar displays a single calendar month. By default, the current month of the Web server is the month that is displayed. You can configure the appearance of the calendar by setting the properties of the Calendar control.

In Visual Studio .NET, you can insert the Calendar control directly in the HTML code, or drag and drop the control from the Web Forms tab in the Toolbox. Because the control is an ASP.NET control, the name of the control includes the prefix asp followed by the word, calendar. The runat property must be assigned to server, and you should assign a value to the ID property. The code following this paragraph is the code to manually insert the Calendar control.

```
<asp:Calendar id="MyCal" runat="server" />
```

## Supported Properties, Methods, and Events

The Calendar control supports several style properties that you can configure when you insert the control. You also change these properties dynamically in the code behind the page. Most of the style properties can modify the background color; text color; font face, size, and style; alignment; width and height; wrapping; and border style. You can also assign a style using a class defined in the **CSSClass property**. Then, you configure the class from an external cascading style sheet.

The various Calendar control style properties that can be configured are as follows:

- **DayHeaderStyle:** Sets the style for the days of the week
- **DayStyle:** Sets the style for the individual dates
- **NextPrevStyle:** Sets the style for the navigation controls in the heading
- **OtherMonthDayStyle:** Sets the style for dates that are not in the current month
- **SelectedDayStyle:** Sets the style for the dates that are selected
- **SelectorStyle:** Sets the style for the month date selection column
- **TitleStyle:** Sets the style for the title in the heading
- **TodayDayStyle:** Sets the style for the current date
- **WeekendDayStyle:** Sets the style for weekend dates

Other properties that allow you to modify the Calendar control's appearance include the following:

- The **ShowDayHeader property** is used to show or hide the days of the week heading row.
- The **ShowGridLines property** is used to show or hide the gridlines that divide the days of the month.
- The **ShowNextPrev property** is used to show or hide the navigation controls. The navigation controls are used to navigate to the next or previous month.
- The **ShowTitle property** is used to show or hide the title in the heading.

Note that there are several methods and events exposed by the Calendar control. The Calendar control visually indicates to the user which date is selected. When the user clicks a new date, the SelectionChanged event occurs. This event changes the selected date to a new selected date. The value in the SelectedDate property then becomes the new selected date.

You can write different event handlers to intercept events and execute your own custom code. For instance, when the user clicks the next or previous month hyperlinks, the VisibleMonthChanged event occurs. If you create an event handler for the VisibleMonth-Changed event, you also pass the MonthChanged event handler object as a parameter to the event handler. The MonthChanged event handler object contains several properties. For example, when you click the next or previous month, the Calendar control displays the new month in the Web page. The NewDate property is the current date in that new month.

# Creating a Program to Interact with the Calendar Control

You can build code within the code behind that page to interact with Calendar controls. For instance, each date is displayed as a hyperlink. You can assign a default selected date using the SelectedDate property. When the user clicks a date, you can create an event handler to capture the selected date. You can retrieve the current date or a date that the user selects by clicking the hyperlink using the SelectedDate property. (*Note*: The Date data type is equivalent to the .NET Framework DateTime data type.) You can refer to each date selected by its position within the **SelectedDates object**. An example of how to retrieve the collection of selected dates is MyCalendar.SelectedDates(). You can also refer individually to each date in the collection of selected dates by using MyCalendar.SelectedDate(). You can use the **ToShortDateString property** of the SelectedDate to display the selected date using the short date format, as shown in the following code snippet. (*Note*: The short date format is *mm/dd/yyyy*)

```
Label1.Text = _
Calendar1.SelectedDate.ToShortDateString()
```

The following activity has two parts. In the first part, you will create a Calendar control and modify the properties of the Calendar control. In the second part, you will modify the code behind the page to interact with the Calendar control.

## Setting the Calendar Control Properties

In the following exercise, you will set the properties of the Calendar control.

1. Double-click the **ch5_calendar.aspx** file in the **ch5_calendar folder** to open the page in the main code window. Click the **Design** tab. Click the **Calendar** control to select it.

2. In the Properties window, click the **plus sign** in front of DayHeaderStyle to expand the properties. Change the BackColor property to **#E0E0E0**. This turns the background color a light shade of gray. Click the **ForeColor** property drop-down list arrow, click the **Web** tab, and then click **Firebrick** to change the ForeColor property to **Firebrick**. Click the **plus sign** next to the Font property to expand the Font properties. Change the Name property to **Verdana**. Change the Size property to **Medium**. Click the **minus sign** in front of DayHeaderStyle to collapse the properties.

3. Click the **plus sign** in front of DayStyle, and then click the **ForeColor** property drop-down list arrow. Click the **Web** tab, and then click **Maroon**, which changes the ForeColor property to Maroon. Change the HorizontalAlign property to **Center**. Click the **plus sign** in front of the Font property to expand the Font properties. Change the Name property to **Verdana**. Change the Size property to **Small**. Click the **minus sign** in front of DayStyle to collapse the properties.

4. Click the **plus sign** in front of NextPrevStyle, and then click the **plus sign** in front of Font. Change the Font Name property to **Trebuchet MS**. Click the

**ForeColor** property drop-down list arrow, click the **Web** tab, and then click **Firebrick** to change the ForeColor property to **FireBrick**. Click the **minus sign** in front of NextPrevStyle to collapse the properties.

5. Click the **plus sign** in front of TitleStyle, and then click the **plus sign** in front of Font. Change the Font Name property to **Comic Sans MS** and the Font Size property to **X-Large**. Change the BackColor property to **#FFE0C0**. Change the ForeColor property to **Firebrick**. Click the **minus sign** in front of TitleStyle to collapse the properties.

6. Click the **Save All** button.

## Creating a Page to Interact with the Calendar Control

In the exercise that follows, you will add the code behind the page to the calendar.aspx page. You will create an event handler to detect when the user clicks a new date, and display a message in the Web page indicating the value of the new date. You will use an If-Then control structure to determine if the date selected is the current date. If the date selected is the current date, you will display a different message in the Label control.

1. Double-click the **Calendar** control. This opens the code behind the page and places the cursor in the Calendar1_SelectionChanged procedure.

2. Type the code as shown in Figure 5-5. This code executes when the user clicks a new date. The code changes the Text property of a Label control named Label1. The message displayed includes a string message.

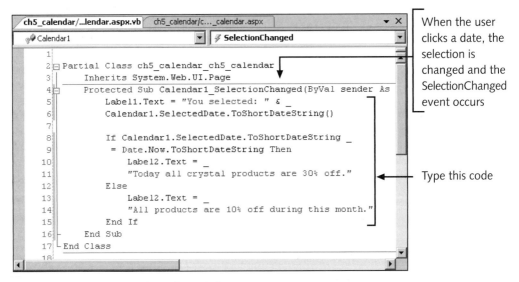

**Figure 5-5**   Retrieving the selected date

3. Click the **Save All** button.

4. Click the **calendar.aspx** tab, and then click the **Design** tab to return to Design view. Right-click the page, and then click **View in Browser**. Click the link for next Monday.

5. Click the link for today. The message should appear as shown in Figure 5-6.

6. Close all of the pages.

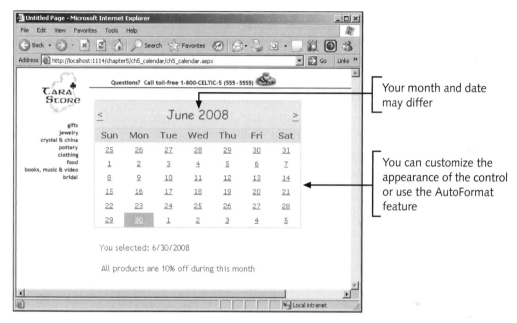

**Figure 5-6**    Interacting with a Calendar control

## Working with Multiple Dates

When the visitor clicks multiple dates, such as when he or she selects the entire week, you can retrieve the values selected with the **SelectedDates property**. The SelectedDates property contains a collection of dates. The **Count property** provides the number of dates that were selected. (You will use a **For-Next loop** to iterate through each date that was selected.) You can refer to each date selected by its position within the SelectedDates property. An example of how to refer to each date selected is `MyCalendar.SelectedDates(i)`. The position within the object is often called the **index position**. The first index position in all arrays and collections in Visual Basic .NET is 0. The value of the last index position in the SelectedDates property is equal to the value of Count property minus 1. You can use a **loop counter** to keep track of how many times the looping structure repeats.

Once you finish retrieving the SelectedDates property, you can loop through the list of dates by looping through the SelectedDates collection. The loop counter is declared as an integer outside of the loop. The counter is initialized at a beginning value such as 0. Because the loop counter started with the number 0, the loop should repeat until the counter reaches the value of the Count property minus 1. If there are three dates selected, the Count property equals 3. Because the first element in the array is at index position 0, the loop counter begins at 0. The loop displays the first date. During the second loop, the loop counter is 1, and the second date is displayed. During the third loop, the loop counter is 2, and the third date is displayed. During each loop, the loop counter is also used to retrieve the ToShortDateString property of the SelectedDate. The loop ends when the loop counter reaches the value of the Count property minus 1. You need to include the minus 1 so that the loop will continue to run the code for the last iteration.

The sample code in Figure 5-7 shows you how you can iterate through the list of selected dates. This code should be placed within the SelectionChanged event procedure for the Calendar control. The dates selected are displayed in a Label control.

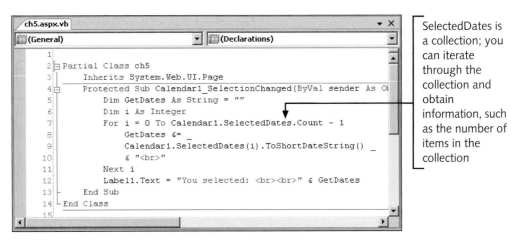

SelectedDates is a collection; you can iterate through the collection and obtain information, such as the number of items in the collection

```
ch5.aspx.vb
(General)                                    (Declarations)
1
2  Partial Class ch5
3      Inherits System.Web.UI.Page
4      Protected Sub Calendar1_SelectionChanged(ByVal sender As O
5          Dim GetDates As String = ""
6          Dim i As Integer
7          For i = 0 To Calendar1.SelectedDates.Count - 1
8              GetDates &= _
9              Calendar1.SelectedDates(i).ToShortDateString() _
10             & "<br>"
11         Next i
12         Label1.Text = "You selected: <br><br>" & GetDates
13     End Sub
14  End Class
15
```

**Figure 5-7**   Retrieving multiple dates

## USING THE FILEUPLOAD CONTROL

The **FileUpload control** allows you to upload a file to a Web server. There are many uses for a FileUpload control, such as the following:

- In an online store, the store manager is often required to complete an online form when adding a product to the store database. You can use a FileUpload control to allow the manager to upload a graphic image of the product.

- Community and volunteer organizations often have several people who submit materials such as monthly newsletters and event flyers to be placed on the Web site. By using a FileUpload control, the members can upload the documents to the Web site without having to learn how to use a Web editing tool or a file transfer program.

- Businesses often share documents with other businesses. These documents can be delivered through e-mail as attachments. Some types of files such as graphics are very large, however. If the document is delivered to a large number of employees or a mailing list, the mail server could have difficulty storing the files and could crash. Because of this, businesses have limited the size of the files that can be sent through e-mail attachments to their company mailing lists. In order to make these documents accessible, you can use the FileUpload control to upload the file to the Web server. Then, you can create a Web page that will provide employees with the ability to view or to download the document.

In versions of HTML before ASP.NET originated, you had to use the HTML server control known as the **File Input control** (now referred to as the HtmlInputFile control) to browse your network and locate a file for uploading. The File Input control consisted of a browse button that allowed you to search your network and locate both the file and the text box that stored the URL of the file. The form tag required you to set the **Enctype attribute** to multipart/form-data to indicate to the Web server that there is a file attached to the URL request. While this control allowed you to select and store the URL of the file, it did not allow you to upload the file to the Web server. To actually upload the file, you had to use a file upload component to handle the file upload. For instance, you had to use third-party file upload components such as SA-FileUp by Software Artisans (*www.softwareartisans.com*) or Posting Acceptor from Microsoft. Both of the file upload components had to be installed on the Web server.

Fortunately, the file upload capability is now completely built into the ASP.NET runtime and available to all ASP.NET applications without third-party file upload components. You can now use the FileUpload control to upload files such as Web pages, PDF documents created with Adobe Acrobat, word processing documents, spreadsheets, and databases.

The key to building an upload feature into your Web site is the FileUpload control, which is a Web control. The FileUpload control class is the `System.Web.UI.WebControls.FileUpload`. Thus, you cannot only browse your file system and select a file, but also upload the file to the Web server.

**NOTE**
When you modify the Web page to allow uploading a file, you do not need to modify the attributes of the Form tag. ASP.NET will convert the FileUpload control into the appropriate HTML code on the client.

In the following sections, you will modify a Web page so that it will allow an end user to upload a file to your Web application.

## Uploading a File with the FileUpload Control

The FileUpload control, created with the `<asp:FileUpload />` tag, allows the user to browse through their file system and locate their file. You always should verify the user's credentials before allowing them to upload the file. You can allow the file to keep the same file name or you can allow the user to change the file name. For example, you can allow them to select a new file name from a drop-down list or allow them to enter the name in an input TextBox control.

The FileUpload control contains several properties that you may access before you upload the file:

- The **HasFile property** specifies if the FileUpload control contains a file. You always should verify that a file has been selected.
- The **FileName property** retrieves the complete file name on the client's computer.
- The **FileBytes property** identifies actual bytes in the file stored as an array.
- The **FileContent property** is a stream output of the file contents.

### Uploading the File with the HttpPostedFile Class

To save the file on the Web server, you must call the **PostedFile.SaveAs method** from the HttpPostedFile class and pass the path to the file on the client's computer. **HttpPostedFile class** provides a **PostedFile object**, which handles the file and allows you to upload the file, manipulate the file, and retrieve information about the file. For example, as shown in Figure 5-8, you can obtain information about the file size and type. This is useful to provide information to the user that their file was uploaded successfully.

**TIP** You must determine where you want to store your images. If you store them in the server's file system, it is more difficult to manage the files. If you store the images within the database, the images are stored in a central location, and are therefore easier to maintain. When you store images in a database, however, they are stored as BLOB objects (Binary Large Objects). Not all databases support BLOBs. When you store binary files in a database, the physical size of the database may become very large, requiring more hard drive space and memory on the database server.

## Creating the File Upload Page

You may want to enable only authenticated users to upload a file. In the following exercise, you will create a login form. After the user is authenticated, you will show the File Upload control on the user's screen. Then, you will allow the user to upload the file to the Web server.

1. Expand the **ch5_upload** folder, right-click **ch5_upload.aspx** in the Solution Explorer window, and then click **View Code**. Type the code to retrieve the value from the FileUpload control and upload the file, as shown in Figure 5-9.

2. Click the **Save All** button.

3. Right-click the **ch5_upload.aspx** in the Solution Explorer window, and then click **View in Browser**.

The Server control contains a MapPath method to map the path to a file; you can also hardcode the path directory

You can retrieve the file name using Path.GetFileName(FilePath)

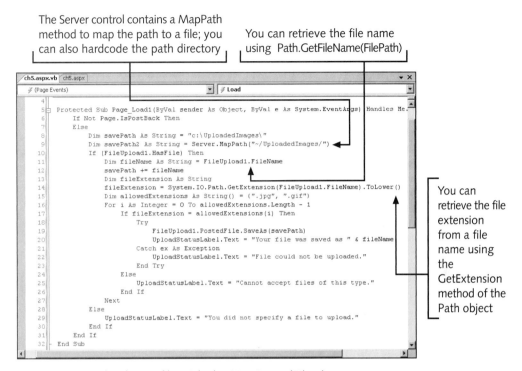

You can retrieve the file extension from a file name using the GetExtension method of the Path object

**Figure 5-8**   Uploading a file with the HttpPostedFile class

Many methods exist to retrieve and construct a file path

Type this code

Unless you know your server URL will not change, you should use relative URLs

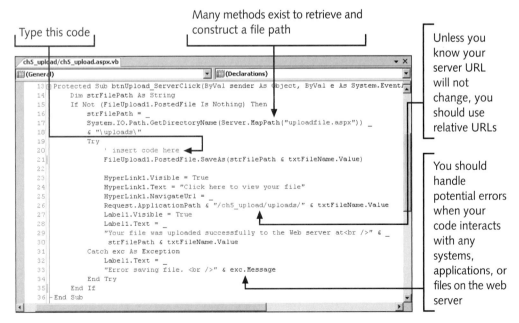

You should handle potential errors when your code interacts with any systems, applications, or files on the web server

**Figure 5-9**   Uploading a file with the HttpPostedFile class

4. Click the **Browse** button to locate a file in your chapter5\images folder named, uploadimage.gif. Click the **Open** button. The file name and path appear in the text box. Enter **uploadimage.gif** in the File Name text box. Click the **Upload the Image** button.

5. Read the message that is displayed; it indicates that the image was not uploaded. The message says "Error saving file. Access to the path 'c:\inetpub\wwwroot\ chapter5\ch5_upload\uploads\uploadimage.gif' is denied". This means that you do not have permission set to upload a file. In the next exercise, you will learn to set the security permissions to upload a file. (*Note*: If you have already set your permissions correctly, you will not see an error message.)

6. Close any open pages.

# Changing Security Permissions to the Upload Folder

Security is a complex topic because there are two types of security that can be implemented with Web applications. The first type is page level security, which affects only a single page. The second is application level security, which applies to an entire Web application, such as the chapter5 project. You can layer page security and application level security by programming login methods within the application. In large companies, you may be the Web server administrator and have to work with a network administrator who may not agree to modify the security permissions for the server.

You need to perform two distinct sets of steps to allow the ASP.NET Machine user account to upload files from a browser. The following sections will discuss each in turn.

## Display Security Permissions in Windows Explorer

First, you will need to make sure your files support displaying the NTFS information in the Windows Explorer application. To do this, complete the following steps:

1. Click the **Start** menu, and then click **Run**.

2. Type **%SystemRoot%\explorer.exe** in the Open text box, and then click **OK**. (The variable %SystemRoot% is the location of your windows files. For most users, this is C:\windows, so you would enter C:\windows\explorer.exe.)

3. The Windows Explorer application opens. Click the **Tools** menu, and then click **Folder Options**. Click the **View** tab.

4. Scroll down to and, if necessary, uncheck the **Use simple file sharing (Recommended)** check box.

5. Click the **OK** button.

## Set Permissions for the ASP.NET User Account

You can set security at the Web server using the Internet Information Server administration tools. You can also set the security level within Windows using NTFS. NTFS is the Windows

NT file system that allows you to assign permissions to individual files and folders based on the user account. The default user account for the Web browser is the **anonymous user**, which is **IUSR_MACHINENAME**. If your machine was named KALATA, then your anonymous user account is IUSR_KALATA. You do not need to change permissions for this account with ASP.NET. You do need, however, to modify permissions to allow the ASP.NET Machine user account to access the files and folders. The **ASP.NET Machine** user account is the account that ASP.NET Web applications use to communicate with the operating system.

By default, the user cannot upload pages because the user does not have NTFS permissions to write to the uploads directory. The following steps will allow you to set the permissions for the ASP.NET Machine user account.

1. Open **Windows Explorer**, if necessary. Navigate through Windows Explorer in the folders pane until you find the Uploads directory. (*Note*: By default, it is located at C:\Inetpub\wwwroot\chapter5\Ch5_upload\Uploads.)

2. Right-click the **Uploads** folder and then select **Properties**.

3. Click the **Security** tab. This tab allows you to add Windows user accounts and set the NTFS permissions for each user. A message may appear that says the following: "The permissions on Uploads are ordered incorrectly, which may cause some entries to be ineffective. Press OK to continue and sort the permissions correctly, or Cancel to reset the permissions." Click **OK**. (*Note*: If you click Cancel, the permissions will be reset to allow the Everyone account to have full access to the folder, which is a security risk.)

4. Click the **Add** button. In the lower text box, enter the full name for the ASP.NET Machine user account called MACHINENAME\ASPNET. The full name consists of the name of your machine and "\ASPNET". For instance, if the name of the machine were KALATA, then the full name would be KALATA\ASPNET.

5. After you enter the full name for the ASP.NET Machine user account, click the **OK** button.

6. In the Properties window, verify that the ASP.NET Machine user account is selected. If not, select it in the top list box.

7. Then, click the Allow check boxes labeled **Modify**, **Read & Execute**, **List Folder Contents**, **Read**, and **Write** in the Permissions panel.

8. Click the **OK** button and close Windows Explorer.

9. View the **ch5_upload.aspx** page in the browser. Upload the uploadimage.gif file again as instructed in the previous exercise. A new message will appear stating that the file has been uploaded successfully as shown in Figure 5-10. Click the hyperlink to view the image in the browser. Close the browser window. (*Note*: If you receive an error message, you should contact your system administrator or Web administrator to request the NTFS permissions to be set for the Uploads folder.)

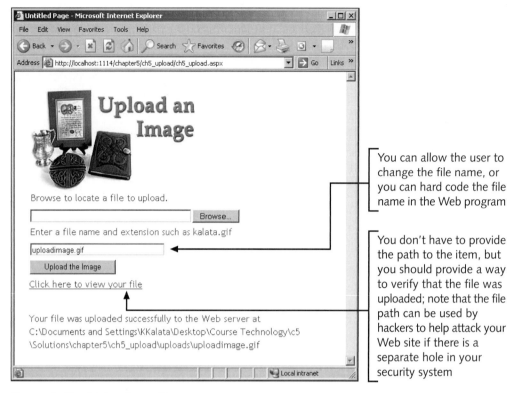

**Figure 5-10**   Uploading a file

**TIP**

You should always check with your system administrator or Web administrator for the company policy on uploading files before implementing the ability for users to upload files. If you include a login page, make sure to inform your users that login names and passwords on Web Forms are case sensitive.

## SENDING E-MAIL FROM THE WEB PAGE

Often you will want to generate a customized automated e-mail reply that uses form data. This automated reply may, for instance, send an order confirmation to a customer. To send outbound e-mail from a Web page, you must use an e-mail server, along with an e-mail object or application to communicate with the e-mail server. In the following sections, you will learn how to identify security issues related to sending e-mail messages, describe the role of the e-mail server, configure the e-mail server, describe the e-mail object, and finally send e-mail from your Web application. You will also learn how to troubleshoot problems that may occur when you send an e-mail message.

## Security and Privacy Issues Related to E-Mail

E-mailing is the process of sending messages through e-mail servers. These e-mail messages are primarily text-based, but may contain additional content such as HTML, images, and attached files. E-mail widely was used in universities prior to the World Wide Web, and has now become one of the primary functions of end users on the Internet.

With the use of e-mail in the business community, Web developers must take precautions to ensure that their systems do not participate in delivering viruses through e-mail. In addition, system administrators must use virus protection programs to ensure that files are not infected on their systems.

A major privacy issue related to e-mail is spam. **Spam** is unauthorized delivery of e-mail messages. The bulk of e-mail today on the Internet is spam. Because there is virtually no cost to deliver spam, it is commonly used as a marketing tool to attract customers. A vast amount of spam also consists of proliferation of pornographic and illicit material, such as advertisements of drugs. Some spam poses as legitimate e-mail and use hyperlinks to lure end users onto Web sites that download viruses and steal information such as passwords, bank account numbers, and credit card information.

## The Role of the E-Mail Server

Web developers must ensure that their Web applications do not allow unauthorized users to send e-mail through their Web application or e-mail server. The e-mail server, known as the SMTP server, is included when you install the IIS Web server. The **SMTP server** provides an easy way to transmit Internet e-mail messages. **Simple Mail Transfer Protocol (SMTP)** is a protocol, or set of rules, used to transfer mail between servers. The SMTP server contains several default folders, including Pickup, Queue, Badmail, Drop Route, Mailbox, and SortTemp. These folders are located by default in C:\Inetpub\MailRoot\. The Pickup folder is used to store outgoing mail messages. These messages are sent from the SMTP server to other servers. The default port for the SMTP server is 25. Mail messages can be placed in this directory by hand or by other software applications.

E-mail servers are not available with all operating systems.

In the following exercise, you will verify that the e-mail server on your computer is installed and running. The property pages and configuration settings for the SMTP server will vary between Windows XP and other operating systems.

1. To verify that the SMTP services are running, click **Start**, and then click **Control Panel**. If nessary, click **Classic View** in Windows XP to show the Administrative Tools icon. Double-click the **Administrative Tools** icon.

Double-click the **Services** icon. The Services window opens with the list of running and stopped services.

2. Scroll down the window until you locate the Simple Mail Transfer Protocol (SMTP) service in the Name column. The Status column should say that the Simple Mail Transfer Protocol (SMTP) has been Started. (*Note*: If it is stopped, you can right-click the Simple Mail Transfer Protocol (SMTP) name and click Start.)

3. Close the Services window by clicking the **Close** button and then close the Administrative Tools folder.

Pausing a server will gracefully stop the server without interrupting active connections. You will prevent only new client connections; the server will continue to process existing connections and deliver queued messages.

You can right-click the Simple Mail Transfer Protocol (SMTP) service to access the SMTP server properties. You can configure the service to start automatically when the server is booted by setting the startup type to Automatic. You can also identify what action you want to take if the service has failed. For example, you can run a file, restart the service, or reboot the computer. Your Webmaster or system administrator is usually the one responsible for configuring your e-mail server.

## Configuring the E-Mail Server

The Microsoft Management Console (MMC) is the main interface to the administrative programs such as IIS and SMTP. You can access the SMTP server and IIS through the same Microsoft Management Console (MMC). (*Note*: You can open an MMC with no snap-ins using C:\WINDOWS\system32\mmc.exe. You would have to add the IIS and SMTP snap-ins to the console.) In the following exercise, you will view the SMTP settings through the MMC.

1. To open the Microsoft Management Console (MMC), click **Start**, and then click **Control Panel**. Double-click the **Administrative Tools** folder, and then double-click **Internet Information Services**. The Internet Information Services window opens.

2. Click the **plus sign** next to the computer icon to expand the list of FTP sites, Web sites, and SMTP servers available. (*Note*: You can also double-click the name of the computer or the computer icon to expand the menu.)

3. Click the name of the server. (*Note*: IIS places the Web sites and FTP sites in folders.)

4. Right-click the **Default SMTP Virtual Server** icon, and then click **Properties** to open the Default SMTP Virtual Server Properties window. You can configure the server properties on these property pages. Notice that on the General tab, you can enable logging. By default, if logging is enabled, the SMTP log files are stored in the C:\WINDOWS\System32\LogFiles\ SmtpSvc1 directory.

5. Click the check box labeled **Enable logging**. The default format is W3C Extended Log File Format. Click **Properties**. Click the **Extended Properties** tab. The Extended Logging Properties window shows the same options are available for both the Web server and the e-mail server. The default log file monitors the Time (time), Client IP Address (c-ip), Method (cs-method), URI Stem (cs-uri-stem), and Protocol Status (sc-status). Click **Cancel** to close the window.

**TIP**  The Microsoft IIS Log File Format and the National Center for Supercomputer Applications (NCSA) Common Log File Format are used to store fixed log information in an ASCII format. ASCII is a basic text format that can be read by most computers.

**NOTE**  Server versions provide the ability to send IIS, FTP, and SMTP logging to an ODBC-compliant database. A SQL Server script located at C:\WINDOWS\ system32\inetsrv\logtemp.sql is provided to assist you in creating a compatible table named inetlog. This file contains a listing of the required fields and data types.

6. On the General tab, you can configure the number of connections and number of minutes per connection. To verify that the TCP port selected is 25, click **Advanced**. You can add additional IP addresses and modify the port settings here. Click **Cancel**. (*Note*: Services that do not explicitly assign an IP address use the default IP address and can be referred to as localhost. IP addresses are assigned to the network interface card. These addresses must be unique within the local network. If the server is connected to the Internet, the system administrator will configure the server to use a specific Internet address that is assigned to that organization.)

7. Click the **Access** tab. The Access property page allows you to configure which accounts will be allowed to send e-mail through the Default SMTP Virtual Server.

8. Click the **Authentication** button to view the Authentication property page. You can allow the Internet anonymous user account to send e-mail, or restrict access using Basic or Windows authentication.

9. Click **Cancel** to return to the Access tab.

10. Click the **Messages** tab. The Messages property page allows you to configure the size of the message and the session size. The session size is the total size of all of the message body sections within a single connection. The Messages property page allows you to configure the number of messages per connection and the number of recipients per connection. For example, if there are 150 recipients on an e-mail list, the first 100 would be delivered using one connection, and then a new connection would open and deliver the remaining 50 messages. When an e-mail message is not sent, the message is deposited in the Badmail directory, which is located by default at C:\Inetpub\mailroot\ Badmail. You can specify that a Non-Delivery report be e-mailed to you.

11. Click the **Delivery** tab. The Delivery property page allows you to configure how the message is delivered. For example, if the e-mail cannot be sent, you can specify the number of minutes to wait before attempting to e-mail the message again.

**TIP**

The retry interval is the number of minutes the server waits before issuing a failed delivery status message for outbound e-mail messages. Networks can experience delays due to increased traffic. You can use delay notification to configure the server to wait before sending the failure notification. You can use different values for local or remote messages. Local settings would apply to the internal network, such as when you are configuring an intranet application.

12. Click **Outbound Security**. You can configure a different user account to send mail messages. You can use the anonymous account, or authenticate the user with basic authentication or Windows authentication. You also can require the authentication process to use a standard encryption protocol called Transport Layer Security (TLS). TLS is a more secure version of SSL and will encrypt the communication during the authentication process. Click **Cancel**.

13. Click **Outbound connections**. You can limit the number of outbound messages, the time-out property, and the number of connections per domain. You also can change the port number for the mail server. The default port is 25. It is recommended not to use any of the well known port numbers. (*Note*: Refer to Chapter 9 for more information on port numbers.) Click **Cancel**.

14. Click **Advanced**. You can configure which servers can access the Default SMTP Virtual Server to send or relay e-mail messages. Some e-mail servers reject the message if the Mail From line contains an invalid domain address. You can set the Masquerade domain field to a valid fully qualified domain name (FQDN). This will replace the local domain name listed in the Mail From line.

Messages can be routed to a number of servers on the Internet before it reaches its final destination server. Hop count is the number of servers the message is permitted to pass through. You can set the hop count property. If the hop count is more than what is set in the mail server configuration, the message is returned.

You can assign a smart host, which is a fully qualified domain name of a virtual server, instead of sending all of the e-mail messages directly to a domain. This configuration is used to route messages over a connection that may be more direct or less costly than a different route. Click **Cancel**.

15. Click the **LDAP Routing** tab to view the LDAP Routing properties. LDAP stands for Lightweight Directory Access Protocol. LDAP is the primary access protocol for Active Directory. Active Directory is a directory service that stores information about objects on a network. Users can access resources anywhere on the network using a single logon process.

16. Click the last tab labeled **Security**. It allows you to configure who can access and change the SMTP settings. By default, only members of the administrators group can alter the SMTP settings. You should only allow trusted users to alter the SMTP settings. Click **Cancel**.

17. In the MMC, click the **plus sign** next to the envelope icon that represents the Default SMTP Virtual Server.

18. Click **Domains**. In the right window, your Web server is listed under the Domain Name column. The default domain is listed and cannot be deleted. The domain is used for messages that do not have a domain identified. You can delete any domain that you create, but you cannot delete the default domain. You may want to add more domains for Web sites that use multiple domain names for the same Web content. For example, e-mail sent to admin@tarastore.com and admin@tarastore.net would both be delivered to the same mail server. Current sessions allow you to terminate connections with the SMTP server. This may be used when a file that is being delivered is very large and causing problems on the server.

**TIP**

The default domain name is taken from the Domain Name Service (DNS) settings in the Advanced TCP/IP Properties window. To view your settings, go to Start, click Control Panel, and then double-click Network Connections. Right-click your network connection icon and select Properties. Click the General tab. In the list box, select Internet Protocol (TCP/IP) and click Properties. Click Advanced, and then click the DNS tab. The DNS suffixes listed are the domain names available. Domains are configured as local or remote. Examples of domains are course.com and tarastore.net. Check with your system administrator before adding domains to your mail server.

19. Right-click the domain name in the Domain Name column, and then click **Properties**.

20. Click **Cancel** to close the window.

21. Click the **Close** button to close the Internet Information Services window.

22. Close the Administrative Tools window.

**TIP**

The configuration of the e-mail server and network affects how you can send outbound e-mail from your ASP.NET pages. If you have a firewall, or special routing, you must modify your code. For example, in some networks, if your e-mail address is john@yourschool.edu, you might have to explicitly state the domain of the e-mail server. If the e-mail server's name is darkstar, the e-mail address is john@darkstar.yourschool.edu.

You can read more about the SMTP server in the Help files. To open the Help files, go to Start, click Run, type %systemroot%\help\mail.chm, and click OK.

**NOTE**

# CDONTS and E-Mail Objects

An e-mail software component is used in order for the Web page to communicate with the e-mail server. CDONTS is a component provided with the SMTP server to allow third-party applications, such as ASP.NET, to communicate with the SMTP server. The CDONTS component is a scaled-down version of a collection of objects known as **Collaborative Data Objects (CDO)**. CDO is typically used to integrate your applications with active messaging systems such Microsoft Outlook and Microsoft Exchange Services. CDONTS is a collection of objects, properties, and methods that connect the SMTP service with the Web application. CDONTS is located in a file named cdonts.dll, which is located in C:\WINDOWS\system32\, and is made available when you install the Microsoft SMTP server. CDONTS and the SMTP service are available with Windows Server and Windows XP Professional. It is not available with Windows Millennium or Windows XP Home.

You will use the e-mail objects to create and place your message in the Pickup folder. You can obtain the e-mail message information from a database or other data source. The Web application will use the e-mail object to create the e-mail message and copy it in the Pickup folder. The Web application accesses this mail object through the .NET Framework classes. The SMTP server moves the e-mail message from the Pickup folder into the **Queue folder**. If the message recipient is a local account, it places the e-mail message into the **Drop folder**. If the message recipient is on a remote server, it sends the e-mail out to another server. The receiving mail server may accept or reject the e-mail message. The e-mail message is commonly rejected because the user's mailbox is full or the user is not a valid user account. Firewalls, anti-spam software, and virus detection software may also reject an e-mail message. The rejected message is returned to the SMTP server. The SMTP server responds by placing the message in the **Badmail folder** and creating a **Non-Delivery report (NDR)**.

In the following sections, you will learn about .NET mail classes and related class properties. You will need this information because you will need to access these classes to configure your e-mail message before it can be delivered.

## Accessing the E-Mail Object with the .NET Mail Classes

You can access the e-mail object by using three built-in classes within the .NET Framework. The System.Web.Mail namespace provides access to the MailMessage, MailAttachment, and SmtpMail classes. The **MailMessage class** provides access to the properties and methods used to construct an e-mail message. The **MailAttachment class** is used to identify a file that is to be sent with the e-mail message. These attached files often are called **attachments**. The **SmtpMail class** is used to send the e-mail message that is specified in the MailMessage class.

Note the following classes and the properties and methods that they contain:

- **MailAttachment class:** Filename and Encoding properties
- **MailEncoding class:** UUEncode and Base64 properties
- **MailFormat class:** Text and HTML properties
- **MailMessage class:** To, From, Subject, Body, CC, and BCC properties
- **MailPriority class:** Normal, High, and Low properties
- **SmtpMail class:** Send method and SmtpServer property

Other properties that the MailMessage object created by the MailMessage class provides access to include BodyEncoding, BodyFormat, Fields, Headers, Priority, UrlContentBase, and UrlContentLocation. These properties can be set indirectly within the MailMessage object or directly by using the objects that contain the properties.

**TIP**

To actually send e-mail, the Web server must be allowed to send outbound messages from the server, through the internal network, to the Internet. You should contact your system administrator to ensure that the routing permissions have been set up properly for your e-mail server. Some networks have policies against outbound e-mail messages due to the high prevalence of spam. You should provide your system administrator with your policy of how you will ensure that spam will not originate on your server.

## The MailMessage Class Properties for Preparing an E-Mail Message

The MailMessage class allows you to send the body of your message using different formats, such as basic text and HTML. The format of the e-mail message in the MailMessage class can be specified with the **MailFormat enumeration**. The possible enumerated values for e-mail format are as follows:

- The **MailFormat.Text enumeration** means that the format of the MailMessage is plain text. You should use Text when it is important that all e-mail applications be able to read the message. Some e-mail programs do not interpret HTML codes, and so these codes would be visible to the recipient.

- The **MailFormat.Html enumeration** sends the output as HTML. E-mail programs that support the HTML format interpret the HTML commands in the same way that a browser interprets the HTML commands.

The priority of the e-mail message in the MailMessage class is configured with the **MailPriority enumeration**. You can use the MailPriority enumeration to indicate to the e-mail application the importance of the message. Some e-mail applications provide indicators, such as an exclamation point, to indicate that a message has been given a certain priority level. The MailPriority property does affect how quickly a message is sent. The three MailPriority property levels that you can set with the MailMessage class are **MailMessage.Normal**, **MailMessage.High**, and **MailMessage.Low**. The MailPriority is set to Normal by default.

The MailAttachment class provides properties and methods to construct an e-mail attachment. You need to specify the location of the attachment and the encoding format of the attachment. The location of the attachment is specified with the Filename property of the MailAttachment class. The **Filename property** is assigned a string value, which specifies the drive, path, and file name of the attachment. (*Note*: You can use the FileField text box to locate the file name of a local file within an ASP.NET page.) The encoding of the attachment is specified with the **MailEncoding enumerator**. **MailEncoding.UUEncode** is the default encoding format. Some files, such as graphics, must be encoded as binary before they are sent. You can specify binary encoding with the **MailEncoding.Base64 enumeration**.

## The MailMessage Class Properties for Sending an E-Mail Message

The MailMessage class consists of several properties that must be set before the message can be sent. These properties include the recipient, the sender, the subject, and the message body. The **MailMessage.To property** gets or sets the e-mail address of the recipient of the e-mail message. So, you can specify multiple recipients using the To property by separating each e-mail address with a semicolon.

The **MailMessage.From property** gets or sets the e-mail address of the sender of the message. The From property is used to identify the sender. Although it is possible to send anonymous e-mail by omitting the From property entirely, it is not recommended. You should specify a complete e-mail address for the sender. Some e-mail programs do not accept e-mail when the sender's address is not valid. It is useful to change the From property according to the message. For example, if the e-mail is being sent to customers, you might set the From property to "help@mydomain.com". That way, your customer can identify who is sending the e-mail. You cannot specify more than one address using the From property.

You must take precautions when sending e-mail from a Web application. A network administrator is usually the person who is responsible for the network security and for setting up the network servers. Because you can configure the To, From, Subject, Message, and attachments programmatically, it is important to configure your Web server so that it does not support e-mailing visitors without their permission. For example, you should not allow the end user to manually enter the e-mail address of the recipient. It is also important to configure your Web server and SMTP server to disable hackers from sending e-mail from your server. For example, you can configure the mail server not to relay messages from other servers.

The following are some of the required properties that you will configure with e-mail messages:

- The **MailMessage.Subject property** gets or sets the subject line of the e-mail message. You should not leave the subject blank. It is important to pick a meaningful phrase for the Subject property. Because many viruses are sent via e-mail, recipients often delete e-mail from unknown e-mail addresses, or with suspicious subject phrases like "Click here to win a car."

- The **MailMessage.Body property** gets or sets the body of the e-mail message. You can create a variable to hold the entire message, or retrieve the value from a form field. Then, you can assign the contents of the variable or form field to the Body property.

The default encoding, format, and priority level are chosen from the default values of the MailEncoding, MailPriority, and MailFormat enumerations, unless you configure them using the MailMessage class. The MailMessage class also contains properties that you can use to configure the individual e-mail message with the **MailMessage.BodyEncoding**, **MailMessage.BodyFormat**, and **MailMessage.Priority properties**. (*Note*: Each of these properties uses the same values as their counterpart enumerations.)

## The Optional MailMessage Class Properties

There are several optional e-mail properties. The **MailMessage.Attachments property** is a list of attachments that is transmitted with the message that is identified with the MailAttachment class. The **Carbon Copy (MailMessage.Cc) property** gets or sets a semicolon-delimited list of e-mail addresses that receive a carbon copy of the e-mail message. You can separate multiple recipient addressees with semicolons (;).

The **Blind Carbon Copy (MailMessage.Bcc) property** sets a semicolon-delimited list of e-mail addresses that receive a blind carbon copy of the e-mail message. Blind carbon copies are used when you do not want the recipients to know that other individuals have been sent the same message. For example, you could send your customer an e-mail message, and send a blind carbon copy to your manager. The customer would not know that you sent a copy to your manager, and your manager's e-mail address would not be visible to the customer.

You can use the UrlContentBase and UrlContentLocation properties to insert content from another URL into the e-mail message. The **MailMessage.UrlContentBase property** gets or sets the URL base of all relative URLs used within the HTML-encoded body. The **MailMessage.UrlContentLocation property** is used to identify the location of content within the e-mail message. You can use the MailMessage.Headers property of the Mail-Message class to specify custom headers that are sent with the e-mail message. Using the MailMessage.Headers property, you can add additional headers, such as a Reply-To header.

The SmtpMail class provides properties and methods to send an e-mail and attachments using the SMTP e-mail service built into Microsoft Windows operating systems. After the MailMessage class has been configured, you can call the Send method of the SmtpMail class to send the message. The Send method of the MailMessage object creates the message in the required format and writes it to the Queue folder; eventually the message is moved to the Pickup folder. Therefore, all e-mail is, by default, queued, ensuring that the calling program does not block network traffic. The SMTP server then delivers the message. (*Note*: After the message has been sent you should set the object to the keyword, Nothing, to release the object from memory.)

By default, the e-mail is sent using the default local SMTP server. However, you can change the SMTP server used to send the message with the **SmtpServer property** of the SmtpMail class. You can locate the name of the SmtpServer in the property pages of the Default SMTP Virtual Server within the Internet Services Manager console.

You can also configure the MailMessage properties directly when you send the message with the SmtpMail class. You can pass the properties as parameters of the send method instead of defining each property individually. Each of these properties is passed as a string to the send method. The From property is placed first, followed by the To property, the Subject, and the Message Text. The following code illustrates how an e-mail message can be sent in one line of code:

```
SmtpMail.Send("sender@sender.com",
     "recipient@recipient.com", "Subject", "Message")
```

## Sending an E-Mail Message from an ASP.NET Web Page

In the following exercise, you will create a Web page that sends a static message to a single recipient. You must have access to a directory on a computer with a SMTP server running and with CDONTS installed in order to complete this activity.

**TIP**   You should discuss with your system administrator how to connect your pages with your mail server. Some SMTP servers use the same Configuration object to define the configuration settings. Fields in the configuration object, such as sendusing, can be configured to specify where to place the message. You may be required to specify a user name and password to authenticate the send message request.

1. In the Solution Explorer window, right-click the **ch5_email.aspx** page in the **ch5_email** folder and select **View Code**. Type the code as shown in Figure 5-11.

**TIP**   Depending on how your SMTP server is configured to route messages within your network, you may need to use a valid e-mail address for the To and From properties. If you are not allowed to send outbound e-mail messages, you can test the server by changing the second line of the code to MM.To = "student@[ServerName]". This will route the message locally and place the message in the Drop folder.

2. Click the **Save All** button.

3. Right-click on the **ch5_email.aspx** page, and then click **View in Browser**. Type **I have completed the excerise**. in the text box and click the **Send the Message** button.

4. Close the window.

5. On your desktop, double-click the **My Computer** icon, and then double-click the drive on which your Web server is installed. (By default the Web server is installed on drive C.) Double-click **Inetpub**, then **mailroot**, and then **Drop**.

Type this code

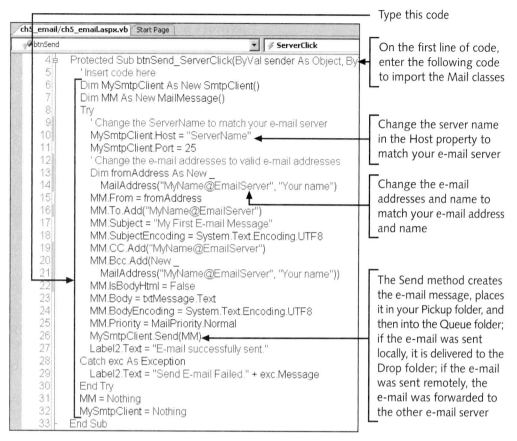

On the first line of code, enter the following code to import the Mail classes

```
ch5_email/ch5_email.aspx.vb    Start Page

btnSend                                    ServerClick

 4   Protected Sub btnSend_ServerClick(ByVal sender As Object, By
 5     ' Insert code here
 6     Dim MySmtpClient As New SmtpClient()
 7     Dim MM As New MailMessage()
 8     Try
 9       ' Change the ServerName to match your e-mail server
10       MySmtpClient.Host = "ServerName"
11       MySmtpClient.Port = 25
12       ' Change the e-mail addresses to valid e-mail addresses
13       Dim fromAddress As New _
14         MailAddress("MyName@EmailServer", "Your name")
15       MM.From = fromAddress
16       MM.To.Add("MyName@EmailServer")
17       MM.Subject = "My First E-mail Message"
18       MM.SubjectEncoding = System.Text.Encoding.UTF8
19       MM.CC.Add("MyName@EmailServer")
20       MM.Bcc.Add(New _
21         MailAddress("MyName@EmailServer", "Your name"))
22       MM.IsBodyHtml = False
23       MM.Body = txtMessage.Text
24       MM.BodyEncoding = System.Text.Encoding.UTF8
25       MM.Priority = MailPriority.Normal
26       MySmtpClient.Send(MM)
27       Label2.Text = "E-mail successfully sent."
28     Catch exc As Exception
29       Label2.Text = "Send E-mail Failed." + exc.Message
30     End Try
31     MM = Nothing
32     MySmtpClient = Nothing
33   End Sub
```

Change the server name in the Host property to match your e-mail server

Change the e-mail addresses and name to match your e-mail address and name

The Send method creates the e-mail message, places it in your Pickup folder, and then into the Queue folder; if the e-mail was sent locally, it is delivered to the Drop folder; if the e-mail was sent remotely, the e-mail was forwarded to the other e-mail server

**Figure 5-11**   Emailing a file from a Web page

6. Right-click the **envelope** icon, and then click **Open with**. In the window, scroll down until you see Notepad. Click **Notepad**, and then click **OK**. Your e-mail message should look similar to the one shown in Figure 5-12. (*Note*: If you select Open, the e-mail message opens in your default e-mail application.)

7. Close the file and close the Drop folder. (*Note*: When your e-mail server is ready, it places the e-mail message in the Pickup folder and sends it. Your e-mail server may not be configured to send the message. Some network settings prevent servers from sending mail via their networks. You should check with your system administrator for the e-mail server settings to send outbound mail through your network. If SMTP is enabled, you won't see the e-mail message. The e-mail will have been sent out for delivery.)

8. If you sent the e-mail to a valid e-mail account, you can now open your e-mail program and verify that you received the e-mail message.

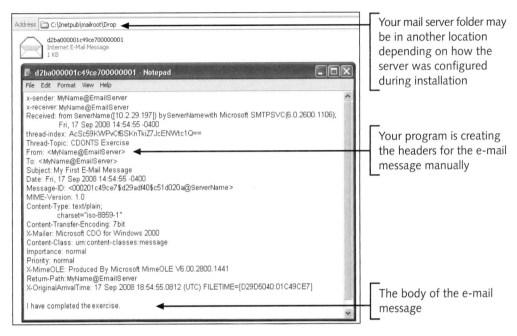

Your mail server folder may be in another location depending on how the server was configured during installation

Your program is creating the headers for the e-mail message manually

The body of the e-mail message

**Figure 5-12**    Viewing an e-mail message

## Troubleshooting the Sending of E-Mail Messages

If you have a message in the browser that says "The SendUsing configuration value is invalid," then you must reconfigure the SMTP settings programmatically and assign a server name before the message is sent:

```
SmtpMail.SmtpServer = "[ServerName]"
```

If you receive an error message that says, "The server rejected one or more recipient addresses," you know that the server response was 550 5.7.1 Unable to relay for [*your-email@your address*]. When you receive this response, you have several options. One option is to change the relay settings to allow your server to relay messages. To configure the server to allow relay messages from your local server, open the IIS MMC, right-click the SMTP server, select Properties, and click the Access tab. On the Access property page, click the Relay button. Make sure to select the radio button labeled "Only the list below," and then click the Add button. Enter the IP address of the server in the Single computer IP address text box, and click OK. The IP address is listed in the Relay Restrictions window as one of the computers that can relay messages. Click OK to close the window. Click OK to close the Access property page and close the MMC.

Another option is to use exception handling and error messages to get to the root of the problem. For example, if you sent an e-mail message to a non-valid e-mail address, the message will be returned with a Non-Delivery report (NDR). This NDR contains information about why the message was not delivered. For example, an e-mail message may not be delivered because the e-mail account did not exist.

Hackers can still attempt to spam servers by spoofing e-mail addresses. Spoofing is where they trick the server into accepting the e-mail as a valid e-mail account. Current technology is being developed by Microsoft and other companies to validate the e-mail addresses using standards that prevent spoofing e-mail addresses.

Not all hosting service providers use the SMTP mail server as their e-mail server. You need to contact your HSP to determine what components interface with their e-mail server. Some hosting service providers may use the SMTP server, but require you to use a different e-mail component.

## STORING AND RETRIEVING DATA IN THE WEB SERVER'S FILE SYSTEM

Another challenging task for Web developers is storing Web information in a file. There are several classes and objects within the `System.IO` namespace that allow you to interact with the Web server's file system. The `System.IO` namespace allows synchronous and asynchronous reading and writing of data streams and files.

The `System.IO` namespace contains several classes, such as File, FileStream, and Directory, that allow you to create, read, and delete files. The **FileSystemInfo class**, however, is the base class for both the FileInfo class and the DirectoryInfo class. The DirectoryInfo and FileInfo classes allow more flexibility and easier access to the file system. The **DirectoryInfo class** allows you to obtain the properties of a directory and its subdirectories. The **FileInfo class** allows you access to the Attribute properties of a file. The attributes listed in the Attribute property consist of one or more FileAttributes, such as ReadOnly or Hidden. In this section, you will learn to work with the DirectoryInfo and FileInfo classes as you learn how to access the directory structure, create and remove directories, and create, read, and delete files.

## Working with Directories and the DirectoryInfo Class

The DirectoryInfo class provides several pieces of information about a directory. When you create a DirectoryInfo object based on the DirectoryInfo class, you must pass the complete path to a directory. The **Attributes property** of the DirectoryInfo class identifies whether the object is a directory. For example, when the Attributes property is 16, the object is a directory.

The **GetDirectories method** of the DirectoryInfo class is used to retrieve the collection of subdirectories. You can use a For-Each-Next loop to iterate through the collection to retrieve information about the subdirectories. Properties of the DirectoryInfo class include Attributes, CreationTime, CreationTimeUtc, Exists, Extension, FullName, LastAccessTime, LastAccessTimeUtc, LastWriteTime, LastWriteTimeUtc, Name, Parent, and Root.

An example for creating a new DirectoryInfo object named DD and retrieving the Name property is shown in the following code:

```
Dim DD As DirectoryInfo = _
     New DirectoryInfo("C:\chapter5\")
Label1.Text = DD.FullName
```

You can iterate through the DirectoryInfo object to retrieve the subdirectory list, as shown in the following code:

```
Dim MySubDirList As String
Dim SubDir As DirectoryInfo
For Each SubDir In DD.GetDirectories()
     MySubDir &= SubDir.Name & "<br />"
     Label2.Text = MySubDirList
Next
```

You can iterate through the FileInfo object to retrieve a list of files. You can use your knowledge of Visual Basic .NET to develop code to modify the display based on the file properties. FileInfo properties include Attributes, CreationTime, CreationTimeUtc, Directory, DirectoryName, Exists, Extension, FullName, LastAccessTime, LastAccessTimeUtc, LastWriteTime, LastWriteTimeUtc, Length, and Name. In Figure 5-13, the .aspx files are displayed as hyperlinks, the .vb and .resx files are not displayed, and all the rest of the files are listed as plain text.

In the following example, you will retrieve the directory properties for your chapter5 project folder, and the list of subdirectories.

1. In the Solution Explorer window, right-click the **ch5_displaydir.aspx** page in the ch5_filesystem folder and click **View Code** to view the code behind the page.

2. Enter the code as shown in Figure 5-14 in the DisplayDirectoryInfo function.

3. Click the **Save All** button.

4. In the Solution Explorer window, right-click **ch5_displaydir.aspx** and select **View in Browser**.

5. In the text box, type **c:\Program Files** and click **go!**. If an error message appears, it is usually because the ASP.NET user account does not have access to all files and folders on the computer. This message is dependent upon the server security settings.

6. In the text box, type the complete path to your chapter5 project folder and click **go!**. The directory information, list of subfolders, and list of files are displayed as shown in Figure 5-15. (*Note*: Because your chapter5 folder may contain different directories your listing may appear different from the listing in Figure 5-15).

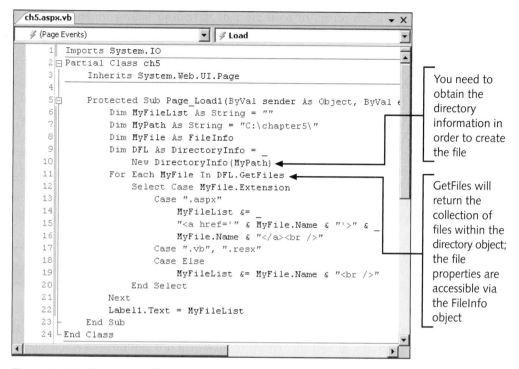

**Figure 5-13**  Retrieving file information with the FileInfo object

Create the DirectoryInfo object

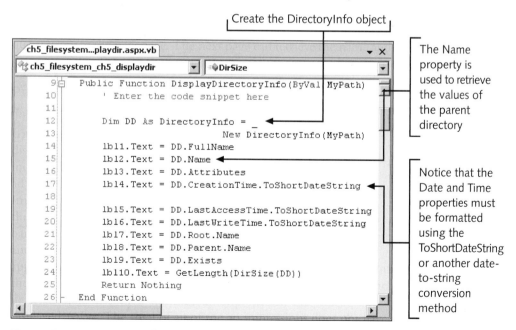

**Figure 5-14**  Retrieving directory information

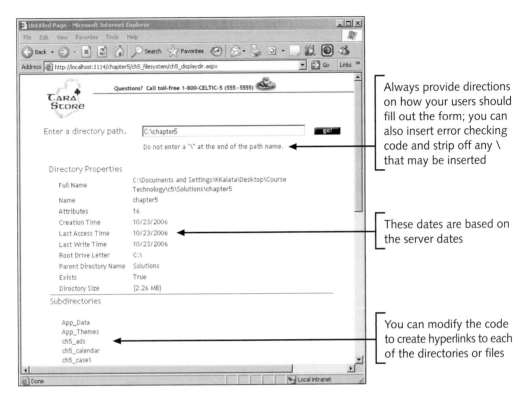

**Figure 5-15** Displaying directory information

7. Close all files.

## Creating and Deleting Directories with the DirectoryInfo Class

You can use the DirectoryInfo class to create and delete directories. For instance, you can use the **CreateSubdirectory method** to create a new directory. You must pass the name of the directory to the DirectoryInfo object. If the path to the directory is too long, or if the directory already exists, an exception may be thrown. You can catch these exceptions using the Try-Catch-End Try structure. The **ArgumentException** is used when you try to create a directory with invalid characters such as <>*?" or \\. If the directory already exists, the **IOException** is thrown. If the name of the path to the directory exceeds 248 characters, the **PathTooLongException** is thrown. If you don't have permission to create the folder, the **SecurityException** is thrown.

When you delete the directory, you use the delete method of the DirectoryInfo object. (If you attempt to delete a directory that does not exist, note that an IOException named **DirectoryNotFoundException** is thrown.) The **Delete method** is used to delete a directory with the DirectoryInfo class.

You can also use the Directory class directly to delete files. You must specify a file, and an optional Boolean value. With the Directory class you specify True or False as a parameter when you call the delete method. If you specify True, then all files and subdirectories are deleted. If you specify False, then if there are any files within the subdirectory, an exception is thrown. (*Note:* You can also use the Directory class within System.IO to create and delete directories.) In the following example, you will create and remove directories with the DirectoryInfo class. You will use a form to retrieve the name of the directory to create and delete.

In the following exercise, you will modify a page so that the web page can create a directory. The page will create the directory, bind the list of directories to the drop-down list, and allow you to delete the newly created directory. You will need to enable simple file sharing; the Security tab is visible only on drives formatted with NTFS. The Security tab may not be visible on a Windows XP computer if simple file sharing is enabled.

1. If you need to enable simple file sharing, click **Start**, and then click **My Computer**. On the **Tools** menu, click **Folder Options**, and then click the **View** tab. In the **Advanced** settings section, clear the **Use simple file sharing (Recommended)** check box. Then click the **OK** button to close the window.

2. If you need to modify the permissions in your Security tab, double-click **My Computer**. Continue navigating in Windows Explorer until you locate and then open the **chapter5** folder. Right-click the **ch5_users** folder, and then click **Properties**. Click the **Security** tab. (*Note:* A warning message may appear on some systems saying that the permissions on ch5_users is incorrectly ordered. If it does, click **OK**. If you click **Cancel**, the security permissions will default to the Everyone group with full control.) Click **Add**. The Select Users or Groups window opens. In the text box, enter **[MACHINENAME]\ ASPNET**. Click **OK**. With the ASPNET Machine Account selected in the Group or user names box , click the **Modify** and **Write** check boxes to select them. Click **Apply**, and then click **OK**.

3. Right-click the **ch5_createdir.aspx** page in the ch5_filesystem folder in the Solution Explorer window and then click **View Code** to view the code behind the page. Type the code in the DisplayDirectory function below the comment as shown in Figure 5-16. This will retrieve the ch5_users subdirectory list and bind it to a DropDownList control.

4. Click the **Save All** button.

5. In the Solution Explorer window, right-click **ch5_createdir.aspx**, and then click **View in Browser**.

6. Type **MyTestFolder** in the text box, and then click the **Create Directory** button, as shown in Figure 5-17. (*Note:* You can try to create an empty subdirectory, or a directory such as MyTestFolder * that contains special characters, and a custom error message will be displayed.)

A Catch clause is used to capture an exception if
the user tries to create a subdirectory without
providing the directory name

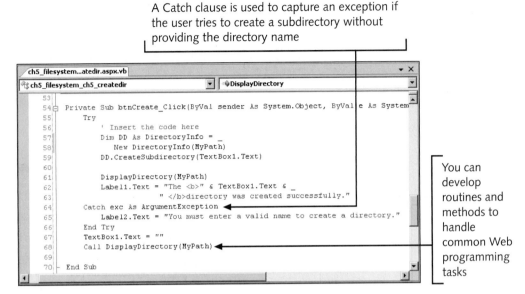

```
ch5_filesystem...atedir.aspx.vb
ch5_filesystem_ch5_createdir                    DisplayDirectory
53
54    Private Sub btnCreate_Click(ByVal sender As System.Object, ByVal e As System
55        Try
56            ' Insert the code here
57            Dim DD As DirectoryInfo = _
58                New DirectoryInfo(MyPath)
59            DD.CreateSubdirectory(TextBox1.Text)
60
61            DisplayDirectory(MyPath)
62            Label1.Text = "The <b>" & TextBox1.Text & _
63                " </b>directory was created successfully."
64        Catch exc As ArgumentException
65            Label2.Text = "You must enter a valid name to create a directory."
66        End Try
67        TextBox1.Text = ""
68        Call DisplayDirectory(MyPath)
69
70    End Sub
```

You can
develop
routines and
methods to
handle
common Web
programming
tasks

**Figure 5-16**   Using the CreateSubdirectory method to create a directory

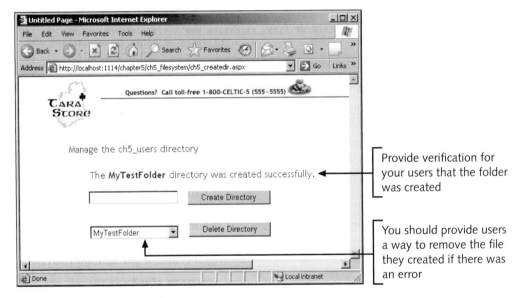

Provide verification for
your users that the folder
was created

You should provide users
a way to remove the file
they created if there was
an error

**Figure 5-17**   Creating a directory

7. Click the **Delete Directory** button. The message that the MyTestFolder directory was deleted is displayed. (*Note:* If you attempt to delete a subdirectory that does not exist, a custom error message will be displayed.)

8. Close any open files.

## Creating and Reading Files from an ASP.NET Page

You use the FileInfo class to create a file, read the contents of a file, and delete a file. The GetFiles method of the FileInfo object returns the files collection. You can retrieve the properties of a file with the FileInfo class. Some of the commonly used properties of the FileInfo class include Attributes, CreationTime, LastAccessedTime, LastWriteTime, Name, FullName, and Exists.

The following is a list of additional properties that can be retrieved using the FileInfo class:

- The Encrypted property identifies that the object is encrypted.

- The Hidden property hides the file in the directory view.

- The Compressed property indicates whether or not a file is compressed.

- The Archive property indicates whether the file has been archived.

- The NotContentIndexed property identifies whether the Index Server will index the page.

- The Offline property identifies whether the file is to be available while the computer is offline.

- The ReadOnly property identifies whether the file is not to be modified by the user.

- The System property identifies whether the file is a system file. You can limit the directory view to avoid displaying system files. Then, the user cannot accidentally modify or remove the system file.

- The Temporary property identifies whether the file is a temp file.

You can use the FileInfo class to create a basic text file or HTML file, copy a file to a new location, move a file to a new location, or delete a file. The **CopyTo method** copies a file from one path to another. The **MoveTo method** copies a file from one path to another, and then deletes the original file. The **Delete method** removes a file from the hard drive.

You can use several objects to create, modify, read, and delete files. The File object contains methods for working with files. The File, Directory, and Path classes are derived from the System.Object class. The DirectoryInfo and FileInfo classes are derived from the System.IO.FileSystemInfo class, however. Both groups of classes allow you to interact with FileStream, BinaryReader, BinaryWriter, StreamReader, and StreamWriter classes, which allow you to read and write to files.

The **CreateText method** returns a **StreamWriter object**. The methods are used to create files. You can create a plain text file or an HTML file. You must pass the path of the new file to the CreateText method. The CreateText method returns the StreamWriter object and opens the file for editing.

The Write method can be used to write HTML contents to the file. If you plan to create an HTML file, and want to display the contents at a later time, you should use the <XMP> tag to ignore the HTML tags in the file. Then, the HTML tags are displayed with the text and not interpreted by the browser. When you create the file, you can specify a relative path or a Universal Naming Convention (UNC) path for a server and share name. For example, the path to the file can be specified as "C:\\*MyDirectory*\\*MyFileName*.txt", "C:\\*MyDirectory*", "*MyDirectory*\\*MySubdirectory*", or "\\*MyServerName*\*MyShareName*".

In the following exercise, you will create a new file, add material to the file from a form, display its properties using the FileInfo class, and delete the file. When you load the page, the default directions appear in the label. When you enter a file name and click the Create File button, the file is created using the name of the file and the CreateText method.

## Creating a Text File

The **Write method** of the StreamWriter object is used to write to the file. When you are finished, you need to use the **Close method** of the StreamWriter object to close the file. You can read the contents of the newly created file with the OpenText method of the FileInfo class. The **OpenText method** returns a **StreamReader object**, which can read through each line from the file. When you are finished, you need to use the Close method of the StreamReader object to close the file.

1. Right-click the **ch5_createfile.aspx** page in the ch5_filesystem folder in the Solution Explorer window and select **View Code**. In the btnCreate_Click event procedure, after the comment, add the code in Figure 5-18 to create the file using the value entered into the text box. (*Note:* The btnDelete_Click event procedure will use the Delete method of the FileInfo object to delete the file. The btnDisplay_Click event procedure will read the file using the file name selected from the drop-down list. The code uses the StreamReader object to retrieve the file from the File object and open the file with the OpenText method. The ReadToEnd method reads the entire file line by line until it reaches the end of the file. The contents of the file are assigned to the Text property of the Label control in the Web page.)

2. Click the **Save All** button.

3. In the Solution Explorer window, right-click the **ch5_createfile.aspx** file and then click **View in Browser**.

4. Type **MyTestFile.txt** in the text box, and then click the **Create File** button.

Store the path to the new file in the
MyFile variable; create the FileInfo
object named MyFileInfo

Create the StreamWriter object
using the CreateText method in
order to create the file and open
the file for writing

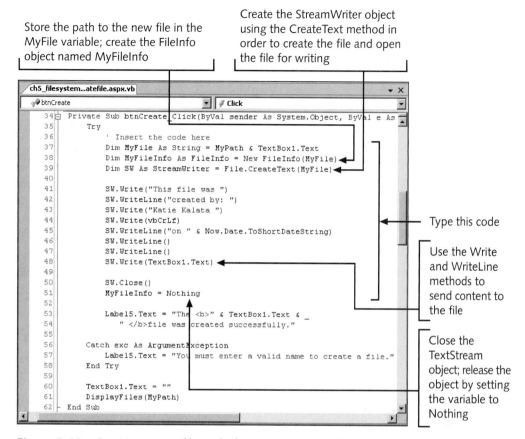

```vb
ch5_filesystem...atefile.aspx.vb
btnCreate                                    Click
34   Private Sub btnCreate_Click(ByVal sender As System.Object, ByVal e As
35       Try
36           ' Insert the code here
37           Dim MyFile As String = MyPath & TextBox1.Text
38           Dim MyFileInfo As FileInfo = New FileInfo(MyFile)
39           Dim SW As StreamWriter = File.CreateText(MyFile)
40
41           SW.Write("This file was ")
42           SW.WriteLine("created by: ")
43           SW.Write("Katie Kalata ")
44           SW.Write(vbCrLf)
45           SW.WriteLine("on " & Now.Date.ToShortDateString)
46           SW.WriteLine()
47           SW.WriteLine()
48           SW.Write(TextBox1.Text)
49
50           SW.Close()
51           MyFileInfo = Nothing
52
53           Label15.Text = "The <b>" & TextBox1.Text & _
54               " </b>file was created successfully."
55
56       Catch exc As ArgumentException
57           Label15.Text = "You must enter a valid name to create a file."
58       End Try
59
60           TextBox1.Text = ""
61           DisplayFiles(MyPath)
62   End Sub
```

Type this code

Use the Write
and WriteLine
methods to
send content to
the file

Close the
TextStream
object; release the
object by setting
the variable to
Nothing

**Figure 5-18**   Creating a text file with the StreamWriter object

5. Select the **MyTestFile.txt** file in the drop-down list. Click the **Display File Contents** button. The contents of the file are displayed, as shown in Figure 5–19.

6. Click the **Delete File** button. Your file is deleted.

7. Close the file and browser.

**TIP**

Notice that the carriage returns are not recognized in the browser. HTML ignores carriage returns and white space such as tabs. WriteLine places a return character at the end of the line, or use the Visual Basic .NET constant vbCrLf to represent a return character. You must use HTML tags to ensure that the contents are placed on the correct line.

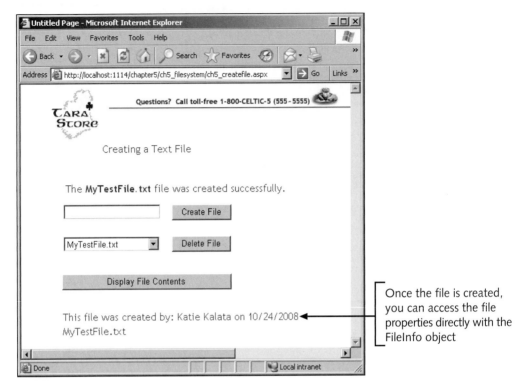

Once the file is created, you can access the file properties directly with the FileInfo object

**Figure 5-19**  Creating a text file

## Creating an HTML Page

In the following exercise, you will create a file named ch5_createhtmlfile.aspx, which includes HTML commands.

1. Right-click the **ch5_createhtmlfile.aspx** page in the Solution Explorer window, and then click **View Code**.

2. In the btnCreate_Click event procedure, after the comment, add the code in Figure 5-20. This will create the file using the value entered into the text box, and set the hyperlink to an empty string so that it is not displayed.

3. Click the **Save All** button.

4. In the Solution Explorer window, right-click the **ch5_createhtmlfile.aspx** and click **View in Browser**.

5. Type **MyTest.htm** in the first text box. In the second text box, type **Welcome to my Web site**.

6. Click the **Create File** button. The file is created and the new hyperlink is displayed, as shown in Figure 5-21.

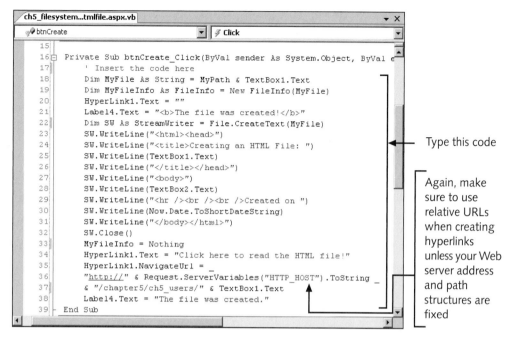

```
ch5_filesystem...tmlfile.aspx.vb                                ▼ ✕
 btnCreate                              ▼   Click                          ▼
15
16  Private Sub btnCreate_Click(ByVal sender As System.Object, ByVal e
17        ' Insert the code here
18        Dim MyFile As String = MyPath & TextBox1.Text
19        Dim MyFileInfo As FileInfo = New FileInfo(MyFile)
20        HyperLink1.Text = ""
21        Label4.Text = "<b>The file was created!</b>"
22        Dim SW As StreamWriter = File.CreateText(MyFile)
23        SW.WriteLine("<html><head>")
24        SW.WriteLine("<title>Creating an HTML File: ")
25        SW.WriteLine(TextBox1.Text)
26        SW.WriteLine("</title></head>")
27        SW.WriteLine("<body>")
28        SW.WriteLine(TextBox2.Text)
29        SW.WriteLine("<hr /><br /><br />Created on ")
30        SW.WriteLine(Now.Date.ToShortDateString)
31        SW.WriteLine("</body></html>")
32        SW.Close()
33        MyFileInfo = Nothing
34        HyperLink1.Text = "Click here to read the HTML file!"
35        HyperLink1.NavigateUrl = _
36        "http://" & Request.ServerVariables("HTTP_HOST").ToString _
37        & "/chapter5/ch5_users/" & TextBox1.Text
38        Label4.Text = "The file was created."
39  End Sub
```

Type this code

Again, make sure to use relative URLs when creating hyperlinks unless your Web server address and path structures are fixed

**Figure 5-20**    Creating an HTML file with the StreamWriter object

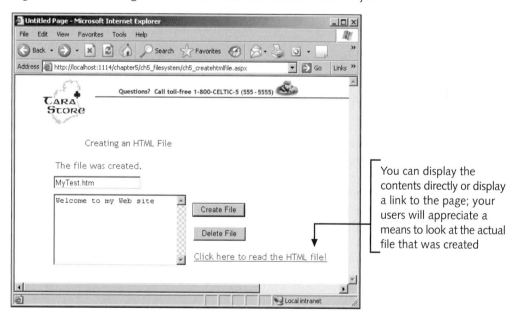

You can display the contents directly or display a link to the page; your users will appreciate a means to look at the actual file that was created

**Figure 5-21**    Creating a file

7. Click the hyperlink to open the page in the browser. The contents of the file are displayed in the browser.

8. Click the **Back** button in the browser.

9. Click the **Delete File** button. Your file is deleted. (*Note*: If you were to refresh the page, the File Not Found error message would appear.)

10. Close the file and the browser.

## Security Issues Related to Building Web Applications

Building a secure and robust Web application takes time and costs more money than a simple one-level HTML Web site. You will need management approval for allocating costs to the project. Many times, company employees don't know the possibilities or the implications of building Web sites. You may need to provide them with suggestions on how to use and how to secure the Web site. Inform them about the technical issues and challenges and then allow them to have input into the policy making decisions. Many institutions will have a network security expert who will review your project requirements and program documentation to determine if there are any security related issues.

As you design your Web sites, you should know the following:

- You can create a login form processed by ASP.NET for Web applications. The hierarchy of files and folders can be modified in IIS using virtual applications and virtual directories. That way, potential hackers would not know the physical paths to files. You can turn off FTP access to your company Web site so that potential hackers cannot upload files using FTP. Newer security methods, such as firewalls, allow you to restrict or allow traffic to specific applications or ports that the applications are listening on. The Web server can be placed outside of the company network, but protected by a firewall. This area is called the demilitarized zone (DMZ).

- Some Web developers have created Web security programs using JavaScripts. JavaScripts run on the client and are not adequate for securing a Web site. As an example of such a situation, consider a not-for-profit company with over 4,000 members in Chicago, Illinois that created online courses for their membership. They hired two programmers who made two major mistakes with respect to their Web site. First, the programmer used Microsoft FrontPage forms to store the end-user data, including credit card numbers and personal information. Microsoft FrontPage extensions allow you to process forms quickly, and store the information in a text file or database. It is up to the Web developer to secure these files, however, by using methods built into Microsoft FrontPage or by configuring NTFS. While it is possible to secure a Web site using Microsoft FrontPage, they didn't have the knowledge to implement it. Second, they used JavaScripts to process the login form. All JavaScripts are client-based, so all Web sites that use them must allow the browser to read the client-program. If the end-user clicks the Escape button quickly, and they have a slower connection to the Internet, it is possible to stop the processing of the redirection scripts, view the JavaScript code, and hack into the Web site.

- In earlier chapters, you learned to create a login script using ASP.NET. If the user was validated, he or she was redirected to a new page; otherwise, he or she was redirected back to the login page. This method needs to be combined with other security methods. Hackers can search the Web site and guess at the names of files in an attempt to hack into the site. To counteract this threat, you must use methods such as Forms Authentication to validate the user. This way, the user must be validated for each ASP.NET resource.

- Access is useful in situations such as displaying non-secure information. An Access file can be downloaded by the end user, however, and although the file can be protected using passwords within the file, hackers can use password detection programs to hack into the file. A better alternative is to use a server-based database program such as Microsoft SQL Server or Oracle. SQL Server provides the ability to create its own set of user names and passwords, such as the default user known as sa.

- An end user can right-click a graphic on your page and save the image locally. Companies that try to protect their graphics by using JavaScript are wasting their time. Copies of these Web pages, including the graphics, are stored locally in the browser's cache directory. End users can browse and copy files from this folder if you block directory browsing. In addition, they can either save the entire page to another location or view the location of the image in the source code and go to the image file directly by typing the URL in the browser location text box.

Fortunately, you can do the following to protect your graphics and resources:

- Adobe's Photoshop (*www.adobe.com*) and other graphics programs allow the graphics designer to embed a watermark in the image. This provides the company with some protections if the case is taken to court. In addition, content that is textual can be presented in PDF format, preventing the ability to cut and paste content quickly into another piece of work.

- Web site management tools that include the ability to upload files are usually provided for employees within the company. Your company can restrict the user of the Web site management tools to be within the company's network and firewall. Your company also may want to restrict which type of files can be uploaded and their maximum file size. You can configure a specific folder where only one user can upload files. One organization that used this method of backing up files was The Midwest Alliance for Nursing Informatics (MANI), which was a not-for-profit group based in Illinois. (*Note*: MANI is now assimilated within the Chicago-based Healthcare Information Management Systems Society called HIMSS.) The MANI board members were allowed to upload certain types of files to their Web site. When they tried to upload the membership directory, the program made a copy of the old directory and then copied the new directory with the same file name as the old directory. This prevented errors when board members modified the file name of the database. In addition, board members were allowed to upload newsletters. The newsletters were contained within a separate directory with different NTFS permissions, however.

## CHAPTER SUMMARY

❏ ASP.NET controls enhance the user interface and increase interactivity within Web pages. Examples of ASP.NET controls are the AdRotator control, and the Calendar control.

❏ The AdRotator control allows you to display rotating banner ads. The banner contains a hyperlink, alternate text, and an image. If you do not specify the height and width, you can display images of varying sizes. The advertisement file is an XML file that is used to store the ad information. The advertisement file can be edited with a text editor, such as Notepad, or an XML editor. The root node is named advertisements. The Impressions property determines the ad's relative display frequency. The Keywords property is used to group banner ads. You can apply a filter and only show some of the banner ads using the KeywordFilter property.

❏ The Calendar control displays an interactive calendar. You can use many properties to format the calendar. The SelectionChanged event allows you to detect when the user clicks a new date. The SelectedDate property indicates the value of the date currently selected. You can retrieve the value of the date that users click, or execute code when they click a particular date.

❏ The File Input control is an HTML Server control that allows you to browse your network to locate a file to upload file to a Web server. The Form Enctype property must be set to multipart/form-data. The upload file field type must be set to file. The FileUpload control is a Web server control that also allows you to browser your network to locate a file to be uploaded to the Web server. On the Web server, you must retrieve the file name. You can change the file name or path on the server in the code behind the page. The SaveAs method saves the file to the Web server.

❏ The SMTP server is the default mail service that is installed with the Internet Information Service Web server. The mail server's default root directory is C:\Inetpub\MailRoot\. The Pickup folder is used to store outgoing mail messages. Mail that cannot be delivered is sent to the BadMail directory. You can configure the SMTP server via the property sheets in the MMC application. The default port for the SMTP server is 25.

❏ The CDONTS object, from cdonts.dll, is installed with the SMTP server and enables you to send outbound e-mail from a Web page. The CDONTS component is only available if the SMTP mail server is installed. You can access the properties of the CDONTS object via the `System.Web.Mail` namespace. The MailMessage class provides the sender and recipient data, as well as the message content. The MailAttachment class is used to identify a file that is to be sent with the e-mail message. The SMTPMail class is used to send the e-mail message. E-mail can be sent as plain text or formatted with HTML. The Send method of the SmtpMail class creates the message in the required format and writes it to the Pickup folder, from where the SMTP server sends it.

❏ The `System.IO` namespace provides you with classes that interact with the Web server's file system. It contains several classes such as File, FileStream, and Directory, which allow you to create, read, and delete files. The newer classes, named DirectoryInfo and FileInfo, are more flexible and provide easier access to the file system.

❏ The DirectoryInfo class allows you to obtain the properties of a directory and its subdirectories.

❏ The GetDirectories method of the DirectoryInfo class is used to retrieve the collection of subdirectories. The CreateSubdirectory method is used to create a new directory. You can capture exceptions when creating directories and files with the Try-Catch-End Try structure.

❏ You can use the FileInfo class to copy a file to a new location, move a file to a new location, or delete a file. The FileInfo class allows you access to the properties of a file, using the FileAttributes. You can use the FileInfo class to create a basic text file or HTML file.

❏ The CreateText and Create methods of the FileInfo class return a StreamWriter object, which is used to create files. The open, OpenRead, OpenText, and OpenWrite methods allow you to open and read the file. The Write method of the StreamWriter object is used to write to the file. The OpenText method returns a StreamReader object, which can read through each line from the file.

## REVIEW QUESTIONS

1. Which Web control allows you to upload a file to a Web server from a Web page?
   a. FileUpload control
   b. Upload control
   c. File control
   d. HTMLFile Upload control

2. Which class is inherited by the FileUpload class?
   a. System.Web.UI.HTMLControl
   b. System.Web.FileUpload
   c. System.UI.WebControls.FileUpload
   d. System.Web.UI.HTMLInputControl

3. Which value is used to identify a file that is attached to the form?
   a. multipart/form–data
   b. type=form–data
   c. attachedFile
   d. type=form/file

4. What is the value of the Type property for the input file field generated by the control used to upload files?
   a. Upload
   b. File
   c. Text
   d. Attached

5. What method is used to perform the upload of the file to the server?
   a. Upload
   b. FileUpload
   c. Save
   d. SaveAs

6. Where is the banner ad information stored?
   a. memory
   b. advertisement file
   c. AdRotator file
   d. Windows Registry

7. Who is responsible for the maintenance of the XML standards?
   a. Microsoft
   b. Sun Microsystems
   c. IBM
   d. W3C

8. In the ads.xml file, what is the name of the root node?
   a. Advertisements
   b. AdSchedule
   c. AdRotator
   d. Products

9. What is the name of the tag used to insert the Calendar control?
   a. table
   b. asp:calendar
   c. xml:calendar
   d. asp/calendar

10. Which property is used to create the hyperlink tag in the banner AdRotator control?
    a. ImageUrl
    b. NavigateUrl
    c. NavigateHref
    d. Href

11. Assume that you have four banner ads, and all four banner ad Impression properties are set to 25. You visit your page 200 times. How many times would you expect to see each banner?

    a. 20

    b. 40

    c. 50

    d. 100

12. What property is used to search for a subset of the banner ads in the advertisement file?

    a. Keyword

    b. KeywordFilter

    c. Advertisement

    d. Impressions

13. What property of the Calendar control is used to capture the date that the user clicked?

    a. VisibleMonthChanged

    b. SelectedDate

    c. DayChanged

    d. SelectionChanged

14. Which word describes the position of an item in a collection?

    a. index position

    b. counter

    c. loop index

    d. counter

15. Which of the following rules is not part of the XML standards?

    a. Element names must not be more than 32 characters long.

    b. All container elements must be closed.

    c. The opening and closing element tags must have the same case.

    d. A child container element can be nested within a parent container element.

16. Which service is used to deliver e-mail to another server?

    a. PopMail Server

    b. Web Publishing

    c. FTP Server

    d. SMTP Server

17. The CDONTS component creates the e-mail message and places the message in which folder?
    a. Pickup
    b. Queue
    c. Drop
    d. Badmail

18. Where is the e-mail message placed after all attempts to deliver the message have failed?
    a. Pickup
    b. Queue
    c. Drop
    d. Badmail

19. Where is the default main e-mail folder located?
    a. c:\Inetpub\Mail
    b. c:\Inetpub\MailRoot
    c. d:\Inetpub\Mail
    d. d:\Inetpub\mailroot

20. Which administrative tool is used to determine if the Simple Mail Transport Protocol (SMTP) has been started?
    a. FTP Server
    b. Exchange Server
    c. Services
    d. SMTP Mail Manager

21. Which class provides access to the properties and methods to construct an e-mail message?
    a. MailMessage
    b. MailAttachment
    c. SmtpMail
    d. System.Web.Mail

22. Which class is used to identify a file that is to be sent with the e-mail message?
    a. MailMessage
    b. MailAttachment
    c. SmtpMail
    d. System.Web.Mail

23. Which property is used to indicate that the output of the message is HTML?
    a. MailFormat.Text
    b. MailFormat.HTML
    c. MailMessage.Normal
    d. MailEncoding.UUEncode

24. Which property is required when creating a MailMessage?
    a. MailMessage.UrlContentBase
    b. MailMessage.From
    c. MailMessage.CC
    d. MailMessage.BCC

25. Which character does not throw an ArgumentException when you create a directory?
    a. <
    b. z
    c. *
    d. ?

26. If you attempt to delete a directory that does not exist, what IOException is thrown?
    a. DirectoryNotFoundException
    b. SecurityException
    c. IOException
    d. PathTooLongException

27. Which of the following is not a property of the FileInfo class?
    a. CreationTime
    b. lastAccessedTime
    c. LastWriteTime
    d. DirectoryKey

28. What property is used to identify if the file is not to be modified by the user?
    a. ReadOnly
    b. Compressed
    c. NotContentIndexed
    d. Archive

29. If you want to copy a file to a new location, and delete the original file, which method of the FileInfo class should you use?

    a. CopyTo

    b. MoveTo

    c. Delete

    d. MakeFile

30. Which method returns a StreamWriter object?

    a. CreateText

    b. Create

    c. CreateFile

    d. Both a and b

31. Compare the classes and methods to create directories and files?

32. What security features should you build into your Web applications when you allow users to send e-mail through a Web page?

33. What security features should you build into your Web applications when you allow users to manage files and folders through a Web page?

34. Describe how you might use a database to populate a Calendar control?

35. Describe possible uses for the AdRotator control?

---

# HANDS-ON PROJECTS

**HANDS-ON PROJECTS**

## Project 5-1

In this project, you configure a Web page to display a rotating banner ad using the AdRotator control. In this exercise, you will use a database as the source of the banner ads.

1. Open your **chapter5** Web site, if it is not open already.

2. In the Solution Explorer window, right-click the **ch5_proj1.aspx** file in the **ch5_proj1** folder and select **View Designer**. Click the AdRotator control located in the right Content control. In the Properties window, set the AdvertisementFile property to **~/ch5_proj1/ads.xml**.

3. Click the **Save All** icon. Right-click the page, and then click **View in Browser**. Click the banner ad image. Either the Michigan or Illinois Web pages will open. Close the browser.

4. Return to the editor and the **ch5_proj1.aspx** page. Click the **AdRotator** control and then in the Properties window, delete the value for the AdvertisementFile property.

5. Click and drag an **AccessDataSource** control from the toolbox to the Web page and place it below the banner ad at the bottom of the Content control. This control is required to connect the Web page to the Access database. Click the **Configure Data Source** hyperlink. In the text box, enter **~/App_Data/ch5_proj1.mdb** and click **Next**. In the SQL Statement text box enter **SELECT * FROM ads**, click **Next**, and then click **Finish**.

6. Click the AdRotator control located in the right Content control. In the Properties window, set the DataSourceID property to **AccessDataSource1**.

7. Click the **Save All** button. Right-click the page, and then click **View in Browser**. Click the banner image. Either the Michigan or Illinois Web pages will open. Close the browser.

8. Return to the editor and the **ch5_proj1.aspx** page. Click the AdRotator control and then in the Properties window, change the KeywordFilter property to **Michigan**.

9. Click the **Save All** button. Right-click the page, and then click **View in Browser**. Click on the banner image. Either the Michigan or Illinois Web pages will open.

10. Click the Back button in the browser. Click the banner image 10 times noting which image is displayed each time. Only properties in Michigan are displayed.

11. Close all of the pages and the browser.

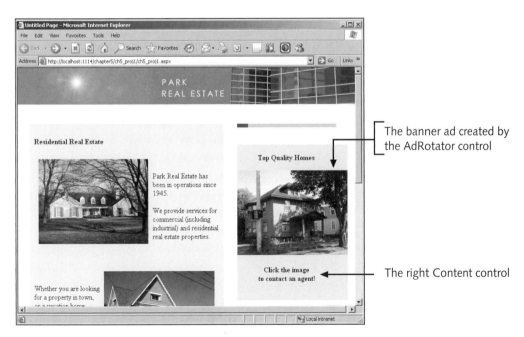

The banner ad created by the AdRotator control

The right Content control

**Figure 5-22**    Configuring the AdRotator with a database

## Project 5-2

In this project, you configure daily events from an array to be displayed in the day cells in the Calendar control.

1. Open your **chapter5** Web site, if it is not already open.

2. In the Solution Explorer window, right-click the **ch5_proj2.aspx** file in the **ch5_proj2** folder and select **View Code**. Type the code as shown in Figure 5-23, which creates the array and populates it with data.

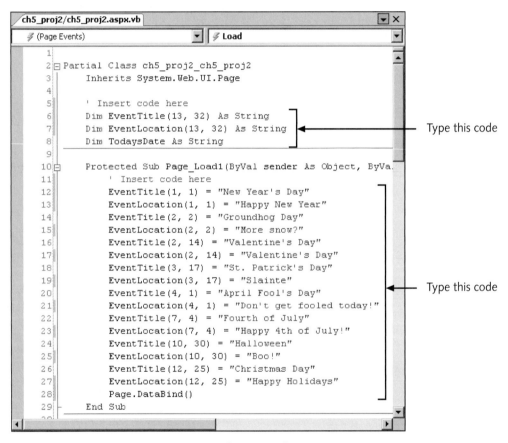

```
ch5_proj2/ch5_proj2.aspx.vb                                    ▼ ×
(Page Events)                          ▼    Load                ▼
 1
 2  Partial Class ch5_proj2_ch5_proj2
 3      Inherits System.Web.UI.Page
 4
 5      ' Insert code here
 6      Dim EventTitle(13, 32) As String          ◄──── Type this code
 7      Dim EventLocation(13, 32) As String
 8      Dim TodaysDate As String
 9
10      Protected Sub Page_Load1(ByVal sender As Object, ByVa
11          ' Insert code here
12          EventTitle(1, 1) = "New Year's Day"
13          EventLocation(1, 1) = "Happy New Year"
14          EventTitle(2, 2) = "Groundhog Day"
15          EventLocation(2, 2) = "More snow?"
16          EventTitle(2, 14) = "Valentine's Day"
17          EventLocation(2, 14) = "Valentine's Day"
18          EventTitle(3, 17) = "St. Patrick's Day"
19          EventLocation(3, 17) = "Slainte"
20          EventTitle(4, 1) = "April Fool's Day"     ◄──── Type this code
21          EventLocation(4, 1) = "Don't get fooled today!"
22          EventTitle(7, 4) = "Fourth of July"
23          EventLocation(7, 4) = "Happy 4th of July!"
24          EventTitle(10, 30) = "Halloween"
25          EventLocation(10, 30) = "Boo!"
26          EventTitle(12, 25) = "Christmas Day"
27          EventLocation(12, 25) = "Happy Holidays"
28          Page.DataBind()
29      End Sub
```

**Figure 5-23**   Create an array to store the event data

3. Scroll down to the Calendar1_DayRender mmethod and type the code as sown in Figure 5-24.

4. Click the **Save All** button.

5. In the Solution Explorer window right-click the **ch5_proj2.aspx** file in the **ch5_proj2** folder and select **View in Browser**. Change the month so it's January. Click the link for January 1st. Note the message displayed on the day cell when it was rendered and when you clicked it.

This is called when the
calendar is rendered

This makes sure no content is
displayed for dates for other months

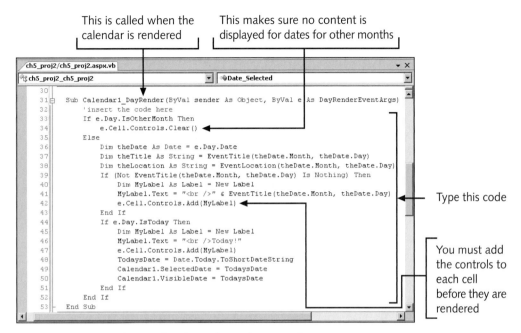

```
ch5_proj2/ch5_proj2.aspx.vb
ch5_proj2_ch5_proj2                                    Date_Selected
30
31    Sub Calendar1_DayRender(ByVal sender As Object, ByVal e As DayRenderEventArgs)
32        'insert the code here
33        If e.Day.IsOtherMonth Then
34            e.Cell.Controls.Clear()
35        Else
36            Dim theDate As Date = e.Day.Date
37            Dim theTitle As String = EventTitle(theDate.Month, theDate.Day)
38            Dim theLocation As String = EventLocation(theDate.Month, theDate.Day)
39            If (Not EventTitle(theDate.Month, theDate.Day) Is Nothing) Then
40                Dim MyLabel As Label = New Label
41                MyLabel.Text = "<br />" & EventTitle(theDate.Month, theDate.Day)
42                e.Cell.Controls.Add(MyLabel)
43            End If
44            If e.Day.IsToday Then
45                Dim MyLabel As Label = New Label
46                MyLabel.Text = "<br />Today!"
47                e.Cell.Controls.Add(MyLabel)
48                TodaysDate = Date.Today.ToShortDateString
49                Calendar1.SelectedDate = TodaysDate
50                Calendar1.VisibleDate = TodaysDate
51            End If
52        End If
53    End Sub
```

Type this code

You must add
the controls to
each cell
before they are
rendered

**Figure 5-24**   Populating the day cells with event data

6. Close all of the pages and the browser.

## Project 5-3

In this project, you create a Web page that uses FileUpload control to upload a Word document file.

1. Open your **chapter5** Web site, if it is not already open.

2. In the Solution Explorer window, right-click the **ch5_proj3.aspx** file in the **ch5_proj3** folder and select **View Code**. Type the code as shown in Figure 5-25, which creates the array and populates it with data.

3. Click the **Save All** button.

4. In the Solution Explorer window, right-click the **ch5_proj3.aspx** file in the ch5_proj3 folder and select **View in Browser**. Type your name in the first text box, **My First Article** in the second text box. Click the **Browse** button and from your ch5_proj3 directory select the file **uploadtest.txt**. Type **Article001** in the last text box. Click the **Upload your article** button. The error message is displayed.

5. From your ch5proj3 directory, select the **uploadtext.doc** file. Click the **Browse** button and from your ch5_proj3 directory, select the file **uploadtest.doc**. Click the **Upload your article** button. The file should be uploaded to the uploads folder.

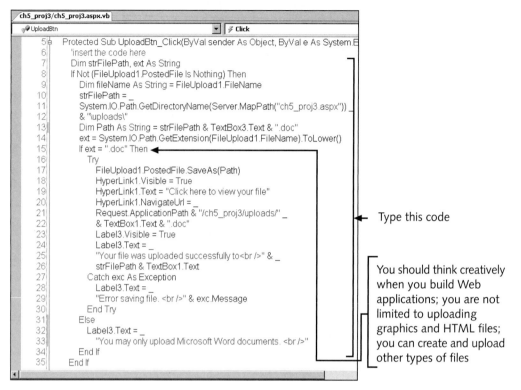

```
ch5_proj3/ch5_proj3.aspx.vb
UploadBtn                                          Click
5     Protected Sub UploadBtn_Click(ByVal sender As Object, ByVal e As System.E
6         'insert the code here
7         Dim strFilePath, ext As String
8         If Not (FileUpload1.PostedFile Is Nothing) Then
9             Dim fileName As String = FileUpload1.FileName
10            strFilePath = _
11            System.IO.Path.GetDirectoryName(Server.MapPath("ch5_proj3.aspx")) _
12            & "\uploads\"
13            Dim Path As String = strFilePath & TextBox3.Text & ".doc"
14            ext = System.IO.Path.GetExtension(FileUpload1.FileName).ToLower()
15            If ext = ".doc" Then
16                Try
17                    FileUpload1.PostedFile.SaveAs(Path)
18                    HyperLink1.Visible = True
19                    HyperLink1.Text = "Click here to view your file"
20                    HyperLink1.NavigateUrl = _
21                    Request.ApplicationPath & "/ch5_proj3/uploads/" _
22                    & TextBox1.Text & ".doc"
23                    Label3.Visible = True
24                    Label3.Text = _
25                    "Your file was uploaded successfully to<br />" & _
26                    strFilePath & TextBox1.Text
27                Catch exc As Exception
28                    Label3.Text = _
29                    "Error saving file. <br />" & exc.Message
30                End Try
31            Else
32                Label3.Text = _
33                "You may only upload Microsoft Word documents. <br />"
34            End If
35        End If
```

← Type this code

You should think creatively when you build Web applications; you are not limited to uploading graphics and HTML files; you can create and upload other types of files

**Figure 5-25**    Uploading a Word document file

6. Close all of the pages and the browser.

## Project 5-4

In this project, you create a Web page that sends an e-mail message to a single recipient. You will retrieve the values for the e-mail message properties from a form.

1. Open your **chapter5** Web site, if it is not already open.

2. In the Solution Explorer window, right-click the **ch5_proj4.aspx** file in the ch5_proj4 folder and select **View Code**. Type the code as shown in Figure 5-26, which creates the array and populates it with data. Make sure to change the name of the mail server from kalata to your mail server name.

3. Click the **Save All** button.

4. Right-click the **ch5_proj4.aspx** file in the ch5_proj4 folder, and then click **View in Browser**. Fill out the form and click the **Send the E-mail** button.

5. Close all of the pages and the browser.

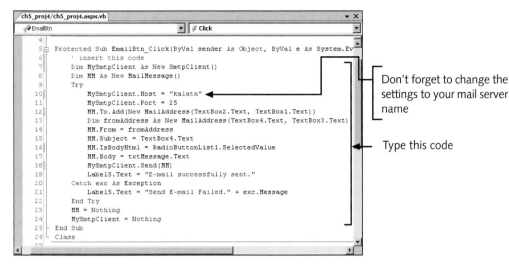

**Figure 5-26** Sending e-mail from a Web page

## Project 5-5

In this project, you create a Web page from the contents of a form.

1. Open your **chapter5** Web site, if it is not already open.

2. In the Solution Explorer window, right-click the **ch5_proj5.aspx** file in the **ch5_proj5** folder and select **View Code**. Type the code as shown in Figure 5-27, which creates the Web page using the values entered in the form.

3. Click the **Save All** button.

4. Right-click the **ch5_proj5.aspx** file in the **ch5_proj5** folder, and then click **View in Browser**. Fill out the form. Enter **Test.htm** in the File Name text box. In the Title text box, enter **Community News**. In the BackgroundColor text box, enter **#99CCCC**. In the Text Color text box, enter **#330099**. In the Body text box, enter **Welcome to my Web site.** Click the **Create File** button. Click the hyperlink to open the page in the browser. The contents of the file are displayed in the browser.

5. Close all of the pages and the browser.

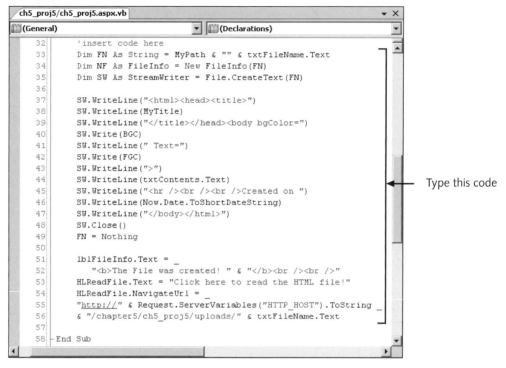

Figure 5-27   Creating the Web page from a form

## CASE PROJECTS

**CASE PROJECTS**

## Project 5-1

The marketing manager at Tara Store has sold contracts to several other Irish Web sites to allow them to display their banner on the Tara Store Web site. Create a page named ch1_case1.xml that contains the ads, using data from Table 5-1.

**Table 5-1**   Ad information

| ImageURL | NavigateURL | AlternateText | Keyword | Impressions |
|----------|-------------|---------------|---------|-------------|
| Images/5a.jpg | http://www.ireland.ie | Ireland.ie | Store | 10 |
| Images/5b.jpg | http://www.rootsweb.com/~irish | The Irish Genealogical Society-International | Culture | 15 |
| Images/5c.jpg | http://www.aoh.com | Ancient Order of Hibernians | Culture | 20 |
| Images/5d.jpg | http://www.ireland.com | The Irish Times | News | 25 |

**Table 5-1**  Ad information (continued)

| ImageURL | NavigateURL | AlternateText | Keyword | Impressions |
|----------|-------------|---------------|---------|-------------|
| Images/5e.jpg | http://home.iol.ie | Ireland On-Line | News | 30 |
| Images/5f.jpg | http://www.irelandseye.com | Ireland's Eye | Culture | 35 |
| Images/5g.jpg | http://www.irishamhc.com | Irish American Heritage Center | Culture | 25 |

Create a page named ch5_case1.aspx in the ch5_case1 folder. Add an AdRotator control to the page. Filter the ads to show only culture-related links. Enhance the page with text, color, and graphics. View the page and print out the Web pages and the ASP.NET source code. View the page 10 times. Tally the number of times each culture-related link is displayed.

**CASE PROJECTS**

## Project 5-2

The store manager needs a method to display a calendar to his employees in order to schedule employee vacation time. Create a Web page with the Calendar control named ch5_case2.aspx in the ch5_case2 folder. Create two buttons labeled Start Date and End Date. When the user clicks a date, then clicks the Start Date button, display a message confirming the start date of the vacation. When the user clicks a date, then clicks the End Date button, display a message confirming the end date of the vacation. Display the start and end dates to the user using Label controls. Add your company logo, graphics, color, and content to enhance the appearance of the calendar and page. Print out your Web page, the source code for the ASP.NET page, and the code behind the page.

**CASE PROJECTS**

## Project 5-3

You have been asked to create an administration tool for the shopping cart on the Tara Store Web site. Open the chapter5 Web site in your Web editor. Create a login form that authenticates the user. Save the page as ch5_case3.aspx. If the user is validated, allow the user to upload the file. If the user is not authenticated, redisplay the form. Add the File Upload control to the page. Allow the user to enter a new file name in a text box. (*Note*: The user must enter a valid file name and extension.) Allow only the store manager to upload only image files to the ch5_case3 directory. (*Note*: Using the Accept property feature may only work in some browsers.) His user name is StoreMan and his password is GalwayBay. Enhance the page with text, color, and graphics. Provide a link to the ch5_case3 folder so that users can browse the folder and view their uploaded image. Print your Web pages and the source code for each ASP.NET page and the code behind the page.

## Project 5-4

Your manager at Tara Store has asked you to create a feedback form page. He wants the form to go to the support team. Create a Web page named ch5_case4.aspx in the ch5_case4 folder. Add a form that collects the To, From, Subject, and Message data. The subject should be Customer Feedback. Make the To field have a value of your e-mail address, and make the subject read-only so that the visitor cannot change the value of the field. Add a submit button that says, Send My E-Mail Message. When the user clicks the button, configure the e-mail objects and send the e-mail message. Set the priority of the e-mail message to high. Enhance the appearance of the form with color, fonts, content, and graphics. Print the form, the source code, and the results from the e-mail message.

## Project 5-5

Your manager has heard that it's more effective to manage files on the Web than to use a file transfer program (FTP) to create and upload files to the Web server. Create a simple Web-based file management system. Create the initial page as ch5_case5.aspx. Allow the end user to enter the name of the file or directory. The path should be hard-coded as your chapter5\ch5_users\ directory. Add buttons that allow you to create and delete directories as well as files. The buttons should be named Create Directory, Delete Directory, Display Directory, Create File, Delete File, and Read File. Add a hyperlink to view the Web page in a browser. The directory information should be displayed in a Label control in the same page. When the Read File button is clicked, the file contents should be displayed in the Label control. Save your Web pages in your ch5_case5 directory. Enhance the Web pages with graphics, color, and text. Print the page and the source code.

CHAPTER

# 6

# SECURING THE ASP.NET APPLICATION

---

**In this chapter, you will:**

◆ Build security and privacy policies

◆ Validate data from a Web Form using Validation controls

◆ Create web pages that maintain state with and without HTTP cookies

◆ Maintain state in an ASP.NET application using session data

◆ Configure the application using configuration files

◆ Use membership services to manage user authentication and authorization

◆ Implement ASP.NET controls to build a secure login form

---

One of the responsibilities of a web developer is to create and process secure web applications. Visitors need to trust that the web site will protect their personal information. In the past, web pages were created using HTML, and processed and validated using client-side scripts. These forms, however, were not secure and could be easily altered before the user submitted the form. In this chapter, you will learn to validate data on the web server; validation on the server ensures both security and browser independence.

Companies need to trust that their information is protected. Membership and employee areas of Internet, intranet, and extranet web sites contain sensitive information that needs to be protected. In some applications, web developers protected the web pages, but not the non-web contents of the folder, which included PDF and graphic files. In this chapter, you will learn to build a secure login and authentication system that will protect your sensitive information. You will also learn how to configure your web site and folders to prevent users from listing and viewing all files.

In previous chapters of this book, you learned how to process forms and share data across web pages using session variables. In previous versions of ASP, session data could not be transferred across web servers, which meant that when a web server crashed, the session data no longer existed. As a result, a customer could place an order in his or her shopping basket, but if the server crashed, all of the items in the basket could be deleted. In this chapter, you will learn how to maintain session data and implement security using forms authentication. Forms authentication allows you to maintain form information and other data throughout an individual user's session, across the entire application, across multiple sessions, and across multiple servers. You will also learn how to create a web application that does not rely on HTTP cookies to establish sessions.

## BUILDING INFORMATION MANAGEMENT SECURITY POLICIES

Security is becoming increasingly important as more information is being made web accessible. Because of this accessibility, the information is becoming the target of hackers, competitors, and disgruntled employees. Web developers and system administrators who specialize in security are a hot commodity today. The reality is that security has always been a problem, as there will always be individuals who try to circumvent the system for their own agendas. Only recently have the news media, and the common user, have become aware of the security issues with respect to the Internet and computer technologies. The problem that web developers and system administrators face today is the existence of ever-evolving operating system software, applications, and business requirements, and the need to develop commensurate security policies to handle the changing technologies and information systems.

Privacy and security are tied together. Security includes protecting resources, and the information they contain. The media has written many stories about private information collected about individuals that has been sold to companies. Breaches in web security has contributed to the lack of trust between consumers and companies with respect to employee and consumer data. It is important to have a privacy policy that clearly demonstrates the company policy about how they handle customer information. Companies must also enforce this policy within their organization.

In the following two sections, you will learn more about security policies and privacy policies. It is important that security be at the forefront of discussions when the web application is being designed.

 Companies need to develop policies for what data they need to collect, and how they will validate the data. When a user is on a computer surfing the Internet and is bombarded with multiple questionnaires and feedback forms, don't be surprised if these individuals complete forms with fake data. Even validating the format of an e-mail address doesn't ensure that the e-mail is a real address. Many users have multiple e-mail addresses and may only provide a "junk" e-mail address to companies who require their e-mail address or for online contests.

## Security Policies

Hackers today have multiple methods to attack web sites. Hackers send malicious program code through e-mail by which they can obtain information from users such as their passwords, cookies, and other private information. One of the more recent methods is cross-site scripting. **Cross-site scripting** occurs when the hacker inserts malicious code through forms and query strings.

ASP.NET contains an **Encode method** that can be used to force dangerous characters such as < and > to be encoded as &lt; and &gt;. If your security policy requires and enforces the use of the Encode method, the hacker cannot execute code from within the form fields using the browser without the < > characters.

The following is sample code that uses the Encode method to protect the contents entered in the web page from being executed in the browser:

```
Dim strName As String
strName = txtName.ToString
message.Text = "Welcome " & HTTPUtility.Encode(strName)
```

You should provide information on your site to educate users to install virus checking programs and firewalls, and keep their virus data files up to date. You should educate them about cookies, privacy, and security issues, and have your privacy and security policies accessible from your home page. Third-party companies will provide security checks for your web site. You can post your results on your home page for your customers, which will alleviate their concerns about transacting business with your site.

Security policies can also dictate how you will ensure that users enter valid data, how you will ensure that the correct information is displayed to the authenticated user, and how you will ensure that unauthorized users do not have access to resources.

A web developer can do the following to make a web site more secure:

- Use Validation controls to validate user input and prevent cross-site scripting
- Use Web Forms to manage posting back data
- Use cookies only for non-private information
- Encrypt values stored within cookies
- Encrypt user data sent in a login form using SSL
- Encrypt user data stored in configuration files
- Develop a cookieless application for users who don't support cookies
- Use Web controls to develop login forms
- Use roles to assign permissions to resources
- Avoid using the guest account or anonymous user
- Avoid installing sample applications on live servers

- Avoid using default configuration on live servers
- Use virtual applications and folders to store protected data
- Move the web root directory to a volume separate from the volume that contains the operating system files
- Back up the files regularly
- Log user activities
- Download the log files onto storage media
- Maintain documentation on configuration setup and any changes
- Monitor the network activity using log files and network utilities
- Maintain policies for when suspicious network activity occurs
- Store file-based databases such as Access outside of the web root directory
- Use a server-based database instead of a file-based database
- Use stored procedures to interact with the databases

As you consider the security policies for your company, it is important to consider the Windows security model. This model includes multiple cumulative layers of security. Web application and web server security protects access to web resources, and Windows security protects access to file system resources.

The web server uses web configuration files to implement security policies. If a user is permitted access, Windows verifies that the user has permission to access the resource by checking the user's access control list. If the user is permitted, the page is displayed; otherwise an error message appears.

The Windows file system that allows you to protect files and folders is called Windows NTFS. Older operating systems may not use NTFS. When you installed your operating system, you should have selected NTFS as the file format. User accounts are assigned to individual users, groups, and services running on Windows such as ASP.NET. These accounts are assigned permission to resources using access control lists (ACLs). If a file is stored within a folder, and the user has the ability to read the folder contents, the user inherits the permission to read the file. Fortunately, this inherited permission can be overwritten at any time by changing the security permissions to the file. This overwriting task should be a standard security policy at your organization.

Web applications that integrate with other applications, such as a database, will have additional layers of security. For example, a web application that accesses a SQL server will need to send a connection string to the server that contains the user name and password, or the application will use integrated Windows authentication to allow the web application to access the database. Even if the web server and Windows allow access to the web page, the web page could still be denied access to the data by the SQL server.

## Privacy Policies

In today's marketplace, it is important for businesses to maintain integrity. A **privacy policy** is often used to inform the user about the type of information being collected and about what is being done with that information. When companies change their privacy policies, they should inform the user. One way to inform the user is to provide a date with the privacy policy link on the home page. Then, the end user can see that the policy has changed. Another method is to display the new policy before the user accesses resources using a simple pop-up window. Many users concerned about their privacy do not want web sites to keep information about them. Your privacy policy should flow from your business strategy.

The following is a list of web sites that discuss privacy issues and privacy policies related to Internet communications:

- TRUSTe—*www.truste.org*

- Electronic Frontier Foundation—*www.eff.org*

- Center for Democracy & Technology (CDT)—*www.cdt.org*

- Federal Trade Commission for the Consumer (FTC)—*www.ftc.gov/bcp/menu-internet.htm*

- Watchdog—*http://watchdog.cdt.org*

Platform for Privacy Preferences (P3P) standards provide a way for browsers to obtain the privacy policy for any particular web site. Currently only Internet Explorer version 6 or higher can automatically display the privacy policy. (*Note*: To view the privacy policy, select the View menu and then click Privacy Report. Then, double-click the web site that contains the privacy policy you would like to view.)

Many tools are built into the .NET Framework, ASP.NET, and your ASP.NET web development editor that will make security easier to implement. In the next section, you will learn how to validate data passed from a Web Form using ASP.NET.

## Passing Valid Data from a Web Form

Form fields are used to pass data. The code behind the page retrieves this data as strings. Form fields often collect data that has to be arranged in a particular format. For example, a phone number may be required to be entered as 999-999-9999, (999) 999-9999, or a custom data format. It is important to ensure that the data passed in from the form be received in the format intended. When the data is in the intended format, it is called valid data.

Valid data, or the lack thereof, can become important because this data is often inserted into databases, used by other applications, or misused by hackers to gain access to your web server. For instance, recall that you can create a web page using the contents in a form. You do not want a hacker to insert code into the form fields. To keep him or her from doing this, you may want to verify that your visitor doesn't enter any HTML tags, special characters, or client-scripts in the form. Likewise, if your form allows the user to upload a file, you may want to prevent the user from entering the file name *and* an extension for the file he or she wants to upload. A hacker may attempt to upload a web page that contains programming code that could be run from a web browser and give the hacker access to your web server files.

Let's consider another example. Assume that you are using form data to populate records in a database. In this case, you may want to make sure the data is in the format that will be used in the data fields, and that the content of the text boxes does not contain data programming commands. You will want to do this because if the text boxes contained programming commands, these commands could be executed by the database server.

In the following subsections, you will learn how to use Validation controls to validate the format of the data entered in form fields. You will also learn how to use Regular Expressions to validate custom data formats. Then, you can validate the data, before the data is processed or inserted into the database. You will then use the Validation controls to validate the form field data.

## Understanding Validation Controls

Client-side programming using JavaScript was often used to validate form data. Browsers vary in their support for standardized XHTML and JavaScript, however. Validating data on the client can be manipulated by hackers. Therefore, web developers started to validate the form data on the server. Although you can use Visual Basic .NET string functions to validate form field contents, a more efficient method to manage validation of form contents is the use of Validation controls. **Validation controls** are Web controls that use rules to validate the contents of form fields. A rule can contain a variety of requirements. For example, the rule may require that the control contain any value or a specific form of data such as alphabetical or numeric. The rule may also specify that data must be contained within a range of two values. The rule may be general, or it may be very specific and require formatting, such as uppercase letters and periods.

There are five built-in Validation controls and a control to display a summary of the validation errors. All five controls can be added to your web page using the **Validation tab** on the Toolbox or entering the code manually in the source code view of the web page. These controls are used in combination with other form controls. When you insert a Validation control, you configure the control that needs to be validated, and what the rules are for entering data. The five Validation controls and the validation summary are:

- *RequiredFieldValidator*—Makes sure a form field is not left blank (`<asp:Required FieldValidator>`)

- *RangeValidator*—Makes sure a field's value falls within a given range (`< asp: RangeValidator>`)

- *CompareValidator*—Compares a field's value with other values or other fields' values ({BEG CODE}<asp:CompareValidator>)

- *RegularExpressionValidator*—Evaluates data against a Regular Expression (< asp: RegularExpressionValidator>)

- *CustomValidator*—Evaluates data against custom criteria (<asp:Custom Validator>)

- *ValidationSummary*—Displays a summary of validation errors (<asp: Validation Summary>)

## Error Messages

The Validation controls inherit from the BaseValidator class in the WebControls namespace, which inherits from the Label class. Therefore, all Validation controls can display custom error messages using labels. They all support common appearance properties and methods such as ErrorMessage, Text, and ForeColor as shown in Figure 6-1. There is a subtle difference between the ErrorMessage and Text properties. If you configure the ErrorMessage property and not the Text, the ErrorMessage is displayed when the user tries to enter an invalid value and when the form is submitted. Likewise, if you configure a value for the ErrorMessage and Text property, the Text will be displayed when the user tries to enter an invalid value and when the form is submitted. If you use a ValidationSummary control, however, this control will use the ErrorMessage.

You need to control where the error message will be displayed on the web page seen by the user because this can affect the layout of your web page. You can control the location by using the **Display property**. For instance, when the Display property is set to dynamic and validation fails, space for the error message is dynamically added to the page. The Validation control is inserted into the page and assigned to a hidden field. This error message takes up space in the page, which can offset your HTML elements in an undesirable manner. In contrast, if the Display property is set to static, then space for the validation message is allocated in the page layout. If the validation does not fail, then no message is sent to the browser. The space for the message is still reserved on the page, however. Finally, if the Display property is set to none, then the validation message is never displayed in the browser. You would use this setting in situations such as when you use a Summary control to display all of the error messages in one location.

Validation controls that perform comparisons also inherit from the BaseCompareValidator base class in the WebControls namespace, and therefore inherit additional properties as shown in Figure 6-2.

## The Validate Method and IsValid Property

Each of the Validation controls inherits the **Validate method**, which performs validation on the associated Input control and updates the IsValid property.

The Validation control is visually displayed in Design view with the ErrorMessage displayed unless you configure the Text property

You can apply CSS styles to any Validation control

You can see the name of the class that is used to create the Validation control

Display allows you to configure the space reserved for the Validation control

ErrorMessage is the text message displayed when the field is invalid

The ForeColor property sets the color of the error message; the default ForeColor property value is Red

The Text property assigns a text message that is displayed before the control is validated to indicate what the user should enter

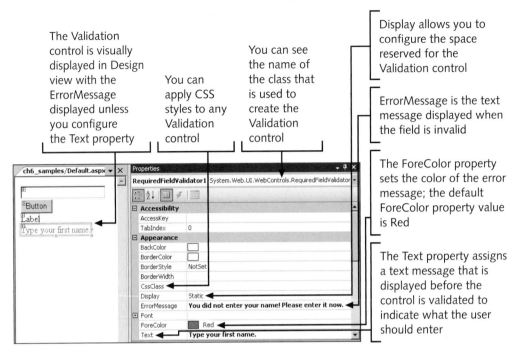

**Figure 6-1**  Appearance properties of Validation controls

The ControlToValidate property assigns the Input control that will be validated by this Validation control

The EnableClientScript property allows you to configure the validation to occur on the client and server

The SetFocusOnError property assigns the focus back to the Input control that contains the error and is therefore invalid

You can optionally assign Validation controls to separate validation groups with the ValidationGroup property

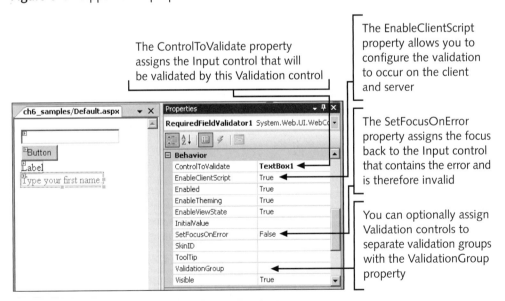

**Figure 6-2**  Behavior properties of Validation controls

The code sample in Figure 6-3 shows how you can check if all of the Input controls in the web page are valid.

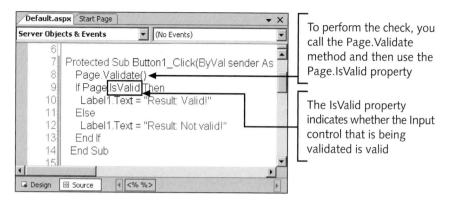

**Figure 6-3**   Validation methods and properties

## RequiredFieldValidator Control

The **RequiredFieldValidator control** is used to determine whether the end user has entered or selected any value at all. The **ControlToValidate property** specifies the Input control to validate. This will be the Input control that the RequiredFieldValidator control will validate.

This control can be combined with other controls. For example, you can use it to detect whether an end user typed in a number for a credit card, but you would use the RegularExpressionValidator control to check whether the number is actually a valid credit card number.

## RangeValidator Control

The **RangeValidator control** checks whether the value of an Input control is within a specified range of values. As shown in Figure 6-4, you must assign the **MinimumValue** and **MaximumValue properties** to specify the minimum and maximum values of the valid range. Then, the value entered in the field is compared against these two values.

## CompareValidator Control

The **CompareValidator control** inherits from the BaseCompareValidator class. This control compares the value entered by the user into an Input control, such as a text box, with the value that is already contained in another Input control, or with a constant value.

If you want to compare a specific Input control with another Input control, set the **ControlToCompare property** to specify the comparison control. If you want to compare the Input control with a constant value, you can specify the constant value with the **ValueToCompare property**. As shown in Figure 6-5, you must use the **Operator property** to specify the type of comparison to perform between the Input control and the ControlToCompare or ValueToCompare property. In the next section you learn how to create a custom Regular Expression to represent a specific date format, but you could use the CompareValidator control to validate a date. If you select Date as the value for the Type

For any Validation control, you can enter basic text or even
HTML tags within the ErrorMessage and Text properties

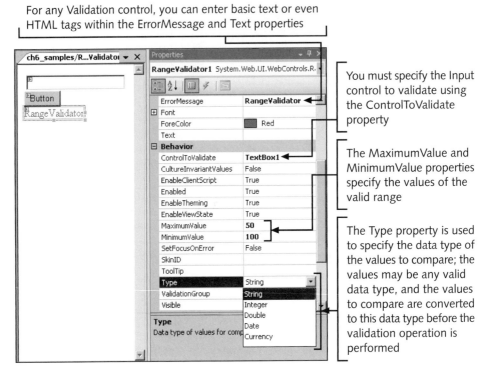

You must specify the Input
control to validate using
the ControlToValidate
property

The MaximumValue and
MinimumValue properties
specify the values of the
valid range

The Type property is used
to specify the data type of
the values to compare; the
values may be any valid
data type, and the values
to compare are converted
to this data type before the
validation operation is
performed

**Figure 6-4**    Configuring the RangeValidator control

property, and the DateTypeCheck for the Operator property, you can allow the user to enter
the date formatted as MM/DD/YYYY or MM/DD/YY using forward slashes or hyphens.
The day or month optionally can have a leading zero, but, the month has to be between 1
and 12 and the days have to be between 1 and 31. This will also validate the correct number
of days in the month, including leap year. Therefore, 11/31/2009 and 2/29/2009 would be
invalid but 2/29/2008 would not. If you plan to store the date in a database and perform
comparisons, you may want to use a Validation control that allows you to create your own
custom Regular Expressions.

## Building Regular Expressions

Before you learn about the other Validation controls, you need to learn about Regular
Expressions. You can create your own validation rules by building a Regular Expression. A
**Regular Expression** is a rule that describes values that are permitted or are not permitted.
The Regular Expression isn't a programming language, but it is a language that describes a
pattern of one or more groups of characters. These characters can be alphanumeric or
symbols, such as the comma. There are several standard Regular Expressions already built in
to Visual Studio .NET:

- *Social Security Number*—/\d{3}-\{2}-d{4}/
- *Internet E-Mail Address*—\w+([-+.]\w+)*@\w+([-.]\w+)*\.\w+([-.]\w+)*

You must configure the ControlToCompare or ValueToCompare property

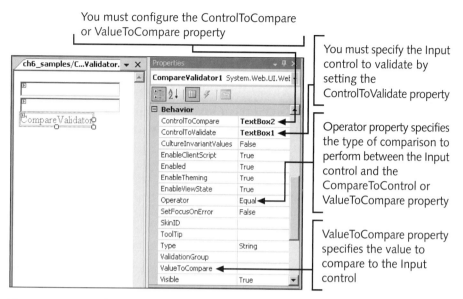

You must specify the Input control to validate by setting the ControlToValidate property

Operator property specifies the type of comparison to perform between the Input control and the CompareToControl or ValueToCompare property

ValueToCompare property specifies the value to compare to the Input control

**Figure 6-5**    Configuring the CompareValidator property

- *Internet URL*—http://([\w-]+\.)+[\w-]+(/[\w- ./?%&=]*)?
- *U.S. Phone*—((\(\d{3}\) ?)|(\d{3}-))?\d{3}-\d{4}
- *U.S. Zip Code*—\d{5}(-\d{4})?
- *Phone Number*—\d{3}-\d{2}-\d{4}

You can also create your own custom Regular Expression. The components of a Regular Expression can be individual characters, sets of characters, ranges of characters, choices between characters, or any combination. You can use any of these rules in combination. You can construct a custom Regular Expression by putting the various components of the expression pattern between delimiters. The backslash is used to insert a pattern or rule into the expression.

In the Regular Expression, certain characters such as the curly braces, parentheses, brackets, and slashes, along with the question mark, dollar sign, plus sign, period, caret, vertical line, and asterisk, do not represent themselves. You can also insert additional characters such as a blank space using the hexadecimal equivalent such as \x20. These characters are called **metacharacters** because they have an additional meaning with Regular Expressions. As you can see from the previous list, Regular Expressions use characters such as d to represent single digits. The number of digits required is listed within the curly braces. Therefore, the Regular Expression \d{5} means that the value had to consist of 5 digits such as 12345. You can use a vertical line (|) to combine expressions and parentheses to combine expressions. So, \d{(5|6)} would allow either a 5-or-6 digit number.

TIP

In JScript, the delimiters are a pair of forward slash (/) characters. Each programming language provides rules for Regular Expressions that may vary.

There are many ways to configure a Regular Expression. Some characters, such as lowercase d, represent a rule that requires a single digit from 0 through 9 in that character. You can also represent this rule, however, by inserting brackets and the range of digits allowed, such as [0–9]. To set the rule not to allow a digit or space, you can use the caret to signify not to allow that character. To not allow a single digit or space, you could use an uppercase D character or [^0–9]. Words are made up of alphanumeric characters. In a Regular Expression the word characters are represented as a lowercase w, or [A–Za–z_0–9]. You can be more specific and only require uppercase letters by using [A–Z] or lowercase with [a–z]. Again to change the rule not to allow a word character, you could use the uppercase W, or the caret, as in [^A–Za–z_0–9]. The lowercase s represents a white space character, and the uppercase S represents a non–white space character. A white space character consists of any of the special characters, such as \n that is used to insert a new line, \t that is used to insert a tab space, and \r that is used to insert a carriage return.

After you identified the type of character allowed in the position, you need to identify the **quantifier**, which indicates how many characters this rule will apply to. There are three patterns to the quantifier. If you specify just a single number, then that rule is applied for just that number of items. In the example of \d{5}, 5 would be the quantifier and there would be 5-digit characters required. For example, \[A–Z]{2} could be used to require 2 uppercase letters for a state abbreviation. If you specify a single number followed by a comma as the quantifier, then you will repeat the rule that number of times. For example, \[A–Za–z]{1,} could be used to require 1 alphabetical character at a minimum such as in a name. The length of the name is variable, so you don't want to put a cap on the number of characters. The third pattern to apply to the quantifier is the minimum number of digits, followed by a comma and the maximum number of digits. For example, there may be 4 to 6 numbers in a product model number. The quantifier would be {4, 6} and the complete rule would be \d{4, 6}.

There are many ways to modify the Regular Expression rules. For example, you can also use wild card characters in a Regular Expression. The question mark represents zero or one repetitions of the rule. So, the d? rule allows zero or more digits, and –? means you can have zero or more hyphens. The plus sign means one or more repetitions, and the asterisk means zero or more repetitions. For example, if you place a sequence of letters within brackets, such as [party], the value that would be allowed would have to match party. If you used [party]/i, the i allows you to match either uppercase or lowercase values, so both party and PARTY would be allowed. If you placed a carat before the pattern, then the left starting value must match that pattern. So, if the pattern was [^birthday], then values that would match include birthday or birthday party but not happy birthday. If you place a dollar sign after the pattern, then the value must match the pattern rule at the end of the value. So, if the pattern was [birthday$], then values that would match include happy birthday or birthday, but not birthday party. In a more practical example, if you need to allow the user to insert a date using either hyphens or forward slashes, you can include this in the rule. The ? is used to allow the user to enter the year using a 2-or-4 digit format. There are many ways to format the date; however, you need to consider what formatting rules you require. For example, (\d{1,2})(?:st|nd|rd|th) validates the 28th of the month, but it also validates incorrectly the 35th, and 28th. You can correct this by only allowing the st after 1, and th only after digits 0, and 4 through 9. A few examples of how you can format the date are shown below to help give you ideas on what techniques can be applied to formatting a date:

- *28<sup>th</sup> Sep 2009*— `^(\d{1,2})(?:st|nd|rd|th)\x20(Jan|Feb|Mar|Apr|May|Jun|Jul|Aug|Sep|Oct|Nov|Dec)\x20(\d{4})$`

- *Sep 28<sup>th</sup>, 2009*— `^(Jan|Feb|Mar|Apr|May|Jun|Jul|Aug|Sep|Oct|Nov|Dec)\x20(\d{1,2})(?:st|nd|rd|th)(,)\x20(\d{4})$`

- *09/28/2009*—`([0-2]\d)/([0-3]\d)/(\d{4})\d\d)[-|/](\d\d)[-|/](\d{2|4})(`

- *09/28/09*—`(\d\d)[-|/](\d\d)[-|/](\d{2|4})`

Regular expressions can be applied to many types of web applications. In an e-commerce application, you often need to validate the shipping cart, order, shipping, and payment data. Credit card numbers can be validated with Regular Expressions. This does not ensure that the number matches the user's name, or that the use of the credit card is authorized, or that the credit charge will be accepted by the credit card company. Rather, the validation only tells you that the number used follows an approved numbering scheme. The prefix has to do with the type of industry that issued the credit card. A prefix of 3 is used by travel and entertainment, 4 or 5 for banking and financial industries, and 7 for petroleum industries. In total, the first 6 digits represent the issuer of the card. Digit 7 until the second to last digit represents the individual account number. The last digit is a checksum digit used to make sure the user entered a valid number.

Each company has its own requirements such as the number of characters and type of numbers required, and a check digit algorithm as shown:

- *American Express*—prefix 34 or 37, length 15 digits, mod 10

- *Mastercard*—prefix 51–55, length 16 digits, mod 10

- *Visa*—prefix 4 or 13, length 16 digits, mod 10

Below are sample credit card numbers that you can use to test your web pages. These, however, are not valid credit card accounts that you can make charges to!

- *American Express*—3111111111111117, 340000000000009, 343434343434343

- *Mastercard*—5105105105105100, 5111111111111118, 5500000000000004

- *Visa*—4007000000027, 4012888888881881, 4111111111111111

You can certainly validate the number on the server using Visual Basic .NET programming statements and using third-party credit card Validation controls. In addition to validating that the user entered a number, you can also validate the credit card number using Validation controls. For example, the Regular Expressions for several types of credit cards where no hyphens are allowed could be:

- *American Express*—`3[4,7]\d{13}$`
- *Mastercard*—`^(51|52|53|54|55)\d{14}$`
- *Visa*—`^(4)\d{14}$|^(13)\d{13}$`

The Mastercard and Visa credit cards allow an optional hyphen between each group of four digits. You can insert the hyphens and combine all three Regular Expressions using `^((4\d{3})|(5[1-5]\d{2}))-?\d{4}-?\d{4}-?\d{4}|3[4,7]\d{13}$`. It is important, however, in a production web site to work with your credit card company to determine which credit cards you can accept, and what their requirements are for your web site.

**TIP**
A global **RegExp object** is used for creating pattern-matching expressions called Regular Expressions. The Regular Expression pattern is stored in the **Pattern property** of the RegExp object. So, in Visual Studio .NET, you can use this object when you want to create Regular Expressions in your programming code, outside of the Validation controls.

## RegularExpressionValidator Control

The **RegularExpressionValidator control** inherits from the BaseCompareValidator class. This control validates whether the value of an Input control matches a pattern defined by a Regular Expression. A Regular Expression can be used to check for predictable sequences of characters, such as those in Social Security numbers, e-mail addresses, telephone numbers, and postal codes.

When using a Validation control, make sure the clientTarget property is set to downlevel. If it is not set to this, the validation will occur on the client and the server. Also, it is important to note that the validation will succeed if the Input control is empty. Therefore, you should use the RequiredFieldValidator in conjunction with this control. As shown in Figure 6-6, you can select a standard expression or insert your own Regular Expression.

## The Use of JScript

You can set the location of the validation to occur on the client, if the client supports JScript, or on the server. If the validation occurs on the client, then JScript Regular Expression syntax is used. If the validation occurs on the server, then the `System.Text.RegularExpressions.Regex` syntax is used. Because the JScript Regular Expression syntax is a subset of the `System.Text.RegularExpressions.Regex` syntax, it is recommended that you use the JScript Regular Expression syntax in order to obtain the same results on both the client and the server.

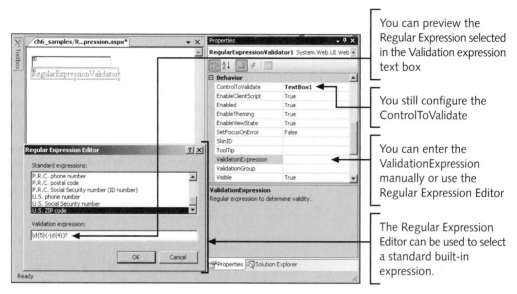

You can preview the Regular Expression selected in the Validation expression text box

You still configure the ControlToValidate

You can enter the ValidationExpression manually or use the Regular Expression Editor

The Regular Expression Editor can be used to select a standard built-in expression.

**Figure 6-6**    Configuring the RegularExpressionValidator control

## ValidationSummary Control

The **ValidationSummary control** is used to summarize the error messages from all validator controls on a web page, in one location. The Validation controls, including the ValidationSummary control, are created by classes that inherit their properties and methods from the WebControl class.

In addition to the basic properties and methods inherited from the WebControls class, the ValidationSummary control has properties such as DisplayMode, ShowSummary, ShowMessageBox, and HeaderText. You can display the message summary as a list, a bulleted list, or a single paragraph by setting the **DisplayMode property** to BulletList, List, or SingleParagraph. You can format the validation summary list and the error messages as shown in Figure 6-7.

**NOTE**    If none of the Validation controls discussed thus far is applicable to your form field, you can create your own validation functions on the client or server using the **CustomValidator control**. The benefit of using the Validation controls is that the single control works for multiple browsers and you don't have to write the client-side scripts. Even if you select client-side validation, the data is still validated on the server.

# Validating Form Data with Validation Controls

The following exercise demonstrates how to use Validation controls to validate form data on a web page.

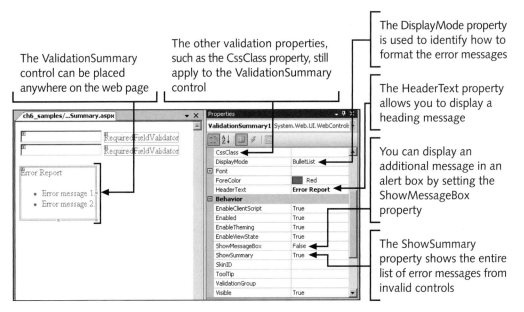

The ValidationSummary control can be placed anywhere on the web page

The other validation properties, such as the CssClass property, still apply to the ValidationSummary control

The DisplayMode property is used to identify how to format the error messages

The HeaderText property allows you to display a heading message

You can display an additional message in an alert box by setting the ShowMessageBox property

The ShowSummary property shows the entire list of error messages from invalid controls

**Figure 6-7**   Configuring the ValidationSummary control

1. Start your web editor application and then open the chapter6 web site.

2. In the Solution Explorer window, select the **ch6_validate** folder, and then double-click **ch6_validateform.aspx**.

3. Expand the **Validation** tab in the Toolbox. The Validation controls will be placed in the third column of the table as shown in Figure 6-8.

4. Drag and drop the **RequiredFieldValidator** control from the Validation tab in the Toolbox to the third table cell on the row where the first name label is displayed as shown in Figure 6-8. Change the Display property to **None**. Change the Text property to **\*** and the ErrorMessage property to **your first name**. Change the ControlToValidate property to **txtFirstName**.

5. Drag and drop the **RegularExpressionValidator** control from the Validation tab in the Toolbox to the third table cell on the row where the phone number label is displayed. Change the Display property to **None**. Change the ErrorMessage property to **the phone number as (999) 999-9999** and the Text property to **Please submit the phone number as (999) 999-9999**. Change the ControlToValidate property to **txtPhone**. Click the **ValidationExpression Build** icon in the Properties window, and from the Regular Expression Editor select **U.S. phone number**, and then click **OK**.

6. Drag and drop the **CompareValidator** control from the Validation tab in the Toolbox to the fifth table cell on the row where the today's date label is displayed. Change the Display property to **None**. Change the ErrorMessage property to **today's date as 99/99/9999** and the Text property to **Please**

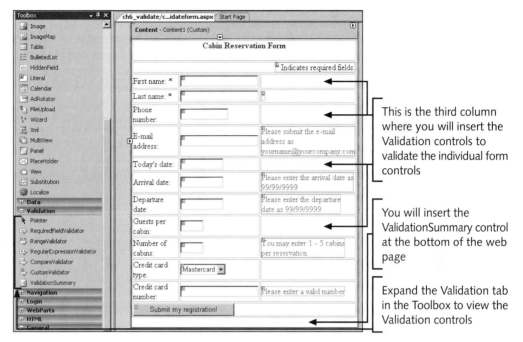

**Figure 6-8**    Placement of the Validation controls on the Web Form

**enter today's date as 99/99/9999**. Change the ControlToValidate property to **txtToday**. Change the Operator property to **DataTypeCheck** and the Type property to **Date**.

7. Drag and drop the **RangeValidator** control from the Validation tab in the Toolbox to the eighth table cell on the row where the guests per cabin label is displayed. Change the Display property to **None**. Change the ErrorMessage property to **1 – 5 guests per cabin** and the Text property to **You may enter 1 – 5 guests per cabin**. Change the ControlToValidate property to **txtGuests**. Change the MaximumValue property to **5** and the MinimumValue property to **1**. Change the Type property to **Integer**.

8. Drag and drop the **ValidationSummary** control from the Validation tab in the Toolbox to below the table. Change the HeaderText property to **Please enter:**. Change the ShowMessageBox property to **True** as shown in Figure 6-9**.**

9. Click the **Save All** button. Right-click the page, and then click **View in Browser**. Enter values for the form fields as shown in Figure 6-10. Click the **Submit my registration!** button. A message box will appear with the error messages, and the page will display the error messages Click **OK** to close the message box. Close each of the pages you created.

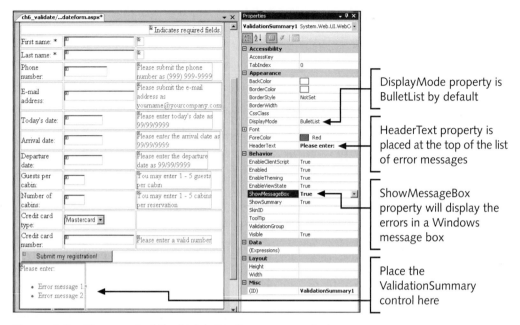

**Figure 6-9**    Placement of the ValidationSummary control

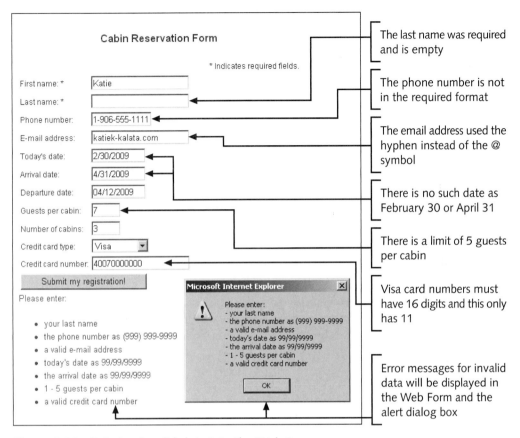

**Figure 6-10**   Entering invalid data into the Web Form

## MAINTAINING STATE

Today, web developers need to be able to identify the user with each subsequent page visited. They need to be able to use information throughout the entire time the user visits the web site. The individual person visiting the site may or may not be identifiable, depending on what data is maintained. Maintaining this information across each page is known as **maintaining state**. The state information is any data that is maintained while the browser is connected to the web site.

There are several techniques that you can use to maintain state information in your Web site. In this section, you will learn how to maintain state with client-side cookies, with HTTP cookies, and without HTTP cookies. All three methods use a unique identifier to recognize the user across web pages.

## Maintaining State with Client-Side Cookies

A common method for maintaining state information in early Internet development was client-side cookies. Client-side cookies maintain information about an individual user across sessions. A **cookie** is a small piece of information that is stored in a file on a client's local computer and is sometimes known as a client-side cookie. Client-side cookies often are also referred to as persistent cookies, because they remain on the user's computer in a file. The **Cookies collection** is a group of cookies that are sent by the server through the header to the client. The browser application on the client receives the cookie and writes the cookie to the client's file system. Storing the cookies with the client provides a means of automating client-side activities, such as the login process form's completion. All web servers have the ability to create a client-side cookie. Each browser may store the cookies in different locations on the client's hard drive. For example, in Internet Explorer, each cookie is stored in a separate text file. In Windows XP, Internet Explorer stores cookies in C:\Documents and Settings\[*UserID*]\Cookies.

### Concerns with Client-Side Cookies

End users often misunderstand the purpose, value, structure, and security of cookies. You should always create a web page on your site that informs the user of the privacy and security policies. In this page, you should provide a definition of cookies, inform the user whether the site uses cookies, and if so, indicate what information is stored in the cookie and for what the cookie is used.

Cookies are limited in size to 4 KB. Most cookies are about 100 to 200 bytes in size. The maximum number of cookies allowed is currently 300, with no more than 20 cookies from the same domain name. The Internet Engineering Task Force (IETF) sets the requirements for cookies in the RFC 2109 specifications. If the limit is reached, the oldest cookies are deleted. The maximum disk space for cookies is 1.2 MB, which is about the size of a floppy disk. Today, hard disk drives are available that can hold gigabytes of data. Therefore, cookies do not "eat up" a client's hard drive space. (*Note:* It is more likely that large amounts of hard drive space are used by the browser cache file, which contains all of the graphics and web pages that the client has visited.) An example of a cookie is shown in Figure 6-11.

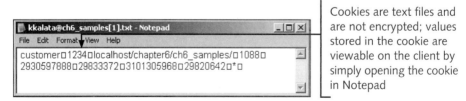

Cookies are text files and are not encrypted; values stored in the cookie are viewable on the client by simply opening the cookie in Notepad

**Figure 6-11**   Viewing a client-side cookie in Notepad

One of the concerns users have is that their personal information can be tracked across multiple web sites. Some web sites have agreements with third-party companies to provide advertising. These companies provide third-party cookies. Each browser has different methods to disallow third-party cookies. In Internet Explorer, you need to set the browser privacy settings to configure which types of cookies you choose to allow as shown in Figure 6-12. Although Figure 6-12 shows Internet Explorer 7, version 6 also provides the same capabilities to manage cookies.

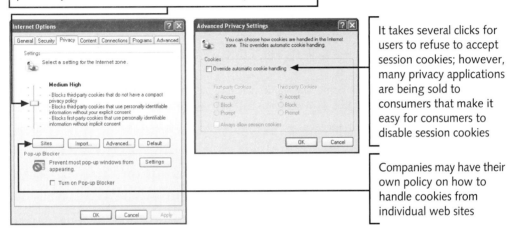

**Figure 6-12**   Changing the cookie setting

## Reading and Writing Client-Side Cookies Using JavaScript

The browser supports a Document Object Model (DOM) with its own set of objects, properties, and methods. The Document object allows you to set and retrieve properties for the web page. The **Cookie property** of the Document object allows you to store and read client-side cookies associated with the document.

To create a cookie, assign the document.cookie property to the cookie name and a value, separated by an equals sign. For example, you can create a cookie named customer with the value of 1234 by writing document.cookie = "customer=1234";. You can also assign the cookie an expiration date as shown in Figure 6-13. To delete the cookie, simply rewrite the cookie using a past date in GMT format such as Monday, 15-Jan-01 12:00:00 GMT. Some web developers prefer dynamically to set this date to yesterday by retrieving the current date, and subtracting one day. You can create a new date to store the date such as var exp = new Date("January 1, 2010") and then convert the date to GMT time using exp=date.toGMTString();. (*Note*: Each browser handles JavaScript, cookies, and dates differently.)

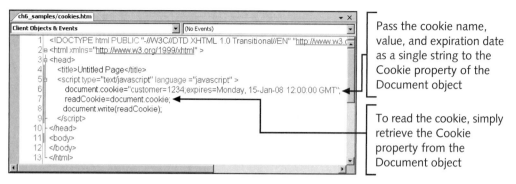

Pass the cookie name, value, and expiration date as a single string to the Cookie property of the Document object

To read the cookie, simply retrieve the Cookie property from the Document object

**Figure 6-13**   Creating a client-side cookie with JavaScript

**TIP**   Each cookie name and value pair is separated by a semicolon. You need to separate each pair of cookies, and then separate the name and value.

In the following exercise, you will modify a web page to create and display client-side cookies. When the user fills the form and clicks the Create Cookie button, the Create-Cookie function is called. This writes the cookie using the values passed in the form and then displays the cookie in an alert message box.

1. In the Solution Explorer window, right-click **ch6_clientcookies.aspx** in the **ch6_cookies** folder and then click **View Markup**.

2. Type the code as shown in Figure 6-14.

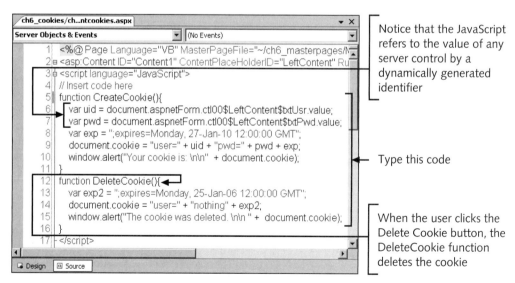

Notice that the JavaScript refers to the value of any server control by a dynamically generated identifier

Type this code

When the user clicks the Delete Cookie button, the DeleteCookie function deletes the cookie

**Figure 6-14**   Creating and deleting a client-side cookie with JavaScript

3. Click the **Save All** button. Right-click **ch6_clientcookies.aspx** and select **View in Browser**.

4. In the User name text box, type **Fred**, and in the Password text box, type **Gwinn**. Click the **Create Cookie** button. An alert message box appears with the value of your cookie. (*Note:* Your alert box may display the per session cookie known as the ASP.NET SessionID.) Click **OK** to close the alert message box.

5. Click the **Delete Cookie** button. An alert message box appears indicating that the client cookie has been deleted.

6. Close any open pages.

## Maintaining State with HTTP Cookies

Another method was storing the identification information in a temporary object on the server. ASP.NET uses Application and Session objects to store data. The **Session object** allows you to store information on the server, but still requires the browser to support a temporary cookie, called the HTTP cookie. This session information is volatile, however. If the web server crashes, the session information is unrecoverable. **HTTP cookies** are cookies created by the web server rather than the browser. They are used to enable the web server to identify the client. The SessionID is the value of the HTTP cookie that identifies the client's session. This same **SessionID** is used to identify a Session object on the server. The Session object can be used to store session variables such as the user's e-mail address, contact information, purchasing habits, browser properties, and personal preferences.

 HTTP cookies are also known as **per session cookies** because they identify the session. HTTP cookies are only used during the client's session, and are deleted when the session ends.

**NOTE**

By default, ASP.NET applications are configured to use HTTP cookies. The HTTP cookie is sent in the HTTP header. The HTTP cookie can be retrieved as an HTTP server variable called HTTP_COOKIE. You can view the value of the HTTP cookie and the client cookies when the web page Trace property is turned on. The following is the syntax for retrieving a cookie from the HTTP header using the server variable HTTP_COOKIE from a web page using the server variables:

```
<% Request.ServerVariables("HTTP_COOKIE") %>
```

### Concerns with HTTP Cookies

In some browsers, users can disable client-side cookies and still allow HTTP cookies. In Internet Explorer version 6.0 and 7.0, the cookie settings are stored in the Privacy Settings. You cannot assume that the client supports HTTP cookies or client-side cookies. Remember that the client can change these settings in the browser, but the programmer can't. (*Note:*

If you are configuring an intranet web site, your system administrator may have a policy about what types of cookies are allowed.)

Today, many web sites track user information. Users want to allow many of their favorite web sites to use cookies to provide them with capabilities such as automatic logons. After being bombarded with cookies and pop-up messages, however, they may decide simply to turn off their cookies. As an alternative to totally turning off cookies, users can specify which domains are (and are not) allowed to read and write cookies to their computers.

## Creating HTTP Cookies with ASP.NET

There are two types of HTTP cookie collections within ASP.NET; both can be accessed via the Cookies object. The first type contains cookies that are passed by the client to the web server from the Cookies header. The second contains cookies that have been generated on the server and transmitted to the client in the **Set-Cookie header**.

Following this paragraph is the syntax for writing a simple cookie using an absolute date. You can specify the number of days from the current date that you want the cookie to expire. If you expect your visitors to visit daily, then you can set the cookie to expire in `Date.Now.Today.AddDays(1)` days. If your visitors visit monthly, you can set the cookie to expire in `Date.Now.Today.AddDays(30)` days. If you want the browser to delete the cookie, you can specify a date in the past such as `Date.Now.Today.AddDays(-1)` or `July 4, 1776`. The browser then deletes the cookie because the cookie has expired.

```
<% Response.Cookies("myCookie") = "value" %>
<% Response.Cookies("myCookie").Expires = "MM DD, YYYY" %>
```

Notice that the Response object, and not the Write method, writes the cookie. The Write method is used to write the value of a string to the web page. The Response.Cookies method actually sends the cookie to the browser, which in turn writes the cookie to the client's file system.

The named group of cookies is also referred to as a dictionary cookie, and the individual cookies within it are sometimes referred to as cookie keys. The following is the syntax for writing a group of cookies named GroupID, where the cookie expires *N* days from today:

```
<% Response.Cookies("GroupID")("Cookie_1")="value"%>
<% Response.Cookies("GroupID")("Cookie_2")="value"%>
<% Response.Cookies("GroupID")("Cookie_n")="value"%>
<% Response.Cookies("GroupID").Expires=_
   "Date.Now.Today.AddDays(N)" %>
```

You can retrieve a cookie's value—whether from a simple cookie or from a group of cookies—by using the Request object. To retrieve a simple cookie with one value, specify the name of the cookie. One of the benefits of using ASP.NET over client-side scripting is that the Request object parses out the cookie names and values for you. It is easy to retrieve the value of a cookie with one line of code.

The following is the syntax for retrieving a simple cookie with one value:

```
<% Request.Cookies("CookieName") %>
```

To retrieve the value of a single cookie from a group of cookies, you must identify the name of the cookie group as well as the name of the individual cookie. Below is the syntax for retrieving a single cookie from a group of cookies named GroupID. CookieName_$n$ represents the name of the single cookie. A group cookie can contain multiple cookies, each with a different cookie name.

```
<% Request.Cookies("GroupID")("CookieName_n") %>
```

You can add additional cookies to the HTTP cookies. You can create an additional cookie with the Response object, read the value of the HTTP cookie using the Request object, and display it in a web page.

In addition to the Request and Response objects, you can use the HttpCookie Collection to create and read cookies. The sample code that follows this paragraph shows how to write a cookie named CookieEmail with the value from a text box named txtEmail. MyCookie is then added to the Cookies Collection using the Add method of the Response object.

```
Dim MyCookie As New HttpCookie("CookieEmail")
MyCookie.Value=txtEmail.Value
Response.Cookies.Add(MyCookie)
```

## Maintaining State with Cookies

In the following example, the web page that maintains state with HTTP cookies is using the Response and Request objects.

1. In the Solution Explorer window, right-click **ch6_servercookies.aspx** in the **ch6_cookies** folder and then click **View Markup**.

2. Type the code as shown in Figure 6-15.

3. Type the code as shown in Figure 6-16.

Type this code

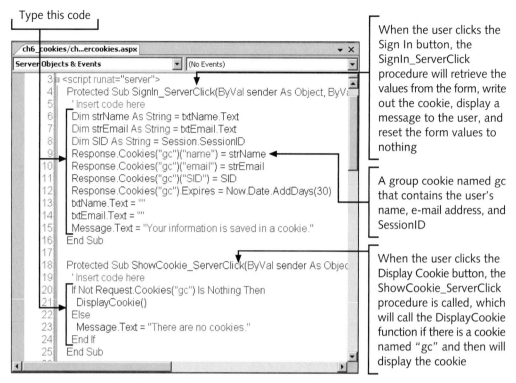

When the user clicks the Sign In button, the SignIn_ServerClick procedure will retrieve the values from the form, write out the cookie, display a message to the user, and reset the form values to nothing

A group cookie named gc that contains the user's name, e-mail address, and SessionID

When the user clicks the Display Cookie button, the ShowCookie_ServerClick procedure is called, which will call the DisplayCookie function if there is a cookie named "gc" and then will display the cookie

**Figure 6-15**   Creating an HTTP cookie

Type this code

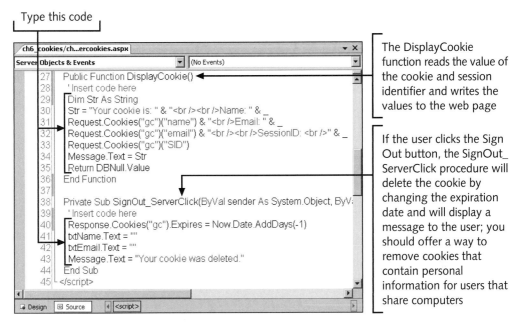

The DisplayCookie function reads the value of the cookie and session identifier and writes the values to the web page

If the user clicks the Sign Out button, the SignOut_ServerClick procedure will delete the cookie by changing the expiration date and will display a message to the user; you should offer a way to remove cookies that contain personal information for users that share computers

```
27    Public Function DisplayCookie()
28        'Insert code here
29        Dim Str As String
30        Str = "Your cookie is: " & "<br /><br />Name: " & _
31        Request.Cookies("gc")("name") & "<br />Email: " & _
32        Request.Cookies("gc")("email") & "<br /><br />SessionID: <br />" & _
33        Request.Cookies("gc")("SID")
34        Message.Text = Str
35        Return DBNull.Value
36    End Function
37
38    Private Sub SignOut_ServerClick(ByVal sender As System.Object, ByV:
39        'Insert code here
40        Response.Cookies("gc").Expires = Now.Date.AddDays(-1)
41        txtName.Text = ""
42        txtEmail.Text = ""
43        Message.Text = "Your cookie was deleted."
44    End Sub
45    </script>
```

**Figure 6-16**   Deleting an HTTP cookie

4. Click the **Save All** button. Right-click the **ch6_servercookies.aspx** page and select **View in Browser**.

5. Fill in the form with *your name* and *your e-mail address*, and click the **Sign In** button. Click the **Display Cookie** button. (*Note*: If a Windows dialog box asks if you want the system to remember the password for this page, click **Cancel**, or **No** in Windows XP.) The text box displays the value of your cookies and the SessionID.

6. View the cookie. If you are using Internet Explorer, open the C:\Documents and Settings\[*user name*]\Cookies folder using Windows Explorer. The cookie that you created should be named [*user name*]@*localhost[1].txt* and is usually the first cookie file listed. You can sort the cookies by the date they were last modified, if necessary, if you cannot locate the cookie. You can open this by double-clicking the file. Your cookie will contain a mixture of text and control characters. Close the cookie file and Windows Explorer windows, and return to the ch6_servercookies.aspx page in the browser.

7. Click the **Sign Out** button. Click the **Display Cookie** button. Your cookie has been deleted. Close any open pages.

## Maintaining State without HTTP Cookies

Previous versions of ASP required client support for HTTP cookies. Using ASP.NET you can create cookieless applications. **Cookieless applications** do not require the user to support client-side or server-side cookies. These HTTP cookies were used to link the client's session to the Session object using the session identifier called the SessionID. The session identification data is passed with the query string appended to the URL.

ASP.NET applications use the HTTP session cookie by default to maintain session data. The web application sets the **Cookieless property** in the sessionState node in the web.config file to determine if the session key requires cookies. The Cookieless property is set to false by default, which means that the default application requires cookies to maintain session state. Because users can refuse to accept HTTP cookies, the configuration can be set up to support session key management without requiring HTTP cookies. You can configure the application to use cookies or be cookieless, but you can't use both settings within the same application.

You can modify your web application to support sessions without requiring HTTP session cookies. The process of creating a cookieless application is known as **cookie munging**. When the Cookieless property is set to true, the web server appends the SessionID to any requested URL. The SessionID does not contain the session data. The session data is still maintained by the web server, or outside the web server. When the next page is requested, the web server can use the SessionID, which is attached to the URL, to identify the client without requiring the client to have a cookie.

In the following example, you will modify your application to support visitors who do not accept HTTP cookies.

1. In the Solution Explorer window, double-click **web.config** in the **chapter6** folder.

2. Type the code that is shown in Figure 6-17.

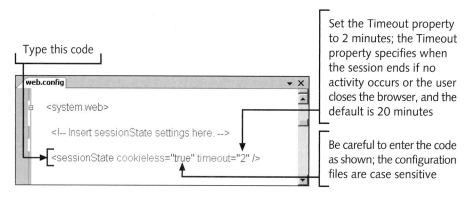

**Figure 6-17**   Creating a cookieless Web application

3. Click the **Save All** button.

4. In the Solution Explorer window, right-click the **ch6_ cookieless.aspx** page in the **ch6_cookies** folder and then select **View in Browser**.

5. Fill in the form with *your name* and *your e-mail address* and click the **Sign In** button. Click the **Display Cookie** button as shown in Figure 6-18.

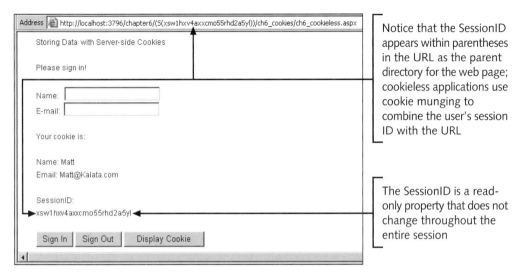

Notice that the SessionID appears within parentheses in the URL as the parent directory for the web page; cookieless applications use cookie munging to combine the user's session ID with the URL

The SessionID is a read-only property that does not change throughout the entire session

**Figure 6-18**   Using cookie munging to pass the SessionID in a cookieless application

6. Return to the web.config file, and delete the entire sessionState node.

7. Click the **Save All** button and close any open pages.

## STORING SESSION DATA

One of the biggest challenges in creating interactive web pages is maintaining the state of the user. It is important to understand web architecture and how state is maintained across web servers. In previous chapters of this book, you learned how to process forms and share data across web pages using session variables. Companies use Web servers networked together to create a web farm. Load balancing servers manage the traffic across multiple web servers within the web farm. In a Web farm, load balancing servers will redistribute the clients based on the workload on the servers. If one server crashes, the clients are redirected to a new server. If the user is directed to web server A, and web server A shuts down, the user can be automatically and seamlessly redirected to web server B. By storing information about the users session outside the web server A, web server B can use the information and pick up where web server A left off. This method allows for companies to expand their web sites by simply adding more web servers. Some companies may choose to expand their web site across multiple computer processing units (CPUs), within a single physical server. This configuration is known as a web garden.

When you visit an interactive web site, the site maintains information about your session, such as your IP address, what pages you clicked and when, when you visited the site, what browser you are using, and your preferences. User information can be tracked across user sessions and across the entire application. Some of this information is retrieved from the HTTP headers using the ServerVariables collection, which is exposed via the Request object, and some is retrieved from the properties of the Session object, such as the SessionID, a unique identifier that identifies each session. In the next two sections, you will learn how to store and retrieve session data within the user's current session, and how to configure your web application to store session data so that it will persist even if the user disconnects from the Internet.

## Storing and Retrieving Session Data

The **session state** maintains information across a single user's session. In the next section, you will learn how to retrieve the session identifier and how to store and retrieve session data across web pages.

### SessionID

The SessionID is a number whose value is determined by several factors, including the current date, and the IP addresses of the client and server. You cannot change the value of the SessionID property. A special session cookie is used to maintain the session information. When the session ends, the cookie is discarded. If the user opens a new session, a new SessionID is issued. Therefore, a SessionID can be used to track a user across a single session, but not across multiple sessions. To track a user across multiple sessions, the SessionID can be stored in a client-side cookie or in a database that contains the identity of an individual. Some of the information web sites track is retrieved from forms submitted by users. Once the user logs on with a user ID, the information collected can be correlated with past visits. The syntax for retrieving the SessionID property of the Session object is `Session.SessionID`.

### Session Object

The Session object is used to maintain session state. In ASP.NET, the Session object can be configured to store the data outside of the web server, without requiring HTTP cookies. The Session object contains properties that allow it to store session variables as a HashTable of key and value pairs. The **session variables** are used to store information, and are also stored in the server's memory. If the session ended, the session data contained within the Session object was also lost. Session variables can only be accessed within the session that declared and assigned the session variables, however. When the session ends, the session variables are released from memory. Figure 6-19 shows examples of how to retrieve the session identifier, and create and retrieve session variables.

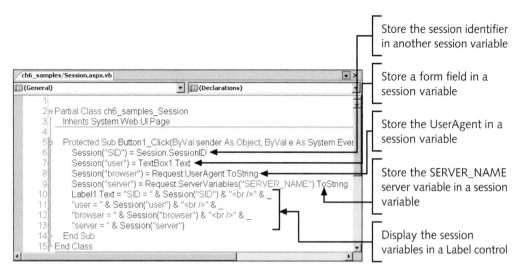

Store the session identifier in another session variable

Store a form field in a session variable

Store the UserAgent in a session variable

Store the SERVER_NAME server variable in a session variable

Display the session variables in a Label control

**Figure 6-19**    Creating and retrieving session variables

**TIP**    You cannot store a built-in object in a Session object. Therefore, you should retrieve the information desired as a string and then assign it to a session variable.

In this exercise, you will view the ch6_sessionvariables.aspx page, which shows the SessionID and all of the session variables and their values. At first, there will be no values assigned to the session variables. Then, after you log in, the session values will be assigned to the session variables. You can then display the SessionID and all of the session variables and their values. When you delete the session variables, all of the variables are reset. The SessionID will remain unchanged, however.

1. In the Solution Explorer window, right-click **ch6_sessionvariables.aspx** in the **ch6_session** folder and then select **View Markup**.

2. Type the code as shown in Figure 6-20.

3. Click the **Save All** button. In the Solution Explorer window, right-click the **ch6_sessionvariables.aspx** page and then select **View in Browser**.

4. Type *your name* and *your e-mail address* in the Name and E-mail text boxes. Click the **Set Session Variables** button.

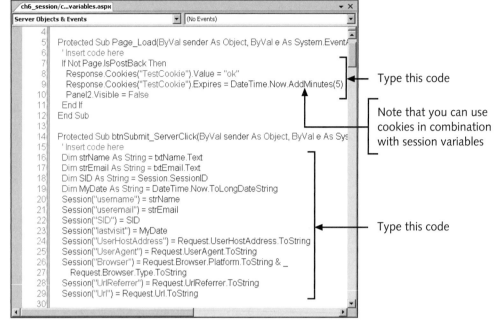

**Figure 6-20**   Using session variables

5. Click the **Display Session Variables** button. The session variables are displayed with their values, as shown in Figure 6-21.

6. Click the **Delete Session Variables** button, which will delete all of the values for the session variables and refresh the page.

7. Close any open web pages.

## Storing Session Data

You can configure where the web server stores the session data. In the machine.config and the web.config files, the **sessionState node** allows you to configure the session management. You can use the **Mode property** to identify which storage method should be used to store session data. The Mode property can be set to InProc, SQLServer, StateServer, Custom, or Off. Note that turning the mode to Off turns off session management, and Custom is used to configure the web application to store session data in a custom data store.

The session data that is being stored is specific to the ASP.NET application. For example, session IDs and session variables are stored as session data. Of course, browsers that don't accept HTTP cookies can't take advantage of session state. Therefore, if your visitors are likely to turn off HTTP cookies, you should build your application without using HTTP cookies. You can then create your own custom session management application and store the data in the database.

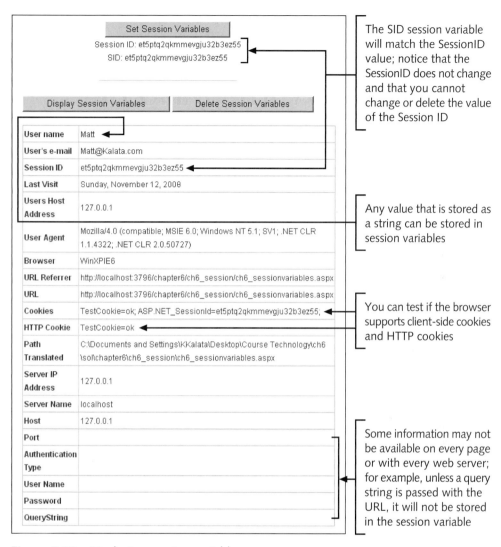

**Figure 6-21**   Displaying session variables

A good resource that discusses the business application of state management is located at *http://msdn2.microsoft.com/en-us/library/ms978631.aspx*.

**TIP**

## Using the Web Server Process to Manage Session State

When the Mode property is set to InProc, the data is stored in the web server process. Because the data is not being sent out of process, this method provides the best performance. You should use this method if you are hosting your web site on a single server, and if your session data is not critical. If the web server crashes, the data is lost. This method is not appropriate for a web farm because the user's request can be redirected to another web server if the web server load values change and the session data would not travel with the request. If you stop and restart the web server service, all session data from all sessions will be lost. Furthermore, session data can be lost if the application domain or the aspnet_wp.exe process (or the w3wp.exe process for IIS version 6.0) has to restart. The application domain (known as AppDomain) is restarted when the configuration files or the bin directory are modified, when the memory limit setting listed in the processModel node in the configuration file has been reached, or if virus scanning software has modified the configuration files. The **processModel node** allows you to configure the idleTimeout, memoryLimit, and other server process related properties.

The following is a sample sessionState setting to run the state management within the web server process:

```
<sessionState mode="InProc"
    cookieless="false" timeout="20" />
```

## Using State Server to Manage Session State

You can set the Mode property to "StateServer" to store the data with a Windows service called **aspnet_state service** or simply the State Server. The State Server program is located at %systemroot%\Microsoft.NET\Framework\[version]\aspnet_state.exe.

You can start the State Server by using the DOS commands or the Windows Services utility program. The **stateNetworkTimeout** property is used to specify the number of seconds that the connection between the web server and the State Server can be idle before the session is dropped. Because the service is run out of process from the web server, the session data is reliably stored. Although the State Server is reading the data out of process, generally it is located on the same server. Therefore, the performance is better than if the session data is sent to an external State Server. The State Server service can be used across multiple web servers.

If you select the mode as StateServer, you must also provide the stateConnectionString. The connection string may vary with your server. The **stateConnectionString** identifies the TCP/IP connection to the State Server. Each network interface card (NIC) is assigned an IP address and up to five port numbers. The **TCP port number** is the connection where applications listen for messages sent to them. For example, the default port for the web server is 80. So, the web server listens on port 80 for HTTP messages.

**NOTE**

You should not use port numbers below 1024 because they are **well-known ports** that have been assigned to commonly used services by the Internet Assigned Numbers Authority (IANA). Ports 1024 through 49151 are registered to commonly used applications such as the State Server. Because the port used by the State Server is the "well-known" port number, it is an easy target for attack by a hacker. You can change the port number by changing the TCP/IP settings. If you assign a port in this range, you must ensure that the port assignment does not conflict with other applications running on the computer. It is recommended to use the default port number, or select a number between 49152 through 65535.

6

The following is a sample sessionState setting to run ASP.NET state management on a local State Server:

```
<sessionState mode="StateServer"
    stateConnectionString="tcpip=127.0.0.1:42424"
    stateNetworkTimeout="10"
    cookieless="false" timeout="20" />
```

**TIP**

If you intend to use the same State Server for multiple web servers, you must change the TCP/IP settings in the stateConnectionString in the web.config file so that each of the web servers points to the same State Server. You cannot use the loopback IP address. You must also configure the machine key on each server. The machine key is used to encrypt the data going to the State Server. In order for the web servers to be able to encrypt the session data, they must all have the same machine key.

To start the State Server using the command prompt window:

1. Open the command prompt window by clicking **Start**, then clicking **Run**.

2. Type **cmd** in the text box, and then press **Enter**. The command prompt window opens.

3. Type **net start aspnet_state**, and then press **Enter** to start the service. A message will be displayed when the service has been started successfully.

4. Type **net stop aspnet_state**, and then press **Enter** to stop the service. A message will be displayed when the service has been stopped successfully.

5. Close the command prompt window.

**TIP**

The localhost is considered a trusted web site by the browser. Therefore, web pages will allow the localhost to save cookies, use session cookies, and perform other activities unless you specifically configure your browser (in the Internet Options window) not to trust the local computer.

State Server is a Windows service and can therefore be accessed via the Windows Services applet. In the following activity, you will start State Server using the Windows Services window:

1. Click **Start**, click **Control Panel**. Switch to **Classic View**, if necessary, to change your view to Classic View.

2. Double-click **Administrative Tools**.

3. Double-click **Services**.

4. In the Name column, double-click **ASP.NET State Service**.

5. To start the State Server service, click the **Start** button as shown in Figure 6-22. The keyword started in the status service column shows that the service has been started. (*Note:* You can also click the **Start** button on the Services toolbar. You can also open the ASP.NET State Service dialog box by right-clicking the **ASP.NET State Service** name and selecting **Properties**.)

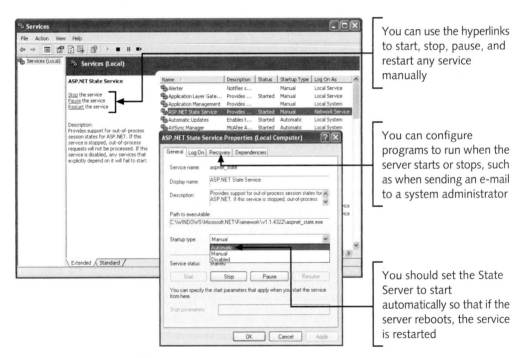

You can use the hyperlinks to start, stop, pause, and restart any service manually

You can configure programs to run when the server starts or stops, such as when sending an e-mail to a system administrator

You should set the State Server to start automatically so that if the server reboots, the service is restarted

**Figure 6-22**   Starting the State Server

6. You can set the service to start manually or automatically by selecting the value in the Startup type drop-down list. Automatic startup means that the service automatically starts whenever the server is restarted. Click **OK**, and then close the Services window.

7. Return to your ASP.NET application in your web editor. Edit the **web.config** file to support the session state parameters. Type the code and set the mode to **stateServer** as shown in Figure 6-23.

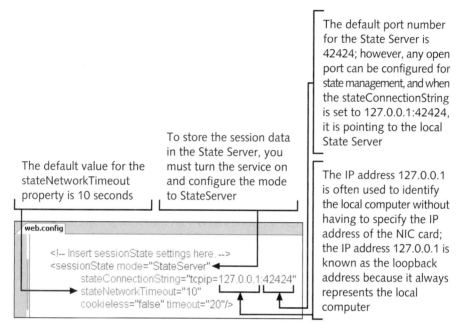

**Figure 6-23** Configuring the web application to store session data in the local State Server

8. Click the **Save All** button.

9. Change the mode in the web.config file session state mode to **InProc**.

10. Click the **Save All** button.

11. Open the command prompt window by clicking **Start**, then clicking **Run**. Type **cmd** in the text box, and then press **Enter**. Type **net stop aspnet_state** in the command window, and then press **Enter** to stop the service. A message will be displayed when the service has been stopped successfully. Close the command prompt window.

12. Close any open pages.

## Using the SQL Server to Manage Session State

If you set the Mode property to SQLServer, you can also use a SQL Server to store your session data. SQL Server is run out of process, which means that the SQL Server application runs outside of the Web Service, in its own memory space. Although using SQL Server to store session data does not provide the same performance as using the StateServer or InProc configuration, it does offer reliable storage of session data.

SQL Server can be run on the same Windows server or another Windows server. To do so, you must identify the connection string used to connect to the SQL Server. The connection string identifies the TCP/IP address and the authentication data required to connect to the database. The connection string must be a valid System.Data.SqlClient.SqlConnection string, minus the Initial Catalog.

**TIP**

Even if you use SQL Server or State Server to manage your session state, session data may be lost in a load balanced web farm environment unless you configure the application path of the web site to be the same for all of the web servers in the web farm. The application path is case sensitive.

The following is a sample sessionState configuration setting to run ASP.NET state management on a local SQL Server:

```
<sessionState mode="SQLServer"
sqlConnectionString="datasource=MACHINENAME\SQLEXPRESS;
userid=sa;password=password"
cookieless="false" timeout="20" />
```

SQL Server can authenticate the user by verifying a user name and password or by using Windows integrated security. **Integrated security** represents that the SQL Server will use integrated Windows security to authenticate requests to access the database. Within the sqlConnectionString property, you must pass a user ID and password, or insert "Integrated Security=SSPI. The following is an example of using Windows integrated security as the authentication method for SQL Server:

```
<sessionState mode="SQLServer"
sqlConnectionString="datasource=localhost;
    Integrated Security=SSPI;"
cookieless="false" timeout="20" />
```

You must configure the sessionState configuration setting to run ASP.NET state management on a local SQL Server. The default TCP port number for SQL Server is 1433. If you have changed the SQL Server port number, you will have to insert the port number into the sqlConnectionString. You can pass the user ID and password, or you can use integrated Windows authentication by setting the sqlConnectionString property to "datasource=localhost; Integrated Security=SSPI;. The data source is the name of the SQL Server. You can then pass the full name of the server or the IP address. If the SQL Server is the only SQL Server on the local machine, you can pass the loopback address (127.0.0.1) or the keyword localhost. You can also use MACHINENAME\SQLEXPRESS to identify the default SQL Server that may have been installed with your web editor.

## APPLICATION CONFIGURATION

A **web application** is a group of files and folders (including virtual folders) located under the web application's root directory. A web application is defined by the web server software. Internet Information Server (IIS) has the capacity to define multiple web applications on the same computer. In IIS, the root directory of a web application may be configured as a virtual web. A **virtual web** is a web application that is stored outside of the C:\Inetpub\wwwroot folder. A web application can be configured to include one or more virtual directories. A **virtual directory** is a directory stored outside of the web application folder or the wwwroot folder.

You can maintain information across the entire web application with the Application object. The **Application object** stores the application variables in the server's memory, and any user can access them from any page within the web site. The application variables are released from memory only when the web application is stopped, when the web server is stopped, or when the server is stopped.

In the past versions of ASP, the configuration of the web site was contained primarily within a data structure called the **Metabase**, and some additional data was stored in the registry. The registry is where Windows applications typically store their configuration settings. The web developer typically accessed the application settings via the web server's snap-in application for the Microsoft Management Console (MMC) application, or by using the **Windows Scripting Host (WSH)** to create scripts to access the Metabase. The web site could be configured locally using the MMC.

Today, you can configure the web server using the property pages within the Microsoft Management Console (MMC) application, in the ASP.NET web configuration files, or in the Web Site Administration Tool (WSAT). Therefore, in the following subsections, you will learn about the properties that can be configured using the MMC, properties that can be configured using the configuration files, and properties that can be configured using the WSAT.

## Viewing and Understanding the Web Server Property Sheets

Both Visual Studio .NET 2005 and Visual Web Developer Express 2005 come with a built-in web server. You cannot configure this web server using property sheets, however. While you are learning ASP.NET, you may or may not have access to a professional web server such as Microsoft Internet Information Server. In order to view the web server property sheets, you have to have a professional web server running. It is important for web developers to know what properties can be configured. This section describes how to view the property sheets, and provides an overview of the property sheets.

If you have Microsoft Internet Information Server installed and running, you can view the property sheets for the web server by completing the following steps:

1. Click the **Start** button and then open the **Control Panel**.

2. Double-click the **Administrative Tools** icon. Double-click the **Internet Information Services** icon.

3. Double-click the computer name. Double-click **Web Sites**.

4. Right-click **Default Web Site**, and then click **Properties**. The web site property sheets open.

The **Web Site** property sheet as shown in Figure 6-24 contains information that identifies the web site, such as the IP address and TCP port.

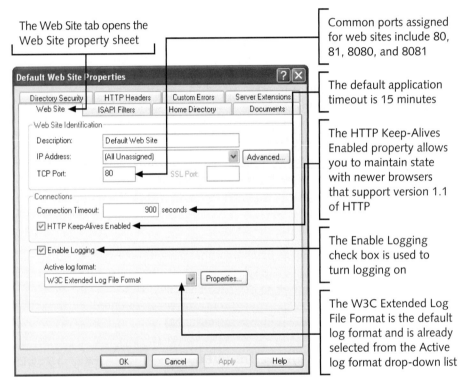

**Figure 6-24**   Web Site property sheet

**TIP**     All of the applications created within the web site log connections are within the same log file. You can disable logging for the log site, however, by deselecting the Log visits check box on an application's Directory property sheet.

Each log format contains different information. The **W3C Extended Log File Format** contains extended properties that can be logged such as the Client IP Address, the User Name, the Method invoked, the HTTP Protocol Version, the User Agent, the Cookie, and the Referer. (*Note*: In this case Referer is spelled referer.) Each log file name is named after the date. The default location for the web server log files is %WinDir%\System32\LogFiles, as shown in Figure 6-25.

The default
directory for
the default
web site log
files is W3SVC1

You can create new
log files daily, or
set a file size limit

Extended properties
allow you to log
extra information
such as the date
and user name

The default naming
scheme is exyymmdd.log,
where yymmdd represents
the last two digits of the
year, the month, and the
day; single values, such as
2, are preceded by a 0; for
example, the default log
file name created on
September 28, 2010, is
ex100928

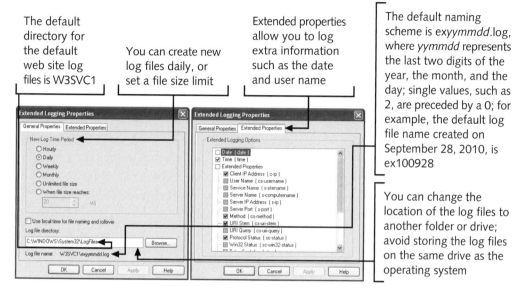

You can change the
location of the log files to
another folder or drive;
avoid storing the log files
on the same drive as the
operating system

**Figure 6-25**   The default extended logging properties

**TIP**

It is recommended that you not allow the log files to increase in size without monitoring them closely. If the log files are on the C: drive and the hard drive disk space fills up, the system will crash. If you set the New Log Time Period to "When file size reaches," the file will overwrite itself when it reaches the specified limit. These files may be required in an investigation or may need to be submitted to a court of law as evidence. Therefore, you should maintain copies of all of the log files on a backup device such as a CD or DVD disk.

**TIP**

The date and time logged in the file is based on the local time zone. If you leave the "Use local time for file naming and rollover" option unchecked, the log files will use the GMT time zone. This makes it easier to compare log files across a large organization that spans time zones.

1. The log file is a text file that can be opened in a text editor. The three-digit number next to each entry indicates an HTTP status message code as shown in Figure 6-26. Some resources such as the images within a web page are also logged when the page is downloaded.

2. There are many applications that can be used to display the log file in a graphical format. You can also import the log file into a word processing document, a spreadsheet, or a database. Or, you can create your own application to display the log files in a graphical format. Commercial applications that

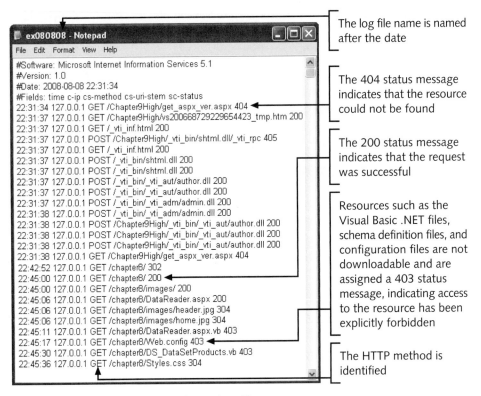

**Figure 6-26**    Raw data in a web site log file

include log file report writers include Analog (*www.analog.cx*), WebTrends (*www.netiq.com/webtrends/default.asp*), and Livestats (*www.deepmetrix.com*). These applications parse raw log files into visual and tabular reports that can be used to analyze your web site traffic.

3. The **Home Directory** property sheet, as shown in Figure 6-27, allows you to configure the web site so that it exists in another directory, hard drive, or web server, or the browser is redirected to another URL.

The **Documents** property sheet allows you to select a different name for the default document. The default document is displayed when the requested URL ends with a folder and not a file name. In ASP.NET, the default name is default.aspx. You can also enable a footer that will appear throughout your entire web application using the IIS Document Footer property.

The **HTTP Headers** property sheet allows you to enable content expiration. You can force the web application to have the page expire immediately after it is delivered, or configure a relative or absolute date and time for the page content to expire. (*Note*: The references on the HTTP Headers property page are no longer current. In 1999, the Recreational Software Advisory Council RSAC was incorporated into the Internet Content Rating Association

Script source access
allows visitors to access
your script source code

The location of the default
web site can be changed to
a different path

Log visits property allows
the log file to log visits to
the web site; indexing this
resource property enables
Index Server to include this
web resource in the Index
Server search engine
catalogues

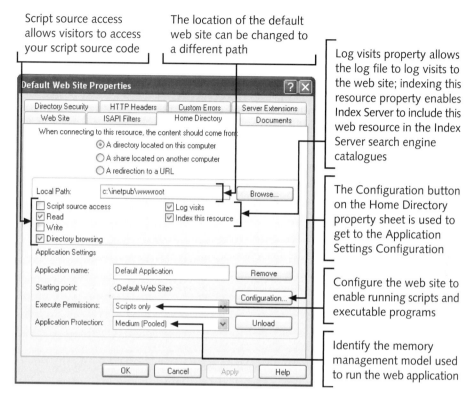

The Configuration button
on the Home Directory
property sheet is used to
get to the Application
Settings Configuration

Configure the web site to
enable running scripts and
executable programs

Identify the memory
management model used
to run the web application

**Figure 6-27** The default Home Directory property sheet

(ICRA). The ICRA's goal is to preserve free speech on the web, while protecting children from potentially harmful content.) Not all content is appropriate for all ages. It is useful to end users to place information about the web site content in a conspicuous place on the home page.

The **Custom Errors** property sheet can configure custom error pages within IIS. The default error pages are located at %systemroot%\help\iisHelp\common\.

The **Directory Security** property sheet allows you to enable anonymous access, basic authentication, or Windows authentication to secure the entire web application. You can enable IP address and domain name restrictions if you are running your web server on a Windows Server. You can also configure client and server certificates within this property sheet.

# Understanding Application Configuration Files

In addition to the web server property pages, web applications contain a series of XML-based configuration files that can be edited in a simple text editor such as Notepad. This text-based configuration file system allows web server and ASP.NET application settings to be easily replicated across web servers. This allows web administrators to add a new web server to the web farm easily. Furthermore, web developers can create their own applications to access the web settings. They can access the web settings remotely via the configuration files.

Because the file is XML compliant, the nodes, elements, properties, and values within the file are case sensitive. You can add comments to the file using the HTML comment tags. Nodes contain properties that are also referred to as **attributes**. Any node that does not contain any content can be written as a minimized tag. The configuration file does not require any particular order for the nodes. The nodes must be nested according to XML rules, however.

Web applications can be configured in the global machine configuration file (machine. config) or from within the application configuration files. The application configuration for the web site is contained in a file named web.config. The application-level web.config file is created by default when you create a web application. The web site configuration is located in the root directory of the application; the entire application inherits the settings configured in this file. It is possible to override these settings by placing a web.config file within a subdirectory, or by configuring the settings within the ASP.NET web page.

In Windows XP the machine-level configuration file is located by default in C:\WINDOWS\Microsoft.NET\Framework\[*version*]\CONFIG\machine. config. This XML-compliant file contains configuration settings for the .NET Framework, Windows applications, and web applications.

You have already used the configuration files in several exercises within this book. The following subsections will review some of the common configuration elements that have not been covered such as the appSettings, pages, httpRuntime, trace, and customErrors elements.

### The appSettings Element

You can use the **appSettings element** to configure custom key/value pairs known as **application variables**. This element allows you to store data such as connection strings that can be used across the entire application. The key is used to retrieve the value at a later time. In the sample code following this paragraph, a key named CompanyName is created with a value of Course Technology. This is also an example of a minimized element.

```
<appSettings>
  <add key="CS1" value="Course Technology" />
</appSettings>
```

Within the web page, you can easily retrieve the values of the application variables. In the following code, the application variable CompanyName is written to the web page:

```
Dim CN As String
CN=ConfigurationSettings.AppSettings("CompanyName")
Response.Write("Company Name: " & CN)
```

## The Pages Element

The **pages element** allows you to configure settings that control how content is delivered to the web page. Many of these settings are often configured at the page level. Using the pages configuration node, you can modify the, enableSessionState, enableViewStateMac, enableViewState, maintainScrollPositionOnPostBack, and buffer attributes.

The **enableSessionState attribute** allows you to use the session capabilities of ASP.NET. You must enable sessions to have access to session variables, session IDs, and HTTP cookies. If you do not plan to use sessions, you can disable this attribute by setting it to false. You can also set the attribute to read-only so that you can use sessions, but cannot create new session data.

The **enableViewStateMac attribute** is used to validate data. This attribute indicates that ASP.NET should run a machine authentication check (MAC) on the encoded version of the view state to ensure that the data has not been altered on the client. The enableView-StateMac attribute is set to false by default because the validation method requires substantial server resources.

The **enableViewState attribute** is used to enable the web page to store data in the __VIEWSTATE hidden form field in the web page.

The **buffer** is an area in memory on the server. As a request is processed, the data generated from the response is stored in the buffer. Setting the buffer attribute to true allows you to store the entire response from the request on the server, until the request has completed processing. If there is an error in your code, buffering the code will help prevent sending an incomplete page out to the browser. If the **buffer attribute** is set to false, the end user sees content generated by the server faster. As a result, the end user perceives that the server has a faster response time. There is no increase in the actual performance of the web server when you change the buffer attribute to false. Once content has been sent to the client, however the header content is also sent. You cannot change the header content once content has been sent to the client. When you want to redirect the user to another page, the header content must be modified. Therefore, if you have code in your page that redirects the user to another page, you cannot set the buffer to false.

When the page reloads after a postback, the page normally loads at the top of the page. In ASP.NET 1.1, the smartNavigation page property allowed the page to return to the previous location in the page. The **maintainScrollPositionOnPostBack element** replaces smart-Navigation and will allow the page to return to the same position in the client browser when pages are posted back to the server.

## The httpRuntime Element

The **httpRuntime element** sets the executionTimeout, maxRequestLength, and use FullyQualifiedRedirectURL attributes. The **executionTimeout attribute** is the time that a resource is allowed to execute before the request times out. The default executionTimeout value is 90 seconds. The **maxRequestLength attribute** is the number of kilobytes that can be accepted from an HTTP request. The default maxRequestLength size is 4096 kilobytes (4 MB). Configuring this attribute will help you prevent users from uploading large files using HTTP.

**TIP** Some hackers have been known to send a large number of requests to a web server to keep the web server busy. These attacks are called denial of service (DOS). By sending many requests, they stop the web server from responding to legitimate requests. If you set the maxRequestLength to a smaller number, the hackers won't be able to send a large number of requests to the server.

The **useFullyQualifiedRedirectUrl attribute** is used to fully qualify the URL when the client has been redirected to a new page. For example, the code `Response.Redirect ("/login.aspx")` redirects the user to a login page using a relative address (/login.aspx). Many clients, such as mobile phones, require fully qualified URLs when they are redirected, however. Therefore, if the useFullyQualifiedRedirectUrl attribute is set to true, when the client is redirected, the absolute URL is sent to the client, even if the code in the page identifies a relative address.

## The Trace Element

Tracing is the ability to retrieve data to help identify the data that was communicated during the request or response. The **Trace property** can be turned on in the page, or in the configuration files in the **trace element**. The following is an example of how you would set the Trace property within the Web Form:

```
<%@ Page Trace="true" %>
```

Within the web configuration file, tracing can be customized. The **enabled attribute** allows the application to turn on tracing. In the machine configuration file, the enabled setting is set to false by default. On a production server, you do not want to display the trace results to the visitor. To avoid this, you can set the **localOnly attribute** to true, so tracing results are only displayed to the localhost and not on other computers. To view the trace results, you access the web site using the URL *http://localhost/*.

**TIP** The Trace property will append the trace information below the web page when the page layout uses FlowLayout. If the page uses GridLayout and dynamic positioning, the trace information displayed is intermixed with the page content. In these cases, it is useful to use the trace utility program to obtain the trace information.

The **pageOutput attribute** allows you to display the trace results with the web page. If the pageOutput attribute is set to false, then the output is not displayed with the page. Instead, you can access the tracing data using a trace utility program. The trace results are stored in memory and can later be accessed using the trace utility program.

The trace element will store the data in the **trace stack**, which can be read by the trace utility program. The .NET class that enables these tracing capabilities is the **TraceContext class**. You can configure your application to send additional data to the trace stack. The **Write method** is used to send information to the trace utility program. The syntax to use the Write method is `Trace.Write("CategoryName","Value")`. CategoryName argument is a string that contains the text label to be displayed in the trace output. The Value argument is a string that contains the value of CategoryName argument. You can use an expression to generate CategoryName or Value. The **Warn method** is used to send information to the trace utility program. The difference between the Write method and the Warn method is that the Warn method sends the output as red text. Therefore, the messages are easily viewed.

To view the trace data, you can insert the Trace property in the page directive and have the trace information appended to the page, or use the trace utility program called **TraceTool**. The values that you add using the Write method appear in the Category column, and their corresponding values appear in the Message column. The tool provides the trace stack information along with the physical directory of the page being traced.

You can enable the Trace feature on any page in any directory even if the enabled property is turned off in the configuration file. It is usually recommended that you disable trace for production applications once the application has been deployed. If you have statements that use Trace.Write, you can leave the commands in the page without having an impact on performance. Later, you may want to use those statements again if you have to debug the application. In the following exercise, you will set the Trace feature for the entire application and then view a web page that sends information to the trace stack when the total calculation is less than or equal to $0, or greater than $1000. Then, you will view the trace stack using the TraceTool program.

1. In the Solution Explorer window, double-click **web.config**.

2. Set the trace node, as shown in Figure 6-28.

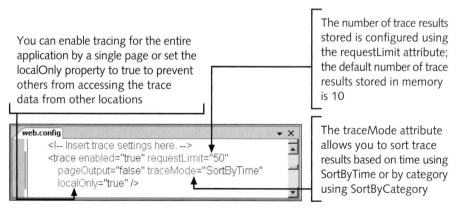

**Figure 6-28**   Setting the trace node in the web configuration file

3. Click the **Save All** button.

4. In the Solution Explorer window, right-click the **ch6_trace.aspx** page in the **ch6_trace** folder and then select **View in Browser**.

5. In the text box, type **0** and then click the **Buy** button. Your screen should resemble Figure 6-29.

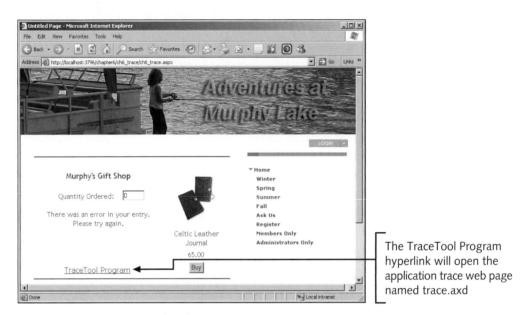

**Figure 6-29** Previewing the ch6_trace.aspx page

6. Click the hyperlink labeled **TraceTool Program**. The TraceUtility program appears with two entries for the ch6_trace.aspx page, as shown in Figure 6-30. The first entry was created when the web page was first viewed. No trace messages would have been written to this entry.

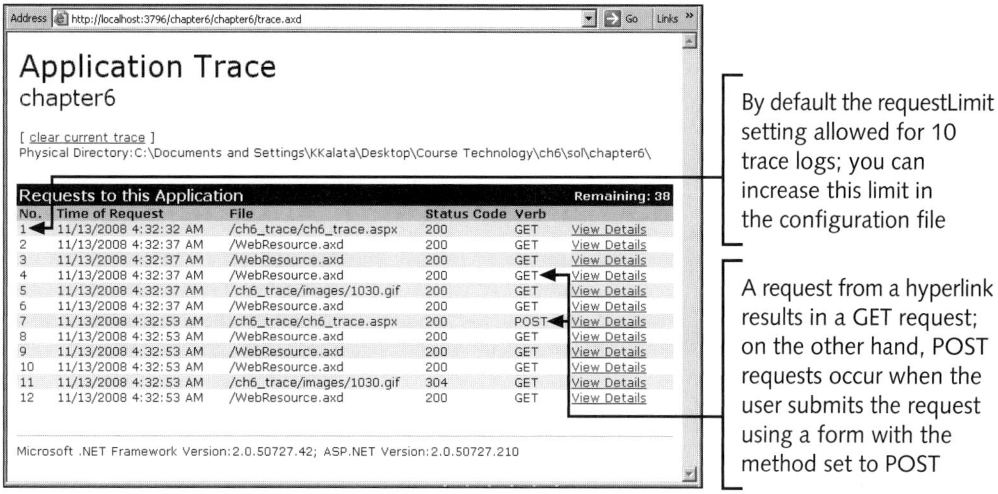
Address http://localhost:3796/chapter6/chapter6/trace.axd
Go
Links
Application Trace
chapter6
[ clear current trace ]
Physical Directory:C:\Documents and Settings\KKalata\Desktop\Course Technology\ch6\sol\chapter6\
Requests to this Application
Remaining: 38
No. Time of Request File Status Code Verb
1 11/13/2008 4:32:32 AM /ch6_trace/ch6_trace.aspx 200 GET View Details
2 11/13/2008 4:32:37 AM /WebResource.axd 200 GET View Details
3 11/13/2008 4:32:37 AM /WebResource.axd 200 GET View Details
4 11/13/2008 4:32:37 AM /WebResource.axd 200 GET View Details
5 11/13/2008 4:32:37 AM /ch6_trace/images/1030.gif 200 GET View Details
6 11/13/2008 4:32:37 AM /WebResource.axd 200 GET View Details
7 11/13/2008 4:32:53 AM /ch6_trace/ch6_trace.aspx 200 POST View Details
8 11/13/2008 4:32:53 AM /WebResource.axd 200 GET View Details
9 11/13/2008 4:32:53 AM /WebResource.axd 200 GET View Details
10 11/13/2008 4:32:53 AM /WebResource.axd 200 GET View Details
11 11/13/2008 4:32:53 AM /ch6_trace/images/1030.gif 304 GET View Details
12 11/13/2008 4:32:53 AM /WebResource.axd 200 GET View Details
Microsoft .NET Framework Version:2.0.50727.42; ASP.NET Version:2.0.50727.210
By default the requestLimit setting allowed for 10 trace logs; you can increase this limit in the configuration file
A request from a hyperlink results in a GET request; on the other hand, POST requests occur when the user submits the request using a form with the method set to POST

**Figure 6-30** The TraceTool Program

7. Click **View Details** for the second entry. This entry was created when the user clicked the button, as shown in Figure 6-31. The price, quantity, and total are all stored in the trace stack. The total is displayed in red text, however.
8. Close all open pages.

## Request Details

### Request Details

| | | | |
|---|---|---|---|
| Session Id: | ygou5m45hhhxr255mwmrxq55 | Request Type: | POST |
| Time of Request: | 11/13/2008 4:32:53 AM | Status Code: | 200 |
| Request Encoding: | Unicode (UTF-8) | Response Encoding: | Unicode (UTF-8) |

### Trace Information

| Category | Message | From First(s) | From Last(s) |
|---|---|---|---|
| aspx.page | Begin PreInit | | |
| aspx.page | End PreInit | 0.000263161938179294 | 0.000263 |
| aspx.page | Begin Init | 0.000292774640352335 | 0.000030 |
| aspx.page | End Init | 0.000480228632409985 | 0.000187 |
| aspx.page | Begin InitComplete | 0.000504254032286226 | 0.000024 |
| aspx.page | End InitComplete | 0.000524088955439867 | 0.000020 |
| aspx.page | Begin LoadState | 0.000543365148363828 | 0.000019 |
| aspx.page | End LoadState | 0.0262273557114102 | 0.025684 |
| aspx.page | Begin ProcessPostData | 0.0262762446065073 | 0.000049 |
| aspx.page | End ProcessPostData | 0.0756355905569004 | 0.049359 |
| aspx.page | Begin PreLoad | 0.0756906254845239 | 0.000055 |
| aspx.page | End PreLoad | 0.0757364413633576 | 0.000046 |
| aspx.page | Begin Load | 0.0757590699376597 | 0.000023 |
| aspx.page | End Load | 0.0758141048652832 | 0.000055 |
| aspx.page | Begin ProcessPostData Second Try | 0.0758370128047 | 0.000023 |
| aspx.page | End ProcessPostData Second Try | 0.0758629937603802 | 0.000026 |
| aspx.page | Begin Raise ChangedEvents | 0.0758836667788783 | 0.000021 |
| aspx.page | End Raise ChangedEvents | 0.0772195907580433 | 0.001336 |
| aspx.page | Begin Raise PostBackEvent | 0.0772469685392976 | 0.000027 |
| Price | 65.00 | 0.160379601318045 | 0.083133 |
| Quantity | 0 | 0.160436591801472 | 0.000057 |
| Total | 0 | 0.160572642612399 | 0.000136 |
| aspx.page | End Raise PostBackEvent | 0.161719157043702 | 0.001147 |
| aspx.page | Begin LoadComplete | 0.161745976094727 | 0.000027 |
| aspx.page | End LoadComplete | 0.16176692847834 | 0.000021 |
| aspx.page | Begin PreRender | 0.161786763401494 | 0.000020 |
| aspx.page | End PreRender | 0.162135131699699 | 0.000348 |
| aspx.page | Begin PreRenderComplete | 0.162160274560035 | 0.000025 |
| aspx.page | End PreRenderComplete | 0.162183461864567 | 0.000023 |
| aspx.page | Begin SaveState | 0.163719690631072 | 0.001536 |
| aspx.page | End SaveState | 0.163942623992714 | 0.000223 |
| aspx.page | Begin SaveStateComplete | 0.16396664939259 | 0.000024 |
| aspx.page | End SaveStateComplete | 0.163989277966892 | 0.000023 |
| aspx.page | Begin Render | 0.164009112890046 | 0.000020 |
| aspx.page | End Render | 0.166313875087476 | 0.002305 |

**Figure 6-31** A web page with tracing enabled

### The customErrors Element

When the user requests a page, the web server provides the page, and an HTTP status message code indicates the status of the request. This is the same status message code that you saw earlier in the log files. The web server and ASP.NET can be configured to send a web page to the user indicating that an error has occurred, as shown in Figure 6-32.

Both ASP.NET and IIS provide error pages that describe the error, error codes, and error messages. The IIS web pages are located in the C:\winnt\Help\iisHelp\common\ directory. ASP.NET provides a variety of additional error messages that are not part of IIS. You can use web server MMC to configure custom error pages. Because this tool was often not available to web developers, custom error pages were seldom used. You could have created a virtual directory named CustomErrors in which to store your default error pages, and then point the IIS custom error configuration and the ASP.NET configuration to this folder. Then, your application uses a common error message for both ASP.NET and IIS errors.

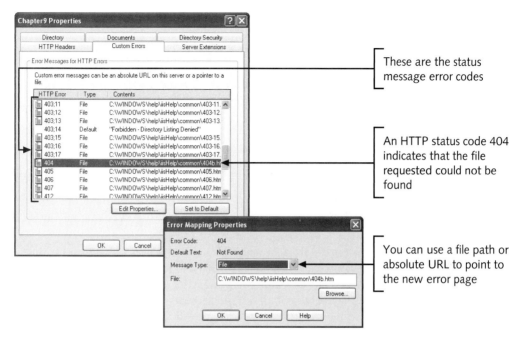

These are the status message error codes

An HTTP status code 404 indicates that the file requested could not be found

You can use a file path or absolute URL to point to the new error page

6

**Figure 6-32** Configuring error messages

Instead of displaying static error messages, ASP.NET provides a rich error page. When an error occurs, the error page provides detailed information about stack traces and compilation errors. You can use this information to help determine where the error occurred, and how to correct the error. You may not want your visitors to see this information, however. You can configure the **customErrors element** to set the mode to **RemoteOnly**, so that the rich error pages are only displayed locally. The RemoteOnly settings can be set to On or Off.

- If the RemoteOnly setting is **On**, then the application contains custom error pages.

- If the RemoteOnly setting is **Off**, then the detailed ASP.NET error pages are displayed.

The error messages can still be displayed when viewing the web site using the localhost. But, if the user visits the web site and an error occurs, the user is redirected to a default error page or a custom error page. (*Note*: It is recommended that you set the RemoteOnly property to RemoteOnly or On in a production web server.) You can also set the **defaultRedirect attribute**, which sets a default error page to be displayed if no applicable custom error page is configured. (*Note*: If an error occurs on the defaultRedirect page, the page does not continually redirect to itself.)

You may want to have access to multiple computers to test the custom error configuration techniques.

You can configure ASP.NET to use a custom error page for each HTTP status code by using the customErrors element. The **statusCode attribute** indicates the status code of the error message. The **Redirect attribute** indicates the page to redirect the user to when the error is detected. The following sample code shows how to configure the default error page and a custom error page for the HTTP status code 404:

```
<customErrors mode="RemoteOnly" defaultRedirect="~/error.aspx"/>
<error statusCode="404" redirect="/error404.aspx"/>
</customErrors>
```

ASP.NET provides the ability to send messages to the Windows error logs. You can use the Application_OnError event handler to send the message to the Windows Event Log. Developers may want to send error messages to the Windows log files because it makes troubleshooting errors easier. You can see how the errors interact with other messages and services.

## Web Application Memory Models

Web applications need to run within a process that runs within an assigned memory space, as illustrated in Figure 6-33. The **Internet Service Manager (ISM)** is used to configure the location of the process that runs the application. The **Component Services** management tool allows you to view how processes are organized. The Application Protection property represents the type of process memory allocation that is used for the application processes. The **Application Protection property** can be set to Low (IIS Process), Medium (Pooled), or High (Isolated).

When the Application Protection property is set to Low (IIS Process), the process runs within the web server's memory. The applications run in this model are called **IIS In-Process Applications** because they run within the web server's process. If the Web application crashes, the web server will also crash, leaving all web sites unavailable. By default, the Application Protection property for web applications is set to **Medium (Pooled)**, which means that the applications are pooled together to run in a single common process known as the **pooled Web application process** or the **IIS Out-of-Process Pooled Applications Process**. Then, if one of the pooled web applications crash, the entire pooled Web application process crashes, but the web server does not crash. If the Application Protection property is set to **High (Isolated)**, the application runs in its own **isolated process**. Then, if the application crashes, none of the other applications or the web server will crash.

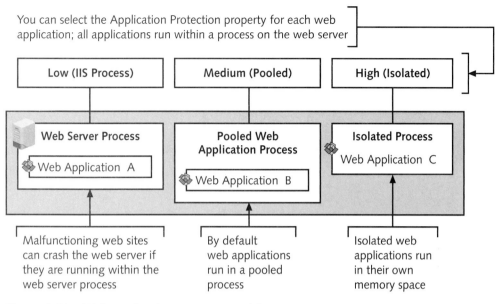

You can select the Application Protection property for each web application; all applications run within a process on the web server

| Low (IIS Process) | Medium (Pooled) | High (Isolated) |

**Web Server Process**

Web Application  A

**Pooled Web Application Process**

Web Application  B

**Isolated Process**

Web Application  C

Malfunctioning web sites can crash the web server if they are running within the web server process

By default web applications run in a pooled process

Isolated web applications run in their own memory space

**Figure 6-33**  Web application memory models

## MEMBERSHIP SERVICES

The two main principles of security are authentication and authorization. **Authentication** is the process of validating the identity of the request. When a user browses a web site, the web server determines if the user is permitted access to the web page using authentication. If he or she is not, an access denied error message appears. The web server uses configuration files to determine if the user has access to the web pages.

**Authorization** is the process of ensuring that you can only access the resources made available to you by the system administrators. The Windows NTFS file system allows you to set permissions on individual files and folders using an **access control list (ACL)**. The system administrators assign the ACL permissions to provide you access to resources.

## Implementing Authorization

The two basic ways that developers implement authorization are role-based and resource-based. Both are discussed in the following subsections.

### Resource-Based Authorization

With **resource-based authorization**, individual resources are assigned specific permissions using the Windows NTFS permissions. For example, in an intranet application, a file named salary.aspx containing sensitive information would be explicitly assigned read access for the manager of a department. Each employee would then be assigned no access, so they would not be able to read the data in the file. Resource-based authorization is not scalable and cannot take advantage of connection pooling, so it will use up more of the server memory resources.

## Role-Based Authorization

Rather than assign permissions to the file for each user, you can use **role-based authorization**. Users are assigned to groups, which are then assigned permission to resources. Therefore, the manager would be in one group, and all the employees would be in a second group. In addition to being a more scalable solution, this is also a better solution for managing users. In the case of a school, for example, students enroll and drop classes throughout the semester. The application can assign students when they enroll to membership in the students group. Then, they would not have to change permission to the student resources each time a student enrolled.

The recommended strategy for role-based authorization is to authenticate the user in the front end of the Web application. Users, when they are entered into the system, are mapped to roles. These roles are assigned to operations such as accessing an application, database, or folder. They are not usually assigned specific permissions to individual resource files. In this way, if files change within the application, you do not need to modify the permissions.

# Authenticating Users with Forms Authentication

**Forms authentication** is a cookie-based authentication method. Every packet of information over the web is sent with a host header, which contains information about the sender and the request. When you log in using an ASP.NET form, the web server checks the IP address and domain in the host header of the request. Once the web server has validated the user's IP address, the web server determines if the anonymous account is enabled. If the anonymous user account is enabled, then the web server passes the request to ASP.NET. ASP.NET determines if a **FormsAuthentication cookie** is present in the header packet. If there is no FormsAuthentication cookie, the client is redirected to the login page. The user must then submit credentials and be authenticated. Once the user has been authenticated, a FormsAuthentication cookie is added to the header packet. After a user has been authenticated, the FormsAuthentication cookie is used to identify future requests. After the user is authenticated, ASP.NET checks to see if the user is authorized to access the resource. If the user has been authorized, the resource is sent to the client.

The user may be validated using the credential list within the configuration files, or the request may be validated against an XML file, a database, an in-memory structure, an LDAP directory, or even a new web-based application called a web service.

In the next section, you will learn how to use the Web Site Administration tool to create a membership and role management system for your web site. You will use this tool to create and manage both users and roles.

## Understanding the Web Site Administration Tool

Today when you use forms authentication, the Web Site Administration Tool provides a way to create users and roles, and to configure the authentication and authorization of resources within your Web application. The WSAT is located at http://localhost:[your port number]/ asp.netwebadminfiles/ and allows you to configure some, but not all, of the web server properties. The information is stored by default in an Access database, but can be stored in other structures such as SQL Server. A SQL script is available to create the compatible SQL database. A built-in data provider called **AspNetSqlProvider** provides your application access to the data. Once you have the database created, you can use one of the built-in controls for allowing users to log in and log out to your application, recover their passwords, or create their accounts. You can use a built-in wizard or programmatically create and manage roles and users, and secure web folders and resources.

## Using the WSAT to Configure Access Rules for Members and Administrators

In the following exercise, you will use the ASP.NET Configuration using the Web Site Administration tool to set up the users, roles, and access rules for the chapter6 web application. You will only be able to do the exercises related to the WSAT if you have SQL Server installed and running.

1. In the Solution Explorer window, click the **ASP.NET Configuration icon**. It is located on the far right toolbar in the Solution Explorer window.

2. Click the **Security** tab.

3. Click the **Select authentication type** link. Select the **From the internet** radio button and click the **Done** button in the lower-right corner of the window.

4. If necessary, click the **Enable roles** link.

5. Click **Create or Manage roles** link.

6. In the **New role name** text box, type **Members** and click the **Add Role** button.

7. In the **New role name** text box, type **Administrators**, click the **Add Role** button, and then click the **Back** button.

8. Click the **Create user** link. In the text boxes, enter **member** for the user name, **Technology\*** for the password, **kkalata@course.com** for the e-mail, **What color is the sky?** for the security question, and **Blue** for the security answer. Check the **Members** check box in the user's role, and then click the **Create User** button. After the user has been created, click the **Continue** button.

9. In the text boxes, enter **administrator** for the user name, **Technology\*** for the password, **katie@course.com** for the e-mail, **What color is the sky?** for the security question, and **Blue** for the security answer. Check the **Administrators** check box in the user's role, and then click the **Create User** button. After the user has been created, click the **Continue** button and then click the **Back** button.

## Using the WSAT to Configure Application Settings

You will now configure access rules for members only to access the ch6_members folder, and administrators can access the ch6_admins folder. If you set the authorization to deny for a user, and he or she attempts to access the resource, the application will return a 401 status code error message.

1. Click the **Create access rules** link. Click the **ch6_members** directory in the left pane. In the right pane, the Administrators are already selected in the drop-down list. Click the **Allow** radio button, and then click the **OK** button.

2. Click the **Create access rules** link. Click the **ch6_members** directory in the left pane. In the right pane, select **Members** from the drop-down list, click the **Allow** radio button, and then click the **OK** button.

3. Click the **Create access rules** link. Click the **ch6_members** directory in the left pane. In the right pane, select the **Anonymous users** radio button, and the Deny radio button is already selected. Click the **OK** button.

4. Click the **Create access rules** link. Click the **ch6_admin** directory in the left pane. In the right pane, the administrators are already selected in the drop-down list. Click the **Allow** radio button, and then click the **OK** button.

5. Click the **Create access rules** link. Click the **ch6_admin** directory in the left pane. In the right pane, select **Members** from the drop-down list, and the Deny radio button is already selected. Click the **OK** button.

6. Click the **Create access rules** link. Click the **ch6_admin** directory in the left pane. In the right pane, select **Anonymous users** radio button, and the Deny radio button is already selected. Click the **OK** button.

## Using the WSAT to Configure the Default Error Page

You will now configure the application settings and a default error page.

1. Click the **Application** tab. Click the **Create application settings** link. In the name and value pair text boxes, enter **ResortName** and **Murphy Lake Resorts**, click the **Save** button, and then click the **OK** button.

2. Click the **Define default error page** link. Click the radio button labeled **Specify a URL to use as the default error page**, click the **ch6_error.aspx** page in the left pane, and then click the **Save** button in the lower-right side of the window. Click the **OK** button.

3. Click the **Configure debugging and tracing** link. If necessary, check the **Capture tracing information** check box. Do not make any changes here. These properties are the same ones you configured previously in the web configuration file in the trace element.

4. Click the **Provider** tab and then click the **Select a different provider for each feature (advanced)** link. Notice that the providers can be different for the Role and Membership services.

5. Close the page.

## Verifying Configuration Settings

You will now view the changes in your web configuration files and test the new security settings.

1. Double-click the **web.config** file in the **chapter6** folder, which is the root folder. Locate the changes in the file. AppSettings element has a key added named ResortName. Role Manager has been enabled. The trace, compilation, and the customErrors elements are configured. The mode in the authentication element has been changed from Windows to Forms.

2. Double-click the **web.config** file in the **ch6_members** folder. The authorization element has been modified. Users in the Administrators and Members roles are allowed, but the anonymous user represented with the question mark is denied access. The asterisk represents all authenticated users.

3. Double-click the **web.config** file in the **ch6_admin** folder. The authorization element has been modified. Users in the Administrators roles are allowed, but the anonymous user and users in the Members role are denied access.

4. In the Solution Explorer window, right-click the **Default.aspx** page and select **View in Browser**. Notice that you are not logged in, because the LOGIN button is displayed. Click the **Members Only** link. Because you are not authenticated, you are redirected to the login page.

5. Enter **member** for the user name, **Technology\*** for the password, and then click the button labeled LOGIN. You are redirected to the Members home page. Notice that you are logged in, because the logout button is displayed.

6. Click the **Administrators Only** link. Because you are not authenticated as an administrator, you are not allowed access, and you are redirected to the login page. But, because you are an authenticated user, you do not have to login again. The login form is not displayed. Click the **Logout** button.

7. Click the **Administrators Only** link. Because you are not authenticated, you are redirected to the login page. Enter **administrator** for the user name, **Technology\*** for the password, and then click the **Log In** button. You are redirected to the Members home page. The login form is configured to redirect all authenticated users to the Members home page. Click the **Administrators Only** link and the Administrators home page is displayed.

You have seen how the WSAT can help you create and manage the users and roles. In the next section, you will learn how you can create programs to interact with the Membership and Role API's in lieu of working with the WSAT.

## The Membership and Role APIs

An application programming interface (API) is used to allow programmers to interact programmatically with the Membership data source, instead of having to use the WSAT. You can create code to not only retrieve membership and role information about a specific user, and for all users, but you can also change this information.

The Membership class contains properties about the Membership data source, properties related to the specific user, and methods to retrieve a specific user from the data source. Below are some of the properties of the Membership class.

- *ApplicationName* returns the path to the current application, and is usually represented as a forward slash.

- *GetNumberOfUsersOnline* provides the number of users currently logged in.

- *UserIsOnlineTimeWindow* shows the number of minutes since their last activity.

- *Provider* is by default System.Web.Security.SqlMembershipProvider and identifies the provider used to communicate with the data source.

- *MinRequiredPasswordLength* is 7 by default and provides the minimum number of characters required in a password.

- *RequiresQuestionAndAnswer* is True by default and identifies if a question and answer are required when the user is created.

- *MaxInvalidPasswordAttempts* is 5 by default and is the number of attempts that is allowed before the user temporarily is locked out.

- *PasswordAttemptWindow* is 10 by default and is the number of minutes that is allowed when invalid attempts are made before the user is temporarily locked out.

- *EnablePasswordReset* is True by default and is used to determine if the current user can reset their password.

- *EnablePasswordRetrieval* is False by default and is used to determine if the current user can retrieve their password.

- *HashAlgorithmType* is SHA1 by default and is the algorithm used to code passwords using a method called hashing.

- *PasswordStrengthRegularExpression* is empty by default and is the Regular Expression used to evaluate the password.

When no user is identified, the GetUser method in the Membership class retrieves the current user. You can also retrieve a specific user by passing the user name to the **GetUser** method, or the e-mail to the **GetUserByEmail** method. Once the user is retrieved, you can retrieve and change the PasswordQuestionAndAnswer and the Password, and update the Membership database. A valid password must be passed to make these changes. To retrieve a collection of all the properties for each user in the Membership database, use the GetAllUsers method. You can bind this data collection to any of the Web controls that support data binding, such as the DataList, DetailsView, and GridView controls. The DetailsView will only show just the first user by default. You can use a GridView to show all the users at one time.

The Role API also allows programmers to interact programmatically with the Role data source, instead of having to use the WSAT. You can create code to retrieve role information directly from the Role class, or user-related role information via the Membership class.

## Using the Membership and Role APIs

In the following exercise, you will view several pages that display the properties for the Membership class, and information maintained on the current user and the member user. This exercise also demonstrates how to change the data for the member user and displays the properties for the administrator user. You will also review the properties for the Role class, and list the roles and the users within each role. You will see how the API can be used to create users, and add them to a role.

1. In the Solution Explorer window, right-click the **Default.aspx** file in the **ch6_membership** folder and then select **View in Browser**. This page contains links to several demonstration pages. Click the **Membership Properties** hyperlink. You can see the defaults for the Membership data as well as the password management default settings. The default provider for Membership management is SqlMembershipProvider. Click the **Go back to the Default.aspx page** link.

2. Click the **Role Properties** link. Notice that the cookie that contains the role information is named ASPXROLES. The default provider for Role management is AspNetSqlRoleProvider. Click the **Go back to the Default.aspx page** link.

3. Click the **Manage Roles** link. This page demonstrates how to create and delete roles using the API. In the text box, enter **Guest** and click the **Create Role** button. Click the **List All Roles** drop-down list to verify the Guest role was added. Click the **Go back to the Default.aspx page** link.

4. Click the **Display Member Users** link. Notice that page displays information only for the member user. This uses the Membership. GetUser("member") statement to retrieve information by passing the user name. Click the **Go back to the Default.aspx page** link.

5. Click the **Display Administrator Properties** link. This code uses the Membership.GetAllUsers method to retrieve information about all of the users. Only one record can be displayed at a time with the DetailsView control, however. This control was used here to demonstrate the list of items stored in the membership for a specific user, including the LastLoginDate and LastActivityDate. Click the **Go back to the Default.aspx page** link.

6. Click the **Current User Properties** link. This page will display the membership data for the current user. If you are not currently logged in, an error message will be displayed. If you are logged in, then the user information will be displayed. Click the **Go back to the Default.aspx page** link.

7. Click the **Change User Properties** link. This page allows you to change the user properties for the member user. The ChangePasswordQuestionAndAnswer, and ChangePassword require you to provide the current user password. Before the changes are made, the code must call the UpdateUser method. In the text boxes, type **Technology\*** for the current password, **Computers\*** for

the new password, **What is the name of the resort?** for the PasswordQuestion, and **Murphy** for the answer. Click the **Submit** button. Click the **Go back to the Default.aspx page** link.

8.  Click the **Change User Roles** link. This page allows you to change, add, or remove a role that is associated with the member. Change the user drop-down list from administrator to **member**. In the Select from all roles drop-down list, select **Guest** and click the **Add User to Role** button. This role now appears in the drop-down list box that contains all the roles associated with this user. Guest already should be selected. Click the **Delete User From Role** button and the role is no longer associated with this user.

9.  Close the open files.

Now that you have seen how to use the WSAT and API to change the membership and roles, you will learn how to modify the authorization and authentication elements directly in the web configuration file.

## The Authorization Element

The **authorization element** in the web configuration file is used to identify which resources can be accessed after the user is authenticated. Although you can use the WSAT to manage your authentication and authorization, both the membership and roles can be manually managed by modifying the web site configuration files.

- The **allow element** configures users that are allowed to access the application.

- The **deny element** configures users that are not allowed to access the application.

- The **users attribute** is used to identify the user. A wild card or a complete user name may be provided to explicitly configure a user's access to the application's resources.

- The **roles attribute** is used to identify a group of users. Groups of users are defined as a role in the Windows Active Directory. You can configure several users at the same time by separating the list of users with a comma, as shown in the code that follows this paragraph.

```
<authorization>
 <allow users="Joan, John" roles="Admins, Customers"/>
 <deny users="?" roles="BlackList"/>
</authorization>
```

- The **verb attribute** is for adding additional security based on the type of HTTP request. The verb attribute identifies the HTTP verbs to which the tag applies. Possible values for the verb property include GET, HEAD, and POST.

```
<authorization>
    <allow verb="GET" users="*"/>
    <allow verb="GET" users="kkalata"/>
    <allow verb="POST" roles="BUILTIN\Administrators"/>
    <deny verb="POST" users="*"/>
</authorization>
```

You can explicitly assign the user or group by specifying the [*domain name*]\[*user name*]. The users and roles configured in the authorization node are Windows accounts. Your applications will be more scalable if you use roles to assign access permissions. If you use Active Directory to store your user data, you can display your user names and group names using the X.500 format, as shown in the following code:

```
<authorization>
  <deny users="jeffrey@sales.corp.course.com" />
  <allow roles ="CN=Murphy Lake,CN=FTE_northamerica,
  CN=Users, DC=sales,DC=corp, DC=course, DC=com" />
</authorization>
```

## Implementing Authentication

In the following subsections, you will learn about Windows authentication, file and folder security permissions, and how to configure these permissions in the web configuration files.

### Windows File and Folder Security Permissions

Specific NTFS permissions are used to assign users or groups to resources. System administrators should maintain detailed documentation about the permissions assigned to users and groups. When ASP.NET was installed, a user and a group were created to be assigned the permissions related to processing ASP.NET requests. When you attempt to interact with the file system, or an Access database, the files and their parent folder must be configured to allow the ASP.NET user and group modify permissions. You may have to work with your network administrator to set these permissions.

You can manually set the authentication and authorization using a combination of the web configuration files, the MMC application, and setting NTFS permissions for files and folders. These permissions identify if you have the rights to read, write, modify, and delete resources. Each user who accesses a resource on the server is using a valid Windows account, as shown in Figure 6-34. If the user does not log into the web site, they are by default assigned to the anonymous user account and only have the rights of an anonymous user.

The authentication method is configured in the authentication element in the web configuration file. The **Mode attribute** is assigned to one of the authentication methods listed below:

- **None**—no authentication is required.
- **Anonymous authentication**—uses the **Internet Guest Account** to verify the user.
- **Basic authentication**—user will need to enter their Windows user name and password in the login window. Their account information, however, is sent as clear text over the Internet, which could be intercepted over the Internet by hackers using tools such as packet analyzers. Only set the permissions to basic authentication if you use SSL to encrypt the login page.

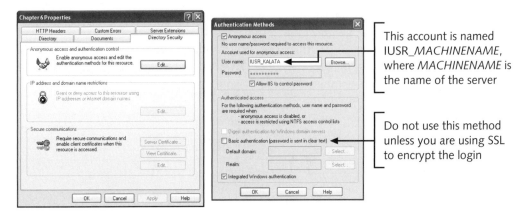

**Figure 6-34**   Windows authentication methods

- **Windows authentication**—allows the system administrator to set the folder and file properties using NT File System (NTFS) permissions. If you are setting access permissions on a folder, the access permissions by default will apply to all the items and subfolders. This would also be applicable to active directory.

NTFS permissions are as follows:

- **Full Control**—modify, add, move, and delete files, their properties, and directories; change permissions settings for all files and subdirectories
- **Modify**—view and modify files and file properties; add and delete files
- **Read & Execute**—run executable files; run scripts such as server-side VBScript and JavaScript
- **List Folder Contents**—view a listing of a folder
- **Read Users**—view files and file properties
- **Write Users**—write to a file; used to publish with FrontPage extensions
- **No Access**—no access to the resource

When the **requireSSL attribute** in the authentication element is set to true, the browser is required to send information using Secure Sockets Layer (SSL). The data, such as the value of cookies, is sent to the server and encrypted, the latter of which protects hackers from intercepting them and reading them over the Internet transport layers. If the **slidingExpiration attribute** is set to true, the authentication cookie is reset on each subsequent request so that the user would not have to be reauthenticated.

## The Authentication Element

The **authentication element** in the web configuration file is used to identify how the user is authenticated. When you use the WSAT to manage authorization, you are using forms authentication. You can manually manage authentication by modifying the mode attribute in the authentication element within the web site configuration files. You can build your own custom authentication method by changing the mode attribute to None. The mode attribute can also be set to Passport. Passport is a single sign on passport identity system created by Microsoft that is called Windows Live ID in .NET Framework 3.0.

The mode attribute can be set to Windows. Windows is the default mode for the authentication mode in both the application and machine configuration files. Windows authentication is best used for intranet web sites where users already have user accounts on the Windows server. You can configure the server to disable the anonymous user so that all visitors must be authenticated by the server using their own valid Windows user accounts. The user must use the Microsoft Internet Explorer browser to view the web site. Only this browser supports the Windows authentication mode. Users will view a login screen requesting their Windows account user name and password. If you use Windows authentication, the user name and password are not sent over the Internet. Instead the information is used to generate a hash value that is sent over the Internet. The server knows the user name and password and can therefore re-create the hash value. If the values are equal, the user is authenticated. If the user attempts to log in with an invalid user account or password, the web browser will display the "Access is denied" error message. There are several ways you can set the application to use Windows authentication:

- NTFS file and folder security properties using Windows Explorer
- Web site security properties using the Internet Information Services management tool
- Web application settings using the web and machine configuration files

Once the user has logged in using his or her Windows account, you can use the WindowsIdentity object to obtain details about the user account. The System.Security.Principal namespace contains the WindowsIdentity object and must be imported in your code. The WindowsIdentity.GetCurrent method provides the current user account, as shown in the following code:

```
Dim WinID As WindowsIdentity
WinID=WindowsIdentity.GetCurrent
```

Various properties about the user can be retrieved, such as the authentication type, authenticated status, and name, as shown in the following code:

```
Label1.Text=WinID.AuthenticationType.ToString
Label2.Text=WinID.IsAuthenticated.ToString
Label3.Text="Windows Account: " & WinID.Name
```

You can also identify the user's name and authentication type:

```
Label4.Text="Welcome : " & Context.User.Identity.Name
Label5.Text="Authentication Type: " & _
Context.User.Identity.AuthenticationType.ToString
```

The **WindowsPrincipal object** provides access to methods that interact with the Windows security system, such as IsInRole. The **IsInRole method** will allow you to check if the user is a member of a specific role. You can determine if the user is a member of a role using the role name or the numeric value that represents the role, as shown in the following code:

```
Dim wp As New WindowsPrincipal(WinID)
Label6.Text="Administrator"   & _
wp.IsInRole(WindowsBuiltInRole.Administrator)
Label7.Text="Backup Operator" & wp.IsInRole(551)
```

**TIP**

If the user is logged on using Windows, you can also retrieve user information using the Request.ServerVariables("AUTH_USER") property.

## The Identity Element

The configuration files contain an **identity element** that can be used to impersonate a Windows user account. The **impersonate attribute** is used to indicate if impersonation is allowed. Impersonation is disabled by default in the machine configuration file. Because the client does not have to log in with a separate account, this is considered a security risk. If you set impersonate to true, you will need to rely on Microsoft Internet Information Services to authenticate the user. You can pass a userName and password attributes in the identity element. If the userName is an empty string, it automatically implies that the application will use the web server (IIS) user account, [IUSR_MachineName].

## The MachineKey Element

The **machineKey element** is used to identify a value and method to encrypt data on the server. The machineKey element allows you to set the values for encryption and decryption. The **validationKey** attribute is used as part of the hash algorithm, so only ASP.NET applications that have the validationKey can use the data. Using the validationKey guarantees that the data is valid. The length of the validationKey must be between 40 and 128 hexadecimal characters. The validation attribute identifies what type of hash is to be created. Possible values for the validation type include MD5, SHA1, and 3DES. 3DES is the strongest algorithm for creating a hash value. The **decryptionKey** attribute is used to guarantee that nontrusted sources can't read the text.

---

# USING WEB CONTROLS TO MAINTAIN SECURITY

There are several built-in Web controls that can be used to maintain security within your web application. These controls contain classes that were designed to interact with membership and role security, so the web developer did not have to create the security infrastructure from scratch. These controls are available to all of your applications. You can use these controls with a customized membership and role provider.

## The Login Control

The **Login control** (`<asp:Login>`) is used to provide a predefined interface to the built-in authentication API's and can be placed on any page. When the user is attempting to access a protected folder that requires authentication, however, they are redirected to the login.aspx page in the root folder. The login.aspx page can use techniques such as server-side redirection to redirect the request to another login page. The Login control allows you to customize the header message, and to include links to resources such as a help page.

You can set the **VisibleWhenLoggedIn property** to false so that a visitor would not see the login form if they already have logged in. The **DestinationPageUrl property** is used to identify the page that the visitor is redirected to if they successfully log in. This would occur for all valid users. Once the user has logged in, his or her information can be saved locally on the client's computer in a cookie.

The **DisplayRememberMe property** displays a check box that can be used to allow the visitor to select his or her preference for storing his or her login information in a cookie. The **RememberMeText property** should be used to tell the visitor that the information would be stored in a cookie. The **FailureText property** is used to display a message for users when their login attempt fails. You may want to remind them how many login attempts are allowed before their account is locked.

Some membership systems allow the users to sign up without assistance, and some allow the users to retrieve a lost password independently. If you allow your users to retrieve a password, you should use the **PasswordRecoveryUrl property**, which directs them to the page that would contain information about how they can retrieve their login information. The **PasswordRecoveryText property** can be used to link to the password recovery page. The **TitleText property** can be used to include a custom message at the top of the login form. You can customize the appearance of the form using properties within the Login control, or using one of the built-in style properties.

## The Password Recovery Control

The **Password Recovery control** (`<asp:PasswordRecovery>`) is used to allow the user to retrieve or reset his or her password. Like the Login control, this control contains text properties, style properties, and built-in styles that can be used to customize the appearance. The user will answer his or her password reminder question. You can customize messages for the user when he or she succeeds or fails. The maildefinition attribute is used to identify the server that sends the message. You can configure the subject and from fields.

## The Login Status Control

The **Login Status control** (`<asp:LoginStatus>`) is useful to identify if the user is currently logged in. You can display custom text or images when the user is logged in, or not logged in. When the user logs out, you can redirect them to a page identified in the login status control. Like the other controls, you can customize the appearance of the control using properties or styles.

## Using the Login Control

You have already seen what it looks like to log in to the site and access resources. In the following exercise, you will modify the code in the login status control to display custom text.

1. Right-click the **login.aspx** page in the **ch6_home** folder and select **View Markup**.

2. Change the value of the Help attribute to **Help**.

3. Right-click the **MasterPage.master** page in the **ch6_masterpages** folder and select **View Markup**.

4. Change the LoginText and LogoutText properties to **Login** and **Logout**.

5. Click the **Save All** button.

6. Right-click the **home.aspx** home page in the **ch6_home** folder and select **View in Browser**. Notice the changes in the login form properties.

7. Close all pages.

## CHAPTER SUMMARY

- ❏ Validation controls are a form of ASP.NET controls that allow you to assign validation rules to other controls. You can build custom validation rules to validate your form fields, or use one of the standard Validation controls with a custom Regular Expression.

- ❏ A cookie can be used to maintain information across multiple sessions for a specific user. The cookie is a text file that is stored on the client's computer. Your web sites should educate and inform users about the use of cookies, and about how the cookie affects their computer system. The cookie is passed in the HTTP header with the other HTTP server variables. Cookies can store single values, and multiple cookies can be stored in a named group of cookies. The cookie is written using the Response object, and retrieved using the Request object. The group of cookies is stored in the HTTPCookieCollection.

- ❏ The SessionID property is assigned by the server, and provides a way to identify the client during the user session. Sessions require the user to support HTTP cookies. You can store session data within the web server process, the State Server, or a SQL Server database. State Server is a Windows service that must be turned on before session data can be stored in the State Server. If the web server crashes, any session data within the State Server or SQL Server persists. The State Server and SQL Server can be used to store session data for a web farm if the web servers are configured to use the same server and machine key. The machine encrypts and decrypts data on the server.

- ❏ A web application is a group of files and folders. The IIS web server software configures the web application using the MMC with the WSAT, or you can configure it via the web application configuration files. Each Web application runs in a process. Web applications that run in an isolated process are more protected than a web site that runs in the web server process. A web site that runs in the web server process is more efficient, however. Most web applications are run in a pooled process, outside of the web server process.

❏ The web.config file configures the web application. The configurations that are commonly configured in the web.config file include state management, application timeout, application variables, globalization settings, default compiler language, trace mode, and custom error pages. The machine.config file maintains information that is used across .NET applications.

❏ Authentication is the process of validating the identity of the request. Authorization is the process of validating the user access privileges to the resources.

❏ Authorization within an ASP.NET application is conducted via the web.config file, WSAT, or via the Windows NTFS permissions.

❏ You can configure web applications to support various types of authentication. Anonymous authentication means that the user does not have to log in with a special account. The Internet Guest Account represents the client. Basic authentication sends the login data as clear text. Windows authentication allows the user to log in without sending his or her login over the Internet. Forms authentication is a new technique in ASP.NET to protect the web application. You can configure forms authentication in the web.config file.

## REVIEW QUESTIONS

1. Which method of authentication is available with ASP.NET?
   a. forms authentication
   b. Windows authentication
   c. basic authentication
   d. all of the above

2. Which form of cookies is also known as HTTP cookies?
   a. response cookies
   b. client-side cookies
   c. permanent cookies
   d. session cookies

3. A group of files and folders located under the web server root directory (wwwroot) is called a _____ .
   a. web application
   b. virtual directory
   c. virtual application
   d. web server

4. A(n) _____ is a unique identifier created by the web server to maintain the identity of the client.

   a. Session GUID

   b. SessionID

   c. e-mail address

   d. CookieID

5. A(n) _____ is used to inform the user about the type of information that is being collected about the user, and to inform the user what is being done with that information.

   a. privacy policy

   b. security policy

   c. access policy

   d. all of the above

6. Which tool configures the web server using text files?

   a. web.config

   b. MMC

   c. Windows Security Monitor

   d. all of the above

7. What log format provides extended properties?

   a. W3C Extended Log File Format

   b. ODBC

   c. Microsoft IIS Format

   d. all of the above

8. _____ is the default directory for the log files for the IIS web server.

   a. Window\LogFiles

   b. Documents and Settings\LogFiles

   c. Window\System32\LogFiles

   d. WINNT\System32\LogFiles

9. Which permission is required to run ASP pages?

   a. Write

   b. Script

   c. Execute

   d. Both a and b

10. The _____ file is the machine configuration file for the web server for ASP.NET applications.

   a. machine.config

   b. web.config

   c. global.asa

   d. machinecfg.ascx

11. The _____ is the root node in the web application configuration file.

   a. configuration node

   b. System.Web node

   c. web node

   d. WebConfigurationNodes node

12. The enableSessionState function is configured in the _____ node configuration.

   a. Pages

   b. HTTPRuntime

   c. AppSettings

   d. Globalization

13. The _____ function is used to store data in the __VIEWSTATE hidden form field.

   a. enableViewState

   b. enableViewStateMac

   c. enableSessionState

   d. autoEventWireUp

14. The default value for executionTimeout is _____ .

   a. 20

   b. 90

   c. 404

   d. 4096

15. Which of the following would create a new application setting?

   a. <add key="StoreName" value="Tara Store"/>

   b. <add key.value="StoreName" text="Tara Store"/>

   c. <add field="StoreName" value="Tara Store"/>

   d. <add name="StoreName" text="Tara Store"/>

**6**

16. Which code sample retrieves an application setting named StoreName?

    a. ConfigurationSettings.AppSettings("StoreName")

    b. AppSettings("StoreName").GetText

    c. ConfigurationSettings("StoreName").GetText

    d. ConfigurationSettings("StoreName").AppSettings

17. The _____ property is used to restrict trace results to the web server console.

    a. localhost

    b. localOnly

    c. disabled

    d. pageOutput

18. The HTTP status message code _____ indicates the success of the HTTP request.

    a. 200

    b. 202

    c. 404

    d. 500

19. Your UserID is KALA9876. Client-side cookies written by Internet Explorer are stored in the _____ directory.

    a. C:\Documents and Settings\KALA9876\Cookies

    b. C:\Windows\Cookies\KALA9876\

    c. C:\Program Files\Internet Explorer\KALA9876\Cookies

    d. C:\KALA9876\Cookies

20. The _____ object represents the client's cookie variables.

    a. HttpCollection

    b. ResponseCookieCollection

    c. CookiesCollections

    d. HttpCookieCollection

21. The Windows service used to store session data is called _____ .

    a. SQL Server

    b. Oracle

    c. Session Server

    d. State Server

22. Your computer's name is DarkStar. The name of the Internet Guest Account is
    _____ .

    a. IUSRDarkStar
    b. localhost
    c. IUSR_Guest
    d. IUSR_DarkStar

23. Which type of authentication sends the user name and password as clear text over the Internet?

    a. anonymous authentication
    b. basic authentication
    c. Windows authentication
    d. all of the above

24. Which value is used to turn off the display of a Validation control error message?

    a. dynamic
    b. none
    c. static
    d. off

25. Which Validation control is the best choice to ensure that zip code values entered in a form are all numeric?

    a. RequiredFieldValidator
    b. RangeValidator
    c. CustomValidator
    d. RegularExpressionValidator

26. Compare client-side with server-side form validation. Explain three benefits and three disadvantages of each method.

27. List the five most important items that you would include in your security policy. Explain what they are and why they are important.

28. Compare the advantages and disadvantages of using windows authentication versus web server authorization.

29. Describe five actions that you can implement to manage errors in your web application.

30. Describe how you would store session data in your web application. Explain your choices.

## HANDS-ON PROJECTS

### Project 6-1

In this exercise, you create an ASP.NET page that processes and validates form data.

1. In your browser, open the page named **ch6_proj1.aspx** located in the **ch6_proj1** folder. This page processes and validates form data.

2. Add at least four Validation controls that validate the form fields as follows. The user must enter a name and not leave the field blank. The user must fill out the form using a standard e-mail address and U.S. format (999) 999-9999. The user should not be allowed to enter a non-alphanumeric number into the product name field. The number of products ordered must be between 5 and 10 inclusively. Configure the Validation controls to display messages to the user if there is an error.

3. If the form is valid, display a message "**Your order has been processed.**" in the page using a Label control. (*Hint:* You can detect if the entire page is valid by using the IsValid property of the Page class.)

4. Save and then view the page in the browser. Complete the form with fictitious and invalid data in each field. Print the page. Then complete the form with fictitious but valid data, and print the page again.

### Project 6-2

In this project, you will create a page that educates the user about cookies.

1. Research the Internet to learn more about cookies. Visit five web pages that discuss cookies.

2. Create a web page called **ch6_proj2.aspx** in the **ch6_proj2** folder.

3. Add a heading that says **What You Should Know About Cookies**.

4. Write a paragraph that describes what a cookie is, what a cookie is used for, and what you will do with the information contained in the cookie. Describe the security information that relates to reading and writing cookies.

5. Add a heading that says **Cookie Resources**. Then, create a list of links to five or more web pages on the Internet that discuss cookies. Format the list as a bulleted list.

6. Add a heading formatted as Heading 2, centered-aligned that says **Your Cookie**.

7. Create a group cookie named myCookie and assign the name cookie to your name. Display the cookie in the web page using a Label control.

8. Modify the web page's layout and appearance with your favorite fonts, colors, and images.

9. Save the web page. View the web page in the browser. Print out the web page.

## Project 6-3

In this project, you will create a privacy policy and a security policy.

1. Visit the TRUSTe web site (*www.truste.com*). Go to Privacy Policies page at *www.truste. org/about/privacy_guidelines.php*. Click each link and read the document. Read the Model Privacy Policy Disclosures at *www.truste.org/docs/Model_Privacy_Policy_ Disclosures.doc*. Read the Privacy Whitepaper at *www.truste.org/pdf/ WriteAGreatPrivacyPolicy.pdf*.

2. Visit at least four web sites that discuss privacy.

3. Locate at least three web sites that contain privacy policies.

4. Open your **chapter6** web site in Visual Studio .NET and create a web page named **ch6_proj3.aspx** in the **ch6_proj3** folder.

5. Add a heading that says **Privacy and Security Policy Resources**. List the sites you visited.

6. Add a heading that says **Sample Privacy and Security Policies**. Then add a bul-leted list of sample policies on the Internet.

7. Add a heading that says **Our Privacy Policy**. Then add at least three paragraphs describing your web site's privacy policy.

8. Add a heading that says **Our Security Policy**. Then add at least three paragraphs describing your web site's security policy.

9. Modify the web page's layout and appearance with your favorite fonts, colors, and images.

10. Save the web page as **ch6_proj3.aspx**.

11. View the web page in the browser. Print the web page and the HTML code.

## Project 6-4

In this project, you will create a page with a registration form. The page that processes the form writes the form field values to a cookie. The browser is redirected to a page that retrieves the cookie values, assigns them to session variables, and displays the session variables.

1. Create a web page called **ch6_proj4.aspx** in your **ch6_proj4** folder.

2. Add a heading that says **Registration Form**.

3. Add two text box form fields named **name** and **pass**, with the labels named **user name** and **password**.

4. Use the following code to add a hidden field named **sid**. The value of the field is the SessionID.

```
<INPUT type="hidden" id="sid"
value="<% = Session.SessionID %>" runat="server">
```

5. Add a label named **message**.

6. Add a button. In the button, display the text **Register Me!.**

7. Double-click the button to edit the code behind the page. Use the code that follows this paragraph to retrieve the form values in the code behind the page and write them to cookies. The cookie group name should be **sc**. Assign the current date to a cookie named **mydate**. Assign the server variables HTTP_REFERER and REMOTE_ADDR to cookies named **referer** and **ip**, as shown in Figure 6-35.

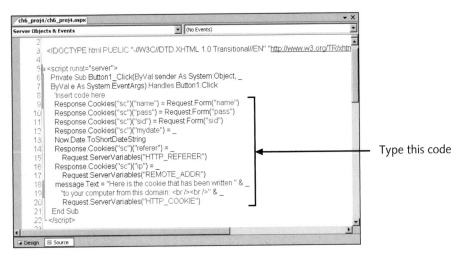

Figure 6-35    Creating cookies

8. Modify the web page's appearance using your favorite fonts, colors, and images. Use line breaks, block quotes, tables, or other HTML tags to format the page layout.

9. Save the page and view the web page in the browser. Type **student** and **password** in the user name and password text boxes, and click the **Register Me!** button. The HTTP cookie is displayed. Click the **Register Me!** button again, and the entire cookie is displayed. Print the web page, the HTML source code, and the code behind the page.

---

# CASE PROJECTS

CASE
PROJECTS

## Project 6-1

Your project manager has asked you to create a form on the web site that allows the visitor to enter contact information. Use the Validation controls to validate the form. Modify the error messages to indicate the error to the visitor. Once the page is validated, display a thank you message to the visitor. (*Hint:* You can use the IsValid property to detect if all of the

Validation controls have been used successfully.) Save the web page as ch6_case1.aspx in the ch6_case1 folder. Print your web pages and the source code.

## Project 6-2

Your manager has decided that the web site should allow the user to log in to the web site using the Login control. The login page should be named ch6_case2_login in the ch6_case2 folder. Within this folder, create the login help page, password recovery page, and a home page. On the home page, display the login status for the user with the LoginStatus control. Modify the web configuration file to support forms authentication. You may need to change the redirection code in the login.aspx file in the chapter6 folder, to the new login page. Allow the user to reset his or her password or to have the password sent to the user. Add graphics and content to enhance the web page. Print the web page and the source code. When you are finished, change the authorization back to Windows and allow all users to access the site.

## Project 6-3

Create a web page that validates the user against a customer XML file. Create an XML file that contains the user name and password. Save the file as ch6_case3.xml in the ch6_case3 folder. (*Note:* The @ character has a hexidecimal value of 0 x 40 and cannot be included in a name of a node in an XML document.) Create a web page named ch6_proj3_login.aspx. Add a login form with User name and Password text boxes. Use the User name and Password fields from the XML file to validate the user. Change the forms authentication in the web configuration file to point to the XML file. Create a web page named ch6_case3. aspx. Insert content to welcome the user. Enhance the appearance of the page with images and style sheets. Include a button that will allow the user to log out. Save all the pages, and view the ch6_case3.aspx page in the browser. You will be redirected to the ch6_case3_login.aspx page. Test the validation by entering a name and password from the XML file and submit form. Print the web page and the source code, the XML file, and the web configuration file. Change the web configuration settings back to Windows authentication, and allow all users access to the web site and save the file.

## Project 6-4

Your supervisor has requested you to create a web page that validates the user against a customer database named ch6_case4 database located in the ch6_case4 folder. The CustomerID is the primary key and an integer. The other fields include CustomerName, EmailAddress, Password, and MembershipLevel. The CustomerName is required, and the CustomerID column is an identity field that increments by one. Create a web page named ch6_ case4.aspx. Add a login form with the txtEmail and textPWD text boxes to collect the user's login information. Use the EmailAddress and Password fields from the database to validate the user. Add graphics and content to enhance the appearance of the page. Change the forms authentication in the web.config file to point to the database. Save the page, build the solution, and view the page in the browser. Test the validation by entering a name and a password from the Customers table. Print the web page, the HTML code, the code behind the page, and the web.config file. Change the web.config settings back to Windows authentication and allow all users access to the web site.

# 7

# MANAGING DATA SOURCES

## In this chapter, you will:

- Identify characteristics of relational database applications
- Use Visual Studio .NET to create a SQL Server database
- Build and execute views and queries using Structured Query Language (SQL)
- Create SQL statements using Visual Studio .NET
- Create and run stored procedures using Visual Studio .NET
- Manage a database using the Visual Studio .NET database tools

In order to develop flexible, effective data-driven Web applications, you must use multiple tools to access data from many sources. Internet applications often integrate web pages, style sheets, multimedia with web servers, e-mail servers, e-commerce servers, certificate servers, application servers, and authentication servers in addition to databases and database servers. As the number of available web development tools increases, the task of integrating data and Web applications becomes more complex. Visual Studio .NET integrates many of these web development tools into one development environment. In this chapter, you will learn how to create, manage, and access web data using the tools available in Visual Studio .NET.

## WORKING WITH DATABASE APPLICATIONS

Data can be stored and formatted using a variety of tools and technologies. A relational database management system (RDBMS) is a system that stores data in related tables. An RDBMS may contain additional tools to help create and manage tables, and provide an interface for programmers to develop applications that can communicate with the database. In this part of the chapter, you will learn about the characteristics of a relational database and how relationships exist between tables.

## Characteristics of a Relational Database

The relational database stores data in tables and organizes the data in rows and columns. These are not the only characteristics of relational databases, however. Edgar Codd devised a listing of 12 rules that describe characteristics of a relational database management system. For example, the information rule requires that the data is represented by its position in the rows and columns of a table. Another rule requires that the relational database management system provides at least one relational language to provide access to the data.

**NOTE**

Many relational databases today don't support all of Codd's rules, but they are still loosely considered relational databases.

For the purposes of learning ASP.NET, you will be working with databases that provide the ability to store data in related tables. These tables have rows and columns and provide programming access to the database through a language known as **Structured Query Language (SQL)**.

In a relational database, the information is held in one or more tables. Each table is designed to store data on one topic or subject. For example, in a product database, one table might contain product information and another table might contain inventory information about the products. Each row in a table represents a single entity. The entity might be, for instance, a product. In the product information table, each row represents a unique product. In the inventory table, each row represents the inventory information for a single product. Each column represents a characteristic about the entity. For a table that contains product information, each row might represent a product and the columns could be the product identification, category identification, model number, model name, product image, and unit cost. In Figure 7-1, the products table consists of four products. For the inventory table, each row could represent the product inventory information, and the columns could be the number of that product in inventory, the number of items on order, and the minimum number of items the company requires to have on hand.

The first step of designing and creating a database is to identify what data you need to store. You then need to organize the data into separate entities. You can use visual tools to help you model these entities; that is, as the database becomes more complex, it's useful to have

Most tables include one column, which contains a unique value for each row; this provides a method to differentiate each row of data

Each column is just one characteristic of the product; database applications usually indicate the column using the column name listed in the first row of the table

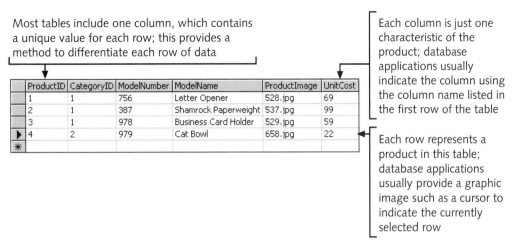

| | ProductID | CategoryID | ModelNumber | ModelName | ProductImage | UnitCost |
|---|---|---|---|---|---|---|
| | 1 | 1 | 756 | Letter Opener | 528.jpg | 69 |
| | 2 | 1 | 387 | Shamrock Paperweight | 537.jpg | 99 |
| | 3 | 1 | 978 | Business Card Holder | 529.jpg | 59 |
| ▶ | 4 | 2 | 979 | Cat Bowl | 658.jpg | 22 |
| ✳ | | | | | | |

Each row represents a product in this table; database applications usually provide a graphic image such as a cursor to indicate the currently selected row

**7**

**Figure 7-1**    Rows and columns in a database table

a visual guide to understand what each table represents in the database. As shown in Figure 7-2, each entity corresponds to a table in the database.

The next step is to create the individual tables. You will need to identify what each of the columns will be named, and what type of data will be stored in each column. You also will need to identify which columns will be required to contain a unique value for each row of data, and that columns can contain no values. A null value means that the column contains no value. Null values in columns need to be processed differently in your web program than a column that contains a blank space. You will need to identify which columns are indexed. Indexed columns allow the database to process searches faster. So, if you know the web program will need to search for the customer by last name, you would want to set up an index for the column that stores the last name data.

## Relationships Between Tables

While you are setting up your database, you will want to set up logical relationships between each of the tables in the database. The process of designing the logical database design is called **normalization**. In Figure 7-1, the data was stored in a single table. You may include multiple tables within a single database. When you normalize the database, you design how tables are related to each other logically. For example, you may want a table to store the orders data separate from a table that stores the customer data. By storing data in multiple tables, you can improve the performance of the database and maintain data integrity.

### Data Redundancy

The first reason to store data in multiple tables is to reduce redundancy. Redundancy occurs when you repeatedly store the same data in one table. For example, suppose your customer, Mr. William Platt, is a distributor of your products and ordered 12 red shirts today from your online store. If all the data was stored in a single table called CustomerOrders, you would

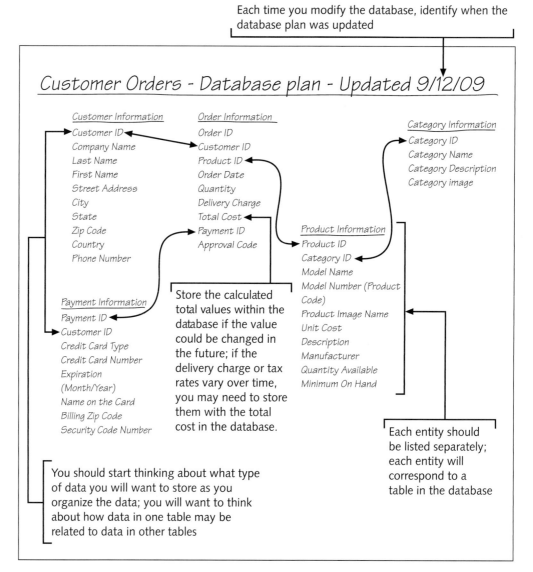

Each time you modify the database, identify when the database plan was updated

*Customer Orders - Database plan - Updated 9/12/09*

*Customer Information*
*Customer ID*
*Company Name*
*Last Name*
*First Name*
*Street Address*
*City*
*State*
*Zip Code*
*Country*
*Phone Number*

*Order Information*
*Order ID*
*Customer ID*
*Product ID*
*Order Date*
*Quantity*
*Delivery Charge*
*Total Cost*
*Payment ID*
*Approval Code*

*Category Information*
*Category ID*
*Category Name*
*Category Description*
*Category image*

*Product Information*
*Product ID*
*Category ID*
*Model Name*
*Model Number (Product Code)*
*Product Image Name*
*Unit Cost*
*Description*
*Manufacturer*
*Quantity Available*
*Minimum On Hand*

*Payment Information*
*Payment ID*
*Customer ID*
*Credit Card Type*
*Credit Card Number*
*Expiration (Month/Year)*
*Name on the Card*
*Billing Zip Code*
*Security Code Number*

Store the calculated total values within the database if the value could be changed in the future; if the delivery charge or tax rates vary over time, you may need to store them with the total cost in the database.

Each entity should be listed separately; each entity will correspond to a table in the database

You should start thinking about what type of data you will want to store as you organize the data; you will want to think about how data in one table may be related to data in other tables

**Figure 7-2** Organizing data into entities

have to insert his delivery information, payment information, and order information in the CustomerOrders table.

On the next day, suppose that Mr. Platt orders 15 black shirts. The new order would need to include the new order information and the *same* delivery and payment information that Mr. Platt entered yesterday. Each time you insert a new row into the database, the file size of your database application will increase. You can calculate the size of the row of data by adding the column size for each column in the table. The amount of memory required to store each column will vary depending on what type of data is stored in that column, what database application you are using to create the database, and what type of indexes are used within each table. For a store that handles only a small volume of online transactions, duplicate rows of data would only have a slight increase in the size of the database file. If you were a large online store with thousands of customers and orders, however, the database files would be quite large. Fortunately, if you stored Mr. Platt's delivery and payment information in a separate table, then only the new order information would need to be inserted into the database.

## Data Integrity

When you store the same data in multiple locations, you also run the risk of storing inaccurate data. If Mr. Platt had to re-enter his delivery and payment information with each order, it would be easier for Mr. Platt to enter the information different from the day before. For example, with the first order he may have sent the item to 435 South Maple Street. With his second order, he may have sent the item to 435 S. Maple. In some cities, there may be a South Maple Avenue and a Maple Road. Inconsistencies can cause problems with credit card payments as well as with fulfillment and delivery of the products. Many credit card companies require the information provided to match exactly to the information in the credit card company database. Therefore, to promote consistency of the data within the application, you would want to store the data in one location in the database. With our described system, Mr. Platt would have to enter his delivery and payment information only once, which would increase the reliability of the information; that is, the information that would be used to process and deliver his orders would be consistent across every order.

The company must be able to rely on the quality of the data stored in the database. When you design the database, you must consider how you will enforce the integrity of the data within each column. The database design should attempt to prevent the user from entering inaccurate data. For example, when Mr. Platt enters his zip code, he should be required to enter only numeric data consisting of exactly five numbers. This could prevent Mr. Platt from entering a zip code such as 1ZE45-4573, or leaving the column with a null value. By restricting the data types and possible values, the database design can maintain the quality of the data in the database.

## Primary and Foreign Keys

In a relational database, it is important to be able to create multiple related tables. A relational database uses primary and foreign keys to create a logical link between the data in one or more tables. A **primary key** is used to identify one column as a unique column for each row. Each value for each row must be unique within this column. All rows must have a value for this column. No record that contains a null value will be allowed in this column. Most database applications such as Microsoft Access and SQL Server indicate the primary key by placing an icon that looks like a key in the row selector. In a relational database, a **foreign key** is a primary key that exists in another table. These keys create the relationship between the two tables.

## A Relationship Diagram

Most database applications provide the ability to create visually the relationships between tables. The relationship diagram can be used to enforce the relationship. A line is drawn from a field in one table to a field in another table to indicate which fields are used to define the relationship between the tables. The endpoints of the line indicate whether the relationship is one-to-one or one-to-many. If a relationship has a key at one endpoint and an infinity symbol at the other, it is a one-to-many relationship. If the relationship has a key at each endpoint, however, then it is a one-to-one relationship. Figure 7-3 shows the relationships defined among five tables.

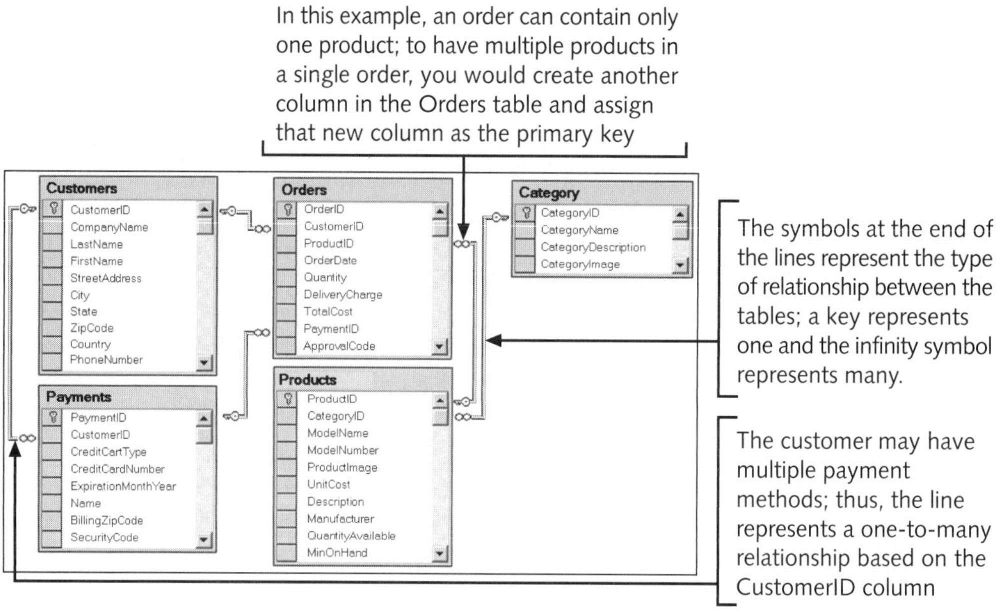

In this example, an order can contain only one product; to have multiple products in a single order, you would create another column in the Orders table and assign that new column as the primary key

The symbols at the end of the lines represent the type of relationship between the tables; a key represents one and the infinity symbol represents many.

The customer may have multiple payment methods; thus, the line represents a one-to-many relationship based on the CustomerID column

**Figure 7-3**    Relationships defined among multiple tables

TIP — If no column can be identified as the primary key, you can create a column that indicates the row number, and assign that column to be the primary key. You can set the column to increment the value of the column by one each time a new row is added, which will guarantee that each value in the column will be unique. Another alternative is to assign two or more columns to be a **composite key**. When the two values in the columns are combined, they must create a unique value that is not repeated in any other row.

## Relationship Integrity

Enforcing relationships is another way to maintain data integrity. For example, suppose there is a relationship between the Orders and Customers tables. A row of data cannot be inserted into the Orders table until the customer data is entered into the Customers table. You can configure the database to enforce this rule to maintain the integrity of the data relationships. This enforcement of referential integrity is used to ensure that no order could be placed without the customer information.

## Applications That Store Relational Data

Many types of applications can be used to store data in a relational database format. Microsoft Access, Microsoft SQL Server, and Oracle, are all examples of popular relational databases. Note the following differences among these databases:

- Microsoft Access is a popular database format for Windows-based applications and is available in several versions. Microsoft Access 2007 stores the data in a file with the extension .accdb, while older versions use .mdb. Microsoft Access, however, stores the information in a single file, can only handle a few concurrent connections through the web, and is less secure than SQL Server. Because Microsoft Access is file based, the data can be downloaded by typing the URL of the database in the browser, if it's stored within an unprotected web directory structure. Note also that the Internet Guest Account (IUSR_*MACHINENAME*) on the web server needs to have read permission to the database in order to retrieve the data and display the data in the web page. Because the file has read permission, the end user can download the Microsoft Access database. Thus, you should store your data folders outside of your web server directories. Some users use the password feature within Microsoft Access to protect the database. Then, when the user downloads the file, he or she needs to enter an additional password to retrieve the data. This does not provide absolute protection of the data, however. Because of these limitations, web developers will create the application using Microsoft Access, and then convert the database to a SQL Server using a process called **upsizing**.

- Microsoft SQL Server is a robust database application that also allows you to create stored procedures and supports transactions. Stored procedures allow you to store data commands in the database. Transactions allow you to group commands so that if one command does not execute successfully, all of the commands will roll back to their previous state. Microsoft SQL Server uses a version of the SQL language called Transact SQL that has been modified to provide additional capabilities. Microsoft SQL Server is available in several versions on the Windows platform. With SQL Server, the database is stored by SQL Server and is not downloadable from the browser. Therefore, you can use SQL Server for secure transactions, such as shopping carts. Microsoft provides SQL Server 2005 Express Edition with Visual Web Developer 2005 Express, which can be used when you develop your Web applications. When the application is deployed, however, the database will need to be upgraded to a production version of SQL Server. It's important for you to know that SQL Server is the name of the application that stores the data. You will use this information to identify the database in the Web application.

- Oracle Database 10*g* is another robust database application that is available in multiple versions. The Oracle Database 10*g* Express Edition is used by developers for training and development. Oracle Database 10*g* is available for both UNIX and Windows platforms. ASP.NET applications will work with Oracle databases. Oracle databases commonly are used with Web applications built with Java and PHP technologies.

## Visual Studio .NET Built-in Database Tools

A variety of Visual Studio .NET tools allow you to create and manipulate a database. With these tools, you can create the database from scratch or convert the data from an existing format into a relational database. You can also import data from a spreadsheet into a Microsoft Access database. In addition, you can convert a Microsoft Access database to a SQL Server database.

Before you work on this chapter, you already should have SQL Server 2005 Express Edition installed or have access to another version of SQL Server. In this book, SQL Server is used to represent all versions of SQL Server unless the version specifically is indicated. Your databases will be stored in the App_Data folder within your project folder. SQL Server allows you to create a SQL Server database file in your project and attach it to your version of SQL Server. To do this, you will need to know the name or IP address of your version of SQL Server. Normally, the SQL Server 2005 Express Edition has a named instance of .\SQLEXPRESS. You can also enter *Machine*\SQLEXPRESS, where *Machine* is the name of your computer. If you have the full version of SQL Server 2005, the default instance is usually (local).

### Creating a SQL Server Database in Visual Studio .NET

Visual Studio .NET provides a graphical user interface that you can use to create a connection to a database. When you create the database, you need to know the type of authentication required for access to the SQL Server. You can use the authentication built within Windows NT, or SQL Server authentication.

You should check with your database administrator to obtain the login values for your server. If you are provided with an additional login window, select the option for Windows Integrated Security. Note that you must have permission to create the database. Within SQL Server, a user ID identifies users, and controls which users can access the database objects. Each user has roles that identify if he or she are able to create or modify a data object.

You can create the database in either the Database Explorer window or the Solution Explorer window. If you create the database in the App_Data folder in the Solution Explorer window, then both the SQL Server data file and the transaction log are stored in the App_Data folder. If you wanted to move this database to another SQL Server, you would simply detach the database from this instance of SQL Server and reattach it to another instance of SQL Server. This is an important feature because web developers can easily move their Web applications across servers and Internet Service Providers.

In the following exercise, you will create a basic database named Chapter7.

1. Open the **Chapter7** folder in your application.

2. In the Solution Explorer window, right-click the **App_Data** folder and then click **Add New Item**.

3. In the Add New Item window, click **SQL Database**. Replace the text in the Name field type with **Chapter7.mdf** and then click the **Add** button.

4. Double-click the **Chapter7.mdf** file in the App_Data folder and the Database Explorer window opens. Chapter7.mdf appears as a database in your Data Connections.

7

# Using the Table Designer

Once you have created your database, you will want to add tables and stored procedures. You can add a table using the Table Designer. The **Table Designer** allows you to create the schema for the table and enter the data. The **table definition**, which is also called the schema, identifies the columns in a table and their properties. Table Designer has two views. In **Table Design view**, you can create new columns and modify the properties of the columns. In **Table Data view**, you can create a new row, modify an existing row, or delete a row. Table Data view is discussed later in the chapter.

## Table Design View

In Table Design view, the top half of the Table Designer allows you to create the structure of the columns within the table. You define the name of the column and the data type. Each column is defined within a row in the Table Designer. Each row contains a row selector box and the following fields: Column Name, Data Type, Length, and Allow Nulls.

The currently selected row in Table Designer can be identified by the triangle in the row selector box. The **row selector** is the gray square located next to the column name. The row selector can also be used to select the current row. The lower half of the Table Designer allows you to modify the properties of the column. The properties within the second half of the Table Designer vary with the data type selected. Most of the data types provide a description property and a default value for the column length property.

## Specifying Column Names

When you create a new column you must specify a name for the column and a data type. Do not use any blank spaces or special characters in a column name other than an underscore. It is best to keep the column name short, but descriptive. For example, the column name LastName describes a field that might contain customer last names. If the column name is LN, however, it's not clear what information is stored in the column. In addition, you must select a data type from a drop-down list. You must also provide the length of each column in bytes, and whether the column requires a value. If a column does not contain a value for a particular record, a null value is returned.

## Specifying Data Types

You must specify a data type when you create each column. The .NET providers convert the SQL Server data types to .NET data types when you retrieve your data using .NET. Many data types are defined within SQL Server. For example, the int data type is used to identify an integer. The possible data types for SQL Server are as shown in Table 7-1 that follows.

**Table 7-1**   Possible data types for SQL Server

| Category | Data Type | Description |
|---|---|---|
| Exact Numerics | bigint | Bigint is used to store very large numbers and requires 8 bytes of memory (+/-9,223,372,036,854,775,808). |
| | int | Int is the primary integer data type and takes up 4 bytes (+/-2,147,483,647). |
| | smallint | Smallint stores values between +/-32,767 and requires 2 bytes of memory. |
| | tinyint | Tinyint stores values from 0 to 255 and requires 1 byte of memory. |
| | bit | Bit stores values as 0 or 1. The string values TRUE and FALSE are converted to 1 and 0, respectively. The amount of memory required to store a column with a bit data type is 1 byte. Up to 8 columns are stored within 1 byte. For each additional 8 columns that store data as bits, the data requires an additional byte of memory. |
| | numeric | There can be a total of 38 digits in a numeric value. The default is 18, which requires 9 bytes of memory. The two parts to the numeric data type are integer portion and the decimal value. The number of digits to the right of the decimal point is called the scale and is 0 by default. |
| | decimal | The decimal data type is the same as the numeric data type except the scale is 0. |
| | money | Money is used to represent currency values and can range from +/-922,337,203,685,477.5808 and requires 8 bytes of memory. |
| | smallmoney | Smallmoney is also used to represent currency values, but the values range from +/-214,748.3648 and require only 4 bytes of memory. |

**Table 7-1**   Possible data types for SQL Server (continued)

| Category | Data Type | Description |
|---|---|---|
| Approximate Numerics | float | Float represents floating point numeric data. Because not all values in the data type range can be represented exactly, the memory requirements may vary between 4 and 8 bytes. |
| | real | Real data type represents floating point numeric data and requires 4 bytes of memory. |
| Date and Time | datetime | The datetime is used to store dates between January 1, 1753 and December 31, 9999 and has an accuracy of 3.33 milliseconds. The datetime values are rounded to increments of .000, .003, or .007 seconds. The datetime value is stored as two 4-byte integers. |
| | smalldatetime | The smalldatetime stores dates between January 1, 1900 through June 6, 2079 and the time in 1 minute increments. If the number of seconds is 29.998 or less, the smalldatetime is rounded down to the nearest minute. The smalldatetime value is stored as two 2-byte integers. |
| Character Strings | char | The char data type contains non-Unicode character data. The length is fixed but can be between 1 and 8,000. |
| | varchar | The varchar data type contains non-Unicode character data. The length is variable but can be between 1 and 8,000. |
| | text | The text data type is used for non-Unicode character data. The length is variable with a maximum of 2,147,483,647 characters. |
| Unicode Character Strings | nchar | The nchar data type contains Unicode character data. Unicode data types are used to support multiple languages to minimize character conversion issues. The length is fixed but can be between 1 and 4,000. The storage size is two times the number of bytes. |
| | nvarchar | The nvarchar data type contains Unicode character data. The length is variable but can be between 1 and 4,000. The storage size is two times the number of bytes. |
| | ntext | The ntext data type is used for Unicode character data. The length is variable with a maximum of 1,073,741,823 characters. To calculate the memory required, multiply the number of characters by two. |
| Binary Strings | image | The image data type contains a variable-length binary data from 0 to 2,147,483,647 bytes. |

7

**Table 7-1**   Possible data types for SQL Server (continued)

| Category | Data Type | Description |
|---|---|---|
| | binary | The binary data type contains fixed-length binary data with a length from 1 through 8,000 bytes. Set the column data type to binary when the sizes of the column values are consistent. |
| | varbinary | The varbinary data type contains variable-length binary data with a length from 1 through 8,000 bytes. Set the column data type to binary when the sizes of the column data are inconsistent or when the data exceeds 8,000 bytes. |
| Other Data Types | uniqueidentifier | The uniqueidentifier data type is used to guarantee that rows are uniquely identified across multiple copies of the table. The format of the uniqueidentifier is xxxxxxxx-xxxx-xxxx-xxxx-xxxxxxxxxxxx, in which each x is a hexadecimal digit. Hexadecimal digits range 0–9 or a–f. For example, 63F614EF-C286-A481-B352-0EE0DAC7348F is a valid uniqueidentifier value. |
| | xml | The xml data type is used to store xml data. The XML column properties include allowing you to identify if the column is an XML document and a schema collection. You can pass the XML data as a fragment or document, but they must be well-formed. The column size cannot exceed 2 gigabytes. |

You can set the default column properties such as column length using the Visual Studio .NET Options window as shown in Figure 7-4.

## Setting Properties and Creating a Table

The properties that can be set for the column will depend on the data type selected. For example, most data types provide properties for setting a default value or allowing null values. Properties are set in the Properties pane in the Table Designer.

In the following exercise, you will create a table named Products and create the columns using the Table Designer.

1. In the Data Connection in the Database Explorer window, click the **plus sign** next to the Data Connection for the Chapter7.mdf database file. Right-click the **Tables** icon, and then click **Add New Table** to open the Table Designer.

2. In the first row, type **ProductID** as the column name. Select **int** as the data type from the drop-down list. The length should be 10. Click the **Allow Nulls** check box to deselect it, because all products are required to have a ProductID. In the properties at the bottom half of the window, scroll down the

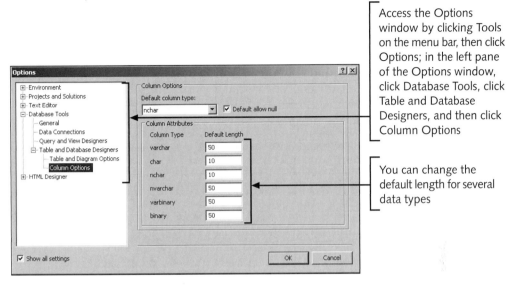

Access the Options window by clicking Tools on the menu bar, then click Options; in the left pane of the Options window, click Database Tools, click Table and Database Designers, and then click Column Options

You can change the default length for several data types

7

**Figure 7-4**   Default column options

window if needed, click the **plus sign** next to the Identity Specification property, and then change the (Is Identity) from No to **Yes** using the drop-down list arrow. Changing this value will change the Identity Seed set to 1, and the Identity Increment to 1. This setting will trigger the database to create a new value for each new record entered in the database.

3. Right-click the **ProductID** row selector, and then click **Set Primary Key**. A yellow key appears at the side of the column name to indicate that this column is the Primary Key column as shown in Figure 7-5.

4. Add the other columns as shown in Figure 7-6. You can leave the default properties for each column.

5. Click the **Save All** button and close the window. The Choose Name dialog box opens. Enter **Products** as the table name, and then click **OK**. Close the Table Designer window.

6. The Products table should appear under the Chapter7 Tables icon in the Data Connections in the Database Explorer window.

7. Click the **plus sign** to expand the Products table and view the columns that you created in Step 4.

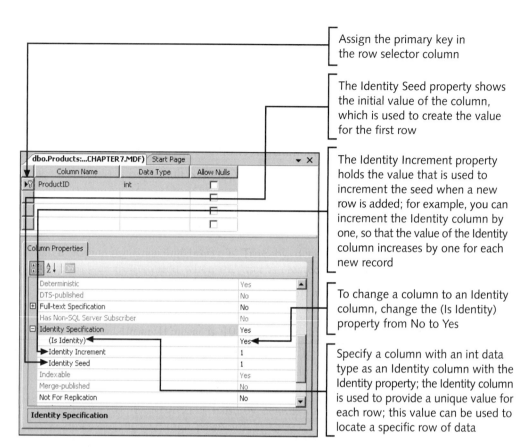

Assign the primary key in the row selector column

The Identity Seed property shows the initial value of the column, which is used to create the value for the first row

The Identity Increment property holds the value that is used to increment the seed when a new row is added; for example, you can increment the Identity column by one, so that the value of the Identity column increases by one for each new record

To change a column to an Identity column, change the (Is Identity) property from No to Yes

Specify a column with an int data type as an Identity column with the Identity property; the Identity column is used to provide a unique value for each row; this value can be used to locate a specific row of data

**Figure 7-5**   Creating an identity column

| Column Name | Data Type | Allow Nulls |
|---|---|---|
| ProductID | int | ☐ |
| CategoryID | int | ☐ |
| ModelNumber | nvarchar(50) | ☑ |
| ModelName | nvarchar(50) | ☑ |
| ProductImage | nvarchar(50) | ☑ |
| UnitCost | money | ☑ |
| Description | nvarchar(50) | ☑ |
| Manufacturer | nvarchar(50) | ☑ |
| QuantityAvailable | int | ☑ |
| MinOnHand | int | ☑ |
|  |  | ☐ |

Create these columns

**Figure 7-6**   Creating the Chapter7.mdf Products table

In the following exercise you will add data for four records into the table.

1. Right-click the **Products** table name, and then click **Show Table Data**. The table opens in Data view. You can enter data for each record in Table Data view. Enter **1** for CategoryID. If prompted, enter your user name and password.

2. Add the values for the other fields using the information in Table 7-2. Leave the other fields empty and press **Enter**. SQL Server assigns the value for the ProductID table after the record is created.

3. Enter the other three records. The data for all of the records is shown in Table 7-2. The ProductID field has been assigned a value of 1, 2, 3, and 4 by the database.

**Table 7-2**   The Products table data for the Chapter7.mdf database

| Column Name | Row 1 Data | Row 2 Data | Row 3 Data | Row 4 Data |
|---|---|---|---|---|
| ProductID | 1 (to be filled in by the database) | 2 (to be filled in by the database) | 3 (to be filled in by the database) | 4 (to be filled in by the database) |
| CategoryID | 1 | 1 | 1 | 2 |
| ModelNumber | 756 | 387 | 978 | 979 |
| ModelName | Letter Opener | Shamrock Paperweight | Business Card Holder | Cat Bowl |
| ProductImage | 528.jpg | 537.jpg | 529.jpg | 658.jpg |
| UnitCost | 69 | 99 | 59 | 22 |
| Description | Letter Opener | Shamrock | Business Card | Cat Bowl |
| Manufacturer | Waterford | Waterford | Waterford | Bradshaw |
| Quantity Available | 10 | 5 | 50 | 25 |
| MinOnHand | 5 | 10 | 25 | 10 |

**TIP**   If you do not enter a value, the column will display <NULL>. If you make a mistake, you can delete the value you entered and configure the column to display <NULL>. When you press the Ctrl key and 0 while inside the column, the contents of the column will be replaced with the <NULL> value.

4. Click the **Save All** button and close the window.

5. Create a second table by right-clicking **Tables** and clicking **Add New Table**. The table has two columns. The name of the first column in the new table is CategoryID. Type **CategoryID** in the Column Name column in the Table Designer window, and assign it as an integer (**int**) data type that has a length of **10** bytes. Click the **Allow Nulls** check box to deselect it. A CategoryID is required for all categories. In the properties at the bottom half of the window, click the **plus sign** next to the Identity Specification property and change the

(Is Identity) from No to **Yes** using the drop-down list arrow. The Identity Seed is set by the database to 1, and the Identity Increment is set to 1. This creates a new value for each new record entered in the database.

6. Right-click the **CategoryID** column name in the row selector, and then click **Set Primary Key**. A yellow key appears at the side of the column name to indicate that this column is the Primary Key column.

7. The name of the second column in the database is Category Name. Type **CategoryName** in the Column Name column in the Table Designer window. Enter **nvarchar** as the data type and the length as **50** bytes. The CategoryName column is allowed to have null values, so leave the Allow Nulls check box checked.

8. Click the **Save All** button. The Choose Name dialog box opens. Enter **Categories** for the table name, click **OK**, and then close the window.

9. Open the table and add two records. Right-click the **Categories** table in the Data Connections in the Database Explorer window and select **Show Table Data**. In the first row, press the **Tab** key to move to the CategoryName column. The database server adds the CategoryID for you. Type **Waterford** as the CategoryName. If prompted, enter your user name and password.

10. Press the **Tab** key twice to get the CategoryName for the second row. Type **Pottery**, and then press **Enter**.

11. Click the **Save All** button. Close the window.

# Creating a Relationship with the Database Diagram

In Visual Studio .NET, the Database Diagram is used to identify relationships between tables. After you create a database diagram, you can use the **Database Designer** to define relationships between tables using columns. In the Database Designer, each table contains a **title bar**, which displays the name of the table. If the table has an owner, the owner's name is shown in parentheses on the title bar after the table name.

## Changing the View

By default the tables are displayed in the Database Designer showing the table names on the title bar and the column names. This view of the table is called the **Column Names view**. You can change the view from Column Names by right-clicking the table, selecting Table View, and then selecting another view name. Your view name choices are:

- The **Standard view**, which displays the column names and the schema for the columns.

- The **Keys view**, which displays the names of the tables on the title bar and the names of the primary key columns.

- The **Name Only view**, which displays only the names of the tables on the title bar.

- The **Custom view**, which allows you to add any of the properties to the view.

## Creating a Database Diagram

In the following exercise, you will use the Database Designer to create a relationship between the Categories table and the Products table.

1. In the Data Connections window, under the Chapter7.mdf data connection, right-click **Database Diagrams**, and then click **Add New Diagram**. When the alert box appears, click **Yes**. The Data Diagram Editor opens along with the Add Table dialog box. Select both the **Categories** table and the **Products** table by holding down the **Shift** key while you make the selections. Click the **Add** button and then the **Close** button. The tables are added to the Database Designer. You may move any table by clicking the table name and dragging on the table to a new location.

2. Click the **row selector** next to the CategoryID column in the Categories table and drag the row to the row selector next to the CategoryID column in the Products table. The Tables and Columns window opens. The CategoryID is assigned as the primary key in the Categories table and as the foreign key in the Products table.

3. Click **OK** and when the next window opens, click **OK** again. The line now indicates a one-to-many relationship between the two tables. Only one CategoryID value is in the Categories table. Many products can have the same CategoryID value.

4. Click the **Save All** button to save the view. In the Choose Name dialog box, type **Category_Products** as the name of the view, and then click **OK**. A warning message may appear indicating that the tables will be saved to the database. Click **Yes**. The table relationship is shown in Figure 7-7.

5. Close the window.

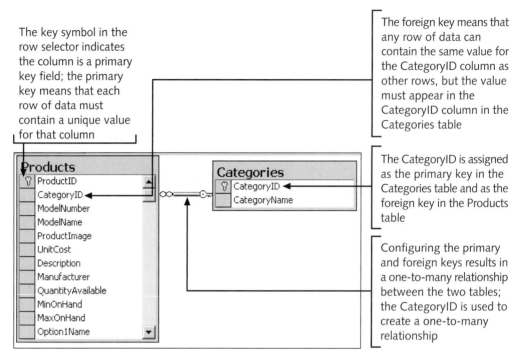

The key symbol in the row selector indicates the column is a primary key field; the primary key means that each row of data must contain a unique value for that column

The foreign key means that any row of data can contain the same value for the CategoryID column as other rows, but the value must appear in the CategoryID column in the Categories table

The CategoryID is assigned as the primary key in the Categories table and as the foreign key in the Products table

Configuring the primary and foreign keys results in a one-to-many relationship between the two tables; the CategoryID is used to create a one-to-many relationship

**Figure 7-7**   Using the Database Diagram to create table relationships

## VIEWS AND QUERIES

The Visual Studio .NET SQL Editor is used to create and edit views, SQL scripts, and stored procedures. Views and queries allow you to retrieve information from the database. Queries are SQL commands that retrieve data from the database. You can run the commands when you create the query, or save the query as a view, and run it at a later time. SQL scripts and stored procedures may contain the same SQL commands used in queries and views. They can also be used to perform additional tasks to manage the database, such as creating a new table.

## Using Views and Queries

It's important to understand that queries and views can both be used to retrieve data from the database. Because queries and views have so many similarities, it is easy to overlook their differences.

A view is an SQL statement that is saved with the database as part of a database design. View Designer is used to create and manage views and works only with SQL Server. SQL contains commands such as select, insert, delete, and update, which are used to manage the data. Views can contain only select statements, which means that views can retrieve data. They cannot be used to create, update, or delete data.

Some subsets of data are of interest to many users. As you design a database, you can include views in the design to establish a particular subset of data that can be used by a database user. Views can also be used to conceal base tables. For instance, you can disallow all user access to database tables, requiring users to manipulate data through views only. Such an approach can prevent users and application programs from modifying data. You cannot create parameters for a view, but you can sort a view result if the view includes the TOP clause.

**NOTE** A **query plan** is an internal strategy by which a database server tries to create result sets quickly. A database server can establish a query plan for a view as soon as the view is saved.

A query is an SQL statement that is saved with a Visual Studio database project and not with the database. The Query Designer is similar to the View Designer, but it will work with nearly any data source. Query Designer allows you to design, select, insert, update, and delete SQL statements that means that the Query Designer can be used to create, update, and delete data. You can sort any query result, and you can create parameters for a query. A database server cannot establish a query plan until the query is actually run; that is, until the user explicitly demands the result set.

## Building a View with the Query and View Designer

There is a Query and View Designer for creating database queries. The Query and View Designer allows you to create a query or view within Visual Studio .NET. You can use the visual tools to create the SQL commands, or insert the SQL commands manually. (*Note*: If you have other versions of SQL Server, you may have tools such as Query Analyzer that can be used without Visual Studio .NET to create and manage databases.)

To aid you in creating views and queries, there are four windows called **panes** displayed within the Query and View Designer. The top pane is the Diagram pane. (*Note*: In previous versions this was also called the Table pane.) In the **Diagram pane**, you can add tables and select which columns to include in the query or view. The query or view is displayed visually with icons next to the columns, which represent pieces of the SQL command. For example, if you sort the table based on a column, a sort icon is placed next to the column name in the Diagram pane. This provides a quick method for viewing the query or view.

The second pane is the Grid pane. You use the **Grid pane** to select columns and criteria. The **Column** option is used to identify the name of the column and the **Table** option indicates where to retrieve the values for the column. The **Output** option indicates if the column should be visible in the results when the query is executed. The **Sort Order** option is used to specify one or more columns for sorting the results. You can number the sort order to specify which column should be sorted first. (*Note*: The sort order with the lowest number is sorted first.) You can specify the sort order as ascending or descending by using the **Sort Type** option. The **Alias** option is used to display an alternate name in the results. Because the field names do not contain spaces or special characters, it is sometimes useful to provide a more readable alias name for the end user. You use the **Criteria** option to create a conditional statement that must be met before the record can be retrieved. The **Or** option indicates an alternate condition that could be met for the record to be retrieved.

The third pane is the SQL pane. The **SQL pane** generates the SQL for you based on the Diagram pane and Grid pane. You can edit the SQL commands directly within the SQL pane. The Grid pane and Diagram pane are updated automatically when you make a change to the SQL pane. It is not recommended to edit the SQL pane manually because you may introduce a syntax or typographical error.

The last pane is the Results pane. (*Note*: In previous versions this was called the Output pane.) In the **Results pane**, the output from the query or view is displayed. Therefore, you can test your views and queries from within Visual Studio .NET before you place them in your web pages.

## Using the Query and View Designer

In the following exercise, you will use the Query and View Designer to create a view that will display the products from the Waterford manufacturer.

1. In the Data Connections in the Database Explorer window, under Chapter7.mdf data connection, right-click **Views**, and then click **Add New View**. The Query and View Designer opens along with the Add Table dialog box. You need to select which tables you would like to add to the view. Select the **Products** table, click the **Add** button, and then click the **Close** button. The Products table is added to the Diagram pane.

2. In the Diagram pane, click the **check box** next to the following column names to select them: **ProductID**, **CategoryID**, **ModelName**, and **Manufacturer**. This places the column names into the view in the Grid pane and the SQL pane. (*Note*: You may have to scroll down the Table Fields list in order to view and select some of the fields.)

3. In the Grid pane, go to the Sort Type property for the ModelName column, and select **Ascending** from the drop-down list. The sort order is entered as **1**, which indicates that this is the first column to be sorted.

4. In the row that represents the Manufacturer column, enter **=N'Waterford'** in the Filter property.

5. Right-click the **Diagram pane**, and then click **Execute SQL**. The three Waterford products are displayed with the Business Card Holder displayed first. If prompted, enter your user name and password.

6. Click the **Save All** button to save the view. In the Choose Name dialog box, enter **DisplayWaterford** as the name of the view, and then click **OK**. The view is shown in Figure 7-8.

7. Close the Query and View Designer.

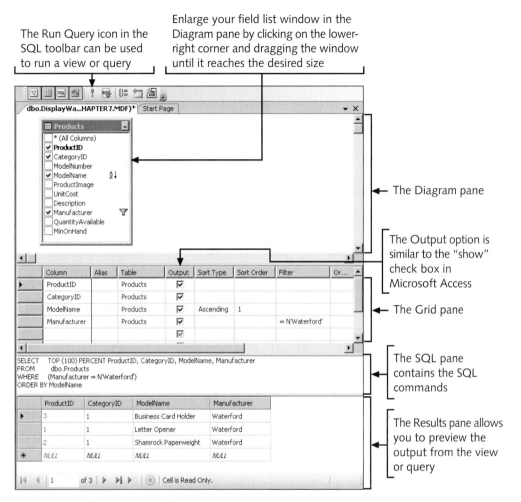

The Run Query icon in the SQL toolbar can be used to run a view or query

Enlarge your field list window in the Diagram pane by clicking on the lower-right corner and dragging the window until it reaches the desired size

The Diagram pane

The Output option is similar to the "show" check box in Microsoft Access

The Grid pane

The SQL pane contains the SQL commands

The Results pane allows you to preview the output from the view or query

**Figure 7-8**    The Query and View Designer

8.  To rerun the view, first click the **plus sign** next to the Views icon under Data Connections in the Database Explorer Window to display the list of views.

9.  Right-click the **Display Waterford** view, and then click **Show Results**. The view runs and displays the results, but it does not display the Query and View Designer. If prompted, enter your user name and password.

10.  Close the window.

# SQL Statements

You can build and modify the SQL commands to retrieve a select group of records. To retrieve all the records in the Products table, you can use the SQL command following this paragraph. The asterisk is a wildcard character, which indicates that all columns are selected. The keyword FROM is used to indicate the name of the table where the data is retrieved. (*Note*: With SQL Server databases, you can also specify the owner of the table, such as dbo.products.)

```
SELECT * FROM Products
```

In the Chapter 7 table, you can retrieve the list of manufacturers by using the Select statement. Some manufacturers would be listed multiple times, however. The keyword DISTINCT will provide you with a list of discrete values for a column. In the code following this paragraph, the keyword DISTINCT is used to retrieve a single list of manufacturers from the Products table.

```
SELECT DISTINCT Manufacturers FROM Products
```

As you can see in the following code, the view can use the keyword TOP to retrieve a subset of the records in the table. Notice that the percentage was 50, which means that only the top half of the records were returned.

```
SELECT TOP (50) PERCENT * FROM Products
```

## Creating Search Conditions

Retrieving all columns and rows will increase the time required to process the command. With Web applications where you may run queries with each web page request, retrieving unnecessary data can also degrade the database server performance. You can use keywords to qualify a subset of records and columns to retrieve. You can customize the SQL statement with a search condition to retrieve only some of the records. A **search condition** is a SQL clause, which identifies the criterion that is used to filter the records. A search condition evaluates either to true or false. The search condition uses the keyword WHERE to identify the search condition.

The SQL clause WHERE Manufacturer=N'Waterford' would evaluate to true or false. For records in which the user name is John, the record is returned in the data set. In Access and SQL, you can create more complex queries using multiple search conditions within the same clause. When the keyword AND is used to separate conditions, both search conditions must be resolved to true. If the keyword OR is used to separate conditions, only one of the search conditions needs to be resolved to true. Below is the SQL command that you created in the Waterford view:

```
SELECT TOP (100) PERCENT ProductID, CategoryID, ModelName,
Manufacturer
FROM dbo.Products
```

```
WHERE (Manufacturer=N'Waterford')
ORDER BY ModelName
```

## The WHERE Clause of a Search Condition

The WHERE clause of a search condition consists of the keyword WHERE, an expression, a comparison operator, and another expression. An expression can be simple, such as the name of a field, or it can be a string, a number, or a value passed from a form. If the expression is a string, the string must be enclosed within quotation marks. Strings are case sensitive when used as expressions. So, "product" and "PRODUCT" are not evaluated as equal expressions. A comparison operator is used to evaluate the expression. Valid comparison operators include +, <, >, <>, IS, and ISNOT. The syntax to create search criteria in a SQL statement is as follows:

```
WHERE [expression1] [comparisonoperator] [expression2]
```

You can use a static value as the comparative expression or use a variable that contains a value. If the value is a string, single quotes are used around the value. If the value passed is a number, the value must be passed without any quotes.

By using the keywords AND and OR, you can combine multiple search criteria within the same SQL statement. For example, you can create a query that lists the product names of any product where the number of items is less than five. This information could be provided to the person in charge of ordering new supplies. You don't need to order discontinued products, however. By using combination queries, you can combine all of these search criteria into one SQL statement. The sample code that follows this paragraph contains valid expressions that use multiple search criteria and data types:

```
WHERE User='George' AND Password='Thunderbowl'
WHERE state='CA' OR state='TX' AND People>=10000
WHERE LastVisit>#12/31/2009# OR Member='New'
WHERE Member='Staff' AND Salary>55000
WHERE Birth=IS NULL OR Email=IS NULL
```

TIP     Note that an expression that contains a date must append the pound sign (#) before and after the date. While strings use quotes, the dates use pound signs, and the numbers, variables, and constants do not use quotes.

TIP     The keyword NULL can be used to search for empty fields. An empty string is not the same as a NULL field, because NULL fields do not contain any data. The word NULL is used as the expression.

## The GROUP BY and ORDER BY Clauses

The GROUP BY clause allows you to aggregate the records based on the values of one of the columns. For example, you might want to list each of the products, but group the list by the category.

```
SELECT *FROM Products GROUP BY CategoryID
```

The ORDER BY clause allows you to sort the results based on one or more columns. You can separate multiple sort columns with a comma. When there are multiple sort columns, the rows will be sorted by the first sort column, then the second, and so forth. You can specify the sort order as ascending with ASC or descending with DESC. The sample SQL statement that follows this paragraph displays a list of category names. The rows returned are sorted by CategoryName in ascending order.

```
SELECT CategoryName FROM Categories
ORDER BY CategoryName ASC
```

## Joining tables with JOIN Clauses

There are many ways to use JOIN clauses to combine one or more tables into a single set of records. The INNER JOIN clause uses a comparison to compare the value between columns in different tables. Inner joins are used when you want to combine the data from two related tables. Inner joins will not include records where the fields in the where clause have a null value. Outer joins will use the OUTER JOIN keywords and to include all records from both tables. If the records with null values in the left table should be returned use the LEFT OUTER JOIN keywords. If the records with null values in the right table should be returned use the RIGHT OUTER JOIN keywords. In the query SELECT DISTINCT* FROM employee LEFT OUTER JOIN Department ON Employee. DepartmentID = Department.DepartmentID all of the employee records would be retrieved even if the value of Department.Department is null. The ON keyword is used to identify which fields should be matched in both tables. As shown in Figure 7-9, the INNER JOIN keywords are used to create the connection between the two tables. The keywords INNER JOIN are located in the FROM clause or the WHERE clause. When you join tables, you should refer to each column name prefixed by the name of the table followed by a period. This will prevent errors from the database application retrieving the data from the wrong column.

# Building SQL Queries to Insert, Update, and Delete Data

You can use the following keywords in SQL statements to insert, update, and delete records:

- INSERT to add a new record
- UPDATE to modify one or more rows of data
- DELETE to delete one or more rows of data

The following sections will discuss each.

To use the INNER JOIN,
you must start with two
related tables

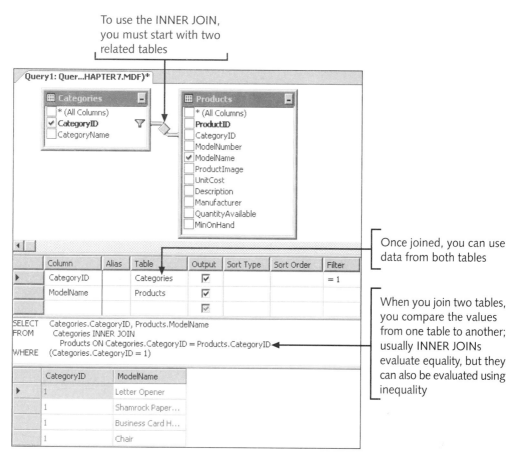

Once joined, you can use
data from both tables

When you join two tables,
you compare the values
from one table to another;
usually INNER JOINs
evaluate equality, but they
can also be evaluated using
inequality

Figure 7-9   Viewing a query created with an INNER JOIN clause

## The INSERT Statement

In SQL, you must create an INSERT statement in order to create a new record. Insert queries can be performed only on one table at a time and only one record at a time can be inserted. Furthermore, you must specify a value for every field. If no value is available, you can substitute the keyword NULL for the value. You must enter strings using quotation marks. If you enter the fields without specifying the field names, you must enter them in the order that the fields appear in the database structure. If you have used an autonumber field in Access or an identity field in SQL Server, you can't enter a value in that field. The database automatically inserts a value when the record is added.

The syntax for inserting a new record into a table that has only five fields using SQL is listed after this paragraph. The values are entered sequentially in the table. In the example, the string 'chair' is placed in the first column and 153.29 is placed in the second column:

```
INSERT INTO Products
VALUES ('chair',153.29,#12/1/2009#,NULL,'furniture')
```

You can specify the field names in parentheses after the table if you plan to enter values for only a subset of fields. The sample code that follows this paragraph demonstrates how to enter only the product name and price. It is better to specify the field names because if the order of the columns is changed, then the SQL query will have to be changed.

```
INSERT INTO Products(name, price)
VALUES('chair',153.29)
```

## The UPDATE Statement

The SQL statement uses the UPDATE statement instead of the SELECT or INSERT statements to modify a record. The UPDATE statement needs to know which table to update as well as which fields and values. The keyword SET is used to assign the values to the field names. If you do not specify a search condition using the WHERE clause, the value is updated for all records in the database.

The code snippet following this paragraph assigns the entire SQL statement to a variable named SQL. Note that the SQL statement is stored as a string and therefore must be enclosed within double quotation marks. If you write the code across multiple lines, you will have to concatenate the SQL statement using multiple strings. It is easier to read the code by concatenating in a pattern for each line, such as name=value. (*Note:* This is a common place in which inattentive developers make typographical errors.) By using a standard format, you will decrease the number of typographical and syntax errors.

```
SQL="UPDATE Products SET " & _
" ProductName='Claddagh Ring'," & _
" UnitCost=25.45 WHERE ProductID=353"
```

To use the SQL statement with variables, you can replace the static values with variables that contain values, as shown in the sample code that follows this paragraph. (*Note:* It is important to make sure the single quotation marks are included for strings, and the pound sign for dates. You will have to concatenate the variable between the set of strings such as SQL="FieldName='" & VariableName & "'," .)

```
SQL="UPDATE Products SET " & _
" ProductName='" & MyProduct & "'," & _
" UnitCost=" & MyCost & _
" WHERE ProductID=" & MyProductID
```

## The DELETE Statement

The SQL DELETE statement is used to delete records within the database. When you use the DELETE command, you must specify which records to delete and the name of the table. If you do not specify a specific record or set of records using the WHERE clause, the entire set of records is deleted. The following sample code passes a value to the SQL DELETE statement so that only a single record is deleted.

```
SQL="DELETE FROM Products " & _
" WHERE ProductID=" & MyProductID
```

Before you run an UPDATE, INSERT, or DELETE statement you should first run the SQL statement as a SELECT query to ensure that you are operating on the correct data source. It's useful to display the data to the user and confirm his or her intent to modify the database before the SQL statement is executed.

# SQL Stored Procedures and SQL Server Scripts

Both stored procedures and SQL Server scripts provide the ability to expand the functionality of your SQL Server database. Stored procedures can be used to create an SQL command that is stored within the database. Because the command is stored with the database server, it already has been parsed and compiled by the server. Therefore, the stored procedure is more efficient than an SQL statement. Prior to Visual Studio .NET, you had to create the stored procedure from within an SQL Server tool such as Query Analyzer or Enterprise Manager. Today, you can create your stored procedure from within Visual Studio .NET.

As you work through this part of the chapter, note that SQL Server scripts provide you with the ability to store SQL commands in an external text file. The SQL Server script can be run from within SQL Server. SQL Server scripts are often used to create and backup your SQL Server databases. In this section, you will learn how to create more advanced SQL statements using parameters, store the information as stored procedures, and then run the stored procedure. Then, you will learn how to use built-in stored procedures and views, and how to create SQL Server scripts.

## Input and Output Parameters

You can use a stored procedure to run an SQL statement. You do not want to continually create stored procedures for every SQL statement, however. A better technique is to pass values to the stored procedure that can be used in the SQL statement. The values that are passed to and from the stored procedure are called parameters. You can create a stored procedure that uses input and output parameters. The name of any parameter within a stored procedure always begins with the @ symbol.

An **input parameter** is a value that is passed to the stored procedure when it is called. The data type and length of this value must match the data type and length that is specified within the stored procedure. Any of the values within the SQL statement can be replaced with the input parameters. Usually, the input parameter is compared to a value. Then, a new record is created, or a subset of matching records is retrieved, modified, or deleted. You can specify a default value for the parameter in the stored procedure. Therefore, if the user does not enter a parameter, the default is used. The default value must be a constant, or it can be null. You can return values of integer, money, and varchar, but not text.

The other type of parameter is the output parameter. **Output parameters** can send values back to the object that called the stored procedure. (*Note:* Text, ntext, and image parameters can be used as output parameters.) Output parameters are often used to retrieve the value of the identity column for a newly inserted row.

## The Return Code

You can have a return value passed back to the stored procedure call. The return code is indicated with the keyword RETURN and is often used to indicate the status of the query. By default the return value is set to 0, which means the query execution was successful. When the value is 1, the required parameter value was not passed to the query. When the value was 2, the parameter passed was not valid. This occurs when the data type or length of the value passed does not match the data type or length of the parameter defined in the query.

The return code is often used for queries that don't return columns, such as an INSERT query. You can specify information such as the number of records affected in the return value. By setting the keyword RETURN to @@Identity, the query will retrieve the Identity column when the stored procedure is run.

**NOTE**    Visual Studio .NET provides a **SQL Editor** to create and edit SQL scripts and stored procedures. Although the SQL Editor does not have IntelliSense prompting, it does color-code SQL keywords, which helps minimize syntax and spelling errors. You can change the editor's default behaviors, such as tab size, word wrapping, and line numbers, by selecting Options on the Tools menu.

## Creating Stored Procedures with the SQL Editor

In the following exercises, you will create stored procedures using the SQL Editor. The first procedure will retrieve all the records from the table where the QuantityAvailable column is less than MinOnHand. This creates a listing of products that must be reordered because there are not enough units available.

1. In the Data Connection in the Database Explorer window, under the Chapter7.mdf data connection, right-click **Stored Procedures**, and then click **Add New Stored Procedure**. The stored procedure document opens with the default text for creating the stored procedure.

2. Replace the text dbo.StoredProcedure1 with **dbo.sp_ReorderProducts**.

3. Under the keyword AS, insert a new line and type the code as shown in Figure 7-10. The code retrieves all the columns from the database where the QuantityAvailable column is less than or equal to the MinOnHand column.

4. Click the **Save All** button. The stored procedure is saved. The first line of the SQL command changes from CREATE PROCEDURE to ALTER PROCEDURE. This means that the procedure has been created. At this point, you only can change the procedure using the ALTER PROCEDURE command. Close the window.

5. Click the **plus sign** next to Stored Procedures in the Data Connection in the Database Explorer window. Right-click the **sp_ReorderProducts** stored procedure and then click **Execute**. The results are displayed in the **Output window** as shown in Figure 7-11. There should be one row returned, which

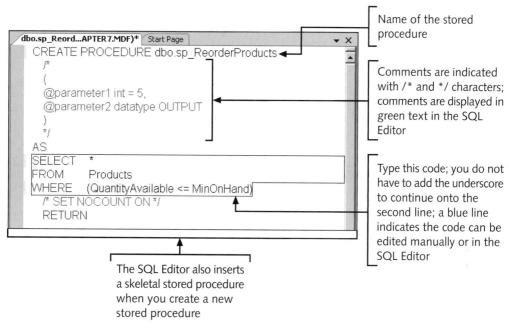

**Figure 7-10**    Creating the sp_ReorderProducts stored procedure

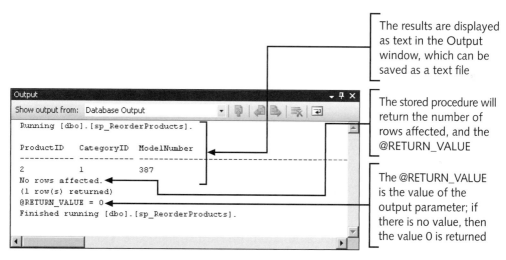

**Figure 7-11**    Viewing the results of the sp_ReorderProducts stored procedure

contains ProductID 2. The results will return the number of rows affected, which is 1, and the @RETURN_VALUE, which is 0. Close the window. If prompted, enter your user name and password.

## Creating a Stored Procedure with an Input Parameter

Now you will create a stored procedure that returns the products that match an input parameter value. In this example, you will use the visual editor to run the stored procedure and pass the input parameter to the database.

1. In Data Connection in the Database Explorer window, under the Chapter7.mdf data connection, right-click **Stored Procedures**, and then click **Add New Stored Procedure**. The stored procedure document opens with the default text for creating the stored procedure.

2. Replace the text dbo.StoredProcedure2 with **dbo.sp_DisplayProduct**.

3. Type the code as shown in Figure 7-12. You must supply the name of the product when the stored procedure is called.

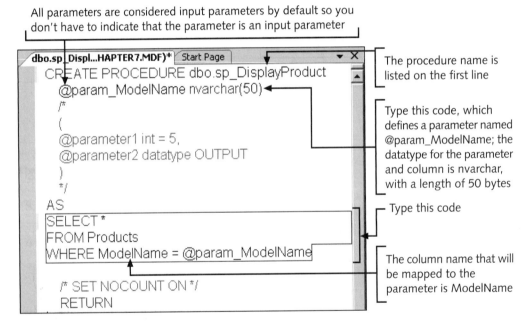

**Figure 7-12**   Creating the sp_DisplayProduct stored procedure

4. Click the **Save All** button. The stored procedure is saved. The first line of the SQL command changes from CREATE PROCEDURE to ALTER PROCEDURE. This means that the procedure has been created. At this point, you can only alter the procedure, using the ALTER PROCEDURE command.

5. Right-click the **sp_DisplayProduct** stored procedure, and then select **Execute**. The Run Stored Procedure window appears. (*Note:* You can have multiple input parameters listed here.) In the Value column for the

@param_ModelName procedure, delete <DEFAULT> and type **Letter Opener**, as shown in Figure 7-13.

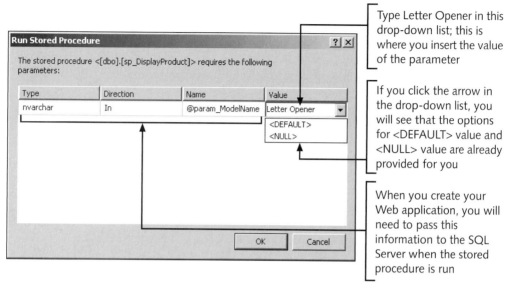

Type Letter Opener in this drop-down list; this is where you insert the value of the parameter

If you click the arrow in the drop-down list, you will see that the options for <DEFAULT> value and <NULL> value are already provided for you

When you create your Web application, you will need to pass this information to the SQL Server when the stored procedure is run

**Figure 7-13**    Inserting a value for a parameter

6. Click the **OK** button. Only one column matches the criteria. The columns listed for the first record are displayed in the Output window, as shown in Figure 7-14.

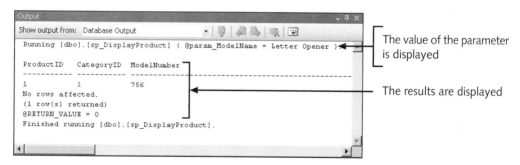

The value of the parameter is displayed

The results are displayed

**Figure 7-14**    Viewing the results of the sp_DisplayProduct stored procedure

7. Close the output window and the stored procedure.

## Inserting a New Record with a Stored Procedure

In the following exercise, you use the SQL Editor to create a stored procedure that will insert a new record in the Categories table and return the value of the Identity column.

1. In the Data Connections in the Database Explorer window, under the Chapter7.mdf data connection, right-click **Stored Procedures** and then click **Add New Stored Procedure**. The stored procedure document opens with the default text for creating the stored procedure.

2. Replace the text dbo.StoredProcedure3 with **dbo.sp_InsertCat**.

3. Type the code as shown in Figure 7-15.

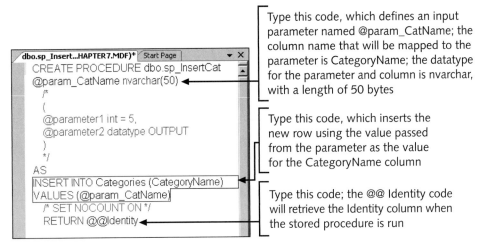

Type this code, which defines an input parameter named @param_CatName; the column name that will be mapped to the parameter is CategoryName; the datatype for the parameter and column is nvarchar, with a length of 50 bytes

Type this code, which inserts the new row using the value passed from the parameter as the value for the CategoryName column

Type this code; the @@ Identity code will retrieve the Identity column when the stored procedure is run

**Figure 7-15**   Creating the sp_InsertCat stored procedure

4. Click the **Save All** button and close the window. The stored procedure is saved in the SQL Server database.

5. Right-click the **sp_InsertCat** stored procedure, and then click **Execute**. The Run Stored Procedure window opens. In the Value column for the @param_CatName procedure, type **Jewelry**, and then click the **OK** button. If prompted, enter your user name and password.

6. Right-click the **Categories** icon under the Tables list for the Chapter7.mdf database in the Data Connections window, and then click **Show Table Data**. The Jewelry entry should be listed in a new record in the third row.

7. Close all the windows.

## Using Wildcard Characters to Search for a Matching Value in a Column

In the following exercise, you will create a stored procedure that searches a field in the database for a matching value. You will search a text string under the ModelName field, and then display the results.

1. In the Data Connection in the Database Explorer window, under the Chapter7.mdf data connection, right-click **Stored Procedures**, and then click **Add New Stored Procedure**. The stored procedure document opens with the default text for creating the stored procedure.

2. Replace the text dbo.StoredProcedure4 with **dbo.sp_SearchProducts**.

3. Enter the code as shown in Figure 7-16.

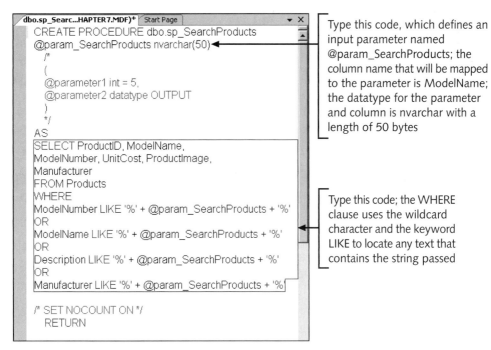

**Figure 7-16**  Creating the sp_SearchProducts stored procedure

4. Click the **Save All** button and close the window.

5. Right-click the **sp_SearchProducts** stored procedure, and then click **Execute**. The Run Stored Procedure window opens. In the Value column for the @param_SearchProducts procedure, type **Letter**, and then click the **OK** button. Only one column matches the criteria. The columns listed for the first record are displayed.

6. Run the stored procedure again with a different value entered for the input parameter. Right-click the **sp_ SearchProducts** stored procedure, and then click **Execute**. The Run Stored Procedure window opens. In the Value column for the @param_SearchProducts procedure, type **Waterford**, and then click the **OK** button. Now all three columns match the criteria.

7. Close the windows.

## Modifying a Stored Procedure with the SQL Editor

The SQL Query Builder has the same user interface as the Query and View Editor that you used earlier. The code to create the query, however, is stored in the stored procedure. Within the stored procedure, you can edit the blocks of code that are enclosed within a blue line, via the SQL Query Builder. You only need to right-click the block and select Design SQL Block. In the following exercise, you will modify a stored procedure using the SQL Query Builder.

1. In the Data Connection in the Database Explorer window, under the Chapter7.mdf data connection, double-click the **sp_ReorderProducts** stored procedure. The stored procedure script you created earlier opens.

2. Right-click the blue-outlined block of code, and then click **Design SQL Block**. This opens the block of code within the SQL Query Builder.

3. In the Grid pane in the Filter option, change the QuantityAvailable criteria from <= MinOnHand to **<=10**. Click **OK**.

4. Click the **Save All** button.

5. Right-click the **sp_ReorderProducts** stored procedure, and then click **Execute**. There should be two records displayed in the Results pane.

6. Close the window.

## Using Built-in Views and Stored Procedures

Built-in views and stored procedures allow you to retrieve information about your database. For example, you might want to retrieve a list of tables in the database. The sp_tables built-in stored procedure would return a list of tables in the database. The sp_columns built-in stored procedure would return the list of columns for the name of the table that is passed as a parameter to the stored procedure. You can access the stored system views and stored procedures in the Database Explorer. In the next activity, you will run a built-in stored procedure to do this.

1. In Database Explorer, right-click the **Chapter7.mdf** file, select **Change View**, and then select **Schema**.

2. Expand the **System-supplied Objects** and then **System Views**.

3. Scroll down until you see tables. Right-click **tables** and then select **Show Results**. The tables view provides a list of tables in the database. There are three tables listed. The sysdiagrams table stored information for your database diagram you created earlier.

4. Expand the **System Stored Procedures** to view the list of built-in stored procedures. Right-click **sp_columns**, and then select **Execute**. In the Run Stored Procedure window, enter **Products** as the value for the @table_name parameter, and then click **OK**. Information about all 10 columns is displayed in the Results pane. Close the results pane.

5. In Database Explorer, right-click the **Chapter7.mdf** file, select **Change View**, and then select **Default**.

6. Close the windows.

Some of the built-in stored procedures can be used maliciously if your SQL Server security has been breached. Therefore, it is important to provide strong security for the SQL server, and in some cases, some of the built-in stored procedures may have to be removed or disabled.

## Using and Building SQL Server Scripts

The SQL script file is a text file that contains SQL statements. If you create this file manually, you must be careful to use the correct SQL syntax or the file may not execute properly. SQL scripts are often used to create databases and objects such as tables and stored procedures. You can create these files in a basic text editor, such as Notepad, or within Visual Studio .NET. With the full version of SQL Server, you will have access to a command line utility called sqlcmd and the SQL Server Management Studio, which contains more robust tools for creating and managing SQL Server scripts. (*Note:* A list of tools is located at *http://msdn2. microsoft.com/en-us/library/8czxd086(VS.80).aspx.*) Note, however, that you will not be able to create the SQL Server scripts with the express editions of SQL Server or Visual Studio .NET. You also cannot use the command line prompt with the express edition because the express version of SQL Server 2005 does not permit remote connections. An example of a SQL Server script is shown in Figure 7-17.

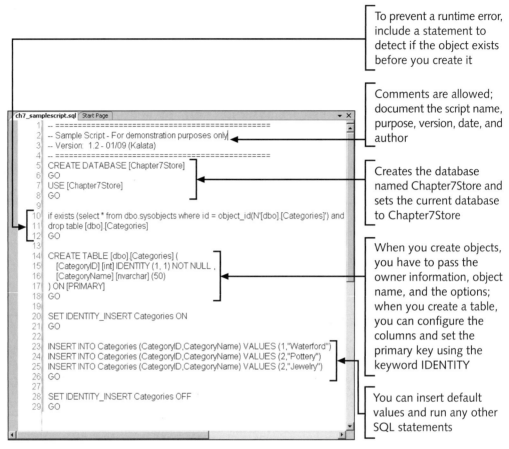

**Figure 7-17**    A sample SQL Server script

## DATABASE CONNECTIONS

So far, you have been working with Visual Studio .NET to create and manage your database. Now it is time to create a connection to the database. In the following sections, you will identify parts of a connection string, store a connection string in the web configuration file, create a connection to the database from a web page, identify how to create connections to other databases, and describe how to move data from Access to SQL Server.

## Understanding the Connection String

To create the connection to the database, your Web application will need to know how to locate your database. The **connection string** is a piece of text that contains the location of your database and any additional information required to access the database. The connection string format is different for each database because each database has different connection string requirements. When you use Visual Studio .NET to create a connection to a database, you will fill out the connection information using a dialog box, and the software will create the connection string for you.

The following code is a sample of a connection string to a SQL Server database. This string must be placed on one line in your Web application. The Data Source is the name of the SQL Server instance. The AttachDbFilename identifies the location of the database. Because the database uses Windows authentication, the Integrated Security property is set to true and no user identification or password information needs to be provided. The name of the SQL Server provider, which is the software used to connect the Web application to the database server, is SQLOLEDB.1. Every database application requires a different provider. You do not include the name of the SQL Server provider because it is selected by default.

```
Data Source=.\SQLEXPRESS;
AttachDbFilename="C:\[Your student
folder]\Chapter7\App_Data\Chapter7.mdf";
Integrated Security=True;
```

**7**

## Storing Connection Strings in the Web Configuration File

It's useful to store the connection strings in a central location because they can be used across web pages and components. You can include many connection strings within the Web. config file. By default, Visual Studio .NET creates a configuration file named Web.config. The Web.config file, which is stored at the root level of the web site, is a global configuration file. There are two methods to store connection strings in the configuration file. First, you can create a global application variable that is available to the entire application. The connection string is stored as key and value pairs. The key represents the name of the connection string, which you use later to retrieve a connection string. You can add many pairs of keys and values within the add tag. Second, you can include the connection strings within the connectionStrings element of the web configuration file. (*Note:* You can include connection strings within Web.config files that are stored in subdirectories.) In Figure 7-18, the connection string to the Chapter7.mdf database is stored in the web configuration file as a global variable and as a connection string element.

To access the connection strings, you can assign the values to a variable or access them directly. The sample code in Figure 7-19 assigns the connection string to a property of a Web control.

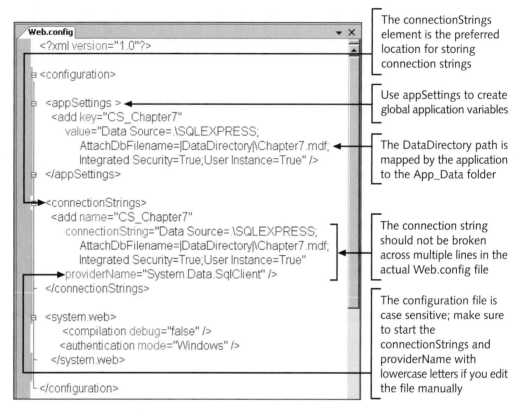

**Figure 7-18**   Storing the connection string in the web configuration file

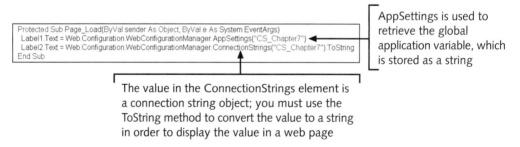

**Figure 7-19**   Retrieving the connection string from the web configuration file

You can also assign the value of the connection string directly to a data source control. A data source control is used by your Web application to connect to the database. In Figure 7-20, the SQL data source control has a ConnectionString property that is assigned to the value of the connection string stored in the web configuration file.

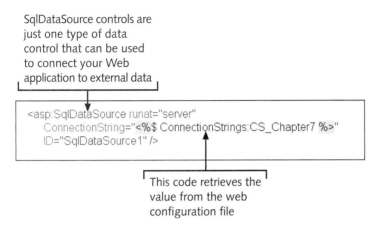

SqlDataSource controls are just one type of data control that can be used to connect your Web application to external data

```
<asp:SqlDataSource runat="server"
    ConnectionString="<%$ ConnectionStrings:CS_Chapter7 %>"
    ID="SqlDataSource1" />
```

This code retrieves the value from the web configuration file

**Figure 7-20**   Assigning the connection string to a data source control

**TIP**   You may include a tilde (~) character to indicate the path of the database file based on the root directory of the Web application. For example, ~/database/file.mdb represents that the database is located in the database folder underneath the root web folder. The tilde character is used to represent the built-in server.mappath function, which is used to map the physical root folder of the Web application. You can locate the complete physical path to the current file using server.mappath(Request.ServerVariables("PATH_INFO")).

## Creating a Connection to a Database from a Web Page

In the following exercise, you will create a connection to the database from a web page, and you will modify the configuration file to create a new global connection string named CS_Chapter7. The CS_Chapter7 connection string contains the connection string to your database.

1. In the Solution Explorer window, right-click the **ch7_SQL.aspx** page, and then click **Open**. If you are not in the Design view, click the Design tab.

2. In the Toolbox, expand the Data section, and then click and drag the **SqlDataSource** to the web page.

3. In the SqlDataSource Tasks smart tag, click the **Configure Data Source** link.

4. In the Configure Data Source dialog box, select **Chapter7.mdf** from the drop-down list. Click the **plus sign** next to the connection string to view the connection string as shown in Figure 7-21. Click the **Next** button.

5. In the text box, change ConnectionString to **CS_Chapter7** as shown in Figure 7-22, and then click **Next**. This will store the connection string in the web configuration file for you.

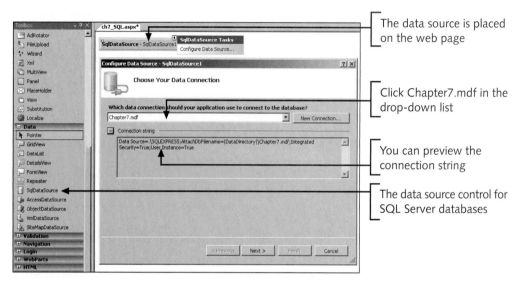

The data source is placed on the web page

Click Chapter7.mdf in the drop-down list

You can preview the connection string

The data source control for SQL Server databases

**Figure 7-21** Inserting an SqlDataSource control in the web page

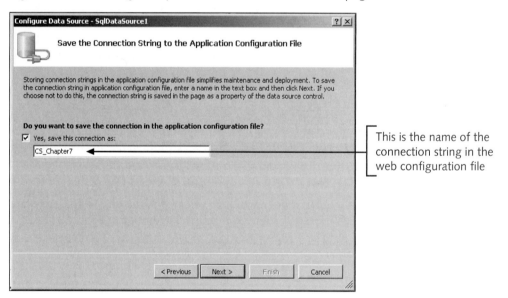

This is the name of the connection string in the web configuration file

**Figure 7-22** Saving the connection string in the web configuration file

6. In the drop-down list, select the **Products** table. Click the **asterisk (\*)** check box to include all of the fields in the query as shown in Figure 7-23. Notice that each time you make a change, the SQL statement is displayed. Click the **WHERE** button.

7. In the Column drop-down list, select **CategoryID**. In the Source drop-down list, select **None**. In the Parameter properties Value text box, type **1** as shown

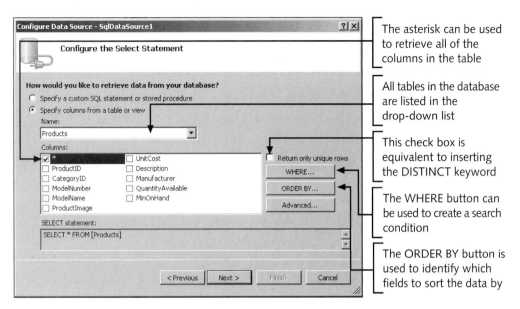

The asterisk can be used to retrieve all of the columns in the table

All tables in the database are listed in the drop-down list

This check box is equivalent to inserting the DISTINCT keyword

The WHERE button can be used to create a search condition

The ORDER BY button is used to identify which fields to sort the data by

7

**Figure 7-23**   Configuring the SQL statement

in Figure 7-24, and then click the **Add** button. The WHERE clause has been generated for you and is displayed. Click **OK**. The new SQL statement is displayed.

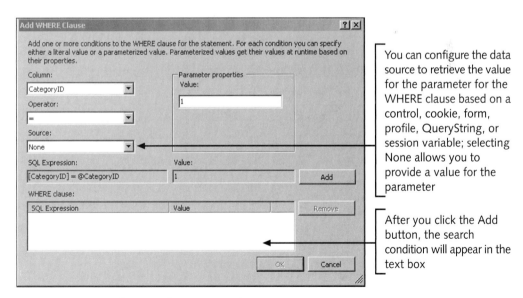

You can configure the data source to retrieve the value for the parameter for the WHERE clause based on a control, cookie, form, profile, QueryString, or session variable; selecting None allows you to provide a value for the parameter

After you click the Add button, the search condition will appear in the text box

**Figure 7-24**   Configuring the WHERE clause

8. Click the **ORDER BY** button in the Configure Data Source window. In the Sort by drop-down list, select **ModelName** as shown in Figure 7-25, and then click **OK**. The new SQL statement is displayed.

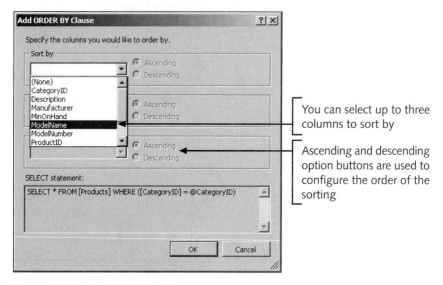

**Figure 7-25**   Sorting the columns

9. Click the **Advanced** button in the Configure Data Source window. Check the check box labeled **Generate INSERT, UPDATE, and DELETE statements** as shown in Figure 7-26. Click **OK**, and then click **Next**.

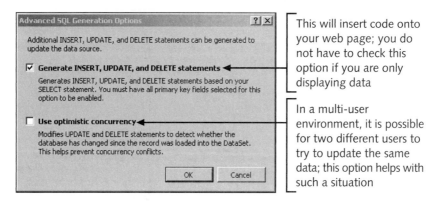

**Figure 7-26**   Generating the SQL statements

10. Click the **Test Query** button, and then click **OK**. Three records are returned as shown in Figure 7-27. Click **Finish**.

11. Click the **Save All** button.

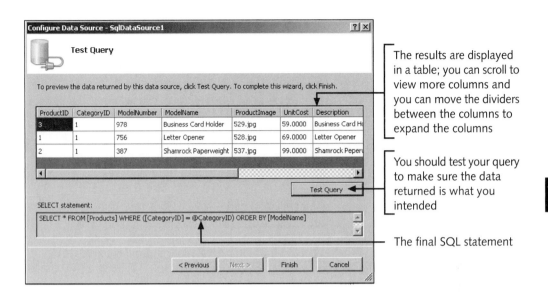

The results are displayed in a table; you can scroll to view more columns and you can move the dividers between the columns to expand the columns

You should test your query to make sure the data returned is what you intended

The final SQL statement

**Figure 7-27**    Previewing the results of the query

12. Click the **Source** tab at the bottom of the window to view the code. The SqlDataSource control contains the ConnectionStrings property that is set to the value of the CS_Chapter7 connection string in the web configuration file.

13. Double-click the **Web.config** file in the Solution Explorer window. The connection string has been added to the file and can now be reused across the entire web site. Notice that the ProviderName property was assigned the value System.Data.SqlClient. This is the data class that contains the SQL Server provider.

14. Close all the windows.

## Creating a Connection to a Microsoft Access Database

Visual Studio .NET uses a data source control to make the connection. The five Data controls that are used to create the data connections are shown in Figure 7-28. The SqlDataSource control is used to connect to SQL Server databases. The other Data controls are used to connect to other types of data sources.

You can create a connection and a connection string to other databases the same way that you created the connection to the Chapter7 SQL Server database. This activity allows you to connect to a Microsoft Access database using the AccessDataSource control. (*Note:* This database was created with Microsoft Access 2003 that cannot open Microsoft Access 2007 files.)

1. In the Solution Explorer window, right-click the **ch7_Access.aspx** page, and then click **Open**. If you are not in the Design view, click the Design tab.

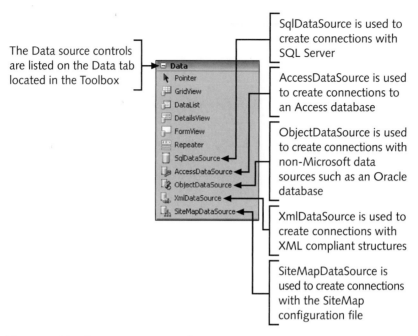

The Data source controls are listed on the Data tab located in the Toolbox

SqlDataSource is used to create connections with SQL Server

AccessDataSource is used to create connections to an Access database

ObjectDataSource is used to create connections with non-Microsoft data sources such as an Oracle database

XmlDataSource is used to create connections with XML compliant structures

SiteMapDataSource is used to create connections with the SiteMap configuration file

**Figure 7-28**   Data source controls

2. In the Toolbox, expand the Data section, and then click and drag the **AccessDataSource** to the web page.

3. In the AccessDataSource Tasks smart tag, click the **Configure Data Source** link.

4. Click the **Browse** button to locate the Residential.mdb database. Click the **App_Data** folder as shown in Figure 7-29, and then click on **Residential.mdb**. Notice that the drop-down list identified the file as a Microsoft Access Database. Click **OK**. The path to the file is inserted as ~/App_Data/Residential.mdb. Click **Next**.

5. The ads table is already selected. Click the **asterisk (*)** to include all the fields in the query. Click **Next**, and then click **Finish**.

6. Click the **Save All** button. You were not asked to save the connection string to the web configuration file.

7. Click the **Source** tab to view the connection string displayed within the HTML source view as shown in Figure 7-30.

8. Close all the windows.

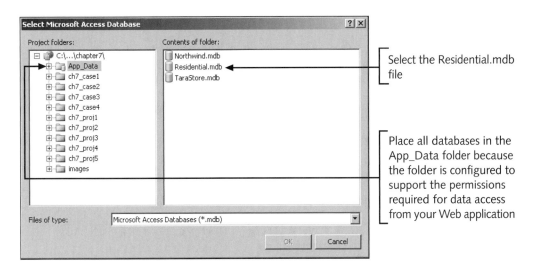

Select the Residential.mdb file

Place all databases in the App_Data folder because the folder is configured to support the permissions required for data access from your Web application

7

**Figure 7-29**  Browsing for databases in the App_Data folder

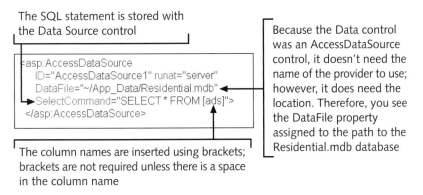

The SQL statement is stored with the Data Source control

Because the Data control was an AccessDataSource control, it doesn't need the name of the provider to use; however, it does need the location. Therefore, you see the DataFile property assigned to the path to the Residential.mdb database

The column names are inserted using brackets; brackets are not required unless there is a space in the column name

**Figure 7-30**  Configuring the connection string for the Access Data Source control

## Creating a Connection to XML Data

In Chapter 3, you learned how to use the XML control to display XML data. Note, however, that the XML control displays only the XML data with the XSL Stylesheet applied. Fortunately, you can also use the XmlDataSource control to manage the connection to the XML and XSL files. This would allow you to bind the XML data to different Data controls. The following activity allows you to connect to an XML file using the XmlDataSource control.

1. In the Solution Explorer window, right-click the **ch7_XML.aspx** page, and then click **Open**. If you are not in the Design view, click the **Design** tab.

2. In the Toolbox, expand the Data section, and then click and drag the **XmlDataSource** to the web page.

3. In the XmlDataSource Tasks smart tag, click the **Configure Data Source** link.

4. In the Data file text box, type **~/ch7_XML.xml**, and in the Transform file text box, type **~/ch7_XML.xsl** as shown in Figure 7-31. Click **OK**.

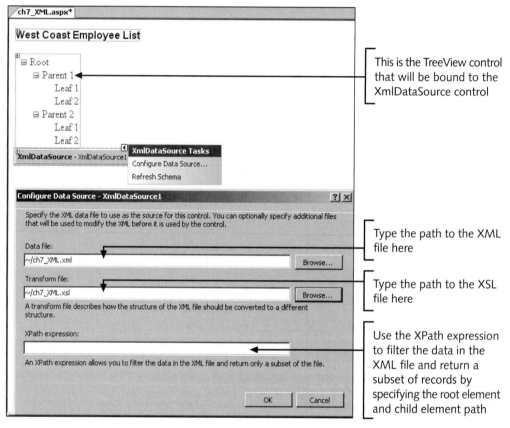

**Figure 7-31**    Configuring the XmlDataSource control

5. Click the **Save All** button.

6. In the Solution Explorer window, right-click the **ch7_XML.aspx** page, and then click **View in Browser**. The page should appear as shown in Figure 7-32.

7. Close all the windows.

## Moving Data to SQL Server

You can convert and move your data application to the SQL Server in many ways. For instance, if the data is in Microsoft Excel, you can import the data into Microsoft Access and then use the Upsizing Wizard to convert the database to a SQL Server database. Note that you also can use the Upsizing Wizard within Microsoft Access to upgrade to SQL Server.

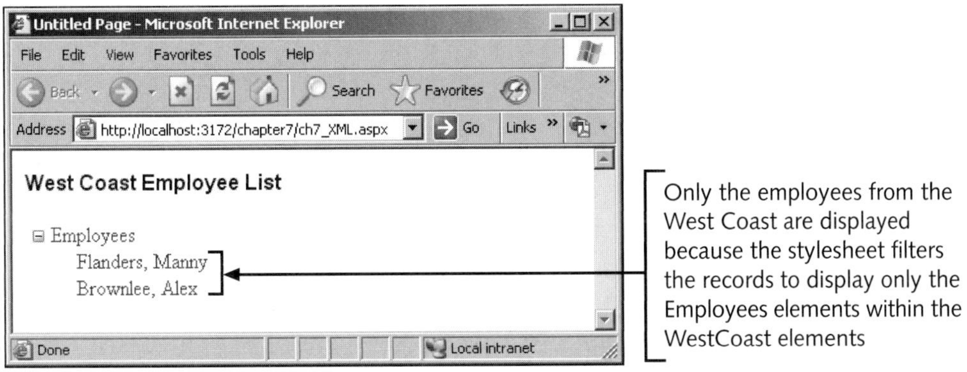

Figure 7-32   Displaying XML data with the XmlDataSource control

**NOTE** The Upsizing Wizard is available in Microsoft Access 2007 and is also available in earlier versions. When you upsize the database, the wizard may only upsize the table structure and data and not include some queries such as crosstab queries, action queries that take parameters or contain nested queries, union queries, or queries that reference values on a form.

After you have upsized the database, Microsoft Access provides a report that contains information about the new database, which you should keep as a reference for what data types were converted. In the following exercise, you will upsize a Microsoft Access database to a SQL Server. Your user account needs **write** permission to the Microsoft Access database in order to upsize the database. When you upsize a database, the new database is placed in the default database directory, which is not in your Web application. The default database directory for SQL Server 2005 Express Edition is C:\Program Files\Microsoft SQL Server\MSSQL.1\MSSQL\Data.

In the following exercise, you can upsize the TaraStore database to Ch7_TaraStoreSQL.

1. Start **Microsoft Access**. (On most computers, you click **Start**, point to **All Programs**, click **Microsoft Office**, and then click **Microsoft Office Access 2007**.)

2. Click the **Office Button** and click **Open**. In the Open dialog box, navigate to [*Your student folder*]\Chapter7\App_Data folder, select the file **TaraStore.mdb**, and then click **Open**.

**NOTE** The layout of Microsoft Office is significantly different from previous versions. Microsoft Office 2007 does not use menus. Therefore, there are no menus with Microsoft Access 2007. You can locate most commands taht used to be in the File menu by clicking on the Microsoft Office button in any Microsoft Office 2007 application. The menus were replaced with contextual tabs and a ribbon. When you click on a tab, the ribbon shows you only the tasks that are available. This layout makes it easier for you to locate a task.

3. Click the **Database Tools** tab, and then click the **SQL Server** button in the Move Data section. Enable content if necessary at the top of the Access window.

4. Verify that the option button labeled Create new database is selected, and then click **Next**.

5. In the drop-down list box, select **.\SQLEXPRESS** for the name of the SQL Server database. Leave the Windows authentication set to **Use Trusted Connection.** (*Note:* You must use a user account with CREATE DATABASE privileges.)

6. In the last text box, delete the text, type **Ch7_TaraStoreSQL** as the name of the new SQL Server database, and then click **Next**.

7. In the Upsizing Wizard dialog box, click the **>>** button to select all the tables in the database to be exported to SQL Server. Click the **Next** button to advance to the next step. The next window allows you to modify how the table attributes are exported. Change the drop-down list for the timestamp option to **No, never**. Click the **Next** button to advance to the next step.

8. The next window allows you to export an Access application. There is no application with this database, so the No application changes option button is already selected for you. (*Note*: If this option has not been selected for you, select the option button labeled No application changes.) Click the **Next** button to advance to the next step.

9. Click the **Finish** button. The Upsizing Wizard upsizes the database, and then produces a report, which contains information about the tables and objects upsized to the SQL Server. (*Note:* You can print or export the report to another application.)

This process will store the database by default with the other SQL Server data files in the default data directory, which is usually located in C:\Program Files\Microsoft SQL Server\MSSQL.1\MSSQL\Data. This does not create a SQL Server file that can be attached and detached to your web project. This method will work if you need to share this data with another SQL Server, however, because it can be copied to the other server.

10. Click the **More** button in the Data section on the ribbon, and then select **HTML Document**. Click **Browse**. Navigate to [*Your student folder*]\Chapter 7 folder, if needed. In the File name text box, type **TSUpsizeReport**. Click **Save**, and then click **OK**. In the HTML Output Options window, click **OK**. Do not save the Export steps. .

11. In Visual Studio .NET, open your Chapter7 folder, right-click the folder, select **Refresh**, right-click the **TSUpsizeReport.html**, and then select **View in Browser**. At the top of the page is the name of the SQL Server database and

the original Access database. You can view the data types that were changed when the data fields were updated to SQL Server.

12. Close the web page and the Upsizing Wizard Report window.

13. Close the database and Microsoft Access.

**TIP**

When you upsize the database, a field named upsize_ts is added to each of the tables with a date and time stamp. You can use this information to determine which data was updated.

7

## Chapter Summary

❏ Relational databases store data related tables. Tables consist of rows and columns. When you create the column, you must identify the data type, the file size, and if the column allows null values. Relationships between tables are defined in the Database Diagram. The primary key column contains a unique value for each row of data and is used to create the relationship in other tables. When values of primary keys are stored in other tables, they are called foreign keys. Normalization is the process used to design databases, which will reduce redundancy, promote data integrity, and improve database performance.

❏ You can use the Visual Database Tools within Visual Studio .NET to create and maintain your databases. The Table Designer allows you to create tables and enter data. If you want to store large amounts of data in a column, you should use the varchar, nvarchar, and varbinary data types. The Query and View Designer allows you to create queries called views. Views are stored in the database and only are used with select statements. Queries must be executed manually but can contain INSERT, UPDATE, and DELETE statements.

❏ The SQL Editor allows you to create stored procedures. Stored procedures are SQL commands that are stored with the SQL Server, and then compiled. Therefore, stored procedures run faster than SQL commands that are stored on a web page. The SQL Query Builder allows you to use the visual tools to build your stored procedures. SQL Server scripts are files that contain SQL statements and are often used to create new databases and back up existing databases.

❏ You can store the connection strings in the root level Web.config application configuration file making them available from any web page in the application using global application variables or the connectionStrings element. The connection string syntax varies with each type of database. The connection string contains the information needed to identify the type of database, the location of the database, the software provider required to communicate with the database, and user permissions required to access the data in the database.

❏ You can convert a Microsoft Access database to SQL Server using the upsizing wizard. ASP.NET allows you to create connections to non-Microsoft data sources such as XML files.

## REVIEW QUESTIONS

1. Which is a required characteristic of a relational database?

    a. It must be created in Microsoft Access.

    b. It must contain at least two rows of data.

    c. It must not contain a column that has no data value.

    d. It must have unique values for the primary key field.

2. If there is no unique value in the ProductID field, and you need to create a relationship between the product and inventory tables, you should _____ _____ .

3. True or False. A composite key is the combination of the primary key and foreign key.

4. What is used to ensure that no duplicates can appear in a column?

    a. foreign key

    b. primary key

    c. connection string

    d. relationship

5. True or False. SQL is an abbreviation for SQL Server 2005 Express Edition.

6. True or False. You can create the SQL Server database in either the Solution Explorer or Data Connection windows.

7. _____ is another name for the table definition.

8. You identify that each row is unique. You should configure the _____ property for the primary key field.

9. Which of the following is not a data type in SQL Server?

    a. int

    b. nvarchar

    c. char

    d. array

10. Which SQL command is used to create a new record in the database?

    a. Update

    b. Insert

    c. AddNew

    d. Add

11. What is/are stored in the column when there is no value?

 a. Null

 b. False

 c. Empty

 d. Nothing

12. If the relationship in the database diagram has a key at each endpoint, then what type of relationship is it?

 a. one-to-two

 b. many-to-one

 c. one-to-one

 d. many-to-many

13. Which object is used to create the connection to an XML data structure?

 a. AccessDataSource

 b. SQLDataSource

 c. XmlDataSource

 d. ObjectDataSource

14. What is the keyword used to identify the name of the server within a connection string?

 a. Database

 b. Data Source

 c. Service

 d. Data Store

15. What is the name of the property that is used to identify the connection string that is passed to the SqlDataSource control?

 a. Connection

 b. ActiveConnection

 c. ConnectionObject

 d. ConnectionString

16. What is the tool used to create a new table in Visual Studio .NET?

 a. Table Designer

 b. Database Designer

 c. SQL Builder

 d. Query and View Editor

7

17. Which pane in the SQL Editor shows the criteria as visual icons?

   a. Table pane

   b. Grid pane

   c. SQL pane

   d. Results pane

18. Where can you store the connection string so that it is available to all pages within your application?

   a. Global.netx

   b. Web.config

   c. Config.web

   d. Default.aspx

19. What symbol is used to identify the parameter in a stored procedure?

   a. @

   b. $

   c. #

   d. *

## HANDS-ON PROJECTS

### Project 7-1

The Northwind database is a database created by Microsoft to help developers learn how to work with database applications. In this project, you will use Visual Studio .NET to learn more about the Northwind database. The Northwind database is located in your App_Data folder. You then will modify a web page named **ch7_proj1.aspx** that will be used to display your answers to the questions in Steps 1 through 4.

1. Look at the database contents within the Database Explorer tool and answer the questions in the following list. Type your answers in the Ch7_Proj1.aspx page in the space provided in the table.

   ❑ What are the names of the tables in the Northwind database?

   ❑ How many records are in the Customers table? (*Hint:* You can count them manually or create a stored procedure that will return to you the number of records.)

   ❑ What is the primary key column for the Customers table?

   ❑ Which data types are used in the Customers table?

   ❑ Which columns are required to have a value?

   ❑ Which field(s) must contain unique values within the column?

2. Look at the **Products by Category** view. Type your answers to the questions in the following list on the Ch7_Proj1.aspx page.

   ❑ What are the two tables that are joined together in the query?

   ❑ What is the relationship between the tables?

   ❑ What field is used to establish a relationship between the tables? How many records are displayed in the view?

3. Look at the **Ten Most Expensive Products** query. Type your answers to the questions in the following list on the Ch7_Proj1.aspx page.

   ❑ What is the name of the table being used?

   ❑ What part of the SQL statement is used to select only the top ten most expensive products?

   ❑ What are the keywords used to sort the data?

4. Look at the **Alphabetical List of Products** query. Type your answers to the questions in the following list on the Ch7_Proj1.aspx page.

   ❑ What are the names of the tables being used in the query?

   ❑ What keywords are used to describe the relationship between the two tables?

   ❑ How would you change this into a view in SQL Server?

   ❑ How would you change this into a stored procedure named DiscontinuedProducts in SQL Server where the Discontinued value is passed as a parameter named Discontinued?

   ❑ What symbol is used to identify the parameter?

   ❑ What is the data type of the parameter? Is the parameter an input or output parameter?

   ❑ After you create the procedure, why does the stored procedure say ALTER PROCEDURE instead of CREATE PROCEDURE?

5. Save the Ch7_Proj1.aspx page. Print the web page.

# Project 7-2

In this project, you will create a customer database using Visual Studio .NET.

1. In Visual Studio .NET, create a SQL Server database named **Ch7_Proj2** in your App_Data folder.

2. Use the information in Figure 7-33 to create the columns and configure the column names, data types, lengths, and properties.

3. In the properties at the bottom half of the window, change the Is Identity for the CustomerID column from No to **Yes** using the drop-down list arrow. The Identity

| Column Name | Data Type | Allow Nulls |
|---|---|---|
| CustomerID | int | ☐ |
| CustomerName | nvarchar(50) | ☑ |
| EmailAddress | nvarchar(50) | ☑ |
| Password | nvarchar(50) | ☑ |
| ▶ MembershipLevel | int | ☑ |
| | | ☐ |

**Figure 7-33** Create the Customers table in the Ch7_Proj2 database

Seed should be set to 1, and the Identity Increment should be set to 1. This creates a new value for each new record entered in the database.

4. Right-click the **CustomerID** column name and select **Set Primary Key**. A yellow key appears at the side of the column name to indicate that this column is the primary key column.

5. Click the **Save All** button and save the table as **Customers**.

6. Enter the data listed in Figure 7-34. Let the database assign the values for the CustomerID column.

**Customers: Qu...H7_PROJ2.MDF)**

| CustomerID | CustomerName | EmailAddress | Password | MembershipLevel |
|---|---|---|---|---|
| 1 | Joyce Roloff | JR@parkrealestate.com | Cranberry | 1 |
| 2 | Johnny Brown | JBrown@parkrealestate.com | Stuffing | 2 |
| 3 | Brad Granger | BGranger@parkrealestate.com | Loyola | 3 |
| 4 | Cathy Lase | CLase@parkrealestate.com | Forest | 2 |
| 5 | Kylie Whistler | KWhistler@parkrealestate.com | Crypto | 3 |
| 6 | Boris Chapman | BChapman@parkrealestate.com | Plastic | 2 |
| 7 | Freida Burkart | FBurkart@parkrealestate.com | Trust | 3 |
| 8 | Cynthia Walters | CWalters@parkrealestate.com | Playground | 2 |
| 9 | Fred Munson | FMunson@parkrealestate.com | Worry | 1 |
| ▶ 10 | Mia Chen | MChen@parkrealestate.com | Boardroom | 2 |
| * NULL | NULL | NULL | NULL | NULL |

10 of 10

**Figure 7-34** Inserting data in the Customers table

7. Print the table and the schema. (*Note:* You can print the screen by pressing the **PrntScrn** key. You can also copy the screen shot by pressing the **Shift** key and the **PrntScrn** key at the same time. Then, you can paste this into a word processing document.)

8. In the ch7_proj2 folder, open the **ch7_proj2.aspx** page. Drag the appropriate SQL Server Data Source control onto your web page and configure the connection. Save the connection string as **CS_Ch7_Proj2**. Select all of the records and all the columns for customers who have a **MembershipLevel** of **2** and order the results based on the **CustomerName** column in ascending order. Print the markup view of the ch7_proj2.aspx page.

9. Open and print the web configuration file. Close all files when you are finished.

## Project 7-3

In this project, you will create a stored procedure in the TaraStore database using Visual Studio .NET.

1.  Create a new stored procedure named **sp_Ch7_Proj3** in the Chapter7.mdf database.

2.  Create the Ch7_Proj3 stored procedure as shown in Figure 7-35. Only display records from the Jewelry category and sort the records by the ModelName in descending order.

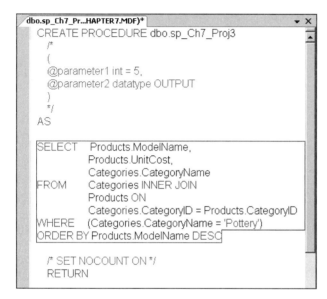

```
dbo.sp_Ch7_Pr...HAPTER7.MDF)*                          ▼ ×
   CREATE PROCEDURE dbo.sp_Ch7_Proj3
    /*
    (
    @parameter1 int = 5,
    @parameter2 datatype OUTPUT
    )
    */
   AS

   SELECT    Products.ModelName,
             Products.UnitCost,
             Categories.CategoryName
   FROM      Categories INNER JOIN
             Products ON
             Categories.CategoryID = Products.CategoryID
   WHERE     (Categories.CategoryName = 'Pottery')
   ORDER BY Products.ModelName DESC

    /* SET NOCOUNT ON */
   RETURN
```

**Figure 7-35**   Create the Ch7_Proj3 stored procedure

3.  Run the stored procedure. Print the results displayed in the Results window. Save the results as **Ch7_Proj3.txt** in the Ch7_Proj3 directory.

## Project 7-4

In this project, you will create three stored procedures that allow you to insert and delete records in the Products table in the Chapter7.mdf database using Visual Studio .NET.

1.  Create a stored procedure named **sp_Ch7_Proj4_Insert1** in the Chapter7 database. Use the code in Figure 7-36 to insert a static value. Save and execute the stored procedure.

2.  Create a stored procedure named **sp_Ch7_Proj4_Insert2** in the Chapter7 database. The input parameter is named CatName and is of data type nvarchar(50) and the output parameter is CategoryID and is an int data type. The stored procedure should insert the new record given the CatName input parameter, and then create the value for the CategoryName. The CategoryID should be created automatically. Return the CategoryID value in the CategoryID parameter.

```
dbo.StoredPro...HAPTER7.MDF)*                    ▼ ✕
   CREATE PROCEDURE dbo.sp_Ch7_Proj4_Insert1       ▲
      /*
      (
      @parameter1 int = 5,
      @parameter2 datatype OUTPUT
      }
      */
   AS
   INSERT INTO Products (CategoryID, ModelNumber,
      ModelName, ProductImage, UnitCost, Description,
      Manufacturer, QuantityAvailable, MinOnHand)
   VALUES ('1',132,'Chair',NULL,231.99, 'Rocking Chair',
   'Chester Manufacturing', 10, 3)

   /* SET NOCOUNT ON */
      RETURN
```

**Figure 7-36**   Create the Ch7_Proj4 stored procedure

3. **Save** and **execute** the stored procedure using **Furniture** as the CategoryName. Re-run the procedure creating the categories: **Food**, **Gifts**, **Sports**, and **Holiday**. Make sure to choose **Null** for the value for the CategoryID or you will get an error message.

4. Create a stored procedure named **sp_Ch7_Proj4_Insert3** in the Chapter7 database. Use the following code to delete a static value. Save and execute the stored procedure.

   ```
   DELETE FROM Categories
   WHERE CategoryName = 'Holiday'
   ```

---

## CASE PROJECTS

### Project 7-1

Your boss has asked you to create a database application for an online grocery store. Your first step is to set up a sample database. Create a database named Ch7_Case1 using your local SQL Server. Design a relational database that is normalized. Create at least four tables with at least four columns in each table. Each table must have a primary key. Create the database diagram using the Database Diagram Designer. Establish a relationship between the tables using the primary and foreign keys. Each table must be related to at least one other table. Save the database diagram as Ch7_Case1. Enter sample data for at least three records into each of the tables. Print the database diagram, the table schema, and the data for each table.

## Project 7-2

Your boss has heard that it's more efficient to use a stored procedure than an SQL query. He would like you to create and run several queries using stored procedures. Using the Northwind SQL Server database, create a new stored procedure named sp_Ch7_Case2_SP1. Retrieve the records for all customers in the USA. Sort the results based on the Region and CompanyName columns. Run the stored procedure and print out the results. Create a stored procedure named sp_Ch7_Case2_SP2 to enter a new product. Create a stored procedure named sp_Ch7_Case2_SP3 to enter a new employee. There is already a view for Category Sales for 1997. Create a stored procedure named sp_Ch7_Case2_SP4, which allows you to input the year and retrieve the same information as the view. Create a stored procedure named sp_Ch7_Case2_SP5 to change the shipped date from null to a date provided as a parameter. Save and print each stored procedure. Execute the stored procedures and print the results. Save the results to your ch7_case2 folder.

## Project 7-3

Your company sometimes uses eBay to purchase certain office equipment. You are developing a database named Ch7_Case3 that can be used to track your eBay purchases and sales. There should be one products table that lists all of the products bought and sold, a category table that lists the types of categories for the products, a users table that identifies authorized users within your company, and a department list table that lists the departments in the company. You should make sure to document with each purchase or sale, the name of the product, the cost, the name of the person making the transaction, the department name requesting the transaction, and the date of the transaction. You may add other columns as necessary. Create a data diagram using the Database Designer. Name the data diagram Ch7_Case3 Diagram. You should create relationships between each of the tables. Make sure to insert at least five rows of data for each table. Print the database diagrams and the schemas and data for each of the tables. Create a stored procedure named ch7_case3_purchase to display all of your purchases within the last three months. Create a stored procedure named ch7_case3_sell to display all of your sales within the last six months. Create a stored procedure named ch7_case3_department to display all of sales and purchases within the past six months for a given department. You will need to use input parameters to configure which department data to display. Create a stored procedure named ch7_case3_user to display all of the transactions for a specific user sorted by date. You will need to use input parameters to configure which user data to display. Save and print each stored procedure. Execute the stored procedures and print the results. Save the results to your ch7_case3 folder.

## Project 7-4

Your company is creating a Web application for a medical office. You are responsible to create a web database application to store the billing information. You are going to need to create the database, tables, and stored procedures to manage the application. Create the SQL Server database named Ch7_Case4 in your App_Data folder. Create a table to store the patient data and another table to store information about their office visit such as the date,

7

the purpose of the visit, which doctor they visited, and which diagnosis was made. In another table you will create a list of diseases and illnesses that the doctors commonly treat and the hourly charge for the visit for that diagnosis. For example, a patient with the diagnosis of pneumonia may be charged $50, but a patient with diabetes may be charged only $35. (*Note:* You may use the Internet to locate information about various illnesses and medical diagnoses.) You may add other columns and tables as necessary. Create a data diagram using the Database Designer. Name the data diagram Ch7_Case4_Diagram. You should create relationships between each of the tables. Print the database diagrams, the schemas, and the data for each of the tables. Create a stored procedure named ch7_case4_patients to display all of the patient visits for the past month, sorted by the patient name. Create a stored procedure named ch7_case4_diagnosis to display a distinct list of diagnosis and illnesses that were treated over the past month. Create a stored procedure named ch7_case4_charges to display all of the bills within the past six months for a given patient. You will need to use input parameters to configure which patient data to display. Create a stored procedure named ch7_case4_newpatient to insert a new patient record. Create a stored procedure named ch7_case4_deletepatient to delete a patient record for a specific patient. Create a stored procedure named ch7_case4_doctors, which lists the doctors that saw patients this month. Save and print each stored procedure. Execute the stored procedures and print the results. Save the results to your ch7_case4 folder.

CHAPTER

# 8

# BINDING DATA TO WEB CONTROLS

**In this chapter, you will:**

♦ Design a Web data application in the .NET framework

♦ Discuss data access components

♦ Describe methods used to bind data to Web controls

♦ Bind data to Web controls and Data controls manually

♦ Use automatic binding to bind data to Data controls

♦ Identify errors and methods for correction

♦ Learn about the ADO.NET model

♦ Retrieve data in the .NET framework

One of the challenges that web developers face is the variety of data sources and ways in which data can be displayed in Web applications. For example, a data source can be a simple hash table, an array, an XML file, or a database. In previous chapters, you learned to bind data sources such as an XML file or SiteMap file to a Web control to display a menu. XML files and sitemaps are just a few of the types of data sources that can be bound to Data controls. Data can be displayed using different types of output, such as a simple list, a drop-down list, or a table. A web developer must be able to use various techniques to build data-driven Web applications. Using ASP.NET, you can separate the data source from the presentation of the data. In the previous chapter, you learned how to connect to and manage a database.

In this chapter, you will learn how to work with various controls to display data in your Web applications. You will learn how to bind different types of data to many different types of ASP.NET controls. You also will learn basic data binding techniques, and then will change the data source to a database. You will use the .NET DataAdapter, DataSet, and DataView objects to retrieve data from a database. By the end of this chapter, you will have learned a variety of data binding techniques.

# Designing a Web Data Application in the .NET Framework

In the past, database management systems were proprietary; that is, stored data could be accessed only via the program that was used to create the database. Programs could not share data unless you built an interface to the database application. Today, business needs demand flexible database management systems. This flexibility has been achieved by means of the **data access model**, which provides a method whereby data can be shared across different applications and platforms.

As shown in Figure 8-1, there are several tiers represented in a distributed application. These tiers are logical. The actual components that make up the tiers may be located on different physical computers. In Chapter 7, you learned to create a SQL Server database using Visual Studio .NET. Data can be stored in many forms, not just as databases. **Data source** is a term that represents the data. The application data source can be a simple data structure, XML data, a file database such as Microsoft Access, or stored in a data server such as SQL Server or Oracle. Databases such as Microsoft Access and SQL Server are examples of relational data sources, where the data structure is in tables made up of rows and columns. Data can be in the form of a single item, such as the name of an image, or it can be in the form of multiple items, such as a list or an array containing the names of many images.

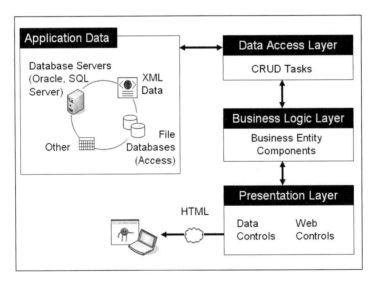

**Figure 8-1**   Common tiers of a distributed application

The **data access layer**, also called the data tier or middle tier, interfaces with the data source. The data access layer contains the ability to manage the data source using one of the CRUD methods. CRUD represents an acronym for the four methods performed on the database. The four CRUD methods are creating a new record, reading records, updating records, or deleting records. When you are designing your Web application in the .NET framework, you will use programming code and tools to create the interface from the data access layer to the data source.

The **business logic layer** provides the interface between the Web application and the data access layer. Although the Web application can interact with the data access layer directly, the additional layer of abstraction provides for better maintenance, performance, and scalability. The business logic layer configuration may vary. Many enterprise Web applications develop complex systems that define business entities and the business components that interact with the data source. In these cases, the business components interact with the data access layer, which maintains the interface to the data source. Often this layer consists of a business entity component with or without the CRUD methods. Often, the data you are retrieving is not just a discrete set of numbers, but data that represents a business entity, such as a customer address or an order. **Business entity components** are objects that can call the underlying data access layer. These can be simple classes stored within the App_Code folder, XML data, or datasets. Business entities are defined within the business entity components and are used to represent logical groups of data within the application. For example, the customer table may represent the customer business entity. The business entity component would manage the interface to the tables that make up the customer business entity. The customer business entity is modeled by the customer table data. One way to create the models for business entities is in your application Unified Modeling Language (UML). UML allows you to build a visual model of your data structures, business processes, application architecture, and user interactions.

If you choose XML data to represent the business entity, the XML data can be a static file, or an XML string that conforms to the XML Document Object Model. An XML file is a type of **hierarchical data source**, where all of the data is nested within a single node structure. Once the file is bound, the attributes of the XML elements are treated like data-bindable fields and then can be bound to Web controls and Data controls. You need to set the **XPath** to identify the first level of the XML file hierarchy that you want to expose. Then, you can use the XPath attribute in an expression in the template of the Data control. XML data can be converted to a DataSet using built-in methods.

You may also choose to represent the business entity with a dataset. The **DataSet object** is a cached set of records retrieved from a database or XML data file. DataSet works like a virtual data store because it is disconnected from the original database source. The DataSet consists of one or more tables in memory, is stored in the memory of the web server, and can be strongly or loosely typed. A **loosely typed dataset** derives the schema or data definitions for the data from the columns returned from a query. A **strongly typed dataset** inherits from the DataSet class methods, events, and properties that can be used to access the tables, columns, rows, and data. The data for the strongly typed dataset is typed based on a defined database schema. When you refer to a column in a loosely typed dataset, you will need to reference the column name using a string or index number. When you reference a strongly typed dataset, you can reference the column name by the column properties directly.

The **presentation layer** of your application, which is also known as the presentation tier, often consists of Web Forms containing Web controls and Data controls that will interact with the data access layer. These controls will generate the output as XHTML to the web page.

Separating the layers allows you to upload one layer with no impact on the other layers. For example, when you can create Data controls on the web page, they are bound to the data source defined within the data component. If the web site owner decides to change the appearance of the web page, the web developer can make the change on the web page, without affecting the data layer.

Sometimes you may need to modify more than one layer. You can create stored procedures in the business logic layer to collect data from the database. When a database administrator decides to change a field name, the database administrator can also make the change in the stored procedure. The data access layer is separate from the business logic and presentation layers. Although you may need to change the code within the business logic layer, no changes need to be made to the presentation layer in the Web application.

**TIP**    Microsoft provides several enterprise applications to assist developers in learning to work with distributed Web-based applications. You can read more about how to download the Duwamish 7.0 and Fitch and Mather 7.0 enterprise samples at *http://msdn2.microsoft.com/en-us/library/aa301548(VS.71).aspx.*

## Data Access Components

Built-in data access layer components that can retrieve and store multiple data records at a single time include the DataSet and DataReader.

- The **DataSet object** can contain one or more DataTable objects. The **DataTable object** contains one or more rows of data with one or more columns. Because there can be multiple tables included in a single DataSet, you must identify the table members with the DataMember property of the DataSet. The **DataMember property** is the control that binds to one or more tables within a DataSet object. A **DataView object** contains a subset of rows of data from a DataTable object. You can use a DataView to retrieve a subset of data temporarily without returning to the data source.

- A **DataReader object** is a read-only, forward-only stream of data from the database. A DataReader object is similar to the DataView object because it returns one or more rows of data. The DataReader object, however, is not a disconnected source of data. The data connection remains open while the DataReader object reads the data, row by row. The DataReader object provides better performance than the DataView or DataSet objects. If you use the DataReader object, you can read the rows only once. You might choose to use the DataReader when you want to retrieve data that does not change with the client. As a result, you cannot create multiple controls with the data returned from the DataReader object. In other words, after you iterate through the list of rows displaying the data, to retrieve the first row again would require you to re-read the data in the database.

You can create the DataReader and DataSet objects programmatically or allow the DataSource objects to create and manage these objects. By default, the AccessDataSource and SqlData-Source objects return a DataSet. The DataSet is required when you want to sort and page features of the GridView control. You can configure the object to use a DataReader by modifying the DataSourceMode property. The **DataSourceMode property** is used to identify how the AccessDataSource and SqlDataSource objects retrieve the data from the database. The possible values for the DataSourceMode property are DataReader and DataSet.

## Creating DataSets and DataAdapters

The DataSet is usually not connected to the database directly. Rather, a DataAdapter object is used to manage the connection and queries. In the following exercise, you will create a typed DataSet using the DataAdapter Configuration Wizard.

1. Start your web development editor.

2. Click **File** on the menu bar, and then click **Open Web Site**. This opens the Open Web Site window. Locate the **chapter8** folder from your student folder and click **Open**.

3. In the Solution Explorer window, right-click the **App_Code** folder and select **Add New Item**. Click **DataSet** in the Add New Item dialog box. In the Name text box, replace DataSet1.xsd with **Ch8_ProductListSubcat47.xsd** and then click the **Add** button. The TableAdapter Configuration Wizard opens.

4. Click the **New Connection** button. If necessary, select **Microsoft Access Database File** in the Choose Data Source window, and then click **Continue**. In the Add Connection window, click the **Browse** button. Navigate to the **App_Data** folder in your Chapter8 web site, select the **TaraStore.mdb** file, and then click the **Open** button.

5. Click the **OK** button. Click the **plus sign** next to the Connection string label. The connection string that is stored in the web configuration file appears as shown in Figure 8-2. Click the **Next** button.

6. The wizard will store the connection string in the web configuration file as TaraStoreConnectionString. Notice that the wizard will not allow you to create or edit a stored procedure, because Access does not support stored procedures. Use SQL statements is selected by default. Click the **Next** button.

7. Click the **Query Builder** button. In the Add Table window, click **Products**, click the **Add** button, and then click the **Close** button. If necessary, enlarge the Query Builder window.

8. In the diagram pane, click the check boxes for **ModelName** and **SubCategoryID**. In the filter for the SubCategoryID, enter **=47**. Click the **Execute Query** button. The results are shown in Figure 8-3. Thirteen records are returned. Click the **OK** button.

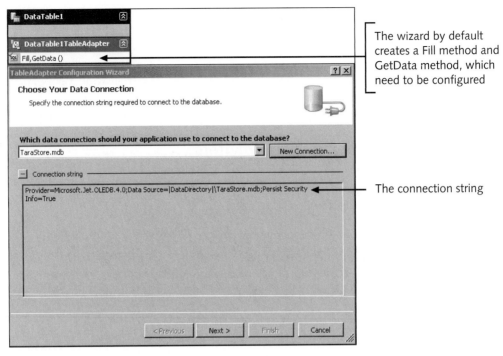

The wizard by default creates a Fill method and GetData method, which need to be configured

The connection string

**Figure 8-2**    Using the TableAdapter Configuration Wizard to create a DataSet

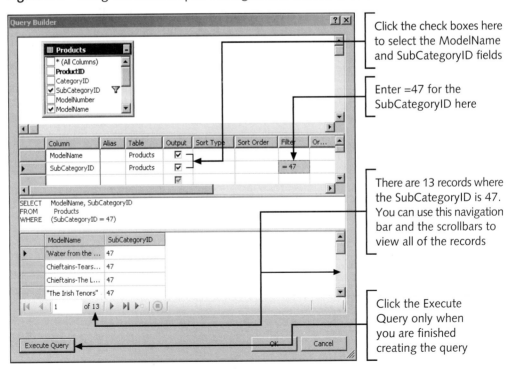

Click the check boxes here to select the ModelName and SubCategoryID fields

Enter =47 for the SubCategoryID here

There are 13 records where the SubCategoryID is 47. You can use this navigation bar and the scrollbars to view all of the records

Click the Execute Query only when you are finished creating the query

**Figure 8-3**    Creating the select query

9. Click the **Advanced Options** button. The options available are used to create the CRUD methods and to create methods to avoid concurrency issues as shown in Figure 8-4. Click the **Cancel** button.

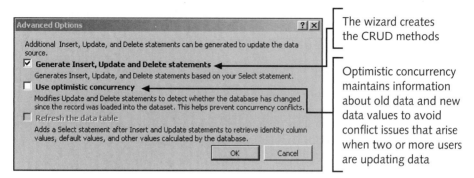

**Figure 8-4**   Creating the CRUD methods

10. Click the **Next** button. You can configure the Fill and GetData methods as shown in Figure 8-5. Click the **Next** button.

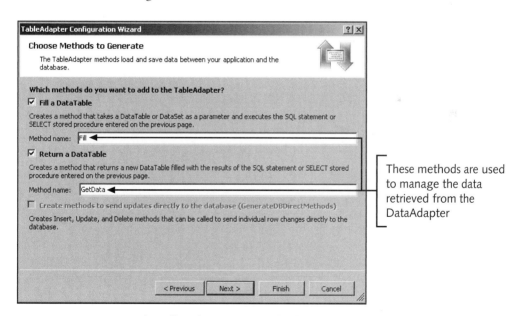

**Figure 8-5**   Creating the Fill and GetData methods

11. The message as shown in Figure 8-6 is used to inform you that the rows of data in the DataSet table cannot be identified because no primary key from the database was selected. This prevents you from accurately updating the database.

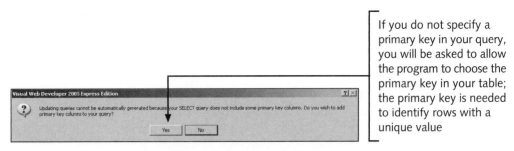

If you do not specify a primary key in your query, you will be asked to allow the program to choose the primary key in your table; the primary key is needed to identify rows with a unique value

**Figure 8-6**  Adding a primary key to the DataSet table

12. Click the **Yes** button. A message appears displaying the methods created as shown in Figure 8-7. Click the **Finish** button.

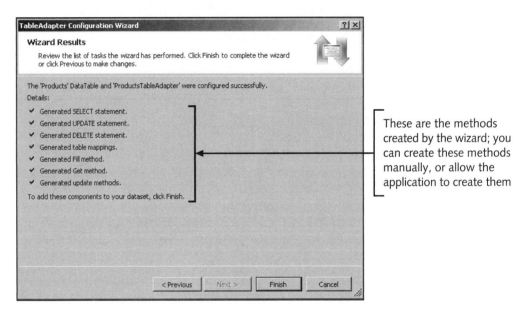

These are the methods created by the wizard; you can create these methods manually, or allow the application to create them

**Figure 8-7**  Creating the DataAdapter methods

13. In the Solution Explorer window, right-click the **Ch8_ProductListSubcat47 .xsd** file in the App_Code folder and then select **View Code**. The connection, schema, and the methods are stored in this file. Close the file.

14. In the Design view of the DataSet, right-click the **Fill( ), GetData( )** methods in the configuration table and then select **Preview Data**. Click the **Preview** button. After the data is displayed, click the **Close** button. Close the file. When you are asked to save the changes, click **Yes**.

**TIP**

The Query Builder in the Data Source Configuration Wizard can fail if the user permissions are set incorrectly or the connection is not available. If you receive an error message that the Query Builder cannot be launched, you can rerun the wizard, and make sure the database user permissions are set up correctly. If this does not work, you can manually enter the query comments in the Data Source Configuration Wizard. Another tip is to restart your web editor or reboot the computer.

DataAdapters can store multiple queries. In the following exercise, you will add a query to the DataAdapter.

1. In the Solution Explorer window, right-click the **Ch8_ProductLists.xsd** file in the App_Code folder. Select **Open**.

2. Right-click the **Fill( ), GetData( )** methods in the Design view, select **Add**, and then select **Query**. Click the **Next** button. The first button already is selected, which will return rows of data. Click the **Next** button.

3. Click the **Query Builder** button. In the filter for the SubCategoryID, enter **=?**. Click the **Execute Query** button. In the value box, enter **47** and then click the **OK** button. The data is displayed. Click the **OK** button. Click the **Next** button. Notice the default named for the Fill and GetData methods are FillBy and GetDataBy. Click the **Next** button and then click **Finish**. The FillBy and Get-DataBy methods are displayed in the DataTable1TableAdapter methods list in Design view as shown in Figure 8-8.

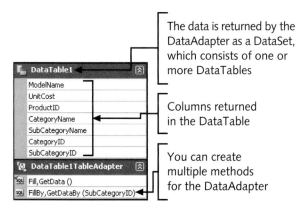

**Figure 8-8**   Creating the DataTable1DataAdapter methods

4. Right-click the **DataTable1TableAdapter** in the Design view and then select **Preview Data**.

5. In the drop-down list at the top of the window, the methods are displayed. Select **Ch8_ProductLists.DataTable1.FillBy, GetDataBy (SubCategoryID)**. In the Value box, enter **47** and then click the **Preview** button. The data is displayed as shown in Figure 8-9. After the data is displayed, click the **Close** button. Close the file. When you are asked to save the changes, click **Yes**.

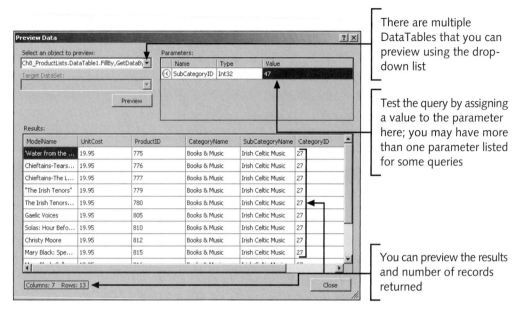

There are multiple DataTables that you can preview using the drop-down list

Test the query by assigning a value to the parameter here; you may have more than one parameter listed for some queries

You can preview the results and number of records returned

**Figure 8-9**    Passing parameters to the DataAdapter methods

## Data Binding Techniques

The data from the data source can be retrieved but the data needs to be used by the Web application. This data can be used in the program code or displayed in the browser. Web controls can be bound to data. When you bind a control to data, the data will be used by that control to configure the value of a property. The process of assigning the data source to a Web control is called **data binding**. The two types of data binding are single-expression binding and repeat-expression binding. The data source can be single expressions or repeated expressions.

When a single piece of data or a single expression is bound to a control, it is called **single-expression binding**. Single-expression binding sometimes is used to store single values such as constants and read-only properties. For example, a single expression data source may be an image name such as home.gif. The Image control can assign this data source as the value for the ImageUrl property. When the page is requested the browser would display the home.gif image.

**Repeat-expression binding** allows you to bind your control to multiple rows of data. Examples of repeated expressions include hash tables, array lists, databases, or other data structures. Data binding usually occurs when the page is first loaded, or when the data has changed. Some Web controls, such as RadioButtonLists, CheckBoxLists, DropDownList, and List controls, can display multiple values. These controls contain a collection of items. The values and text displayed can be obtained from various types of data sources, such as array lists, hash tables, and databases. Web controls that are commonly used to display bound data are called **Data controls**. They have additional properties beyond Web controls. The

Data controls are located in the Toolbox on the Data tab. You can also use this method to bind to middle-tier business objects or a DataSet, which is created in code stored within the Bin or App_Code folders.

You can bind some controls directly to certain types of data, such as Hashtables and ArrayLists. With most Web applications, however, you will be working with databases. To use the data in the database, the Web application needs to connect to the database, pass one of the CRUD methods, and then receive the data. The data access model provides objects to perform these tasks programmatically. In ASP.NET, there are built-in objects that provide these functions. As shown in Figure 8-10, the data source objects can be used to perform the data access logic and business layer logic functions. Then, the Web controls and Data controls are bound to the DataSource objects. The Web and Data controls then are used to display the data in the Web application. The choice of control used to display the data is independent of the data being retrieved.

8

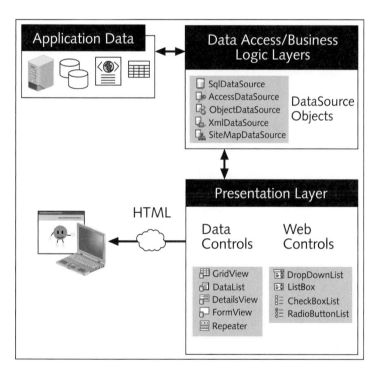

**Figure 8-10**  Binding data sources to a variety of controls

## Binding Data to Web Controls

In a Web application, there are many advantages to binding data to Data or Web controls. If the data changes, the control automatically reflects the change. Data binding allows you to get records **synchronously**, which means the ability to retrieve records is not tied to the page loading process. As a result, the whole page is more responsive and loads quicker. Data binding results in fewer trips to the server, because you normally will not need to interact with the server once the requested data has been downloaded. Any interaction with the database requires a round trip to the server to refresh the page, which ensures total browser compatibility. You can improve performance when interacting with the database by storing the requested pages on the server through a process called caching.

In the following subsections, you will learn how to bind single and repeated expressions to Web controls.

## Single-Expression Binding

Single-expression binding is used to bind a single value or expression to a Web control. To bind a single expression to an ASP.NET control, you use the pound sign (#) before the expression's name. The expression is enclosed within inline server tags (<% %>). No other code can be placed inside the tags, as shown in the following code. The ImageURL variable stores the location of the image. Later in the page, the image location can be retrieved and used to display the image.

```
<% Dim ImageURL As String = "logo.gif" %>
<img name="Logo" src="<%# ImageURL %>" alt="Logo" />
```

The data that is being bound can be in the form of a property, procedure, or expression. You can use the bound expression to display the value on a web page, to store a value, or to use the value in another expression. The data is not bound until the **DataBind method** is called from the page or the control. This is important because the data is stored separately from the control. The data is integrated into the control only when the control is created in the Web Server's memory. If the data has changed before the data is bound to the control, the most recent data will be used.

In ASP.NET 2.0, you do not call the DataBind method if you are binding the data to one of the built-in data sources. If you are going to create custom data binding methods, however, you will need to call the DataBind method manually. The DataBind method for the page is called using Page.DataBind(). The Page.DataBind procedure is often called within the Page_Load event handler so the data is bound before the page is displayed. You can also bind the expression to a single control by calling the DataBind method of an individual control, such as Logo.DataBind().

In this chapter, you will insert code both manually and by using the wizards. There is a greater chance for programming errors to occur when web developers type in the code. Make sure to double-check the spelling and syntax when you enter your code, especially for connection strings and while working in HTML view. Using the wizards when possible will also decrease the chance of making typographical errors.

In the following exercise, you edit a web page and will create a function that will return the filename of an image. You will bind all the Web controls to this data using Page.DataBind(), and then display the data-bound Web controls on the web page. The Label and Text Box controls are bound to the value from the ImageURL property. The Image Button control is bound to the value returned by the GetImageURL function. When the page is rendered, the controls are bound to the values, and displayed on the web page, as shown in the following exercise.

1. In the Solution Explorer window, right-click **ch8_singlebind.aspx**. Then click **View Code**. Type the code as shown in Figure 8-11.

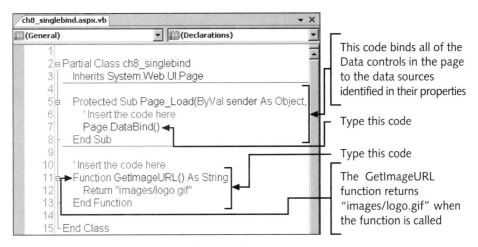

**Figure 8-11**   Using the DataBind method

2. Click the **Save All** button. Click the **ch8_singlebind.aspx** tab to edit the ch8_singlebind.aspx page, if necessary. Open the ch8_singlebind.aspx page, then click the Design button.

3. To select the first control, open the Properties window if needed, click the drop-down list arrow at the top, and select the control **lblImageURL**. (*Note*: This drop-down list contains all of the controls within the page. This is an alternative way to select controls.) In the Text property, add the code **<%# GetImageURL()%>**. This code will insert the image name into the label control when the page is rendered.

4. Click the **Code** button to edit the markup code. Locate the txtImageURL TextBox Web server control. After the id="txtImageURL" code property, add a blank space and the code **Text="<%# GetImageURL()%>"**. Click the **Design** button to return to Design view.

5. Click the last control, which is below the second, to select it. Verify that the ID of the Image Web Server control is imgImageURL. Change the ImageUrl property to **<%# GetImageURL() %>**. This will create the binding expression for the imgImageURL control. (*Note*: If you add the image path here, instead of in the function, the binding expression is returned. Therefore, it is better to have the path included in the function or property, and not in the ASP.NET control.)

6. Click the **Save All** button. Right-click the page in Design view and then click **View in Browser**. Your page should look like the one in Figure 8-12.

7. Close any open pages.

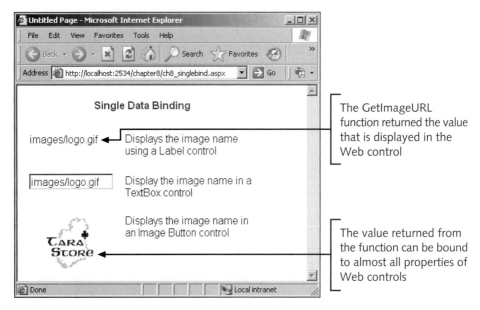

**Figure 8-12**   Binding Web controls to a single expression

## Repeated-Expression Binding

Binding a set of data to an ASP.NET control is called repeated-expression binding. There are several Web controls that you can use to bind to repeated expressions. Because they are inherited from the same classes, they share many properties. When you learn to work with templates for the GridView control, you will use similar templates for the DataList control. All of these controls contain a DataSource property that can be set to a data expression. When the DataBind method of the page is called, the control is bound to the data in the DataSource property. The repeated expression, which is bound to the Data control, can be a collection or another type of data structure. What's new with ASP.NET 2.0 is that these controls can be bound to the control without having to explicitly call the DataBind method. In the next section, you will learn about binding repeated expressions to Web controls and Data controls.

## BINDING DATA TO WEB CONTROLS AND DATA CONTROLS

Web controls and Data controls can be bound to different types of data sources. The Web controls and Data controls determine how the data is displayed on the web page. The most commonly used Web controls and Data controls bound to repeated expressions include the following:

- The **CheckBoxList** and **RadioButtonList controls** both display the data using the XHTML input tag with the type set to check box or radio. These controls are often used to represent Boolean data values in the database.

- The **DropDownList** and **ListBox controls** both display the data using the XHTML select tag. The DropDownList control usually only displays one value at a time, however, while the ListBox control generally displays all the values at the same time.

- The **Repeater control** is a small, lightweight control. The Repeater control displays the data using controls that you can define. No visible interface or formatting is available with the Repeater control; it simply repeats the content that you define.

- The **DataList control** displays the data as a basic list. You can modify the layout of the list by changing the number of horizontal or vertical columns.

- The **GridView control** repeats content you define once for each data row. When the control is rendered, the page places the data in a table.

- The **DetailsView control** displays content in a table like the GridView control, but only for one data row. It is often used to display information about a record that has been selected from a GridView control.

- The **FormsView control** repeats content you define once for each data row. The FormsView control uses templates to render the content. The FormsView control is often used to create custom forms to insert, edit, and delete records.

In the next section, you bind data in collections to a Web control and then to a Data control.

## Binding Data in a Collection to a Web Control

You manually can bind a collection object to the Web controls on the web page. This same procedure could be used to bind ListBox, RadioButtonList, and CheckBoxList controls and other Web controls. The step sequence in this part of the chapter demonstrates that the DropDownList control can be bound to a variety of data sources. In the steps, the data source is identified with the **DataSource property** of the DropDownList control. You must specify which item is displayed on the web page using the **DataTextField property**. You use the **DataValueField property** to specify the value property of the DropDownList items, which is displayed only in the HTML source view of the rendered web page. The DataValueField property corresponds to the value property of the HTML <option> control. The value is formatted using the **DataTextFormatString property** of the DropDownList control. The formats are entered using the standard format string rules, such as {0:c} for currency. The zero represents the formatting applied to the first item, and the c represents the format rule, which is currency.

In the following exercise, you will bind the ArrayList and HashTable to the DropDownList controls. Then, you will use the DataBind method to bind the data to the controls.

1. Right-click the **ch8_dropdownlist.aspx** page icon in the Solution Explorer window and then click **View Code**.

2. Immediately after the comment "Insert the code here", type the code shown in Figure 8-13. Click the **Save All** button.

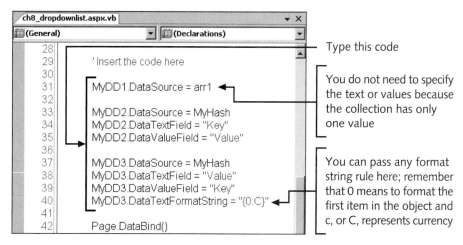

**Figure 8-13**   Binding Web controls to a single expression

3. Right-click the **ch8_dropdownlist.aspx** page in the Solution Explorer and then click **View in Browser**. Select **Shamrock Paperweight** from the first drop-down list. Select **Belleek Colleen Vase** and **$22.00** from the last two drop-down lists. Click **Submit**. The values selected are displayed in the Label control. Your page should look like the one shown in Figure 8-14.

4. Close any open pages.

## Binding Data to a Data Control

The Repeater control is a Data control designed to bind data to a data source. Because the Repeater control has no default appearance, you must use the markup view to modify the control. The Repeater control allows more control over the data output. You can modify the layout of the list or table using templates. The templates available to the Repeater control include the header, footer, alternating, item, and separator templates. Therefore, the Repeater can be used to create tables, comma-delimited lists, bulleted lists, and numbered lists. The data-binding instructions are stored within the templates.

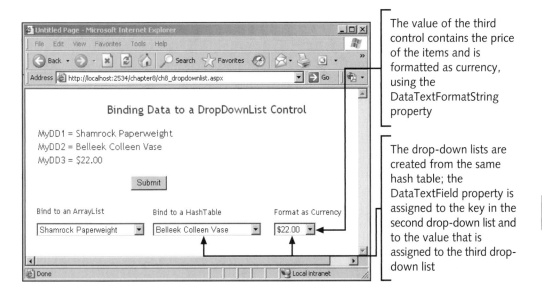

The value of the third control contains the price of the items and is formatted as currency, using the DataTextFormatString property

The drop-down lists are created from the same hash table; the DataTextField property is assigned to the key in the second drop-down list and to the value that is assigned to the third drop-down list

**Figure 8-14**   Binding data to a DropDownList control

**TIP**

In order to position the Repeater control, you must use additional controls such as the XHTML <div> tag or Panel control.

The Data controls require you to configure an **ItemTemplate** within the control in order to display the data. Within the ItemTemplate is the **DataItem property**. (*Note:* This same DataItem property is also applied to other Data controls.) The **DataRow property** is referenced as a DataItem object within the container control and the field.

## Data-Binding Methods

Data-binding methods identify how to bind the data to an expression. The **DataBinder.Eval method** is used to bind data one way, which means that the data can be read from the database. The **Bind method** is used to provide two, way binding, which means that the data can be read from the database and the data will be uploaded to the database if the value changes.

The DataBinder.Eval method is often referred to as the Eval method. The Eval method can include formatting instructions. The Eval method applies the formatting rule to the data so that the formatting is applied at run time before the data is sent to the XHTML code. For example, if a product cost 25 U.S. dollars, but you wanted to display the data as $25.00, you could format the data using XHTML after the data is bound.

Up to three arguments are passed for Web controls that display lists of data. The DataList, DataGrid, and Repeater controls use templates to display and format the data. These controls must use the **Container.DataItem** naming container to store the results as the first argument.

The Container.DataItem represents each item within the data source. The second argument is usually the name of the data element, which is passed within quotation marks. The third argument passed is the formatting instructions, which are also passed within quotation marks. For example, with "{0:c}", the 0 represents the data element and the c represents currency. Both C and c represent currency. P, or p, represents percent. In the latter case, the value is converted to a percent value and the percent sign is appended to the data.

The following sample code inserts a Repeater control into the page. The data is inserted into the Repeater control with an ItemTemplate. The content in the ItemTemplate is duplicated for each row of data retrieved. The Container.DataItem.Key property passes the key from the data source. The Container.DataItem.Value property passes the value from the data source. You can add XHTML tags to format the ItemTemplate of the Repeater control. You can format the value of the Container.DataItem as currency using the same format as the DropDownList control. (*Note*: The ItemTemplate is used with all of the Data controls to display the data.)

```
<asp:Repeater id="Repeater1" runat="server">
  <ItemTemplate>
    <b><%# Container.DataItem.Key %></b>
    (<%# Container.DataItem.Value %>)<br/>
    (<%# DataBinder.Eval(Container.DataItem, "Value","{0:C}") %>)
  </ItemTemplate>
</asp:Repeater>
```

## Manually Binding Data to a Repeater Control

The following step sequence shows you how to insert a simple Repeater control onto a web page. The Repeater control is bound to a hash table. The bold tags are used to format the name of the product and the product price is formatted as currency. The Repeater control was bound to the same data using the same method as you would with a DropDownList control.

1. Double-click the file **ch8_repeater.aspx** in the Solution Explorer window to open the page. On the Data tab in the Toolbox, click and drag the **Repeater** control to the page and place the control inside the Panel control named Panel1.

2. Click the **Source** tab to edit the HTML code. Between the opening and closing Repeater tags, type the code shown in Figure 8-15.

3. Right-click the page and then click **View Code**. Immediately after the comment "Insert code here", add the following code to bind the Repeater control named Repeater1 to the Hashtable. Bind the data expressions to the DataSource property of the Repeater control. Notice that here the DataBind method is called specifically for the Repeater control:
   ```
   Repeater1.DataSource = MyHash
   Repeater1.DataBind()
   ```

4. Click the **Save All** button. Right-click **ch8_repeater.aspx** in the Solution Explorer window, and then select **View in Browser**. Your page will look like Figure 8-16.

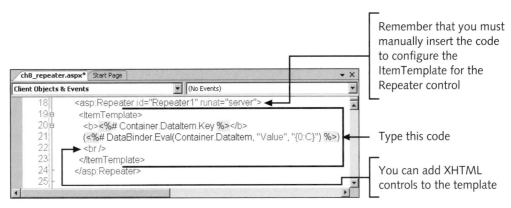

Remember that you must manually insert the code to configure the ItemTemplate for the Repeater control

Type this code

You can add XHTML controls to the template

**Figure 8-15**   Modifying the ItemTemplate of a Repeater control

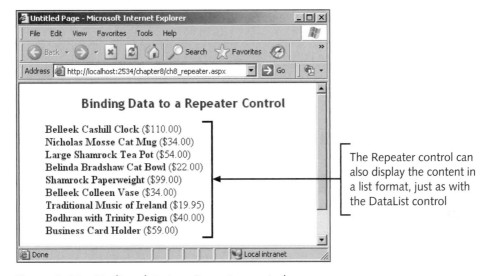

The Repeater control can also display the content in a list format, just as with the DataList control

**Figure 8-16**   Binding data to a Repeater control

5. Close any open pages.

In the next section, you will learn to use the Data controls to bind automatically to a data source.

## Automatic Binding Techniques

One of the new features of ASP.NET is to allow controls automatically to bind to data sources. When you add a Data control to the page, the smart tag appears that is identified by the arrow in the upper-right corner of the control. The smart tag can be used to configure the control, and the DataSource property. While you manually can bind a Data control such as the DataList to a data source, you can bind these controls to data sources using automatic binding. **Automatic binding** allows you to use the built-in wizards and bind to data sources such as a Microsoft Access or SQL Server database, XML file, sitemap file, or business object. You do not have to call the DataBind method automatically. Remember that all of these controls support both manual and automatic binding, and can be bound to a variety of data sources.

In the following subsection, you will learn how to bind data to the DataList control and the GridView control.

# Binding Data to a DataList Control

The DataList control allows you to display values as a simple list. When you add the DataList controls, you need to identify the columns to bind to the data. DataList and GridView controls support templates to configure the appearance of the control and the values bound to the controls. The code to insert a DataList control is as follows:

```
<asp:DataList id="MyDL1" runat="server" />
```

In the previous exercise, you had to add tags within the ItemTemplate to format the output of the Repeater control. One of the advantages of using the DataList control rather than the Repeater control is that the DataList control can be used to create multiple columns of data without using the table tags in the ItemTemplate. You can alter the number of columns displayed and the direction or layout. The number of columns is the number of columns of data displayed across the web page. The number of columns repeated is formatted using the **RepeatColumns property**. The RepeatColumns property must be an integer. The **RepeatDirections property** stores the direction of the columns. If the columns repeat horizontally, then the value is RepeatColumns.Horizontal. If they repeat vertically, then the value is RepeatColumns.Vertical. These are properties of the DataList control, and not the template.

## Binding Hierarchical Data to a DataList Control

In the following exercise, you will bind a DataList control to an XML file using the automatic binding method. Because the XML data is stored in a hierarchical structure, you will need to configure the XPath to the starting node. You will use the smart tag to configure the DataSource properties of the DataList control. You can use templates to modify the DataList control. In the following exercise, you will display the data using the DataList control formatted as multiple columns. Within the DataList control, you can use the table tags to format the output more precisely. You need to make sure that the width of the tables is specified in order to ensure that the entire output is visible. In this example, you are going to create the data objects using the automatic data binding method.

1. Double-click **ch8_datalist.aspx** in the Solution Explorer window to open the page. If necessary, click the **Design** tab.

2. Click the **DataList control**. Click the **smart tag**. In the Choose Data Source drop-down list, select **New data source**. Click the **XML File** icon. The data source will be listed as XmlDataSource1. Click the **OK** button.

3. In the Data file text box, type **~/ch8_products.xml**. In the XPath expression text box, type **/productlist/product**, and then click the **OK** button.

4. Click the **Source** tab. Type the code as shown in Figure 8-17.

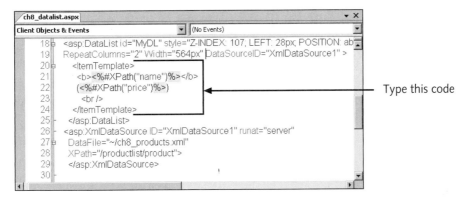

**Figure 8-17**    Using the XPath attribute to retrieve the data from the XML File

5. Click the **Save All** button.

6. Right-click the page, and then click **View in Browser**. The page should appear as shown in Figure 8-18.

7. Close any open pages.

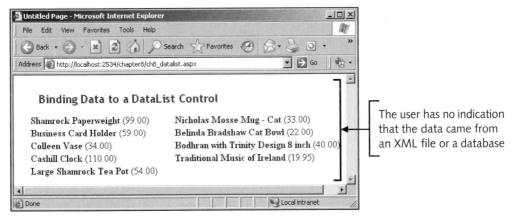

**Figure 8-18**    Using the RepeatColumns property to format the DataList control

**NOTE**    In Chapter 9, you will learn to use templates to modify the appearance of the Data controls. They allow you another way to customize the appearance of your Data controls.

## Binding Relational Data to a GridView Control

The GridView control can be bound to various data sources. The GridView control contains many properties to help format the bound data, and the properties include the following:

- The **AutoGenerateColumns property** does not allow you to specify the columns that you want to bind to your data source. (*Note*: You do not have to bind all of the data columns in your data source to the GridView control.)

- The **HeaderText property** allows you to change the string displayed at the top of the column headings. (*Note*: You can include HTML tags in the headings if you also set the HtmlEncoded property to false.)

- The **DataFormatString property** is used to display currency and is applied to the values displayed within the GridView control.

- The **AllowSorting** and **AllowPaging properties** allow you to configure the GridView control to support sorting and paging features. This capability is built into the control with no additional programming required. Both features can be turned on concurrently.

- The **NullDisplayText property** is used to set an alternate message if a field's value is null; otherwise, by default an empty string ("") is displayed for the value. For individual bound columns, you can specify that the ConvertEmptyStringToNull property be set to true, which will also set the string to null when it returns to the database.

The DataFormatString can be passed to any of the format methods such as {0:c}, or a custom format such as {0:MM/dd/yyyy}. Some hackers will try to attack your site using cross-site scripting attacks. To prevent a cross-site scripting attack, by default the value in the Data control column is encoded with the **HtmlEncoded property** before the DataFormatString format is applied to the value. So, to apply these formats you must change the HtmlEncoded property to false.

### Binding Relational Data to a GridView Control

When you configure the GridView control to use the database, the wizard inserts an AccessDataSource control. Therefore, you do not have to create the underlying data access layer logic. The **AccessDataSource control** is used to manage the connection to a Microsoft Access Database. The connection string, and all of the other data logic tools, are built into the AccessDataSource control. You do not have to specify the provider used to connect the Data control to the database. The **DataFile property** is used to identify the relative or absolute URL for the database. The **SelectCommand property** is used to identify the SQL SELECT statement that should be executed. The code to insert a GridView control is as follows:

```
<asp:GridView id="MyGV1" runat="server" />
```

In the following exercise, you will bind a GridView control to a table in a Microsoft Access database.

1. Right-click **ch8_gridview.aspx**, then click **View Designer** in the Solution Explorer window to open the page. On the Data tab in the Toolbox, click and drag the **GridView control** to the page and place the control below the Label control.

2. Click the **smart tag** for the GridView control. In the Choose Data Source drop-down list, select **New data source**. Click the **Access Database** icon and then click the **OK** button. Type **~/App_Data/TaraStore.mdb** in the Microsoft Access data file text box, and then click **Next**.

3. Select the **Specify a custom SQL statement or stored procedure** radio button, and then click **Next**.

4. In the SQL statement text box, type **SELECT ProductID, ModelNumber, ModelName, ProductImage, UnitCost FROM Products WHERE SubCategoryID = 8**, click the **Next** button, and then click **Finish**.

5. In the smart tag window, click the check boxes labeled **Enable Paging** and **Enable Sorting**.

6. In the smart tag window, select **Auto Format**. The left pane in the Auto Format dialog box contains preformatted schemes, and the right pane allows you to preview individual schemes. In the left pane, select **Clover Field**, and then click **OK.** The format scheme is applied to the GridView control.

7. Click the **Save All** button.

8. Right-click the **ch8_gridview.aspx** tab in the Solution Explorer window, and then click **View in Browser**. Click the ModelName heading text. The table is sorted based on the name of the product. Your page should look like the one shown in Figure 8-19.

9. Close any open pages.

## Generic Database Connection Error Messages

Most types of errors in Web database applications are related to database connections. If your Web application is on a remote server, you may have to configure the permissions for the ASP.NET Machine account to manage the file. The **ASP.NET Machine account** is used by the web server to run ASP.NET pages and allow them to interact with the web server. By default, the user cannot modify a file-based database because the ASP.NET Machine user does not have NTFS permissions to manage the database.

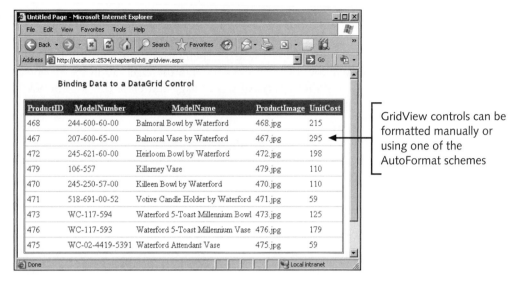

**Figure 8-19**   Binding hierarchical data to a GridView control

## Microsoft Access Database Connection Error Messages

After you change permissions, you may still receive other error messages. You may receive an error message that says "Could not lock file." Although the error points to an OleDbDataAdapter1 object, the problem is the ability for the object to open a connection to the database. There are several reasons that this may occur:

- This often happens if the file has been opened in Microsoft Access and the file was not closed properly.

- Another possibility is that the locking mode permissions have been set to restrict editing the record. A Microsoft Access database is created in Microsoft Access XP 2003. The Open Mode property has been set to share by default. The Record Locking property has been set to no locks. Databases are opened with record-level locking. To view the Open Mode and Database Record Locking properties in Microsoft Access, open the database in Microsoft Access XP 2003. Select the Tools menu, and then select Options. In the Options window, select the Advanced tab.

- If you have an error involving permissions, you may have to reset your NTFS directory permissions. You should make sure the account that runs your ASP.NET Web application has write permissions to the directory that contains the database. The ASP.NET Machine account must be able to create a Microsoft Access LDB lock file in the directory. The Microsoft Access LDB lock file is named after the database (databasename.ldb). Change the user permissions to allow the user to have permissions to that directory. Then, Access can create the Microsoft Access LDB lock file when the file is opened. If you set the permissions at the folder level, the permissions will be inherited by the files within the folder. If you did not place the database in the App_Data folder, it is better to place the databases into folders separate from your Web Forms so that the permissions can be set for the databases separately from the permissions for the Web Forms.

# OVERVIEW OF THE ADO.NET DATA MODEL

Web developers must create Web applications that can coexist with evolving data structures. With the .NET Framework, the ActiveX Data Object .NET Model (also referred to as ADO.NET or simply .NET) provides objects that allow you to interface with the database. The .NET model allows you to retrieve data from a variety of sources, including XML data. By using these technologies together, you can exchange data across products and platforms. If you are working with basic web databases, then you should use the built-in data sources and Data controls. These data sources and Data controls provide a user-friendly interface to the .NET framework. It is important to understand that this framework allows programmers to customize their data access layer and business logic layer by programming directly against these built-in objects. You have seen how to use the various data sources to connect to different data. The objects in the .NET framework allow you to bypass the built-in data sources and customize your programming code.

As you can see in Figure 8-20, data can be stored in a variety of formats, from flat files to relational databases.

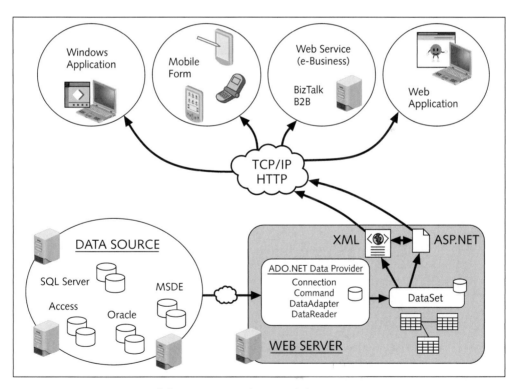

**Figure 8-20**    Overview of the ADO.NET data model

Although you have access to wizards and visual tools, you can create the code and bind your data manually. You can create connections to various data sources, such as collections and databases. The process of manually binding the data is the same regardless of the data source. To bind the data source to the control manually, you must assign the data source to the DataSource property of the Data control, and then call either the DataBind method of the control or the DataBind method of the page.

In the next subsections, you will learn about the use of ODBC drivers and OLE DB providers and the providers used for .NET applications.

## ODBC and OLE DB

In the United Nations, many members need to communicate with members from other countries. They use translators to translate their language into another language. A member who speaks American English would use a translator who could speak French. The French prime minister would receive the message in French, and respond with a return message in French. The translator would translate the message from French to American English. When applied to databases, this kind of simultaneous translation allows you to interact with a database using its own proprietary interface. You can use a standard such as Open Database Connectivity (ODBC) or Object Linking and Embedding Database (OLE DB) to translate commands between your application and the database.

In 1992, the standard known as **Open Database Connectivity (ODBC)** was created to provide a common interface to relational database systems. ODBC drivers are used to provide access to a legacy ODBC-compliant database. Using ODBC drivers, an application can access a database without an application- or database-specific interface. You do not need to know how the database application stores the data in order to access the data. The **ODBC drivers** provide the low-level interface to the database applications. ODBC drivers are available for most legacy Database Management Systems (DBMSs), including Access, SQL Server, and Oracle. Therefore, if you want to create an application that accesses a legacy Access database, you would use the .NET Provider objects to create a connection to the database via the ODBC driver.

Relational databases store data in a collection of rows of data. Some database programs store nonrelational data in a different format. The method for accessing relational database stores, as well as these nonrelational data stores, is called **Object Linking and Embedding Database (OLE DB)**. OLE DB providers allow your application to access a database without an application- or database-specific interface. In other words, you do not need to know how the database application stores the data in order to access it. OLE DB providers are available for most common data stores, including Access, SQL Server, and Exchange Server. Microsoft provides an OLE DB provider that will interface with the ODBC driver in order to support legacy database applications. For example, if your database application does not have an OLE DB provider, but does have the ODBC driver, you can use the OLE DB provider for ODBC to access the database.

The ODBC drivers and OLE DB providers reside on the server, not the client. The Web application interacts with objects built within the ADO.NET model. Then .NET Data Providers interface with the database via the ODBC and OLE DB. Your Web application interfaces with the data objects.

# .NET Providers

Visual Studio .NET includes a new set of Data Providers, known as Managed Providers or .NET Providers. The **.NET Providers** are responsible for providing the connection to the data source, executing commands, and returning data results.

The .NET Provider establishes a connection to a specific data source using the Connection object. The .NET Provider contains a Command object that executes a command against a data source. The Command object exposes Parameter objects, which can be used to send information with the command. For example, the command might be to retrieve all of the employees within a particular state. A Parameter object can be used to send data representing a specific state, such as Michigan. Then, the command would only retrieve employees who live in Michigan.

When you use the .NET Provider, you can access the data source using built-in objects. Within the web page, the ASP.NET Data controls are bound to the DataReaders or DataSets. The data returned can be processed directly by the .NET Provider, placed into an object such as a DataSet, or sent to another tier of an application. The .NET Provider contains a DataReader object, which reads a forward-only, read-only stream of data from a data source. The .NET Provider also contains a DataAdapter object that will populate a typed DataSet. Once the DataSet is populated, the data remains disconnected from the database. Changes can be made to the data within the DataSet. The DataAdapter will update the DataSet with the data source. The DataAdapter manages the changes between the DataSet and the original source of data. Therefore, the .NET Provider is often referred to as a Managed Provider.

It is important to note that lower-level communication is still maintained by the set of generic data access software, such as ODBC drivers and OLE DB Providers. The .NET Provider is used to create a more uniform way to access and manage the data within your applications. You don't need to be familiar with this lower-level software, only with the .NET Providers themselves.

## Using .NET Providers

There are four versions of the .NET providers available by default:

- The **SQL Server .NET Provider** is used to connect to an SQL Server database.
- The **OLE DB .NET Provider** is used to connect to any other data source that can be accessed via the OLE DB interface.
- The **ODBC .NET Provider** is used to access data using the ODBC interface.
- The **Oracle Provider** is used to access an Oracle database.

There are some important differences between the SQL Server .NET Provider and the OLE DB .NET Provider. The SQL Server .NET Provider uses a native communication method to communicate with SQL Server. The SQL Server .NET Provider does not have to convert the COM data types from the OLE DB Providers to the .NET data types in the SQL Server .NET Providers.

.NET Providers, as shown in Figure 8-21, are available for most common data stores, including Access, SQL Server, and Oracle. They all contain a Connection, Command, DataReader, and DataAdapter object. The names of the .NET objects contain a prefix that identifies the type of data source that is managed by the .NET Provider. For example, SQL Server Provider objects contain the "Sql" prefix. So SQL Server and .NET Provider objects include the SqlConnection, SqlCommand, SqlDataReader, and SqlDataAdapter objects.

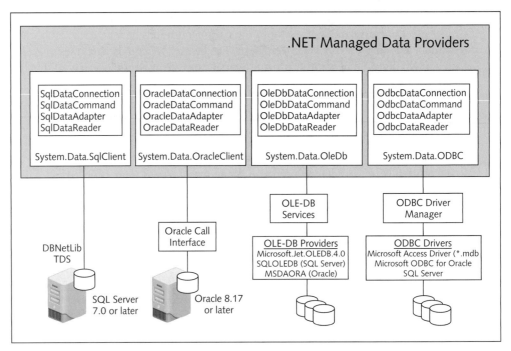

**Figure 8-21**   .NET Managed Data Providers

## The Connection Object

The **Connection object** provides the connection to the database. The connection string format is different for each .NET Provider because each provider has its own name. When you create a connection to a database, you will fill out the connection information using a dialog box, and the software will create the connection string. Within the data connection, you must specify the location of the database, the access permissions, and any additional required parameters using a **connection string**. The connection string must contain the following:

- The provider, which is identified with the keyword **Provider**.
- The name of the server, which is identified as the **Data Source**.

- The User ID and Password, which identify the authentication data required to connect to the database.

- The name of the database, which, in SQL Server, is identified as the **Initial Catalog**. The name of the SQL Server OLE DB Provider is Provider=SQLOLEDB.1.

The Connection object provides access to the **Transaction object**, which allows you to group data commands together as a logical transaction. If any command within the transaction fails, the entire transaction fails, and all data is returned to the original values. Transactions are often used with credit card processing.

## The Command Object

The **Command object** is used to identify an SQL command or a stored procedure. SQL is the **Structured Query Language** that is used to identify what records to add, delete, or modify within the database. **Stored procedures** are SQL commands that are stored within the database. It is not recommended in a production application to prefix the name of stored procedures with sp_. The server will look for the stored procedures with this prefix in the master database first, before looking in the current database. This additional step will reduce performance of your application.

The following are the additional properties exposed by the Command object:

- The **Parameters collection** is exposed by the Command object and can be used to apply parameters, which are passed to stored procedures.

- The **Connection property** defined the connection used by the Command object.

- The **CommandText property** defines the command.

- The **CommandType property** is used to indicate the type of command being executed. The CommandType property is **Text** by default, which indicates that the command is an SQL text string. The CommandType property can also be **TableDirect**, which specifies the name of a table to return, or **StoredProcedure**, which specifies the name of a stored procedure.

- The **Execute method** of the Command object executes the command and passes the results to the DataReader object.

- The **ExecuteNonQuery method** does not return rows because it is used to insert, modify, and delete data. Therefore, the method returns an integer representing the number of rows affected by the command.

## RETRIEVING DATA IN THE .NET FRAMEWORK

The .NET framework provides objects that are used to retrieve the data from the data source. In the following subsections, you will learn to use the DataReader and DataSet objects to retrieve data from a database, use a DataSet object to retrieve data from an XML file, and use the DataView object to retrieve a subset of data.

## Using the DataReader to Retrieve Data from a Database

The DataReader object is used to deliver a stream of data from the database. It is included in order to provide a high-performance method of accessing read-only data, as shown in Figure 8-22. The DataReader object provides a read-only, forward-only stream of data from the database, and requires continual access to the database. Therefore, you cannot make changes to the database directly. You can make changes to the database with the DataReader object by using the Command object.

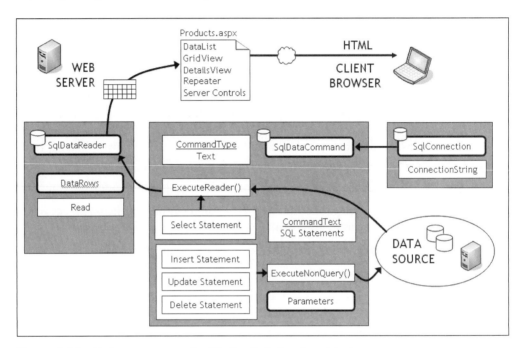

Figure 8-22    Data management with the DataReader object

When you call the **ExecuteReader method** of the Command object, the DataReader object opens a connection to the database and then retrieves rows of data as they are located in the database. The **Read method** of the DataReader object returns a single row and caches each row in memory only once. It then moves the current record pointer to the next record or row. You must remain connected until you have finished reading the stream of data. When you are finished, you need to close the connection using the **CommandBehavior property** of the Command object. If you set the CommandBehavior to **CloseConnection**, the connection closes automatically when the **Close method** of the DataReader object is called. You must call the Close method to close the DataReader object and release the references to the row set.

In the following exercise, you use the DataReader object to retrieve data and display a listing of categories in the TaraStore database.

Assign the contents of the MyCat variable to the Text property of the label named lblCat. The label displays the results from the DataReader on the web page.

1. Right-click the **ch8_datareader.aspx** page icon in the Solution Explorer window and then select **View Code**.

2. Within the Page_Load procedure, type the code shown in Figure 8-23.

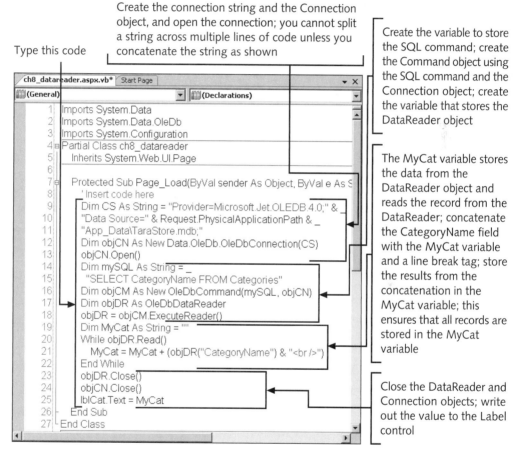

Create the connection string and the Connection object, and open the connection; you cannot split a string across multiple lines of code unless you concatenate the string as shown

Type this code

Create the variable to store the SQL command; create the Command object using the SQL command and the Connection object; create the variable that stores the DataReader object

The MyCat variable stores the data from the DataReader object and reads the record from the DataReader; concatenate the CategoryName field with the MyCat variable and a line break tag; store the results from the concatenation in the MyCat variable; this ensures that all records are stored in the MyCat variable

Close the DataReader and Connection objects; write out the value to the Label control

```
ch8_datareader.aspx.vb*   Start Page
(General)                              (Declarations)
1   Imports System.Data
2   Imports System.Data.OleDb
3   Imports System.Configuration
4   Partial Class ch8_datareader
5       Inherits System.Web.UI.Page
6
7       Protected Sub Page_Load(ByVal sender As Object, ByVal e As S
8           ' Insert code here
9           Dim CS As String = "Provider=Microsoft.Jet.OLEDB.4.0;" & _
10          "Data Source=" & Request.PhysicalApplicationPath & _
11          "App_Data\TaraStore.mdb;"
12          Dim objCN As New Data.OleDb.OleDbConnection(CS)
13          objCN.Open()
14          Dim mySQL As String = _
15              "SELECT CategoryName FROM Categories"
16          Dim objCM As New OleDbCommand(mySQL, objCN)
17          Dim objDR As OleDbDataReader
18          objDR = objCM.ExecuteReader()
19          Dim MyCat As String = ""
20          While objDR.Read()
21              MyCat = MyCat + (objDR("CategoryName") & "<br />")
22          End While
23          objDR.Close()
24          objCN.Close()
25          lblCat.Text = MyCat
26      End Sub
27  End Class
```

**Figure 8-23**   Configuring the DataReader object

3. Click the **Save All** button.

4. In the Solution Explorer window, double-click the **ch8_datareader.aspx** page to open it. Right-click the page, and then click **View in Browser**. Your page should look like the one in Figure 8-24.

5. Close any open pages.

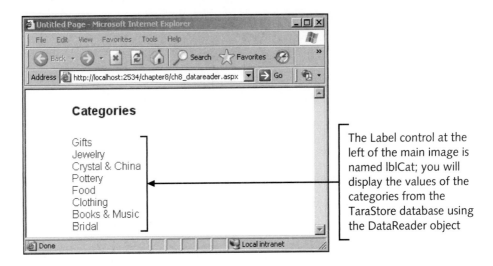

**Figure 8-24** Using the DataReader object to display data from an Access database

## The DataAdapter and DataSet Objects

The **DataAdapter object** primarily is used to populate a DataSet object, as shown in Figure 8-25. The DataAdapter object provides four commands that you can use to access the DataSet object:

- **SelectCommand** is used to retrieve data. When you use SelectCommand, the data must be inserted into the DataSet object. The **Fill method** of the Data-Adapter object inserts the data returned from the SelectCommand into the DataSet object. The DataSet object is effectively a private copy of the database, and does not necessarily reflect the current state of the database. If you want to see the latest changes made by other users, you can refresh the DataSet object by calling the appropriate Fill method of the DataAdapter object.

- **InsertCommand** is used to add a new record.

- **UpdateCommand** is used to modify the data within an existing record.

- **DeleteCommand** is used to remove a record from the database permanently. (*Note*: If no records are returned, then the command returns a count of records affected.)

These four commands are used to manage the data within the DataSet object. The **DataSet object** is a disconnected collection of one or more tables that are stored in memory on the server. Because the DataSet object is disconnected, there must be methods used to maintain the original set of data and the changes. When the code has completed making changes to the DataSet object, there must be a method to upload the changes to the database. The DataSet object contains the methods required to maintain the list of changes made to the DataSet object.

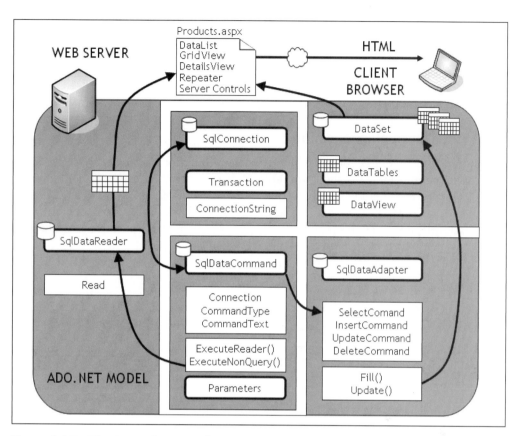

**Figure 8-25**   The DataAdapter and DataSet objects

Usually, the DataAdapter, DataSet, and DataView objects are used together to retrieve data from the database. The DataSet object does not know the source of the data. Only the DataAdapter knows where the data is located. The DataAdapter object represents a database connection and a set of commands used to manage the data within the DataSet object. The Fill method of the DataAdapter object is used to get the data from the database and populate the DataSet object. The DataAdapter object connects to the database and reconciles changes made to the data in the DataSet object with the data source when the Update method is called. The **Update method** is used to update the records in the original database with the values changed in the DataSet.

When you use the wizards, the DataAdapter object commands are automatically generated via the **CommandBuilder object**. So, the DataAdapter object provides the bridge between the DataSet object and the data source. The DataSet object is a passive container for the data. To actually fetch data from the database, and (optionally) write data to the database, use the DataAdapter object.

When accessing data from a database, you can access the data from multiple tables. These tables are received as a DataSet object. A DataSet object contains a DataTablesCollection. Individual DataTable objects within the DataTablesCollection can have relationships defined between the DataTable objects. You can use the DataTable object to specify the subset of tables and records that you want to access. The DataView object is used to retrieve a subset of one of the tables within the DataSet. The results always are received by the RecordSet object as a single table, however. With a DataSet object, the data can be received as a group of one or more related tables. The DataBind method is used to bind the DataSet or DataView objects to the Data control.

## The DataTablesCollection

The DataSet object consists of the DataTablesCollection and the DataRelationsCollection. As shown in Figure 8-26, the **DataTablesCollection** is a collection of one or more **DataTable objects**. Each DataTable object consists of a DataRowsCollection, a DataColumnsCollection, and a ConstraintsCollection. The DataRowsCollection and DataColumnsCollection store information about the rows and columns of data. (*Note*: The column is also referred to as the field.)

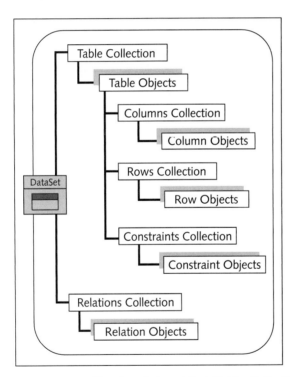

**Figure 8-26**   The DataSet and DataTablesCollection

The **ConstraintsCollection** includes information about the primary and foreign keys, and constraint rules. A primary key is used to ensure that no duplicate records appear in a column. Therefore, if one customer has a specific customer number, no other customer can have that number. The **constraint rules** are used to ensure that the field contains the correct data type and values. The UniqueConstraint and ForeignKeyConstraint are constraints used to create the relationships. The **DataRelationsCollection** contains the data required to maintain relationships between the DataTable objects. Relational data can be exposed via ADO.NET because relationships can be made between DataTable objects. The tables are joined using the primary and foreign keys that are defined in the DataTable object. The **ExtendedProperties property** of the DataSet object allows you to specify information that can be stored with the DataSet object and later retrieved. The ExtendedProperties can be used to store the date the DataSet object was generated, the SQL statement, or any other data.

## Using the DataSet to Retrieve Data from a Database

In the following exercise, you bind the DataSet object to a Data control to display the data. (*Note:* For any page that you will insert the code manually, there must be a reference to import the Data classes used on the page. In code view, if you use an Access database you will see at the top of the code Imports System.Data.OleDb and Imports System.Data. In these exercises, this code has been inserted for you.)

1. Right-click the **ch8_dataset.aspx** page icon in the Solution Explorer window, and then select **View Code**.

2. Type the code as shown in Figure 8-27.

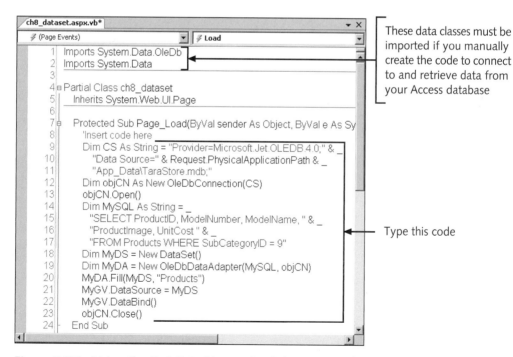

**Figure 8-27** Using the DataSet object to bind data in a GridView control

3. Click the **Save All** button.

4. In the Solution Explorer window, double-click the **ch8_dataset.aspx** page to open it. Right-click the page, and then click **View in Browser**. Your page should look like the one in Figure 8-28.

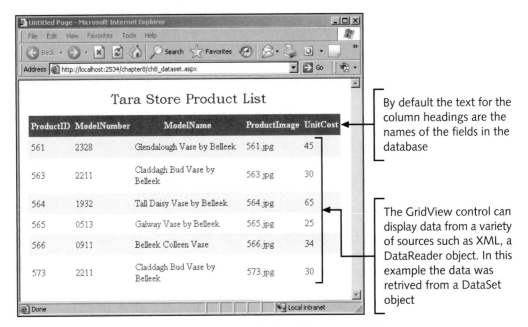

Figure 8-28    Using the DataSet object to display data in a GridView control

5. Close any open pages.

## Using the DataSet Object to Retrieve Data from an XML File

Several ways exist to retrieve the hierarchical data and insert it into the DataSet object. The following exercise shows how to read the XML file into a DataSet object using the ReadXML built-in method of the DataSet object. The **ReadXML method** will transform the data from a hierarchical file to a DataSet object.

1. Right-click the **ch8_dataset_new.aspx** page icon in the Solution Explorer window, and then select **View Code**.

2. Type the code as shown in Figure 8-29.

3. Click the **Save All** button.

4. In the Solution Explorer window, double-click the **ch8_dataset_new.aspx** page to open it. Right-click the page, and then click **View in Browser**. Your page should look like the one in Figure 8-30.

5. Close any open pages.

Type this code

These classes must be imported if you interact with the file system

XML data can be stored in a file, or in a stream; use the StreamReader object to retrieve the XML data as a stream, which can be read by the DataSet object

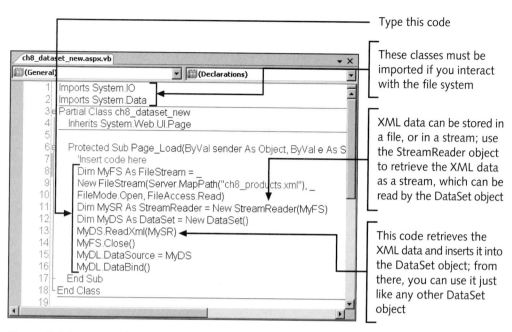

This code retrieves the XML data and inserts it into the DataSet object; from there, you can use it just like any other DataSet object

**Figure 8-29**   Using the DataSet object to bind XML data in a DataList control

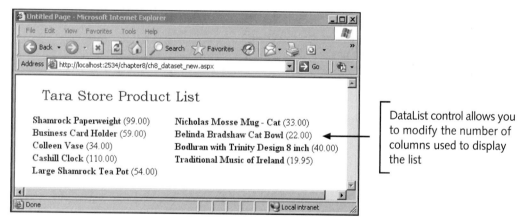

DataList control allows you to modify the number of columns used to display the list

**Figure 8-30**   Using the DataSet object to display XML data in a DataList control

## The DataView Object

A **DataView object** contains the data from the DataSet object for a single DataTable object or subset of records from a table. The DataTable object has a DefaultView property that returns all the records in the DataTable object. You can select a subset of records from a table. You also can add columns to the DataColumnsCollection as well as filter and sort the data in a DataView object.

Two of the commonly used properties of the DataView object are:

- The **RowFilter property** of the DataView object allows you to filter a subset of the DataView object.

- The **Sort property** of the DataView object allows you to sort the data based on a specific criterion in one or more of the columns.

When you use the RowFilter property, use the single apostrophe around strings. You can retrieve the value for the RowFilter property from a control or other data source and create the RowFilter property by concatenating the strings. The following is an example of how to implement the RowFilter:

```
MyDV.RowFilter = "SubCategoryID=9";
MyDV.RowFilter = "ModelName='" + MyDL.SelectedItem.Text + "'"
```

The DataView object is a collection of data from the DataSet object. The default DataView object for the DataSet object for a specific table is the collection of all the records in the table. Many DataView objects can be retrieved from a DataSet object. The ASP.NET Data controls, for example the DataGrid control, are bound to the DataView object. Visual Studio .NET contains visual controls to create the DataAdapter, DataSet, and DataView objects.

## Populating the DataView Object

The DataAdapter object is used to populate the DataSet object. The DataSet object can consist of multiple related tables. When you create the DataAdapter object using the DataAdapter Wizard, you are creating a SQL command and identifying the Connection object. Then, you must identify the DataSet object to be filled with data manually when the Fill method is called. After you fill the DataSet object, you use a DataView object to identify which subset of the DataSet object you want to access. If there is only one table involved, then you can simply use the default DataView object, or you can identify the table or SQL statement to use to retrieve a table for the DataView object.

The following code sample shows how you can fill the DataSet object with data using the Fill method of the DataAdapter object. Then, you can create a DataView object from the DataSet object, which is a subset of one of the tables within the DataSet object. In this example, the default DataView object contains all of the rows from the Categories table. Then, the DataGrid control is bound to the DataView object using the DataBind method of the DataGrid control.

```
SqlDataAdapter1.Fill(MyDS)
Dim MyDV As DataView = New DataView(MyDS, "Categories")
MyDG.DataSource = MyDV
MyDG.DataBind()
```

You can refer to the DataTable object in the DataView object by the table name or by its index position within the Tables collection. The DataTablesCollection is a series of tables within the DataSet object. When you create the DataView object, you are referring to one of the tables within the Tables collection. DefaultView returns all of the data within the DataTable object. But you must identify which table to retrieve. The index position is the number that represents the DataTable object within the Tables collection. The sample code that follows this paragraph shows how to retrieve all of the data within the first table of the Tables collection from the MyDS DataSet object. The DataView object is then bound to the MyDG DataGrid control.

```
Dim objDV As New DataView()
objDV = MyDS.Tables(0).DefaultView
MyDG.DataSource = objDV
MyDG.DataBind()
```

The DataAdapter object also has other methods and properties. The **SelectCommand method** allows you to identify the command used to retrieve the records. When the Fill method is called, the DataAdapter object uses the SQL command identified by the SelectCommand property, to determine which records to retrieve. In the following sample code, the DataAdapter object is used to fill a DataSet object using the Categories DataTable object:

```
Dim CN As New SqlConnection(CS)
Dim MySQL As String = "Select * From Categories"
MyDS = New DataSet()
MyDA = New SqlDataAdapter(MySQL, CN)
MyDA.Fill(MyDS, "Categories")
```

The DataAdapter object contains a Command Builder method to generate commands automatically to insert, modify, and delete data. The database tables must have primary keys defined in order to use the Command Builder method. Although you can write the code to access the Command Builder method manually, it is much simpler to use the DataAdapter Wizard to activate the Command Builder method. The Command Builder method creates the SelectCommand, InsertCommand, and DeleteCommand.

## Using the DataSet Object to Retrieve Data from a Database with a DataView Object

Once you create the DataAdapter object and fill the DataSet object, you define a DataView object that will be bound to your Data control. In the following exercise, you use Visual Studio .NET to create a DataAdapter object, add a DataSet object, generate the DataSet methods, and create a DataView object. You will bind the DataView object to an ASP.NET Data control to display the data.

1. Right-click the **ch8_dataview.aspx** page icon in the Solution Explorer window, and then select **View Code**.

2. Type the code as shown in Figure 8-31.

3. Click the **Save All** button.

4. In the Solution Explorer window, double-click the **ch8_dataview.aspx** page to open it. Right-click the page, and then click **View in Browser**. Your page should look like the one in Figure 8-32.

5. Close any open pages.

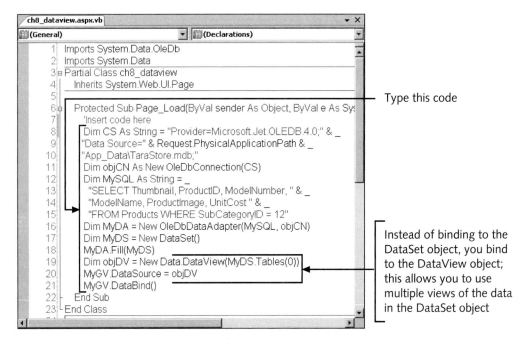

**Figure 8-31**    Using the DataView object to display data in a GridView control

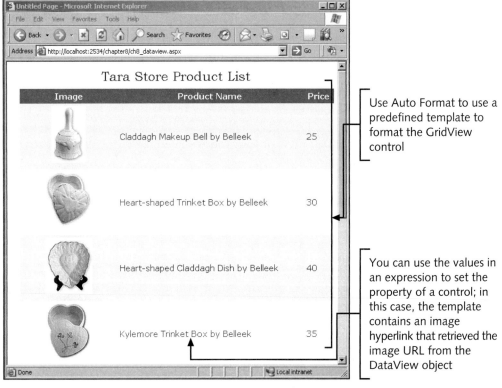

**Figure 8-32**    Using the DataView object to display data in a GridView control

**TIP** This app_offline.html file is used by ASP.NET as a placeholder if your web site is taken down. The app_offline.htm in the root of the application allows you to bring down your ASP.NET application while you make changes to it. If this file exists, ASP.NET shuts down the app-domain for the application. Simply removing or renaming the file will allow the application to restart. You may view the app_offline.html file in your chapter8 data folder. The file was named app_offline1.html to prevent the page from displaying while you worked on the chapter exercises.

## CHAPTER SUMMARY

❑ The Data Access Model provides a way to organize a data application logically. The data can be stored in various formats, including XML, database files, and database servers. The data access layer provides the ability to connect to and manage the CRUD methods within the data source. The business logic layer is often used to separate business logic such as business components from the data access layer. The presentation layer is used to generate the output to the user. All three layers interact together and may overlap. A well-defined Web application will provide logical layers to provide maximum efficiency and maintenance of the application.

❑ The DataSet object is a disconnected set of data that is stored in memory. The DataSet object created by the DataAdapter object maintains the changes in the DataSet object and pushes the changes to the server.

❑ The DataSet object consists of a DataTablesCollection and DataRelationsCollection. The DataTable object can consist of many DataView objects.

❑ A DataView object is a subset of data from a single DataTable object. A DataSet object can be persisted as an XML document. You can import XML data into a DataSet object, or store the DataSet object as an XML document.

❑ A DataReader object is a read-only, forward-only stream of data from the database. The data connection remains open while the DataReader object reads the data.

❑ Single-expression binding is used to store single values such as constants and read-only properties. Repeated-expression binding is used to bind multiple rows of data to a control. You can use Data controls that automatically bind to the data, or you manually can configure the controls to bind to the data with the DataBind method.

❑ Data can be displayed using Web controls and Data controls. The DropDownList, ListBox, CheckBoxList, and RadioButtonList controls inherit from a ListControls class. The DropDownList control usually only displays one value at a time, while the ListBox control generally displays all the values at the same time.

❑ Web controls use the DataSource property to identify the data to be bound. The DataTextField property is used to identify which values should be displayed by the control, and the DataTextFormatString property identifies how to format the control. The DataValueField property specifies the Value property of the control, which is displayed only in the HTML source view of the rendered web page.

❑ The DataList control uses an ItemTemplate to display the values. When you use a template such as the ItemTemplate to display the data, use the DataItem property.

❑ While the DataBinder.Eval method is used for one-way data binding, you need to use the Bind method for two-way data binding so the data can be read from the database and the data will be uploaded to the database if the value changes.

❑ The GridView control allows you to create bound and unbound columns. Bound columns contain a value that is bound to a value in the database.

❑ The DataList and GridView controls use templates to create the header, footer, and item sections of the Data control. You can format these controls using the Auto Format templates.

❑ The Repeater control must be edited manually in HTML view. No graphical tool exists to edit the Repeater control.

❑ In the ADO.NET model, you connect to data sources using Managed Providers. These providers maintain the interface with the lower-level providers and drivers that communicate directly with the data source.

❑ You can write your application to interface directly with the ADO.NET framework, or use the built-in DataSource objects and Data controls.

❑ The ADO.NET object model consists of four primary objects: Connection, Command, DataAdapter, and DataReader. Each of the .NET Providers contains its own version of these four ADO.NET objects. The DataAdapter object serves as a bridge between the DataSet object and the data source. The DataReader object is a high-performance object that provides a stream of data. The data is read-only and forward-only.

# REVIEW QUESTIONS

1. Which of the following controls cannot be used to display data in a web page?
   a. DataList
   b. DataView
   c. DataGrid
   d. Repeater

2. What method can be used to bind the DG1 control to a hash table?
   a. DG1.Bind()
   b. Page.Bind()
   c. DG1.DataBind()
   d. Bind.Page()

3. Which method provides two-way data binding?
   a. Eval()
   b. DataBinder.Eval()
   c. Bind()
   d. DoubleBind()

4. In a tiered application, which layer interfaces directly with the data source?

    a. data access layer

    b. business logic layer

    c. presentation layer

    d. all of the above

5. Which object provides a read-only, forward-only stream of data from the database?

    a. DataReader

    b. DataSet

    c. DataView

    d. ArrayList

6. Which Data control displays one value at a time?

    a. ListBox

    b. DropDownList

    c. DataList

    d. DataGrid

7. Which control cannot be bound automatically to a repeated-expression?

    a. DataGrid

    b. DataList

    c. CheckBoxList

    d. Label

8. Which property of the Data control identifies where to get its data?

    a. DataView

    b. DataSource

    c. DataTable

    d. DataTextField

9. What property allows you to format a value as currency?

    a. FormatCurrency

    b. Format $C

    c. DataTextFormatString

    d. DataTextField

10. Which property is used to identify the column to be displayed in a DropDownList control?

    a. DataValueField

    b. DataTextFormat

    c. DataTextFormatString

    d. DataTextField

8

11. Which property must be set to False before you can change the displayed DataGrid columns?

   a.  Auto FormatColumns

   b.  FormatColumns

   c.  AutoDataColumns

   d.  AutoGenerateColumns

12. In the template that contains the value, which expression returns a value from a column named "thumbnail"?

   a.  <%# Container.DataItem("thumbnail") %>

   b.  <%# Columns.DataItem("thumbnail") %>

   c.  <%# Columns ("thumbnail") %>

   d.  <%# Columns.thumbnail %>

13. Compare the steps to bind data using the manual and automatic methods.

14. Compare the use of the DataView and DataTable.

15. Describe how to refer to a data field from a database inside a Web control.

16. Compare the use of one-way and two-way data binding.

17. Describe the method used to convert XML to a DataSet control.

18. Describe the steps to bind a Web control to a collection such as a HashTable.

19. Describe the steps to bind a Data control to a collection such as a HashTable.

20. Describe the steps to bind a Data control to a database.

21. Describe the difference between the four .NET Providers.

22. Compare manual and automatic data binding in a .NET application.

23. List the five DataSource objects that are used in automatic binding in .NET applications.

# HANDS-ON PROJECTS

**HANDS-ON
PROJECTS**

## Project 8-1

In this project, you will create a web page that displays data from an ArrayList in a DropDownList control.

1. Start your web editor and open your **chapter8** solution if it is not already open.

2. Create a page named **ch8_proj1.aspx** in the ch8_proj1 folder.

3. Add an **ASP.NET Label** control, DropDownList control named **MyDD1**, and a **Submit** button to the page.

4. In Code view when the page loads, create an array named **arr1** that has seven items. Insert the following values into the array: **Detroit, Escanaba, Iron Mountain, Kalamazoo, Lansing, Marquette,** and **Munising**.

5. If the page previously has not been visited, populate the MyDD1 control with the values in the array, and bind the values to the control. If the page has already loaded, display a message in the Label control.

6. Add headings, graphics, fonts, and colors to enhance the appearance of the page.

7. Click the **Save All** icon. View your web page in the browser. Print the web page, the code view, and the source code from the browser.

HANDS-ON
PROJECTS

## Project 8-2

8

In this project, you will create a web page that binds a Repeater control to a database and displays the data in an image. A DropDownList control is used to display the state choices. When the user selects a state, the page should display the images of the houses available in that state.

1. Start your web editor and open your **chapter8** solution if necessary.

2. Open a web page named **ch8_proj2.aspx** in the ch8_proj2 folder.

3. Add the **Repeater control** to the bottom of the page. Configure the connection and query using the Configure Data Source Wizard. The SQL select statement should retrieve all of the columns from the **homes** table for all records. Configure the WHERE clause to locate only records where the State column is equal to the value selected from the DropDownList1 control.

4. In Code view, configure the ItemTemplate in the Repeater control to display the image and location of the houses in that state. You first will display the value from the **City** column and a line break tag. Remember to use the Eval() method and Container.DataItem to retrieve the values.

5. Insert an image tag. Set the **src** property to the ImageUrl column. The images are located in the **/chapter8/images/Houses/** folder. You will need to insert this into the src property before you retrieve the value of the ImageUrl column.

6. Configure the **height** and **width** properties to equal the values from the Height and Width columns.

7. Configure the **alt** property to equal the value from the City column. Include a line break that clears all returns after the image tag.

8. Add headings, graphics, fonts, and colors to enhance the appearance of the page and the templates.

9. Click the **Save All** icon. View your web page in the browser. Print the web page and the markup code.

## Project 8-3

In this project, you will create the code to bind a DropDownList control and a GridView control to a SQL Server database. You will configure the bound columns in the GridView control.

1. Start your web editor and open your **chapter8** solution if necessary.

2. Open the web page named **ch8_proj3.aspx** in the ch8_proj3 folder.

3. Add a **DropDownList** control to the page and place it to the left of the Submit button. Use the Configure Data Source Wizard for the DropDownList to configure a connection to the Chapter8 SQL Server database and to create the SQL query. The connection is already stored in the configuration file as CS_Chapter8, which will show up in your connection string drop-down list. The SQL select statement should retrieve the CategoryID and CategoryName fields from the **Categories** table.

4. Add a **GridView** control to the page and place it below the house graphic. Configure the connection to the Chapter8 database and SQL query using the Configure Data Source Wizard. The SQL select statement should retrieve all of the products from the **Products** table where the CategoryID is equal to the value in the DropDownList1 control.

5. In Markup view, modify the BoundColumn for the UnitCost column. Insert the DataFormatString property and assign the value to "{0:c}". Insert the HtmlEncode property and assign the value to "False".

6. In Markup view, change the HeaderText properties for the three bound columns to **Category ID**, **Product Name**, and **Price**.

7. In Design view, right-click the GridView control and select **Auto Format**. Select **Mocha** as the scheme and then click **OK**.

8. Add headings, graphics, fonts, and colors to enhance the appearance of the page and the templates.

9. Click the **Save All** icon. View your web page in the browser. Print the web page and the markup code.

## Project 8-4

In this project, you will create manually the data objects and bind a database to a Repeater control. The page will display all the columns in the Products table for all of the products.

1. Open **ch8_proj4.aspx** in the ch8_proj4 folder.

2. Add a **GridView** control to the page below the Label control.

3. In the code behind the page, below the "Insert the code here" comment, add the code to create the **connection** to the TaraStore database. You can concatenate the connection string using the Request.PhysicalApplicationPath and the relative URL of the database as you did in the chapter exercises, or you can create a static connection string.

4. Create a **variable** to store the SQL statement. The SQL variable contains the SQL statement that selects all of the products in the database.

5. Create a **Connection** object and pass the connection string variable when the new object is created.

6. Create a **DataAdapter** object and pass the Connection object and the SQL variable when the new object is created.

7. Create the **DataSet** object.

8. Call the **Fill** method of the DataAdapter object and pass the DataSet object and the "Products" table.

9. Create a **DataView** object. Assign the DataView object to the DefaultView property of the first table in the DataSet object.

10. Assign the DataView object to the DataSource property of the GridView1 control

11. Call the DataBind method for all of the objects on the page.

12. In Design view, right-click the GridView control and then select **Auto Format**. Select **Mocha** as the scheme and then click **OK**.

13. Add headings, graphics, fonts, and colors to enhance the appearance of the page.

14. Click the **Save All** icon. View your web page in the browser. Print the web page and the source code.

## CASE PROJECTS

### Project 8-1

**CASE PROJECTS**

Your manager has asked you to provide information about the various Web controls and Data controls that can be bound to data sources. Go to the Help menu within Visual Studio .NET and search for the Web controls and Data controls listed in this chapter. If you do not have Visual Studio .NET Help installed, you can search for the information at *http://msdn.microsoft.com*. Create a web page that describes at least five controls. List at least three properties that you can configure with each control. Provide an example of the syntax used to insert each control on the web page. List at least three properties that you can configure with each control. On the same page, use one of the controls to display data from a database. You may use the TaraStore, Residential, Chapter8 databases, or create your own database. Add headings, graphics, fonts, and colors to enhance the appearance of the page. Save the page as Ch8Case1.aspx. Print the web page.

### Project 8-2

**CASE PROJECTS**

Your boss would like you to manage the company employee list. Create a database named ch8_case2 using Access or SQL Server that holds the employee first and last name, employee ID, user name and password, home address, department name, position, hire date, and salary. Create a page to display the users in a drop-down list. When the manager selects an employee in the drop-down list, and then clicks the Submit button, the page will display the employee information for the employee selected in the drop-down list, in a GridView control. The employee information that is displayed should include first and last name, employee ID, user name and password, home address, department name, position, hire date, and salary. Format the employee salary as currency. Format his or her hire date as mm/dd/yyyy. His or her password should be displayed in a web server Label control and all of the users and passwords should be displayed in a DataList control. Add headings, graphics, fonts, and colors to enhance the appearance of the page. Save the page as Ch8Case2.aspx. Print the web page.

CASE
PROJECTS

## Project 8-3

Your boss has asked you to create a web site to display products available in the store. In the first phase, you must create a database named ch8_case3 that contains the product information. Place the database in your project data directory. You can use SQL Server, Access, or another database application to create the database. Include the name of the product, price, description, product ID, and product image name. Insert some sample data. There should be at least five categories and five products in each category. Create a web page that displays the categories in a DataList control and the products data using a GridView control. Format the GridView control using the Property Builder. Change the HeaderText property for each of the columns and format the GridView control with one of the Auto Format schemes. Add headings, graphics, fonts, and colors to enhance the appearance of the page. Save the page as Ch8Case3.aspx. Print the web page and the source code.

CASE
PROJECTS

## Project 8-4

Your boss has asked you to create a Web application to display train schedules. You may pick a city and use the data for the train schedules if they are posted publicly, or make up your own train schedule. Create a database named ch8_case4 that contains the train schedule information. Place the database in your project data directory. You can use SQL Server, Access, or another database application to create the database. Include the name of the city, the train departure and destination points, and the times the train departs and arrives. Provide the price for the ticket and a field that will identify if a snack car or handicap services are provided with each route. Insert some sample data. Create a web page that allows the user to select his or her departure location and destination location. Display the schedules sorted by destination time, if the route provides the snack car or handicap service, and the ticket price formatted as currency. Make sure to format the time for departure using hh:mm. Add headings, graphics, fonts, and colors to enhance the appearance of the page. Save the page as Ch8Case4.aspx. Print the web page and the source code.

CHAPTER

# 9

# CUSTOMIZING DATA WITH WEB CONTROLS

---

### In this chapter, you will:

- ♦ Learn about the various Data controls to display data
- ♦ Modify the Data controls using templates and styles
- ♦ Use the GridView control to display data
- ♦ Build a master-detail page with the GridView control and DetailsView controls
- ♦ Create custom templates

---

One of the challenges that web developers face is the variety of layouts for web sites, and the frequency at which web designers modify the web site appearance. You already have learned how to modify the web site design using style sheets, themes, and skins. You have also learned that some controls have styles and templates that can be used to modify the appearance of the control. In the last chapter, you learned how to bind data to commonly used Data controls. In this chapter, you will learn how to modify their style properties and use templates to configure the appearance of the Data controls. You will also learn about the GridView control, which essentially has replaced the DataGrid control found in previous versions of ASP.NET. The GridView control allows you to display, sort, page, and filter records within the table. Another common feature in a web database application is the ability to display data based on the record selection by the users. This is known as the master-detail page. In this chapter, you will learn how to allow the user to select a record in a GridView control, and retrieve and display the results in the DetailsView control. Lastly, you will learn about ways to create your web pages efficiently by using custom templates.

## Templates and Styles Available to the Data Controls

In this section, you will learn to use different types of columns, templates, and column style properties in order to modify the content and appearance of the data within the Data controls. You will also learn how to apply templates and styles to the DataList control. Many of the techniques can also be applied to the other controls because they inherit the same classes.

## Templates Available to Data Controls

When you bound data to a DropDownList control, the data simply was displayed in the control. With other types of controls, however, you can modify how the data is displayed. For example, if you display the data in a GridView control, you may want to modify the column headings using the HeaderText property. To be able to control how the data is displayed, you can use a template. A template is used to format Data controls. The **templates** in your Data control are the parts of the control that determine how to display specific data. As you saw in Chapter 8, templates are used to bind data to individual areas within the control and to format the areas within the control. These special areas include the header, footer, and item sections. For example, the ItemTemplate would contain the data for the record. A Footer-Template might be used to display the total number of records in the table. The appearance of these templates and others can be modified manually in the markup Source view, by using the Property Builder, or by editing the templates in Design view. Using the editing templates instead of editing the code manually may help you be more efficient and accurate in your web programming. No matter which version you choose to edit the templates, however, the end result will be the same.

Details of these templates are as follows:

- **HeaderTemplate** is used to configure the data contained within the header section. Instead of using the HeaderText property for the column control, you will use HeaderTemplate to modify contents of the header cell. Therefore, you can use these templates to display images as well as textual content.

- **FooterTemplate** is used to configure the data contained within the footer section.

- **ItemTemplate** is used to configure how the row will appear in display mode. The data is actually displayed in read-only mode in this template. The GridView and DetailsView controls allow you to format the rows of data using columns. In the ItemTemplate, the data is generally bound to the field in the database. Instead of inserting the name of a graphic, you can insert an image control and set the src property to the name of the graphic. Then, the image would be displayed in the row in display mode.

- **EditItemTemplate** allows you to configure the columns in edit mode. Therefore, the user can change the values of the data. Instead of editing the data using text boxes, you can use other types of controls such as check boxes and drop-down lists to edit the data.

- **AlternatingItemTemplate** allows you to configure every other row of data.

- **SeparatorTemplate** allows you to configure the row that is displayed between each row of data.

- **SelectedTemplate** allows you to configure the row that is currently selected.

- **PagerTemplate** allows you to configure a custom template for the page navigation controls. The Data control may display one or more records on a page. The page navigation controls allow you to change which page of records is displayed. By default, for a GridView control, 10 records are displayed on the page. If there were 20 records, you could view the first 10 records on the first page and then use the page navigation controls to move to the next set of 10 records.

- **EmptyItemTemplate** allows you to provide alternative content in case your query returns no records.

Not all of the templates are available for all of the Data controls. By default, the GridView control allows you to modify only the PagerTemplate and EmptyItemTemplate, as shown in Figure 9-1. If you have modified the GridView control to contain custom columns, then you may have access to additional templates.

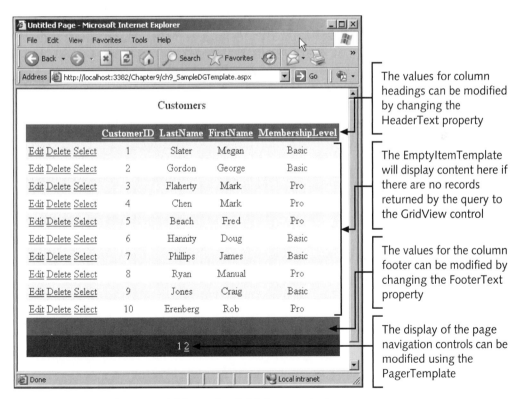

**Figure 9-1**   Templates available to the GridView control

The DetailsView control allows you to modify the HeaderTemplate and FooterTemplate in addition to the PagerTemplate and EmptyItemTemplate, as shown in Figure 9-2. If you have modified the DetailsView control to contain custom columns, then you may have access to additional templates.

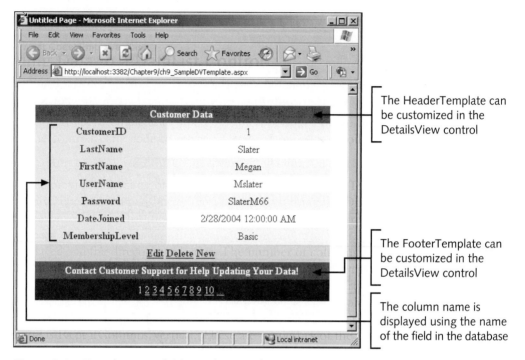

The HeaderTemplate can be customized in the DetailsView control

The FooterTemplate can be customized in the DetailsView control

The column name is displayed using the name of the field in the database

**Figure 9-2**   Templates available to the DetailsView control

The DataList control allows you to modify all of the templates except for the PagerTemplate and EmptyItemTemplate, as shown in Figure 9-3.

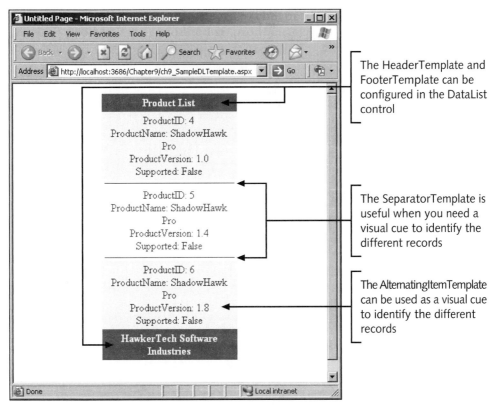

The HeaderTemplate and FooterTemplate can be configured in the DataList control

The SeparatorTemplate is useful when you need a visual cue to identify the different records

The AlternatingItemTemplate can be used as a visual cue to identify the different records

**Figure 9-3**   Templates available to the DataList control

As you can see in Figure 9-4, you can modify the templates for the DataList control in Design view. The GridView and DetailsView controls also allow editing of the templates in Design view.

As you can see in Figure 9-5, you can modify the templates for the FormView control in Design view. The FormView control differs from the other controls because it also has an InsertItemTemplate. This is important because the FormView control contains the ability to insert new records with built-in templates.

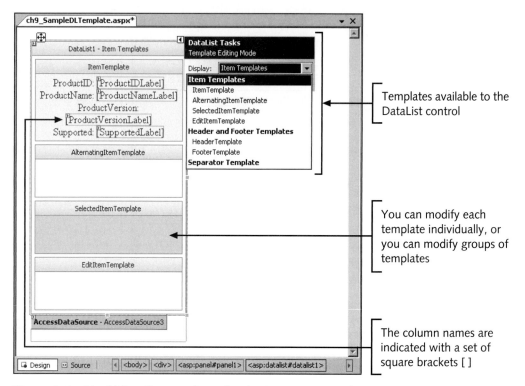

Templates available to the DataList control

You can modify each template individually, or you can modify groups of templates

The column names are indicated with a set of square brackets [ ]

**Figure 9-4**   Modifying the templates for the DataList control

Not all templates are available to all Data controls; the FormView control has an InsertItemTemplate which is used for creating a new record in the database; the InsertItemTemplate is not available in the DataList control

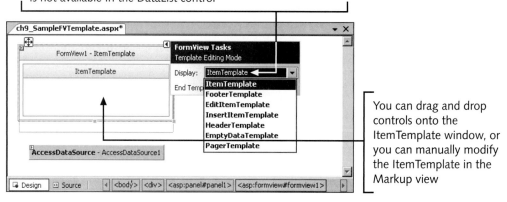

You can drag and drop controls onto the ItemTemplate window, or you can manually modify the ItemTemplate in the Markup view

**Figure 9-5**   Modifying the templates for the FormView control

The ShowHeader and ShowFooter properties of any Data control inserted into a web page needs to be set to true for the information in the header and footer to be displayed.

## Styles Available to Data Controls

Once you have a template created, you can format the Data control using styles. The following list describes the styles that can be used to modify the DataList controls:

- *AlternatingItemStyle*—Identifies the style for alternating rows.

- *EditItemStyle*—Identifies the style for a row being edited; the EditItemStyle is used in conjunction with the EditItemTemplate in the Data control.

- *FooterStyle*—Identifies the style for the footer row.

- *HeaderStyle*—Identifies the style for the header row.

- *ItemStyle*—Identifies the style for individual items within the list or control.

- *SelectedItemStyle*—Identifies the style for the currently selected item.

- *SeparatorStyle*—Identifies the style for content that is between each item.

The FooterStyle and HeaderStyle are also available with the GridView controls. The GridView control allows you to configure the style of the Pager controls. **Pager controls** are used when the number of rows exceeds the number of rows that can be displayed on the web page. The numbers of rows that are displayed on the web page are configured using the PageSize property of the Data control. The following list describes other styles that can be used to modify the GridView controls:

- *AlternatingRowStyle*—Identifies the style for alternating rows.

- *EditRowStyle*—Identifies the style for a row being edited.

- *EmptyDataRowStyle*—Identifies the style applied when there is no data in the row.

- *PagerStyle*—Identifies the style for the page navigation controls with GridView and DataList controls.

- *RowStyle*—Identifies the style for content that is between each item.

- *SelectedRowStyle*—Identifies the style for content that is between each item.

You can apply individual styles to a specific column in a GridView control. For example, in a shopping cart, you have a list of all of the products purchased. Each row contains a product the user selected. You may want the column that contains the cost of the item to have a total at the bottom of the column. In that case, you could use the FooterStyle to format just that footer table cell, and not the rest of the GridView control.

## Modifying the DataList Control Using Styles

Styles can be configured using the graphical user interface through the Properties window, or manually edited in the source code view of the ASP.NET page. In the following exercise, you will modify a page similar to one you created in the last chapter. Your modifications, which will be done in the Properties window, will allow the DataList control to support styles.

1. Open the **Chapter9** project in your web development editor if it is not already open.

2. Right-click the **ch9_DataList.aspx** file in the Solution Explorer window, and then click **View Designer** to open the page.

3. Change HeaderStyle font properties to **Trebuchet MS** and the size to **Large**. Change the color of the text to **#004040**, using the ForeColor property. Change the HorizontalAlign property to **Center**, as shown in Figure 9-6.

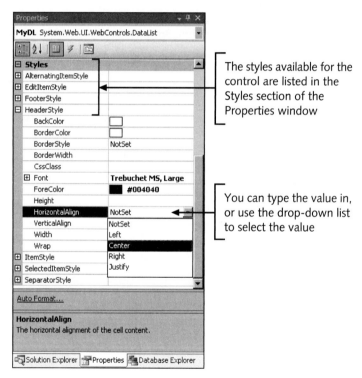

**Figure 9-6**  Using the Properties window to configure styles

4. Change the background color of the AlternatingItemStyle to **#400000**. The text color property is ForeColor.

5. Change ItemStyle font properties to **Arial** and the size to **Small**. Change the color of the text to **#004040** using the ForeColor property.

6. Click the **Source** tab to view the code, as shown in Figure 9-7. Notice that each of the templates and styles is identified using tags.

The three styles are available for editing manually; the names for the font properties are not the same as the name identified in the Properties window; however, styles and templates support IntelliSense; if you click the Spacebar while editing the tag, you can select the property name from the list of properties displayed

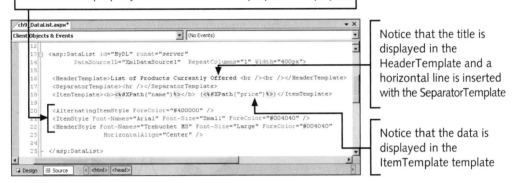

Notice that the title is displayed in the HeaderTemplate and a horizontal line is inserted with the SeparatorTemplate

Notice that the data is displayed in the ItemTemplate template

**Figure 9-7**   Configure styles manually in Source view

7. Click the **Save All** icon. Right-click the page in the Solution Explorer window and then select **View in Browser**. The page is displayed, as shown in Figure 9-8. Close the browser.

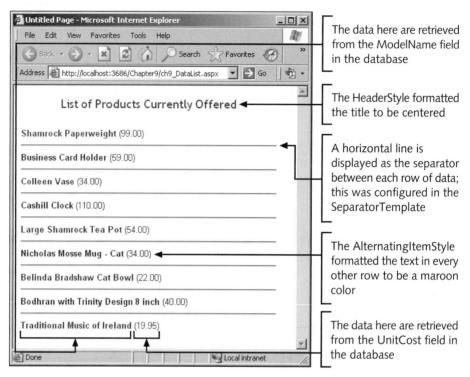

The data here are retrieved from the ModelName field in the database

The HeaderStyle formatted the title to be centered

A horizontal line is displayed as the separator between each row of data; this was configured in the SeparatorTemplate

The AlternatingItemStyle formatted the text in every other row to be a maroon color

The data here are retrieved from the UnitCost field in the database

**Figure 9-8**   Viewing a page that uses styles to format a Data control

**TIP**

Do not forget that you can also use Cascading Style Sheets (CSS), themes and skins to control the appearance of the Data control. The style sheets will only format the HTML markup. Skins support modifying the properties of any Web control or Data control directly. Styles may conflict with one another. For example, you may configure the ForeColor property of the GridView control to display the text as blue. When you configure the ForeColor property in the HeaderStyle of the same GridView control, you might configure the text color as green. The GridView control and each of the styles can be configured to use CSS classes by assigning a class to the CssClass property. If your CSS style sheet modifies the text color to be red, there will be a conflict between the CSS style and the styles defined in the GridView control. Therefore, you need to be cautious when applying styles using a variety of techniques. To minimize the potential conflicts between styles, you should either configure the styles using CSS classes or configure the style properties in the Properties window.

## MODIFYING DATA CONTROLS USING TEMPLATES

In this section, you will learn to use different types of columns, templates, and column style properties in order to modify the content and appearance of the data. Many of the techniques can also be applied to the other controls because they inherit the same class. You will learn how to apply templates to the Repeater and DataList controls.

## Using Templates to Modify the Repeater Control

You can use templates to modify the Repeater control. Remember that the Repeater control repeats only once for each row of data. You cannot configure the Repeater control in Design view. You must modify the control manually in the Source code view of the web page. The Repeater control is used when you want to have the most flexibility for displaying and managing your data.

In the following example, you will create a header template that contains the heading graphics. You will use a footer template to create an area that contains a company logo and links to the home page. In the body of the web page, you will use an ItemTemplate object, which is bound to the data in the database. You will use the product image names to display the product images, and create hyperlinks. Within the ItemTemplate object, you can retrieve the values of the data columns using `<%# Container.DataItem("ColumnName") %>`, where ColumnName is the name of the column in the database. You can format the output using any of the standard HTML tags.

1. In the Solution Explorer window, right-click the file **ch9_RepeaterTemplate.aspx** and then select **View Code**.

2. Immediately after the closing SeparatorTemplate tag, add the code to create the ItemTemplate template, as shown in Figure 9-9.

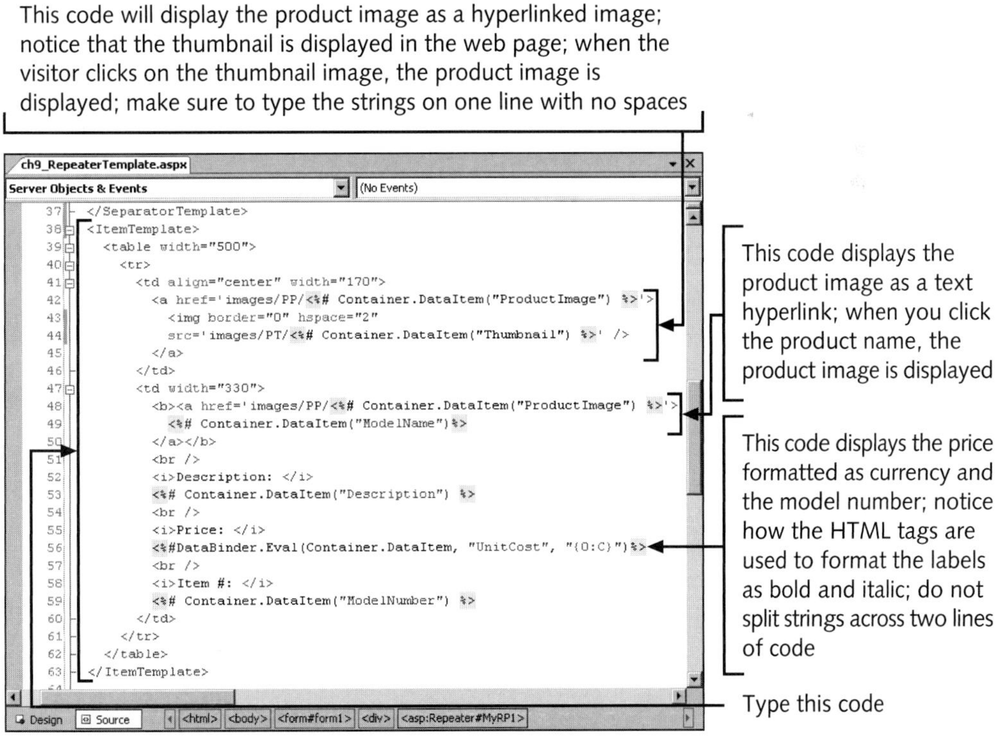

This code will display the product image as a hyperlinked image; notice that the thumbnail is displayed in the web page; when the visitor clicks on the thumbnail image, the product image is displayed; make sure to type the strings on one line with no spaces

This code displays the product image as a text hyperlink; when you click the product name, the product image is displayed

This code displays the price formatted as currency and the model number; notice how the HTML tags are used to format the labels as bold and italic; do not split strings across two lines of code

Type this code

**Figure 9-9**   Configuring ItemTemplate in a Repeater control

3. Click the **Save All** button. Right-click the page, and then click **View in Browser**. The page should appear as shown in Figure 9-10.

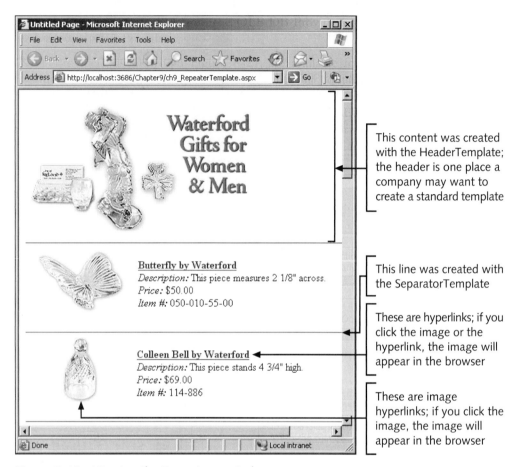

**Figure 9-10**   Viewing the Repeater control

4. Close any open pages.

**TIP**

You can replace DataBinder.Eval(Container.DataItem, "field") with a shorter expression that benefits from a new public method called Eval, which is available from the Page class. The new expression looks like Eval("field"). Internally, Eval calls the static Eval method on the DataBinder class and determines the correct binding context to use. The Eval method only reads the data in the field and returns it as a string. The Bind method is also used to retrieve the values from the database. However, the Bind method will submit the values back to the database when the Update method is called.

## Using Templates to Modify the DataList Control

In the previous exercise, table tags were used within the ItemTemplate to format the output of the Repeater control. One of the advantages of using the DataList control rather than the Repeater control is that the DataList control can be used to create multiple columns of data without using the table tags in the ItemTemplate.

As you complete this exercise, note that you can alter the number of columns displayed and the direction or layout. The number of columns is the number of columns of data displayed across the web page. The number of columns repeated is formatted using the **RepeatColumns property**. The RepeatColumns property must be an integer. The **RepeatDirections property** stores the direction of the columns. If the columns repeat horizontally, then the value is RepeatColumns.Horizontal. If they repeat vertically, then the value is RepeatColumns.Vertical. These properties are properties of the DataList control and not the template.

In the following exercise, you will display the data using the DataList control formatted as two columns and configure the HeaderTemplate and FooterTemplate.

1. In the Solution Explorer window, right-click **ch9_DataListTemplate.aspx** and then select **View Code**.

2. Change the RepeatColumns property in the DataList tag to **2**.

3. After the opening DataList tag and above the opening ItemTemplate tag, add the code shown in Figure 9-11 to create the HeaderTemplate and the Footer-Template templates.

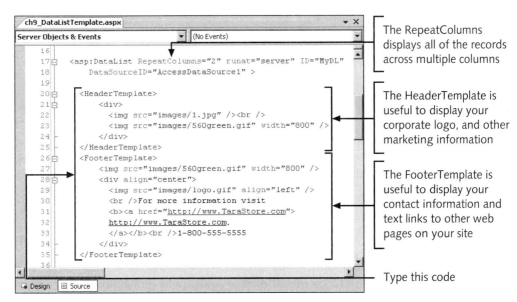

**Figure 9-11**   Configuring templates in a DataList control

4. Click the **Save All** button. Right-click the page, and then click **View in Browser**. Figure 9-12 shows how the page appears in the browser.

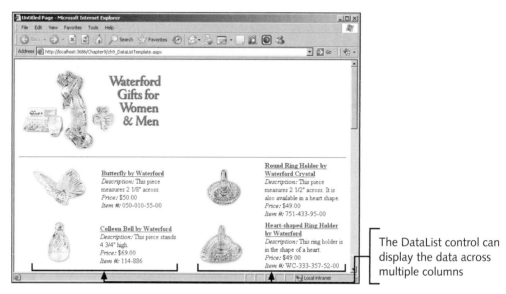

The DataList control can display the data across multiple columns

**Figure 9-12**   Viewing templates in a DataList control

5. Close any open pages.

## USING THE GRIDVIEW CONTROL TO DISPLAY DATA

The GridView control is a Data control that allows you to display data in a table. The GridView control allows you to bind data to individual columns or to create custom columns. In this section, you will learn about the different types of columns, the column properties, the data in the columns, and what templates and styles are available to configure for the GridView control. You will also learn how to customize filtering, paging, and sorting of data in the GridView control.

### GridView Columns

The GridView control contains a collection of columns. Each column can contain different types of information. Some columns are bound to specific fields in the database in order to display and manage data from the database.

Columns can be bound to data in the record or unbound. When a column is bound to data, it means that the data is retrieved from the data source for the current record, and displayed in that column. If the GridView control allows you to edit the record, a bound column will automatically update the database with the new value for the current record.

The following is a list of column types used by the GridView control:

- **BoundFields** are used to insert a button that can activate row-specific procedures. You can modify the button's text and type using the **LinkButton** or **Button properties**. You can use the **CommandName property** to identify a procedure that is called when the button is clicked. The **ItemCommand event** is raised when any button is clicked within a GridView control.

- **TemplateFields** allows you to customize the columns in both display and edit modes.

- **HyperLinkFields** displays a hyperlink that you can customize. You can hard code the text displayed and the URL of the hyperlink, or set these properties with values from the data.

- **ButtonFields** allow you to insert buttons that will be used to execute custom commands.

- **CommandFields** contains three predefined buttons that allow you to change the mode of the row from display to edit.

- **ImageFields** allows you to bind data to image controls.

- **CheckBoxFields** allows you to customize the value as a check box.

**NOTE**

Note that in previous editions of ASP.NET these "fields" were referred to as "columns."

Bound columns are referred to as **BoundFields**. A BoundField is used to retrieve and display the data. In the previous chapter, you used BoundFields to display the data in display mode. **Display mode** is a state where you are only displaying the data. **Edit mode** allows you to modify data. In this chapter, you will work with display mode. In the next chapter, you will learn how to edit the GridView control in edit mode.

Some limited formatting with styles can be applied to the data within a BoundField. You can modify the text, font, and color of the column header and footer, the column width, and format the data. The data in the column can be set to **read-only** so that the data cannot be modified when the other fields are updated. The benefit of using BoundFields is that the GridView control maintains the connection between the field and the data. This means that you do not have to write the code to retrieve the value from the page, and then insert the value into the field in the database. This saves you programming time and will decrease the likelihood of syntax errors. With BoundFields, you can use the built-in tools to support inserting, deleting, and editing data. With unbound columns, data manipulation must be programmed manually.

## Column Properties

**BoundFields** are columns used to manage the display and updating of data in the GridView control. All BoundField columns also allow you to specify the **DataField** property, which identifies the column from the data source bound to the column, and the **DataFormatString property**, which identifies the formatting rules for the contents of the BoundField object. You must set the ReadOnly property to true for fields where you modify the DataFormatString property. The **ReadOnly property** is used with BoundField objects to stop the user from editing a column when the GridView control is in edit mode. Many times you may want to show the user data while they are editing the record, but you do not want them to be able to edit certain fields. For example, if the user will be editing customer information, you may want to display the customer identification number, but you do not want the user to be able to edit the customer identification number.

All columns within the GridView control allow you to configure the appearance of the column, along with the **HeaderText**, **HeaderImageURL**, and **FooterText properties**. You can also set the **Visible property** for a column, which allows you to show or hide the column. The **SortExpression property** can be used to identify the column from the data source that is used when sorting the column.

The **TemplateField column** is used to provide additional content, such as HTML. The column can contain bound data as well as unbound data. You can configure the **EditItemTemplate property** to be used when the GridView is in edit mode. The **HeaderTemplate** and **FooterTemplate objects** appear at the top and bottom of the TemplateField, respectively, and may contain HTML elements and controls. The **ItemTemplate column** contains HTML elements and controls within the column.

A **HyperLinkField column** is used by the GridView control to bind a hyperlink to data. It often is used to select a value, such as the CategoryID from a GridView control that displays the category list, and open a related set of data such as the list of products for a particular category. The following are some of the properties that can be configured with the HyperLinkField:

- The **Text property** identifies the text of the hyperlink, which is formatted with the **DataNavigateUrlFormatString property**.

- The **DataTextField property** is the value of the data source that is displayed as text, and is formatted by the **DataTextFormatString property**.

- The **NavigateUrl property** and the **DataNavigateUrlFields property** both identify a URL the client is redirected to when the hyperlink is clicked. If both properties are set, NavigateUrl takes precedence.

- The **Target property** identifies in which window the web page will open. The value of Target can be _Top, _New, _Parent, or _Blank.

A **ButtonField column** is used by the GridView control to insert a user-defined button. You can use the buttons for adding and deleting records, and to execute other commands. By default the buttons created for you in a ButtonField or Command column are

**LinkButtons**. They appear as hyperlinks, but have additional functionality similar to a physical button. You can also specify that the ButtonType property for the ButtonField column be **PushButton**, which means that the appearance of the button would be similar to a physical button.

## Column Data

It is important to understand how the GridView control refers to the data in case you need to access the data programmatically. In the update procedure, when you pass a request to retrieve the contents of a cell in a bound column, the request is passed as an argument. So, when you update a BoundField column, the contents of the columns are sent using **GridViewCommandEventArgs**; the arguments in the column are represented with the variable $e$. When you want to access a specific cell within a column, you must use the **Item property** of the e object. The e.Item property contains an indexed Cells collection that contains one Cell object for each column in the GridView control. The column in the GridView are numbered starting with 0. So, e.Item.Cells(0) would represent the first column in the GridView control. You may have more than one control within the cell. Template columns frequently have more than one control in a cell. For a bound control, the data is found in the first control in the Controls collection of the cell. The first control in the Controls collection of the cell is represented by 0.

The following sample code retrieves the contents as a string from the TextBox control that is displayed in the second column:

```
Sub UpdateItem(ByVal sender As Object,
   ByVal e As GridViewCommandEventArgs)
 Dim MyData As String
 Dim MyTB As TextBox
 MyTB = CType(e.Item.Cells(1).Controls(0), TextBox)
 MyData = MyTB.Text
End Sub
```

When you pass a request to retrieve the contents of a cell in a TemplateField object, the request is also passed as an argument. The e.Item property in the TemplateField object also contains an indexed Cells collection that contains one cell for each column in the GridView control. The data is contained in the controls you created within the template. Because there are multiple controls in the column, you may not know which control represents the data. You can use the **FindControl method** and the control's name to retrieve the data within the cell.

The sample code that follows retrieves the data from the TextBox control by using the Name property of the control. The name of the control requested is "ProductName," which is found in the second column of the GridView control.

```
Sub UpdateItem(ByVal sender As Object,
   ByVal e As GridViewCommandEventArgs)
Dim MyData As String
Dim box As TextBox
MyTB = CType(e.Item.Cells(1).FindControl("FirstName"),
```

9

```
    TextBox)
MyData = MyTB.text
End Sub
```

## Modifying the GridView Control Columns and Templates

In this example, the categories and products data are displayed using two different GridView objects. Each GridView is bound to a different DataSource object that was derived from the same Microsoft Access database. When the user clicks the category, the Category ID is passed in the QueryString back to the page. The other GridView control displays the list of products for that category.

In the web page, an AccessDataSource object called AccessDataSource2 is used to display the list of categories. AccessDataSource1 is used to display the list of products. The AccessDataSource1 control uses a filter to select a subset of the data that has been downloaded from the database. The CategoryID parameter passed in the QueryString is used to filter the data from the database. This is a temporary filter that can be easily inserted and removed, without having an impact on the data. This is one alternative to using parameters with a SELECT query.

The Categories GridView object uses the ItemTemplate object within the TemplateColumn object to display the categories as a hyperlink. The HyperLinkField is created using the <asp:HyperLink> <asp:HyperLink> tags. The hyperlink will refresh the current page and pass a parameter in the QueryString object. The AccessDataSource control will use the parameter from the QueryString to filter the data which will then be displayed in the Products GridView object.

1. Right-click the file **ch9_GridViewTemplate.aspx** in the Solution Explorer window and then select **View Code**.

2. Enter the code as shown in Figure 9-13 for the HyperLink tag for the Products Gridview. The code you enter will create the TemplateField column.

The zoom image and hyperlink were inserted using the TemplateField object

It is important to enter this code on a single line or the web page will not display correctly in the browser; you cannot break this code across multiple lines

The Count property of the Rows Collection within the GridView object is used to display the total number of records displayed in the FooterTemplate object

Type this code

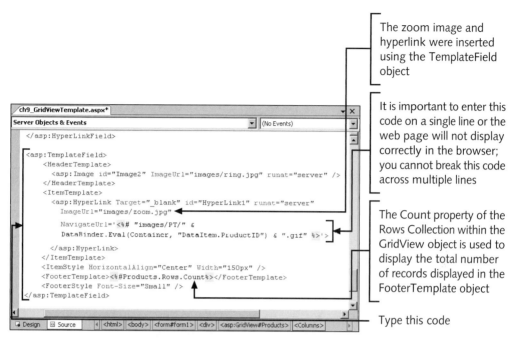

```
ch9_GridViewTemplate.aspx*
Server Objects & Events                              (No Events)
    </asp:HyperLinkField>

    <asp:TemplateField>
        <HeaderTemplate>
            <asp:Image id="Image2" ImageUrl="images/ring.jpg" runat="server" />
        </HeaderTemplate>
        <ItemTemplate>
            <asp:HyperLink Target="_blank" id="HyperLink1" runat="server"
            ImageUrl="images/zoom.jpg"
                NavigateUrl='<%# "images/PT/" &
                DataBinder.Eval(Container, "DataItem.ProductID") & ".gif" %>'>

            </asp:HyperLink>
        </ItemTemplate>
        <ItemStyle HorizontalAlign="Center" Width="150px" />
        <FooterTemplate><%#Products.Rows.Count%></FooterTemplate>
        <FooterStyle Font-Size="Small" />
    </asp:TemplateField>

Design   Source   <html> <body> <form#form1> <div> <asp:GridView#Products> <Columns>
```

**Figure 9-13**   Configuring columns in a GridView control

3. Click the **Save All** button. Right-click the page, and then click **View in Browser**. A list of 102 items are displayed.

4. Click the **JEWELRY** link. There are 15 products listed. Notice the footer displays the total number of items in the Products table, as shown in Figure 9-14.

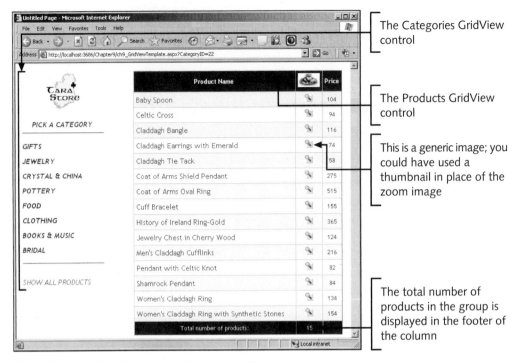

The Categories GridView control

The Products GridView control

This is a generic image; you could have used a thumbnail in place of the zoom image

The total number of products in the group is displayed in the footer of the column

**Figure 9-14**  Viewing the GridView control

5. Click the **CLOTHING** link. A list of 36 items will appear. Click the second magnifying glass. A window opens with the product thumbnail image. Close the window.

6. Click the **Dark Blue Donegal Tweed Cap** link. The ch9_Products.aspx page opens, which retrieves the QueryString object and displays the product image and product ID. Click the **Back** button.

7. Click the **SHOW ALL PRODUCTS** link. There are 444 products listed.

8. Close any open pages.

In the next section, we will move away from the display of data to selecting data. The GridView control allows you to create a column that supports selecting a single record. This information then can be used to query the database again and display the record in the DetailsView control.

# BUILDING A MASTER-DETAIL PAGE WITH GRIDVIEW AND DETAILSVIEW CONTROLS

It is very common that in a web database application, a user will want to search for a particular record, and then display details about that record. The type of web page that supports this type of display is known as a **master-detail** page. Once you learn the technique to bind a control to the value in another Data control or other source, you easily can modify the steps to work with a variety of data sources and Data controls. In a master-detail page, you configure the master control to pass the value to the detail control. Often the master control is the GridView control and the detail control is the DetailsView control.

In this section, you will learn to create and bind a drop-down list to a field. Then when the user selects a value, another list is generated. Finally, the user selects a record from a GridView control, and the specific record data is displayed in a DetailsView control. This method will also work with values that are retrieved from other sources, such as QueryString. In this example, the data and DataSource controls have already been inserted for you. You will use the Task List to configure the controls to pass the selected values so that the data can be queried again using a different parameter.

1. Right-click the **ch9_ MasterDetails.aspx** file in the Solution Explorer window, and then click **View Designer**. The AccessDataSource1 control is already configured to retrieve the categories list from the Categories table and the data is bound to the DropDownList1 control.

2. Click the **smart tasks** icon on the **AccessDataSource2** control and then select **Configure Data Source**. The TaraStore database has already been selected. Click **Next**. Click the **Next** button and then click the subsequent **Next** button.

3. In the Parameter source drop-down list, select **Control**. In the ControlID drop-down list, select **DropDownList1**, as shown in Figure 9-15. Click **Next** and then click **Finish**.

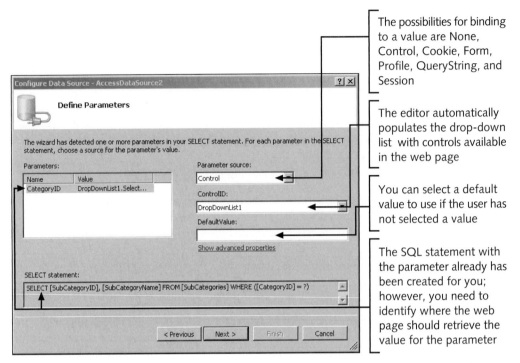

The possibilities for binding to a value are None, Control, Cookie, Form, Profile, QueryString, and Session

The editor automatically populates the drop-down list with controls available in the web page

You can select a default value to use if the user has not selected a value

The SQL statement with the parameter already has been created for you; however, you need to identify where the web page should retrieve the value for the parameter

**Figure 9-15** Binding data from a DropDownList to another DropDownList control

4. Click the **smart tasks** icon on the **AccessDataSource3** control and then select **Configure Data Source**. The TaraStore database has already been selected. Click **Next**. Click the **Next** button and then click the subsequent **Next** button.

5. In the Parameter source drop-down list, select **Control**. In the ControlID drop-down list, select **DropDownList2**. Click **Next** and then click **Finish**. (*Note*: If you are asked to Refresh Fields and DataKeys control, click **No**.)

6. Click the **smart task**s icon on the **AccessDataSource4** control and then select **Configure Data Source**. The TaraStore database already has been selected. Click **Next**. Click the **Next** button and then click the subsequent **Next** button.

7. In the column drop-down list, select **ProductID**. Leave = as the operator. In the Parameter source drop-down list, select **Control**. In the ControlID drop-down list, select **GridView1**. Click **Next** and then click **Finish**. (*Note*: If you are asked to Refresh Fields and DataKeys the control, click **No**.)

8. Click the **Save All** button. Right-click the page, and then click **View in Browser**. In the first drop-down list, select **Jewelry**. In the second drop-down list, select **Men's Jewelry**. Click the **Buy!** link in the GridView table for the

**Men's Claddagh Cufflinks**. The product information is displayed in the DetailsView control, as shown in Figure 9-16.

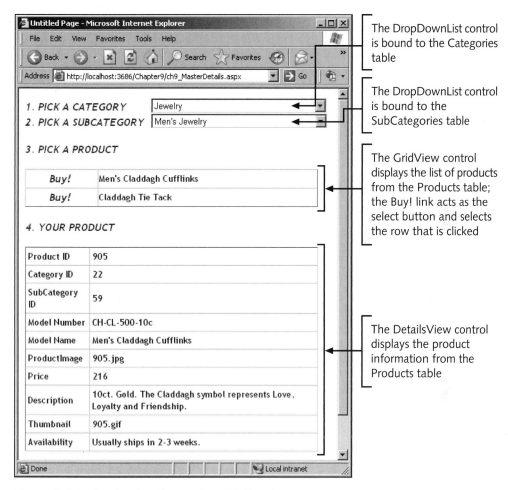

**Figure 9-16**   Previewing the master-detail web page

9. Close any open pages.

# CREATING CUSTOM TEMPLATES

It is important to be efficient when you build your web sites. You have learned how to use snippets and the Toolbox to store reusable code. Another tool to improve your efficiency with web programming is custom templates. In order to understand how to customize templates, you need to understand how templates are created and where they are stored. Visual Studio allows the user to create item templates and project templates. (*Note:* These are not the same templates that are used to configure Data controls.) Visual Studio stores user defined templates separate from the application templates. User templates are templates that are only available to the individual user. When Visual Studio was installed, a folder was created for the user; this folder contains user-specific files such as the user templates. Visual Studio stores the user defined templates at C:\Documents and Settings\[*UserName*]\My Documents\Visual Studio 2005\Templates.

Note the following:

- Item templates will appear in the list of items when you add a new item to your project. When you add an item to your project, the application will look in the C:\Program Files\Microsoft Visual Studio 8\Common7\IDE\ItemTemplates\Web\VisualBasic\1033 folder for item templates.

- Project templates will appear in the list of project types when you create a new project.

Both the ProjectTemplates folder and the ItemTemplates folder are shown in Figure 9-17.

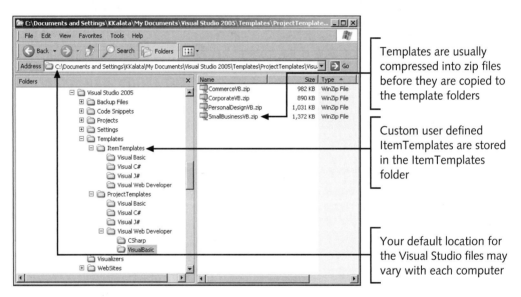

**Figure 9-17**   Visual Studio folders

In the following exercise, you will create a custom item template and use the template to create a web page in your Web application.

1. In the Solution Explorer window, right-click **ch9_CustomTemplate.aspx** and then select **View Code**.

2. Change the content in the author meta tag from *Your Name* to your real name.

3. Click the **Design** button. Right-click the **GridView** control and then select **Properties**. In the Properties window, expand the **Pager Settings** and change the Mode to **NextPreviousFirstLast**, as shown in Figure 9-18.

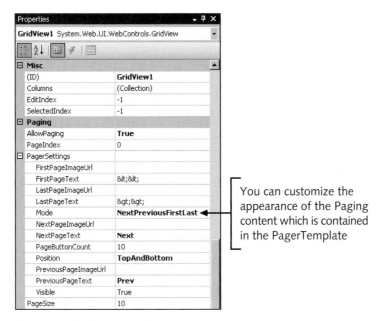

You can customize the appearance of the Paging content which is contained in the PagerTemplate

**Figure 9-18**  Pager settings

4. Click the **Save All** button. Click the **File** menu, and then select **Export Template**. Click the **Item template** radio button. Change the language category drop-down list to **Visual Basic**. Click the **Next** button.

5. Scroll up the window and click the check box labeled **ch9_CustomTemplate.aspx**. Click **Next**, and then click **Next** again.

6. Change the template name to **CustomGridView** and enter **CustomGridView** in the template description text box. Click **Finish**. Your user item templates folder will open with a CustomGridView.zip file displayed. This file contains the template. Close the window. A copy of the file also is placed in C:\Documents and Settings\[*User Name*]\My Documents\ Visual Studio 2005\My Exported Templates.

7. Right-click the **Chapter9** folder in the Solution Explorer window and then select **Add New Item**. Select **CustomGridView** and click **Add**. The CustomGridView.aspx page is added to the project and is opened for editing.

8. Close any open pages.

## CHAPTER SUMMARY

❑ The DataList, Repeater, and GridView controls use an ItemTemplate to display the values. The DataList and DataGrid controls use templates to create the header, footer, and item sections of the Data control. You can format these controls using the graphical Style Builder tool or manually. The Repeater control must be edited manually in HTML view. There is no graphical tool to edit the Repeater control.

❑ Styles are used to format the appearance of the control. You can format the control using style sheets or formatting properties within the control. You can also use individual style objects to format the controls. Templates are used to display the content within the control. There is header, footer, item, alternating item, and other specialized templates for each of the Data controls. You can modify the templates manually or using the graphical user interface within the web editor.

❑ The GridView control allows you to create a collection of bound and unbound columns. Bound columns contain a value that is bound to a value in the database. Bound columns are referred to as BoundFields. Other types of columns include HyperLinkFields and TemplateFields. TemplateFields allow you the most flexibility. Even though the column is not bound, you can still retrieve and display the data in the column.

❑ Master-detail pages provide a way to retrieve data that is based on a selection that the user makes in another Data control. The DataSource control uses this data to create a parameter query and binds the new data set to the Data control. Other types of data, such as a QueryString or session parameter, can also be used as a parameter for the DataSource control.

## REVIEW QUESTIONS

1. Which of the following Data controls cannot be used to display data in a web page?
   a. DataList
   b. DataView
   c. GridView
   d. Repeater

2. Which Data control displays one value at a time?
   a. ListBox
   b. DropDownList
   c. DataList
   d. DataGrid

3. Which property of the Data control identifies where to get its data?
   a. DataView
   b. DataSource
   c. DataTable
   d. DataTextField

4. What property allows you to format a value in a field as currency?

a. FormatCurrency

b. Format $C

c. DataTextFormatString

d. DataTextField

5. Which property is used to identify the column to be displayed in a DropDownList control?

a. DataValueField

b. DataTextFormat

c. DataTextFormatString

d. DataTextField

6. Which property must be set to False before you can change the displayed GridView columns?

a. AutoFormatColumns

b. FormatColumns

c. AutoDataColumns

d. AutoGenerateColumns

7. What ASP.NET tag is used to format a bound column in a GridView control?

a. <asp:BoundField>

b. <Columns>

c. <ASP:Columns>

d. <asp:BoundColumn>

8. Which template includes the values from the database?

a. HeaderTemplate

b. FooterTemplate

c. AlternatingTemplate

d. ItemTemplate

9. In the template that contains the value, which expression returns a value from a column named "thumbnail"?

a. <%# Container.DataItem("thumbnail") %>

b. <%# Columns.DataItem("thumbnail") %>

c. <%# Columns ("thumbnail") %>

d. <%# Columns.thumbnail %>

**9**

10. Which template allows you to configure the columns in edit mode?

a. EditTemplate

b. ItemTemplate

c. EditItemTemplate

d. EditColumn

11. Which style is used to format every other row of data in a GridView control?

a. AlternatingItemStyle

b. AlternatingRowStyle

c. ItemStyle

d. RowStyle

12. Which style is used to format the page navigation controls with GridView and DataList controls?

a. SelectedItemStyle

b. EditItemTemplate

c. PagerStyle

d. PageTemplate

13. Which property identifies a URL the client is redirected to when the HyperLinkField is clicked?

a. Target property

b. DataNavigateURLFormatString

c. DataTextField

d. DataNavigateURLFields

14. What type of column allows you to customize the column and insert custom commands?

a. BoundFields

b. CommandFields

c. HyperlinkFields

d. TemplateFields

15. A(n) _____ object is used by the GridView control to insert a user-defined button?

a. ButtonField

b. EditCommandColumn

c. HyperLinkButton

d. ButtonType

16. What property is used to create a temporary filter for the data returned by the SQL query?

    a. FilterRows

    b. FilterExpression

    c. EditParameter

    d. Filter

17. Which data source cannot be used to bind to a DataSource using the GridView Tasks?

    a. Control

    b. Cookie

    c. Profile

    d. Application

18. Which data source can be used to bind to a DataSource to the value passed in the address bar in the browser?

    a. Session

    b. QueryString

    c. Form

    d. None

19. What is the name of the mode that is a state where you are only displaying the data?

    a. Edit mode

    b. Read-only

    c. Static mode

    d. Display mode

20. The appearance and content of a Data control can be configured with which of the following tools?

    a. Styles

    b. Templates

    c. Cascading Style Sheets

    d. all of the above

21. Choose two Data controls and compare the styles, templates, and columns available.

22. Discuss how you would setup Visual Studio to enable developers to share templates.

23. Describe five types of objects that can be passed as parameters to an SQL query.

24. Compare five similarities and five differences between styles and templates.

25. Describe four types of columns available to the GridView control.

26. Which Data control(s) would you use for inserting new records? Explain why.

27. Which Data control(s) would you use for editing existing records? Explain why.

28. Describe how to refer in code to the control in the third column named "ClientName."

29. If you were the architect for a Web application, how would you setup the web site to maintain the same presentation layer throughout the site for all the Data controls?

30. Describe the purpose of a master–detail page.

---

## Hands-On Projects

**HANDS-ON PROJECTS**

### Project 9-1

In this project, you will create a web page that binds a database to a DataList control. You will modify the Repeater control using templates. The Residential database is located in the App_Data folder. The images are in the ../images/residential folder.

1. Start your web editor and open your **Chapter9** solution if necessary. Add a web page named **ch9_proj1.aspx**.

2. Create the data source to the **Residential** table. Make sure to change the SQL Select statement to choose all the records in the **residential** table that are **houses** with **5** or **6 bedrooms**. (*Hint:* When you select the parameter, pick **None**, and enter **5** in the Parameter Properties Value text box. Then, go back and add another parameter and enter **6** in the Parameter Properties Value text box. You will have to change the keyword AND to **OR** in the SELECT statement in code view.)

3. In Design view of the web page, add a **DataList** control to the page. Assign the DataSourceID to the **AccessDataSource1** control. Set the RepeatColumns to **3** and RepeatDirection to **Horizontal**. Set the ItemStyle-VerticalAlign to **Top** and ItemStyle-HorizontalAlign to **Left**.

4. Insert a **HeaderTemplate** that contains an image **800** pixels wide and is located at **../images/560green.gif**. Insert a **FooterTemplate** that contains an image **800** pixels wide and is located at **../images/560green.gif**.

5. Insert an **ItemTemplate**. Display the image of the houses using the **HousePicture** field. The image width is **250** and height is **150** pixels. You can set the properties with the Style Property Builder in the Properties window. Insert the **HouseID**, **Bedrooms**, **Bath**, **Price**, **State**, and **Agent** information. Format the appearance of the labels, as shown in Figure 9-19. Format the price as currency. When you modify the DataFormatString property for a field, you must set the ReadOnly property to true. Format the font style as **Arial** and **small**.

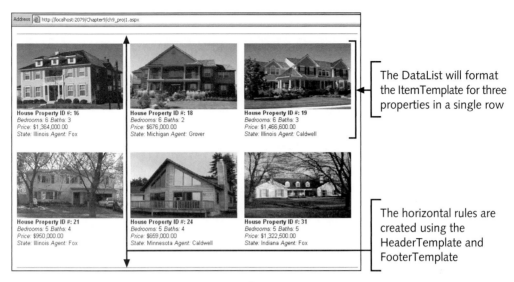

The DataList will format the ItemTemplate for three properties in a single row

The horizontal rules are created using the HeaderTemplate and FooterTemplate

**Figure 9-19**   Formatting a DataList control in Project 9-1

   a.  Modify the page by adding your own formatting styles and additional content.

   b.  Save your page and view your web page in the browser.

**HANDS-ON PROJECTS**

## Project 9-2

In this project, you will create a web page that binds a database to a GridView control. You will modify the GridView control using templates. The Residential database is located in the App_Data folder. The images are in the ../images/residential folder. You will create a TemplateField that contains a hyperlink. When the user clicks the hyperlink, an image of the house will be displayed.

1.  Start your web editor and open your **Chapter9** solution, if necessary. Add a web page named **ch9_proj2.aspx**.

2.  Create the data source to the **Residential** table. Make sure to change the SQL Select statement to choose all the records in the **residential** table. Insert a **GridView** control that uses the data source and **enable paging**.

3.  To open the Fields dialog box, click the Smart Tasks of the GridView control and then select **Edit Columns**. Change the **HousePicture** bound field to unbound **TemplateField**, as shown in Figure 9-20, and then click **OK**.

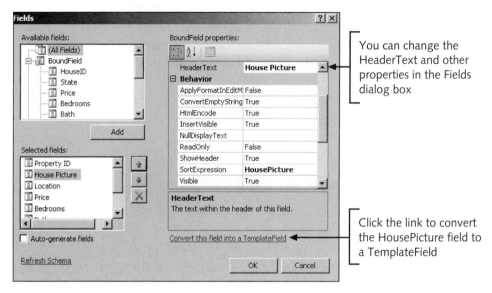

You can change the HeaderText and other properties in the Fields dialog box

Click the link to convert the HousePicture field to a TemplateField

**Figure 9-20**    Formatting a DataList control in Project 9-2

4. Click the **Source** tab to edit the code. Delete the entire **EditItemTemplate**. Change the Label control to a **Hyperlink** control. Change the Text property to use the **DataBinder.Eval** instead of Bind method. Change the **NavigateUrl** property to the path of the HousePicture image. (*Hint*: You can concatenate the image page (../images/residential/) and the HousePicture value. You can retrieve the value using the DataBinder.Eval method and passing the DataItem.HousePicture value as you did earlier in the chapter.)

5. Modify the page by adding your own formatting styles and additional content.

6. Save your page and view your web page in the browser.

HANDS-ON PROJECTS

## Project 9-3

In this project, you will create a master-detail page. The Residential database is located in the App_Data folder. The images are in the ../images/residential folder. The page will display the type of housing first, either apartments, or houses. After the user makes their selection, they are provided a list of the states where there are houses for sale. When the user selects a state, a list of houses appears, sorted by price. The user can click the house, and view a picture of the house and details about the house such as the number of bedrooms and baths.

1. Start your web editor and open your **Chapter9** solution, if necessary. Add a web page named **ch9_proj3.aspx**.

2. Create four data source objects that connect to the **Residential** table. The **AccessDataSource1** will retrieve all the records for types of housing using the **ClassifyHA** field. You must bind the value in the Housing DropDownList1 control. **AccessDataSource2** will retrieve all the records for the states where housing is available

using the **State** field. You must bind the State to the **DropDownList2** control. Then, you will use the state value to create the parameter for the **AccessDataSource3** control, which will retrieve all of the properties in the state for that type of housing. Then you will use the house ID parameter to retrieve the data on a specific house. (*Hint:* You will have to retrieve the value for both the RadioButtonList controls.) Use the **AccessDataSource4** control to bind to the Data control. You will then use the value the user selected to view the property details including a picture. (*Hint:* The picture is created within a TemplateField object.)

3. Create the labels and two RadioButtonList controls. Bind the RadioButtonList controls to the **AccessDataSource1** and **AccessDataSource2** controls. Create a GridView and DetailsView control and bind them to the **AccessDataSource3** and **AccessDataSource4** controls. Change the HeaderText of the columns so the heading is clear, and format the price as currency. Remember that you must set the ReadOnly property to **true** for fields that you modify the DataFormatString property.

4. Change the HousePicture field in the DetailsView control to a **TemplateField**. Remove the **InsertItemTemplate** and **EditItemTemplate**. Change the Text property to **AlternateText**. Insert the **ImageUrl** property and set it to the path to **../images/residential/** concatenated with the value returned from the **HousePicture**.

5. Modify the page by adding your own formatting styles and additional content. You may use a table to layout the controls. A sample of what your page may look like is in Figure 9-21.

6. Save your page and view your web page in the browser.

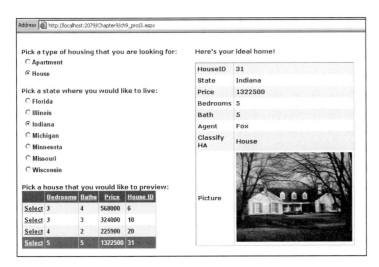

**Figure 9-21**    Formatting a DataList control in Project 9-3

## CASE PROJECTS

### Project 9-1

Your boss has asked you to create a shopping cart application. In the first phase, you must create a database named Ch9_Case1 that contains the product information. Place the database in your project data directory. You can use SQL Server, Access, or another database application to create the database. Include the name of the product, price, description, product ID, and product image name. Insert some sample data. Create a web page that displays the data using a GridView control. Format the GridView control using the Property Builder, styles, and Cascading Style Sheets. Format the GridView control using the header, footer, item, and alternating row templates. Change the font color, background color, cell alignment, font name, and font size for HeaderTemplate and ItemTemplate for each of the columns. Change the background color of the alternating rows. Add headings, graphics, fonts, and colors to enhance the appearance of the page. Save the page as Ch9_Case1.aspx. Print the web page and the source code.

### Project 9-2

Your boss has asked you to create a shopping cart application. In the first phase, you must create a database named Ch9_Case2 that contains the product information. Place the database in your project data directory. You can use SQL Server, Access, or another database application to create the database. Include the name of the product, price, description, product ID, and product image name. (*Note:* If you created the database in the previous case, you can reuse that database.) Insert some sample data. Create a web page that displays the data using a DataList control. Format the DataList control using the header, footer, item, separator, and alternating item templates. Change the font color, background color, cell alignment, font name, and font size for the HeaderTemplate and the ItemTemplate for each of the columns. Change the background color of the alternating rows. Change the display so that there are always two columns of data displayed on one page. Add headings, graphics, fonts, and colors to enhance the appearance of the page. Save the page as Ch9_Case2.aspx. Print the web page and the source code.

### Project 9-3

Create a database named Ch9_Case3 that contains your data. Place the database in your project data directory. You can use SQL Server, Access, or another database application to create the database. Insert some sample data. Create a web page that displays the data using a GridView control. Format the GridView control using the header, footer, item, and alternating row templates. Change the font color, background color, cell alignment, font name, and font size for the HeaderTemplate and the ItemTemplate for each of the columns. Include a custom template column, command column, hyperlink column, and button column. Change the background color of the alternating rows. Add headings, graphics, fonts, and colors to enhance the appearance of the page. Save the page as Ch9_Case3.aspx. Print the web page and the source code.

## Project 9-4

Your boss has asked you to create a web page that retrieves the customers from the CustomerService database. The database is located in your App_Data folder. Select a Data control to display the list of customers by last name alphabetically in ascending order. Based on the value the user selected, display the products that the customer has purchased using a DetailsView control. Create a second page that displays the product names. Based on the user's selection, display the versions that are still supported using a DetailsView control. Format the GridView and DetailsView controls using style sheets, styles, and templates. Change the font color, background color, cell alignment, font name, and font size for the HeaderTemplate and the ItemTemplate for each of the columns and labels. Change the background color of the alternating rows. Add headings, graphics, fonts, and colors to enhance the appearance of the page. Save the pages as Ch9_Case4a.aspx and Ch9_Case4b. aspx. Print the web pages and the source code.

9

CHAPTER

# 10

# MANAGING DATA
# WITH ASP.NET

**In this chapter, you will:**

- ◆ Insert, modify, and delete records using the GridView, DetailsView, and FormView controls
- ◆ Use stored procedures and parameter collections to manage inserting, modifying, and deleting data
- ◆ Insert, modify, and delete other types of data using Data controls
- ◆ Provide security for your data, maintain data integrity, and detect database errors

**W**eb data management is an ever-evolving component of web development. Businesses must quickly create Web data-driven applications that display data, allow the user to customize the data displayed, allow the administrator to manage the data remotely, and provide data security. Data security includes data integrity, as well as preventing unauthorized access. The .NET Framework provides new data objects that you can use to manage your data connections, and new Data controls that you can use to manage your data within the web page. These new Data controls can also be used to allow the end user to manipulate the data from the web page. In this chapter, you will learn how to insert, modify, and delete records using the GridView and FormView controls. You will learn how to manage your data using stored procedures and Data controls. You will also learn methods that can be used to secure your data and identify database errors.

## INSERTING, MODIFYING, AND DELETING RECORDS

To maintain a database you must be able to create new records, modify existing records, and delete records. You can accomplish this by using SQL commands or by using the methods built into the Data controls. You either can use the Command Builder method built into the GridView, DataList, and Repeater controls to help you build methods and procedures to maintain the database, or you can create your own methods to interact with the Data controls and database.

## Using the GridView Control to Maintain a Database

The GridView control allows you to bind data to the columns in the database. You can use the GridView control to insert, modify, and delete data. In the last chapter, you learned that the GridView control allows you to create columns such as the BoundField, TemplateField, ButtonField, CommandField, and HyperLinkField columns. The GridView control contains properties such as AutoGenerateDeleteButton, AutoGenerateEditButton, and AutoGenerateSelectButton that when set to True, will insert a delete, edit, or select button at the beginning of each row. These buttons have built-in properties and methods that will be used to manage the database.

Remember that when a request is made to retrieve the contents of a cell in a bound column, the request is passed as an argument. When the GridView control creates the table, each item in the cell is a control. In a bound column, there is only one control. By default when you use bound columns, the input editing is automatically performed using text boxes. The **InsertItemTemplate template** is used to display the bound data in a read-only format. You can modify the template to change how the data is displayed, however. The **EditItemTemplate template** is used to format the controls that are available in edit mode. You can modify the controls used to edit the field using different Web controls by manually modifying the EditItemTemplate template. For example, for a column named chkActive that contains Boolean data, it may be fine to display the values True and False to the user. When the user wants to edit the row of data, however, the user should be able to click a check box or radio button. The user should not have to type True or False. The GridView control provides a CommandField column that can be used to include hyperlink buttons that will be used to select a row. Two styles often used with the GridView control in edit mode are the SelectedItemStyle and EditItemStyle. The **SelectedItemStyle** identifies the style for the currently selected row. The **EditItemStyle** identifies the style for the row that is currently being edited.

In ASP.NET 1.1, the DataGrid control was used to display and manage data in a table structure. Filtering, sorting, and searching within the control, however, required significant additional programming. In ASP.NET 2.0, the GridView control replaces the DataGrid control. While the DataGrid control is maintained for backwards compatibility, you should use the GridView control in all new Web applications. The GridView control is more stable and does not require extensive programming code to filter and search within the control.

The GridView control allows you to support sorting of data automatically from many DataSource objects without extensive programming.

## Filtering Data with the GridView Control

A common scenario is to want to pass the value of a control as the parameter to the SQL query. In previous versions of ASP, programmers concatenated values with the SQL clause. Although you can still manually create a concatenated SQL query, new ways to filter data were built into the DataSource control. In the last chapter, you learned that the parameter for a select query could be set to the value of a control. Parameters passed to the Select statement are called SelectParameter objects and are collectively called the SelectParameters collection. There are also InsertParameter, UpdateParameter, DeleteParameter, and FilterParameter objects for the insert, update, delete, and filter queries. These parameter objects are properties of the DataSource control. Therefore, the parameters are written in code as child elements of the DataSource object. It's important to understand that the FilterParameter collection is applied after the data has been retrieved from the data from the database. The parameters defined within the SelectParameters, InsertParameter, UpdateParameter, and DeleteParameter collections are applied at the database before the database records are retrieved.

The value of a drop-down list was used as the value of the SelectParameter object. To use a value from a control such as a drop-down list or text box, you configure the ControlParameter property of the Parameter object allowed to the value of the control. Each of these Parameter objects is stored in a collection. For example, the parameter value was passed to the SelectParameter object in the SelectParameters collection. Although there can be multiple collections of Parameter objects, you will only be working with individual Parameter objects such as the ControlParameter object and FilterParameter object. You can retrieve the parameter from the value from any of the following sources:

- **ControlParameter:** Allows you to retrieve the value from a property of a server control on a web page using the PropertyName property.

- **CookieParameter:** Allows you to retrieve the value from an HTTP cookie using the CookieName property.

- **FormParameter:** Allows you to retrieve the value from a form control on a web page using the FormField property.

- **ProfileParameter:** Allows you to retrieve the value from the user profile using the ParameterName property.

- **QueryStringParameter:** Allows you to retrieve the value from a QueryString using the QueryStringField property.

- **SessionParameter:** Allows you to retrieve the value from a Session variable using the SessionField property.

All parameters have a **Name property** to identify the property. Each parameter identifies the data type with the **Type property**. For example, a text box may pass the value as a string type, or convert the string to an integer and pass the value as an int32 type. The type must correspond to typed defined to the corresponding fields in the database.

In the following exercise, you will use the select records displayed in a GridView control based on the value selected from a drop-down list.

1. Open the **Chapter10** project with your web editor if necessary.

2. Right-click the **ch10_GridViewFilter1.aspx** page in the Solution Explorer window and then select **View Code**. Locate the SQL statement for the AccessDataSource2 control. Notice that the clause WHERE ([LastName] = ?) is used to identify the parameter.

3. Type the code as shown in Figure 10-1 to create the ControlParameter parameter.

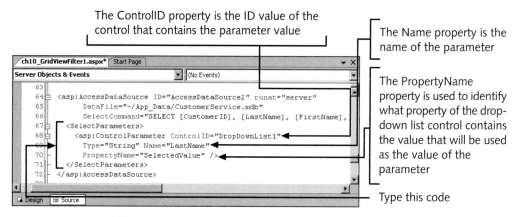

**Figure 10-1** Select data using a ControlParameter parameter

4. Click the **Save All** icon. Right-click the **ch10_ GridViewFilter1.aspx** page in the Solution Explorer window and then select **View in Browser**. In the drop-down list, select **Morgan**. The data for the customer is displayed in the GridView control.

5. Close the browser and the page in your editor.

**TIP**

You can pass a parameter value to a SQL query by concatenating the value to the SQL statement. Alternatively, the FilterParameter property and the FilterExpression property of the DataSource control can be used to identify the parameter or expression used to filter the data. The **FilterExpression property** is set to the value of a valid SQL WHERE clause without the WHERE keyword such as `"CategoryID = '"` & `CatID.ToString` & `"'"`. For this example the code that would be inserted into the page would be `FilterExpression =` `"CategoryID = '"` & `CatID.ToString` & `"'"`. The FilterExpression property uses the same syntax as the RowFilter property of the DataView object that you learned about in Chapter 8. You only need to enclose a string within a pair of single quotation marks. This filter is then applied to the data. Be cautious when entering concatenated SQL statements. It is easy to mistake where a single or double quotation is located. Let's look at the SQL statement, `"CategoryID = '"` & `CatID.ToString` & `"'"`. In this example, the single quotation mark follows the equal sign and a double quotation mark follows the single quotation mark. At the end of the statement, a single quotation mark is surrounded by a pair of double quotation marks. When the CategoryID is 21, the concatenated SQL statement should read CategoryID = '21'.

**10**

The **FilterParameter object** is set to the value of a parameter used in a FilterExpression. The FilterParameter is defined in the DataSource control as a Parameter object. Both the FilterExpression property and FilterParameter object can be defined within the DataSource object or programmatically. Both of these properties are applied to a parameter that is defined in the FilterParameter collection of the DataSource object. In other words, a SQL query can have multiple Parameter objects that are stored in a Parameter collection.

Filtering data only is supported if the Select statement returns a DataSet, DataTable, or DataView object but not with the DataReader object. When filtering is applied to a DataSource object, a filtering event occurs. You can intercept the filtering event and create your own custom event handler and set the filter parameters programmatically. You must combine the use of the FilterExpression property and FilterParameter object. The Filter-Expression property would set the value of the parameter to the name of a parameter. With SQL Server, the name of the parameter may be preceded with the @ symbol. In the previous example, the code to insert a parameter as the FilterExpression property would be `FilterExpression = "CategoryID = @CatID"`. You also could have inserted the parameter directly into Select statement such as `"SELECT * FROM Categories WHERE CategoryID = @CatID"`. (*Note:* You can optionally place square brackets ([ ]) around column names in SQL queries.)

**TIP**

Microsoft Access uses the question mark to represent the name for unnamed parameters. Therefore the Name attribute refers to the database column that the parameter applies to. The @ symbol is used to identify parameters in SQL Server databases.

Alternatively, you can pass an anonymous parameter placeholder, such as the question mark. However, you would have to be careful when using multiple parameters to identify the correct order that the parameters should be inserted into the SQL query. In the previous example, the code to insert a parameter as the FilterExpression property would be `FilterExpression = "CategoryID = ?"`.

When you retrieve a value from a control such as a drop-down list that allows you to select multiple values, multiple values may be passed as parameters. You can identify the order of the parameters using the syntax `{'i'}` where i represents the sequential order of the parameter. In the previous example, to select the first item selected in the drop-down list, the FilterExpression would be written as `FilterExpression = "CategoryID = '{0}'"`. You can also use complex expressions such as `FilterExpression=" CategoryName LIKE '{0}' AND SubCategoryName LIKE '{1}'"`.

After creating the FilterExpression property, you would use the FilterParameters property to create your parameters. The FilterParameters property identifies where the parameter values are retrieved. You can also identify the value for the parameter by programmatically assigning a value to the FilterParameter object. In the previous example, to retrieve the value from the CategoryID control the code would be `<asp:ControlParameter Name="CategoryID" ControlID="CategoryID" PropertyName="SelectedValue" />`. Notice that the value for the PropertyName property was assigned to the SelectedValue property of the CategoryID DropDownList control. However, you can assign the value to any of the properties of a control.

In the following exercise, you will use the GridView control to filter records using the FilterExpression property and the FilterParameter object. The first two examples use the AccessDataSource control to retrieve data from the CustomerService.mdb database and the last example uses the SqlDataSource control to retrieve data from the Residential.mdf database.

1. Right-click the **ch10_GridViewFilter2.aspx** page in the Solution Explorer window and then select **View in Browser**. All of the data for the customers in the CustomerService.mdb database is displayed. Close the browser window.

2. Right-click the **ch10_GridViewFilter2.aspx** page in the Solution Explorer window and then select **View Code**. (*Note*: Because there is no code file, the Markup view for the page is displayed.)

3. Type the code as shown in Figure 10-2 to create the FilterExpression parameter. The code should be inserted above the Select statement.

4. Click the **Save All** icon. Right-click the **ch10_GridViewFilter2.aspx** page in the Solution Explorer window and then select **View in Browser**. Only the data for the customer named Slater is displayed in the GridView control. Close the browser window.

5. Right-click the **ch10_GridViewFilter3.aspx** page in the Solution Explorer window and then select **View Code**. Type the code as shown in Figure 10-3 to create the Parameter object in the FilterParameters property.

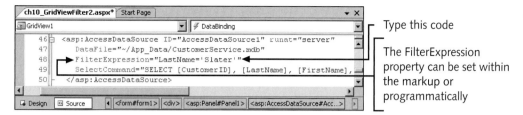

**Figure 10-2**    Filter data using a FilterExpression property

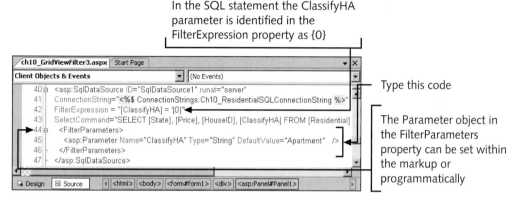

**Figure 10-3**    Select data using a Parameter object in the FilterParameters property

6. Click the **Save All** icon. Right-click the **ch10_GridViewFilter3.aspx** page in the Solution Explorer window and then select **View in Browser**. Only the data for the housing classification as Apartment is displayed in the GridView control.

7. Close the browser and the page in your editor.

**TIP**
In this example the Price was formatted using `DataFormatString="({0:C0})"`. The additional 0 after the C meant that the decimals were dropped from the formatted display. If you want to convert the bound column, which contains a non-string data type such as DateTime or a Decimal to other formats, you need to first set the HtmlEncode property to False for that BoundField. By default for bound columns the HtmlEncode property is set to True. The Html-Encode property converts the value of the cell to a string before the Data-FormatString is applied.

# Sorting Data with the GridView Control

The GridView control can easily be configured to support sorting data from the DataSource object by setting the AllowSorting property to True. By default, each column heading in the GridView control will be displayed as a hyperlink when sorting is enabled. When the user clicks the hyperlink, the data in the GridView control is sorted by that column in ascending order. Clicking the hyperlink a second time sorts the data in descending order.

By default, the GridView control displays all the columns retrieved from the DataSource object. You can display only a selected list of columns by changing the AutoGenerateColumns property of the GridView control to False. Then insert bound columns using the BoundFields controls. For each of the bound columns, set the DataField property to the name of the column in the DataSource object. Then, for each bound column in the GridView control assign the SortExpression property to the name of the column that you want to be sorted. Usually the value of the SortExpression property is the same as the DataField property.

In the following exercise, you will use the built-in methods of the GridView control to sort records.

1. Open the **Chapter10** project in your web editor if necessary.

2. Right-click the **ch10_GridViewSort.aspx** page in the Solution Explorer window and then select **View in Browser**. The data is sorted by the CustomerID values. The column headings are text labels. Close the browser window.

3. Right-click the **ch10_GridViewSort.aspx** page in the Solution Explorer window and then select **View in Designer**. Click the <smart> tag on the GridView object. In the GridView Tasks window, click the check box next to **Enable Sorting**.

4. Click the **Save All** icon. Right-click the **ch10_GridViewSort.aspx** page in the Solution Explorer window and then select **View in Browser**. The column headings now are all hypertext links.

5. Click the **Customer ID** column heading. The customers are sorted based on that column in ascending order. Click the **Customer ID** column heading again. The customers are sorted based on that column in descending order.

6. Close the browser and the page in your editor.

## Editing a New Record with the GridView Control

You can write custom code to insert, edit, or delete records, or you can use the methods built into the Data controls. In the following exercise, you will use the built-in methods of the GridView control to modify records.

1. Right-click the **ch10_GridViewEdit1.aspx** page in the Solution Explorer window and select **View in Designer**.

2. Click the <smart> tag to open the Task List for the **AccessDataSource1** control and select Configure Data Source. The TaraStore database already is selected. Click **Next**. Make sure the **Categories** table is selected in the drop-down list. Click the check box for the asterisk (*   ). Click the **Advanced** button. Click the first and second check box. The first check box will create the procedures and SQL statements for inserting, deleting, and modifying records in the Categories table. The editor will insert the code to create the parameters and the

SQL statements. (*Note:* You can remove the code for InsertParameters, InsertCommand, DeleteParameters, and DeleteCommand if you do not allow insertion or deletion of records using the GridView control.) The second check box is used to maintain data integrity and prevent others from modifying the data while you are editing the record. The check box will not become active until you check the first check box. Click **OK**, click **Next**, and then click **Finish**.

3. Click the <smart> tag to open the Task List for the **GridView** control and then click Auto Format. Select the **Mocha** scheme and click **OK**.

4. Click the <smart> tag to open the Task List for the **GridView** control and then in the Choose Data Source text box select **AccessDataSource1** from the drop-down list. Then, click the check box labeled **Enable Editing**. This inserts a CommandField that contains hyperlinks for editing, deleting, and canceling your editing requests. Then, click the **Edit Columns** hyperlink. In the lower-left text box, click **Edit, Update, Cancel**. The properties for this CommandField column appear in the right of the window. Change the ButtonType property from Link to **Button** as shown in Figure 10-4. Click **OK**.

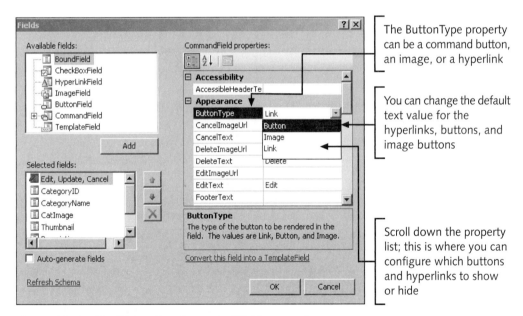

**Figure 10-4**   Modifying the CommandField properties

5. Click the **Save All** icon. Right-click the page in the Solution Explorer window and then select **View in Browser**. Click the **Edit** button for the Bridal category. Change the value of the description to **Bridal Gifts** as shown in Figure 10-5. Click the **Update** button. The change should be immediately displayed in the table.

When editing a GridView control it is useful to
display each row using a different style to prevent
users from selecting the wrong row

You can set the ReadOnly
property for any column
to True to prevent the user
from modifying the values

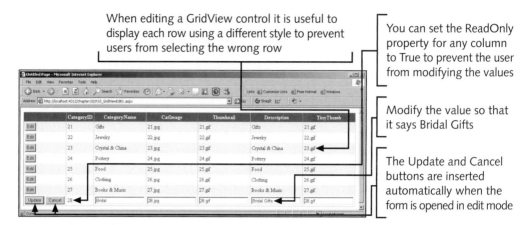

Modify the value so that
it says Bridal Gifts

The Update and Cancel
buttons are inserted
automatically when the
form is opened in edit mode

**Figure 10-5**    Using the GridView control to modify data

In the following exercise, you will convert a BoundField to a TemplateField.

1. Right-click the **ch10_GridViewEdit2.aspx** page in the Solution Explorer
   window and select **View in Designer**.

2. Click the <smart> tag to open the Task List for the **GridView** control and
   then select **Edit Columns**. Click the **Thumbnail** field in the lower-left text
   box and then click the hyperlink labeled **Convert this field into a
   TemplateField**. Click **OK**.

3. Click the **Source** tab. Locate the **ItemTemplate** for the Thumbnail
   TemplateField. Delete the Label control in the ItemTemplate. Enter the code
   for the Image control in the ItemTemplate as shown in Figure 10-6.

The Eval method is used here for the Text property; the Bind method
is used in the template for two-way data binding for updating the
database when the value has been changed; if you modify the
format for the control, you can pass the formatting method directly
with the Eval method; you will also need to set the HtmlEncode
property to False in order to use this formatting method

Type this code

**Figure 10-6**    Modifying the ItemTemplate of the GridView control

4. Let's modify the EditItemTemplate to allow you to select the value from a
   drop-down list. Click the **Design** tab. Click the <smart> tag to open the Task
   List for the GridView. Click **Edit Templates**. Change the Display drop-down

list from ItemTemplate to **EditItemTemplate**. Delete the Textbox control from the template window. Drag a **DropDownList** control onto the template window from the Toolbox as shown in Figure 10-7.

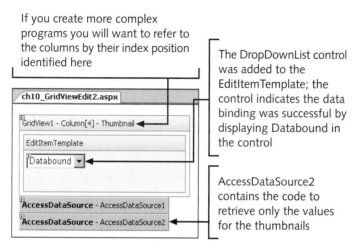

If you create more complex programs you will want to refer to the columns by their index position identified here

The DropDownList control was added to the EditItemTemplate; the control indicates the data binding was successful by displaying Databound in the control

AccessDataSource2 contains the code to retrieve only the values for the thumbnails

ch10_GridViewEdit2.aspx

GridView1 - Column[4] - Thumbnail

EditItemTemplate

Databound

AccessDataSource - AccessDataSource1
AccessDataSource - AccessDataSource2

**10**

**Figure 10-7**    Modifying the EditItemTemplate of the GridView control

5. In the task list, click **Choose Data Source**. In the first drop-down list, select **AccessDataSource2** as the data source. Click **OK**. (*Note:* The Thumbnail field will be populated into the other two drop-down lists. These are used to determine the value to display and send from the drop-down list. If the Thumbnail field does not appear, click the Refresh Schema hyperlink or select it from the drop-down lists. If you view the source code, you will see that this simply added the DataTextField, DataValueField, and DataSourceID properties to the DropDownList control. This could also have manually been inserted.)

6. Click the <smart> tag to open the task list for the DropDownList. Click **Edit DataBindings**. Click the **Refresh Schema** hyperlink. In the Field binding Bound to drop-down list, select **Thumbnail** as shown in Figure 10-8. Verify that the **Two-way databinding** check box is checked. Click **OK**.

7. Click the <smart> tag to open the task list for the GridView control. Click **End Template Editing**.

8. Click the **Save All** icon. Right-click the page in the Solution Explorer window and then select **View in Browser**. Notice the thumbnail images are displayed. Click the **Edit** button for the Bridal category. Change the value of the thumbnail from 28.gif to **21.gif** in the drop-down list as shown in Figure 10-9. Click the **Update** button. (*Note:* The change should be immediately displayed in the table. This only changes the value in the table. It does not remove the image from the web site. You cannot insert the value back into the list using this method. You can use a text box when you want them to be able to modify the values in the control.)

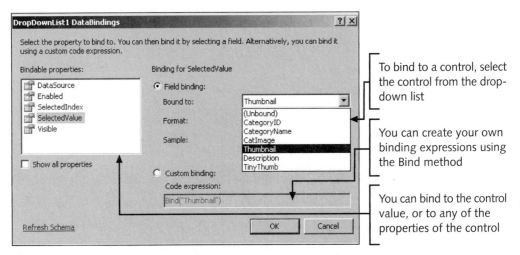

**Figure 10-8**    Modifying the EditItemTemplate of the GridView control

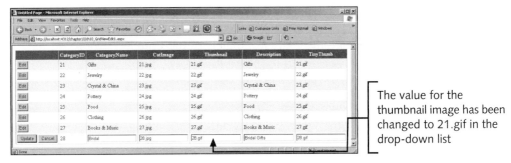

**Figure 10-9**    Using the DropDownList for editing a GridView control

9. Click the **Edit** button for the Bridal category. Notice that you do not have the option to choose 28.gif because the drop-down list retrieved the value from the table.

10. Right-click the **ch10_GridViewEdit1.aspx** page in the Solution Explorer window and then select **View in Browser**. Click the **Edit** button for the Bridal category. Change the value of the thumbnail to **28.gif**. Click the **Update** button and the data should be changed in the table.

11. Close the browser and any open pages in your editor.

In this example, you used the graphical user interface and modified the code to use the Bind method to bind the data to the control. You could also have written this code in the web page, however.

You do not always have to use a TemplateField to bind to alternative controls. You can insert other types of controls to bind to data, such as the **CheckBoxField** control directly in the Columns collection. Simply identify the field to bind to by using the **DataField** property of the control.

```
<asp:CheckBoxField HeaderText="Contract" DataField="contract" />
```

You do not have to specify the parameters on the parameter collection of a data source control when you are using the graphical tools to help build your queries and bind the controls.

## Deleting a New Record with the GridView Control

You can write code to delete records in the GridView control, as shown in the following exercise. This process is similar to editing the GridView control.

1. Right-click the **ch10_GridViewDelete.aspx** page in the Solution Explorer window and select **View in Designer**. The GridView and AccessDataSource controls already have been inserted for you.

2. Click the <smart> tag to open the Task List for the GridView control. Click **Enable Editing** and **Enable Deleting**.

3. Click the **Save All** icon. Right-click the page in the Solution Explorer window and then select **View in Browser**.

4. Click the **Delete** hyperlink for the Bridal category. The record should be deleted immediately. Close the browser window and the web page in your editor.

Although you can create code to insert a new record with the GridView control, the **ShowInsertButton** for the control is set to False by default. Using the insert methods with the GridView control would require additional programming and is not as flexible as using the DetailsView control to insert a new record. The controls were purposely designed to work together. Therefore in the next section, you will work with the DetailsView control to insert a new record.

## Inserting a New Record with the DetailsView Control

You can write code to insert or delete records, or you can use the methods built into the Data controls. The DetailsView control is essentially the same as the GridView control, except it only displays one record at a time. In the following exercise, you use the DetailsView control to create new records.

1. Right-click the **ch10_DetailsViewInsert.aspx** page icon in the Solution Explorer window and select **View in Designer**.

2. Click the <smart> tag to open the Task List for the DetailsView control. Click the **Enable Paging**, **Enable Inserting**, **Enable Editing**, and **Enable Deleting** check boxes. Notice that a new set of hyperlink controls is enabled at the bottom of the control.

3. Click the **Save All** icon. Right-click the page in the Solution Explorer window and then select **View in Browser**.

4. In the browser, click the **New** hyperlink. The CurrentMode property changes to insert mode. Insert the values for the Bridal record. Category ID (**28**), Category Name (**Bridal**), Image (**28.jpg**), Thumbnail (**28.gif**), Description (**Bridal Gifts**), and Tiny Thumbnail (**28.gif**) as shown in Figure 10-10.

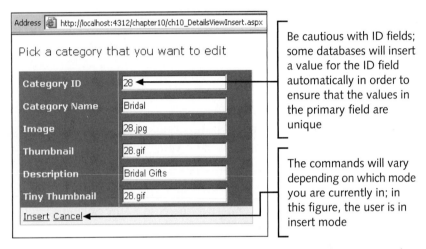

**Figure 10-10**   Using the DropDownList for editing a GridView control

5. Click the **Insert** button. The CurrentMode property changes back to display. Click the **8** hyperlink in the pager row at the bottom of the GridView control to verify that the record was inserted.

6. Close the browser and the web page.

## Using a FormView Control

You can use a Data control, such as a DropDownList or RadioButtonList, to retrieve the record that you want to edit. You can also use the **pager row** to allow users to page through each record to locate the record that they want to edit. With large record sets, however, this is impractical. Therefore, you should learn how to bind a value returned from the Data control to the query for retrieving a record in the FormView control. In the first part of this exercise, you will bind the data to the FormView control. In the second part, you will learn how you can modify the FormView control's styles and templates to improve the appearance of the FormView control.

1. Right-click the **ch10_FormView.aspx** page in the Solution Explorer window and then select **View in Browser**.

2. In the drop-down list, select **Bridal**. The bridal data appears as shown in Figure 10-11.

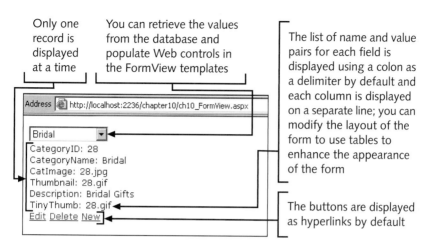

**Figure 10-11**    Using the FormView control to display data

3. Click the **Edit** hyperlink. Notice that the format and layout as shown in Figure 10-12 could be confusing for some users because the text boxes are not aligned and the user must type the values into the text boxes. Click the **Cancel** hyperlink.

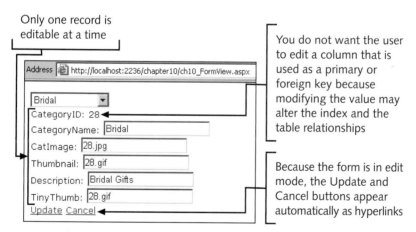

**Figure 10-12**    Using the FormView control to edit data

4. Click the **New** hyperlink. The InsertTemplate appears similar to the EditItemTemplate. Click **Cancel**.

5. Close the browser and the web page.

**TIP**

A great way to learn more about data and data binding is by using the walkthroughs within Visual Studio .NET. These walkthroughs are tutorials that help you learn the more complex tasks within the program. Several walk-throughs on using and editing the GridView control are available at *http://msdn2.microsoft.com/en-us/library/sbxx05zk(VS.80).aspx.*

By default the FormView control is displayed in display mode. There are several ways to change the default mode. The FormView control has a **DefaultMode property** that can be set inside of the FormView tag. The **CurrentMode property** is used to identify the current mode. You can also change the mode programmatically. You can assign the value using the **ChangeMode method** of the FormView control, (FormView.ChangeMode(FormViewMode.Insert) ) or you can explicitly change the DefaultMode property ( FormViewMember.DefaultMode = FormViewMode.Insert ). Both methods accept the FormViewMode enumeration for Insert, ReadOnly, and Edit. The default DefaultMode is ReadOnly {0}.

## Using Templates and Styles with the FormView Control

You can see that the default values for the FormView control are very bland and unprofessional. In this second part, you will learn how you can modify the FormView styles and templates to improve the appearance of the FormView control. This process is the same for the FormView control as it was with the DetailsView, GridView, DataList, and Repeater controls. Just a review will be covered here.

1. Double-click the **ch10_FormViewTemplates.aspx** page in the Solution Explorer window. The AccessDataSource, DropDownlist, and FormView controls already have been inserted and configured for you. A Cascading Style Sheet is also linked to the page that changes the default text format to 10 pt and Verdana.

2. Right-click the **FormView1** control and select **Properties**. In the Properties window, modify the FormView properties. Expand the **HeaderStyle** properties in the Properties window. Change the BackColor to **#6B696B**, ForeColor to **White**, and Width to **500px**.

3. Expand the **EditRowStyle** properties in the Properties window. Change the BackColor to **#6B696B**, ForeColor to **White**, and Width to **500px**. (*Note*: You can change the other styles using this same technique.)

4. Change the template to the **EditItemTemplate**. Notice that the links are difficult to read. (*Note*: The EditRowStyle is what changes the background color to a shade of maroon. Once you insert a new record, the web page puts you immediately into edit mode by default and will use the EditRowStyle. You can avoid this conflict by using an InsertRowStyle if you use an InsertItemTemplate.)

5. A class called EditItemLink will change the hyperlink color from the default blue to white. Click the **Update** hyperlink. In the Properties window, change the CSSClass property to **EditItemLink**. Click the **Cancel** hyperlink. In the Properties window, change the CSSClass property to **EditItemLink**.

6. Change the template to the **InsertItemTemplate**. Click the **Insert** hyperlink. In the Properties window, change the CSSClass property to **EditItemLink**. Click the **Cancel** hyperlink. In the Properties window, change the CSSClass property to **EditItemLink**.

7. Click the <smart> tag to open the Task List for the **FormView** control. Click **End Template Editing**.

8. Click the **Save All** icon. Right-click the page in the Solution Explorer window and then select **View in Browser**.

9. In the drop-down list, select **Bridal**. The bridal data appears as shown in Figure 10-13.

**10**

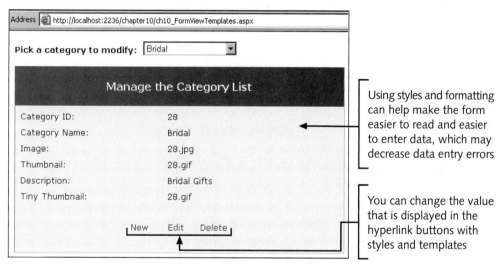

**Figure 10-13**    Using styles and templates to modify the FormView control

10. Close the browser and the web page.

You can see that it is easy to manage your data through a web interface. You may want to use stored procedures with your Web applications, however. In the next section, you will learn to use other data utilities, such as stored procedures, to enhance your Web application.

## DATA MANAGEMENT

With Visual Studio .NET, you can create SQL queries and stored procedures. **Stored procedures** are SQL queries that are stored with the database and can be reused. They can contain SQL commands and can be as simple as a Select statement. Stored procedures are queries that reside on the database server, and because they are compiled by the database server, they are more efficient. Stored procedures execute faster and are more secure than passing SQL queries. Once you create the stored procedure in the database, you can call it from a web page and cause it to execute. Popular databases, such as Oracle and Microsoft SQL Server, support stored procedures. Not all databases support the concept of stored procedures. Microsoft Access does not support stored procedures.

In SQL Server, SQL queries can be saved in stored procedures. Stored procedures in SQL Server are more efficient to run and more secure then SQL queries because stored procedures are compiled. Both AccessDataSource and SqlDataSource controls can be configured to pass parameters to an SQL query or to a stored procedure. In Microsoft Access, a stored procedure is called a **parameter query**. You can use parameterized queries with Access using the AccessDataSource control as shown earlier in this chapter. For example, you can develop a SQL statement that selects all records where the state field contains a value that matches a variable called strState. This SQL statement can be saved as a stored procedure and executed at a later time. When the stored procedure is called, you can then pass the value of the state, such as "IL," to the state variable strState.

In this section of the chapter, you will learn how to call the stored procedure from the web page and pass input parameters to the stored procedures.

## Using Stored Procedures with a GridView Control

The purpose of this activity is to call a simple stored procedure from the web page. You will also call a stored procedure and pass parameters to the stored procedure. The name of the database you will work with in this activity is Ch10ResidentialSQL, and it is located in the App_Data folder. In the following activity you need to have a local version of SQL Server Express running.

1. Right-click the **ch10_GridView_DisplaySP.aspx** page in the Solution Explorer window and select **View in Designer**. The SqlDataSource, DropDownList, and GridView controls already have been inserted and configured for you.

2. Click the <smart> tag to open the Task List for the **SqlDataSource2** and then select **Configure Data Source**. Select **Ch10_ResidentialSQLConnectionString** from the drop-down list. Click **Next** to continue. (*Note*: Remember that the web editor will pick up any data connection strings that are defined within your web configuration file.)

3. Do not select a table. Instead, select the radio button labeled **Specify a custom SQL statement or stored procedure**. Click **Next**. Click the radio button

labeled **Stored procedure**. In the drop-down list, select **Ch10_Display_ AllPropertiesByState** as shown in Figure 10-14. Click **Next**.

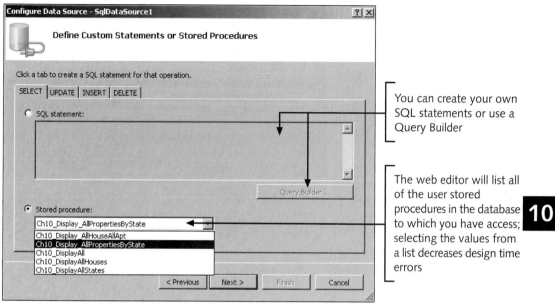

Figure 10-14    Configuring a DataSource object to use a stored procedure

4. In the Parameter source drop-down list, select **Control**. In the ControlID drop-down list, select **DropDownList1** as shown in Figure 10-15. Click **Next** and then click **Finish**. (*Note*: If a window opens that asks if you want to refresh fields and keys for GridView1, click **Yes**. This message appears when you reconfigure the AccessDataSource control that has been assigned as the data source for a GridView control.)

5. If necessary, click the smart tag to open the Task List for the **GridView** control. In the Choose Data Source drop-down list, select **SqlDataSource2**.

6. Click the **Source** tab. Locate the code for the Price BoundField column. Insert the **DataFormatString** and **HtmlEncode** properties as shown in Figure 10-16.

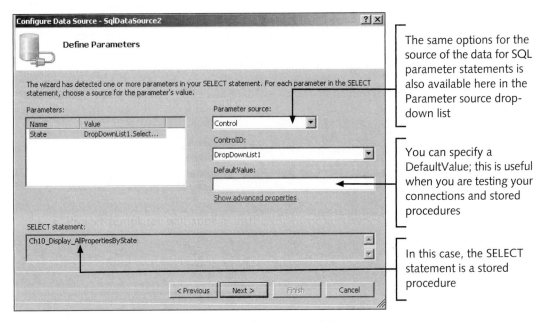

**Figure 10-15**    Selecting a Data control as the source of the parameter value

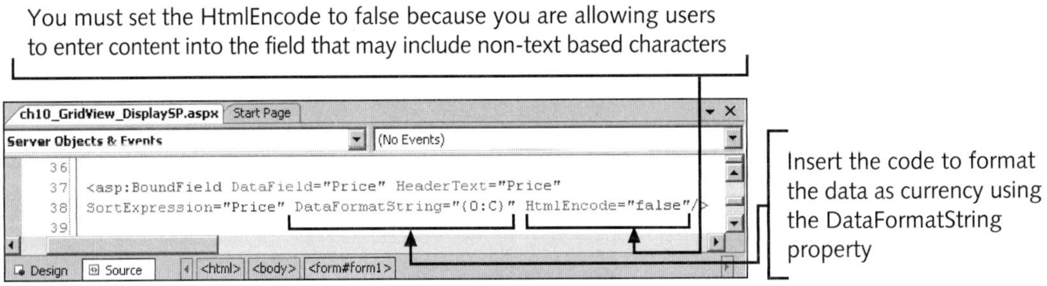

You must set the HtmlEncode to false because you are allowing users
to enter content into the field that may include non-text based characters

**Figure 10-16**    Formatting the Price BoundField column as currency

7. Click the **Save All** icon. Figure 10-17 shows the Ch10_Display_
   AllPropertiesByState stored procedure for your reference. Notice that the
   value from the control will be used as the @State input parameter.

8. Right-click the web page in the Solution Explorer window and then select
   **View in Browser**.

9. In the drop-down list, select **Michigan**. The data appears as shown in
   Figure 10-18.

10. Close the browser and the web page.

If you allow the users not to pass a value in the field when the record is created or updated,
this can cause problems with your data integrity. You may want to use Validation controls to

You insert comments in the stored procedure within the /* */ characters; it is useful to document acceptable values in the stored procedure and to test the stored procedure with a value before you execute it in your application

The parameter is identified with the @ symbol; if there are multiple parameters, separate them with a comma

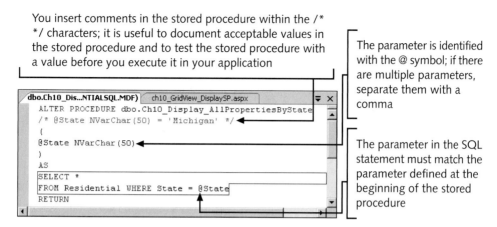

The parameter in the SQL statement must match the parameter defined at the beginning of the stored procedure

**Figure 10-17**   The Ch10_Display_AllPropertiesByState stored procedure

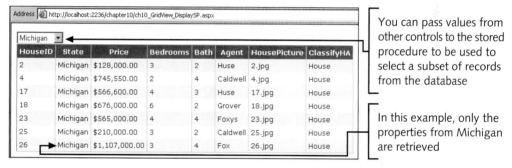

You can pass values from other controls to the stored procedure to be used to select a subset of records from the database

In this example, only the properties from Michigan are retrieved

**Figure 10-18**   Displaying data using a parameter and a stored procedure

make sure that the controls allow only valid data to be entered into the database. If no value is entered, the lack of the value is called **Null**. Null is not the same thing as an empty string. It represents that no information has been entered into the cell.

Note that the SqlDataSource object has been configured to retrieve the data from the Ch10ResidentialSQL.mdf file in your project App_Data folder using a connection string stored in the web configuration file as Ch10_ResidentialSQLConnectionString. If you do not use the default settings, you may have to modify the connection string or the connection for the DataSource object. If you do not have a local version of SQL Server Express, you may replicate this activity with SQL Server. Your data connection properties will vary, however. You can upsize the Residential and TaraStore Microsoft Access databases in the App_Data folder to a SQL Server database or attach the databases to another version of SQL Server 2005.

## Using Stored Procedures with a FormView Control

In this section, you will learn to modify the web page to support SQL Server and parameter queries. This example uses SQL Server Express. Although you can use the visual tools, it is also useful to know how to modify the code manually. This exercise will demonstrate how to call the stored procedures manually.

1. Create the stored procedures to select and update the database as listed in Figure 10-19. You will have to create each one individually in the Data Explorer window. (*Note:* To create a stored procedure, expand the database, right-click the **Stored Procedures** folder, and then select **Add New Stored Procedure**. Type the code as shown, and save the stored procedure.)

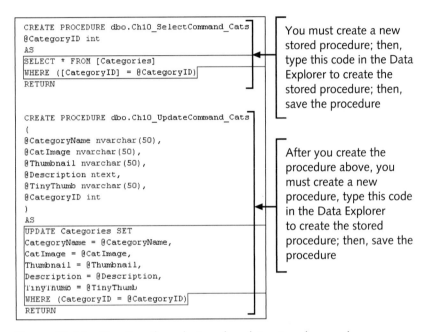

**Figure 10-19**   Creating the select and update stored procedures

2. Create the stored procedures listed in Figure 10-20. You will have to create and save each one separately.

3. Right-click the **ch10_FormView_InsertSP.aspx** page in the Solution Explorer window and then select **View Code**. The SqlDataSource, Drop-DownList, and FormView controls already have been inserted and configured for you.

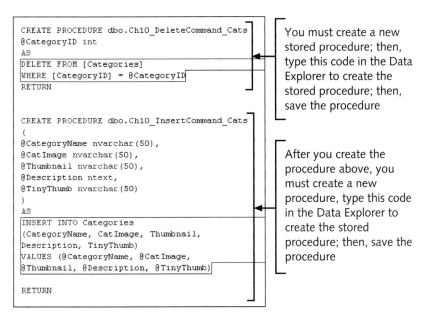

```
CREATE PROCEDURE dbo.Ch10_DeleteCommand_Cats
@CategoryID int
AS
DELETE FROM [Categories]
WHERE [CategoryID] = @CategoryID
RETURN
```

You must create a new stored procedure; then, type this code in the Data Explorer to create the stored procedure; then, save the procedure

```
CREATE PROCEDURE dbo.Ch10_InsertCommand_Cats
(
@CategoryName nvarchar(50),
@CatImage nvarchar(50),
@Thumbnail nvarchar(50),
@Description ntext,
@TinyThumb nvarchar(50)
)
AS
INSERT INTO Categories
(CategoryName, CatImage, Thumbnail,
Description, TinyThumb)
VALUES (@CategoryName, @CatImage,
@Thumbnail, @Description, @TinyThumb)

RETURN
```

After you create the procedure above, you must create a new procedure, type this code in the Data Explorer to create the stored procedure; then, save the procedure

**10**

**Figure 10-20**   Creating the delete and insert stored procedures

4. Locate the SqlDataSource1 control. Enter the code as shown in Figure 10-21.

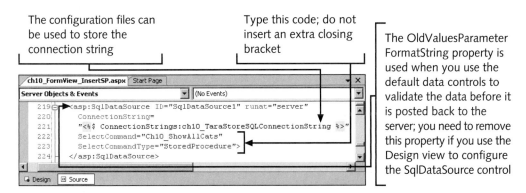

The configuration files can be used to store the connection string

Type this code; do not insert an extra closing bracket

The OldValuesParameter FormatString property is used when you use the default data controls to validate the data before it is posted back to the server; you need to remove this property if you use the Design view to configure the SqlDataSource control

```
ch10_FormView_InsertSP.aspx  Start Page
Server Objects & Events                    (No Events)
219   <asp:SqlDataSource ID="SqlDataSource1" runat="server"
220       ConnectionString=
221       "<%$ ConnectionStrings:ch10_TaraStoreSQLConnectionString %>"
222       SelectCommand="Ch10_ShowAllCats"
223       SelectCommandType="StoredProcedure">
224   </asp:SqlDataSource>
Design    Source
```

**Figure 10-21**   Binding a SqlDataSource control to a stored procedure

5. Locate the SqlDataSource2 control. Enter the code as shown in Figure 10-22. Figure 10-23 displays the insert, delete, and update parameters that have been inserted for you.

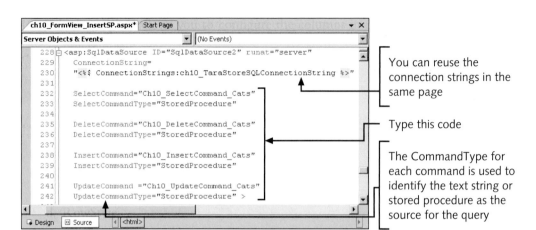

You can reuse the connection strings in the same page

Type this code

The CommandType for each command is used to identify the text string or stored procedure as the source for the query

**Figure 10-22**   Configuring the SqlDataSource control to support stored procedures

The select stored procedure will use the value from the drop-down list to locate the record

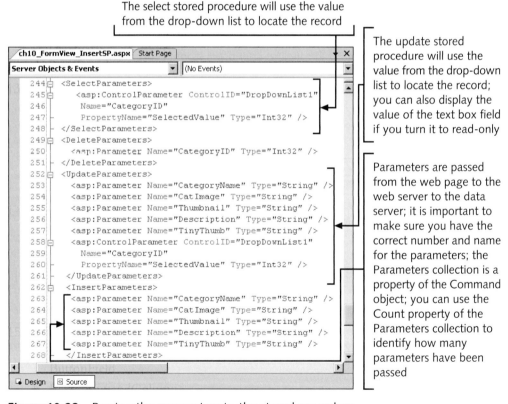

The update stored procedure will use the value from the drop-down list to locate the record; you can also display the value of the text box field if you turn it to read-only

Parameters are passed from the web page to the web server to the data server; it is important to make sure you have the correct number and name for the parameters; the Parameters collection is a property of the Command object; you can use the Count property of the Parameters collection to identify how many parameters have been passed

**Figure 10-23**   Passing the parameters to the stored procedure

6. In the script section located at the top of the web page, type the code after each comment as shown in Figure 10-24.

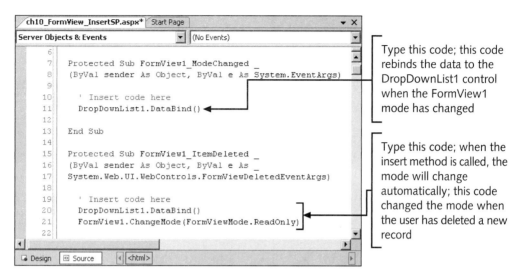

Type this code; this code rebinds the data to the DropDownList1 control when the FormView1 mode has changed

Type this code; when the insert method is called, the mode will change automatically; this code changed the mode when the user has deleted a new record

**Figure 10-24** Changing modes

7. Click the **Save All** icon. Right-click the page in the Solution Explorer window and then select **View in Browser**.

8. Click the **New** hyperlink. Insert a new record. Set the CategoryID to **33**, the CategoryName to **Magazines**, the CatImage to **33.jpg**, the Thumbnail to **33.gif**, the TinyThumbnail to **33.gif**, and the Description to **Weekly Magazines**. Click the **Insert** hyperlink.

9. In the drop-down list, select **Magazines**. Click the **Edit** hyperlink. Change the description to **Monthly Magazines**. Click the **Update** hyperlink. In the drop-down list, select **Magazines**. Click the **Delete** hyperlink. The entry is removed from the drop-down list.

10. Close the browser and the web page.

You can see that it is easy to manage your data with stored procedures and ASP.NET. You must also make sure that your data is stored securely on the server, however, and it passed security between the client and server. In the next section, you will learn to use other methods to secure the data in your Web application.

## SECURING DATABASES

In this next section, you will learn more about securing your databases and how to detect database errors.

## Securing Databases

You have learned how to create SQL queries and stored procedures with Visual Studio .NET. Once you create the stored procedure, you can call it from an ASP.NET page and cause it to operate. The ability to execute stored procedures or SQL queries from a web page, increases the risk of exposing the network to security breaches and other malicious attacks.

**Hackers** are people who intrude into another person's software. Their intentions may be to expose, modify, or delete the data or files on your network. Therefore, it is important to prevent them from gaining access to the SQL Server database. One of the main reasons for implementing stored procedures is to prevent SQL injection. **SQL injection** is a technique that is used by hackers to attach SQL statements to an existing SQL query in order to run additional commands. When a user enters data within a text box that is combined with an SQL statement, the hacker can insert additional SQL statements within that text box. This action injects the hacker's own SQL commands. For example, suppose your SQL statement requires the user to enter a parameter into a text box. The user could append the value with a semicolon and insert a new SQL statement. The semicolon indicates the end of one SQL statement. The SQL Server would execute both SQL statements. While most of the SQL statements you have seen so far are used to retrieve or manage data, there are many SQL statements that can be used to create or delete SQL objects such as tables. The create table [table name] will create a new table. The drop table [table name] will delete a table from the database. If the parameter passed is ; drop table Products, then the Products table would be deleted from the database.

To prevent SQL injection, always use stored procedures with sensitive data. You can read more about SQL injection at *http://msdn2.microsoft.com/en-us/library/ms161953.aspx*. Additional information on how to build secure SQL Server Web database applications can be found at *http://msdn2.microsoft.com/en-us/library/ms998271.aspx* and *http://msdn2.microsoft.com/en-us/library/bb355989.aspx*.

You can secure your SQL Server database by not leaving your password blank and by also using a strong password. A **strong password** uses a combination of numbers and special characters to make it more difficult to guess. Your system administrator, web administrator, or database administrator will provide you with the user ID and password required to connect to a database.

TIP    You can use Query Analyzer to manage your database, create stored procedures and SQL scripts, and run ad hoc SQL queries. SQL scripts are a series of SQL statements stored in a plain text file that can be run within Query Analyzer. They are often used when building the database, populating the database with data, and backing up the database. In the Enterprise version of SQL Server, the software comes with an administration tool called Enterprise Manager. This tool allows you to add user roles to a database, change user passwords, and manage databases. There is an HTML version of Enterprise Manager available for download free from Microsoft. You should ask your system administrator which SQL Server tools are available to manage your SQL Server databases. In many large companies, a database administrator is responsible for creation, maintenance, and deletion of databases, stored procedures, and SQL scripts.

# Detecting Database Errors

When you edit a record, you should try to determine if the record was added successfully, or if there was an error. If the record is not added successfully and an exception is triggered, the web page can catch the exception as an Exception object. The **Exception object** contains information about the error, such as the exception number, which helps you determine the type of error that occurred. For example, if you try to add a record and the primary key already exists, the exception number returned is 2627. If you are updating a record and do not correctly form the SQL command, the exception number returned might be 137.

In order to determine if an exception occurred, you can enclose the code within a Try-Catch construct. The **Try-Catch construct** allows you to place code in the Try section that you want to execute. If an exception is thrown within this code, the code within the Catch section runs. The exception can be caught and stored as an object in a variable. You can access the exception number using the Number property of the Exception object. In the following exercise, you will modify the GridView control to edit a record and use the Try-Catch construct to detect if there was an error when you attempted to update the database.

The sample code shown in Figure 10-25 shows how to add the Try-Catch construct. In the Try section, you add the code to open the connection, execute the SQL update command, rebind the data to the GridView control, close the connection, and reset the EditItemIndex to **-1**. Also, you change the Text property of the label to indicate that the record was successfully updated. If its exception number is 2627, the code displays a message indicating that the record was not added because the primary key cannot have a duplicate value in the table. Otherwise, the code displays a general error message. (*Note:*You can use this technique to send e-mail to the database administrator, run a program, or perform other functions.)

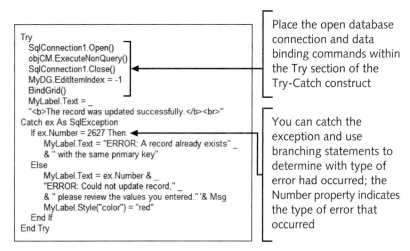

```
Try
    SqlConnection1.Open()
    objCM.ExecuteNonQuery()
    SqlConnection1.Close()
    MyDG.EditItemIndex = -1
    BindGrid()
    MyLabel.Text = _
    "<b>The record was updated successfully.</b><br>"
Catch ex As SqlException
    If ex.Number = 2627 Then
        MyLabel.Text = "ERROR: A record already exists" _
        & " with the same primary key"
    Else
        MyLabel.Text = ex.Number & _
        "ERROR: Could not update record," _
        & " please review the values you entered." '& Msg
        MyLabel.Style("color") = "red"
    End If
End Try
```

Place the open database connection and data binding commands within the Try section of the Try-Catch construct

You can catch the exception and use branching statements to determine with type of error had occurred; the Number property indicates the type of error that occurred

**Figure 10-25**   Exception handling

**TIP**   You can write the MySQL variable out in the Catch section. It is useful to write out the SQL command statement and any variables when you are trying to determine why an error occurred.

There are many types of issues that will arise when you program server-side Web applications. Many of these already have been addressed in the book. You will learn that there are many areas that can be viewed as a weakness in your web server program, however. For example, when you are working with databases, the DataSource control maintains the original primary key values for the fields specified in the **DataKeyNames** property. This property allows the control to identify the key row of data you are selecting, editing, or deleting. This information is stored in the ViewState control. As you know, the ViewState control is maintained with the page in an encoded but hidden variable. Because this is not encrypted, the information could be decoded. If your primary key values contain sensitive or personal information, such as an employee ID number, bank account number, or Social Security number, you should encrypt the contents within the ViewState control. To encrypt the ViewState control, set the page property called **ViewStateEncryptionMode** to Always.

## CHAPTER SUMMARY

- Data controls can be bound to a variety of data sources. You can dynamically display the data by controlling when the BindData method is called. You can bind all of the controls at once or do so individually.

- Data can be filtered using the SQL statement with the WHERE clause, or using a parameter, such as a FilterParameter, or using the FilterExpression property.

❑ The EditItemTemplate property is used to format the controls that are available in edit mode. The EditItemStyle identifies the style for the row that currently is being edited. You can bind the controls using a variety of controls, such as the TemplateField, HyperLinkField, and CheckBoxField.

❑ The CommandField contains an Edit, Update, and Cancel hyperlink for editing, deleting, and canceling your editing requests. You can change the hyperlink to a button with the ButtonType property. You need to enable editing and deleting for the GridView control. The methods are built into the control, however. Therefore, you do not have to write custom code for basic web database management.

❑ The DetailsView or FormView controls should be used for inserting new records instead of the GridView control. The InsertTemplate is used to configure the columns and values to insert into the new record.

❑ The DefaultMode for the FormView control is ReadOnly. You can programmatically modify the mode using the ChangeMode method, or by explicitly modifying the DefaultMode or CurrentMode property. The **EditItemLink** is used to format the hyperlink controls that control the **CurrentMode property** in the FormView control.

❑ Stored procedures can improve efficiency within your program, decrease maintenance requirements, decrease design time errors, and improve data integrity and security. Both Visual Web Developer Express and Visual Studio .NET provide support for graphical user interfaces to create stored procedures and configure your Data controls to implement stored procedures. When you select the Return only unique rows, the program places the keyword Distinct in the query.

❑ Data controls can be bound to a variety of data sources. You can dynamically display the data by controlling when the BindData method is called. You can bind all of the controls at once or do so individually.

❑ Data security is one aspect that should be included in your company information systems security policy. Try-Catch can help identify and handle errors with database applications. SQL injection is a technique that is used by hackers to attach SQL statements to an existing SQL query in order to run additional commands.

10

## REVIEW QUESTIONS

1. Which Data control is best used to insert a new record?
   a. DataView
   b. DataReader
   c. FormView
   d. GridView

2. What method is used to place the data into the Data control?

   a. Fill

   b. GenerateData

   c. FillAdaptor

   d. Bind

3. Which types of button(s) can be used with the GridView EditCommandColumn?

   a. Link

   b. Button

   c. Image

   d. All of the above

4. Which property allows you to change the LinkButton type in a GridView control?

   a. ButtonType

   b. LinkButton

   c. Button

   d. GridButton

5. Which property allows you to specify the column that identifies the unique record in a GridView control?

   a. DataKeyField

   b. UpdateCommand

   c. EditItemIndex

   d. ItemIndex

6. Which is not a feature of the GridView control?

   a. HeaderText

   b. HeaderImage

   c. SortExpression

   d. AcceptButton

7. Which SQL command is used to create a new record in the database?

   a. Update

   b. Insert

   c. AddNew

   d. Add

8. What is/are stored in the field when there is no value?

   a. NULL

   b. Nothing

   c. " "

   d. All of the above

9. Where can you store the connection string so that it is available to all pages within your application?

   a. Global.ASP

   b. Web.config

   c. Config.Web

   d. Default.asp

10. What is the value assigned to the CommandType parameter when the Data control requests a stored procedure?

   a. Procedure

   b. StoredProcedure

   c. CommandProcedure

   d. SQLProcedure

11. What template is used to modify a new record in a GridView control?

   a. EditHyperLink

   b. SelectedField

   c. EditItemTemplate

   d. InsertTemplate

12. What property needs to be set before you can apply the currency format?

   a. HtmlEncode

   b. Container.Databind

   c. Eval

   d. HtmlDecode

13. Which binding method supports two-way binding?

   a. Bind

   b. Eval

   c. Container.Eval

   d. Update

**10**

14. What keyword is used to select unique values within a field?

    a. UNIQUE

    b. GUID

    c. ID

    d. DISTINCT

15. What is the default mode for the FormView control?

    a. Design

    b. Insert

    c. Edit

    d. ReadOnly

16. What symbol is used to identify the parameter value in a stored procedure?

    a. @

    b. %

    c. #

    d. *

17. Which is the best example of a strong password?

    a. HappyDays2

    b. WorldWideWeb*

    c. *Donuts

    d. &GeT*MoLaSSeS#

18. What property is used to identify the primary key value in the Data control?

    a. DataKey

    b. DataKeyNames

    c. RecordKeys

    d. getDataKeys

19. Where is the primary key information stored when the information is passed to the server?

    a. HTTP header

    b. message body

    c. __ViewState object

    d. CommandField

20. What is a technique that is used by hackers to attach SQL statements to an existing SQL query in order to run additional commands?

   a. SQL injection

   b. GetSQL

   c. Set SQL

   d. HackSQL

21. Compare the ability to select, insert, delete, and update data with the GridView, FormView and DetailsView controls.

22. Define six different types of parameters. Describe what conditions you would not send the parameter using the QueryString parameter and explain why.

23. Explain the Name and Type properties used in an InsertParameter.

24. Identify which character(s) can be used to identify parameter values in a Select statement with an AccessDataSource control and a SqlDataSource control.

25. Compare the difference between the FilterParameters and FilterExpression property and using the Where clause in a Select statement.

26. Select the GridView or FormView control. Provide five ways to modify the Data control to prevent data entry errors.

27. Explain the purpose of the DataKeyNames property.

28. Explain the purpose of the HtmlEncode property.

29. Provide five ways to modify the Web application to prevent data connection errors.

30. Describe two ways to prevent SQL database errors.

31. Describe two ways to prevent SQL database injection attacks.

32. Visit the SQL injection at *http://msdn2.microsoft.com/en-us/library/ms161953.aspx*. Additional information on how to build secure SQL Server Web database applications can be found at *http://msdn2.microsoft.com/en-us/library/ms998271.aspx* and *http://msdn2.microsoft.com/en-us/library/bb355989.aspx*. Describe five ways to prevent SQL injection.

# HANDS-ON PROJECTS

## Project 10-1

In this project, you will use the Northwind Traders database and display the data in the Customers table using the GridView control. You will configure the GridView control using Styles and Templates.

   1. Start your editor and open your **Chapter10** solution if necessary. Create the **ch10_proj1.aspx** page in your ch10_proj1 folder.

2. Insert an **AccessDataSource** and configure the connection to the Northwind Traders database. Configure the data source control to use a SELECT query to retrieve all of the fields in the Customers table.

3. Insert a **GridView** control to display all of the fields in the Customers table. Set the DataSourceID to the **AccessDataSource** control.

4. Configure the GridView control to **Enable Paging** and **Enable Sorting**.

5. Modify the GridView control. Put the name of the company, **Northwind Traders**, in the HeaderTemplate. Put the total number of customers in the FooterTemplate. Modify the PagerStyle properties to say **Next** and **Previous**.

6. Modify the HeaderTemplate, AlternatingRowTemplate, ItemTemplate, and Footer-Template using the **HeaderStyle**, **AlteratingRowStyle**, **ItemStyle**, **FooterStyle**, and **PagerStyle**. Use different font family, size, and style characteristics as well as a different background and text color.

7. Click the **Save All** icon. Right-click the **ch10_proj1.aspx** page in the Solution Explorer window and then select **View in Browser**.

**NOTE**    Microsoft provides sample databases with Access and SQL Server. Northwind Traders is provided with Microsoft Access. For information on how to convert the database to SQL Server, visit *http://office.microsoft.com/en-us/access/HP051886201033.aspx*.

**HANDS-ON PROJECTS**

## Project 10-2

In this project, you will use the Northwind Traders database. You will modify a web page to support editing the Customers table with the GridView control.

1. Start your editor and open your **Chapter10** solution if necessary. Create the **ch10_proj2.aspx** page in your ch10_proj2 folder.

2. Insert an **AccessDataSource** and configure the connection to the Northwind Traders database. Configure the data source control to retrieve all of the fields in the Customers table. Use the wizard to create the insert, update, and delete queries.

3. Insert a GridView control. Configure the GridView control to **Enable Editing** and **Enable Deleting**.

4. Configure the GridView control format and style. Select **Auto Format** and format the GridView control with the **Mocha** style.

5. Change the **EditItemTemplate** so that the user must pick the country from a drop-down list of all the current values for the country.

6. Use the Validation controls to validate the contents of the **PostalCode** and **Phone** fields. Use the required field Validation control to validate that the user has entered values for the **CompanyName**, **ContactName**, and **ContactTitle**. (*Hint*: You may want to refer to your previous chapters on how to use a Validation control.)

7. Click the **Save All** button. Right-click the **ch10_proj2.aspx** page in the Solution Explorer window and then select **View in Browser**.

## Project 10-3

In this project, you will use the Northwind Traders database and the FormView control to insert, edit, and delete data from the Products table. You will display the left cell products using a RadioButtonList. In the right cell, you will use a FormView control to manage the data.

1. Start your editor and open your **Chapter10** solution if necessary. Create the **ch10_proj3.aspx** page in your ch10_proj3 folder.

2. Create a table with two cells. Configure the border to **0**, cellpadding and cellspacing to **5** and **0**, and **center** the table. Configure the cells vAlign property to **top**.

3. Insert an **AccessDataSource** below that table and configure the connection to the Northwind Traders database. Configure the Data Source control to retrieve a list of all the products. Sort the products alphabetically in ascending order.

4. Insert a **RadioButtonList** and display the list of products in the left table cell. Configure the Data control to retrieve a list of products from the AccessDataSource using the **DataSource** property. Display the **ProductName** and pass the **ProductID** as the value of the option.

5. Insert an **AccessDataSource** below the table and configure the connection to the Northwind Traders database. Configure the Data Source control to retrieve all the fields in the **Products** table. Only retrieve the record, however, where the user has selected a value from the RadioButtonList control. Use the wizard to create the insert, update, and delete queries.

6. Insert a FormView control in the right table cell. Configure the FormView control to **Enable Editing, Enable Inserting**, and **Enable Deleting**.

7. Configure the FormView control format and style. Select **Auto Format** and format the FormView control with the **Mocha** style.

8. Change the **EditItemTemplate** so that the user must pick the country from a drop-down list of all of the current values for the country.

9. Use the Validation controls to validate the contents of the **PostalCode** and **Phone** fields. Use the required field Validation control to validate that the user has entered values for the **CompanyName**, **ContactName**, and **ContactTitle.** (*Hint*: You may want to refer to your previous chapters on how to use a Validation control.)

10

10. Modify the **ItemTemplate**, **EditItemTemplate**, and **InsertItemTemplate** so that the fields are displayed in tables. The tables should have the borders turned off. Modify the tables so that the width of each table is fixed to **500** pixels.

11. Create a program to rebind the data and then redisplay the RadioButtonList when a new record is inserted or deleted.

12. Click the **Save All** button. Right-click the page in the Solution Explorer window and then select **View in Browser**.

## Project 10-4

In this project, you will use the ch10_TaraStoreSQL database and use stored procedures to maintain the Products table.

1. Start your editor and open your **Chapter10** solution if necessary. Create the **ch10_proj4.aspx** page in your ch10_proj4 folder.

2. Create a stored procedure to insert a new product, update an existing product, and delete an existing product. Create a stored procedure to display all of the products.

3. Create a table with two cells. Configure the border to **0**, cellpadding and cellspacing to **5** and **0**, and **center** the table. Configure the cells vAlign property to **top**.

4. Insert an **AccessDataSource** below that table and configure the connection to the database. Configure the Data Source control to retrieve a list of all of the products in the **Products** table. Sort the products alphabetically in ascending order by their product name.

5. Insert a **RadioButtonList** and display the list of products in the left table cell. Configure the Data control to retrieve a list of products from the AccessDataSource using the **DataSource** property. Display the product name, and pass the product ID as the value of the option.

6. Insert an **AccessDataSource** below the table and configure the connection to the database. Configure the Data Source control to retrieve all the fields in the **Products** table. Only retrieve the record, however, where the user has selected a value from the RadioButtonList control. Do not use the wizard to create the insert, update, and delete queries.

7. Insert a FormView control in the right table cell. Configure the FormView control to **Enable Editing, Enable Inserting**, and **Enable Deleting**.

8. Configure the FormView control format and style. Select **Auto Format** and format the FormView control with the **Mocha** style.

9. Display the thumbnail image of the product in the **ItemTemplate**. Create a hyperlink from the name of the product to the large product image.

10. Provide a method for the user that allows the user to upload an image for the thumbnail and product image. (*Note:* You may want to review how to use the File-Upload control presented in an earlier chapter.)

11. Modify the **ItemTemplate**, **EditItemTemplate**, and **InsertItemTemplate** so that the fields are displayed in tables. The tables should have the borders turned off. Modify the tables so that the width of each table is fixed to **500** pixels.

12. Create a program to rebind the data and then redisplay the RadioButtonList when a new record is inserted or deleted.

13. Click the **Save All** button. Right-click the page in the Solution Explorer window and then select **View in Browser**.

## CASE PROJECTS

### Project 10-1

You work as a web developer at a small web hosting company. A local company called Northwind Traders has asked you to create a web database application to manage its entire database that consists of eight tables. Your job is to create a functional web database management system and design a site that is easy to navigate and has a consistent and professional appearance. You may use a TreeView or other navigation control. You can create a page for each table that allows you to edit, update, and insert the data all on one page. Or, you may choose to combine the entire table editing features for all tables in a single page. Make sure to use Validation controls so that the user is required to fill in all of the required fields. If the data type is a string, make sure the user cannot insert data that is over the limit of the field length. Use Validation controls or conversion methods to make sure the user has entered the correct data type in the forms.

Create web pages to display the data from the tables to a visitor. Use styles, templates, and Cascading Style Sheets to format the design of the web site. Save the home page to your application as ch10_case1.aspx in your ch10_case1 directory. Protect your web database management system using authentication methods such as a login form. Provide documentation for your application in ch10_case1_docs.aspx. Print the web page, your source code, and the code behind the page.

### Project 10-2

You work as a web developer at a small web hosting company. A local company called Tara Store has asked you to create a web database application to manage its entire database. Your job is to create a functional web database management system and design a site that is easy to navigate and has a consistent and professional appearance. You may use a TreeView or other navigation control. You can create a page for each table that allows you to edit, update, and insert the data all on one page. Or, you may choose to combine the entire table editing features for all tables in a single page. Make sure to use Validation controls so that the user is required to fill in all of the required fields. If the data type is a string, make sure the user cannot insert data that is over the limit of the field length. Use Validation controls or conversion methods to make sure the user has entered the correct data type in the forms.

CASE PROJECTS

10

Allow the users to upload graphic images as they enter the product information. Provide them with the ability to select information from existing data in a drop-down list. For example, they should be able to select the category and subcategory properties with the product information through a drop-down list. Then, it would be less likely that they would make a data entry error.

Create web pages to display the data from the tables to a visitor. Use styles, templates, and Cascading Style Sheets to format the design of the web site. Save the home page to your application as ch10_case2.aspx in your ch10_case2 directory. Protect your web database management system using authentication methods such as a login form. Provide documentation for your application in ch10_case2_docs.aspx. Print the web page, your source code, and the code behind the page.

**CASE PROJECTS**

# Project 10-3

You work as a web developer in a small department at CMS. Create a web database to manage the web page content in your web site. Create a table to store the page characteristics, such as the author, date created, category, and title, and a page that contains the page contents, such as the HTML code. Your job is to create a functional web database management system and design a site that is easy to navigate and has a consistent and professional appearance. You may use a TreeView or other navigation control. Create a page for each table that allows you to edit, update, and insert the data all on one page. Make sure to use Validation controls so that the user is required to fill in all of the required fields. If the data type is a string, make sure the user cannot insert data that is over the limit of the field length. Use Validation controls or conversion methods to make sure the user has entered the correct data type in the forms.

Allow the users to upload graphic images as they enter the product information. Provide them with the ability to select information from existing data in a drop-down list. For example, they should be able to select the author name through a drop-down list. Then, it would be less likely that they would make a data entry error.

Create web pages to display the data from the tables to a visitor. For the web page contents table, display the HTML code in the page but also create a page to preview the code in the browser so the users can see the results of their work.

Use styles, templates, and Cascading Style Sheets to format the design of the web site. Save the home page to your application as ch10_case3.aspx in your directory. Protect your web database management system using authentication methods such as a login form. Provide documentation for your application in ch10_case3_docs.aspx. Print the web page, your source code, and the code behind the page.

# CHAPTER
# 11
# ADVANCED WEB PROGRAMMING

## In this chapter, you will:

- Build reusable code
- Build a complete Web application
- Describe innovations in ASP.NET tools and technologies
- Deploy your Web application to a live web server

**B**usinesses have learned through experience that they need to develop applications that fulfill their business needs. In the 1990s, many web development and technology companies created innovative Web applications, but had no business plan and resources to support them. Today, companies are more savvy about matching the technologies they choose for their business ventures. Companies chose different technologies to solve some specific need. A key business concept, however, that was often left out of the equation is leveraging. Companies need to leverage current resources, applications, and data across systems in order to not only fulfill their business needs, but also to provide efficiencies across the organization. A second key business concept often left out is vision. Leaders within companies may have a vision for the company, but it is not integrated with the technologies within, or available to, the organization. Information technology leaders and web developers need to work with leaders in the company to integrate the web development within the vision of the company. Web developers will work with other information technology professionals alongside other company employees to design and develop Web applications that fulfill the company vision. In this chapter, you will learn how to leverage your Web applications through building reusable components and expanding on third-party applications. You will learn how to plan and build a complete Web application. You will also learn about the latest developments and tools using ASP.NET technologies. Lastly, you will learn to deploy your Web application to a live web server.

## BUILDING REUSABLE CODE

In earlier chapters of this book, you learned how to build individual web pages. Further, if you wanted to replicate the same programming code across web pages, you learned you could use tools such as user controls and master content pages. If you want to replicate the same behaviors and programming across applications, however, you would have to create the code in each application.

To help you deal with leverage technologies, ASP.NET technologies give you the ability to create and reuse classes and assemblies. In this section, you will learn how to create reusable code with shared classes, call a class from a web page, create and use classes in your Web application, create snippets, compile your application, and use third party components.

## Creating Reusable Code with Classes

You have learned how to create classes using Visual Basic .NET. Remember that an object is an instance of the class created at run-time based on the structure defined in the class. You have already learned that you can create classes and store them in the App_Code folder. Did you know that you can create class files and source code files and place them in the App_Code folder without directly compiling them? That is right — class files written in VB have a .vb extension, and any code within the App_Code folder will be automatically compiled at runtime.

You can create classes that can be shared across the application. These shared classes are stored in class files that are located in the App_Code folder and are often called **components**. The App_Code folder is a special folder that is configured to allow classes to be compiled dynamically when the application is first run. If there is a change in the files detected, the files are re-compiled automatically. When you create a class based on another class, the new class is called a **derived class**. A derived class can extend or add additional properties, methods, variables, and events. When the application first is accessed, the code in the App_Code folder is compiled with any additional code in the application, into an assembly. Your application can include references to third-party assemblies or you can create your own assembly. You must store the compiled assemblies in the bin directory. The file extension for compiled assemblies is .dll. Your application can then reference the programming stored within the assembly. The classes and assemblies can be written and compiled in any of the .NET programming languages, and implemented within your Web applications.

The process of creating a shared class works like this:

1. When you create your class in the editor, you will identify the program language that will be used to create the class. The program will save classes written in C# with the .cs file extension. Classes written in Visual Basic will be saved with the .vb file extension.

2. After you create and save the class file, you can run the Web application by viewing one of the web pages in a browser.

3. The first time the Web application is run, the program recognizes the file extension for classes defined in the App_Code folder and compiles the classes and adds them to the Web application assembly. The compiler used to compile the class depends on the file extension of the class.

4. Classes that could be written in multiple languages, such as XML schemas (.xsd), will be compiled with the default compiler configured in the compilation element of the Web application or machine configuration file.

You can organize your source code in any way including using nested files and folders. You can store these classes within subdirectories within the App_Code folder if you configure the codeSubDirectories element within the web configuration files. At runtime, ASP.NET compiles the entire contents of the App_Code folder into a single assembly. Therefore, you can store programs written in the same programming language in the App_Code folder. Once compiled, you can reuse the code across the entire application.

You may want to use this solution for class files that frequently change with each installation of the program. Let's look at a situation where you might want to use shared classes. You work for the Foster Plastics Manufacturing company as a web developer. Your job is to create a Web application to manage the customer database. You have all of the information on the data types in the database and have created a form to collect and manage the customer data. You recently learned that the company has purchased another plastics company. You know that your application will also need to interface with the other company database. You don't have information about their customer database, however. Although you could create an assembly with the database fields, you could also choose to store them in shared classes. Then, when you obtain the information about the other database fields you could modify the class files.

When you use the class, you must first instantiate an instance of the class, which means that you are instructing the application to use the code in the class to create the structure of the object. Then, *ClassName.FunctionName()* can reference public functions that are created within the class. You can pass parameters to the function. Using this method allows you to store global functions within public classes that can be accessed throughout your application. By having these functions defined in an external file, the functions can be more shared easily and managed within an application.

Within your class definition, you can use members of an already existing class. For example, all of the Web controls are built from existing classes. You can modify and extend these classes instead of creating the class from scratch. Then, you can inherit many of the properties and methods of that object. When you reuse the class, you will create an object based on the new class.

## Calling the Class from the Web Page

After you have created the class, your web page can access the data by simply instantiating the class as a new object from the base class with the keyword **New**, and then calling the function using the new class. Although it will look like you are adding more code than in the original page, this method provides benefits when you are developing large complex Web applications. For instance, the benefit of storing the procedures in an external class is that the entire set of procedures does not have to be stored within each web page. In addition, you can select which procedures to call from your web page. If a stored procedure changes, you need only change the stored procedure within one page, instead of throughout all the pages on your site. Therefore, using classes to store your stored procedures is more efficient than storing them in individual pages.

You already have learned that a class is used to create reusable programming code. A component extends this concept of a class because it is also a class file that contains your reusable programming code. The component goes one step further, however, and includes a visual template with the programming code. This additional feature of a component, means that you can use the graphical tools to add items to your component. That is, you can drag and drop objects onto the component designer, or you can add them manually in the code behind the component page. The process of adding an object to the component is the same as you would add an object to an ASP.NET page. The component contains a class definition named after the component. It is best not to name the component with the same name as the project. Remember that when the Web application is run, the code in the project is compiled into a single assembly. If there are multiple references to objects with the same name, there will be a conflict when the application is run. The Web application will not know which code to execute.

## Creating and Using Classes

One of the benefits of using classes is that they support web architecture referred to as n-tier application development. Recall that n-tiered applications separate the presentation, business logic, and data layers. The business logic may consist of classes that manage the data in the data layer and send the data to the web pages to be displayed to the end user. By using classes, when a change in the data layer occurs, such as an additional field in the database, only the classes in the business logic layer would need to be changed. This helps decrease the time and resources required to maintain the application. Furthermore, companies in certain industries, such as banking and finance, often experience mergers and acquisitions. By separating the presentation and business logic layers, a company would be able to change the presentation layer without impacting the business logic layer. For example, they could change the style, logos, themes, and layout of the web pages without impacting the rest of the Web application.

In the following example, the user will be able to select the state using an image map, and the web page will display the houses that are available in that state. This example also illustrates one way to separate the presentation, business logic, and data layers. In order to build reusable code, you will create two class files. The first class file will define an image map from a class definition, and the second will define an AccessDataSource control. The benefit of creating the image map from a class definition is that the code can be changed without impacting the code in the presentation layer. If the real estate company decides to add listings in a new state, the map can be changed without impacting the presentation layer.

In the class files, you will inherit from the base ImageMap and AccessDataSource classes and create a new object based on the ImageMap and AccessDataSource classes. It is useful to be able to extend classes and one way to do this is through creating a derived class. The new derived class could have additional properties, events, and methods associated with the class that were not defined in the original class.

In this example, you will also create the GridView control and Label controls dynamically within the web page using a **constructor**. The constructor is simply the code to create the object based on the original class. After creating the controls based on the class definition files, or using the constructors, you have to add them to the controls collection on the page, or to a PlaceHolder control. The only controls statically created within the page code are a table to maintain page layout and two placeholder controls. The placeholder controls will be used to identify where to place the ImageMap and GridView controls when they are rendered. In this example, the ImageMap is put into the PlaceHolder1 control and the Label, GridView, and AccessDataSource controls are put into the PlaceHolder2 control. If you do not add the control to one of these collections, the control will not be displayed within the browser.

**11**

1. Open the **chapter11** project and your web editor if necessary.

2. In the Solution Explorer window, right-click the **ch11_GetStatesData.vb** file in the **App_Code** folder and select **Open**.

3. Type the code in Figure 11-1 to creates the AccessDataSource control based on the original AccessDataSource class. (Note: The code to configure the control has already been inserted for you.)

4. Click the **Save All** icon and close the file. As soon as you save the page, the code is integrated within your solution.

5. In the Solution Explorer window, right-click the **ch11_Remap.vb** file in the **App_Code** folder and select **Open**.

6. Type the code in Figure 11-2. This code creates the ImageMap control based on the ImageMap class. (Note: The code to insert the coordinates has already been inserted for you.)

7. Click the **Save All** icon and close the file.

Type this code

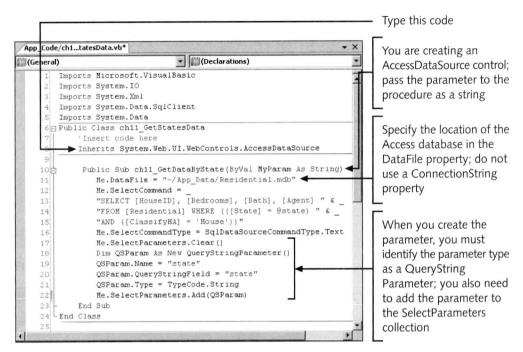

You are creating an AccessDataSource control; pass the parameter to the procedure as a string

Specify the location of the Access database in the DataFile property; do not use a ConnectionString property

When you create the parameter, you must identify the parameter type as a QueryString Parameter; you also need to add the parameter to the SelectParameters collection

**Figure 11-1**    Dynamically create an AccessDataSource control

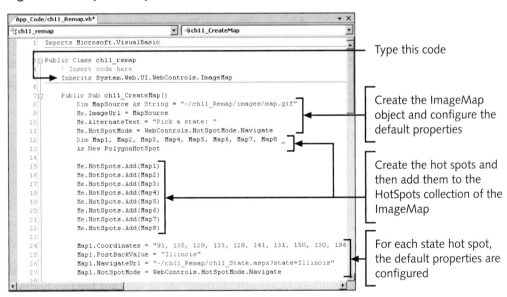

Type this code

Create the ImageMap object and configure the default properties

Create the hot spots and then add them to the HotSpots collection of the ImageMap

For each state hot spot, the default properties are configured

**Figure 11-2**    Dynamically create an ImageMap control

8. In the ch11_Remap folder, right-click the **ch11_State.aspx** file and select **Open**. In the Page_Load event procedure, insert the code to create the ImageMap and AccessDataSource controls and add them to their respective PlaceHolder controls. (Note: The code to create the Label and GridView controls and add them to the page has already been inserted for you.) See Figure 11-3.

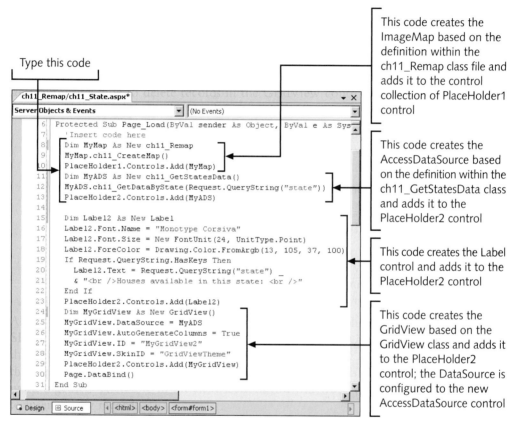

Type this code

This code creates the ImageMap based on the definition within the ch11_Remap class file and adds it to the control collection of PlaceHolder1 control

This code creates the AccessDataSource based on the definition within the ch11_GetStatesData class and adds it to the PlaceHolder2 control

This code creates the Label control and adds it to the PlaceHolder2 control

This code creates the GridView based on the GridView class and adds it to the PlaceHolder2 control; the DataSource is configured to the new AccessDataSource control

```
ch11_Remap/ch11_State.aspx*                    ▼ ×
Server Objects & Events          ▼  (No Events)              ▼
 6    Protected Sub Page_Load(ByVal sender As Object, ByVal e As Sys
 7      'Insert code here
 8      Dim MyMap As New ch11_Remap
 9      MyMap.ch11_CreateMap()
10      PlaceHolder1.Controls.Add(MyMap)
11      Dim MyADS As New ch11_GetStatesData()
12      MyADS.ch11_GetDataByState(Request.QueryString("state"))
13      PlaceHolder2.Controls.Add(MyADS)
14
15      Dim Label2 As New Label
16      Label2.Font.Name = "Monotype Corsiva"
17      Label2.Font.Size = New FontUnit(24, UnitType.Point)
18      Label2.ForeColor = Drawing.Color.FromArgb(13, 105, 37, 100)
19      If Request.QueryString.HasKeys Then
20        Label2.Text = Request.QueryString("state") _
21          & "<br />Houses available in this state: <br />"
22      End If
23      PlaceHolder2.Controls.Add(Label2)
24      Dim MyGridView As New GridView()
25      MyGridView.DataSource = MyADS
26      MyGridView.AutoGenerateColumns = True
27      MyGridView.ID = "MyGridView2"
28      MyGridView.SkinID = "GridViewTheme"
29      PlaceHolder2.Controls.Add(MyGridView)
30      Page.DataBind()
31    End Sub

 Design   Source    <html> <body> <form#form1>
```

**Figure 11-3**  Dynamically create the DataGrid and Label controls

9. Click the **Save All** icon. Right-click the page in the Solution Explorer window and then select **View in Browser**. Click the state of **Wisconsin** in the ImageMap. Your page should look like the one in Figure 11-4.

10. Close the browser and any open pages.

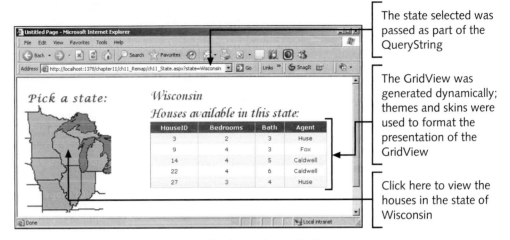

The state selected was passed as part of the QueryString

The GridView was generated dynamically; themes and skins were used to format the presentation of the GridView

Click here to view the houses in the state of Wisconsin

**Figure 11-4** Previewing a page with dynamic content

**TIP** There is extensive documentation on the *www.asp.net* web site and the MSDN Library on how to create custom controls. Basically, you can create a namespace and a class definition that inherits the control class from System.Web.UI. Control. For a class named MyClass, you would change the class definition to `Public Class SimpleVB : Inherits Control`. The next step would be to override the Render method of the control class. The Render method uses the Write method from System.Web.UI.HtmlTextWriter to send the output to the browser. So, your code might look like `Protected Overrides Sub Render(Output As HtmlTextWriter) Output.Write("<H1>My First Custom Control</H1>")`. The end user would register the control as they would any other user control, but he or she would also provide the name of the namespace and the assembly file that contains the namespace.

## Using Code Snippets

You have learned that you can create snippets of code and store them within the Toolbox. You can even create your own tabs to customize the Toolbox. Now that you know these basic programming techniques, you should learn about some of the tools that can help you speed up your Web application development. For instance, the **Code Snippets Manager** is a new tool that allows you to select from some of the commonly used activities from a predefined list. Some of these snippets will be more useful to you when you are developing Windows applications than when creating Web applications. As you develop entire Web applications, however, you may want to use some of these snippets so that you can increase your programming efficiency.

In the following exercise you will use the Code Snippets Manager to insert sample code. Then, you will customize the code for your application. In this exercise, you will create a schema from an XML file.

1. In the Solution Explorer window, right-click the **ch11_CreateSchema.aspx** file and select **Open**. As shown in Figure 11-5, the namespaces and variables required to locate the physical paths to the files already are inserted.

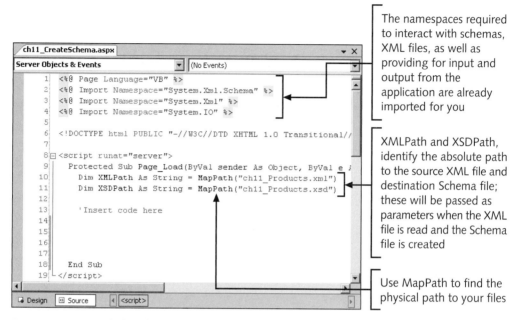

The namespaces required to interact with schemas, XML files, as well as providing for input and output from the application are already imported for you

XMLPath and XSDPath, identify the absolute path to the source XML file and destination Schema file; these will be passed as parameters when the XML file is read and the Schema file is created

Use MapPath to find the physical path to your files

**Figure 11-5**  Find the physical path to your files

2. Place the cursor on the line after the comment. Right-click the page, and then select **Insert Snippet**. The snippet category list will be displayed as shown in Figure 11-6. Double-click the **XML** category.

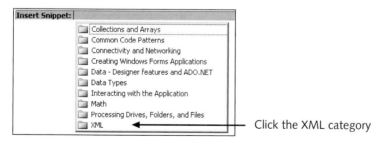

Click the XML category

**Figure 11-6**  Snippet categories

3. Select **Infer and create a Schema from an XML file** as shown in Figure 11-7. In the Page_Load event handler, the code snippet has been inserted by

the Snippet Manager. As shown in Figure 11-8 the snippet template highlights two placeholders, which identify the parameters that you will need to customize.

You can use the built-in methods which
will read the XML file, infer the schema,
and write the schema out to a file

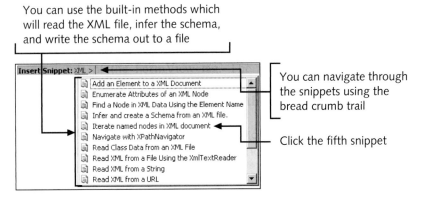

You can navigate through
the snippets using the
bread crumb trail

Click the fifth snippet

**Figure 11-7**   XML snippets

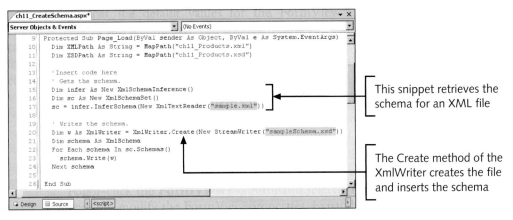

This snippet retrieves the
schema for an XML file

The Create method of the
XmlWriter creates the file
and inserts the schema

**Figure 11-8**   The snippet template

4. Change the path to the source and destination parameters to **XMLPath** and **XSDPath**, as shown in Figure 11-9.

5. Click the **Save All** icon. Right-click the page in the Solution Explorer window and select **View in Browser**. The page will be blank except for a message indicating that the file was created. There is no other output generated to the web page for this exercise. (*Note*: If you get an error message that says "The process cannot access the file '[*drive*:\\*path*\\]\chapter11\ch11_Products.xsd' because it is being used by another process.", you will have to close the project and reopen it.) Close the browser window.

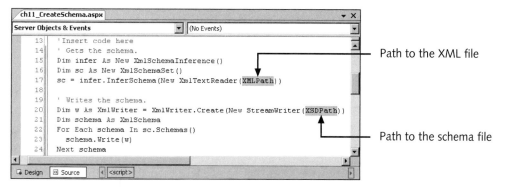

**Figure 11-9**   Customizing the snippet

6. In the Solution Explorer window, right-click the **chapter11** project icon and then select **Refresh Folder**. Click **File** on the menu bar, click **Close Project**, and then reopen the project. Click **File** on the menu bar, point to **Recent Projects**, and then click the Chapter 11 project, which is labeled [*drive*:\*path*\]Chapter11.

7. In the Solution Explorer window, right-click the **ch11_Products.xsd** file and then select **Open**. (*Note:* The file may appear all on one line. To view the entire file, go to the **Edit** menu, select **Advanced**, and select **Word Wrap**.) To improve the file format, go to the **Edit** menu and select **Format Document**. You can see that the schema is now in a more readable, outlined format, as shown in Figure 11-10. (*Note:* The elementFormDefault and xmlns:xs attributes were moved to the subsequent lines to make the figure fit on one page.)

8. Click the **Save All** icon. Close the browser and any open pages.

## Compiling the Application

As previously explained, the class files in the App_Code folder are compiled dynamically at runtime when the application is first called. The source code is available, however. These class files are viewable using a text editor. Therefore, you should always be aware of what code is placed within this folder. If you were to sell your program, the user could view your source code files. This could be a problem because the user could alter the source code. Therefore, in situations such as these, you should compile your class files into assemblies (.dll files). The assemblies are stored within the Bin folder of the web site. Any classes in the Bin folder are automatically referenced in your web site. The Bin folder has the permissions to execute the code within the assemblies. Another reason to precompile the programming code is related to response time. When the application is first requested, the application needs additional time to compile itself. By precompiling the application, the end user will not experience any lag in response time.

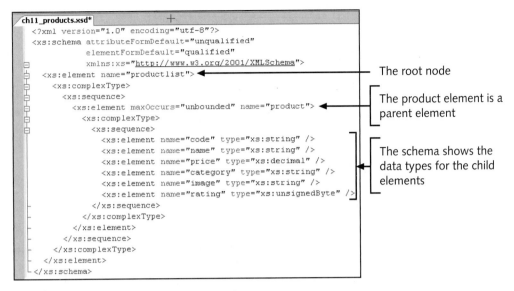

**Figure 11-10**   Formatting a document layout

Class files in the App_Code folder are not the only files you may want to compile. Remember that you can still have source code files within your application that contain programming code. When you compile your Web application, you can remove all of the source code files, including the code-behind files. The code within the ASP.NET page will be compiled if it is within script tags. Inline code, which is located between inline script tags, is not compiled. Non-programming files such as HTML and graphic files are not compiled.

**NOTE**   Many types of files are not compiled, including themes, skins, and web configuration files. Once you have compiled the Web application, to make any changes in the programming code within the Web application, you must change the original files, recompile the entire web site, and redeploy the new files. You may modify the web configuration file without having to recompile the Web application, however.

You can use the command line tool called the ASP.NET Compilation (Aspnet_compiler. exe) to compile your entire Web application before it is deployed, as shown in the following exercise:

1. To run the tool, click the **Start** menu, select **All Programs**, select **Microsoft .NET Framework SDK v2.0**, and select **SDK Command Prompt**.

2. Type **aspnet_compiler –?** in the window and press the **Enter** key. Information on the optional switches for the compiler is displayed such as where the compiled application should be stored.

3. To compile the Web application, type **aspnet_compiler –v** *virtualPath* *targetPath*.

4. You will then transfer the assembly created and the non-compiled files to your live web server using a file transfer program. The assembly is the .dll file created in the target path directory when you compiled the Web application. You need to place this in the bin folder of your Web application on the live web server.

There are different ways to pre-compile your Web application. The v switch indicates that you are using a virtual path to the folder identified in the virtual path. You may use a physical path to the Web application if you change the v switch to p. The target path is the physical path to where you want to store the compiled application. You may include a u switch at the end of the command to indicate if you are compiling the application for deployment and allow limited updates after deployment. This deployment and update option allows you to add and modify controls as long as they do not require programming code. You can also modify colors, fonts, and other elements on the web page.

## Third-Party Components

Although you may choose to create your own assemblies, it is likely that you will want to use an application, component, or assembly that was created by a third party. The **Provider Model** allows you to create new versions of software that easily can be created and plugged into your application. This architectural model results in applications that are more flexible, expandable, customizable, and easier to maintain.

**NOTE** ASP.NET supports many different types of providers including Membership Providers, Role Providers, Site Map Providers, and Data Providers. You can download sample providers and create your own provider for your custom application. Microsoft provides a Provider Toolkit to help developers create their own custom providers.

Over 1500 third-party components are downloadable for free or for purchase at the Control Gallery on the ASP.NET web site. These are available for both ASP.NET 1.0 and 2.0. You can visit this site at *http://www.asp.net/default.aspx?tabindex=6&tabid=31*. Each control will have slightly different procedures for installation and use.

One of the more common controls is FreeTextBox, which is available at *http://freetextbox. com/*. The **FreeTextBox control** is, as its name implies, a free HTML editor. As described in Figure 11-11, you would place this control inside an ASP.NET page, and the user would be able to enter content using a graphical user interface that is similar to Microsoft Office applications. This is a commonly used control that was included in the releases of many products. One such product is DotNetDuke, which is an open source application that developers use as a learning tool and template for beginning web sites.

Like other controls, to use the FreeTextBox control, you must copy the assembly and support files to your application. Then, in your web page you must insert the code to register the control. For example, the code to register the control would be written as `<%@ Register Assembly="FreeTextBox" Namespace="FreeTextBoxControls" TagPrefix="FTB" %>`. Then, in the body section of the web page, you would insert the

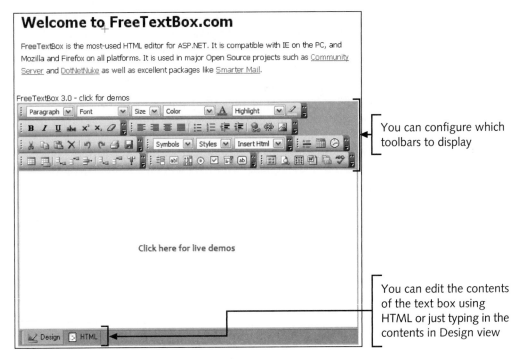

**Figure 11-11**    The FreeTextBox control

control, as shown in Figure 11-12. As you can see there are some properties that you can set, which include the paths to external resources. Depending on the products with which you work, you may have to install additional folders for files and images in your project.

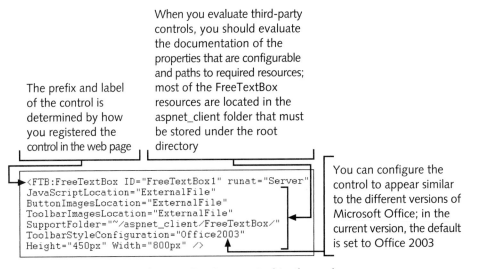

**Figure 11-12**    Inserting the FreeTextBox control in the web page

As a web developer you not only will be programming web sites, but also assisting other professionals in designing the system, understanding the capabilities of the Web application, and implementing the system. When you are designing the system, you must determine which components are essential to be developed internally, and which portions, if any, can be outsourced or licensed. While many developers would prefer to create the application from scratch, this sometimes is not possible. In a situation such as this, you may want to purchase or license third-party software, components, or applications. Some third-party providers allow you to purchase a license for the source code. With the source code, you can customize the code for your company. It is critical that the integration is well documented and implemented so that the company can later swap out the third-party tools for another product, or insert their own program at a later date.

In early versions of web development it was common for web developers to use third-party components for features such as chat rooms, forums, discussion threads, and email management. In the past, some of these companies have merged or went out of business. The third-party components were no longer supported. Therefore, many companies want only to use code that they have created and/or own. Because major technology innovations occur routinely, it is important to assess the tradeoff between not using a third-party component or creating your own component. You may determine that your company may not want to implement a solution now, because of the current limitations of technology, and will wait for the new technology to be developed. Or, your company may choose to implement a phased or pilot approach. In this phased approach, they may decide to use a third-party component for the Web application now, and then build in plans to swap out the third-party component at a later date. This provides a company with time to develop the custom components, without having to delay implementing the solution. Sometimes in Web applications, this phased or pilot approach often works better than implementing a company-wide solution. Individual departments could implement their own solutions, which would later be integrated when the company has the resources available.

## BUILDING A COMPLETE APPLICATION

In earlier versions of ASP.NET, Microsoft partnered with several companies and generated complete Web applications to be used as starting templates and learning tools for web developers. Today, there are many sample applications, which are called **starter kits**. The Microsoft ASP.NET team has created a basic Personal Web Site, Club Web Site, Time Tracker Web Site, and Classifieds Site. All of these are starter kits. In the next section, you will learn about starter kits. You will also learn how to plan your Web application, including how to analyze the Web application requirements, plan the design, implement the development process, and test and maintain the Web application.

## Starter Kits

The ASP.NET community has also developed more advanced Starter Kits, including TheBeerHouse: CMS & E-commerce Starter Kit, PayPal eCommerce Web Site, DotNetNuke® Portal Web Site, Job Site Starter Site, and the Media Library Starter Kit. The latest addition is the Small Business Starter Kit, as shown in Figure 11-13. This starter kit can be used as a business promotion web site for small- and medium-sized businesses. The advanced features within this starter kit include integration with SQL Server and XML data sources for both content and data management. You can view a live version of the site at *http://starterkits.asp.net/SmallBusiness/*.

Starter Kits are often populated with fake data and content for fictitious companies

**Figure 11-13**    The Small Business Starter Kit

Although many starter kits are used solely as learning tools, the DotNetNuke Starter Kit also has been used as the template for many live web sites. The available open source code, ongoing community support (over 335,000 registered users), and international support has made it one of the more commonly used starter kits.

DotNetNuke has an extensive content management system. In addition, it has an unrestricted Open Source BSD license and is free for use in both non-commercial and commercial environments. DotNetNuke (known as DNN) is referred to as a Web Application Framework because there have been many modules and extensions released since the project was first available. Its scalability and extensibility is well documented. Currently, there are over 25 modules that are distributed with DotNetNuke. These modules extend the functionality of the DotNetNuke Web application. Many hosting service providers will install the core DotNetNuke modules for developers.

**NOTE**

DotNetNuke can be previewed at *http://dotnetnuke.com/*. In 2007, support for ASP.NET 2.0 became available with DotNetNuke version 4.41.

## Planning Your Web Application

Because of the complexity of the web development projects, you will want to incorporate a team approach. The first thing you should do is plan your web site and gather your web development team. Who is on the web development team varies with the size, scope, and type of project, the size and type of company, and the technologies used. In a small company, some members of the team may take on multiple roles. In large enterprise applications, you may have many web developers and programmers involved in the project. Only a few of them may be members on the web development team, however.

At some phases, the team members may have varying degrees of responsibilities, as outlined in the following list:

- The **customer** may be an individual or company. The company may use their own resources and personnel to create the Web application or outsource some or all of the Web application development.

- The **business systems analyst** usually helps coordinate the communication as well as project management. The business systems analyst will also help identify the project scope, mission, and project statements, and the goals and measurable objectives of the project. The business systems analyst identifies member roles and sets up communication channels. Sometimes an additional account manager is used to work directly with the customer.

- The **software architects** may be one or more advanced web developers or network specialists. They have advanced skills and training in Web application, database, and network architecture and security. They help design the infrastructure and Web application programming standards. The network engineer and information architect may have oversight authority on the project in order to guarantee that the application is secure and robust.

- A **marketing research specialist** is used to help identify current trends and technologies used in related fields that help identify key components to the Web application.

- A **graphic designer** is used to provide the presentation layer, including page layout, design, navigational, and graphical elements. They may use existing media or create custom media and graphics for the web site.

- **Web developers** may range from entry-level HTML programmers to web database programmers. They will perform the actual coding of the Web application. You may also want to hire additional employees for data entry and content editing. These activities can be labor intensive but do not require the technical skills of a web developer.

11

- **Windows developers** may also be required. Some Web applications are integrated with intranet applications that are Windows-based. Therefore, although the user interfaces may be different, the underlying business logic and data access layers may be shared across the web and Windows applications.

- A **database administrator** manages the database management system and may also set up the database and database permissions.

- A **quality control specialist** is often used to promote consistency across the Web application and across other applications that may already exist. They also ensure that the requirements and standards are met. They may perform testing on the web site to determine performance and functionality.

- A **documentation specialist** is often used to create help systems and documentation for the Web application. There needs to be internal documentation for the web development team, and external documentation for the end user.

- A **network administrator** will have ongoing use to ensure that the Web application remains functional and available at all times. A network security specialist may also be called in to work with the network administrator to ensure that the file, folder, and database permissions are secured along with securing the Web application.

- There may be a **trainer** involved to help the customer or end user understand how to deploy, use, and maintain the Web application.

The software development life cycle for web development is an ongoing development process for web development projects. As you can see in Figure 11-14, the process starts with analysis, design, develop, test, deploy, and maintain.

## Analyzing Project Requirements

Usually the business systems analyst is the primary contact for the client and maintains the documentation, including the non-disclosure agreements, contracts, and scope of work documents. The analysis phase often cannot start until a non-disclosure agreement (NDA) is signed. In a **non-disclosure agreement**, the parties are contractually obligated to not share information from the project with other companies or the public at large.

At the start of the process, you will want to analyze your project requirements, which consists of the business goals and resources, target audience goals and capabilities, and technologies available. A **needs assessment** is performed to quantify the objectives, requirements, target audience, and deliverables. The needs assessment and project requirements typically are written up in a report called the **project requirements document**. The acronym **SMART** often is used to identify that the outcomes from the project must be specific, measurable, attainable, realistic, and time limited. The project requirements must be supported with marketing research. You can also perform your own focus groups. **Focus groups** use small numbers of users to try to obtain answers to questions about their products

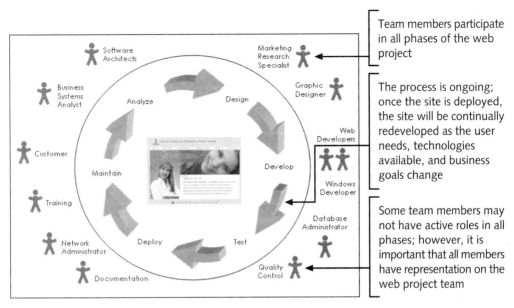

Team members participate in all phases of the web project

The process is ongoing; once the site is deployed, the site will be continually redeveloped as the user needs, technologies available, and business goals change

Some team members may not have active roles in all phases; however, it is important that all members have representation on the web project team

**11**

**Figure 11-14**   Web development life cycle

and services. If you use a focus group, make sure to include the typical user, and possibly some users who aren't computer or Internet savvy.

**NOTE**   You can also look to industry sites such as *www.WebMergers.com* to determine what trends are occurring in the industry.

Your next step is to qualify your customers based on the corporate goals and the strategic plan. You should identify the type of Internet connection of the end user who will be using the Web application. Slower connection speeds impact performance and you may need to limit client-server communications. You should identify the end user's browser, platform, support for plug-ins, and monitor resolution from market research and existing log files. You should identify constraints related to user technology.

Next, identify the technical requirements and infrastructure required. Remember to include backup of the data and program files, security requirements, and client support. Do you intend to have support on your site through e-mail, user groups, list server, or telephone support? How will you handle unplanned outages or other technical and security problems? Do you have an emergency disaster plan? You will need to plan for your Web application to be scalable. What is your level of use and throughput? For example, can your site support a sudden increase of 10,000 orders per day? As your web audience grows, you should be able to handle the increased volume without having to rewrite your entire application.

A good example of not accurately identifying technical requirements correctly is the Toys-R-Us web site. When they opened their online store, many users were greeted with a message stating that the site was too busy and to try again later during the holiday season. There were many other toy stores that sprouted on the web that year that were able to accommodate end users. Eventually, the maintenance of the Toys-R-Us web site was transferred to Amazon.com. Other companies like Victoria Secret and Quixtar also under-estimated their number of visitors and had to redesign their programming and networking systems. In 1999, Victoria Secret advertised on the SuperBowl and their online audience for their Victoria's Secret Fashion Show drew 1.5 million viewers. By turning potential customers away, they lost not only revenue, but also their reputation. Quixtar, a multi-level marketing company, had total sales of $1.058 billion for fiscal year 2005. When their site went live in 1999, their site was also unreachable by many of their customers. Because their customer base consisted largely of distributors, however, the down-time had less long-term effects on their business.

In the project requirements documents, you will include a study of the current financial, technical, and human resources available, Internet technologies and services available, issues related to the intranet, and impact on other operations. You will also prepare a project schedule and budget. The budget should also show the return on investment (ROI). ROI is often used by administrators to determine which projects to undertake. Essentially, the revenue generated by the project needs to be greater than the cost. Note, however, that many companies set higher limits, such as 20 percent above costs, before they approve a project.

## Designing the User Interface and Programming Requirements

Once the analysis is completed, you will want to provide a **creative brief** that outlines the design of the site. The creative brief provides the information needed to provide the user interface and will be included in the project requirements document. This process will involve the creative and technical teams. The creative teams generally include graphic designers and the technical teams generally include web developers. You will want the web designer to help provide a concept that can link the site together. This sets the tone for the user experience. For example, if your web site is about tourism in a village, you may want to use a street pole with street signs to navigate across the web site. You will want to provide documentation on the visual design for the site. Many graphic web designers create the web pages in Adobe PhotoShop before they create sample pages. Then, if they need to make a change, it is simpler to edit in Photoshop than it is with a web graphic file. The technical team will help provide guidance to the creative team. For example, the creative team may design a navigation bar that spans diagonally across the page. If technically this can't be done in this application, the technical team would communicate this to the creative team. By working together, you can decrease time used to develop designs that are unworkable.

Designing the site is not just about creating graphics, banners, and menus. It is about selecting the right layout and navigation for your target audience. You will design a user interface and provide a plan for including interactivity within the web site. Companies such as Yahoo! Shopping provide data on how your customers click through each page in your site. As a business manager, you can use this data to help develop models of what your customers prefer and what patterns emerge.

Note that graphic art and multimedia can be labor intensive and therefore expensive to develop. Create criteria of what your expectations are for the graphics and multimedia within your budget. In the Joy of Ireland e-commerce site, the time to edit the product photo was used to determine the hourly rate and quantity of work assigned to the graphic designer.

Web sites use a variety of web site navigation strategies. That is, some sites focus more on functionality and others focus on convenience as perceived by the customer. You should provide documentation that describes the layout of the page and the web site navigation. A **site diagram** provides information or a visual representation of how the pages are related through hyperlinks. A **web page schematic** provides an overview of the elements and content on the web page, including where they are placed.

Prepare a project specification including the functional/technical specifications, site architecture, site map, schematics, and design of the site. As you can see in the site map in Figure 11-15, the user enters the site on the default page, but can end the experience on a different page. This type of diagram is fine for small sites but not for large sites. For a large site, you can instead provide visual diagrams of possible and probable patterns of visits. This will help the architect understand how the visitor will use the site. For example, once the user has registered, the user should be automatically redirected back to their previous page, or forwarded to the membership page. A prototype may be useful in large sites with multiple navigation strategies and users. The prototype may be created in a web page editor, or in multimedia or presentation software.

**11**

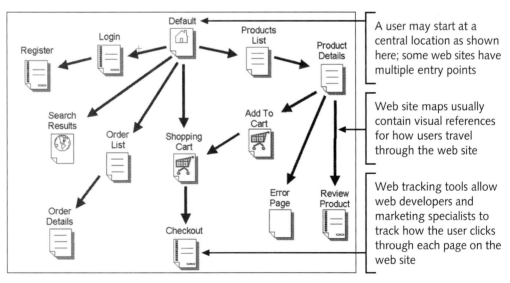

**Figure 11-15**   Sample site map

Another major part of the design process is the architecture of the Web application. There are individuals who specialize in designing Web applications for large corporate environments, where the information, accessibility, extensibility, and scalability are critical to the success of the project. Software solution architects often focus on Windows-based single user or multi-user applications, or on internal network applications. Today, software architects who specialize in Web application development have additional specialized skills in networking, security, web programming and web databases, web marketing, e-commerce, internationalization, and web development.

You will have specific production or programming guidelines before you start coding. For example, you will be provided with the information on the database format and structure. This may include details on the tables, fields, data directory, and possibly sample data. It is useful to have a data diagram of the relationships between the tables, as shown in Figure 11-16.

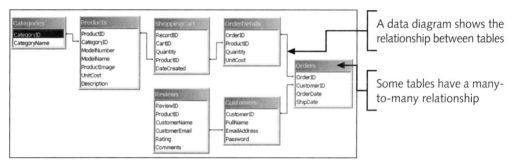

A data diagram shows the relationship between tables

Some tables have a many-to-many relationship

**Figure 11-16**   Data diagram to view relationships between tables

Remember to have the client sign off on the project requirements document in a contract before any production is started. Sometimes this is referred to as a **Marketing Requirements Document**, **Marketing Proposal**, **Service Delivery Agreement**, or **Scope of Work**. Provide the charges, but not the actual cost of building the site. Often a deposit is provided when the scope of work is signed. It is useful to have some of the sample layouts, designs, and sample content included with the contracts. Make sure to address under what conditions changes can be made in the contract and deliverables. Provide a detailed work breakdown structure, which consists of the key elements, tasks, and subtasks in the site. Some companies prefer to develop in workgroups, and in other companies the developers work independently on self-contained modules, providing documentation on the interface between modules.

## Developing the Web Application

Once the plan is identified, the web development process begins. You will want to make sure to provide instruction to the web developers on the project requirements related to directory structure, file names, and coding and scripting requirements. Some companies provide development servers for web developers to work with. You will want to provide sample templates, and track the development process. There are many project management software applications available such as Microsoft Project. This software allows you to track key events in the development process. If a critical component of the process is delayed, the software can help identify the impact of the project timelines and deadlines.

## Testing the Web Application

During and after development, you will perform multiple assessments or tests. A quality control specialist creates the test plan before the tests begin. Often these tests are determined at the beginning of the project and correlate directly with the outcomes defined in the **project requirements documentation**. The tests need to be specific and provide **metrics** to measure the features and functionality.

Testing of business outcomes is often called **requirements testing**. You need to be able to verify that the code you develop accomplishes the goals identified in the plan, follows the plan, and is implemented correctly. Quality testing of the code may be performed at various levels, from **page level testing** and **modular testing** to an integrated testing process where the servers simulate a realistic situation, such as a large increase in numbers of visitors. Testing may include performing function tests to determine what happens when the user progresses through the web site. Each testing scheme is known as a test case or **use case**. You may test multiple use cases in the testing phase.

Testing is critical when the application is integrated with other components, modules, databases, third-party tools, and other internal systems. Testing may be used to detect errors called bugs, but can also be used to determine if the project requirements were met. If errors occur, a report should be made and the errors should be corrected before the project is deployed. Sometimes, companies will deploy projects that have minor bugs, provided the project requirements were met. They later release patches for the bugs as soon as the release is available. This iterative process requires that the quality control workers determine if tests are required with each release. You don't test for everything, but you should test for common problems that can be disruptive to the system and that are potential security risks.

**NOTE** **Capacity testing** is measured in requests per second. You will want to perform additional testing to verify the server configuration, processing, servicing concurrent requests, load balancing capabilities, and data backup and recovery features.

Once the testing has been successfully completed, the application is deployed. Once you have deployed the application, you may want to repeat a final test before the site is available to the public. For example, you need to make sure all of the links work properly, the forms process correctly, the data web pages are able to access and modify data, and the site can handle additional volume.

## Maintaining the Web Application

An ongoing maintenance plan is put in place not only to detect problems, but also to prevent problems. You will also want to implement marketing and web site promotion strategies. For instance, Google provides ways to pay for the placement of an advertisement on a page when the user enters a special keyword. For example, The Junior League of Evanston-North Shore used **Google Ad Words** to provide a link to their web site when a Google user entered the keywords Junior League or Evanston. Affiliate programs, banner exchanges, and partnerships are additional ways web sites drive traffic to their web site.

Ongoing redevelopment will occur as needed. For example, your web site may need to upsize from Microsoft Access to SQL Server based on the numbers of users visiting the web site. You may need to provide additional features on the site that were not part of the initial plans. You can use tools such as web server log files, performance analysis tools, web site traffic analysis, purchasing and personalization trends, feedback forms, and click trails to determine problems that customers may be experiencing. Thus, as you can see from these examples that the life cycle for a web development application is an ongoing, collaborative process.

## New Tools and Technologies

Many new technologies are being developed every day that expand on the .NET platform and ASP.NET technologies. These technologies are often focused on a specific technology feature. Some of the longest running issues in web development are client-side performance and compatibility, server side performance, and resource utilization. Performance on the client is impacted by the client's connection, network and Internet access, Internet traffic, and server capabilities. In intranet Web applications, you may be able to require users to obtain and use specific hardware and software; however, in most situations, you cannot control the client resources and capabilities. On the web server, there may be other applications running and the web server may also have interaction with other types of servers. The web server is also handling a magnitude of client requests simultaneously. Technologies such as IFRAMES and Java Applets were not capable of solving the core problem.

In the following sections, you will learn about AJAX, which was developed to manage client-server interactions more efficiently, and Atlas, which integrated AJAX with ASP.NET applications.

## AJAX

Web developers have to create cross-browser applications. Currently, many of the user interface features require round trips to the server, which regenerates the client-side code. With each browser request, the request is sent via HTTP to the web server. AJAX (Asynchronous JavaScript XML) is an architecture that allows the application to save a complete round trip to the server on post back. That is, with AJAX you can refresh your portion of a web page without refreshing the entire whole page. With AJAX, you can build more complex applications with less client-side code. The processing occurs on a client's computer using some scripting, with data being exchanged with the server. Essentially the client-side code is making a remote call to the server for another resource.

AJAX uses a combination of client-side XMLHTTPRequest object, HTML, client scripting (JavaScript and Jscript), and CSS. The **XMLHTTPRequest object** is used to manage the exchange of data asynchronously with the web server. All of these standards are openly available. ECMAScript standards are the standards used for JavaScripts and are maintained by ECMA. The W3C maintains standards for HTML and XHTML, XML, and CSS.

The need to use JavaScript is one reason for web developers not to choose AJAX. If JavaScript is disabled in the browser, or the user has a device that does not support JavaScript, then AJAX won't work. Then the web developer is back to delivering multiple content for multiple platforms. AJAX also violates the purpose of layered architectures (n-tier) by intertwining the presentation logic and presentation layers.

AJAX is used in multiple web sites today such as Google Suggest and Google Maps. Third-party tools allow you to place ASP.NET controls inside of the AJAX container that automatically enables AJAX for the controls.

## Atlas

Microsoft Atlas was the initial code name for framework for using ASP.NET with AJAX. Atlas popularity and interest is evident as over 250,000 downloads occurred in 2006. With Atlas you can develop interactive, cross-browser Web applications. Atlas works across a variety of browsers with no additional modifications, including IE, Firefox, Mozilla, and Safari.

Atlas is free from Microsoft. When you download Atlas, you also receive a plug-in for Visual Studio .Net that allows you to create a blank Atlas application. The server-side functionality of Atlas is contained within Microsoft.Web.Atlas.dll, which resides in the Bin folder.

There are three versions of Atlas:

- Microsoft AJAX Library is the client-side JavaScript library that works with any browser, and supports any backend web server including PHP and ColdFusion.

- ASP.NET 2.0 AJAX Extensions is the server-side functionality that integrates with ASP.NET. In early release versions of Atlas, the tag prefix for the Atlas was `<atlas:>`; Atlas will be built-into the next version of ASP.NET as `<asp:>`.

- ASP.NET AJAX Control Toolkit (formerly known as the Atlas Control Toolkit) provides free, shared source controls and components to help developers use ASP.NET AJAX Extensions more effectively.

In practice, when you created master content pages, the pages were merged into a single page on the server. With AJAX, you can selectively modify a part of a page displayed by the browser, and at a future time update it without the need to reload the whole document. Ajax would be effective if you use multiple images and menus that would normally require multiple downloads on the client each time a page was requested.

**11**

## Integrating ASP.NET into Current Business Applications

Some companies wait until the technology settles before integrating the technology into their applications and others are early adopters. In one institution, the network administrator didn't notify the developer that the servers were upgraded to the .NET Framework 2.0. The developer was not familiar with the 2.0 version, although it had been released to the public for over a year. The department application he was responsible for was written in version 1.0 and was not working. Rather than fix the old version, the author recommended that the developer upgrade the application, which took less than a week. The improvements included increased performance, increased functionality, and reduced development time.

Although this situation worked out fine, the developer in question should have been aware of the technologies available and how they could have impacted the systems and Web applications. Keeping abreast of technology isn't difficult; in fact, there are many forums and user groups dedicated to ASP.NET for web developers. These focus on the technical questions surrounding ASP.NET. The difficulty lies in the time required for the developer to read the updated technical support documents, participate in forums, and practice using the new technologies.

Once a web developer has conquered the technical issues surrounding ASP.NET, he or she should then address the business case and application for ASP.NET. Often the web developer is educated formally in computer science and not business. Microsoft provides support for developers to help them analyze technologies. Case studies provide a foundation for beginning the discussion for best practices for web developers. Microsoft publishes a web site that displays case studies that use ASP.NET technologies. You can view case studies on the following:

- Mobile Web applications: *http://msdn.microsoft.com/mobility/casestudies/default.aspx*

- Microsoft Servers: *http://www.microsoft.com/windowsserver/facts/casestudies/default.mspx*

- ASP.NET technologies: *http://msdn2.microsoft.com/en-us/asp.net/aa336563.aspx*

- Web sites running ASP.NET: *http://msdn2.microsoft.com/en-us/asp.net/aa336566.aspx*

**NOTE** According to Microsoft, "ASP.NET 2.0 developers accomplished 113% more tasks in the same amount of time as ASP developers" and "ASP.NET 2.0 developers created web content pages up to 357% faster than ASP developers." (*http://msdn2.microsoft.com/en-us/asp.net/aa336674.aspx*). This article provided a detailed analysis of the practical application of ASP.NET to a typical web site application.

## Deploying an ASP.NET Web Application

In previous versions of ASP, before a component would work, you had to stop the web service, log into the web server locally, copy the component software to the server, register the component using the **RegServ32.exe application**, and then restart the web service.

This required access to the physical web server, or to run a program such as Telnet to provide command line access to run RegServ32.exe. Most developers do not have physical access or Telnet access to their web servers because of security restrictions. Furthermore, once a component was installed, it was available to other installed applications on the server. A license for the component may be for only one web site. It would be difficult to block other web developers from accessing the component in their Web application, however. In addition, it was very difficult to install multiple versions of the same application on the same server. So, you could not install different versions for different developers.

In the current version of ASP.NET, deployment of Web applications is simpler and does not require registration of the component or stopping the web service. You can install multiple versions of the same component and can restrict the use of the component to one or more Web applications. In ASP.NET, the component is the DLL file that contains the application logic, and is known as the assembly. The two locations for storing assemblies are the local application cache and the global assembly cache.

The **local application cache** is the default location for the assemblies for the local application. The local application cache is the bin directory located under the root directory of the application. Only the local application can access the assembly in the local application cache.

The **AppDomain class** manages the application process, and controls the assemblies and threads, such as loading and unloading assemblies. To install a compiled assembly, simply copy the .dll file to the bin directory of the application. The AppDomain class creates an in-memory shadow of the DLL file. The original .dll file is never locked. Therefore, any current connections with the in-memory shadow remain open. Any new connections are started with the new in-memory shadow. When there are no more connections with the current in-memory shadow, it is removed from memory. Any time the AppDomain detects a change in the .dll file, the in-memory shadow is replaced with the new version.

The **global assembly cache** is the default location for assemblies that are available to the entire server. Therefore, the global assembly cache can be shared by multiple applications. A hosting service provider may install several versions of the same application in the global assembly cache. The .dll file is stored on the server, but registered with the global assembly cache with the GacUtil.exe utility. Because there may be multiple versions of the same assembly, the GacUtil.exe utility registers the assembly and keeps track of the version of the assembly. The GacUtil.exe specifies the default version of the assembly. Applications are allowed to override the default settings.

Publishing your Web application on the Internet is as simple as copying files in Windows Explorer or another XCOPY application. Your web hosting provider may provide you with a file transfer protocol (FTP) account that allows you to transfer the files quickly to the web server. Usually, the FTP folder when you log in is mapped to the root folder of your web site. You can download an FTP program to transfer your files using the FTP account. If you have created an assembly, all you need to do is copy the assembly to the bin directory on the server. If you have compiled your Web application, there is no need to include the source code files, such as the class files located in the App_Code folder and the code behind the page files. You will want to transfer the .aspx pages, configuration files, and graphics or resource files to the server.

## CHAPTER SUMMARY

❏ Create class files and source code files and place them in the App_Code folder without directly compiling them. ASP.NET compiles the entire contents of the App_Code folder into a single assembly. Within your class definition, you can use members of an already existing class. Create custom controls by creating a namespace and create a class definition that inherits the control class from System.Web.UI.Control.

❏ Code Snippets Manager is a new tool that allows you to select from some of the commonly used activities from a predefined list. InferSchema reads through the XML file and infers the data schema from the node and leaf structures and data. The Create method of the XmlWriter creates the file and inserts the schema.

❏ Assemblies are stored within the bin folder of the web site. The Bin folder has the permissions to execute the code within the assemblies. The Provider Model allows you to create new versions of software that easily can be created and plugged into your application, which results in applications that are more flexible, expandable, customizable, and easier to maintain.

❏ Many third-party components work with Asp.NET. FreeTextBox is a free HTML editor. DotNetDuke is an open source application that developers use as a learning tool and template for beginning web sites.

❏ The Web development life cycle includes the tasks: analyze, design, develop, test, deploy, and maintain.

❏ AJAX is an acronym for Asynchronous JavaScript XML. AJAX is an architecture that allows the application to save a complete round trip to the server on post back. AJAX uses a combination of client-side XMLHTTPRequest object, HTML, client scripting (JavaScript and Jscript), and CSS. The XMLHTTPRequest object is used to manage the exchange of data asynchronously with the web server. Microsoft Atlas was the initial code name for framework for using ASP.NET with AJAX.

## REVIEW QUESTIONS

1. Which ASP.NET special folder is used to place code files that will be compiled at runtime?

   a. App_Data

   b. App_Code

   c. Local_Resources

   d. Bin

2. What class does a custom control inherit?

   a. System.Web.UI.Control

   b. System.Web.UI.Data

   c. System.Web.UI.SimpleVB

   d. System.Web.UI.HtmlTextWriter

3. Which tool allows you to select from some of the commonly used activities from a predefined list?

   a. Code Snippets Manager

   b. IntelliSense

   c. Toolbox

   d. MyTools

4. Which tool is used to find the physical path to your files?

   a. MapPath

   b. Path

   c. GetPath

   d. VirtualPath

5. Which method reads through the XML file and infers the data schema from the node and leaf structures and data?

   a. InferSchema

   b. GetSchema

   c. HtmlTextWriter

   d. XMLHTTPRequest

6. Which command line tool is used to compile your entire Web application before it is deployed?

   a. ASP.NET Compilation

   b. HtmlTextWriter

   c. Visual Basic .NET Compiler

   d. Framework SDK

7. Which third party control allows users to enter content similar to entering content in Microsoft Word?

   a. I Buy Spy

   b. TheBeerHouse

   c. FreeTextBox

   d. DotNetDuke

**11**

8. Who is the primary contact for the client, and maintains the documentation?

   a. account manager

   b. web designer

   c. network administrator

   d. information architect

9. Which is not a phase of the web development life cycle?

   a. analyze

   b. design

   c. test

   d. terminate

10. Which is not part of the acronym SMART?

    a. specific

    b. money

    c. attainable

    d. realistic

11. Which provides information or a visual representation of how the pages are related through hyperlinks?

    a. site diagram

    b. story board

    c. web page

    d. non-disclosure agreements

12. Which site provides data on how your customers click through each page in your site?

    a. Yahoo! Shopping

    b. Google Ad Words

    c. Forrester Research

    d. DotNetNuke

13. Where are project requirements communicated to the customer?

    a. Marketing Requirements Document

    b. Marketing Proposal

    c. Scope of Work

    d. all of the above

14. Each testing scheme is known as a test case or _____ .

    a. use case

    b. bugs

    c. black ox testing

    d. all of the above

15. Testing of business outcomes often is called _____ .

    a. Requirements Testing

    b. Group Testing

    c. Facilities Testing

    d. Substitute Testing

16. What does the acronym AJAX stand for?

    a. Adjusted Java XML

    b. Java XML Technologies

    c. Additional JavaScript Extras

    d. Asynchronous JavaScript XML

17. Which object is used to manage the exchange of data asynchronously with the web server?

    a. XMLHTTPRequest

    b. XML

    c. HTTPRequest

    d. HTTP Post

18. What is the name of the client-side JavaScript library provided by Microsoft for AJAX development?

    a. Microsoft AJAX Library

    b. Microsoft J# Toolkit

    c. Microsoft J# Library

    d. Microsoft ASP J# Library

19. Which technology(s) are required to support AJAX?

    a. HTML

    b. client-side scripting

    c. style sheets

    d. all of the above

20. What technology is required to publish your Web application on the Internet?

    a. local application cache

    b. RegServ32.exe

    c. AppDomain

    d. XCOPY

21. Compare the use of DHTML and AJAX to develop dynamic Web applications.

22. Pick one starter kit mentioned in this chapter. Visit the Microsoft and/or ASP.NET web site and read about the starter kit. Describe the architecture and features of the starter kit. List five types of Web applications that might use the starter kit. List five things that are not useful in the starter kit.

23. Visit one of the web sites in the Control Gallery list on the ASP.NET web site at *http://www.asp.net/default.aspx?tabindex=6&tabid=31*. Describe the control, identify the requirements, and list four benefits of using this component in a Web application. Provide the name of the component and the URL for the web site that contains the component.

---

# HANDS-ON PROJECTS

HANDS-ON
PROJECTS

## Project 11-1

In this project, you create a class that retrieves multiple sets of data from a database and publishes the data to the web page. You will also pass parameters from the web page to the class before you create the Web controls dynamically in the web page. You will use constructors to create a RadioButtonList, DropDownList, GridView control, DetailsView control, and AccessDataControls.

1. If necessary, start your web editor and open your **chapter11** project.

2. Open the **ch11_Proj1.vb** file in the App_Code folder. Below the first comment, insert the code to inherit from the System.Web.UI.WebControls.AccessDataSource class.

3. After the second comment, insert the code to create a new procedure named **ch11_GetSubCatID**.

4. In the subprocedure, insert the code to configure the AccessDataSource properties. The DataFile should be set to [author will fill this information in after copyedits]. The SelectCommand should be set to **SELECT [SubCategoryID], [SubCategoryName], [CategoryID] FROM [SubCategories] WHERE [CategoryID] = 27**. The SelectCommandType should be set to **SqlDataSourceCommandType.Text**.

5. Save and close the class file.

6. Open **ch11_Proj1.aspx** in the **ch11_Proj1** folder.

7. After the first comment, insert the code to create an AccessDataSource control named **MyADS**. Call the GetSubCatID method of the MyADS control.

8. After the second comment, insert the code to create a drop-down list named **MyDDL**. Set the AutoPostBack property to **True**, the DataTextField property to **SubCategoryName**, and the DataValueField to **SubCategoryID**. Set the DataSource property to **MyADS**. Add the control to the **PlaceHolder1** control collection.

9. Call the **DataBind** method for the web page class.

10. Click the **Save All** icon. Right-click the page in the Solution Explorer window and select **View in Browser**. The list of categories should populate the drop-down list. Close the browser and any open pages.

## Project 11-2

In this project, you use code snippets to help you create a page that interacts with the file system.

1. If necessary, start your web editor and open your **chapter11** project.

2. Open **ch11_Proj2.aspx** in the **ch11_Proj2** folder.

3. Use code snippets to help you create the code to read text from a file named **ch11_Proj2Input.txt** and write text to a file named **ch11_Proj2Output.txt** in the **ch11_Proj2** folder. Modify the code snippets as needed. You will have to replace the default values with **Proj2Input.txt** and **Proj2Output.txt**. Use the **MapPath** method to store the location of the path to the files.

4. Click the **Save All** icon. Right-click the page in the Solution Explorer window and select **View in Browser**. A message appears showing you the contents of the ch11_Proj2Output.txt file.

5. Close the browser and any open pages.

## Project 11-3

In this project, you include a FreeTextBox control in your Web application. You will download and install the assembly, and integrate your Web application with the FreeTextBox namespace and classes.

1. If necessary, start your web editor and open your **chapter11** project.

2. Download the FreeTextBox control at *http://freetextbox.com/download/* to a folder named FTB on your desktop. The latest version is 3.1.6. You will need another browser other than IE 6.0, or you can change the file extension from .aspx to .zip. Unzip the downloaded file and extract the file contents into the FTB folder. Open, read, and print the **readme.txt** file.

3. Copy the appropriate **FreeTextBox.dll** from Framework-2.0 folder into your **bin** folder in your **chapter11** project.

4. In your web configuration file shown in Figure 11-17, modify the code to support the httpHandlers for the new assembly.

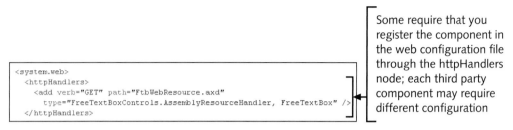

Some require that you register the component in the web configuration file through the httpHandlers node; each third party component may require different configuration

```
<system.web>
  <httpHandlers>
    <add verb="GET" path="FtbWebResource.axd"
      type="FreeTextBoxControls.AssemblyResourceHandler, FreeTextBox" />
  </httpHandlers>
```

**Figure 11-17**   Modifying the web configuration file

5. Open **ch11_Proj3.aspx** in the **ch11_Proj3** folder. Add the code to the top of the page to register the FreeTextBox control.

```
<%@ Register TagPrefix="FTB" Namespace="FreeTextBoxControls"
Assembly="FreeTextBox" %>
```

6. In the body section of the page, include this code to insert the FreeTextBox control.

```
<FTB:FreeTextBox id="FreeTextBox1" runat="Server" />
```

7. A label control has already been inserted into the page. The label will redisplay the contents from the FreeTextBox control when the user clicks on the submit button. Click the **Save All** icon.

8. Right-click the page in the Solution Explorer window and select **View in Browser**. Enter a welcome message into the text box control and click the **Submit** button.

9. Close the browser and any open pages.

# Case Projects

CASE
PROJECTS

## Project 11-1

Your manager has asked you to develop a file management Web application by the end of the working day. The default page is named ch11_case1.aspx and all pages should be accessible or linked from this page. Use code snippets to help create the file management Web application. In your application, you need to be able to copy files, list the directory contents, determine if a file or folder exists, determine the available space, create and delete files, create and delete subdirectories, rename a file or directory, read a file in the My Documents, search the directory for a file, search a file for an expression, determine the size and properties of a file, and compare the contents of two files. You may format the Web application using additional graphics, content, fonts, and color to enhance the appearance of the page. Use themes, skins, and Cascading Style Sheets to provide additional formatting. Save the files in the ch11_Case1 folder.

## Project 11-2

Your manager has asked you to develop a content management Web application by the end of the working day. The default page is named ch11_case2.aspx and all pages should be accessible or linked from this page. Use a third-party component such as FreeTextBox to help create the content management Web application. In your application, you need to create an authentication system to validate your user. Each user will have permission to create web pages in their folder. User folders should be named after the user ID. If the user is authenticated, allow them to create a new page in their folder. They also should be able to upload graphic files to their folder or images subfolder. You should also provide the ability for the user to delete a file or folder, except for their main folder. You can configure the FreeTextBox control using various properties available. You may format the Web application using additional graphics, content, fonts, and color to enhance the appearance of the page. Use themes, skins, and Cascading Style Sheets to provide additional formatting. Save the files in the ch11_Case2 folder. View each web page in your browser.

11

## Project 11-3

Your manager has asked you to develop a web database application by the end of the working day. The default page is named ch11_case3.aspx and all pages should be accessible or linked from this page. Use classes to help create the web database application. You may use the Northwind Traders, TaraStore, or Residential database, or create your own. There should be at least three tables that have a relationship defined. In at least one of the tables, there should be at least one field with currency information, one field which contains the name of a graphic file, and one field with a hyperlink address. Create a combination of queries using SQL statements and stored procedures to display the records. Create a stored procedure that takes an input parameter. Create a class that uses an input parameter to retrieve a set of records. Display the records in the web page. Create a web page that allows the user to create a new record with the FormView control. The programming data logic layer should be stored within a class file. Allow the user to upload graphic files to their folder or images subfolder. Use a Data control that displays the graphics in the web page. Create a web page that allows you to edit one of the tables. The data logic should be stored within the class file. Lastly, modify the class to create a GridView control or DetailsView control that does not have the columns auto generated. Create the bound, hyperlink, and template columns dynamically within the class file. (Note: You will want to review the help information in the MSDN Library on constructors for fields.) You should also provide the ability for the user to delete records. You may format the Web application using additional graphics, content, fonts, and color to enhance the appearance of the page. Use themes, skins, and Cascading Style Sheets to provide additional formatting. Save the files in the ch11_Case3 folder. View each web page in your browser.

## Project 11-4

Your manager has asked you to develop a Web application by the end of the working day. The default page is named ch11_case4.aspx and all pages should be accessible or linked from this page. Use a third-party component to help create the Web application. Provide documentation in your Web application to support how you configured your component. Provide a web page that describes the component, provides a link to where you downloaded it, and provides instruction on how to use the component in a Web application. List the features that are available to your application because you implemented the component. You may format the Web application using additional graphics, content, fonts, and color to enhance the appearance of the page. Use themes, skins, and Cascading Style Sheets to provide additional formatting. Save the files in the ch11_Case4 folder. View each web page in your browser.

## Project 11-5

Your manager has asked you to develop a Web application by the end of the working day. The default page is named ch11_case5.aspx and all pages should be accessible or linked from this page. Use third-party components, if necessary, to help create the Web application. Provide documentation in your Web application to support how you configured your component. You may integrate your Web application with a database or the file system to store your data. Provide the ability for the user to login and be authenticated. Users should be allowed to post messages within your blog. They should also be able to upload a graphic to an images folder and to display a hyperlink in the blog to the image. They do not have to be able to display of the image in the actual blog message. You may use a text box or another component to allow them to enter their message. Create a page to display the messages for the current month. Allow the user to change the display of the messages by selecting a different month. Provide the ability for the end user to sort the messages by date, author, and topic. You may format the Web application using additional graphics, content, fonts, and color to enhance the appearance of the page. Use themes, skins, and Cascading Style Sheets to provide additional formatting. Save the files in the ch11_Case5 folder.

# EXTENDING WEB APPLICATIONS

> **In this chapter, you will:**
>
> ♦ Describe how Web services communicate
> ♦ Learn how to apply Web services to business applications
> ♦ Identify Web service standards and protocols required to implement Web services
> ♦ Create a Web service using Visual Studio .NET
> ♦ Describe the SOAP protocol
> ♦ Create a web page that consumes a Web service using Visual Studio .NET
> ♦ Web service
> ♦ Explore the security methods used to protect a Web service
> ♦ Build a Web application that can deliver content to a mobile device

**W**eb services are one of the two main applications that are built using ASP.NET technology. While Web Forms deliver web content from a web server to a web-enabled client such as a web browser, Web services can deliver content to any device, application, or platform that supports XML Web services. Web services primarily target computer-to-computer interactions as a way to remove costly human contacts between organizations. In the past, building complex interfaces between multiple computer systems was expensive and laborious. Today, Web services allow you to build an interface quickly that can be reused by multiple computer systems.

One example of a Web service is the business application developed between Dollar Rent-a-Car and Southwest Airlines. Many airlines share a common airline reservation system of which Southwest Airlines is not a part. Dollar Rent-a-Car created an application to provide reservations from within this airline reservation system. Without Web services, Southwest would have had to join the airline reservation system in order to work with Dollar Rent-a-Car's system. Instead, Dollar Rent-a-Car and Southwest Airlines developed a Web service using ASP.NET that allows their two systems to work together. By using Web services, Southwest saved six months in development time, generated

$10 million in incremental revenue, and saved $250,000 in middlemen's fees. They were able to recoup their initial investment. This is one example of how a company can save time and money by using Web services to connect business systems. Microsoft and Dollar Rent-a-Car shared this example with developers when ASP.NET was introduced. You will find there are many examples of real applications built with Web services. Web services promise to bring information into applications from the Internet in much the same way that browsers have made information available to end users. In this chapter, you will learn how Web services communicate between applications, which standards and protocols are required for Web services, and how to create, consume, and secure Web services using Visual Studio .NET. You will also learn how to extend your Web application to alternative platforms such as PDAs and mobile devices.

## OVERVIEW OF WEB SERVICES

Web applications consist of a client, which is the browser application, and a web server. The web browser requests a web page from the web server. The web server interacts with other applications, such as a SQL Server database. Then, the web server delivers the web page to the browser. But what if the owner of the web site wants to share the web site's data with another web site? In previous versions of ASP, you would create a custom program on each web server that would allow communication between programs. One program would include a **Remote Procedure Call (RPC)** to call another application on the web server. This is not useful when you need to create applications that work across platforms, however. Integrating systems across multiple platforms is time-consuming, costly, and often ineffective. The .NET Framework introduces Web services as an integral part of the architecture, making it easy for you to create and consume these services with minimal amounts of code written. Web services use open standards and protocols, allowing programs to communicate easily across platforms.

In the following subsections, you will learn how Web services communicate, how businesses are applying Web services to business applications, and how to use your web editor to create and consume Web services.

## Communicating Between Applications with Web Services

With Visual Studio .NET and ASP.NET you can quickly build Web services that expose parts of your Web application to other businesses and applications. The Web service is part or all of a Web application that is publicly exposed so that other applications can interact with it. The program logic that is exposed via the Web service is accessible through standard web protocols such as HTTP, XML, and the Simple Object Access Protocol (SOAP). Therefore, the Web service is platform independent. This means that any client can access the application using standard protocols.

The SOAP calls are remote function calls that invoke method executions on Web service components. The output is rendered as XML and passed back to the user. It is useful to think of Web services as functions you write, that are available to anyone on the Internet, not just locally on your, or a client, computer. Web services can be used to create business-to-business applications, known as B2B. These applications typically communicate without any human interaction. You can also create Web services that are used to communicate data and call methods between a business and consumer. These business-to-consumer applications are also known as B2C.

Because Web services are built using open standards, you can use them to develop applications that can be called from a variety of clients on a variety of platforms. As a result, Web services combine the best aspects of component-based development and web development. (*Note*: Web services are like libraries that provide data and services to other applications. That is also why Web services are sometimes referred to as the Application Programming Interface (API) for the Web application.) Web services make it easier to build distributed Internet applications.

Microsoft provides additional information about Web services at *http://msdn. microsoft.com/webservices*. The .NET platform provides built-in support for invoking standards-based Web services. Unlike other development platforms, you do not need additional tools or SDKs to build Web services with .NET. All the necessary support is built into the .NET Framework itself.

Figure 12-1 shows how the Web service client communicates with the web server. The Web service client can be a Web application, a mobile application, or even a Microsoft Web application. In Figure 12-1, the Web service client is running a Web application. Therefore, in the figure, the Web service client is a web server and the content is delivered to a browser. (*Note*: The Web service client does not have to be running on a web server, unless it is running a Web application.) The browser is a client of the Web application. The browser does not know that the web server is communicating with a Web service. Additionally, the Web service client does not know that the Web service is communicating with any back-end applications or data sources.

The Web service client application does not communicate directly with the Web service application. Rather, it creates a WSDL proxy. WSDL stands for **Web Service Description Language (WSDL)**. The **WSDL proxy** is a class that is used to invoke the Web service. The WSDL proxy will communicate with the Web service application through a WSDL stub. The **WSDL stub** is the code that communicates between the proxy class and the Web service application. The purpose of the WSDL stub is to make the communication with the Web service application simpler and transparent. The developer does not have to know about the inner workings of the Web service application in order to invoke the Web service. Rather, the WSDL stub knows what can be sent into and out of the Web service application.

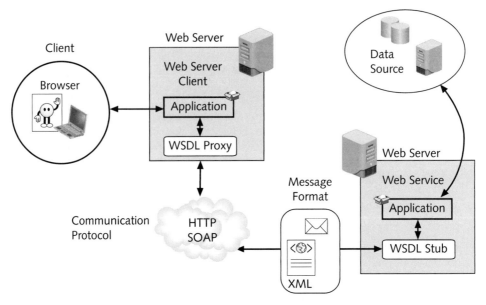

**Figure 12-1**    Web services provide a mechanism for application to communicate with each other

The WSDL proxy and stub can be created manually using the WSDL command-line utility (wsdl.exe), or automatically when you use your editor to create and consume your Web service.

The two applications need to be able to send messages and data back and forth across the TCP/IP network such as the Internet. The messages and data are formatted using XML standards so that both applications can understand them. These messages and data need to be modified to be sent over the Internet using HTTP, however. They are packaged using **Simple Object Access Protocol (SOAP)** as an envelope for the messages and data. Later in this chapter, you will learn more about WSDL and SOAP.

## Applying Web Services to Business Applications

Businesses want to share information across servers over the Internet. You may have seen web sites that list and compare products that are sold across multiple web sites. A recent trend on the Internet is for a web site, we'll call Traders Point, to display books from an online bookstore, we'll call Barney's Books. The Traders Point web site receives money, credit, or other bonuses for referring the user to Barney's Books to purchase the book. To create the link between Traders Point and Barney's Books, you could hard-code the Barney's Books hyperlinks into your application. If Traders Point is a significant business partner to Barney's Books, you could create a custom distributed application to the Barney's Books Web application.

A controversial technique that has been used to retrieve product information across web sites is scraping. **Scraping** a web site is the process of using a program to view a web site and capture the source code. The Traders Point programmer has to create a scraping application that goes to the Barney's Books web site, retrieves the HTML code, and then parses the HTML tags from the product data. Then, the Traders Point programmer has to create a program that integrates the new data now stored on the Traders Point web server into the Traders Point web site. This process would have to be repeated as often as Barney's Books changes. (*Note*: It is important that anyone who uses scraping obtain permission from the web site owner in order to prevent violating copyright laws.) While scraping works, it is labor intensive because any change in the original web site would require reprogramming of the scraping application.

A better solution is for Barney's Books to provide a Web service to its catalog application. Programmers could then use the Barney's Books Catalog Web service within their own Web applications. Barney's Books could limit who has access to the Barney's Books Catalog Web service. They could expose the entire program as a Web service, or only certain parts of the Barney's Books Web application. By making the Barney's Books Web application public with a Web service, any programmer could use Visual Studio .NET tools to integrate his or her web site with the Barney's Books Catalog Web service.

In addition to retrieving data, Web services can also interact with the Web application. In the Barney's Books Catalog Web service, the programmer could expose the ordering functions as a Web service. Then, the Traders Point web site could sell the books without the customer having to leave the Traders Point web site. The Traders Point web site would provide the user interface for the order form. When the customer submitted the form, the Traders Point Web application would order the product via the Barney's Books Catalog Web service. Thus, the Barney's Books Catalog Web service allows the Traders Point web site to act as a distributor for other goods and services on the Internet.

Dozens of ways exist in which Web services can benefit businesses. Let's suppose you work at a security firm in Chicago that manufactures security systems. One of the features of the system is to notify the owner of the property when an intruder has entered a house. You can write a program on the client that calls the web server application when an intruder is detected in the house. In this example, you might only need to pass the customer ID to the web server. The method that would be called on the web server application could then send an email or text message to the owner of the house. This method on the web server is the Web service.

One concept is to stream data, such as stock quotes or the weather forecast. The Web service provides the data, and the client application connects to the Web service to retrieve it. The client could be a browser or another web site. Let's suppose you are working in New York at a firm that manages stock portfolios for multiple firms. Your job is to write programs installed on web server A. You have created a program with a function that will return the current stock quote for your company. This information changes every ten seconds. Your customer, who runs his application on web server B in Houston, needs to display the stock quote on the web page. In the Web application you create on web server A, you would create

12

a method that when called, simply returns the stock price and converts the method to a Web service. The client in Houston would create a Web application on web server B that would connect to the Web service on the web server. The Web application on web server B would receive the stock price from the Web service, and then display the price in the browser.

Another example of a Web service is a real-estate database search application. Assume that several companies list their homes with a multiple listing agent. A real estate company could expose the ability to search for a house in the real estate database. The real estate agents can use the browser to search for homes based on criteria such as the number of bedrooms. The multiple listing service company could allow other web sites to connect to the real estate database Web service. Then, they would be able to allow their customers to search for homes via their web sites. For each sale that originated from the Web service, the real estate company could pay the web site a referral fee. In this case, the data sent by the Web service would be in XML-compatible format or an object that can be serialized such as a DataSet object.

Microsoft offers documentation on several case studies where their enterprise customers create and consume Web services. This documentation is at *http://msdn.microsoft.com/* and *http://www.microsoft.com/casestudies/*.

Web services focus on business-to-business applications. A company can use Web services to develop communication methods between applications within their own systems as well. This would be very useful to companies who must maintain back-end legacy systems. A Web service can be created so that the back-end system can communicate with the newer applications. Because the Web service often can be reused without additional programming, the Web service can be reused across applications. For example, a human resource director in a hospital may desire to have an application that obtains information about a particular employee, but the human resources database may be stored within a mainframe application. The Web service can be used to expose the data from the mainframe. If the human resource application sends the Web service an employee ID, the Web service will communicate with the mainframe and return the employee data. Consider the additional situation in which the nursing administrator needs to be able to access employee data. Instead of building an additional application, the nursing administrator only needs to build his or her application and call the Web service. He or she would not have to rebuild the Web service.

Many other uses of Web services are available. For example, you could use a Web service to deliver educational materials to schools around the country. Each school could integrate the Web service into its own curriculum, instead of purchasing a prepackaged curriculum, or building a custom curriculum.

Web services could also be used to build public service web sites. For example, volunteer organizations share many common areas of interests and needs. A volunteer organization could build a Web service that exposed their resources as a community service directory. The resources could be classified by type of service, such as fundraising, or they could be classified by the age of the targeted group. Then, any volunteer organization could use the same directory, or portions of the directory, within their web site. For example, one organization might want to show only listings for services within its state for children.

Another organization might want to show only services for fundraising in the Midwestern states. By using Web services, a variety of applications can access the data.

Web services could be used to retrieve national statistical data such as the census, or government records. You could build the Web service that contains information about all of the elected government positions. Although all counties in a state have their own governmental bodies, they all share the same state governmental body. Therefore, the counties would be able to access the state-specific data from the Web service. Individual cities and villages could access the county governmental data and their own local governmental data.

As you can see, there are many uses for Web services. To determine if a Web service would be useful, you might start with asking what information would be useful to share with other business or consumer entities. You may also want to ask, if you need to be able to trigger some action by the other business. Like all Web applications, Web services would participate in the same type of project development and team management. What is useful is to have someone on the team who understands what information is needed by the other business or consumer. They should understand both the business aspects and technical skills required for Web service programming.

## Using Web Editors to Create and Consume Web Services

Web services are at the core of the Microsoft .NET vision. Microsoft and IBM worked together to create the initial XML Web services standards. However, Web services can be created using a variety of developer tools and programming languages. The three main parts of building and consuming a Web service are shown in Figure 12-2. As shown in this example, Tara Store has created the Tara Store Web service. They also created a **WSDL contract** that provides information about how to connect to the Tara Store Web service. Tara Store's new partner, MaryKate's Housewares, has contracted to use the Tara Store Web service. They use the WSDL contract to learn how to connect to the Tara Store Web service. They create a proxy client, which connects to the Tara Store Web service. MaryKate's Housewares integrates the data into its own web site. The end user could be using a variety of applications to access the Internet such as a mobile phone or web browser. The client sees only the MaryKate's Housewares web site. They are not aware of the involvement of Tara Store, or the source of the product listing. Although this is an example of a business-to-business-to-consumer application, some Web services will be limited to business-to-business transactions.

### Building a Web Service

The easiest way to build a Web service with .NET is to use your web editor and create an ASP.NET Web service project. Visual Studio .NET creates all the necessary files, including the Web service files. The Web service files are by default called service1.asmx for the web page and service1.asmx.vb for the code behind the page.

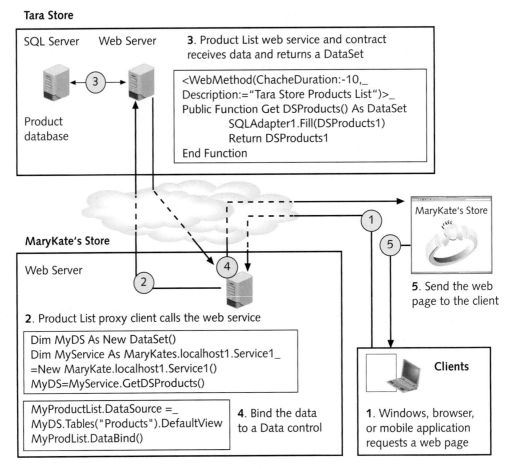

**Figure 12-2**   Building and consuming a Web service

In order to create a Web service, you must create a class method with standard input and output parameters and then mark those classes and the specific methods as exposable over the Internet by using the **WebMethod** keyword.

Three major components make up a Web service:

- The Web service on the server side
- The client application that calls the Web service via a Web reference
- A WSDL Web service description that describes the functionality of the Web service

Several resources for web developers exist on using XML with Web services. You can learn about using XML with Visual Studio .NET at *http://msdn2. microsoft.com/en-us/library/aa301578(VS.71).aspx*. You can locate sample business applications that contain and consume Web services on the *www. IBuySpy.com* web site or at *http://msdn2.microsoft.com/en-us/webservices/ aa740657.aspx*.

## The Web Service

The first part of the Web service is the server application that is exposed. In ASP.NET, the name of the file for the Web service must have the file extension .asmx. This Web service file compiles into a class. So, a Web service is a class that can be called over a TCP/IP network. As with a traditional web page, you can create the source file of the Web service by using a text editor such as Notepad, or a web development tool. If you are creating your code in a text editor, you need to import the System.Web.Services namespace into the source code for the Web service.

The Web service is compiled at runtime similarly to ASP.NET pages. Although the Web service typically is created within a Web application in the same assembly, you can create a separate assembly for the Web service. Web services are part of the ASP.NET application model. Therefore, the Web service must be accessible from a URL that is defined within the web server. Because the Web service was built within the ASP.NET Framework, it has access to the ASP.NET object model and all the ASP.NET objects such as Request, Session, and Application.

The Web service page is also divided into Design view and the code behind the page. The code behind the page can be written in any of the .NET languages. You can specify which parts of the Web service class should be exposed. The keyword, WebMethod, is used to identify the methods that are to be exposed. You can expose properties such as strings, integers, and expressions. The purpose is to allow program calls to the Web service and to be able to return information to the object that called the Web service. Although you can expose objects such as the DataSet object, Web services do not require you to create or expose programmable objects.

12

**TIP**

In the data files for this chapter, there are several projects in subfolders of the chapter12 Data folder. This is because the application that contains the Web services typically is not in the same application as the Web application. The application that contains the Web service can contain multiple Web services. You do not need to create an application for a new Web service. When you create a Web service using your editor, the program will create a default Web service page named **Service1.asmx.vb.** You can create a new item that is a Web service file in the application that stores your Web services. In this chapter, the application that stores all of the Web services is called Chapter12WebService, and the application that calls the Web services is called chapter12. It is important to remember that while you are working on the exercises in this chapter, you are building applications that communicate over http. The editor appends the port number to localhost and randomly changes this value each day. Therefore, if you complete the excises over a period of several days, you may have to edit manually the port number in the web references in the applications. Otherwise, you will see an server error message that says that no connection could be made because the target machine actively refused it. After editing the three files located in the App_WebReferences folder, right-click on the App_WebReferences folder and select Update Web References and then save your project. This will not occur if you are working with a production web server because the port numbers do not randomly change.

In this example, TRS provides credit score information to credit card companies and stores that issue their own credit cards. TRS needs to create a Web service that will use the customer Social Security number to return the customer's credit score.

1. Open the **Chapter12WebService** project.

2. Right-click the project and select **Add New Item**. Click the **Web Service** icon. Change the name in the text box to **TRS.asmx**. Check the **Place code in separate file** check box and then click the **Add** button. (*Note:* The TRS.vb file that is then created is located in the App_Code folder.)

3. Insert the code under the comment, as shown in Figure 12-3, which will create the GetCredit function and expose the code through the Web service. Save your changes.

4. Right-click the **TRS.asmx** file in the Solution Explorer window and then select **View in Browser**. The TRS Web service page appears that will be used to test the TRS Web service.

5. Click the hyperlink **GetCredit** to test the TRS Web service.

6. In the SSN text box, enter **333-33-3333** as shown in Figure 12-4 and then click the **Invoke** button.

7. The results are returned in an XML formatted document displayed in the browser as shown in Figure 12-5. Close this browser window but not the browser window used in Step 5.

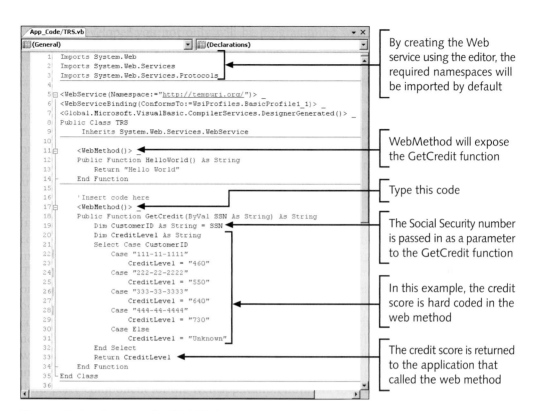

**Figure 12-3**   Creating the TRS Web service

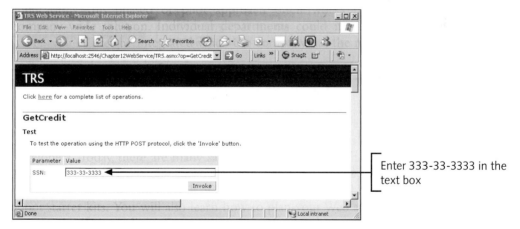

**Figure 12-4**   Testing the TRS Web service

## Locating Web Services

After the Web service is created, developers must be able to locate a discovery file, known as the Web service Description Language (WSDL) document. WSDL is a description language

12

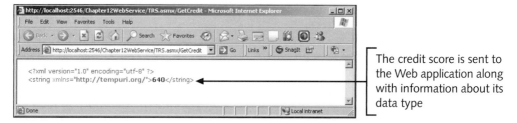

**Figure 12-5**    Returning a value from a Web service

that contains the information on how to interact with the Web service and how to format and send data to the Web service. The WSDL document is an XML document that describes the methods, namespaces, and URL of the Web service. When you use Visual Studio .NET to create your Web service, it automatically will create the WSDL document for you. The WSDL schema is an open standard used to create the WSDL document.

As you can see in Figure 12-6, the Web service client can locate the Web service application in several ways. The directory mechanism is the means to locate a Web service through a Web service **Discovery Directory**. Microsoft and IBM have teamed up to create the **Universal Description, Discovery, and Integration (UDDI)** specification, which can be used to create a third-party Web service Discovery Directory. You can use these UDDI directories to locate Web services and the WSDL document. The UDDI service is now available in the Windows Server 2003 software. You can learn more about the UDDI standards at *http://www. uddi.org*. Microsoft's UDDI server is located at UDDI.Microsoft.Com.

The second mechanism to locate the Web service is known as discovery. The developer can visit the web server and locate a Web Discovery Service file to locate the web server. The **Web Discovery Service** file ends in the file extension .DISCO. The default DISCO file is named default.disco. This file points to all of the Web services within your application and the location of the WSDL document. When you are using .NET development editors, you can use the Server Explorer window to locate the Web services on your server and network by reading the discovery files.

The third mechanism used to locate a Web service is to request the URL of the WSDL document from the owner of the Web service. In the previous exercise, you tested the Web service by simply viewing the Web service home page in the browser. Remember that while you are using the built-in Web service editor, the URL will consist of the web server referred to as localhost, and a port number that will change daily.

## The Proxy Class

Web services can be consumed programmatically or manually, and can be called from within your web or Windows application. Adding a **Web reference** to your application allows you to treat the Web service as a local application. Therefore, you can refer to the Web service class as if it were a local class.

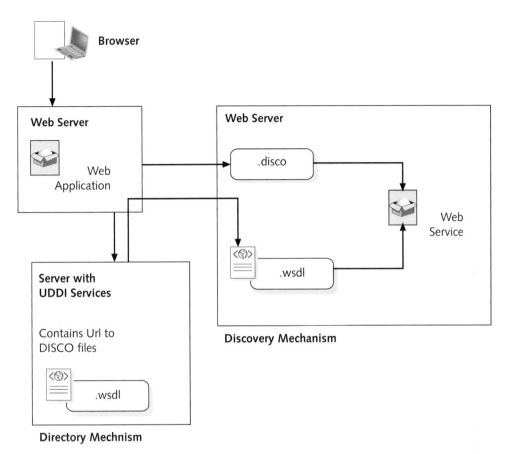

**Figure 12-6**   Locating Web services

Within the .NET development editor, the IntelliSense feature provides access to all of the properties and methods of the Web service class. Even if the Web service was created on a different platform with a different programming language, you can still call the Web service class and create programs that interact with the Web service properties and methods.

The Web service client application does not call the Web service class directly. The application uses the WSDL document to create a **proxy class**. The Web service client application calls the proxy class to invoke the Web service. The proxy class reads the WSDL document and verifies the delivery method. The XML-based request and response messages can be delivered using the HTTPGet method, the HTTPPost method, or SOAP. SOAP calls are remote function calls that invoke method executions on Web service components. The output is rendered as XML and passed back to the Web service client application. SOAP is an important part of creating and consuming Web services—it is the protocol that is responsible for routing the RPC message from the client to the server and returning the result to the client application. SOAP is based on XML and follows a relatively simple design that is easy to implement. SOAP's simplicity has contributed to its widespread support on just about any platform and development environment. As long as a Web service client application has support for SOAP, it can call the remote Web service and return data for it, assuming that the Web service client application is authorized.

If you are sending the message using SOAP, the proxy class creates the **SOAP envelope**, and then passes the envelope to the Web service. The SOAP envelope is used as a wrapper around the messages and provides information about the message format. After the web server receives the SOAP request, it creates a new instance of the Web service. After the Web service has been executed, the return value, indicated by the keyword **Return**, passes the output to the SOAP response. The SOAP response is sent over the HTTP connection to the proxy. The client converts the XML document into a format that is understandable by that client application.

If you think that the data within the Web service will not change frequently, you may want to use caching techniques to increase performance. You can turn on page caching by setting the page caching properties. Caching is not enabled by default for data source controls, but you can enable it by setting the control's **EnableCaching property** to true and setting the number of seconds to wait before refreshing the page using the **CacheDuration property**. If your URL that requested the page contains a query string, you can explicitly enable the page to cache each parameter by using the **@ OutputCache page directive** and adding the **VaryByParam attribute**. The individual Data controls can also be configured to cache their values. Simply set the **EnableCaching property** to True and set the **CacheDuration property** to the number of seconds to wait before recaching the Data control.

Synchronous calls wait for a response from the web server. Your Web service client application performance degrades if you must wait a long time for the response from a Web service. Asynchronous calls request the data from the Web service, and then continue processing the Web service client application. You can configure your application to send asynchronous calls to the Web service to increase the performance of your application. In a production environment, you may not be involved in both creating and consuming the Web service. You may only be creating the Web service and providing its description. Another company creates the Web service client application that uses your Web service description document to create the interface to your Web service application.

In the following example, the Maple Farms grocery store and Harmon Brothers department store both issue credit cards to their customers. In the previous exercise, you created the TRS Web service that will use the customer Social Security number to return the customer's credit score. Both stores will use this information to determine if they will issue a credit card to the customer. Although the credit score scale runs from 300 to 850, the vast majority of individuals will have scores between 600 and 800 with an average around 675. In this example, scores less than 500 will not be issued a credit card by the Maple Farms grocery store and scores less than 660 will not be issued a credit card by the Harmon Brothers department store.

1. Open another instance of your web editor and then open the **chapter12** project.

2. Right-click the **App_WebReferences** folder and then select **Add Web Reference**. In the URL text box, enter **http://localhost:[port number]/Chapter12WebService/TRS.asmx**. Make sure to replace the [port number] with your web server port number. Click **Go**.

3. In the Web reference name text box, enter **TRSWS** as shown in Figure 12-7, and then click the **Add Reference** button.

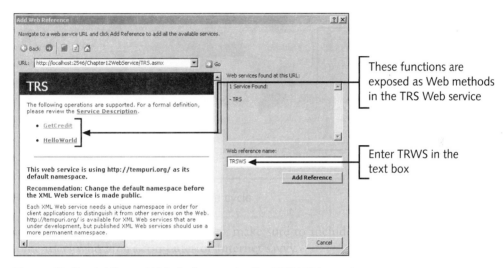

**Figure 12-7**    Adding a Web Reference to the TRS Web service

4. Right-click the **ch12_MapleFarms.aspx** page in the Solution Explorer window and then select **View Code**. Type the code as shown in Figure 12-8. Save your changes.

5. Right-click the **ch12_MapleFarms.aspx** page in the Solution Explorer window and then select **View in Browser**. In the text box enter **333-33-3333** and then click the **Submit my application** button. The page is as shown in Figure 12-9.

6. Close the browser but do not close the two instances of your editors. You will need them in the following exercises.

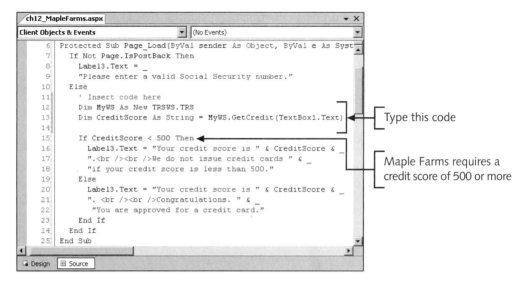

**Figure 12-8**  Calling the TRS Web service

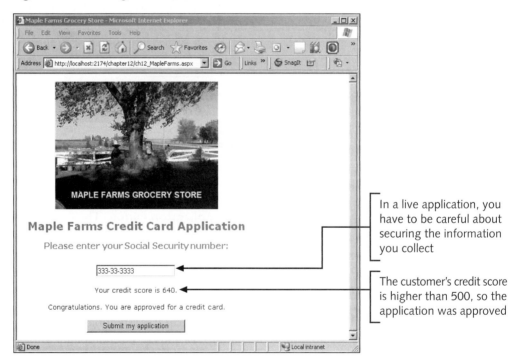

**Figure 12-9**  Using the TRS Web service

# WEB SERVICES STANDARDS AND PROTOCOLS

The HTTP protocol was selected as the primary delivery protocol of Web services because it can be used to deliver documents through proxy servers and firewalls. The three methods used to route the message over HTTP are HTTPGet, HTTPPost, and SOAP. When you create a Web service page such as default.asmx, ASP.NET automatically creates the support for a test page also known as the Service Description page.

In addition to calling the Web service, you can pass parameters to the Web service page with a query string, using the HTTPGet method. The HTTPPost method passes the parameters as a URL-encoded string, which contains the form field variable names and values attached to the body of the message. The SOAP protocol is the default method by which ASP.NET internally calls a Web service.

## Programming Web Services with .NET Development Editors

Web services are fully integrated into the .NET development environment. When you use either Visual Studio .NET or Visual Web Developer Express to create your Web service, the application generates the WSDL document, the DISCO document, and the test web page. You can use the breakpoints within the debugger tool and the tracing features to debug your Web service. When you use a .NET editor to consume a Web service, the application generates a client-side proxy class with both synchronous and asynchronous calls. Then, when you want to access an object, property, or function within the Web service, the local Web application treats the Web service as a local object. As a result, all the features of the .NET development environment, such as IntelliSense and debugging, are also supported.

## The SOAP Contract

The SOAP protocol is an industry standard that is maintained by the W3C. Simple Object Access Protocol (SOAP) is an XML-based protocol used for messaging delivery. SOAP is language independent and platform independent. The SOAP message is a remote procedure call over HTTP using XML. Because it is an XML-based message format, it can easily be transmitted over HTTP through firewalls and proxy servers. Because SOAP can represent remote procedure calls and responses from another application, it allows the client application to call the Web service over HTTP. The SOAP packet contains a SOAP envelope and the response in an XML document. The response may contain the XML data. And, because it serializes the calls and data in XML, SOAP provides a flexible way to express application defined data types. Once the application receives the XML data, the application can deserialize the data into an object such as the DataSet object. So, if you plan to create a Web service that creates objects, you likely will want to call the Web service by using SOAP.

SOAP is a simple protocol for publishing available services. The SOAP contract is an XML-formatted document called the WSDL. The SOAP contract describes the interface to the Web service. You can view the SOAP contract by opening a browser and typing the URL of the Web service followed by "?WSDL". The WSDL file is an XML-formatted file that describes how to call the Web methods using the SOAP protocol. The WSDL document describes the message exchange contract. The WSDL document name has the file extension .wsdl. So, the name of a SOAP contract for a Web service named MyService would be MyService.wsdl.

The SOAP contract uses the XML language to describe the location and interfaces that a particular service supports. The WSDL utility looks at the contract and generates the proxy class based on the contract. The WSDL utility is wsdl.exe. The utility requires you to pass the URL of the description. The parameter ?wsdl is used to generate the proxy. The WSDL utility does not work with the Web service directly, but through a proxy class. Because the default language used to generate the proxy class default is C#, you may want to use the /language or /l parameter to configure the language as Visual Basic .NET. The /protocol parameter is used for communication with the service. The /namespace parameter is used to configure the global namespace.

The default namespace for the proxy class for all Web services is *http://tempuri.org*. This namespace is a generic namespace used in WSDL documents. You can locate more information about the namespaces used in WSDL documents at the *http://tempuri.org* web site. You should change the reference to the tempuri namespace to your namespace when you are ready to deploy your Web application. (*Note*: If you are using Visual Studio .NET to create and consume Web services, you can change the Namespace attribute of the <Web-Method> tag.) After you create the proxy class, you need to compile it and place it inside the assembly cache. You can compile the application directly with the Visual Basic .NET or Visual C# compiler.

The code following this paragraph is a sample of how you can use the WSDL command-line utility to look at the contract and generate the proxy class. The wsdl command is the command to call the WSDL utility, and /language:VB configures Visual Basic .NET as the language of the class. The URL provides the location of the contract to the Web service.

```
wsdl /language:VB http://localhost/Service1.asmx?wsdl
```

The DISCO (discovery) document is not the SOAP contract. Rather, it is a pointer to the location of the Web services within the web project. The DISCO document is an XML document that examines the SOAP contract to describe the method and data formats within the Web service. The DISCO document describes how the proxy class should make calls to the Web service. Although in Visual Studio .NET you can use the tools to create and consume Web services, you can also use command-line utilities without Visual Studio .NET. The wsdl.exe file is used to create the SOAP contract.

You will use the **Visual Basic .NET compiler (VBC.exe)** to create the discovery document. You use the VBC.exe compiler to create the proxy class for a Visual Basic .NET class. Several parameters can be passed when you use the utility. The /username and /password parameters are provided to authenticate the application to the web server. The /domain parameter is the domain name that is needed to access the server. By default, the output from the discovery process is saved to a file in the current directory with the file extension .DISCO. You can specify an alternate directory with the /out parameter. You can suppress the output file entirely with the /nosave parameter. The /nologo parameter will suppress the Microsoft logo. The following sample code uses the Discovery tool to send the discovery information to a file in the temp directory:

```
Disco.exe /nologo /out:c:\temp\disco
http://localhost/websx/services.disco
```

The test page uses the HTTPGet method to test the Web service. Therefore, the names and values are passed with the URL in the query string. Because the HTTPGet method was used, the data is returned in an XML format, and not in a SOAP message. This gives you the opportunity to verify that you can connect to the Web service and retrieve data, however. Because Web services use standard web protocols, they follow typical web rules. For example, Web services are stateless, which means that, even though Web services expose classes, they are more of a remote procedure call interface than a remote class interface. None of the major Web service implementations support properties in any way. You can call methods with parameters rather than storing state in properties between method calls. To maintain state, you will have to use web server-specific functionality, such as the ASP.NET Session object, to store the state and retrieve it on subsequent hits. Furthermore, because Web services use the standard web architecture, the same tools you have used for HTML-based browser applications can also be used in the Web services code.

 A good article on how to consume a Web service using SOAP and Perl is located at *http://msdn2.microsoft.com/en-us/library/ms995764.aspx*.

TIP

**12**

## CREATING A WEB SERVICE

Web services are fully integrated into the .NET development environment. When you use .NET tools to create your Web service, the application generates the WSDL document, the DISCO document, and the test web page. You can use the breakpoints within the debugger tool and the tracing features to debug your Web service. When you create the Web service project, web editor automatically includes references to the System.Data, System.Drawing, System.Web, System.WebServices, and System.XML namespaces. Therefore, you do not have to import these namespaces into your projects

When you create a Web service, there are two parts. When you create a Web service in the .NET development environment, the file automatically will import the WebService namespace at the top of the file. Then, the page class is converted into a Web service by the insertion of the WebServiceAttribute, which means that the WebService keyword is inserted before the class declaration. The use of the WebServiceAttribute is optional. As shown in the code in Figure 12-10, however, you can include several properties with the WebServiceAttribute, including Namespace and Description.

As you can see in Figure 12-10, the namespace, name, and description of the Web service is configured. The **Namespace property** identifies a unique URL that can distinguish your

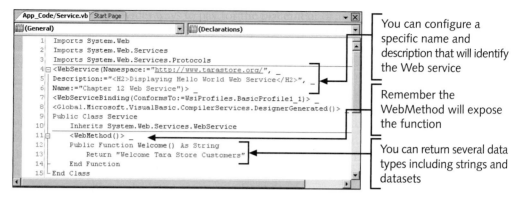

**Figure 12-10**   Modifying the Web service properties

Web service from other Web services on the Internet. The default uses the domain tempuri.org. If you use tempuri.org as the namespace, your Web service home page will display a message reminding you to change the namespace value. It is highly recommended to replace the tempuri.org namespace with your company's domain name. In the code in Figure 12-10, the default properties for the Web service were changed. The default namespace was changed to tarastore.org. The **Description property** can be used to provide information about your Web service. The Description attribute will appear on the Web service home page. Therefore, you can use HTML commands to format the Description attribute. The **Name property** allows you to provide a name for the Web service that will be displayed in the Web service home page.

Within the class defined within the Web service, you will expose one or more methods or functions by using the **WebMethod property**, as shown in the code in Figure 12-11. The WebMethod property provides several properties such as BufferResponse, CacheDuration, MessageName, and Description. The properties of the WebServiceAttribute are separated from the values using a colon and an equal sign. The **BufferResponse property** allows you to store the response on the server until the entire function is processed. Then, the data is returned to the client. By setting the BufferResponse property to true, you will improve your server performance by minimizing the communication required between the web server process and the ASP.NET worker process.

As you can see in Figure 12-11, the CacheDuration, MessageName, and description of the Web service is configured. The CacheDuration property is used to identify in seconds how long to cache results from the Web service. This method often is set when you are sending data from the Web service. The WebMethod will automatically cache the results for each unique parameter sent to the WebMethod. The **MessageName property** allows you to assign a name for the method that will be displayed within the Web service home page. The **Description property** allows you to provide a description for the method that will be displayed within the Web service home page. Because this is a string, you can format the description with HTML.

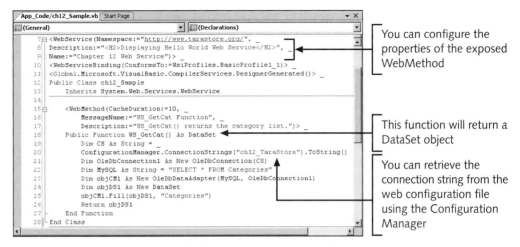

```
App_Code/ch12_Sample.vb  Start Page                                    ▾ × ×
(General)                            ▾   (Declarations)                      ▾
   7  <WebService (Namespace:="http://www.tarastore.org/", _
   8   Description:="<H2>Displaying Hello World Web Service</H2>", _
   9   Name:="Chapter 12 Web Service")> _
  10  <WebServiceBinding(ConformsTo:=WsiProfiles.BasicProfile1_1)> _
  11  <Global.Microsoft.VisualBasic.CompilerServices.DesignerGenerated()> _
  12  Public Class ch12_Sample
  13      Inherits System.Web.Services.WebService
  14
  15      <WebMethod(CacheDuration:=10, _
  16          MessageName:="WS_GetCat Function", _
  17          Description:="WS_GetCat() returns the category list.")> _
  18      Public Function WS_GetCat() As DataSet
  19          Dim CS As String = _
  20          ConfigurationManager.ConnectionStrings("ch12_TaraStore").ToString()
  21          Dim OleDbConnection1 As New OleDbConnection(CS)
  22          Dim MySQL As String = "SELECT * FROM Categories"
  23          Dim objCM1 As New OleDbDataAdapter(MySQL, OleDbConnection1)
  24          Dim objDS1 As New DataSet
  25          objCM1.Fill(objDS1, "Categories")
  26          Return objDS1
  27      End Function
  28  End Class
```

You can configure the properties of the exposed WebMethod

This function will return a DataSet object

You can retrieve the connection string from the web configuration file using the Configuration Manager

**Figure 12-11**   Exposing a method or function using WebMethod

A common task is to put the connection string in the web configuration file. When you place the data access code within a separate class file, you can configure the class to access the web configuration file directly, to retrieve the connection string. This method will prevent the connection string from being accessed through your Web application files. This method is also efficient because if you change the location of your database, you do not have to recompile the Web application. Although you can store the connection strings in variables and separate configuration files, there is no difference in security risk. You should encrypt your web configuration file prior to deployment.

## Creating a Web Service to Display Data from a Database

It is important to understand how to layer the data access layer independent of the presentation layer. In this exercise, you will verify the data connection settings for your application. Most of the issues developers have are with data connections. Before you develop your Web service, if it involves accessing a data source, you should always develop a test page to verify that the data connections can be made successfully before creating the Web service. This will help you validate your code and verify the connection. Remember that the App_Data folder automatically is mapped to the DataDirectory variable in the web configuration file. The Configuration Manager is used to retrieve the connection string from the web configuration file.

In the following exercise, you will create a Web service that when called, will send data from a database. The named ch12_TaraStore connection string to the TaraStore.mdb database already has been configured for you in the web.config file. You create a Web service in the Chapter12WebService application for Tara Store to allow other stores to display its merchandise. The Web service is located in the Chapter12WebService folder, and the Web application that will request the Web service. The Web service called Ch12_WS_ ProductsDS returns data as a DataSet object. You will use the WebMethod in the declaration line to declare the function as a Web service method. There are four functions that will be exposed; each corresponds to functions used in the ch12_CatMenu.aspx page. You will modify the code by inserting the web method. The code creates the Connection String, DataAdapter object, Connection object, Command object, and DataSet object for each of the four functions. When a Web service client application calls the Web service, it will be able to access these four functions and receive a DataSet object with the results.

1. Open the **Chapter12WebService** project, if necessary.

2. Right-click the **ch12_ CatMenu.aspx** page in the Solution Explorer window and then select **View in Browser**. The list of categories and the home image should appear. (*Note*: If the page does not display the category list or the home image, you must verify the connection string and the permissions on the database and folder before proceeding to the next step.) The objects in the ch12_ CatMenu.aspx page call the functions in the ch12_Products.vb page in the App_Code folder that creates a connection string variable, a Connection object, and four functions.

3. Right-click the **Ch12_WS_ProductsDS.asmx** page in the Solution Explorer window and then select **View Code**. The Ch12_WS_ProductsDS.asmx page is the Web service home page.

4. Below the comment that says 'Insert the WS_GetCat()WebMethod here', type the code in Figure 12-12. The code will configure the WS_GetCat() function as a WebMethod. You can refer to Figure 12-12 for the placement of the code.

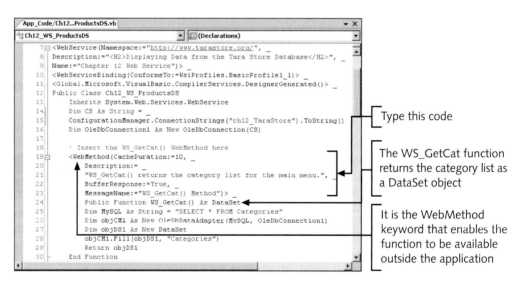

**Figure 12-12**   Creating the WS_GetCat WebMethod

5. Click the **Save All** button.

## Previewing the Web Service Home Page

In the next part of the exercise, you will view the Web service home page in a browser. This will provide you with a list of the functions and properties defined in the Web service. In this example, there are four functions exposed. Clicking the hyperlinks will take you to the test page, where you can test each function. The test page shows sample code that illustrates the sample request and response that is used when communicating with the Web service using SOAP, HTTPGet, or HTTPPost. From there you can test the Web service by invoking the function then and view the output in an XML-formatted document.

1. Right-click the **Ch12_WS_ProductsDS.asmx** page in the Solution Explorer window and then select **View in Browser**. Notice that the Web service Description property is shown in the Web service home page as <H2>Displaying Data from the Tara Store Database</H2>. Refer to Figure 12-13.

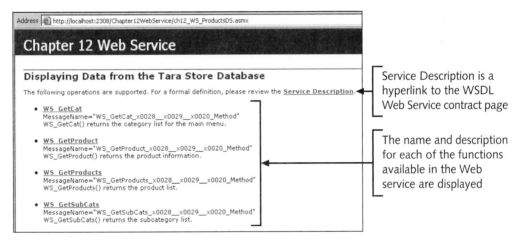

**Figure 12-13**  Web service home page

2. Click the hyperlink named **WS_GetCat**. This hyperlink is the method that was defined in the Web service. See Figure 12-14.

3. Click the **Invoke** button to test the WS_GetCat() method. An XML document is returned that describes the data and contains the data. As shown in Figure 12-15, the top portion of the document describes the data. There are no additional parameters passed with the query string in this example.

4. As shown in Figure 12-16, the lower portion of the XML file contains the product data.

5. Close the browser window that contains the XML document.

6. Click the **Back** button in the browser to return to the Web service home page.

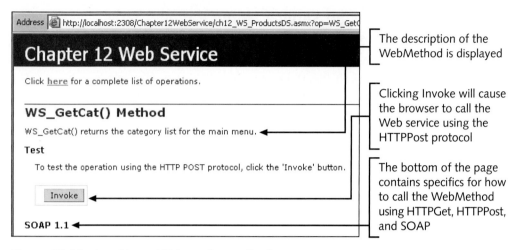

The description of the WebMethod is displayed

Clicking Invoke will cause the browser to call the Web service using the HTTPPost protocol

The bottom of the page contains specifics for how to call the WebMethod using HTTPGet, HTTPPost, and SOAP

**Figure 12-14**    Invoking a Web service method

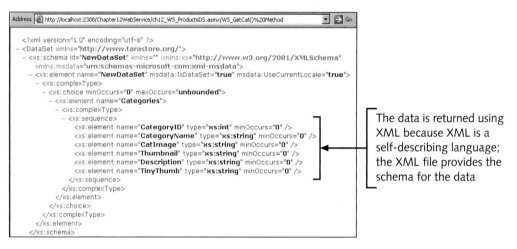

The data is returned using XML because XML is a self-describing language; the XML file provides the schema for the data

**Figure 12-15**    Viewing the schema

7. Click the hyperlink labeled **Service Description** to view the service contract. The URL of the Service Description page is the same as that of the Web service home page with ?WSDL appended, as shown in Figure 12-17.

8. Close the browser window. Return to your web editor. Click the **Save All** button. Do not close the project! This will quit the web server. You will need this project "running" on the web server to access it from the chapter12 Web application.

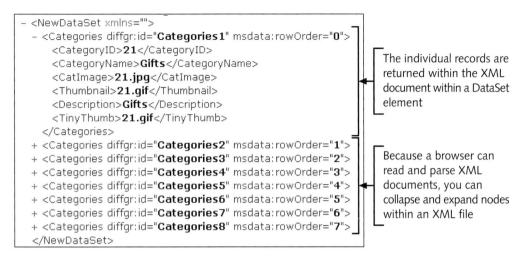

The individual records are returned within the XML document within a DataSet element

Because a browser can read and parse XML documents, you can collapse and expand nodes within an XML file

**Figure 12-16**   Viewing the data

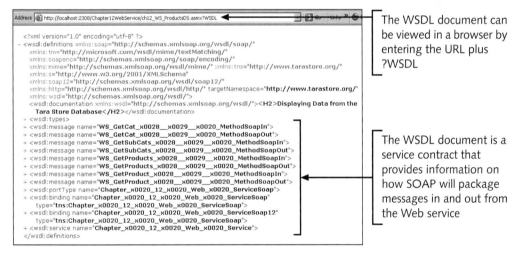

The WSDL document can be viewed in a browser by entering the URL plus ?WSDL

The WSDL document is a service contract that provides information on how SOAP will package messages in and out from the Web service

**Figure 12-17**   Web service description page

**TIP**

You can turn the line numbering feature on or off. The line numbering feature is useful when you want to locate specific lines of code. To configure the line numbering feature, go to the Options command on the Tools menu. Click the Text Editor tab, select All Languages, and then select General. Click the Line numbers check box to turn line numbering on, and then click OK.

## USING A WEB SERVICE

You can call Web services via the HTTPGet and HTTPPost methods, or via SOAP. Although the HTTPGet and HTTPPost methods are limited to sending only primitive data types such as integers and strings, they can also send arrays of these primitive data types. The SOAP protocol allows you to send any structure, class, or enumerator over the Internet. For example, you can send an ADO object, such as a DataSet object, or an array of Data objects.

When you send the information over the Internet, the information is packaged in a format that can travel over a TCP/IP network. **Serialization** is the process of changing an object into a form that can be readily transported over the network. For example, you can serialize the output of a structure, such as a DataSet object, into a string. With Web services, you use HTTPGet or HTTPPost to send an object; then the methods, properties, and values of the object can be rendered as elements of an XML document. The process of converting the object to an XML document is known as XML serialization. Once this has been done, you can use the HTTP Get and Post methods to retrieve the serialized object. You then change the string back into the original structure, which is known as **deserialization**. If the document is in XML format, you can also use the LoadXML method of the XML Document Object Model (DOM) to retrieve the XML data. When you use the .NET development editors to create and consume Web services, the editors will create the code necessary to serialize and deserialize your Web services.

**TIP**    You can learn more about XML Web services and serialization at *http:// msdn2.microsoft.com/en-us/webservices/aa740671.aspx*, *http://msdn2. microsoft.com/en-us/library/ms950721.aspx*, *http://msdn2.microsoft.com/ en-us/webservices/aa740676.aspx*, and *http://msdn2.microsoft.com/en-us/ library/182eeyhh(vs.71).aspx*.

When you use the .NET development editors to consume a Web service, the application generates a client-side proxy class with both synchronous and asynchronous calls. Then, when you want to access an object, property, or function within the Web service, the local Web application treats the Web service as a local object. As a result, all the programming tools, such as IntelliSense and debugging, are also supported with Web services.

The application that calls the Web service is a Web service client. You create a Web service client from an ASP.NET page. The Web service may be called by the HTTPGet and HTTPPost methods, or SOAP. The Server Explorer window allows you to see Web services installed within your local web server.

## Locating a Web Service

A partner of Tara Store is named MaryKate's Housewares. This company wants to distribute Tara Store's products on its web site. The owners hope to increase their market share by expanding their product line. They do not, however, want their customers to know of their relationship with Tara Store. In the exercise following this paragraph, you locate the Web service in the Chapter12WebService application, and add a Web reference to the chapter12 application for MaryKate's Housewares.

1. If necessary, open another instance of your web editor and then open the **chapter12** project.

2. In the Solution Explorer window, right-click the **App_WebReferences** folder, and then click **Add Web Reference**. The Add Web Reference dialog box opens. You can search for local or remote Web services.

3. In the address text box, enter the URL of the home page of the Web service, and then click **Go**. The URL is *http://localhost:[port number]/Chapter12WebService/Ch12_WS_ProductsDS.asmx*. You will have to change the [*port number*] to the port number for your web server from the previous exercise. The home page appears in the left window, as shown in Figure 12-18. (*Note:* You can view the contract and definition within the dialog box.)

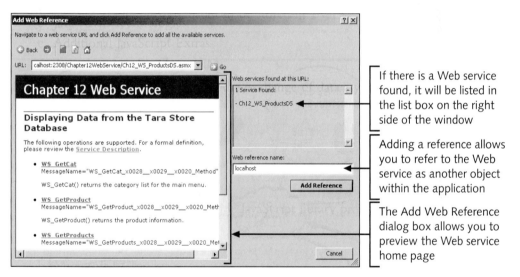

**Figure 12-18**   Adding a Web reference to a Web application

4. Change the Web reference name from localhost to **WR_Chapter12WebService** in the Web reference name text box.

5. Click the **Add Reference** button to add the Web reference to the chapter12 application. (*Note:* A folder named App_WebReferences is already added to the project. The reference to the WR_Chapter12WebService is added to the project App_WebReferences folder. You can refer to more than one Web service. Therefore, the Web reference contains a map with the URL to the Web services, and a copy of the service contract for each Web service.)

## Consuming a Web Service from a Web Page

In the next activity, you will modify a web page to consume the Tara Store Web service and displays Tara Store's products.

1. Right-click **Ch12_DisplayProducts.aspx** in the Solution Explorer window and select **View Code**.

2. Refer to Figure 12-19. Change 2308 to your port number. On the line below the comment that says Insert the code here, type the code as shown in Figure 12-19.

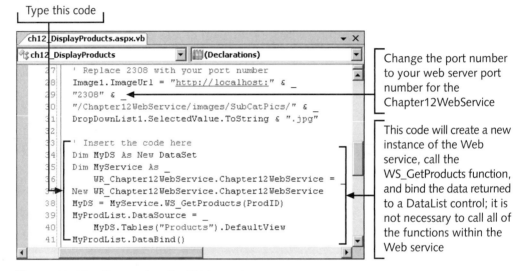

**Figure 12-19**  Consuming the Web service

**NOTE**  The port in the built-in editor will change daily. If at a later time you return to this exercise, you will need to change the port number in each of the files within the Web references folder for the WR_Chapter12WebService Web service, and in the Ch12_DisplayProducts.aspx page and the Ch12_DisplayProducts.vb page.

3. Click the **Save All** button.

**NOTE** The Web services are included within the Web references in the Solution Explorer window. When you bring in a Web reference for the first time, localhost represents that Web service. As you bring in additional Web references, however, the names of the Web reference may vary with the namespace of the Web service. Because you will be importing multiple Web references from the same server, localhost, the .NET development editor will append a number after localhost for each Web service referenced. It is important to make sure that in your code you refer to the Web service using the correct name in the Web reference list.

4. Click the **Ch12_DisplayProducts.aspx** in the Solution Explorer window. Right-click the page, then click **View in Browser**. In the drop-down list box, select **Royal Tara Bone China** and then click the **go!** button. A selection of products within the subcategory is displayed. Your page should look like the one in Figure 12-20.

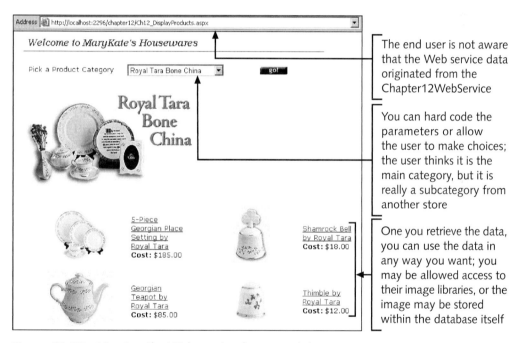

**Figure 12-20**   Viewing the Web service from a web browser

5. Close any open pages. Close both projects and both instances of your web editor.

## Locating Third-Party Web Services

Many third-party Web services are available. The UDDI is a directory service that was initially created by Microsoft and IBM to provide businesses a method for registering and searching for Web services. The UDDI allows you to search for third-party Web services. The home page for UDDI is located at *www.uddi.org*. Additional information about UDDI can also be located on Microsoft's web site at *http://www.microsoft.com/windowsserver2003/ technologies/idm/uddi/default.mspx*. (*Note*: Windows Server 2003 now includes Enterprise UDDI Services, which you can use to run your own UDDI service on your own computers.) When you add a Web reference to your project, instead of typing the URL in the location text box, you can click on the UDDI hyperlink to locate Web services.

In addition to the UDDI, you can find several third-party Web services at *www.xmethods.net*, *www.asp.net*, and *www.gotdotnet.com*. In Figure 12-21, you can see that the XMethods web site provides a listing of SOAP-based Web services. Not all Web services are created on Microsoft Windows platforms. You can easily integrate non–Windows Web services into your application in the same way you would integrate Microsoft Windows Web services.

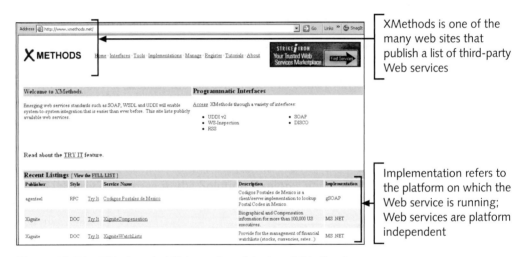

**Figure 12-21**    Third-party Web services listed on XMethods

When you add a Web service, you can locate additional Web services on your local network or server. To locate local Web services, add a Web reference to your project. Instead of typing in the URL of the Web service in the location text box, click the hyperlink Web References on Local Machine. The discovery document points you to where the Web services are located. Notice in the image that the Web service you created earlier will be listed.

The following is a list of web sites that discuss Web services or provide Web services:

- *directory.google.com/Top/Computers/Programming/Internet/Service-Oriented_ Architecture/Web_Services/www.hitmill.com/webservices/direct.asp*

- *www.prairietruckandtractor.com/webserdir.html*

- *www.programming-x.com/programming/uddi.html*

- *www.remotemethods.com*

- *www.soaprpc.com/webservice*

- *www.soapwebservices.com*

- *www.webservicelist.com*

Microsoft provides additional Web services for developers. You can locate the Microsoft Web services at *http://msdn2.microsoft.com/en-us/webservices/aa740657.aspx*. Microsoft.com Web service is an XML Web service that will enable you to integrate information and services from MSDN, TechNet, other Microsoft.com sites, and Microsoft Support. The Web service provides information about top downloads from Microsoft. Microsoft MapPoint allows you to integrate high-quality maps and other location intelligence into your applications. Three additional Web services that are useful for developers are as follows:

- Amazon.Com Web services — *www.amazon.com/gp/browse.html/?node=3435361*

- Google Web APIs Service — *www.google.com/apis/*

- TerraServer Web service — *terraserver-usa.com/webservices.aspx*

# SECURING WEB SERVICES

**12**

In addition to configuring state management, you will want to make sure your Web services are secure. Securing and maintaining security for a web site are important, ongoing responsibilities. Data-driven web sites and Web services often require additional security measures to protect data integrity and prevent malicious acts from hackers. You will want to limit access to your Web services by using an authentication scheme. Although the Web service architecture doesn't provide security for the developer, you can take advantage of the traditional security methods such as HTTP authentication services and SSL.

Creating a secure Web service is an important factor for business-to-business (B2B) and business-to-consumer (B2C) applications. You can secure a Web service by using traditional methods such as IIS Web security, Windows authentication and Windows NTFS file permissions, and Passport authentication. Web services also support the SSL protocol, which is used to encrypt data that is sent using the HTTP protocol. If you need to send the data securely over the Internet, you can also apply HTTPS instead of HTTP. The HTTPS protocol encrypts the message using Secure Sockets Layer (SSL) standards. You can identify when a web site uses SSL because the HTTPS protocol is used as the protocol within the URL.

Microsoft provides the Web services Enhancements (WSE) 2.0 Service Pack 2 for Microsoft .NET, which contains fixes to scalability and functionality; it also contains security tools that can be used to protect your Web service. WSE simplifies the development and deployment of secure Web services and allows developers and administrators to apply security policies on your Web service more easily. You can download WES at *http://www.microsoft.com/downloads/details.aspx?familyid=fc5f06c5-821f-41d3-a4fe-6c7b56423841&displaylang=en*.

The Web service is compiled dynamically with the application into the Web application's assembly that is stored in a dll file in the bin directory. If you precompile the application, the

WebService.vb file does not have to be deployed with the application. When the call is received for the Web service, the dll contains the code to respond.

Access to the Web service requires access to the Web service page. As you recall, this page ends in .asmx. You can protect this file by using the web server authentication tools. In IIS, you can configure access to the web site using the Directory Security tab. The web server allows you to filter users by IP address or domain name. You can require a specific authentication method such as anonymous access, or a specific Windows user account. You can require the client to use a secure communications channel such as SSL. (*Note:* You can read more about IIS security at *http://msdn2.microsoft.com/en-us/library/ms995343.aspx*. You can also learn more about IIS security at *http://support.microsoft.com/default.aspx?scid=kb;en-us;324964*.) In addition, you can protect your Web service by using ASP.NET security methods. To learn more about these techniques, go to *http://msdn2.microsoft.com/en-us/library/ms978378.aspx*.

You can also apply Windows NTFS file or directory security to protect the Web service page. Windows NTFS (Windows NT File System) allows you to protect the file by setting permission to the file for specific users and groups. The code following this paragraph configures the web.config file to use Windows security to authenticate the user. Then, within Windows, you need to set the permissions on the file.

```
<authentication mode= "Windows">
</authentication>
```

You can learn more about Windows security at *http://msdn2.microsoft.com/en-us/webservices/aa740661.aspx*. You can also learn about the best practices for creating a secure server at *http://msdn2.microsoft.com/en-us/library/ms994921.aspx*.

Although you used .NET development editor to create your Web service, there are some web developers who will use other tools, such as the SOAP Toolkit, to create XML Web services. There are several ways to protect Web services using SOAP. SOAP can take advantage of HTTP authentication. You can also use SOAP headers with your own encryption algorithms to secure your Web service. The SOAP header class is a class within the .NET Framework. You can inherit from this class, and then set the properties within the class. You can add data to the header and call methods. The SOAP packet contains a SOAP envelope and the response in an XML document. The response may contain the XML data.

To learn more about what the future of Web services/ASP.Net – 3.0 visit *http://www.oreillynet.com/windows/blog/2006/06/okay_slow_down_what_is_net_30.html*.

# WORKING WITH ALTERNATIVE PLATFORMS: PDAS AND MOBILE DEVICES

Today, a Web application is thought of as a series of web pages viewed with a browser. Each year more consumers are viewing web content via alternative devices such as mobile phones. Several major issues affect the development of a Web application for mobile devices. Because there is a wide range of hardware and software for these devices, not all of them have the same screen size, resolution, color, graphics, and multimedia capabilities. Some devices support a scaled-down version of a browser, and others only support text. Although some users connect directly via a network or wireless LAN, other users connect via modems or cellular phones. This means that web developers have less control over the end-user interface than ever before. Therefore, you should focus on what you can control, which is the content you are providing to the end user.

The main platforms for portable devices are Palm, Windows Pocket PC, and Windows CE. Some platforms, such as the Pocket PC, use a browser to display web pages, and some platforms use other HTML and XML interpreters. There are a wide range of mobile devices and platforms. Displaying web pages is very difficult on a mobile device because of the limited screen size. New technologies, however, have made it easier for developers to create a single mobile application that can be displayed on a variety of mobile devices and platforms. As the telecommunications and network infrastructures are upgraded to newer technologies, more mobile and Internet capabilities will be built into mobile and portable devices. As a result, you will see a greater demand for Web applications to expand to these new markets. Because mobile phones have become more sophisticated and are offering capabilities similar to PDAs, they often are referred to as **SmartPhones** or smart devices. PDAs, on the other hand, have additional capabilities, including phone and messaging.

There are several options for operating systems for these devices and several methods to program for these devices. Many of the new devices have the .NET Compact Framework installed. The .NET Compact Framework is a subset of the .NET Framework that is designed to run on portable and mobile devices. When you write the application using the .NET Compact Framework, the application is running on the client as a stand-alone application.

You can use .NET development editors to create .NET applications for the Pocket PC devices. Some developers may choose to use eMbedded Visual Tools to create their mobile applications. eMbedded Visual Tools is a stand-alone development environment used to create mobile applications. Mobile controls are built into the Microsoft .NET Framework.

In the following subsections, you will learn how to create a WML document, describe how Mobile controls are used to build mobile applications, and learn how to use Mobile controls to create a mobile application.

## Creating a WML Document

The standard used to program on a mobile device is the **Wireless Application Protocol (WAP)**. WAP is an open standard that is available from the Open Mobile Alliance at

12

*www.wapforum.com.* Within the WAP is the **Wireless S Protocol (WSP)**, which is a transport protocol that performs the same functions as HTTP for mobile devices. To work with web content, the WAP standards use an application standard known as **Wireless Markup Language (WML)**. Files that use the WML end with the file extension .wml. These files can contain small programs written in a scripting language such as VBScript. If the file contains programming scripts, the file extension ends in .wmls. Wireless bitmap images end in .wbmp.

When you develop applications for wireless devices, you need to view the results on the device, or use a device simulator. Most mobile devices supply a simulator for developers. Device emulators simulate several devices and allow you to apply different templates, called skins, to the emulator. Each device has its own skin, which you can view on the device emulator. The simulator is installed on your desktop computer to test your applications. The Nokia 7110 phone device simulators are available at *http://www.forum.nokia.com*. You can also use the OpenWave device simulator to test several types of phones. The **OpenWave Simulator** allows you to simulate phones from Ericsson, Mitsubishi, and Samsung. Open-Wave can be found at *http://developer.openwave.com/dvl/*.

NOTE

You can configure your web server to support WML files by adding a MIME Map for the file extension .wml with content type set to text/vnd.asp.wml.

WML is compliant with the XML protocols, and therefore is case sensitive. You must also close each tag, with a closing tag or by adding a forward slash to the end of the opening tag. All WML files contain the MIME type declared in the document type declaration:

```
<?xml version="1.0"?>
<!DOCTYPE wml PUBLIC =-//WAFORUM??DTD WML 1.1//EN
"http:///www.wapforum.org/DTD/wml_1.1.xml">
```

The rest of the document is enclosed in a single pair of WML tags, which serve as the root element of the WML document. The WML card metaphor is used to organize content delivered to a mobile device. So, a WML file consists of a deck of cards. Each card is a screen of content. Although the entire file is sent to the device, only one screen is displayed at a time. Each card is identified with the card tag: <card>. The title attribute of the card is used to provide a description of the content within the card. You can link WML documents using a hyperlink created with an anchor tag <a>. The href property of the anchor tag is used to identify the target in the WML document. You can set the target to an internal target or to another URL. Additional tags, such as the line break, paragraph, and bold tags, commonly are used in mobile devices.

## Building PDA and Mobile Applications in .NET Development Tools

Older versions of Visual Studio .NET required the web developer to download the Mobile Internet Toolkit from Microsoft. The current Mobile controls available within .NET development editors allow you to create mobile applications. These Mobile controls generate WML, compact HTML (cHTML) for Japanese i-mode phones, and HTML 3.2. The selection of what output is chosen is determined when the client connects to the Web application. In other words, two devices could connect to the same mobile application and the Mobile controls would generate a different set of code.

You can create ASP.NET pages that can be displayed on mobile devices. The ASP.NET web pages that contain Mobile controls are known as **Mobile Forms**. The tool within .NET development editors that allows you to create Mobile Forms using a GUI is called the **Mobile Internet Designer**. You do not have to create the WML code. ASP.NET will generate the code that is appropriate for the mobile device. So, if you use ASP.NET, the ASP.NET **Mobile controls** will generate the WML output for your Web application. Just as with Web Forms, you can also create Mobile Forms by using an editor or in a simple editor such as Notepad.

The Mobile controls inherit from the `System.Web.Mobile` namespace. You can add Mobile Forms to an ASP.NET Web application, or create a mobile web project and create the Mobile Forms within it. The Mobile Web Forms tab is shown in Figure 12-22.

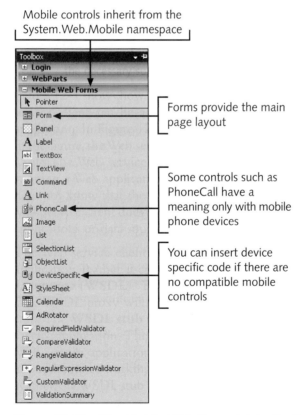

**Figure 12-22**   The Mobile Web Forms tab in the Toolbox

## Using Mobile Controls in an ASP.NET Application

Mobile controls inherit a code behind the page named System.Web.UI.MobileControls. MobilePage. Each web page contains a register directive that is used to register the mobile tag controls with the Mobile control namespace. So, on the first line of code on the web page, you will see the code as shown in Figure 12-23. This code is automatically placed on the Mobile Form by your editor when you create the Mobile Form.

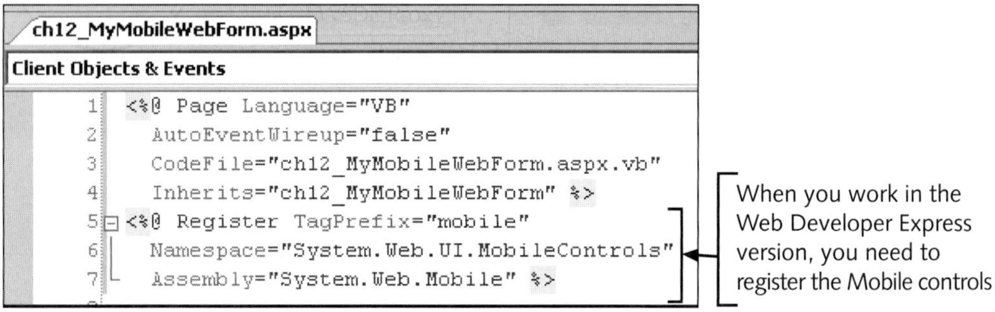

```
ch12_MyMobileWebForm.aspx

Client Objects & Events

1   <%@ Page Language="VB"
2       AutoEventWireup="false"
3       CodeFile="ch12_MyMobileWebForm.aspx.vb"
4       Inherits="ch12_MyMobileWebForm" %>
5   <%@ Register TagPrefix="mobile"
6       Namespace="System.Web.UI.MobileControls"
7       Assembly="System.Web.Mobile" %>
```

When you work in the Web Developer Express version, you need to register the Mobile controls

**Figure 12-23**   Registering mobile Web controls

Mobile controls have similar properties to Web controls. However, they have additional properties that are specifically for mobile devices. For example, for each item within the List control, the **Text attribute** assigns the value and the displayed text. The **Decoration property** identifies the type of list. By default, the List control Decoration property is set to none. The Decoration property may also be assigned to Numbered or Bulleted.

There are many other Mobile Form controls that you can insert into a Mobile Form. You can add AdRotator controls and Calendar controls to the Mobile Forms. You can also create a form with text boxes. The text fields can only exist on one line, however. Multiple-line text boxes are not supported. You can also use TextView control to insert long text blocks. TextView can support some formatting such as bold, italic, and hyperlinks. You can use the Numeric Text controls with WML devices only. The Password Text control displays an asterisk instead of the number in the screen window, but it does not hide the value from the code behind the page. You can use Validation controls to validate the form fields, similarly to how they are used with Web Forms. You cannot use client-side JavaScript to display error messages with the Validation controls. If you use a ValidationSummary control, you must keep the control on a separate form and use the FormToValidate property to assign the control to a Mobile Form. The error messages are not displayed interactively as you move from control to control. Because the List object is created with a control, you can change the list items programmatically. You can insert command buttons that can be used to send a command with the OnItemCommand property for the ItemCommand event.

## Creating a Mobile Form

In the following exercise, you will create a basic Mobile Form using your .NET development editor. Although these controls look similar to ASP.NET Web Form controls, they have additional properties to support Mobile Forms. In the code behind the page, the program binds a list to an array. Because the WML is XML compliant, you can view the document in an XML reader such as Internet Explorer if you do not have a mobile device simulator installed. (*Note:* If you have a device emulator installed, you can also view the page in the device emulator.)

1. Open your **chapter12** solution if it is not already open. Right-click the **ch12_MyMobileWebForm.aspx** file in the Solution Explorer window and then select **View Designer**. The Mobile Form appears smaller on the web page. This is the default width of the form.

2. Drag a **Label** control from the Mobile Forms tab in the Toolbox to the form.

3. With the Label control selected, view the properties in the Properties window. Change the (ID) of the label to **lblStoreName**.

4. Change the font to **Trebuchet MS**, the ForeColor property to **#004040**, the Alignment property to **Center**, and the Bold property to **True**.

5. Change the Text property to **Tara Store Home Page**.

6. Drag a **List** control from the Mobile Forms tab in the Toolbox to the form below the label control.

7. Change the List control properties for the font to **Trebuchet MS** and for the ForeColor to **#004040**.

8. Click the **Source** tab. Notice that the form and each of the form fields are tagged with the mobile prefix.

9. Click the **Save All** button.

10. Right-click the **ch12_MyMobileWebForm.aspx** file in the Solution Explorer window and then select **View in Browser**. The page is displayed as shown in the Internet Explorer window in Figure 12-24.

**Figure 12-24**  Viewing a Mobile Form in a browser

11. View the source code for the web page in the browser. Right-click the page and then select **View Source**. Notice that there is no sign of Mobile Forms or WML. The ASP.NET Web application sent the code that was supported by the device.

12. Close the browser.

In the preceding exercise, not all of the content is displayed on the screen. You must scroll down to view additional content. You can set the **Wrapping property** of the form to NoWrap to stop the control from wrapping. Wrapping allows content that extends over a long line to wrap to the next line. If wrapping is turned off, the user must scroll horizontally to view long lines. You can also set the **TextView property** to enable pagination for large amounts of text. You can set the **Paginate property** for the Mobile Form to true. Using pagination allows you to divide the list into multiple pages. When you create the list, you can display the default pagination properties, or set the values of the displayed text with the **PagerStyle properties**. In the sample code that follows this paragraph, the **PageLabel property** of the PagerStyle properties identifies the number of pages that are available. You can also add the **NextPageText** and **PreviousPageText** PagerStyle elements to your page and assign them a text value to display in the window, as shown in the following sample code:

```
PagerStyle -PageLabel="Page {0} of {1}"
PagerStyle -NextPageText="Continue"
PagerStyle -PreviousPageText="Back"
```

Each card can be represented by a separate Mobile Form within the WML document. You can then create a Link control to link to other cards within the same file, or to another WML file. The **NavigateURL** is used to identify links. The pound sign (#) is used to indicate an internal link.

With the WML file, you easily can insert scripts within the Mobile Form document. You can interact with page events, such as Page_Load. You can detect if the form has any mobile capabilities in the Page_Load event handler or in the Machine.config file. Within the Machine.config file, the <browserCaps> section identifies the support for mobile devices, which are exposed through the MobileCapabilities class. You can also use form templates to provide reusable content, such as the HeaderTemplate and FooterTemplate. Several Mobile Form controls can contain other controls such as the paragraph, line break, bold, italic, and anchor HTML tags.

## Creating Multiple Web Forms

In the following activity, you will modify a page that creates multiple Mobile Forms in the same document.

1. Right-click **ch12_MultipleForms.aspx** in the Solution Explorer window and then select **View Markup**. Insert the code for the last form after the comment as shown in Figure 12-25. (*Note*: The text will not wrap the same as shown in the figure.)

Type this code

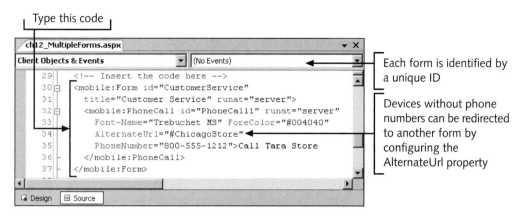

**Figure 12-25**   Creating multiple Mobile Forms

2. Click the **Save All** button. Right-click the page and then select **View in Browser**. (*Note*: If you have a device emulator installed, you can also view the page in the device emulator.) The page is displayed as shown in Figure 12-26.

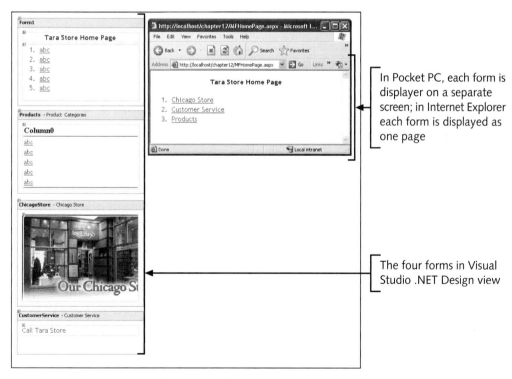

**Figure 12-26**   Viewing multiple Mobile Forms in a browser

3. Click the **Products** link. Click the **Back** button in the browser.

4. Click the **Chicago Store** link. Click the **Back** button in the browser.

5. Click the **Customer Service** link.

6. Click the **Call Tara Store 800-555-1212** hyperlink. The browser is redirected to the Chicago Store page.

7. Close the browser and all the files in your editor. Close the chapter12 Web application.

## CHAPTER SUMMARY

- Web services are used to expose part or all of an application. In ASP.NET, the name of the file for the Web service must end in the .asmx extension. The keyword, WebMethod, is used to identify the methods that are to be exposed.

- The Web Service Description Language (WSDL) schema is used to create a WSDL document that describes the functionality of the Web service.

- Microsoft and IBM have teamed up to create the Universal Description, Discovery, and Integration (UDDI) specification, which is used to locate Web services.

- Web services may be called by the HTTPGet and HTTPPost methods, or by SOAP.

- In Visual Studio .NET, the Web application uses the WSDL document to create a proxy class. The Web application calls the proxy class to invoke the Web service. The proxy class reads the WSDL document and verifies the delivery method.

- The SOAP contract is an XML-formatted document called the WSDL. The test page uses the HTTPGet method to test the Web service.

- You can secure a Web service by using the traditional methods such as IIS Web security, HTTPS with SSL, Windows authentication, and Passport authentication.

- The Wireless Application Protocol (WAP) is an open standard used to create programs on a mobile device. Wireless Markup Language (WML) is the programming language used to create the code for the mobile applications. WML is compliant with the XML protocols. The WML files use cards to organize and divide the structure of the WML document. You can use additional HTML tags within the WML language, such as the anchor tag.

- Device emulators, such as the OpenWave Simulator, allow you to simulate phones from a variety of vendors. The web server must be configured to recognize the mobile application file extensions, and to run the mobile applications. By using .NET developer applications, such as Visual Studio .NET and the Mobile Internet Toolkit, developers can create mobile applications using ASP.NET Mobile server controls. A web page that contains Mobile controls is called a Mobile Form. Mobile controls inherit a code behind the page named System.Web.UI.MobileControls.MobilePage. You can view the output of the WML file within a browser.

# REVIEW QUESTIONS

1. Which method is used to call applications over a TCP/IP network?

   a. RPC

   b. ADO

   c. Web service

   d. Web Form

2. What file extension is used to identify a Web service?

   a. .asmx

   b. .aspx

   c. .asp

   d. .ascx

3. What format(s) is/are used to query the Web service using the autogenerated test page?

   a. HTTPGet

   b. HTTPPost

   c. SOAP

   d. All of the above

4. The default namespace for all Web services is _____ .

   a. *http://tempuri.org*

   b. *http://www.tempuri.com*

   c. *http://www.uddi.org*

   d. *http://www.uddi.net*

5. The _____ keyword(s) is/are used to define a function as a Web service.

   a. Web service

   b. WebService

   c. WebMethod

   d. Web Methods

6. What keyword in the Web service declaration is used to cache the results from the Web service?

   a. CacheDuration

   b. Cache

   c. CacheAll

   d. WebCache

7. What keyword(s) in the Web service declaration is/are used to describe the Web service in the default test page?

  a. Description

  b. Name

  c. ID

  d. All of the above

8. Which URL would provide the Service Description Page?

  a. *http://localhost/WebService/Service1?WSDL*

  b. *http://localhost/WebService/WSDL?*

  c. *http://localhost/WebService/?WSDL*

  d. *http://localhost/WebService/Service1.asmx?WSDL*

9. Which method of the XML Document Object Model (DOM) is used to retrieve the XML data?

  a. GetXML

  b. LoadXML

  c. LoadXMLData

  d. ReadXMLData

10. Which object is used to call the Web service?

  a. Web service Alias

  b. Proxy Service

  c. Proxy Class

  d. Web service Public Class

11. What does SOAP stand for?

  a. Simple Object Access Protocol

  b. Simple Object ASP Protocol

  c. Simple Object Access Pages

  d. Serialized Object Access Protocol

12. What method(s) should be used to call a Web service that accesses a Data object?

  a. HTTPGet

  b. HTTPPost

  c. SOAP

  d. All of the above

13. What company(ies) initiated the UDDI standards?

    a. Microsoft

    b. IBM

    c. Sun

    d. Both a and b

14. The _____ is a directory service that provides businesses with a method to register and search for Web services.

    a. UDDI

    b. ASP

    c. WebServices

    d. ASMX

15. What method(s) can be used to secure Web services?

    a. IIS Web security

    b. Windows authentication

    c. SOAP headers

    d. All of the above

16. What third-party tool(s) from Microsoft provide(s) authentication services?

    a. NTFS

    b. Passport

    c. SSL

    d. All of the above

17. Which tool(s) within Visual Studio is/are used to add a Web service to a Web project?

    a. Web reference

    b. Web service

    c. XML Web service

    d. All of the above

18. What is the file extension of the discovery document that is created when you create a Web service in Visual Studio .NET?

    a. .DCO

    b. .ASMX

    c. .DISCO

    d. .DISC

**12**

19. If your company uses a firewall, when should you use Web services?

    a. Never. You can't use Web services with firewalls.

    b. Use them only if the company uses a proxy server.

    c. Anytime. Web services can send files through a firewall.

    d. Use them only when the firewall supports the SOAP protocol.

20. What type(s) of applications can call a Web service?

    a. Web applications

    b. Window applications

    c. Java applications

    d. All of the above

21. From what namespace do Mobile Web Forms inherit?

    a. System.Web.Form.Mobile

    b. System.Web.MobileForm

    c. System.Data.Web

    d. System.IO.Web

22. What organization maintains the WAP standards?

    a. InterNIC

    b. Network Solutions

    c. World Wide Web Consortium

    d. WapForum.com

23. Which markup language is used to build WAP applications?

    a. WML

    b. ASP

    c. VB.BET

    d. ASP.NET

24. Which prefix is used to create a Mobile control?

    a. mobile

    b. asp

    c. pda

    d. cellular

25. Based on your experience and what you learned in this chapter, compare five things that are different between Windows programs and Web services.

26. Describe three types of applications not presented in this chapter where Web services might be used in a business scenario.

27. Explain how Web service programming provides a new way to encapsulate programming logic.

28. Visit Google, Yahoo!, or another search engine. List three other providers of Web services content. Provide the URL, the company name, the Web service name, and a short description of the Web service.

29. List five things you could do to protect a web site that provides Web services to other companies.

30. Compare and contrast business-to-business and business-to-consumer web sites. Would one be more applicable for either Web services or mobile applications?

31. Explain the challenges for building a Web application that supports multiple PDAs and mobile devices.

---

# HANDS-ON PROJECTS

## Project 12-1

In this project, you create and consume a banner ad Web service.

1. Open the **Chapter12WebService** Web application.

2. Expand the ch12_proj1 folder to be able to right-click the ch12_proj1.asmx files. Right-click the **ch12_proj1.asmx** and then select **View Code**. In Code view, add the code as shown in Figure 12-27. Create the WebMethod, which displays the banner randomly. Then, add the GetAd function to generate a banner ad object with two properties, ImageURL and NavigateURL, which are both strings. Make sure to replace the port number with the one that is current on your computer.

3. Click the **Save All** button.

4. Open another instance of your .NET editor and open the **chapter12** application. Add a **Web Reference** named wr_ch12_proj1 to the new banner ad Web Service at *http://localhost:2308/Chapter12WebService/ch12_proj1/ch12_proj1.asmx*. Make sure to change the port number to your current port number.

5. Right-click **ch12_proj1.aspx** in the Solution Explorer window and then select **View Code**. This file will retrieve one of the banner ads using a hyperlink control named Hyperlink1. Insert the code in the Page_Load event handler to call the Web service and retrieve the image name and URL from the Web service, as shown in Figure 12-28. Make sure to change the port number to your current port number in the code that sets the value for the Ad.ImageURL or the images will not display properly.

6. Save the page. View the page in the browser. Click the **Refresh** button several times to see the banner ad rotate images randomly. Print the web page, your source code, and the source code for the Web service.

12

Type this code

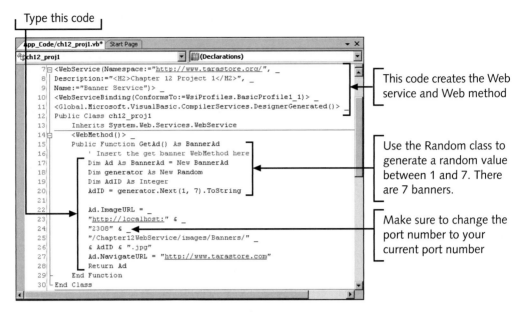

Figure 12-27    Creating the banner ad Web service

Type this code

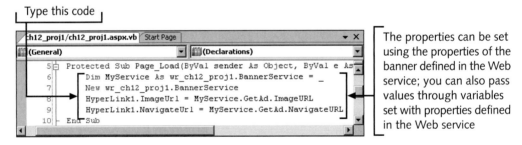

Figure 12-28    Consuming the banner ad Web service

HANDS-ON
PROJECTS

## Project 12-2

In this project, you create a banner ad Web service using the values from the database.

1. Open the **Chapter12WebService** Web application in your .NET editor.

2. Expand the ch12_proj2 folder to be able to right-click the ch12_proj2.asmx file. Open the ch12_proj2.asmx page. Use the **SqlDataSource** to connect to the **Ch12_Banners** SQL Server database in your App_Data folder. Select all of the fields and all of the records within the Banners table. Then, generate a DataSet named **DS_Banners** based on the Banners table, and add the DataSet to the designer. Add a **DataView** and set the Table property to the **Banners** table.

3. Right-click the **ch12_proj2.asmx** page and then select **View Code**.

4. In Code view, add the code as shown in Figure 12-29. This code includes a function to generate a ch12_proj1_BannerAd object with properties for each of the properties in an image hyperlink such as ImageURL, NavigateURL, ImageWidth, ImageHeight, AltText. Make sure to change the port number to your current port number in the code that sets the value for the Ad.ImageURL or the images will not display properly.

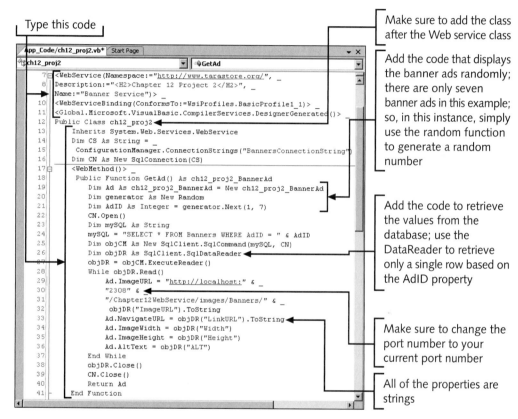

Type this code

Make sure to add the class after the Web service class

Add the code that displays the banner ads randomly; there are only seven banner ads in this example; so, in this instance, simply use the random function to generate a random number

Add the code to retrieve the values from the database; use the DataReader to retrieve only a single row based on the AdID property

Make sure to change the port number to your current port number

All of the properties are strings

```
App_Code/ch12_proj2.vb*  Start Page
ch12_proj2                                    GetAd
  7  <WebService(Namespace:="http://www.tarastore.org/", _
  8  Description:="<H2>Chapter 12 Project 2</H2>", _
  9  Name:="Banner Service")> _
 10  <WebServiceBinding(ConformsTo:=WsiProfiles.BasicProfile1_1)> _
 11  <Global.Microsoft.VisualBasic.CompilerServices.DesignerGenerated()> _
 12  Public Class ch12_proj2
 13     Inherits System.Web.Services.WebService
 14     Dim CS As String = _
 15     ConfigurationManager.ConnectionStrings("BannersConnectionString")
 16     Dim CN As New SqlConnection(CS)
 17     <WebMethod()> _
 18     Public Function GetAd() As ch12_proj2_BannerAd
 19        Dim Ad As ch12_proj2_BannerAd = New ch12_proj2_BannerAd
 20        Dim generator As New Random
 21        Dim AdID As Integer = generator.Next(1, 7)
 22        CN.Open()
 23        Dim mySQL As String
 24        mySQL = "SELECT * FROM Banners WHERE AdID = " & AdID
 25        Dim objCM As New SqlClient.SqlCommand(mySQL, CN)
 26        Dim objDR As SqlClient.SqlDataReader
 27        objDR = objCM.ExecuteReader()
 28        While objDR.Read()
 29           Ad.ImageURL = "http://localhost:" & _
 30           "2308" & _
 31           "/Chapter12WebService/images/Banners/" & _
 32           objDR("ImageURL").ToString
 33           Ad.NavigateURL = objDR("LinkURL").ToString
 34           Ad.ImageWidth = objDR("Width")
 35           Ad.ImageHeight = objDR("Height")
 36           Ad.AltText = objDR("ALT")
 37        End While
 38        objDR.Close()
 39        CN.Close()
 40        Return Ad
 41     End Function
```

**Figure 12-29**   Creating the banner ad Web service using a database

5. Click the **Save All** button.

6. Open the **chapter12** application in another instance of your .NET development editor and add a **Web Reference** named **wr_ch12_proj2** to the new Web service at *http://localhost:2308/Chapter12WebService/ch12_proj2/ch12_proj2.asmx*. Make sure to change the port number to your current port number in the code that sets the value for the Ad.ImageURL, or the images will not display properly.

7. Open **ch12_proj2.aspx.** In Code view, type the code as shown in Figure 12-30.

8. Save the page. View the page in the browser. Click the **Refresh** button several times to see the banner ad rotate images randomly. Print the web page, your source code, and the source code for the Web service.

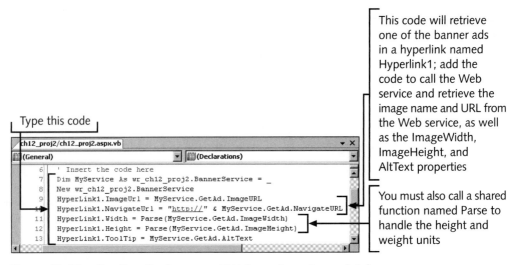

Type this code

This code will retrieve one of the banner ads in a hyperlink named Hyperlink1; add the code to call the Web service and retrieve the image name and URL from the Web service, as well as the ImageWidth, ImageHeight, and AltText properties

You must also call a shared function named Parse to handle the height and weight units

**Figure 12-30** Creating the banner ad Web service using a database

HANDS-ON
PROJECTS

## Project 12-3

In this project, you create a web page that can be viewed on a mobile Web application.

1. Open the **chapter12** application in your .NET editor.

2. Expand the ch12_proj3 folder to be able to right-click the ch12_proj3.asmx file. Right-click the **ch12_proj3.aspx** page in the Solution Explorer window and then select **View Markup**.

3. Type the code as shown in Figure 12-31 after the Selection1 control and the two line breaks. This page creates a Mobile control to display the phone number. The entire page includa selection list that is used to display phone book information stored in a HashTable. The code you will enter will display an active phone number that can be dialed from mobile devices.

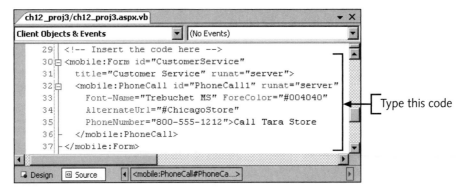

Type this code

**Figure 12-31** Creating an interactive Mobile Form

4. Save the page. Right-click the **ch12_proj3.aspx** page and then select **View in Browser**. The entire page includes a selection list that is used to display phone book information stored in a HashTable.

5. In the drop-down list select **Friend** and then click the **Dial the number** button. The text for the PhoneCall control changes to Dial the phone! 800-555-2222.

6. Close the browser window and all the pages.

## CASE PROJECTS

### Project 12-1

Your boss would like to use a third-party Web service already established on the Internet. Your task is to implement a third-party Web service. Visit a web site such as *www.uddi.org*, *www.xmethods.net*, *www.asp.net*, or *www.gotdotnet.com*, or visit one of the Web services mentioned in the chapter. Locate one Web service that you would like to implement within your web site. Create a web page named ch12_case1.aspx in the ch12_case1 folder in the chapter12 project that consumes the Web service. On your web page, document the information about the Web service such as:

❑ Name of the Web service

❑ URL where you found the Web service

❑ Description of the Web service

❑ Who owns the Web service

❑ The costs required to use the Web service

❑ The requirements to consume the Web service

❑ The procedure for consuming the Web service

Create a web page named ch12_case1_ws.aspx in the ch12_case1 folder in the chapter12 project. Write the code to consume the Web service in this page. Create a hyperlink form the ch12_case1.aspx page to the ch12_case1_ws.aspx page. View the web pages in the browser, and print out the web pages and the source code.

### Project 12-2

Your boss would like you to create a membership database that can be accessed by other companies. You decide to implement a membership Web service named ch12_case2 in the Chapter12WebService application. Create a database named ch12_members that contains member information. You can use Access or SQL Server to create your database. Then, create a Web service named ch12_case2 in the Chapter12WebService application that exposes the membership data. Create a new page named ch12_case2.aspx in the ch12_case2 folder in the chapter12 application. Write the code to consume the Web service and display the membership data. Print out your web pages and the source code.

## Project 12-3

You are the information technology manager for a new corporation. You decide to implement a Web service named ch12_case3 in the Chapter12WebService application. Create a database named ch12_case3 that contains information that you want to expose. You can use Access or SQL Server to create your database. Then, create a Web service named ch12_case3 in the Chapter12WebService application that exposes the data using a parameterized query. Create a new page named ch12_case3.aspx in the ch12_case3 folder in the chapter12 application. Pass a parameter to the Web service to customize the dataset returned. Write the code to consume the Web service and display the membership data. Print out your web pages and the source code.

## Project 12-4

Your customers are starting to use wireless and PDA devices to connect to the web site. Create a series of five Web Forms that display information about the online store. On one of the forms, use a TextBox control to retrieve input from the user. Change the values of a property based on the input value. Use a Validation control to make sure the user entered data into the text box, and use a regular expression Validation control to make sure they entered valid data. Save your Web application to your ch12_case4 folder in the chapter12 folder. Enhance the web pages with graphics, color, and text. Print the web page and the source code.

## Project 12-5

There are many types of Web services available, such as GoogleMaps. Search the Internet for an example of a Web service that is freely accessible. Create a Web application that connects to and uses the Web service. Provide a documentation page on how you created the web programming interface to the Web service. Describe what differences you found between the live examples and the examples in this chapter. Save your Web application to your ch12_case5 folder in the chapter12 folder. Enhance the web pages with graphics, color, and text.

APPENDIX

# A

# .NET DEVELOPMENT EDITOR REQUIREMENTS, SETUP, AND CONFIGURATION

In this book, you will be using one of the .NET development editors to create your ASP.NET applications. To support your use of this book, this appendix will give you detailed information on the hardware, software, and software installation requirements that you will encounter throughout the chapters.

Note that this book was written using the default installation for Windows XP Professional SP2 and Visual Web Developer Express 2005. Although this appendix provides additional information on installation, setup, and configuration, it cannot be used as a definitive guide. You always should read the installation manuals and readme guides that come with your software product. These documents contain the latest information related to software requirements, configuration, installation, and compatibility issues.

## SOFTWARE REQUIREMENTS – IN BRIEF

The following is a short list of the software requirements for this book:

- *Operating system:* Windows XP Professional SP2
- *Web server:* The built-in web server
- *Developer tools:* Visual Studio .NET 2005 Professional or Visual Web Developer Express 2005
- *Documentation:* Microsoft Developer Network Library (MSDN) or access to the online version of the MSDN at *http://msdn.microsoft.com*
- *Database server:* SQL Server Express, or SQL Server 2005
- *Database application:* Microsoft Office XP (Access XP is the required application)

## SOFTWARE REQUIREMENTS – IN DETAIL

This part of the appendix gives you detailed information on the software that you will use to work through the chapters of this textbook.

### Operating System

You can install the .NET development tools on a variety of Windows operating systems. Because you do not need to have access to a remote web server, this book supports a variety of Windows XP Professional and Windows Server family of products. The samples in this book were created on a computer running Windows XP Professional.

As part of the operating system installation, or when you install the editor, you will also be installing support for the .NET Framework. Visual Studio .NET 2005 and ASP.NET 2.0 work with the .NET Framework version 2.0. Because the .NET Framework 2.0 is a proper subset of the .NET Framework 3.0, older applications should be supported in the .NET Framework 3.0.

There are several versions of the Windows XP Professional disks. The version that has been tested with this book is called **Windows XP Professional SP2**. SP stands for service pack. **Service packs (SP)** are add-ons that provide updates to the operating system software. The service packs provide updates to the system that include security updates.

The new Microsoft operating system called Vista has just been released in the business version. Microsoft has provided information specifically on the use of Visual Studio .NET 2005 and Windows Vista at *http://msdn2.microsoft.com/en-us/vstudio/aa948853.aspx*. You will need to run the Visual Studio 2005 Service Pack 1 Update for Windows Vista. One of the major differences with the Vista platform is user management, permissions, and security. Visual Studio 2005 should be run with elevated administrative privileges on the Vista platform.

# Web Server

The editor software comes with a built-in web server for development and testing. When you create your web page, viewing the page in the web server is as simple as right-clicking on the page and selecting View in Browser. Once you are finished viewing the page and close the browser, the instance of the web server is stopped. The web server also only accepts local requests, so it is not a security risk. Your port number for the Web application may change each day you log into the computer, however. Therefore, you should design your Web applications so that they never hard code the port number. This can easily be stored in the web configuration file.

Some courses will have access to a production web server such as Internet Information Server. **Internet Information Server (IIS)** version 6 is the web server software available for Windows XP Professional and Windows server software. Version 5 comes preinstalled with Windows XP Professional. Although ASP.NET and the .NET development editors will work with this version of IIS, this book has not been tested with that version.

# .NET Development Editors

There are different versions of Visual Studio .NET. The activities in this book will work with any of these versions *except* the Visual Studio .NET 2003 Professional or Enterprise Editions. This book is not compatible with any of the Visual Studio .NET 2003 Standard Editions. Students might try to purchase Visual Basic .NET, C#, and C++ separately. It is important to tell them not to purchase this version, however. Any of these standard versions of Visual Studio .NET 2003 will not allow them to create Web applications. The enterprise versions contain additional tools for creating and managing the application architecture and full versions of various server software programs for developing applications. Visual Studio .NET 2005 Professional includes support for Visual Basic .NET, C#, J#, C++, and the Visual Web Developer. This version is provided to schools as part of the Microsoft Academic Alliance (MSDNAA) program. Faculty can distribute Visual Studio .NET 2005 to their students under limited conditions according to the MSD-NAA licensing agreement. Because the MSDNAA program has been implemented successfully at many institutions and because of Microsoft's requirements, we are no longer able to bundle the software with the textbook. You can find out more information on participating in the MSDNAA program at *http://msdn2.microsoft.com/en-us/academic/default.aspx*. Volume licensing is also available for Visual Studio .NET.

A complete listing of the features, product information, and system requirements can be found through the Visual Studio .NET 2005 web site at *http://msdn.microsoft.com/vstudio/*. It is important to understand the difference. For example, if you plan for students to connect to remote database servers or create or modify tables and stored procedures, then you should not use Visual Web Developer Express. If you want to be able to have full support of XSLT in the XML editor, you should use at least the professional version. The following is a list of links to pages that contain more information about Visual Studio .NET.

- Features: *http://msdn.microsoft.com/vstudio/products/compare/default.aspx*
- System requirements: *http://msdn2.microsoft.com/en-us/vstudio/aa718687.aspx*

## MSDN Library

The documentation for Visual Studio .NET Professional is provided in the MSDN Library. The **MSDN Library** contains help files, documentation, and other resources related to most of the Microsoft products, including Visual Studio .NET, the MSDE, SQL Server, Access XP, and IIS.

You can install the MSDN Library software using the disks provided with Visual Studio .NET Professional. You may also have access to more up-to-date versions of the library if you own a subscription to the library. If you have a subscription, Microsoft will send you an updated library disk about four to six times a year. Information about the subscriptions to the library is available at *http://msdn.microsoft.com/*.

The MSDN Library takes up a significant amount of hard drive disk space. If you install the optional MSDN Library documentation, you will need 3.8 GB of hard drive space for full installation of the library and Visual Studio .NET software. Schools may install the MSDN Library in a shared location where all students would have access. You can choose to run the MSDN Library off of the disk media or a network drive. Note, of course, if the library is installed on a network drive, that students would not be able to access these files from an off-campus location.

You can also access much of the .NET documentation online at the MSDN Library at *http://msdn.microsoft.com/library/default.asp*. This book contains many references to online documentation at the MSDN Library. Remember that online versions are subject to being removed, however, so having a local version is always a good idea.

## Database Server

The **SQL Server Express** is a single user version of the Microsoft SQL Server. Information on installation and configuration and troubleshooting data connectivity issues is covered in Appendix B. (*Note*: It is also possible to convert the database to Oracle, and use Oracle as the database server. None of the exercises in the book require Oracle.) If you are using Visual Web Developer Express, you are also provided with SQL Server Express. You can use only the built-in database design tools to create and modify tables and stored procedures, however. Although you can connect to a remote server, you cannot do these specific data management activities on a database on a remote data server.

## Database Application

Some of the exercises use Microsoft Access as the database application. Some of the activities with Access are provided to instruct the developer on the differences in writing applications with Access and SQL Server. Because there are minimal differences between the actual coding of Web applications that use Access and SQL Server, the reader can modify their code to use the database engine that they prefer.

Note that the exercises that are developed with the SQL Server are not provided with differential instructions for Access users. There are some differences between the database engines, such as the syntax of SQL instructions and the ability to use stored procedures that will require the reader to reprogram some of their Web application programming code. Although the reader can reconfigure the applications to work with either database engine, the author recommends using the database engine that is listed in the instructions of the exercises. (*Note:* You can open the file in Access, and then convert the file to an earlier version of Access. The upsizing wizard is available with Access 2000, Access 2003, and Access 2007.)

## HARDWARE REQUIREMENTS

Visual Studio .NET, Microsoft XP Professional (as well as the new Microsoft Vista operating system), and Microsoft Office have specific hardware requirements. The information in this section is a listing of those minimal requirements.

The minimum memory required is 192 MB of RAM with 256 MB recommended. This is also sufficient for installation of Windows XP Professional. It is recommended to have between 512 MB and 1 GB of RAM, however, to complete the activities in this textbook and install all of the required software. The more memory you have, the better performance you will have.

The amount of hard drive space required for the OS varies with how you intend to install the product, which version you are using, and which features you install. If you plan to install the software over a network share, you likely will need additional space. The total amount that is required will vary with the features that you choose during installation. In all cases, Visual Studio .NET 2005 requires 1 GB of available space on the system drive and 2 GB on the installation drive. If you plan to install the full version of the MSDN Library, you will need 3.8 GB of available space on the installation drive during the installation process in addition to the 1 GB requirement for the system drive. Refer to *http://msdn2.microsoft.com/en-us/vstudio/ aa718687.aspx* for additional requirements.

The amount of hard drive space required for the data files will depend on how you install them. If the student completes every activity in the book, this would require about 106 MB of hard drive space, depending on the graphics and databases the student includes within his or her web pages. Some of the databases are provided with extensive data so that students can create additional examples using the database and images. They would focus on the web programming instead of the creation or procurement of graphics.

Note that there are several ways you can modify the installation and configuration to reduce the hard drive space requirements. You can select to only support a single programming language and not install the local MSDN files. Note that some of the book data files, such as the graphics, are used across multiple chapters. By placing them in a central location and reusing these files, you can reduce the disk space requirement. You can create a single solution for the entire book, and then create a single project for each chapter. References to images would be to a central project directory. You would have to change the URL for the images in the web page or programming code, and many of the URLs for the hyperlinks would need to be adjusted. Some chapters will require changes in the web configuration files, however, which may need to be customized by the instructor in this type of setting.

## Visual Studio .NET Professional Installation on Windows XP Professional

In this section, you will learn about the basic choices for installing Visual Studio .NET Professional. Of course, the potential installation media include DVDs, multiple CDs, a network share, or the downloaded installation program. Therefore, the steps to the installation of the program will vary with the type of medium, the version you are installing, and the configuration of your computer system.

Before the program installs, you may need to update your system with the Visual Studio .NET prerequisites, which will update your system with the .NET components and install the .NET Framework. The prerequisites may be included with your installation disks. The entire process can take 1 to 2 hours, depending on the speed of your CD-ROM drive, the speed of your processor, memory, and the components that are selected during the installation process.

After you have installed the software, you should be aware of the changes in your system configuration due to the installation of Visual Studio .NET, as follows:

- Setup registers the file extensions with the ASP.NET engine located at C:\WINDOWS\Microsoft.NET\Framework\v2.0.50727\aspnet_isapi.dll. Notice that the previous version of ASP is still mapped to C:\WINDOWS\System32\inetsrv\asp.dll, allowing previous applications to run concurrently with ASP.NET. Notice that the path for the ASP.NET dll file is within the version of the .NET Framework installed on your computer. Although you can install different versions of the .NET Framework on the same computer, it is not recommended for beginning students. If your file mapping does not appear, you can remap the file extensions.

- If you are running Internet Information Server locally, the setup program registered ASP.NET with the web server so that the ASP.NET file extensions are recognized by the web server. You can verify this by going to the IIS Microsoft management console. You do not need to do this if you are using the built-in web server in the web editor.

In Windows XP Professional, all files, software applications, and server applications require a Windows user account to be assigned to access and run the application and access the files. The VS Developer and Debugger Users groups, and the SQLDebugger user account, were added to this machine. The **VS Developer** group allows developers to create Web applications on the machine. The **Debugger Users** group and the **SQLDebugger** account allows Visual Studio .NET to debug applications locally and remotely. Add only trusted users to these accounts. **Trusted users** would be administrators and developers, but not anonymous users or guests. ASPNET is a user added by the .NET Framework. This user is known as the **ASP.NET**

**Machine Account** because it is used to run the worker process located in aspnet_wp.dll, one of the processes that manage ASP.NET applications on the server. The ASP.NET Machine Account is the account that is used by ASP.NET web pages when they access resources on the computer. For example, to create a new file in a folder on the web server, or to upload a file to the web server, you will need to give permissions to the ASP.NET machine account. Chapter 4 contains detailed instructions on setting permissions for the ASP.NET Machine Account. The following is a list of users that have been added by the .NET setup files:

- SQLDebugger Group
- Debugger Users Group
- ASP.NET User

If you are running your own version of Internet Information Server, the IUSR_ MachineName and IWAM_MachineName were added by the web server software. If your machine name was Kalata, then these users would be named IUSR_Kalata and IWAM_ Kalata. The **IUSR_MACHINENAME** account is called the **Internet Guest Account** and is used for anonymous access to the web server. For example, when a user browses a web page, the connections are logged as occurring by IUSR_MachineName. The **IWAM_MACHINENAME** account is called the **Launch IIS Process Account** and is used to launch applications out of the normal process. If you are running your own version of Internet Information Server, the following is a list of users that have been added by the web server setup files:

To view the users and groups installed on your system, do the following:

1. Click **Start**, and then click **Run**.
2. In the Run window, type **%SystemRoot%\system32\compmgmt.msc /s** in the text box, and then click the **OK** button. (*Note:* You can also enter the absolute path, C:\WINDOWS\system32\compmgmt.msc /s.)
3. In the left pane, click the **plus sign** next to Local Users and Groups.
4. Click **Users**, and the user accounts appear in the right pane.
5. Click **Groups**, and the group accounts appear in the right pane.
6. Click **File** on the menu bar, and then click **Exit** to close the Internet Information Services window.

## Installing Visual Studio .NET on Windows Vista

Remember that with Windows Vista, you will have to run the Visual Studio .NET with elevated administrative permissions. You should make sure that the user assigned to run the Visual Studio .NET application is a member of the Administrators group on the local machine. If you plan to run Visual Studio .NET with normal user permissions, you should read about the issues at *http://msdn2.microsoft.com/en-us/vstudio/aa972193.aspx*. There are still potential issues with running Windows Vista and Visual Studio .NET 2005. You can read about these issues at *http://msdn2.microsoft.com/en-us/vstudio/aa964140.aspx*.

## COMPATIBILITY ISSUES WITH VISUAL STUDIO .NET

One of the benefits of the .NET Framework is that you can install multiple instances of the same application. With Visual Studio .NET, you can even install multiple instances of the .NET Framework itself. ASP.NET and the previous version of ASP can also coexist on the same server. Visual Studio .NET 2005 has major changes over the Visual Studio .NET 2003 version. The features within Visual Studio include enhancements in Web Services, XML, Web database, the development tools, and performance tools.

It is not recommended to run Visual Studio .NET 2003 on the same system as Visual Studio .NET 2005. You may run Visual Studio .NET 2005 and Visual Web Developer Express 2005 on the same computer, however. You can also run SQL Server Express 2005 and full versions of SQL Server on the same local computer.

**TIP**    The asp.dll is the engine that processes ASP pages. As long as that file has not been removed, you can still process ASP pages with scripting languages such as VBScript. This often is used in courses to demonstrate the evolution of ASP and how the web programming model has evolved from a scripting based technology to a server programming technology.

# B

# TROUBLESHOOTING DATA CONNECTIVITY ISSUES

In this book, you learned how to create and manage sample databases using Visual Studio .NET and ASP.NET. This appendix will provide you with additional information about the installation and configuration of the SQL Server database server and how to troubleshoot common database connectivity issues. (*Note*: You must install the SQL Server before you can install and configure the samples that come with the .NET Framework.)

## INSTALLING AND CONFIGURING THE DATABASE SERVER

It is important to understand that there are multiple ways to obtain the SQL Server. The SQL Server contains the desktop data engine and the client connectivity components. These components include the OLE DB Provider for SQL Server, the SQL Server ODBC driver, and the client Net-Libraries. SQL Server Express is automatically installed with both of the .NET development editors. You do not have to install SQL Server independently.

The SQL Server Express is available for free from Microsoft for developing and testing data-driven applications. This version will allow you to build applications for web sites that serve up to 25 concurrent users. It is not meant or licensed for production applications. When you publish your application to a production server, you should upgrade your databases to a production server such as SQL Server or Oracle. If you use the Visual Studio .NET Professional Edition, the Visual Studio Tools For Office, or the Visual Studio Team System, you are provided with the SQL Server 2005 Developer Edition. This is a more robust version of SQL Server.

SQL Server Express has networking protocols disabled so that the database will not connect to other servers. This is done as a security precaution. So, you can only to connect the SQL Server Express through a remote connection. You cannot store the SQL Server Express on one computer, and then access it with Visual Web Developer Express on another computer. You can use a production version of SQL Server to complete any of the activities in this book. The full version and developer versions of SQL Server will support more concurrent connections and come with additional management tools such as Enterprise Manager.

The Microsoft .NET Framework SDK QuickStart is a series of samples and documentation for .NET applications. Many of these samples require SQL Server to be installed. You must be logged in with Administrator privileges to install the SQL Server and sample web sites. (*Note*: You can read the details on the installation and configuration of the Microsoft .NET Framework SDK QuickStart at C:\Program Files\Microsoft Visual Studio 8\SDK\v2. 0\Samples\Setup\html\ConfigDetails.htm. You will need to have at least one network connection enabled.)

If you followed the SQL Server default installation when you installed your .NET development editor, the default name of the instance of the SQL Server will be named SQLExpress. So you will refer to the instance as (local)\SQLExpress or [*Machine Name*]\SQLExpress or .\SQLExpress.

In the past, you would create various named instances for each SQL Server version installed. With SQL Server Express, however, you can store the data and log files in the App_Data folder of your web directory, separate from the SQL Server program files. Then, when the database and application is started, the data is recognized and attached to the SQL Server program. This method is very useful for keeping data contained with the application and makes it easier to deploy the application.

# DATABASE CONNECTIVITY FOR WEB APPLICATIONS

There are two ways to have your Web applications authenticated by the SQL Server database server. First, your Web application can be authenticated using Windows integrated authentication. This means that the Web application must connect to the SQL Server using a Windows account. The SQL Server defaults to integrated authentication. Web applications run using a Windows account called [*MachineName*]\ASPNET. This account needs to be given permission to access the SQL Server. If you accepted the default settings during installation, your SQL Server will use Windows integrated authentication and you do not need to make any changes.

If your Web application authenticates a web database application as SQL Server authentication, however, you may want to change this back to Windows authentication. SQL Server has the ability to manage users and permissions within the SQL Server software. You can also manage users for SQL Server databases. You can assign a user ID and password that the Web application will use to connect to the SQL Server. SQL Server 2000 will use SQL Server authentication by default. You can modify the user permissions using SQL Server Client Tools or Enterprise Manager. Many developers may not have access to these tools. You can access the same database server commands by running a command line program that can be accessed through the command program.

The switch named SECURITYMODE was set to SQL, which changed the default login authentication mode from Windows NT authentication to SQL authentication. If you used the SQL Server setup program defaults to install the SQL Server, however, then the Web application will use Windows integrated authentication on a Windows XP computer. If your Web application uses Windows authentication, you may need to change the permissions for the [*MachineName*]\ASPNET user account each time you create a database on the SQL Server. The ASP.NET process runs under the [*MachineName*]\ASPNET user account. In order for the account to access the SQL Server database, this user must be granted rights to the SQL Server databases. There is another method that can be used to modify the database authentication configuration. The **Registry** stores information about your computer and the applications. You can modify the registration for the database server to change the authentication mode from Windows authentication to integrated SQL Server authentication.

# C

# WORKING WITH PROJECT AND SOLUTION FILES

In this book, you will use Visual Studio .NET 2005 or Visual Web Developer Express to create your ASP.NET applications. This appendix will provide you more detailed information working with projects and solution files and using the data and solution files.

## MANAGING PROJECTS AND SOLUTIONS

When you use the .NET development editors to create a Web application, no project files and solution files are required. You can simply open the web site by locating the root folder. This means that your Web application can be stored on portable devices such as flash drives. This entire book was created using a flash drive to store the data files. Flash drives are removable and portable devices to store data, and often are connected to the computer using a plug and play USB cable.

Remember that new to the .NET development editors is the installation of a local built-in web server. Therefore, your directory can be located anywhere on your network.

If you do install the Internet Information Server, however, here are some additional pieces of information that you should know. The web server available for Windows XP Professional can only accommodate one web site. The default web site is located in the c:\Inetpub\wwwroot folder. You can create multiple Web applications within the web site using subwebs and virtual webs. **Subwebs** are folders beneath the wwwroot directory that are configured as a single Web application. **Virtual webs** are folders outside of the wwwroot directory that are configured as a single Web application. **Virtual directories** are folders within a Web application that are not located in the same physical directory as the Web application. You can configure Web applications using the Microsoft Management Console (MMC) for Internet Information Server (IIS).

## USING THE DATA FILES AND SOLUTION FILES

In each chapter, you will be creating one Web application. Your system may be set up to store the solution files within your user folder such as C:\Documents and Settings\[*Your Windows User Name*]\My Documents\MyClass\Chapter*N*, where *N* is the chapter number.

You must have access to the data files to perform the activities within this book. The data files are available from the Course Technology web site at *www.course.com,* or through your instructor. The solution files are provided to instructors only through the Course Technology web site and with the Instructor's Resource Kit (IRK).

When you create a database using the SQL Server, two files are created. The location of the log file and data files is your App_Data folder within your Web application.

If you decide to delete a project, you first should close your .NET development editor. Then, delete the entire folder.

## SETTING UP ALTERNATIVE CONFIGURATIONS FOR CLASSROOM INSTRUCTION

If you publish your web site to a live web server, the student will need access to a server to post or FTP his or her ASP.NET web pages. There are many ways to install and configure your web development environment. You should plan your class hardware and software configuration, and you would likely benefit from consulting with your network administrator. This person likely will have additional information about the specifications of your network and lab, such as where students save files and preferences. If you are looking for additional information, the Visual Studio .NET MSDNAA Academic Teaching Tools Guide (http://download.microsoft.com/download/f/f/8/ff8c8040-d1a7-4402-90df-5d1aaa7d37af/TeachingToolsGuide.pdf) contains a significant amount of information about various configurations within a computer science lab setting. There are also instructor materials available at the Academic Resource Center at *http://www.microsoft.com/education/facultyconnection/ARC/ResourceCenter.aspx*. You can also access academic materials at the .NET Framework Academic Resource Kit web page at *http://www.academicresourcecenter.net/curriculum/AcademicResKit.aspx*.

The projects within this textbook were created using the default installation and configuration. The web projects were tested with the built-in web server, localhost. The database server used was the local .\SQLExpress. This setup works well when students have access to the computer during class and outside of class. If the students save their Web application on a local drive, however, they may not be able to access the project from another room, or outside of the school.

**TIP**

No matter what configuration is selected, the instructor will need administrative access to the server in order to view and grade homework assignments. The instructor needs to access the code behind the page and the ASP.NET page. One method is to have students simply zip their folder and send it to the instructor because all of the files are self-contained within the folder.

There are different alternatives to publishing your Web application on a local web server. The following is a list of suggested ways to handle the publishing of remote Web applications:

- Name Web application after the student name: *http://[remoteserver]/Student1_Chapter2*

- Create a virtual directory for each student: *http://[remoteserver]/Student1/ Chapter1*

- Create a virtual directory tree for each class: *http://[remoteserver]/CIS220/ Section001/Fall2005/Student1/WebProject1*

- Store project files on a flash disk drive, a rewriteable optical drive, or other removable media: *http://localhost:port/Chapter1*

Students can alter the names of the project to reflect their student identification or user name. For example, the projects would be named Student1_Chapter2, Student1_Chapter3, and so on. The student would create their application as *http://[remoteserver]/Student1_Chapter2*. The instructor would have to change each of the data files to reflect the change in the project name. For example, in the first line of each web page is a reference to the project. This reference would have to be changed to the new project name. The other drawback to this option is that the web directory will become very large.

The instructor can also create a virtual directory for each of the students on the web server. For instance, the instructor could name the folders after the student ID, such as Student1, Student2, etc. The student could create their projects in his or her own directory. When he or she creates a project such as WebProject1, he or she would type http://[*remoteserver*] /Student1/WebProject1 in the location text box in the New Project window. Therefore, the student would be publishing the Web applications in that central directory. The project files are stored in that directory by default. They must be able to access that central directory and the directory where the solution files are located, from the other computers in your labs. The instructor can tell the students that the first time they create a project, their user directory would be created. (*Note*: The instructor may want to create user accounts and passwords for each student so that they cannot alter other students' files. Of course, the instructor would provide them with full control to their own directories.)

The preceding option works well with a small number of students, or where the projects will be deleted each semester. Another option is to create a virtual directory tree where the web project files would be identifiable based on the class, semester, student, and project. For example, *http://[remoteserver]/CIS220/Section001/Fall2008/Student1/Chapter1* could be used to reference a project for a student. Although it is a longer URL for the students to type, it would be easier for the instructors to manage the students' files. In addition, they would be able to remove files based on when they were taught.

In addition, some of the projects within the textbook contain more than a megabyte of data files and images. Storing these files on a single floppy disk is not an option. The instructor can store the images in a central location on the web server, however, and change the data files to point to the central images directory.

**TIP**

In earlier chapters, instructors may want to have the student print out the browser view, the source code from the browser, the .vb file, and the .aspx file. Doing this helps show students that the server code generates the client code. It will also help them debug errors that may be related to client scripting and HTML. The instructor would have to check the code manually for errors. This would be useful in the early chapters where students are still learning how to publish to the class server.

## Web Server Connection Methods Used to Publish Web Projects

There are issues regarding getting access to the web server and allowing publishing of web pages. Two primary methods exist to publish your web pages to the web server. This is the same whether you are publishing to the localhost web server or remote web server. The two methods to connect to the web server and publish the web projects are file share and FrontPage extensions. When students try to create a project, they will be asked which method they would like to use to connect to the web server. The instructor can configure the method used to connect to the web server in the Options menu. Selecting file share indicates that you want to access your project files directly on the web server through a file share. This method does not require FrontPage server extensions to be installed on the server. If you select using a file system as the method to create and publish the application, you can use a simple File Transfer Protocol program (FTP) to copy the files to the server.

# D

# ASP.NET CONTROLS

In this book, you learned about many of the HTML Server controls and Web controls used within ASP.NET applications. This appendix will provide you with additional reference information about these controls and how they are related to each other.

## Control Hierarchy

When you create a project in Visual Studio .NET, references to classes are made in the .NET Framework. For ASP.NET Web applications, the references added include System, System. Web, System.Drawing, System.Data, and System.XML. The System.Web class is required to create the Web Forms and several of the Web controls. Today, these references are inserted into the web configuration file in the pages node. The pages node contains a child node called namespaces. You can add and remove namespaces associated with your application in the namespaces node in the web configuration files.

You can read about the class hierarchy and locate the classes, events, properties and methods by creating an ASP.NET Web application and using the **Object Browser**. The Object Browser contains the hierarchy for your Web application. To view the Object Browser, simply go to the View menu and select Object Browser. The **Class Browser** application provides the hierarchy for all of the .NET classes, events, properties, and methods. You can preview the Class Browser at *http://quickstarts.asp.net/QuickStartv20/util/classbrowser.aspx*.

You can also view more information about hierarchy of controls in the MSDN Library at *http://msdn.microsoft.com/library/*.

**TIP**

The following list contains the URLs to the documentation for the HTML Server and Web controls. These pages link to documentation of the classes, as well as the properties, methods, and events for each control within the class.

- System.Web.UI.HtmlControls Class: *http://msdn2.microsoft.com/en-us/library/system. web.ui.htmlcontrols(vs.80).aspx* and *http://msdn2.microsoft.com/en-us/library/system.web. ui.htmlcontrols.aspx*

- System.Web.UI.WebControls Class: *http://msdn2.microsoft.com/en-us/library/zfzfkea6. aspx* and *http://msdn2.microsoft.com/en-us/library/system.web.ui.webcontrols.aspx*

## HTML Server Controls

You learned about HTML Server controls, their properties, methods, and events. The HTML controls on the HTML tab in the .NET development editor are simple HTML controls. You must change their runat property in order to access the controls on the server. Then, they will be called HTML Server controls. These controls correspond to the basic HTML tags.

The HTML Server controls are created within the System.Web.UI.HTMLControls. That means that they inherit the System.Web.UI.Control class but they are also a member of the System.Web.UI.HTMLControls class. The three subclasses within the HTMLControl class are discussed in the list that follows. Subclasses that create HTML Server controls will inherit the same events, methods, and properties. Some of these properties, such as ID, are inherited through other classes.

- HTMLImage control: The **HTMLImage** control contains the Align, Alt, Border, Height, Src, and Width properties.

- HtmlContainerControl control (HtmlAnchor, HtmlButton, HtmlForm, HtmlGenericControl, HtmlSelect, HtmlTable, HtmlTableCell, HtmlTableRow, and HtmlTextArea): The **HTMLContainerControl** class is used for HTML controls that implement beginning and ending tags. These controls share the properties InnerText and InnerHTML.

- HtmlInputControl control (HtmlInputButton, HtmlInputCheckBox, HtmlInputFile, HtmlInputHidden, HtmlInputImage, HtmlInputRadioButton, and HtmlInputText): The **HTMLInputControl** class shares the Name, Type, and Value properties.

You can reference each of these HTMLControl controls by its fully qualified name. For example, the HTMLAnchor, also called the Hyperlink HTML Server control, would be referenced as System.Web.UI.HTMLControls.HTMLAnchor.

Additional properties are available to Web controls through inheritance. The System.Web.UI.HTMLControls.HTMLControl class inherits from the System.Web.UI. Control class, and the System.Web.UI.Control class inherits from the Class control within the System.Object class. Therefore, these control properties are available to almost any .NET control, including Web controls and HTML Server controls.

## Web Controls

You learned earlier that the tag name for user controls consisted of two parts — the class and the control name. Web controls are also known as ASP.NET controls because their tags are prefixed with "asp:" and followed by the control name. You have seen many of these controls on the Web Forms tab in the Toolbox. ASP.NET controls commonly are referred to as Web controls.

There are several logical groupings of Web controls. These are informal groupings of controls based on their function and that is how they are organized within the Toolbox. They do not have any relationship to the control hierarchy but the structured grouping of controls helps facilitate understanding of how these controls are applied. The following is a list of logical control groupings of Web controls:

- *Form controls*: Button, HyperLink, LinkButton, DataGridLinkButton, Image, ImageButton, TextBox, CheckBox, RadioButton, Label, Panel, Table, TableCell, TableRow, GridViewTable, LiteralControl, TemplateControl, and PlaceHolder, AdRotator, Calendar, XML control, CheckBoxList, RadioButtonList, DropDownList, and ListBox.

- *Data controls*: GridView, DataList, DetailsView, FormView, Repeater, DataGrid, as well as Data Source controls such as SqlDataSource, AccessDataSource, ObjectDataSource, XMLDataSource, and SiteMapDataSource.

- *Validation controls*: BaseCompareValidator, CustomValidator, RegularExpressionValidator, RequiredFieldValidator, and ValidationSummary.

- *Navigation*: SiteMaptPath, TreeView, and Menu controls.

- *Login*: Login forms and login management controls and wizards.

- *WebParts*: WebPartManager and WebPartZone along with other zones.

- *Mobile*: Mobile controls are available when you edit a mobile ASP.NET page.

## The System.Web.UI.WebControls.WebControl Class Hierarchy

Throughout the textbook, you have learned about many Web controls and their properties, methods, and events. Web controls are created within the System.Web.UI.WebControls. WebControl class. That means that they inherit the System.Web.UI.Control class but are also members of the System.Web.UI.WebControls class.

The subclasses within the WebControl class are contained in the list that follows. You can refer to all of these WebControl controls by their fully qualified names. For example, the AdRotator would be referenced as System.Web.UI.WebControls.AdRotator. Some of the classes, such as BaseDataList, do not appear on the Web Forms tab in the Toolbox. This abstract base class contains subclasses, such as GridView and DataList, which are controls listed on the Toolbox. This occurs because both controls require similar events, properties, and methods. Therefore, a class was created to provide common events, properties, and methods.

- *AdRotator control*
- *BaseDataList class:* GridView, DataList
- *Button control*
- *Calendar control*
- *CheckBox control*: RadioButton
- *DataListItem class*
- *HyperLink control*
- *Image control*: ImageButton
- *Label control*: BaseValidator (BaseValidator contains the subclasses BaseCompareValidator, CustomValidator, RegularExpressionValidator, RequiredFieldValidator)
- *LinkButton control*: GridViewLinkButton
- *ListControl class*: CheckBoxList, DropDownList, ListBox, RadioButtonList
- *Panel control*

- *Table control*: GridViewTable

- *TableCell class*: TableHeaderCell

- *TableRow class*: GridViewItem

- *TextBox control*

- *ValidationSummary control*

D

## Properties, Events, and Methods of the System.Web.UI.WebControls. WebControl Class

Subclasses that create Web controls will inherit the same events, methods, and properties. Some of these properties, such as BackColor, can be set through the Properties window when the control is selected. Some of these properties, such as ID, are inherited through other classes. Properties such as ControlStyle are used by developers who work with creating custom controls. Properties such as TagKey are protected and not public. Table D-1 contains some properties available in the System.Web.UI. WebControls.WebControl class. (*Note*: "Get" and "Set" indicate whether you can retrieve or change the value of the property.)

**Table 4-1**    System.Web.UI.WebControls.WebControl properties

| Name Accessibility | Type | Description |
|---|---|---|
| Attributes (Get) | AttributeCollection | A collection of arbitrary attributes used only for rendering that do not correspond to properties on the Web control |
| BackColor (Get, Set) | Color | Background color |
| BorderColor (Get, Set) | Color | Border color |
| BorderStyle (Get, Set) | BorderStyle | Border style |
| BorderWidth (Get, Set) | Unit | Border width |
| ControlStyle (Get) | Style | Style of the Web control |
| ControlStyleCreated (Get) | Boolean | Value indicates whether a Style object has been created for the ControlStyle property |
| CssClass (Get, Set) | String | Cascading Style Sheet (CSS) class rendered by the Web control on the client |
| Enabled (Get, Set) | Boolean | Value indicates whether the Web control is enabled |
| EnableViewState (Get, Set) | Boolean | Value indicates whether the control saves its state for round trips back to the server |
| Font (Get) | FontInfo | Font properties |
| ForeColor (Get, Set) | Color | Foreground color (typically the color of the text) |
| Height (Get, Set) | Unit | Height |

**Table 4-1**  System.Web.UI.WebControls.WebControl properties (continued)

| Name Accessibility | Type | Description |
|---|---|---|
| Style (Get) | CssStyleCollection | A collection of text attributes that will be rendered as a style attribute on the outer tag of the Web control |
| TabIndex (Get, Set) | Int16 | Tab index |
| TagKey | HtmlTextWriterTag | The System.Web.UI.HtmlTextWriterTag value that corresponds to this Web control |
| TagName | String | Name of the control tag |
| ToolTip (Get, Set) | String | Text displayed when the mouse pointer hovers over the Web control |
| Width (Get, Set) | Unit | Width |

Additional properties are available to Web controls through inheritance. The properties listed in Table D-2 are available to Web controls because the System.Web.UI.WebControls. WebControl class inherits from the System.Web.UI.Control class, and the System.Web.UI. Control class inherits from the Class control within the System.Object class. Therefore, these control properties are available to almost any .NET control, including Web controls and HTML Server controls.

**Table 4-2**  Inherited properties of a Web control

| Name Accessibility | Type | Description |
|---|---|---|
| ClientID (Get) | String | The control identifier generated by ASP.NET |
| ID (Get, Set) | String | Programmatic identifier for the control |
| NamingContainer (Get) | Control | Gets a collection of text attributes that will be rendered as a style attribute on the outer tag of the control |
| Page (Get, Set) | Page | A reference to the System.Web.UI.Page instance that contains the control |
| Parent (Get) | Control | The control's parent control in the page control hierarchy |
| TemplateSourceDirectory (Get) | String | The virtual directory of the System.Web.UI.Page or System.Web.UI.UserControl that contains the current control |
| UniqueID (Get) | String | A unique, hierarchically-qualified identifier for the control |
| Visible (Get, Set) | Boolean | Indicates if the control was rendered and therefore visible |

# BUILDING WEB CONTROLS

The ASP.NET Control Gallery at *www.asp.net/Default.aspx?tabindex=2&tabid=31* contains a myriad of third-party Web controls that you can include within your Web applications. You can build custom controls and implement third-party Web controls. The following web sites contain a vast amount of information on how to build controls:

- Authoring Custom Controls: *http://samples.gotdotnet.com/quickstart/aspplus/doc/webctrlauthoring.aspx*

- Building DataBound Templated Custom ASP.NET Server Controls: *http://msdn.microsoft.com/asp.net/using/building/webcontrols/default.aspx?pull=/library/en-us/dnaspp/html/databoundtemplatedcontrols.asp*

- Creating Custom Controls: *http://msdn.microsoft.com/library/en-us/cpguide/html/cpcondevelopingwebformscontrols.asp*

# E

# USING C#

This textbook was tested using Visual Basic .NET. Other .NET languages may be used to create ASP.NET Web applications, however. Many of the online examples are available in C# as well as Visual Basic .NET. (C# is pronounced *C-Sharp.*) C# is a very popular language for web developers because of its similarity in syntax to Java. This appendix gives you information about some of the differences between Visual Basic .NET and C#. For additional information on modifying the samples in the book to use C#, please refer to the Instructor Manual.

## EDITORS TO SUPPORT BUILDING APPLICATIONS

C# is a new language created by Microsoft to allow non–Visual Basic .NET programmers to take advantage of the powerful features of Visual Studio .NET. The syntax of C# is similar to JavaScript and C++. It is important to remember that when the program is compiled by the C# compiler, the code is compiled into the same managed Intermediate Language code as that generated by the Visual Basic .NET compiler.

All of the .NET Framework, the .NET base classes, and the Visual Studio development environment are available across programming languages. So, you can include programs written with C# within your ASP.NET application. In addition, you have access to the same Windows Form tools and ASP.NET Web Form tools. Therefore, the user interface to your application is not language dependent. You can create your Web Form the same way for all .NET programming languages.

**TIP**

It is important to understand that you can add individual content items using different programming languages. If you choose to precompile your application into a separate assembly, however, you will have to use only one programming language. That is because you have to select a single compiler when you compile the application. You can create classes and other programs using different languages, and compile them into separate assemblies, which would both be inserted into the bin directory. This way, you could have multiple languages used within the same project.

**TIP**

In this textbook, you use Visual Basic .NET primarily because most beginning programming courses use Visual Basic. Once you learn one programming language, however, the programming concepts are similar with other languages. It is useful to be aware of the differences between programming languages. In addition, some of the samples you may find on the Internet are written in C#. If you are familiar with some of the structures of the C# application, you can convert the C# code into Visual Basic .NET. When you open the QuickStart web site at *http://www.asp.net/tutorials/quickstart.aspx*, you can specify the samples to be displayed by default using C# by changing the drop-down list box located in the upper-right corner from VB to C#.

One of the first things that you will notice in a C# program is that each statement ends with a semicolon. The semicolon is called the line termination character because it indicates the end of the statement. Therefore, you can write statements that extend across multiple lines without using an underscore, because the program knows that the end of the statement occurs where the semicolon is located. C# uses the plus sign as the concatenation operator instead of the ampersand that is used in Visual Basic .NET. The following sample code shows how to concatenate strings in C#:

```
var s1 : String;
var s2 : String = "Welcome to ";
```

```
s2 += "Tara Store";
s1 = s2 + " !!!";
```

To improve performance, you can use the **StringBuilder class**. The StringBuilder class is available to both Visual Basic .NET and C#. The sample code that follows this paragraph shows how to concatenate strings in C# using the StringBuilder class. The Append method is used to concatenate two or more strings.

```
var s1:StringBuilder = new StringBuilder();
s1.Append("Welcome to ");
s1.Append("Tara Store");
s1.Append(" !!!");
```

One difference between the two programs is that C# is case sensitive. You must be careful about the names of variables, properties, namespaces, functions, and other programming keywords. In C#, you often use lowercase for the names of programming elements within the C# language.

When you assign a value to a variable in C#, you do not have to use the keyword dim to declare it. When you declare a string variable, you must indicate in both languages that the variable is a string data type. In Visual Basic .NET, you use the keywords As String after the variable name. In C#, you specify the data type first, String, then you specify the variable name; do not forget that the data types are different and are transformed to the Common Language Runtime data types at compile time. When you create an object data type in Visual Basic .NET, you declare the object using the keyword dim and the object name. Then, you assign the name using the keyword As to New Object(), where Object is the name of the class that is used to create the new object. In C#, you do not use Dim or As keywords. You specify the data type of the object first, then the name of the object. You use the assignment operator new Object(), where the keyword new is lowercase. If you declare the variable public in Visual Basic .NET, you capitalize the first letter in Public. If you declare the variable public in C#, you use all lowercase letters for the keyword public. The following sample code shows how to declare a variable and assign it a value in C#:

```
String StoreName = "Tara Store";
int counter = 1;
```

Comments in C# are similar to comments in JavaScript. A single line comment is preceded by two forward slashes. A multiline comment begins with a forward slash and an asterisk. After the comment, an asterisk and forward slash mark the end of the comment. The following sample code illustrates how to create a comment in C#:

```
// This is a single line comment
/*
This is a multiline comment
Always document your code
*/
```

When you create an array using C# instead of using parentheses around the index position, use square brackets. Anytime you work with one or more statements, you enclose the code in curly braces. This nesting of code within curly braces is the same in JavaScript and C#.

Certain types of control structures use the curly braces to indicate which blocks of code should be executed. In a Visual Basic .NET If-Then statement, the keyword Then is used to identify the first block of code. Because there are no curly braces, there is also an End If statement to indicate when the function ends. In C#, the If-Then statement does not require the Then or End If keywords because the curly braces indicate which blocks of code are executed when the statement is True or False.

# Index

## Symbols

<> (angle brackets), 9
= (assignment operator), 65–66
\* (asterisk), 382
= (equal to), 95
> (greater than)
>= (greater than or equal to), 95
< (less than), 95
<= (less than or equal to), 95
<> (not equal to), 95
+ (plus sign), 67
# (pound sign), 383, 430
? (question mark), 507, 508
~ (tilde) character, 399
_ (underscore) character, 63, 86

## A

.accdb file extension, 367
Access
    examples using, 630–631
    features of, 367
    parameter queries, 520
    security issues with, 269
    Upsizing Wizard, 406–409
Access databases
    connection error messages, 442
    database connections to, 403–405
AccessDataSource control, 404, 405, 440, 484, 508–509
accessibility issues, with Web sites, 35–36
accessibility validation tools, 35–36
access rules, configuring, 339
Active Server Pages .NET. See ASP.NET
ActiveViewIndex, 167
ActiveX Data Object .NET Model. See ADO.NET data model
AdCreated event, 230
AdCreateEventArgs arguments, 230
Add method, 72
AddRange method, 73
Ad elements, 226
Adobe Photoshop, 269, 560
ADO.NET data model, 443–447
AdProperties value, 230
AdRotator control, 226–233
    advertisement file, 226–230
    inserting, into Web page, 231–233
    integrating, with database, 231
    properties, 230–231
AdType property, 229
advertisement file, 226–230
AdvertisementFile property, 230
Advertisements node, 226
AJAX (Asynchronous JavaScript XML), 564–565
algorithms, hashing, 73
align attribute, 16, 17
allOverride attribute, 190
AllowPaging property, 440
AllowSorting property, 440
alt attribute, 16
AlternateText element, 227
AlternatingItemStyle, 473
AlternatingItemTemplate, 469
AlternatingRowStyle, 473
alternative platforms, 609–616
American Online, 8
American with Disabilities Act (ADA), 35

anchor tags, 17
AND keyword, 382, 383
And operator, 95
angle brackets (<>), 9
annotated ruby text tag, 19
anonymous users, 243
APIs. See application programming interfaces
App_Code folder, 84, 542, 551
app_offline.html file, 459
App_Themes folder, 187, 188
AppDomain class, 318, 567
AppearanceEditorPart control, 208
application configuration, 323–337
application configuration files, 327–337
    appSettings element, 328
    customErrors element, 332–334
    httpRuntime element, 329–330
    pages element, 329
    trace element, 331–334
ApplicationException class, 99
application level security, 242
Application object, 323
application programming interfaces (APIs), 341–344
Application Protection property, 336
application settings, configuring, 340
application variables, 328
appSettings element, 328, 398
architecture, Web application, 82–83, 562
ArgumentException, 260
arguments, 504
ArrayList collection, 72–73, 429
    data binding to, 434
    methods of, 72–73
    populating the, 72
ASCII format, 247
Asc method, 67
.asmx file extension, 585
asp.dll, 634
ASP.NET
    class creation in, 83–84
    creating HTTP cookies with, 308–309
    HTML controls, 41
    integration of, with current applications, 566
    introduction to, 1
    introduction to server programming, 36–45
    Server controls. see Server controls
    Web controls. see Web controls
ASP.NET_Compiler.exe, 37–38
aspnet_state service, 318
ASP.NET applications
    See also Web applications
    cookieless, 311–313
    deployment of, 566–568
    processing, 37–38
ASP.NET Compilation, 552–553
ASP.NET controls. See Web controls
ASP.NET Machine account, 243, 441, 632–633
ASP.NET pages
    See also Web pages
    creating and reading files from, 263–268
    for mobile devices, 610–616
    previewing, 25
AspNetSqlProvider, 339
.aspx file extension, 37
assemblies, 37–38, 542, 544, 551–553, 567
assignment operator (=), 65–66

asterisk (\*) character, 382
Asynchronous JavaScript XML (AJAX), 564–565
Atlas, 565
attachments, 250–251, 252
attributes, 328
Attributes property, 257
authentication, 337
    database creation and, 368
    forms, 338–345
    implementing, 345–348
    user, 269
authentication element, 346–348
authorization, 337
    implementing, 337–338
    resource-based, 337–338
    role-based, 338
authorization element, 344–345
AutoGenerateColumns property, 440, 510
AutoGenerateDeleteButton, 504
AutoGenerateEditButton, 504
AutoGenerateSelectButton, 504
Auto Hide property, 6
automatic data binding, 437–442

## B

background colors, 12
background images, 12–13
badmail folder, 250
banner ads, 226–233
base class libraries, 83
Basevalidator class, 291
best practices, programming, 104–105
bgcolor attribute, 12
bgproperties attribute, 12
bigint data type, 370
big tag, 14
binary data type, 372
binary strings, 371–372
binding expressions, 431
Bind method, 435, 478, 512–515
bit data type, 370
Bitmap class, 89
Blackboard, 214
_blank, 92
Blind Carbon Copy property, 252
blockquote tags, 13
Bobby, 35–36
body section, 10, 12–13
body tags, 12
bold tag, 14
bookmarks, 17
Boolean data type, 70
border attribute, 16
bound columns, 504
BoundFields, 481, 482, 512–515
branch nodes, 29
breadcrumb trails, 155–157
breakpoints, 103, 593
browse mode, 202
Browser property, 77
browsers. see Web browsers
Brushes enumerator, 89
buffer, 329
buffer attribute, 329

BufferResponse property, 596
bugs, 98
built-in stored procedures, 394–395
built-in views, 394–395
bulleted lists, 16
business applications, of Web services, 580–583
business concepts, 541
business entity components, 421
business logic layer, 421
business systems analysts, 557
ButtonField columns, 481, 482–483
ButtonType property, 511
Byte data type, 68

**C**

C# language, 594, 651–654
cache
    global assembly, 567
    local application, 567
CacheDuration property, 590
caching, 590
Calendar control, 233–238
    creating program for, 235–237
    multiple dates and, 237–238
    properties, methods, and events, 234
    setting properties, 235–236
California Online Privacy Protection Act (COPPA), 35
Call keyword, 85
Capacity property, 72
capacity testing, 563
caption tags, 15
cascading priority, 124–125
cascading style sheets (CSSs), 28, 476
    See also style sheets
    class creation, 125–126
    comments within, 124
    creating, 120–128
    vs. inline styles, 121
    Style Builder, 126–127
    style rules, 120–124
case sensitivity, of XML, 10, 28
CatalogZone control, 203–204, 207
CDONTS, 250
Center for Applied Science Technology (CAST), 35–36
ChangeMode method, 518
character encoding, 11–12
characters entities, 18
characters, 18
character strings, 371
char data type, 66, 371
charset attribute, 19
check boxes, binding collections to, 75
CheckBoxFields, 481
CheckBoxList controls, 428, 433
Checked property, 75
Choose Location window, 7
Chr method, 67
chrome type, 204
class attribute, 10
Class Browser, 644
class definition, 84, 543
classes
    calling, from Web page, 543–544
    compiling in assemblies, 551–553
    components, 84
    creating, 83–84, 544–548
    in CSSs, 125–126
    derived, 542, 545
    hierarchy, 644
    instances of, 84, 543
    in .Net Framework, 83
    partial, 62
    proxy, 588–592
    references to, 644
    for reusable code, 542–543
    shared, 542–543
    using, 544–548
    viewing, 89
class libraries, base, 83
clear attribute, 16

Clear method, 72, 73
clickthrough, 229
client applications, 8
client-server programming, 36
client-side cookies, maintaining state with, 304–307
client-side redirection, 11
client-side scripting, 36–37
CloseConnection property, 448
Close method, 264, 448
Codd, Edgar, 362
code, reusable. See reusable code
code behind the page, 62–63
CodeFile property, 62
code snippets, 548–551
Code Snippets Manager, 548–551
colgroup tags, 15
Collaborative Data Objects (CDO), 250
collections
    ArrayList, 72–73, 429, 434
    binding to Web controls, 75, 433–434
    cookies, 304
    DataRelationsCollection, 453
    Forms, 77–78
    HashTable, 73–74, 429, 434
    QueryString, 77–78
    Queue, 75
    SelectParameters, 505
    SortedList, 74
    Stack, 75
    in Web Forms, 75–76
    working with, 71–76
colon (:), 70
color, background, 12
Color Picker feature, 127–128
column names, 363, 369–370
Column Names view, 376
column properties, 482–483
columns
    See also specific types
    data in, 483–484
    modifying, in GridView control, 484–486
    searching, 393–394
    setting properties, 372–374
    sorting, 402
column tags, 15
CommandBehavior property, 448
Command Builder method, 457, 504
CommandBuilder object, 451
CommandField columns, 481, 504
CommandField property, 511
Command objects, 445, 447, 448
CommandText property, 447
CommandType property, 447
comments
    in code, 104
    within CSSs, 124
    in stored procedures, 389
Common Log File Format, 247
compact HTML (cHTML), 611
Compare method, 67
CompareValidator control, 293–294, 300
comparison operators, 95
compatability issues, 634
compilation, 551–553
compiled assemblies, 542, 551–553
compiler tool, 37–38
components
    creating, 542–544
    defined, 84
    third-party, 553–555
Component Services, 336
composite keys, 366
concatenated SQL statements, 507
concatenation, 67
Concat method, 67
concurrency issues, 425
conditional expressions, 94–96

configuration files
    See also web configuration files
    application, 327–337
    machine-level, 328
    Web.config file, 397–399
configuration settings, verifying, 341
Connection object, 445, 446–447, 456
Connection property, 447
connections. See database connections
connection speeds, 559
connection strings, 396–405
    Connection object and, 446–447
    in web configuration file, 597
connectionStrings element, 398
constants, declaring, 66
Const keyword, 66
constraint rules, 452–453
ConstraintsCollection, 452–453
constructors, 545
Container.DataItem, 435–436
container elements, 29
container tags, 13–14
ContainsKey method, 74
ContainsValue method, 74
content pages, 147
    applying themes to, 191
    creating, 148–150
    using, 150
ContentPlaceHolder controls, 147–148
Contents Help, 46
Control Gallery, 553
ControlParameter, 505
controls, 504, 643–649
    See also specific types
    custom, 548
    grouping, with skins, 187
    hierarchy, 644
    parameters for, 505
    positioning, with div tags, 13–14
control statements, 93
control structures
    decision, 93–94
    Do loops, 96
    For Each loops, 97
    If Then statements, 95
    loop structures, 94–97
    nested statements, 97–98
    For Next loops, 97
    Select Case statement, 95–96
    While loop, 96
ControlToCompare property, 293
conversions, data type, 71
cookieless applications, 311–313
Cookieless property, 312
cookie munging, 312
CookieParameter, 505
Cookie property, 305
cookies
    client-side, 304–307
    defined, 304
    FormsAuthentication cookie, 338
    HTTP, 307–311
cookies collection, 304
Coordinated Universal Time (UTC), 69
CopyTo method, 263
CountClicks property, 229
Count property, 72, 73, 237
CountViews property, 229
CreateSubdirectory method, 260
CreateText method, 263
creative briefs, 560
cross-browser applications, 564–565
cross-page posting, 78
cross-site scripting, 287
CRUD methods, 420–421, 429
CSS. See cascading style sheets
CssClass property, 183, 234, 476

currency, 68
CurrentMode property, 518
Custom Color tab, 128
custom controls, 548
customErrors element, 101, 334–336
Custom Errors property sheet, 327
customers, 557
custom templates, 489–491
Custom view, 377

**D**

DashStyle property, 90
data
    *See also* records
    column, 483–484
    deleting, 515
    displaying, 419
        in GridView control, 480–486, 480–486, 506–509
        in MultiView control, 165–168
        Web service for, 597–598
    editing, 510–518
    filtering, with GridView control, 505–509
    inserting, 515–516
    moving to SQL Server, 406–409
    read-only, 481
    saving, using Session object, 80–81
    sorting, 509–510
    writing to files, 263–264
data access components, 422–423
data access layer, 420–421
data access model, 420
DataAdapter Configuration Wizard, 423
DataAdapter objects, 445
    adding queries to, 427–428
    creating, 423–428
    Fill method, 456–457
    populating DataSet with, 450–452
    SelectCommand method, 457
database administrators, 558
database applications
    software requirements, 630–631
    working with, 362–368
database connections, 396–409
    connection strings, 396–405
    creating
        to Access database, 403–405
        from a Web page, 399–403
    error messages, 441–442
    moving data to SQL Server, 406–409
    troubleshooting, 635–637
    Web.config file, 397–399
    to XML data, 405–406
database design, 363–367
Database Designer, 376–378
database diagrams, 376–378
database errors, detecting, 529–530
Database Explorer window, 3, 368, 394–395
database management, 503–505, 520–527
Database Management Systems (DBMSs), 444
databases
    *See also* relational databases
    creating, 362–363, 368–369
    retrieving data from, 447–459
    retrieving records from, 382–387
    searching, 393–394
    securing, 528–530
    upsizing, 406–409
    views, 376–381
database servers, 630, 636
    *See also* SQL Server
database software, 367–368
database tools
    built-in, 368–378
    Database Designer, 376–378
    SQL Server, 368–369
    Table Designer, 369–376
DataBinder.Eval method, 435, 478
data binding
    advantages of, 429–430
    automatic techniques, 437–442

to Data controls, 432–437, 487–489
to DataList control, 438–439
to FormView control, 516–518
to GridView control, 440–442
manual, 436–437
master-detail page for, 487–489
methods, 428–429, 435–436
repeat-expression binding, 432
single-expression binding, 430–432
to Web controls, 429–434
DataBindings property, 161
DataBind method, 430–431, 456
DataColumnsCollection, 455
Data controls, 428–429, 646
    *See also specific controls*
    automatic data binding to, 437–442
    binding data to, 432–437, 487–489
    for data management, 503
    modifying, using templates, 476–480
    in presentation layer, 422
    styles available to, 473–476, 504
    style sheets with, 476
    templates for, 468–473
data conversion errors, avoiding, 104
data diagrams, 562
DataDirectory path, 398
DataField property, 482, 510
DataFile property, 440
data files, 640
DataFormatString property, 440, 482
DataGrid control, 456–457, 504, 547
DataList controls, 433
    applying templates to, 479–480
    binding data to, 438–439
    modifying, using styles, 474–476
    templates available in, 470–471, 472
DataMember property, 231, 422
DataNavigateUrlFields property, 482
DataNavigateUrlFormatString property, 482
Data Protection Act, 35
Data Providers, 445–447
DataReader objects, 422–423
    data retrieval using, 448–453
data redundancy, 363–365
DataRelationsCollection, 453
data retrieval, 382–387, 447–459
    with DataReader object, 448–453
    with DataSet object, 450–459
    with DataView object, 455–459
    DirectoryInfo class, 257–260
    from a form, 77–78
    from header, 77
    with Request object, 77–78
    synchronous, 429–430
    from TextBox control, 215
    from Web server's file system, 257–268
    with Web services, 580–581
data security. *See* security
DataSet objects, 421–423, 445
    creating, 423–428
    data retrieval with, 450–459
datasets, typed, 32
Data Source Configuration Wizard, 427
DataSource control, 398–399, 403–405
    DateKeyNames property, 530
    parameters of, 505, 507
DataSourceID property, 153, 231
Data Source keyword, 446
DataSourceMode property, 423
DataSource objects, 429, 509–510
DataSource property, 433
data sources
    defined, 420
    types of, 419
data storage
    with Web objects, 77–81
    in Web server's file system, 257–268
data streaming, 581–582
Data tab, 3
DataTable objects, 422, 451–452, 455

DataTablesCollection, 452–453
DataTextField property, 74, 433, 482
DataTextFormatString property, 433, 482
data tier, 83
data types, 64
    Boolean, 70
    char, 66, 371
    converting, 71
    DateTime, 69–70, 371
    decimal, 68, 370
    numeric, 67–69
    specifying, 370
    for SQL Server, 370
    strings, 66–67
    text data, 66–67
    working with different, 66–71
data validation
    from forms, 289–303
    Regular Expressions, 294–299
DataValueField property, 74, 433
DataView objects, 422, 455–459
    data dispay with, 457–458
    data retrieval with, 455–459
    populating, 456–457
DateKeyNames property, 530
dates, formatting, 69–70
DateTime data type, 69–70, 371
debugger tools, 103–104
Debugger Users group, 632
debugging, 98
Debug mode, 26
Decimal data type, 68, 370
decision control structures, 83, 93–97
DeclarativeCatalogPart control, 204
Decoration property, 612
default error page, configuring, 340
DefaultMode property, 518
defaultRedirect attribute, 101, 335
DeleteCommand, 450
Delete method, 260, 263
DeleteParameter objects, 505
DELETE statement, 386, 387
delimiters, 296
denial of service (DOS) attacks, 330
deployment, 566–568
derived classes, 542, 545
Description property, 596
deserialization, 602
design
    custom applications, 181–217
    master and content pages, 147–150
    of navigational systems, 151–168, 561
    site, 560–562
    using cascading style sheets, 120–128
    using XSLT stylesheets, 129–146
DestinationPageUrl property, 349
DetailsView control, 433
    building master-detail page with, 487–489
    inserting new records with, 515–516
    templates available in, 470
Diagram pane, 379
diagrams
    data, 562
    database, 376–378
    relationship, 366
    site, 561
Dim keyword, 64, 72, 73, 84
directories
    creating and deleting, 260–262
    retrieving data from, 257–260
    virtual, 323
    working with, 257–260
DirectoryInfo class, 257, 257–262
DirectoryNotFoundException, 260
Directory Security property sheet, 327
Disability Discrimination Act, 35
DISCO (discovery) document, 594
Discovery Directory, 588
Display mode, 481
DisplayMode property, 203, 299

Display property, 291
DisplayRememberMe property, 349
Dispose method, 90
distributed applications, 420–422
div tags, 13–14
.dll file extension, 542, 567
Dockable property, 6
Doctype declarations, 31–32
documentation specialists, 558
DocumentSource property, 145
Documents property sheet, 326
document type definition (DTD) documents, 31
document type definitions (DTDs), 31–32
Dollar Rent-a-Car, 577–578
Do loops, 96
DotNetNuke Starter Kit, 213, 556–557
Double data type, 68
Do Until loops, 96
Do While loops, 96
Dragon Naturally Speaking software, 35–36
DrawString class, 89, 90
DropDownList control, 75, 183, 428, 433–435, 514, 516
DTD documents. See document type definition (DTD) documents
dynamic content, previewing, 548
Dynamic Help, 46
Dynamic HTML (DHTML), 39
dynamic menus, 161
dynamic Web applications, 36–37

E

eCollege, 214
EditItemLink class, 519
EditItemStyle, 473, 504
EditItemTemplate template, 468, 482, 504, 512–513, 518
Edit mode, 481
EditorZone control, 204–205
EditRowStyle, 473
elements, 71
    container, 29
    nested, 28–29
    root, 28–29
    in style sheets, 121
element templates, 132–134
e-mail
    attachments, 250–251, 252
    CDONTS, 250
    .NET mail classes, 250–254
    preparing, 251–252
    rejection of, 250
    security and privacy issues, 245
    sending, 251–256
        from Web page, 244–257
    spam, 245, 251
    troubleshooting, 256–257
e-mail addresses, spoofing, 257
e-mail objects, 250–251
e-mail servers, 244, 257
    configuring, 246–250
    role of, 245–246
embedded styles, 121–122
EmptyDataRowStyle, 473
EmptyItemTemplate, 469
EnableCaching property, 590
enabled attribute, 331
enableSessionState attribute, 329
EnableTheming property, 184, 191–192
enableViewState attribute, 45, 329
enableViewStateMac attribute, 329
Encode method, 287
Enctype attribute, 239
Enterprise Manager, 529
entities, 362–363, 364
equal to (=), 95
Erase method, 73
error detection, 99–100, 529–530
error handling, 98
ErrorPage property, 100–101

error status messages
    common, 100
    configuring default, 340
    custom, 100–103, 332–334
    customErrors element, 332–334
    database connections, 441–442
    e-mail, 256
    validation, 299
    Validation controls, 291
Eval method, 435, 478, 512
_EVENTARGUMENT, 40
event procedures, creating, 86
events, page, 86–87
_EVENTTARGET, 40
_EVENTVALIDATION, 40
Exception classes, 98–100
exception handling, 98–100, 529–530
Exception objects, 529
exceptions, 98, 99–100
Execute method, 447
ExecuteNonQuery method, 447
ExecuteReader method, 448
executionTimeout attribute, 329
Exit Do loops, 96
Exit For loopss, 97
Exit While, 96
Explicit property, 65
ExtendedProperties property, 453
Extensible Markup Language (XML). see XML
Extensible Stylesheet Language (XSL), 28
external cascading style sheets (CSS), 28
ExternalException class, 99
external styles, 122–124, 182–184

F

Failuretext property, 349
field names, 386
FileInfo class, 257, 263–268
File Input control, 239
Filename property, 251
File Not Found (404) error, 100
file permissions, 345–346
files
    copying of, by users, 269
    creating and reading, 263–268
    deleting, 261
    uploading, to Web server, 238–244
file system, data storage and retrieval in, 257–268
FileSystemInfo class, 257
file transfer protocol (FTP), 2, 567–568, 642
FileUpload control, 238–244
file uploads, restrictions on, 269
FillEllipse method, 89
Fill method, 425, 450, 456–457
FillPolygon method, 89
FillRectangle method, 89
FilterExpression property, 507, 508–509
FilterParameter objects, 505, 507–509
FilterParameter property, 507
FindControl method, 483
FireFox, 8
float data type, 371
Floating property, 6
focus groups, 558–559
folders
    applying themes to, 188–189
    permissions, 345–346
Font class, 89
FooterStyle, 473
FooterTemplate objects, 468, 470, 482
FooterText properties, 482
For Each loops, 97
ForeColor property, 476
foreign keys, 365
Format method, 68–70
Form controls, 645

form field data
    accessing, 78
    invalid, 303
    validation of, 289–303
FormParameter, 505
forms
    generating, 15–16
    required fields in, 293
    retrieving data from, 77–78
forms authentication, 269, 338–345
FormsAuthentication cookie, 338
Forms collection, 77–78
FormsView control, 433
form tags, 15–16
FormView control
    styles with, 518–519
    templates with, 472, 518–519
    using, 516–518
    using stored procedures with, 523–527
For Next loops, 97, 237
forward slash (/) character, 9, 70, 296
FreeTextBox control, 213–214, 216–217, 553–554
Friend keyword, 65
FROM keyword, 382
FrontPage, 268
functions, 87

G

GDI+ class, 89–90
General tab, 5
GetData method, 425
GetDirectories method, 257
GetFiles method, 263
GetImageURL function, 431, 432
GetUserByEmail method, 342
GetUser method, 342
.gif file extension, 12
global assembly cache, 567
Google AdWords, 564
graphic design, 560–561
graphic designers, 557
Graphics class, 89–91, 90–91
greater than (>), 95
greater than or equal to (>=), 95
Grid pane, 379–380
GridViewCommandEventArgs, 483
GridView control, 433
    about, 467
    binding data to, 440–442
    building master-detail page with, 487–489
    column data, 483–484
    column properties, 482–483
    columns, 480–481
    creating with constructor, 545
    deleting records with, 515
    displaying data using, 480–486, 506–509
    editing records with, 510–515
    filtering data with, 505–509
    maintaining database with, 504–505
    modifying, 484–486
    sorting data with, 509–510
    styles in, 473
    templates available in, 469
    using stored procedures with, 520–523
GROUP BY clause, 384

H

hackers, 528
hard drive space, 631–632
hardware requirements, 631–633
hashing algorithm, 73
hash keys, 74
HashTable collection, 73–74, 429
    data binding to, 434
header, 77
HeaderImageURL property, 482
HeaderStyle, 473

HeaderTemplate, 468, 470, 471, 478, 482
HeaderText property, 440, 482
heading section, 10–12
heading tags, 13
Height property, 227, 230
Help resources, 46
hierarchical data source, 421
Home Directory property sheet, 326
horizontal lines, 14–15
HoverNodeStyle property, 157
href attribute, 17, 122
hr tag, 14–15
hspace attribute, 16
.htm file extension, 8
HTML. *See* Hypertext Markup Language
HTML 3.2, 611
HTMLContainerControl control, 645
HTML controls, 41, 644–645
HtmlEncoded property, 440
.html file extension, 8
HTMLImage control, 645
HTMLInputControl control, 645
HTML pages
    creating, 266–268
    previewing in browser, 23, 25
HTML Server controls, 644–645
HTML tab, 5
HTML tags, 8–10
    anchor, 17
    attributes of, 9–10
    closing, 9
    form, 15–16
    heading, 10–12, 13
    HTML controls and, 41
    images, 16–17
    IntelliSense and, 20
    list, 16
    opening, 9
    paragraph, 13–14
    for text, 13–15
*http://tempuri.org*, 594
HTTP cookies, 307–311
HTTPGet method, 589, 595
HTTP Headers property sheet, 326–327
HttpPostedFile class, 240, 241
HTTPPost method, 589
httpRuntime element, 329–330
HTTPS protocol, 607
HttpStatusCode property, 100
HTTP Status Message Codes, 100
HyperLink controls, 92
    dynamic creation of, 92–93
    formatting with skins, 186–187
HyperLinkField columns, 481, 482, 484
hyperlinks, 17
Hypertext Markup Language (HTML)
    attributes, 9–10, 12–13, 15, 16
    creating Web page with, 20–22
    introduction to, 8–26
    special characters, 18
    structure, 10–13
    tags. *see* HTML tags

I
id attribute, 9–10
identity columns, 374
identity element, 348
Identity Increment property, 374
Identity Seed property, 374
If Then statements, 95
IIS In-Process Applications, 336
IIS Log File Format, 247
IIS Out-of-Process Applications, 336
IIS Web security, 607–608
image data type, 371
ImageFields, 481
ImageMap control, 544–546
image maps, 16–17, 544–546

images
    background, 12–13
    displaying, with XML files, 35
    Graphics class and, 89–90
    saving of, by users, 269
    storage of, 240
    watermarks on, 269
image tags, 16–17
ImageURL property, 92, 227, 430, 431
impersonate attribute, 348
ImportCatalogPart control, 204
impressions, 229
Impressions element, 227–228
in data type, 370
indentation, of text, 13
Index Help, 46
index number, drop-down lists and, 75
IndexOf property, 73
IndexOutOfRangeException, 99
index position, 237
information management security policies, 286–289
infrastructure, 559
Inherits property, 62
Initial Catalog, 447
inline server code, 62
inline server tags, 430
inline styles, 121, 182
INNER JOIN clause, 384, 385
input parameters, 387, 390–391
InsertCommand, 450
InsertItemTemplate template, 504
Insert method, 72
InsertParameter objects, 505
INSERT statements, 384–385, 387, 388
instantiation, 84, 543
Integer data type, 68
integers, 64
integrity
    data, 365, 503
    relationship, 366–367
IntelliSense, 20, 589
internal anchors, 17
Internet, publishing Web applications to, 567–568, 642
Internet Assigned Numbers Authority (IANA), 319
Internet Explorer, 8
Internet Guest Account, 367, 633
Internet Information Services (IIS), 25, 629
Internet Service Manager (ISM), 336
intranet applications, 564
InvalidCastException, 71
IOException, 260
IsArray function, 73
IsInRole method, 347–348
ISO 8859 character encoding, 11–12
isolated processes, 336
IsValid property, 291–293
italic tag, 14
Item property, 483
ItemStyle, 473
ItemTemplate, 436, 468, 477, 484, 512
item templates, 45
IUSR_MachineName, 633
IWAM_MachineName, 633

J
JavaScript, 39
    AJAX and, 565
    client-side cookies and, 305–307
    security issues with, 268
JOIN clause, 384, 385
.jpg file extension, 12
JScript, 298

K
Keys view, 376
Keyword element, 228
KeywordFilter property, 231

L
Label controls, 42, 545, 547
Language property, 62
language support, 11–12, 18–19
Launch IIS Process Account, 633
LCase method, 67
leadership, 541
leaf nodes, 29
LEFT OUTER JOIN clause, 384
less than (<), 95
less than or equal to (<=), 95
leverage, 541, 542
line break tags, 13, 16
LineCap property, 90
line numbering feature, 601
LinkButtons, 483
link tags, 10, 17
ListBox control, 433
List controls, 428
list item tags, 16
lists
    bulleted, 16
    creating, 16
    numbered, 16
Literal control, 92
local application cache, 567
localhost, 25, 319
localOnly attribute, 331
local variables, 64
location elements, 189–190
log files, web server, 324–326
logical operators, 95
Login controls, 349, 350, 646
login forms, 268
login scripts, 269
Login Status control, 349
Login tab, 4
login values, 368
Logo.DataBind() method, 430
Long data type, 68
loop counters, 237
loops, 94
    Do, 96
    For Each, 97
    Exit For, 97
    For Next, 97, 237
    While, 96
loosely typed datasets, 421
Ltrim method, 67

M
machineKey element, 348
machine-level configuration file, 328
MailAttachment class, 250–251
MailEncoding enumeration, 251
MailFormat enumeration, 250
MailMessage.Attachment property, 252
MailMessage.Body property, 251–252
MailMessage class, 250–254
MailMessage.From property, 251
MailMessage.Subject property, 251
MailMessage.To property, 251
MailMessage.UrlContentBase property, 252
MailPriority enumeration, 250–251
maintaining state, 44–45, 303–313
    *See also* session data
    with client-side cookies, 304–307
    with HTTP cookies, 307–311
    Session objects and, 79–81
    with Web services, 595
    without HTTP cookies, 311–313
maintainScrollPositionOnPostBack element, 329
maintenance, of Web applications, 563–564
Main window, 2–3
Managed Providers, 445–446
marketing research specialists, 557
markup codes, for common XML characters, 28
markup validation, of XML, 30–33, 35

Markup Validation Service, 32
masks, 70
master-detail page, 467, 487–489
MasterPageFile property, 150
master pages, 147
    AJAX and, 565
    applying themes to, 191
    creating, 147–148
    using, 150
mathematical methods, 68
maxRequestLength attribute, 329–330
.mdb file extension, 367
Membership APIs, 342–344
Membership class, 342
membership services, 337–348
memory, buffer, 329
memory models, 336–337
memory requirements, 631
Menu control
    creating, 161–162
    layouts and properties, 163–165
MenuItem control, 163
MenuItemStyle class, 161
menus
    dynamic, 161
    static, 161
MenuStyle class, 161
MessageName property, 596
Metabase, 323
metacharacters, 295
meta tags, 11–12
methods
    calling, 85
    viewing, 89
Microsoft Access. *See* Access
Microsoft Atlas, 565
Microsoft FrontPage, 268
Microsoft IIS Log File Format, 247
Microsoft Intermediate Language (MSIL), 37
Microsoft Internet Information Server, 323
Microsoft Management Console (MMC), 246, 323
Microsoft Office, 407
Microsoft Project, 562–563
Microsoft SQL Server. *See* SQL Server
Microsoft Web services, 607
Microsoft XML Core Services, 27
Microsoft XML schema, 32
middle tier, 83
Midwest Alliance for Nursing Informatics (MANI), 269
Mobile controls, 610–616, 646
mobile devices, development for, 609–616
Mobile Forms, 611–616
Mobile Internet Designer, 611
Mobile Internet Toolkit, 610
Mode attribute, 101, 345–346
Mode property, 316, 317, 318
modular testing, 563
module-level variables, 64
money data type, 370
MoveTo method, 263
MSDN library, 630
MultiView control, 165–168
My Templates section, 45

**N**

name attribute, 9, 17
Named Colors tab, 127
named markup, 18
Name Only view, 377
Name property, 505, 506, 596
Namespace property, 595–596
namespaces, 41, 83
naming rules, for variables, 65
narrowing conversions, 71
National Center for Supercomputing Applications (NCSA), 247
NavigateUrl element, 227, 482

navigational systems
    breadcrumb trails, 155–157
    creating, 151–168
    designing, 151–168, 561
    Menu control, 161–165
    MultiView control, 165–168
    site maps, 151–155, 158–161
    TreeView control, 158–161
Navigation controls, 646
Navigation tab, 4
nchar data type, 371
needs assessments, 558
nested elements, 28–29
nested statements, 97–98
.NET development editors, 593, 629
.NET development environment
    building mobile applications in, 610–611
    creating Web services within, 595–598
    system requirements for, 627–633
.NET Framework, 82
    data management in, 503
    designing Web data application in, 420–432
    multiple instances of, 634
    organization of classes in, 83
    receiving data in, 447–459
    tools and utilities in, 32
    Web services support in, 579
.NET mail classes, 250–254
.NET model. *See* ADO.NET data model
.NET Providers, 445–447
Netscape Browser, 8
.Net Web applications, designing, 82–83
network administrators, 558
New keyword, 84, 543–544
New Web Site window, 7
/nologo parameter, 594–595
Non-Delivery Report (NDR), 250, 256
non-disclosure agreements, 558
normalization, 363
not equal to (<>), 95
Not operator, 95
ntext data type, 371
NullDisplayText property, 440
NULL keyword, 383, 385
NullReferenceException, 99
Null values, 523
numbered lists, creating, 16
numeric data type, 67–69, 370
nvarchar data type, 371

**O**

Object Browser, 89, 644
ObjectDataSource control, 404
Object Linking and Embedding Database (OLE DB), 444–445
object-oriented programming, 61, 83
objects
    creating, 84
    defined, 83–84
ODBC drivers, 444–445
ODBC .NET Provider, 445–446
OleDbException, 99
OLE DB .NET Provider, 445–446
Open Database Connectivity (ODBC), 444–445
Open Mobile Alliance, 609–610
OpenText method, 264
OpenWave Simulator, 610
operating system requirements, 628
OperatorValueToCompare property, 293–294
Options window, 22–24
Oracle, 269
Oracle Database 10g, 368
Oracle Provider, 445–446
ORDER BY clause, 384
ordered list tags, 16
OR keyword, 382, 383
Or operator, 95
OUTER JOIN clause, 384

/out parameter, 594
@ OutputCache page directive, 590
output parameters, 387

**P**

Page_Init event, 86
Page_Load event, 86
Page_PreRender event, 87
Page_Unload event, 87
PageCatalogPart control, 204
Page class
    Request object, 77–78
    Response object, 79
Page.DataBind() method, 430
@Page directive, 45
Page directive
    configuring, 62
    Debug attribute, 103–104
    Explicit property, 65
page events, 86–87
page level security, 242
page level testing, 563
page lifecycles, 86
pageOutput attribute, 331
Pager controls, 473
pager row, 516
PagerStyle, 473
PagerTemplate, 469
pages element, 329
Panel control, 92
panes, 379
paragraph tags, 13–14
parameter queries, 520
    *See also* stored procedures
parameters, 85
    input, 387, 390–391
    multiple values for, 508
    order of, 508
    output, 387
    passing to queries, 507
    passing to stored procedures, 520–523, 526
    setting to value of control, 505
    unnamed, 507–508
Parameters collection, 447
_parent, 92
parenthesis, 19
ParentLevelsDisplayed property, 157
Park University, 216
partial classes, 62
PassordRecoveryUrl property, 349
password feature, in Access, 367
Password Recovery control, 349
passwords, 528
PathDirection property, 157
PathSeparatorStyle property, 157
PathSeparatorTemplate property, 157
Pen class, 90
permissions
    error messages regarding, 442
    file, 345–346
    folder, 345–346
    write permission, 407
personal digital assistants (PDAs), development for, 609–616
Photoshop, 269, 560
Placeholder control, 92, 93, 545
plus sign (+), 67
Pocket PC devices, 609
Point class, 89
PopFrequency property, 229
PopPositionLeft property, 229
PopPosition property, 229
pop-up ads, 229
port numbers, 318–319
postback process, 44–45
PostBackUrl property, 78
PostedFile objects, 240
PostedFile.SaveAs method, 240

pound sign (#), 383, 430
PreInit event handler, 150
presentational tags, 14
presentation layer, 422
    customizing, 182–197
        with skins, 184–187
        with style sheets, 182–184
        with themes, 187–197
presentation tier, 82
primary keys, 365, 373–374, 426
privacy issues, 245, 286
privacy policies, 289
procedures
    *See also* stored procedures
    event, 86
    subprocedures, 85
    using, 85–87
processing instructions, 129–130, 135, 138–144
processModel node, 318
programming
    best practices, 104–105
    configuring Page directive, 62
    constants, 66
    control structures, 93–98
    data types and, 66–71
    integrated, and Web Forms, 62–63
    object-oriented, 83
    variables, 64–66
    with Visual Basic .Net, 83–93
programming models, 62–63
programming statements, 62–63, 83
Project and Solutions options, 24
project management software, 562–563
project requirements document, 558, 563
projects, 639–642
prologue, 27
properties, viewing, 89
Properties window, 2, 4, 474
Property Builder, 468
PropertyGridEditorPart control, 204
Property methods, creating, 88–89
PropertyName property, 506
property sheets, 323–327
Protected keyword, 65
/ protocol parameter, 594
Provider keyword, 446
Provider Model, 553–555
proxy class, 588–592, 594
Public keyword, 64, 85
PushButtons, 483

**Q**

quality control specialists, 558
quantifiers, 296
queries, 378–381, 384–387
    adding to DataAdapters, 427–428
    concatenated, 505
    passing parameters to, 507
Query Analyzer, 379, 529
Query Builder, 394, 427
Query Designer, 379–381
query plans, 379
QueryString collection, 77–78
QueryStringParameter, 505
question mark (?), 507, 508
Queue collection, 75
Queue folder, 250
QuickStart Web site, 46
Quixtar, 560
quotation marks, 507

**R**

RadioButtonList controls, 428, 433
radio buttons, binding collections to, 75
RangeValidator control, 293, 301
Read method, 448
read-only data, 481
ReadOnly keyword, 89, 482, 512

ReadXML method, 454–455
real data type, 371
records
    deleting, 386, 387, 504–505, 515
    editing, 504–505, 510–518
    filtering, 505–509
    inserting, 384–385, 392, 504–505, 515–516
    retrieving, 382–387
    sorting, 384, 509–510
    updating, 386
redevelopment needs, 564
Redirect attribute, 336
redundancy, 363–365
RegExp objects, 298
@Register directive, 199
Registry, 637
RegServ32.exe application, 566–567
Regular Expressions, 294–299
Regular ExpressionValidator control, 300
RegularExpressValidator control, 298
relational data
    applications storing, 367–368
    binding, to GridView control, 440–442
relational database management systems (RDBMs),
        362–368
relational databases
    *See also* tables
    characteristics of, 362–363
    composite keys, 366
    data redundancy in, 363–365
    data sources and, 420
    foreign keys, 365
    primary keys, 365, 373–374, 426
    software, 367–368
relationship diagrams, 366
relationships
    creating, with Database Designer, 376–378
    integrity of, 366–367
    between tables, 363–367
relative address, 12
relay settings, 256
rel property, 122
RememberMeText property, 349
Remote Procedure Calls (RPCs), 578
RemoveAt method, 72
Remove method, 72
RemoveRange method, 73
RenderCurrentNodeAsLink property, 157
RepeatColumns property, 438, 439, 479
RepeatDirections property, 438, 479
Repeater control, 433–437, 476–480
repeat-expression binding, 428–429, 432
Replace method, 67
Request object
    retrieving data from Form with, 77–78
    retrieving data from header with, 77
request status, 332
RequiredFieldValidator control, 293, 300
requirements testing, 563
requireSSL attribute, 346
resource-based authorization, 337–338
Response object, 79
Results pane, 380
retrievable data, value of, 216–217
retry intervals, 248
return code, 388
Return keyword, 388, 590
reusable code, 43, 542–555
    calling from Web page, 543–544
    code snippets, 548–551
    creating with classes, 542–543, 544–548
    third-party components, 553–555
RIGHT OUTER JOIN clause, 384
Role APIs, 342–344
role-based authorization, 338
root element, 28–29
root node, 28–29, 226
root tags, 28
RowFilter property, 456

rows, 363
rtc tag, 19
Rtrim method, 67
ruby base text tag, 19
Ruby markup, 18–19
ruby parenthesis tag, 19
ruby tag, 19
runtime errors, 98

**S**

scaling, 83
schema documents, 31
schemas, 31, 32, 369
scope, variable, 64–65
scraping, 581
scripts, SQL, 378, 387, 395–396, 529
script tags, 10
SDK QuickStart, 636
search conditions, 382–384
Search Help, 46
Secure Sockets Layer (SSL) protocol, 45, 607
security, 285–286
    with building Web applications, 268–269
    client-side scripting and, 37
    of databases, 503, 528–530
    with e-mail, 245
    maintaining, with Web controls, 348–350
    permissions, 242–244
    policies, 286–289
    of Web services, 607–608
Select Case statement, 95–96
SelectCommand method, 457
SelectCommand property, 440, 450
SelectedDates property, 235, 237
SelectedIndex property, 75
SelectedItemStyle, 473, 504
SelectedRowStyle, 473
SelectedTemplate, 469
SelectParameter objects, 505
SelectParameters collection, 505
Select statement, 382
_self, 92
Sender As Object parameter, 86
SeparatorStyle, 473
SeparatorTemplate, 469, 471
serialization, 602
Server controls, 38–40
    applying themes to, 194–197
    code behind the page and, 62
    dynamic creation of, 92–93, 94
    postback process and, 44–45
server programs, 62
server-side programming, 37
server-side scripting, 37
server timeout property, 215
Server.Transfer method, 79
server variables, 77
session data, 285–286
    *See also* maintaining state
    storage of, 313–322
SessionID property, 79–80, 307, 314
Session objects, 79–81, 307, 314–316
SessionParameter, 505
session state, 314
    managing
        with SQL Server, 321–322
        with State Server, 318–321
        within Web server process, 317–318
sessionState node, 316
session variables, 314–316
Set-Cookie header, 308
SET keyword, 386
shared classes, 542–543
shopping carts, 37
Short data type, 68
ShowFooter property, 473
ShowHeader property, 473
ShowInsertButton, 515

ShowStartingNode property, 161
Simple Mail Transfer Protocol (SMTP), 245–246
Simple Object Access Protocol (SOAP), 578–579, 580, 589–590, 593–595
Single data type, 68
single-expression binding, 428, 430–432
site design, 560–562
site diagrams, 561
SiteMapDataSource control, 153–155, 404
siteMapNode elements, 152
SiteMapPath control, 155–157
site maps, 151–155
    code for, 151
    creating, 152–153
    designing, 561
    limitations of, 152
    properties, 152
    SiteMapDataSource control, 153–155
    TreeView control, 158–161
SkinID property, 184–187, 194
skins
    applying, 194–197
    formatting Web Form with, 184–187
slidingExpiration attribute, 346
Small Business Starter Kit, 556
smalldatetime data type, 371
smallint data type, 370
smallmoney data type, 370
SMART, 558
SmartPhones, 608
SmoothingMode property, 90
SMTP. See Simple Mail Transfer Protocol (SMTP)
SmtpMail class, 250–251, 253
SmtpServer property, 252
SMTP servers, 245–246, 250, 257
SOAP. See Simple Object Access Protocol (SOAP)
SOAP contract, 593–595
SOAP envelope, 590
SOAP headers, 608
SOAP Toolkit, 608
software architects, 557
software requirements, 628–631
Solution Explorer window, 3, 368
solution files, 639–642
SortedList collection, 74
SortExpression property, 482, 510
Sort property, 456
source code files, compiling, 551–553
Source Code view, 22–23, 475
Southwest Airlines, 577–578
spam, 245, 257
span tags, 13
special characters, 18
Split method, 67
SQL. See Structured Query Language (SQL)
sqlcmd, 395
SqlDataSource controls, 399, 403, 404, 525–526
SqlDataSource objects, 523
SQLDebugger, 632
SQL Editor, 388–389, 392, 394
SqlException, 99
SQL injection, 528
SQL pane, 380
SQL Query Builder, 394
SQL scripts, 529
SQL Server, 269, 367, 368
    authentication, 637
    connection strings, 397
    creating database with, 368–369
    data types, 370
    installing and configuring, 636
    managing session state using, 321–322
    moving data to, 406–409
    Query Designer, 379–381
    scripts, 387
    software requirements, 630–631
    stored procedures in, 520, 523–527
    View Designer, 378–381

SQL Server 2005 Express Edition, 368, 395
SQL Server Express, 630, 636
SQL Server Management Studio, 395
SQL Server .NET Provider, 445–446
SQL Server scripts, 395–396
SQL statements, 382–387
    concatenated, 507
    DELETE, 386, 387
    INSERT, 384–385, 387
    scripts, 395–396
    search conditions, 382–384
    stored procedures and, 387–395
    UPDATE, 386, 387
src attribute, 16, 17
SSL protocol. See Secure Sockets Layer (SSL) protocol
Stack collection, 75
Standard Generalized Markup Language (SGML), 8
standards
    XHTML, 1, 10
    XML, 10, 26–27
Standard tab, 3, 5
Standard view, 376
starter kits, 213, 555–557
Start Page, 2
state, maintaining. See maintaining state
stateConnectionString, 318
stateNetworkTimeout property, 318
State Server, 318–321
static menus, 161
static Web pages, 8, 10–13
Status Code 200, 100
statusCode attribute, 336
StoredProcedure property, 447
stored procedures, 367, 378, 387–395
    built-in, 394–395
    in business logic layer, 422
    in classes, 544
    Command object and, 447
    creating, 388–394
    defined, 520
    input parameters, 387, 390–391
    inserting records with, 392
    modifying, 394
    output parameters, 387
    to prevent SQL injection, 528
    return code, 388
    using with FormView control, 523–527
    using with GridView control, 520–523
StreamReader object, 264
StreamWriter object, 263, 264–265, 267
Strict property, 71
StringBuilder class, 653
strings, 64, 66–67
strongly typed datasets, 421
strong passwords, 528
structural tags, 14
Structured Query Language (SQL), 362
    See also SQL statements
    Command object and, 447
    queries, 378–381, 384–387, 505, 507
    stored procedures, 387–395, 447
Style Builder
    Color Picker feature, 127–128
    interface, 120
    using, 126–127
Style property, 230
style rules
    building, using Style Builder, 126–128
    cascading priority, 124–125
    embedded, 121–122
    external, 122–124
    inline, 121, 182
styles
    for Data controls, 473, 474–476, 504
    with FormView control, 518–519
StyleSheet controls, 120
style sheets, 10
    See also cascading style sheets; XSLT stylesheets
    cascading style sheets (CSS), 28
    classes, 125–126
    configuring Web pages dynamically with, 182–184

CSS, 120–124
    with Data controls, 476
    external, 182–184
    vs. stylesheets, 120
    themes and, 187–188
StyleSheetTheme property, 188
Sub keyword, 85
subprocedures, 85
sub tag, 14
sup tag, 14
SwitchViewByID, 167
SwitchViewByIndex, 167
@ symbol, 387, 507, 523
System Colors tab, 128
SystemException class, 99–100
Systems.Collection namespace, 72
Systems.Drawing.Graphics class, 89–91
System.Web class, 644
System.Web.UI.WebControls namespace, 42
System.Web.UI.WebControls.WebControl class, 646–648

T

TableAdapter Configuration Wizard, 424
table body tags, 15
table cell tags, 15
Table Data view, 369
table definitions, 369
Table Designer, 369, 369–376
TableDirect property, 447
table footer tags, 15
table heading cell tags, 15
table heading tags, 15
table row tags, 15
tables
    See also relational databases
    accessing data in multiple, 451–452
    composite keys, 366
    creating, 15, 369–376
    data in, 362
    data redundancy in, 363–365
    data types for, 370–372
    deleting records from, 386, 387
    foreign keys, 365
    inserting records in, 384–385, 392
    joining, 384, 385
    normalization of, 363
    primary keys, 365, 373–374, 426
    relationships between, 363–367
    searching, 393–394
    setting properties, 372–374
    updating records in, 386
    views, 376–377
table tags, 15, 17
tags
    body, 12–13
    formatting, 14
    horizontal lines, 14–15
    HTML, 8–10
    table, 15
Target property, 92, 160, 230–231, 482
targets, 92
Task List window, 5
TCP port numbers, 318–319
technical requirements, 559–560
Telerik, 214
TemplateColumn, 484
TemplateField columns, 481, 482, 512–515
templates
    creating item, 45
    custom, 489–491
    for Data controls, 468–473, 476–480
    element, 132–134
    formatting main, with XSLT stylesheets, 129–132
    with FormView control, 518–519
    main, with element templates, 132–134
    modifying, 484–486, 504
tempuri namespace, 594
text, formatting, 14
Text attribute, 612
TextBox control

retrieving data from, 483–484
retrieving information from, 215
text data type, 66–67, 371
Text Editor options, 24
text editors, 2, 8
text files, creating, 264–266
Text property, 92, 447, 482
themes
  applying, 188–189, 191, 194–197
  configuring, 191
  configuring multiple, 189–190
  creating, 192–194
  disabling, 191–192
  style sheets and, 187–188
  using, 187–197
third-party components, 553–555
third-party controls, 213–217
third-party Web services, 605–607
tiered hierarchical framework, 82
tilde (~) character, 399
time, 69–70
timeout errors, 215
tinyint data type, 370
title attribute, 10
title tags, 10
Titletext property, 349
Toolbox window, 3–5, 429
  server controls, 38–40
  Validation tab, 290
ToolTip property, 92, 231
_top, 92
ToShortDateString property, 235
Toys-R-Us web site, 560
TraceContext class, 332
trace element, 331–334
Trace feature, 87
Trace property, 87, 331
trace stack, 332
TraceTool program, 332–334
TrackNavigationUrl property, 229
trainers, 558
Transaction objects, 447
transactions, 367
Transact SQL, 367
TransformArgumentList, 146
Transform property, 146
TransformSource property, 145, 146
TreeView control, 158–161, 406
  creating, 158–160
  properties, 160–161
Trim method, 67
trusted users, 632
Try-Catch construct, 529–530
Try-Catch-Finally statement, 98–99
tt tag, 14
typed datasets, 32
Type property, 122, 505–506

U

UCase method, 67
UDDI, 605–606
underline tag, 14
underscore (_), 63, 86
Unified Modeling Language (UML), 421
Uniform Resource Locators (URLs), 12
uniqueidentifier data type, 372
Unit objects, 43
Universal, Description, Discovery, and Integration (UDDI), 588
Universal Naming Convention (UNC), 264
unnamed parameters, 507–508
unordered list tags, 16
UpdateCommand, 450
Update method, 451
UpdateParameter objects, 505
UPDATE statement, 386, 387
upsizing, 367

Upsizing Wizard, 406–409
useFullyQualifiedRedirectUrl attribute, 331
usemap attribute, 16
user accounts, setting security permissions for, 242–244
user agent, 77
user authentication. See authentication
user authorization. See authorization
User controls, 197–201
  creating and registering, 200–201
  understanding, 198–199
user IDs, 368
user interface
  design of, 560–562
  VWD, 2–5
user roles, 368
user technology constraints, 559
UTF-8, 27

V

Validate method, 291–293
validation
  of form field data, 289–303
  JScript, 298
  Regular Expressions, 294–299
Validation controls, 290–294, 298–303, 646
validationKey attribute, 348
Validation options, 24
validation services, 32–33
ValidationSummary control, 299, 301–302
Validation tab, 4
value parameter, 74
values, assigning to variables, 65–66
varbinary data type, 372
varchar data type, 371
variable declarations, 64
variables
  application, 328
  assigning values to, 65–66
  declaring, 64–66
  local, 64
  module-level, 64
  naming, 64, 65
  retrieving and setting value of, 88–89
  scope, 64–65
  server, 77
  using in Web Forms, 64–66
  using Property method with, 88–89
VaryByParam attribute, 590
Victoria Secret, 560
View controls, 165
View Designer, 378–381
views, 378–381
  building, 379
  built-in, 394–395
  database, 376–377
_VIEWSTATE, 40, 45, 80
ViewState control, 530
ViewStateEncryptionMode, 530
virtual directories, 323
virtual web, 323
Visible property, 482
VisibleWhenLoggedIn property, 349
vision, 541
Visual Basic .Net, 652
  programming with, 83–93
Visual Basic .NET compiler (VBC.exe), 594–595
Visual Studio .NET, 2
  built-in database tools, 368–378
  compatibility issues, 634
  custom templates, 489–491
  installation of, 632–633
  versions, 629
Visual Web Developer Express (VWD), 2–5
visual Web developer tools
  creating Web application with, 6–8
  introduction to, 2–8
  user interface, 2–5
VS Developer, 632
vspace attribute, 16

W

W3C Extended Log File Format, 324
walkthroughs, 518
WAP. See Wireless Application Protocol (WAP)
Warn method, 332
watermarks, 269
Web Accessibility Initiative (WAI), 35
Web application architecture, 82–83, 562
Web applications
  accessing, through Web portals, 211–213
  for alternative platforms, 609–616
  applying themes to, 188–189
  applying Web services to, 580–583
  building complete, 555–564
  communication with Web services, 578–580
  compiling, 551–553
  configuration of, 323–337
  creating, with visual Web developer, 6–8
  cross-browser, 564–565
  custom designing, 181–217
  data, in .NET Framework, 420–432
  database connectivity for, 637
  debugging, 98, 103–104
  deployment of, 566–568
  designing, 82–83
  development of, 562–563
  dynamic, 36–37
  integrating ASP.NET into current, 566
  interaction of, with Systems.Drawing.Graphics class, 89–90
  maintaining, 563–564
  memory models, 336–337
  navigational systems for, 151–168
  planning, 557–560
  previewing, 25–26
  programming requirements for, 560–562
  project requirements for, 558–560
  publishing to Internet, 567–568, 642
  security issues of, 268–269
  starter kits, 555–557
  testing, 563
  user interface design, 560–562
Web browsers
  changing, 25, 26
  common, 8
  lack of scripting support in, 37
  previewing Web service in, 599–601
Web colors, 128
Web configuration files
  applying themes in, 188–191
  authentication element, 346–348
  authorization element, 344–345
  changing, for custom error message, 101–103
  configuring for debugging, 103–104
  connection strings in, 597
  storing connection strings in, 397–399
Web Content Accessibility Guidelines (WCAG), 35–36
WebControl class, 646–648
Web controls, 42–43, 645–649
  See also Data controls; specific controls
  AdRotator control, 226–233
  binding collections to, 75, 433–434
  binding data to, 428–429, 429–434
  building, 649
  Calendar control, 233–238
  configuring, with style sheets, 182–184
  FileUpload control, 238–244
  formatting with skins, 184–187
  groupings of, 645–646
  maintaining security with, 348–350
  third-party, 213–217
  Validation controls, 290–294
Web developers, 557
Web developer tools, visual, 2–8
Web development
  integration of, with business objectives, 541
  life cycle, 559
Web Discovery Service file, 588
Web editors, 8–9
  creating Web pages with, 43–45
  creating Web services with, 583–592
Web farms, 45

Web Forms, 37
 constants in, 66
 creating, using a Web editor, 43–45
 creating graphics for, 90–91
 formatting with skins, 184–187
 integrated programming and, 62–63
 postback process, 44–45
 User controls in, 197–201
 using collections in, 75–76
 variables in, 64–66
 vs. Web services, 577
 XML control in, 144–146
WebMethod keyword, 584, 585, 596, 597, 598
Web objects
 Request object, 77–78
 Response object, 79
 Session objects, 79–81
 storing data with, 77–81
Web pages, 8
 backgrounds, 12–13
 body section, 10, 12–13
 calling classes from, 543–544
 calling stored procedures from, 520–523
 creating, using a Web editor, 43–45
 creating database connections from, 399–403
 creating new, 20–22
 with dynamic content, 544–558
 heading section, 10–12
 HTML structure of, 10–13
 inserting AdRotator control in, 231–233
 loading new, 11
 previewing in browser, 23, 25
 processing request for, 8–9
 publishing, 642
 schematics, 561
 sending e-mail from, 244–257
 static, 8, 9
 using Web services from, 604–605
 writing output to, 138–139
Web Palette tab, 127
Web Part controls, 202–203
WebPartManager control, 202–203, 205, 208
Web Parts, 202–211, 646
 CatalogZone control, 203–204
 configuring, 204–205
 displaying, 203–204
 EditorZone control, 204–205
 managing, 205–211
 viewing, 209
 WebPartManager control, 202–203
WebParts tab, 4
WebPartZone control, 206
Web portals, 202, 211–213
Web references, 588, 591, 603, 606
Web server process, managing session state using, 317–318
Web servers
 communication with Web services, 579–580
 data storage and retrieval in, 257–268
 IIS, 25
 internal, 25
 property sheets, 323–327
 software requirements, 629
 uploading files to, 238–244
Web Service Description Language (WSDL), 579
Web Service Description Language (WSDL) document, 587–588, 593–595, 601
Web services
 applications of, 580–583
 calling, 588–592
 communication between applications and, 578–580
 compiling, 585

components of, 584
 creating, 583–587, 595–598
 to display data, 597–598
 locating, 587–588, 589, 602–603
 overview, 577–592
 platform independence of, 578–579
 previewing home page, 599–601
 programming, with .NET development editors, 593
 properties, 595–596
 proxy class, 588–592
 securing, 607–608
 standards and protocols, 593–595
 third-party, 605–607
 using, 602–607
 using, from Web page, 604–605
 XML with, 585, 608
Web services Enhancements (WSE) 2.0 Service Pack 2, 607
Web Site Administration Tool (WSAT), 101–103, 339–340
Web.sitemap, 151
Web sites
 accessibility of, 35–36
 modifying, 467
WebXACT, 35–36
WebZone controls, 202
well-formed documents, 27, 29–30
WHERE clause, 383–384, 386, 401, 507
WHERE keyword, 382
While loop, 96
widening conversion, 71
Width property, 227, 230
wildcard characters, 382, 393–394
windows
 docking, 6
 moving, 6
 reserved, 92
 storing as tabs, 6
 visibility of, 5
Windows authentication, 346
Windows developers, 558
Windows Integrated Security, 368
Windows NTFS, 288, 608
WindowsPrincipal object, 347
Windows Scripting Host (WSH), 323
Windows Vista, 633
Windows XP Professional, 632–633
Wireless Application Protocol (WAP), 609–610
Wireless Markup Language (WML), 610
Wireless S Protocol (WSP), 610
WML documents, 609–610
World Wide Web Consortium (W3C), 10, 27, 32, 120
WriteFile method, 79
Write method, 79, 263, 264–266, 332
write permission, 407
WSDL. *See* Web Service Description Language (WSDL)
wsdl.exe, 594
WSDL proxy, 579–580
WSDL stubs, 579–580

## X

XForms, 16
XHTML
 bookmarks in, 17
 image tags and, 17
 standards, 10
 tag attributes and, 9–10
 unified standards in, 1
 well-formed, 29–30

XHTML 1.1, 32–33
XMethods, 606
XML
 case sensitivity of, 10, 28
 introduction to, 26–36
 nested elements, 28–29
 prologue, 27
 rules, 27–30
 standards, 26–27
 with Web services, 585, 608
XML characters, 28
XML control, 144–146, 405–406
XML data
 binding, to DataList control, 438–439
 connections to, 405–407
 processing, with XSLT stylesheets, 140–142
 representing business entities with, 421
XmlDataSource control, 404, 405–406, 407
xml data type, 372
XML declaration, 27–28
XML Designer, creating and validating XML documents in, 33–35
XML Document Object Model (DOM), 27, 421
XML documents
 creating and validating, in XML Designer, 33–35
 formatting, with XSLT stylesheets, 129–146
 markup validation of, 30–33
 previewing in browser, 30
XML files
 data retrieval from, 454–455
 displaying images with, 35
XMLHTTPRequest objects, 565
xmlns attribute, 10, 32, 35, 130
XML Schema Definition tool, 32
XML schemas, 32
XMLSiteMapProvider, 151
XML standards, 10
XML Web services, 608
XPath attribute, 421
xsl:attribute, 135
xsl:choose, 140–142
XSL (External Stylesheet Language), 129
xsl:for-each statements, 129–130
xsl:if statement, 142–143
xsl:otherwise, 140–142
xsl:sort command, 142
XsltArgumentList, 146
xsl:text instruction, 138–139
XSL Transformations (XSLT) stylesheets, 129–146
XSLTransform object, 146
XSLT stylesheets, 120, 129–146
 customizing, 135–144
 element templates, 132–134
 formatting main template with, 129–132
 hardcoding location of, 130
 nesting, 137–138
 processing XML data with, 140–142
 using processing instructions with, 142–144
 writing output to Web page, 138–139
 XML control, 144–146
xsl:when, 140–142

## Y

Yahoo! Shopping, 560–561

## Z

zero-based, 72
z-index, 13